Between Renaissance and Baroque

Jesuit Art in Rome, 1565–1610

Between Renaissance and Baroque is a stunning achievement – the first book to be written about the original painting commissions of the Jesuits in Rome. Offering a uniquely comprehensive and comparative analysis of the paintings and stuccoes which adorned all of the Jesuit foundations in the city during their first half century of existence, the study treats some of the most crucial monuments of late Renaissance painting including the original decorations of the church of the Gesù and the Collegio Romano, and the martyrdom frescoes at S. Stefano Rotondo.

Based on extensive new archival research from Rome, Florence, Parma, and Perugia, Gauvin Alexander Bailey's study presents an original, revisionist treatment of Central Italian painting in the last four decades of the sixteenth century, a critical transitional period between Renaissance and Baroque. Bailey relates the Jesuit painting cycles to the great religious and intellectual climate of the period, isolates the new stylistic trends which appeared after the Council of Trent, and looks at the different ways in which artists met the challenges for devotional art made by the religious climate of the post-Tridentine period.

Bailey also succeeds in providing the first ever written reconstructions of the Jesuit churches of S. Tommaso di Canterbury, S. Saba, and S. Apollinare, and the original novitiate complex of S. Andrea al Quirinale, the site of the most complex and original hospital decoration in late Renaissance Italy. Through these reconstructions, Bailey sheds new light on such works as Louis Richeôme's meditation manual on the paintings at S. Andrea, *Le peinture spirituelle*, a lively and detailed treatise on late Renaissance art that has never before been the subject of a thorough study. Ultimately, Bailey provides us with a new understanding of the stylistic and iconographic strands which shortly afterward were woven together to form the Baroque.

GAUVIN ALEXANDER BAILEY is a professor in the Department of Art History at the University of Aberdeen.

Between Renaissance and Baroque

Jesuit Art in Rome, 1565–1610

GAUVIN ALEXANDER BAILEY

UNIVERSITY OF TORONTO PRESS
Toronto Buffalo London

© University of Toronto Press Incorporated 2003
Toronto Buffalo London
Printed in Canada

Reprinted in paperback 2009

ISBN 0-8020-3721-6 (cloth)
ISBN 978-1-4426-1030-9 (paper)

Printed on acid-free paper

Library and Archives Canada Cataloguing in Publication

Bailey, Gauvin A.
Between Renaissance and Baroque : Jesuit art in Rome, 1565–1610 / Gauvin
Alexander Bailey.

Includes bibliographical references and index.
ISBN 0-8020-3721-6 (bound). – ISBN 978-1-4426-1030-9 (pbk.)

1. Jesuit art – Italy – Rome – History.   2. Art, Late Renaissance –
Italy – Rome – History.   3. Art, Baroque – Italy – Rome – History.
4. Christian art and symbolism – Italy – Rome – History.   5. Art,
Italian – History.   I. Title.

N7952.R6B34 2003   704.9′482′09456309031   C2003-900180-6

University of Toronto Press acknowledges the financial assistance to its publishing
program of the Canada Council for the Arts and the Ontario Arts Council.

University of Toronto Press acknowledges the financial support for its publishing
activities of the Government of Canada through the Book Publishing Industry
Development Program (BPIDP).

For Peta and John

Contents

Illustrations follow p. 188

Acknowledgments

A book of this size can never be the work of one person, and even though it does not have the global scope of my last one, I am indebted to just as many kind and generous people, both in North America and in Europe. Above all I would like to acknowledge the extraordinary help and friendship of those to whom I have dedicated the book, Peta Gillyatt and John O'Malley, S.J. Without these two companions the book would never have happened. Peta shared in the adventure of discovering fabulous paintings and helped me at every step of the way with her ideas and encouragement. During our trips to Italy together she joined me enthusiastically on many an exhausting drive or COTRAL bus ride to search out paintings and churches, and she introduced me to the world of *porchetta*. John has given freely of his time and his thoughts and has enriched my understanding of the history of the Jesuits through our many collaborative projects, including our second large conference, 'The Jesuits II: Cultures, Sciences, and the Arts, 1540–1773,' at Boston College in 2002. Some of his help was the practical kind, such as reading the entire manuscript and correcting my translations of Latin, for which I am eternally grateful. The other kind was more fun, such as dinners in Trastevere or Zipoli House, or theatre and opera in New York.

I also feel particular gratitude for two other dear friends, T. Frank Kennedy, S.J., and Pamela Jones, both of whom were extremely encouraging during the writing of this as of the last book. T. Frank has provided much scholarly assistance during our regular conversations about Jesuit culture at lunch at St Mary's, and has also been a great comrade in hunting out fine food and scenery in Rome, Florence, and Chile and at the Villa Vistarenni. Pamela, who agreed to traipse around Rome with us on a Palaeochristian Revival church tour, has been tremendously generous with her time and ideas, especially in reading an earlier draft of the manuscript.

Most of this book was written during a fellowship at the Villa I Tatti in Florence in 2000–1, and I would like to express my thanks to the staff and fellows for their support during that year. Among the staff and research associates I am most grateful to Walter Kaiser, Michael Rocke, Alexa Mason, Allan Grieco, Amanda George, Susan Arcamone, Nelda Ferace, Eve Borsook, Marco Spallanzani, and Giovanni Pagliarulo. I especially would like to thank my fellow *borsisti* and their 'spousal equivalents' not only for their conversation and their ideas but also for their friendship and for making that year a memorable one: Jill Burke and David

Rosenthal, Robert and Marian (and Katherine and Theodore) Maniura, Roni Weinstein and Dorit Lerer, Julia Hairston and Toni de Amicis, Monika Schmitter and Marc Lambert, Meg Gallucci and Michael Rotondi, Anne Stone and Jeff Nichols, Stefano Baldassarri, Sergio Tonelli, Peter Howard, Francesco Facchin, Branko Mitrovic, Jan Stejskal, Giuseppe Palmero, Natascia Tonelli, and Katharine Park and Martin Brody. And I offer a particular word of thanks to Robert and all my other *foosball* associates, to Emiliano Pernice for keeping me up to date on the *calcio* scores, and to the Tatti *gatti* Ettore and Birillo for keeping me awake in the morning.

The research and preparation of this book owe much to the generous help of many individuals. I wish I had the space to say exactly what I owe to each, but restraints demand that I list them alphabetically. I am thankful to Morton Abromson, Eric Apfelstadt, John Atteberry, Maria Giulia Barberini, Miroslava Benes, Maura Giacobbe Borelli, Alison Brown, Michael J. Buckley, S.J., Maristella Casciato, Liana Cheney, Joseph Chorpenning, Richard Clay, James Clifton, Maria Conelli, Joseph and Françoise Connors, Carlos Coupeau, S.J., Peter Davidson, Hester Diamond, Samuel Y. Edgerton, David Ekserdjian, Pierre-Antoine Fabre, Janice Farnham, R.J.M., Bruna Filippi, Marc Fumaroli, Luce Giard, Mina Gregori, Sheldon Grossman, Father Gualtiero, Christine Goettler, Mary Jane Harris, Steven Harris, Alexandra Herz, Randi Klebanoff, Antien Knaap, Françoise Kuester, Lance Lazar, Douglas Lewis, Mark Lewis, S.J., Thomas Lucas, S.J., Michael Maher, S.J., Aliocha Maldavsky, Thomas McCoog, S.J., Martin McHugh, Henry Millon, Franco Mormando, S.J., Jeffrey Muller, Michael and Simone Naify, Marcus Neuwirth, Elizabeth Pilliod, Mario Polia, Ursula Pace, Pierre du Prey, Louise Rice, Volker Remmert, Clare Robertson, Giovanni Sale, S.J., Klaus Schwager, John Shearman, Jeffrey Chipps Smith, Jack Spalding, Antonella Stancati, David Stone, Claudio Strinati, Alain Tapié, Nicholas Terpstra, T. Barton Thurber, Katarzyna Toporska, Anna Maria Traversini, Nuno Vassallo e Silva, Ian Verstegen, Edmund De Unger, Barbara Wisch, Helmut Wohl, and Michael Zampelli, S.J.

I also owe much to the kind assistance of the staff at numerous archives, including the Archivum Romanum Societatis Iesu, the Archivio di Stato di Roma, the Biblioteca Apostolica Vaticana, the Archives of the Venerable English College, the Archives of the German-Hungarian College, the Biblioteca Nazionale in Rome, the Archivio di Stato di Firenze in Florence, the Archivio di Stato di Perugia, and the Archivio di Stato di Parma. Special thanks go to Father Joseph De Cock, S.J., Delia Gallagher, and Arnd Franke.

The initial research for this book in 1998–2001 would not have been possible without the financial assistance of a Renaissance Society of America Robert Lehman Foundation Research Grant, as well as three Higgins School of Humanities Research Grants and two Faculty Development Grants, all from Clark University. I am also grateful to Clark for giving me a sabbatical leave for 2000–1 in which to write.

Publication of this book was assisted by subvention grants from the Renaissance Society of America, the Lila Acheson Wallace–Reader's Digest Publications Subsidy at Villa I Tatti, and the Jesuit Institute at Boston College.

Once again, the book has been much improved through the efforts of the tireless editorial staff at the University of Toronto Press. I thank especially Suzanne Rancourt, Theresa Griffin, Ron Schoeffel, Barbara Porter, and Kristen Pederson, as well as the anonymous peer reviewers.

Other friends and family who made the transitions easier were Sherry Ballantyne, Daina Groskaufmanis and Barry Ditto, Patricia Thomas and Meriwether Rhodes, Annemarie and Todd Whilton, and Bill and Betty Pratt.

Between Renaissance and Baroque

Jesuit Art in Rome, 1565–1610

1

Introduction:
A Time without Art?

> Furthermore I will say this, which will seem incredible to relate to you: neither inside nor outside Italy could you find a single painter.
>
> Giovanni Pietro Bellori, *Le vite de' pittori* (1672), p. 38

The Jesuits have been blamed for the destruction of Renaissance art and the creation of the Baroque. One of the most important patrons of the Catholic world in the sixteenth and seventeenth centuries, the Society of Jesus had an extraordinarily powerful impact on the arts and architecture of Italy and the rest of Catholic Europe, not to mention the world. Through foundations such as the Church of the Gesù in Rome (1568–75), the most prominent religious building to be completed in the city in well over a century and a model for hundreds of churches in the years to come, the Jesuits dictated stylistic trends at a pivotal period in the history of Italian art, and would continue to do so at crucial moments throughout the seventeenth century. By means of their intensive intellectual, theological, and educational activities, disseminated through a prodigious publishing branch, the Jesuits also influenced the tastes, iconographies, and decisions of popes, cardinals, and even rival religious orders. While scholars no longer take seriously the notion that the Jesuits created the Baroque, they acknowlege the critical role played by the Society in its inception and development. They also continue to maintain that as the vanguard of the 'Counter-Reformation' the Jesuits played a leading role in bringing about the demise of the Renaissance. In fact, the Jesuits are seen as bearing significant responsibility for making the later sixteenth century – to put a twist on a term coined by Federico Zeri – a 'time without art.'[1]

Nothing in the history of Italian painting may be as detested as the religious painting of the last four decades of the 1500s. Later Cinquecento sacred art is considered the beleaguered and sanctimonious expression of a century that witnessed the Sack of Rome (1527) and the near collapse of the Catholic church, whose resurgence at the Council of Trent (1545–63) is still popularly regarded as sounding the death knell of Renaissance humanism. Its denigration goes back to Early Modern art critics such as Giulio Mancini (1558–1630) and Giovanni Pietro Bellori (1615–96), and to traditional art history's conception of stylistic change as innovation and progression. The later Cinquecento was damned by these seventeenth-century critics and by nineteenth- and twentieth-century art historians because for them it represented the last stage of a stylistic decline following the High Renaissance, a roughly twenty-year period in which Michelangelo painted his Sistine Ceiling, Raphael his Vatican *stanze*, and Leonardo his *Madonna and Child with St Anne*, an age Sydney Freedberg has called 'the most extraordinary intersection of genius art history has known,' and one that traditional art history depicts as a unified and focused moment of perfection.[2] The first stage in this 'decline' occurred after 1520, when Central Italian painting developed into what is still generally called 'Mannerism,' an elegant tangle of styles characterized by Bellori as the 'destroyer of painting' and seldom loved even today.[3] Yet even 'Mannerism' (and 'Maniera,' or courtly late Mannerism, which lasted from ca. 1530–40 to the 1560s) has enjoyed a sophisticated treatment by scholars since the beginning of the twentieth century – even if they are not always inclined to use the name – and many now recognize its wonders. By contrast, sacred painting from the last four decades of the 1500s is still relegated to a page or two at the end of Renaissance art surveys, and the impression is given that the genius simply ran out until it was rescued in the late 1590s by Annibale Carracci and Caravaggio and the beginning of the Baroque.[4] This omission seriously obscures our understanding of what happened to painting between Maniera and Baroque, especially since the later Cinquecento was one of the most productive eras in the history of sacred art, as popes, cardinals, religious orders, and private patrons scrambled to erect new altars, paint new fresco cycles, and restore existing church interiors, and since many of the stylistic innovations of the early Baroque had already been tested out in the later Cinquecento.

Another reason why the later Cinquecento has been so poorly served by traditional art history is that the history has been conceived of primarily as a history of style, and the devotional art of this period is so eclectic that it verges on stylistic anarchy, with no single movement leading the way. Not knowing what to call it, art historians fumble with a complicated and fussy collection of more or less derogatory terms ranging from 'Late Maniera,' 'Counter-Maniera,' 'Late Counter-Maniera,' 'chastened Maniera,' and 'anti-Maniera' to 'mannered Mannerism,' 'Counter Reformation,' and Zeri's slightly more polite 'art without time.'[5] None of these terms were used by the people who actually made or commissioned the art. Few book-length works have been devoted to the painting of this period, and most of those that have been written are from the 1990s, such as the monographs by Cristina Acidini Luchinat and Andrea Emiliani on the Zuccari brothers and Federico Barrocci.[6] Most scholars working in the period have abandoned the traditional monograph approach to look at this painting in terms of the mechanics of patronage, Pope Sixtus V (1585–90), Pope Clement VIII (1592–1605), and Cardinal Alessandro Farnese (1520–89) being three of the most prominent patrons.[7] As impressive and ground-breaking as these studies are they tend to de-emphasize issues of style, with the result that we now know more about the patrons and their propagandistic goals than about the art itself.

In this book on the early artistic enterprise of the Jesuits, I hope to contribute to this discussion of patronage. I will look at the relationship of the visual arts to Jesuit beliefs and goals and to Early Modern Catholicism broadly stated, in considering iconography and religious history as well as liturgy and devotional practice, and even economics. I will ask how the Jesuits used the visual arts, and what their impact was on their audiences, both those within the order and those outside it. But I will also tackle issues of style, since style was a crucial ingredient of the Jesuits' art policy and of that of their contemporaries. Artists and patrons in late Cinquecento Rome were extremely conscious of style – perhaps more so than ever before – and so must we be if we are to understand them. Contrary to the popular perception, this awareness was especially present in artists producing sacred art, where the very effectiveness of a work as an instrument of devotion was at stake.

The Jesuits and the Visual Arts, and Art and 'Counter-Reformation'

As one of the largest and most intellectual orders of the period, the Jesuits give us unique insight into the cultural and religious climate of Early Modern Catholicism. Founded by Ignatius of Loyola (1491–1556) and his companions and given its ecclesiastical charter in 1540 by decree of Paul III Farnese (1534–49), the pope who called the Council of Trent, the Society of Jesus was a company of priests and brothers with an internal structure and a commitment to mobility that gave them a remarkable unity of purpose around the globe. In addition to the traditional vows of poverty, chastity, and obedience, the Jesuits made a special vow to undertake ministry anywhere in the world on the pope's command. At the same time, the Society practised a flexibility that allowed for extraordinary cultural and regional diversity within the order itself. The Jesuits' contributions to the late Renaissance world were twofold. On the one hand, they became a pre-eminent missionary order, a project that took them farther beyond Europe than any of their contemporaries until modern times and involved them in cultural exchanges with civilizations as varied as those of China and of the Guaraní of Paraguay. In an earlier book I surveyed their artistic activity in the mission field.[8] On the other hand, the Jesuits were the first religious order to operate schools and colleges as a principal and distinct ministry, and their commitment to classical education enriched the lives of many in Italy and throughout the world and was responsible for their being called 'Christian humanists.'[9] Contrary to the popular conception of the Jesuits as intolerant conservatives, they promoted the greatest revival of pagan thought since Lorenzo de' Medici's court in Florence, and arrived at a blending of Christianity with the humanistic tradition of secular writers such as Homer, Virgil, Cicero, and Terence that spoke to the new age. The impact of their colleges on the life of late Renaissance Rome, particularly the great Collegio Romano (today the Gregorian University), the German-Hungarian College, and the Venerable English College, can hardly be exaggerated, and the role played by painting in those institutions forms part of the subject of this book.

The Jesuits have fought a persistent image problem since the seventeenth century, when the anti-Jesuit tract *Monita secreta* (1613) presented the Society as 'devils in a soutane' and as hypocritical, power-hungry propagandists; and even today the Society of Jesus is often regarded as having been the bastion of an orthodoxy that was antithetical of Renaissance humanism.[10] Conspiracy theories can be felt most strongly in the history of art, which has suffered from an anticlerical bias since its beginnings as a field in the nineteenth century. In the 1840s the notion of *Jesuitenstil* (Jesuit style), a superficial and specifically Jesuit manner of painting, sculpting, and building that aimed to control the masses through an appeal to their most mundane instincts, first took hold in the popular imagination. Although the notion of a Jesuit style was largely dismissed by scholars in the first half of the twentieth century, the premise that the Jesuits did little more than reduce art to an instrument of Catholic dogma persists to this day. Perhaps the most damning comment of all was written by Freedberg, in whose classic text *Painting in Italy, 1500–1600* the Jesuits turn up time and again as a foil for Renaissance taste and genius. Freedberg said of the paintings by Scipione Pulzone and Giuseppe Valeriano that adorned the newly-built church of the Gesù in Rome (figs 108–9): 'This slick, intentionally witless form illustrates a content that is deliberately made out of banality and sentiment ... In the measure that this is for didactic piety of such a kind, it is anti-art; it is not altogether a hyperbole to suggest that the means of art are either debased to serve efficiency of piety, or turned into a demonstration of technique, or at best employed to manufacture *beaux morceaux.*'[11] For Freedberg even mere contact with Jesuits can reduce an artist to triteness. He blames a melancholy spirituality in the late work of the Florentine painter Jacopino del Conte (1510–98) on a meeting with the Jesuit founder: 'A macabre pietistic seriousness [was] apparently inspired in him at least in part by a direct contact with Ignatius Loyola.'[12]

Rudolf Wittkower spoke with a different sort of disdain when he wrote in the introduction to *Baroque Art: The Jesuit Contribution* (1972), 'We could easily demonstrate that the Society had scarcely any aesthetic ambitions before 1600 or even in the early decades of the new century.'[13] Thanks to Wittkower and to a group of mid-twentieth-century architecture historians, the Jesuits were seen as having little interest in artistic merit and as being concerned solely with iconography and the use of art to manipulate the viewer. This approach was expressed again in the early 1960s by Howard Hibbard, who wrote that 'none of the Jesuit leaders showed any subtlety of appreciation,' and who in the 1980s dismissed the Jesuits' artistic concerns as 'limited to subject matter.'[14] At about the same time, Maria Calì assumed the Freedbergian mantle, in equating the Jesuits with Trent and blaming them for an artificial and exploitative manner of painting that she contrasts with the genuine religiosity of late Michelangelo: 'The Counter Reformation church had found in [the Jesuit painter Giuseppe] Valeriano its most conscious interpreter, and in his bright and cold rationality the most qualified instrument ... The "timeless" formula of Father Valeriano ... tries to erase all contradictions in its impersonality, to suffocate each contrast and every authentic spiritual movement forever in the "objectivity" of given dogma ... The cubic form of Michelangelo was in that way reduced to serve as a support for Catholic orthodoxy as defined by Trent.'[15] Calì even goes so far as to compare the Jesuits' approach to art with that of the Florentine fire-and-brimstone preacher Girolamo Savonarola (1452–98), characterizing it as a 'rigid, levelling orthodoxy.'[16]

Thanks to this perception that the early Jesuits had no interest in good painting, they are regularly blamed for a 'lack of first-rate artists,' and the story goes that they hired men who could work quickly and produce safely banal art at the least expense.[17] As I hope to demonstrate, the Jesuits used the same painters hired by the other leading patrons of the day, and whatever inconsistencies are found in Jesuit painting projects are found also in the projects of the popes, their cardinals, and the other Catholic religious orders. Undoubtedly, some of the artists who worked for the Society were bad painters. But the Jesuits hired just as many talented ones, and these artists' responses to the diverse audiences and spiritual challenges of the day were frequently revolutionary and cutting-edge. The Jesuits' enthusiasm for the didactic and devotional use of art did not preclude an interest in aesthetics or a concern for quality.

This book is the first survey of pre-Baroque Jesuit painting in Rome. One of the reasons why the Jesuits make an ideal subject is that they were especially keen supporters of the visual arts, even in an age already saturated with imagery owing to the efforts of the renewed Catholic church. The Jesuits zealously promoted devotional art and the use of imagery, whether real (as in paintings and illustrated books) or imagined (as in visionary devotional practices), in both meditation and ministry. Ignatius of Loyola assembled a small collection of devotional pictures, including a *Holy Family* that survives today, to assist him in making his prayer, a practice that would be followed by many of his successors. He believed that sight was the most powerful of the five senses, especially as a tool for memory and devotion. The founder of the Society of Jesus also frequently experienced visions, in what he described in his *Autobiography* as a seeing with 'ojos interiores' (interior eyes); he beheld such things as cloudbursts with rays of sun emanating from them and ghostly human forms without differentiation between arms and legs, as well as more clearly defined images of the Virgin and Child or of Christ carrying the cross.[18] But Ignatius's most important contribution to the visual arts was his manual of meditation *Exercitia spiritualia*, or *Spiritual Exercises* (1548). One of the world's most enduring works of spirituality, this manual draws heavily upon imagery – or, more specifically, the use of the senses to conjure up scenes from Sacred Scripture in a kind of mental exercise called the 'composition of place.'[19] Together with the *Formula of the Institute* (conceived in 1539), the *Exercises* was the foundational text of the Society of Jesus. Written over more than two decades, from 1521 to 1548, the date of first publication, the *Exercises* encapsulated the process of Ignatius's own spiritual conversion in a practical and flexible form intended to guide others in their mystical journeys.

Although the *Exercises* was never intended exclusively for the use of Jesuits, its program of prayer was followed in its entirety by every Jesuit who entered the order, and it formed the template for Jesuit ministries around the globe. As John W. O'Malley comments, 'There is no understanding of the Jesuits without reference to that book.'[20] The *Exercises* also gave the Society a unique focus and served as an expression of the Jesuit 'way of proceeding,' as a neat summary of ideals and methods that had no counterpart in other religious orders, even though aspects of the work derived from earlier manuals. Especially influential were the Carthusian Ludolf of Saxony's (1300–78) *Vita Jesu Christi*, which introduced the notions of contemplation of place and of application of the senses; the medieval Franciscan tract *Meditationes vitae Christi* (late thirteenth to early fourteenth century), long attributed to St Bonaventure; and the late medieval devotional practice known as

Devotio moderna, which focused on Thomas à Kempis's *De imitatione Christi* (fif-teenth century).[21] Like the Jesuit policy toward the fine arts, the *Exercises* held a Catholic legacy in common with other religious orders, but the work was distinctive in the way it coordinated elements of that legacy into an integral and original whole.

The *Exercises* was not meant to be read through in a sitting, but was to be used as a teaching manual, providing a spiritual director with directives and suggestions for leading a participant through what came to be known as a retreat. A collage of short pieces of text, including directives, meditations, prayers, declarations, and rules, the book allows for a sequenced progression from confession of the sins of one's past life toward conversion and the understanding of one's vocation. The sequence is underscored by the names of the four principal sections, called 'Weeks.' The First Week concentrates on sin and the constant love of God, and encourages the participant to turn from his or her past sins toward gratitude and love for God. The Second, Third, and Fourth Weeks strengthen the resolve arrived at during the First, by moving the participant through a methodical meditation on the events of Jesus' life as a way of helping him or her find a vocation and make appropriate life choices. A major theme of the text is the binary relationship between God and Satan (the 'Two Standards'), who battle for our hearts and souls, and the need to choose between two paths in our life's journey, the path of Good and the path of Evil.

The book owed its success to its flexibility and to the priority it gave to freedom of choice, reflecting a Jesuit emphasis on free will and the individual's responsibility for action and salvation that set the order apart from most other Catholic groups. The Exercises were practised across the spectrum of social groups, and ranged from the abbreviated 'light' (*leves*) Exercises – not much more than intensified catechism lessons – to the full-scale thirty-day retreat made in seclusion and under the supervision of a spiritual guide, with many variations in between tailored to individual needs and constraints.[22] In the early days the Exercises were occasionally led even by non-Jesuits. In Parma as early as 1540, large numbers of disciples made the Exercises and then went on to instruct others. Throughout the sixteenth century orphan boys, young students, and women, individually and in groups, made the Exercises, which were widely disseminated through confraternities. It would be difficult to overestimate their popular impact and the breadth of exposure to them in sixteenth- and seventeenth-century Italy.

Of most concern here is the use of imagery in the *Exercises*. Although the book was not illustrated until the seventeenth century and probably was not meant to have pictures, the 'composition of place' exhorts the exercitant to re-create imaginatively the sights, sounds, smells, and feelings belonging to a scene such as the Nativity of Christ or the Presentation of Christ in the Temple in a way that has reminded many scholars of the kind of instructions that would be given to a painter.[23] Art historians for the past century have linked the *Exercises* with an emphasis on sensuality in the work of Baroque artists from Gianlorenzo Bernini (1598–1680) to Caravaggio (1573–1610), with varying degrees of success.[24] Some have seen the impact of the 'composition of place' as authoritarian and monolithic, but such a view ignores the method's remarkable flexibility. The 'composition of place' does not supply a literal and detailed description of what Ignatius wants to be re-created in the mind; it is deliberately vague as to the particulars so that those making the Exercises can tailor their vision to their own needs and idiosyncracies. For the 'mental representation of the place' in the Second Prelude of the Second Contemplation of the First Day of the Second Week, Ignatius exhorts his readers to reconstruct the way from Nazareth to Bethlehem traversed by the Holy Family, as well as the grotto of the Nativity: 'Consider its length, its breadth; whether level, or through valleys and over hills. Observe also the place or cave where Christ is born; whether big or little; whether high or low; and how it is arranged' (par. 112).[25] These brief remarks could never serve as an instruction to a painter, and they certainly do not tell the reader how the scene should look or what to think. Ignatius's desire to allow the maximum flexibility compels readers to become active participants in the meditation, by filling in the blanks and doing the mental sketching themselves. As we will see, the paintings in Jesuit foundations ask the same of their viewers.

Recent work by Pierre-Antoine Fabre has suggested that Ignatius envisioned images as a purgative, something to dislodge the mental images previously housed in a person's imagination.[26] In his *Autobiography*, Ignatius wrote about one image, tellingly, that it had 'effaced all the images that are found painted in one's soul.'[27] The *Exercises* also gave a direct endorsement of pictures in churches, in a passage that supports the cult of the saints: 'We ought to praise not only the building and adornment of churches, but also images and veneration of them according to the subject they represent' (par. 360).[28] This directive echoes the twenty-fifth session of the Council of Trent in 1563, which promoted imagery as an extension of the cult of the saints: 'That the images of Christ, of the Virgin Mother of God, and of the other saints, are to be had and retained particularly in temples, and that due honour and veneration are to be given them.'[29]

But it was the subject matter and structure of the *Exercises* that had the greatest impact on Jesuit art commissions. The Jesuits' early painting cycles all reflect the book's emphasis on modelling oneself on Christ's example (and its concentration on certain specific episodes of his life, such as the Nativity and the Passion). They also recall the book's focus on themes such as the Trinity and hell; its binary notion of Good and Evil; its devotional methods such as those of the Three Colloquies (prayers) to Christ, the Virgin, and God the Father; and its emphasis on self-examination and personal choice. Most of all, the thematic and iconographic arrangement of frescoes and canvas paintings in the first Jesuit churches in Rome were inspired by the organization of the *Exercises* as a sequenced pilgrimage of the soul, with a step-by-step ascent from the sins of one's past toward love of God and the embracing of one's vocation. The *Exercises* are our key to understanding the painting commissions undertaken by the Jesuits in their first half century.

The Jesuit concern with imagery – both real and imagined – can be seen in the work of Ignatius's first companions and his successors, many of whom wrote devotional manuals inspired by the *Exercises* and incorporating their own versions of the 'composition of place.' Francis Borgia (1510–72), the third Father General of the Society of Jesus and an early friend and adviser of Ignatius, may have been responsible for the basic iconographic program of the Gesù. Borgia also made extensive use of sacred pictures when preaching, and in a famous statement he likened images to spices at a meal, something that could pique one's spiritual tastebuds.[30] He wrote his own devotional tract, the *Meditaciones para todas las dominicas y ferias del año* (1563–6, published 1675), the first series of meditations based on the texts of the liturgical year, which include the 'composition of place.'[31] Borgia powerfully influenced the cult of images with his endorsement of the icon of the miraculous Madonna supposedly painted by St Luke in the church of S. Maria Maggiore in Rome. This Italo-Byzantine image, now gloriously housed in the Cappella Borghese, was already one of the most popular icons in Rome (it was credited with allowing the Catholic victory over the Turks at Lepanto) when Borgia recognized its usefulness as a meditative and mission tool. After obtaining permission from Pope Pius V in 1569, Borgia had a copy of the icon made under the supervision of Cardinal Carlo Borromeo in a slightly updated style; the copy itself was copied repeatedly in the following decades and sent to the four corners of the globe – to Brazil, Peru, India, China, Persia, and Poland. By the end of the century it was likely the most widely distributed image on earth.[32] An example of an *acheiropoieton*, or image made without human hands, the icon and its copies alike were believed to possess miraculous qualities that aided spiritual conversion. Of course, Borgia's enthusiasm for the image had less to do with 'art' in the Renaissance and modern sense than with the medieval belief that such images possessed the presence of the original, and that copying it extended its spiritual power.[33] But Borgia's campaign on behalf of this Italo-Byzantine icon nevertheless demonstrates his acknowledgment of the power of sacred imagery.

A more literal contribution to the visual arts was made by the Spanish Jesuit Visitor and companion of Ignatius, Jerónimo Nadal (1507–80). Nadal spent the last decades of his life struggling to publish a series of illustrated meditations on the Gospels, the *Evangelicae historiae imagines* (Antwerp, 1593), a volume that links pictures and meditations to the texts of the liturgical year (figs 12, 13). According to O'Malley the 'earliest such series of the whole of the New Testament of any size or importance ever produced,' Nadal's illustrated Gospels were meant to guide students and Jesuit scholastics 'to goodness and devotion,' in a sequenced pilgrimage very similar in its conception to that of the *Exercises*.[34] Nadal's Gospel illustrations were also circulated around the world and served as a copybook for painters and sculptors from Milan to Peru. They were influential long before the engravings were published, since the preparatory drawings were circulated among Jesuit institutions in Rome as early as the 1550s or 1560s (I will look at these in more detail shortly). Despite some scholars' attempts to prove otherwise, Nadal's series was almost certainly the brainchild of Ignatius himself, and it was also strongly promoted by Borgia.[35] The most compelling evidence for Ignatius's involvement in the conception of the series is to be found in the introduction of the 1595 edition, written by the secretary of the Society of Jesus, Diego Jimenez: 'Father Ignatius one day said to Jerónimo Nadal that it would be a praiseworthy enterprise to propose for prayer and meditation to the students of the colleges of the Society some brief remarks on the evangelists for feast days and Sundays; and not only that, but moreover to illustrate them by affixing images and through commentary.'[36] During the almost three decades it took to design and publish Nadal's work, the Society of Jesus demonstrated an extraordinary commitment to the volume, which was pushed to completion in spite of formidable financial and diplomatic challenges.[37] One of the most innovative features of Nadal's imagery, although it was not the first book to use this approach, was the appearance of letters on the narrative scenes keyed to labels below, a mnemonic meditative device that would be used also in the painting cycles at the Jesuit collegiate churches.[38] In fact, since most of the Roman Jesuit painting cycles, from the Novitiate infirmary to the Gesù itself, are characterized by what might be called 'captioning,' or the use of simple (often scriptural or patristic) quotations directly underneath or over the painting as an aid to the viewer. This captioning was likely inspired at least in part by Nadal's manual, even more than a decade before it actually appeared in print. Nadal's illustrations would also have an impact on the composition and arrangement of the Jesuit painting cycles.

Other early Jesuit proponents of devotional imagery included the great controversialist Cardinal Robert Bellarmine (1542–1601), famous for his sermons at the Collegio Romano vindicating the Catholic church in the face of Protestant criticism. Like Ignatius, Bellarmine had a small picture gallery in his apartments, including motivational portraits of great churchmen like Clement VIII, Cardinal Roberto de' Nobili, and Carlo Borromeo.[39] Bellarmine was also an enthusiastic supporter of the cult of angels, the impact of which reverberated throughout the first Jesuit painting cycles, and of the cause for sainthood of the young Jesuit scholastic Aloysius Gonzaga, whose death during the first years of the Collegio Romano turned him into a patron of education and Jesuit youth and ensured that his image was painted in many of the Society's early foundations. In publications such as his *Disputationes de controversiis christianae fidei* (1588) and *De imaginibus sacris et profanis* (1594), Bellarmine showed great concern to maintain the distinction between images and idols, a definition that echoed the last session of Trent; he wrote that sacred images had the advantage over pagan ones in that they depicted the Truth and not falsehood – a position also maintained by the Oratorian treatise writer Gabriele Paleotti (1522–97).[40] For Bellarmine the legitimacy of sacred images was tied to the legitimacy of the cult of the saints, and truthful images served as evidence of the existence of the saints they depicted. This same concern for the Truth inclined Bellarmine to promote naturalism in the visual arts; together with other theorists of the period he encouraged naturalistic tendencies in contemporary painting and sculpture. He also wrote on the futility of presenting images without explanations, thereby implicitly supporting the sort of captioning Nadal had already introduced and that would become typical of Jesuit decorative cycles.

Another Jesuit intellectual who had a critical impact on sacred art was Antonio Possevino (1534–1611). One of the greatest teachers in Jesuit history, Possevino first served the Catholic church as a diplomat in places such as Sweden and Russia, but found his true calling as a teacher in Padua, where he taught theology between 1587 and 1591. He made a major contribution to Jesuit education with the publication of his *Bibliotheca selecta qua agitur de ratio studiorum* (Rome, 1593), which was a compilation of important authors and texts for use in the curriculum, as well as of teaching and study methods.[41] Chapter XXIII of the *Bibliotheca selecta* was entitled 'Pictura similis poesi' (Painting Is Like Poetry), published separately in 1595 in a little tract called *Tractatio de poesi et pictura*. In these works Possevino proposed that painting was a mute form of poetry and an imitation of nature, especially painting of the human figure, and that it was capable of moving the emotions more quickly than words. Drawing upon a battalion of ancient authors from Plato to Pliny, Possevino stressed the importance of historical accuracy in depicting sacred scenes, and maintained that the painter's task was to depict appropriately the sentiments and emotions of humankind – an approach that emphasized correct knowledge of anatomy and history as well as of the science of optics.[42] More important, Possevino enthusiastically endorsed the use of emblems and allegorical images, and the use of pagan images as models for symbols of a religious nature – a concept introduced by the mid-sixteenth-century treatise writer Giovanni Andrea Gilio da Fabriano and one that echoed the Jesuits' use of classical authors in their education program.[43] Possevino's taste for emblematica was shared by many Jesuits in the 1590s and is best seen in the Jesuit painting cycles at the Novitiate infirmary (chapter 3) and the church of S. Vitale (chapter 5).

Perhaps the most enthusiastic supporter of devotional imagery was the fifth Father General, Claudio Acquaviva (in office 1580–1615), who directed the decorative programs of many of the Roman painting cycles as patron and fundraiser, and probably also intervened as a designer and iconographic guide. Acquaviva's enthusiasm for visual imagery was already evident in his advocacy for Nadal's Gospel cycle. In his plea to the Duke of Parma, written on 9 August 1586, Acquaviva asks the Duke for enough money to pay for the finest printmakers of the day, emphasizing that a work of art must be of high quality if it is to be efficacious: 'With this [letter] Your Highness will be given some information about a work of pictures and meditations on the evangelists for the whole [liturgical] year, made by a father of the Society, which contains the life and miracles of our Saviour, taken from the four evangelists. Since it is the best and largest example of this kind of imagery that has appeared so far, and because of the spiritual usefulness we expect from it, we would like to have it engraved by the best artists that can be found.'[44] The engravers eventually hired the Wierix brothers of Antwerp, ranked among the best in the history of Flemish printmaking, even though the Jesuits initially were reluctant to employ them because they were reputed to be dissolute and to spend all their money in cabarets. The Jesuits' concern for high artistic quality, like their consciousness of style, can be felt throughout their early painting commissions in Rome. Although the personal tastes of individual Jesuits varied, they consistently sought high-profile artists for their more public commissions, as far as their budgets would allow.

Acquaviva wrote his own *Spiritual Exercises* (1571) for the express use of novices, a work that draws heavily on Ignatius's 'composition of place' by encouraging readers to imagine what various biblical scenes looked like. The text is full of exhortations to 'imagine that you see' or 'imagine that you are present in front of' the Madonna and Child, St Joseph, or other figures in the Gospels. Such is his First Meditation before the feast of the Purification, where Acquaviva writes, 'Imagine that you see the most Blessed Virgin in this shed, now kneeling before the Word Incarnate, now taking him to her breast, and sometimes giving him to the glorious St Joseph to hold in his arms,' and his Fifth Meditation on the same feast: 'Imagine that you find yourself before the Temple, and contemplate the great commotion of all these people whom you find when the elderly Simeon, with such devotion and tears, watches over the Son of Mary in his arms.'[45] These passages not only recall the *Exercises*, but also bring to mind Pseudo-Bonaventure's *Meditationes vitae Christi*, which encourages its readers to 'kiss the beautiful little feet of the infant Jesus who lies in the manger and beg His mother to offer to let you hold Him a while. Pick Him up and hold Him in your arms. Gaze on his face with devotion and reverently kiss Him and delight in Him.'[46] I will return to this affinity between the Jesuits and the Observant Franciscans in their use of the senses and of the visual arts as an affective tool. In imitation of his spiritual mentor Ignatius, Acquaviva also had a collection of images of the martyrs and *beati* of the Society of Jesus in his rooms for use in his personal meditation, as we can read in his obituary: 'He had the martyrs and other blessed of the Society illustrated, whose portraits he had in his rooms, and he contemplated and revered them with particular affection.'[47] A similar pantheon of Jesuit heroes was found in the original Novitiate at S. Andrea al Quirinale, a commission undertaken largely under his patronage (see chapter 2). Earlier, Acquaviva's biographer cites a similar example of his devotion to the cult of images, in which the Father General is so attached to the flagellation column in the church of S. Prassede in Rome that he has made the painting *Mysteries of the Passion* to hang in his room and be always before his eyes.[48]

It is important to keep these early Jesuits' enthusiasm for imagery in mind, since the Jesuits of the later sixteenth century have been blamed not only for an indifference to quality but for an almost iconoclastic inclination toward poverty and austerity in the arts that resulted in many bare church interiors. One of the documents most frequently used to support this misconception is the statement on Jesuit buildings made in the First General Congregation of the Society of Jesus in 1558: 'As far as is in our power, we should impose norms for the buildings belonging to our houses and colleges, so that besides other inappropriate developments they may not become at some point palaces befitting the nobility; they must be sound buildings, sturdy and well built, suited to be our residences and the place from which we can discharge our duties; they must be such, however, as to demonstrate that we are mindful of poverty – buildings that are not luxurious, therefore, or too fancy.'[49] Scholars continue to interpret this statement as reflecting a policy endorsing plain church interiors, and as proof that the early Jesuits were anti-classical in their approach to the design and decoration of their religious structures.[50] What they fail to note is the very next line of the decree, which states, 'On the other hand, nothing was said about church buildings, and the entire matter appeared to call for further consideration.' As it happens, the matter never was given further consideration, and the evidence in this book clearly indicates that the early Society greatly admired image-saturated interiors in both churches and residences.

Most denigration of Jesuit art patronage derives from the Society's supposed role as the vanguard of the 'Counter-Reformation,' the Catholic reform movement institutionalized in the twenty-five sessions of the Council of Trent, the last session of which, as we have seen, published a decree on sacred imagery. For Early Modern Catholicism in general, the label 'Counter-Reformation' (i.e., the countering of Protestantism) refers to only one of many aspects of the spiritual crisis that began at the end of the fifteenth century and lasted roughly until the end of the Thirty Years' War (1618–48),[51] and it does not identify the most important of the Jesuits' goals either. In the years since Leopold von Ranke presented what he termed the 'Counter-Reformations' as a unified front (1843), scholars have discovered that the period in fact was characterized by many different reformist movements, and that, far from being a monolithic whole imposed from above, the reform was significantly motivated by grass-roots dissenters, whose causes were vastly different from those of the official Church hierarchy.[52] The era witnessed the attempt by Catholics to revitalize the institutions of the Church by defining doctrine and purging the abuses of the late medieval and Renaissance eras. Far from being solely a reaction against Protestantism (hence the term 'Counter-Reformation'), these attempts were inspired by the same crisis that gave rise to the Lutheran schism, and that had given rise to earlier Catholic dissent such as that of the Dominican preacher Savonarola. Ranke traced the anti-Protestant efforts to three main protagonists, Trent, the papacy, and the Jesuits, thereby making the three into 'Counter Reformation' agents in a fashion that continues to be difficult for historians to refute. Yet the first generation of Jesuits and the imagery they commissioned had much less to do with opposing the Protestant Reformation than with promoting a renewed and triumphant Catholic church. Athough a few of the early Roman paintings of the Jesuits were directed toward the battle with Protestantism in the North, the majority were self-affirming, Palaeochristian, and commemorative in nature. If anything, classical history and the worldwide missions were as important as work on the Northern front.

Nevertheless, if the reforms of the Catholic church were not exclusively a reaction to Protestantism, the approach to the visual arts articulated in the Catholic reform did begin that way. Luther, Calvin, and Zwingli all had condemned sacred images as a form of idolatry and an excuse for licentiousness, in a challenge to Christian iconography that was echoed by the Catholic scholar Desiderius Erasmus (1466/9–1536).[53] Since Protestant reformers were moving in the direction of iconoclasm, the first series of Catholic treatises on sacred art, which appeared in the 1540s, openly opposed iconoclasm and reaffirmed the use of sacred pictures while taking care to prevent the accusation of promoting idolatry. The use of sacred images was affirmed by Trent, which saw them as a necessary extension of the cult of the saints but distinguished their use from idolatry and condemned nudity, superstitions, depictions of revelling and drunkenness, and 'filthy lucre': 'not that any divinity, or virtue, is believed to be in them, on account of which they are to be worshipped; or that anything is to be asked of them; or, that trust is to be reposed in images, as was of old done by the Gentiles who placed their hope in idols; but because the honour which is shown them is referred to the prototypes which those images represent.'[54] Although most scholars have focused on the restrictions announced in this decree, its primary purpose was to expand the role of sacred imagery as never before. It emphasized the didactic function of art as providing an aid to the memory, an example for people to follow, and visual proof of the miracles performed by the saints. These fundamental points, together with a call for clarity and simplicity, historically correct and realistic interpretation, and emotionally arresting art as a stimulus to piety, became the leitmotif of a wave of treatises written by clerics between the 1540s and the first decades of the seventeenth century, including those of Gilio da Fabriano (1564), Carlo Borromeo (1577), Gabriele Paleotti (1582), Jan Molanus (1619), and others.[55] Although much attention has been paid to the few cases in which clerics attacked existing works of art (the most famous being Gilio's censure of Michelangelo's *Last Judgment*), and even though some treatises are extremely exacting in their instructions to artists or architects (such as Borromeo's treatise on church building and Molanus's on painting), the direct impact of Trent or the post-Tridentine treatise writers on artists' work was probably very slight.[56] The treatises were written by churchmen for churchmen, they are usually not specific enough to be of any practical use, their definitions of concepts as seemingly basic as 'naturalism' vary dramatically, and few artists would have taken time to read them.[57] Many of them were mere codifications of reformist practices already undertaken independently by artists. Quite rare was a figure such as Federico Borromeo (1564–1631), the author of *De pictura sacra* (1625), who had a connoisseur's interest in style, but he belonged to a later generation than most of the writers.[58]

But the absence of a direct impact on art does not mean that the artists did not share many of the same concerns as the treatise writers. Scholars too often present clerics and artists as polarized in a rather romantic (and post-Enlightenment) battle between artistic freedom and ecclesiastical dogma. Whether at the behest of their patrons or because of their own spiritual crises, artists throughout Italy tempered the excesses of complexity, decoration, and sensuality in painting and took steps toward the very goals expressed by the clerics – historical accuracy, clarity, sobriety, emotional empathy, and decorum. In some cases these goals reflected a committed, passionately felt spirit of devotion; in others, austerity and archaism were employed as window-dressing. Like the Catholic reform movement itself, this process had begun long before Trent. In the early 1530s the Venetian painter Sebastiano del Piombo (ca. 1485–1547) consciously introduced a dark austerity and piety into his work, with an emphasis on death and on the passion of Christ that reflected the popularity of reformist devotional manuals such as Thomas à Kempis's *De imitatione Christi* (fig. 3). Sebastiano was a major inspiration behind the reformist trends of many later Cinquecento artists, and I will return to him shortly. Michelangelo sought to master an aura of authentic archaism in his early drawings by studying medieval and early Renaissance fresco paintings, and in the years following the Sack of Rome, influenced by his friendship with reformist circles, he translated this interest in archaism into a renunciation of some of the artifice and sensuousness of his past work.[59] Michelangelo's close attention to the traditional iconography of the Man of Sorrows demonstrated a belief that archaistic styles carried a greater aura of spiritual authority and a purity that added to their value as sacred pictures. This enthusiasm for the spiritual effectiveness of naive styles echoed the theoretical writings of the influential Portuguese painter Francisco de Holanda (1517–84), as well as Gilio's treatise on art, which celebrated the awkwardness, frontality, and stiffness of medieval painting, suggesting that a 'regulated mixture' of these purer styles with that of contemporary painting would be ideal for sacred painting.[60] It resulted from a crisis in the relationship between artistic style (which was by nature contemporary, cutting-edge, and increasingly secular) and the nature of the sacred icon (which was eternal and unchanging and possessed divine presence); the dilemma came to a head in the Cinquecento and would re-emerge toward the end of the century with the Palaeochristian Revival movement, an attempt to revive the iconographies and archaistic painting styles of the early Christian period, which reached its apogee in the 1590s (see chapter 4).

From the 1560s onward this quiet revolution in sacred painting took many forms, involving figures as different as Santi di Tito, Girolamo Muziano, and Taddeo Zuccaro. These men were not 'forced' to instil a new piety in their art, but were operating instead on a grass-roots level and according to their own will.[61] The evidence is in their eclecticism. In the decades before 1600 a greater variety of styles was being used than ever before in the history of Central Italian painting, as each artist went in his own direction to reformulate the rules of *arte sacra*.

Jesuit approaches to the arts were similarly diverse and flexible. Far from being the monolithic patrons depicted in traditional scholarship, the Jesuits came from widely different backgrounds and nationalities, and in their early years they rarely had a consensus on issues of devotion and aesthetics. Furthermore, they did not act alone. The Jesuits worked directly with the artists to formulate new styles appropriate for their goals, on a case-by-case basis, sometimes inventing as they went along. I have not found a single Jesuit contract that tells a painter how to paint, or even what to avoid. Jesuit art commissions were not the product of stylistic restraints imposed from above, but of a partnership in which artists' own interpretations of sacred art were encouraged and fostered on the ground. It is significant that the decorations of the Gesù, the most important of all the Jesuit painting cycles, represented the culmination and not the beginning of the Society's Roman experimentation in sacred imagery: the Jesuits had the opportunity to test out their use of pictures in their other churches before they adorned their mother church. But though there is no question of artists being 'forced' to work in certain ways, there is no doubt that the Jesuits preferred the work of certain artists to that of others, and that they encouraged their favourites to paint in ways they had found effective. Almost all the paintings executed for the Society during the first fifty years fell within a distinct range of styles. One of my purposes in this book is to uncover what that range was.

It is important to keep in mind that the Jesuits were not the only major art patrons of their day, and that – original as they were – their art commissions shared many features with those of the popes, the cardinals, and, especially, the other religious orders. The closest similarity is to the commissions of the Congregation of the Oratory, the other high-profile new religious order of Early Modern Rome, and I will return to it often in the chapters ahead. Founded by Filippo Neri in 1575 under Pope Gregory XIII, the Oratorians were a community of secular priests and not a monastic order, and in that respect were very like the Jesuits.[62] In its earliest years the community met at the oratory of S. Girolamo in Rome, from which they acquired their name, and their dramatic services, which combined prayer, music, and elaborate liturgy, were the origin of the modern oratorio. Many scholars have tried to polarize the Jesuits and the Oratorians, and as a result the two orders are often treated as opposites – the pro-Florentine, cultured, and aristocratic Oratorians on the one hand and the pro-Spanish, didactic, and low-brow Jesuits on the other.[63] Yet in reality the two were more alike than different. Like the Jesuits, the Oratorians concentrated on the education of young people and on theological debate. The two orders enjoyed a very close relationship, owing particularly to personal friendships, such as that between the Jesuit Robert Bellarmine and the Oratorian Cesare Baronio. Both orders were also extremely concerned with the didactic potential of the visual arts. The differences between the two orders had mainly to do with structure and with degree of unity: unlike the Jesuits, the Oratorians did not make vows; and whereas the Jesuits were highly centralized, Oratorian houses were largely independent – until 1958 the order had no universal leader in the way the Jesuits had. The Jesuits also owed much of their ability to coordinate complex iconographic programs to the *Exercises*, whereas the Oratorians had no such text to bind together their decorative schemes.

The Oratorians, like the Theatines after them, built a monumental mother church, in the old centre of town, the style, plan, and elevation of which roughly echo those of the Gesù. The Oratorians were given the rights to S. Maria in Vallicella in 1575, and the church was soon rebuilt on a grander scale by Martino Longhi, beginning in 1582, when it became known also as the Chiesa Nuova (New Church). As at the Gesù, the chapel decoration (carried out in two phases, from 1578 to 1583 and then from 1586 to the early 1620s) depended on private patrons. Both orders used their chapels to create a decorative program that eventually embraced the entire church interior, and both kept control of the iconography, and probably also the choice of artists, largely in their own hands.[64] I will revisit the Chiesa Nuova side chapels in greater detail in chapter 6. The Jesuits and the Oratorians also shared a significant number of artists, a fact that should help put to rest the popular notion that the two had vastly different tastes in the visual arts. These men included painters such as Girolamo Muziano, Durante Alberti, Scipione Pulzone, Andrea Lilio, the Cavaliere d'Arpino, Paul Brill, and Peter Paul Rubens, as well as the sculptor Flaminio Vacca.[65]

The most celebrated feature of the Oratorians' taste was their enthusiasm for affective art, particularly the work of Federico Barocci (1535–1612) (figs 8, 57, 117), who painted two altarpieces for the Chiesa Nuova, in 1586 and 1603.[66] Filippo Neri himself had a profound attachment to the work of the *marchegiano* painter, and later Oratorian patrons also favored Barrocci and artists whose work expressed a similar fervour and sentimentality, because they wanted the kind of painting that would elicit an emotional response and cause a transformative experience in the viewer. Ian Verstegen aptly characterizes this affective style as 'sweetness with realism.'[67] The Jesuits never hired Barocci, even though Alessandro

Farnese, the cardinal patron of the Gesù, had hoped to have him contribute to its interior decorations, a plan that probably foundered only because Barocci was notoriously slow and overburdened with commissions.[68] Yet they sought the same affective quality in other artists, such as Gaspare Celio and their own Giuseppe Valeriano, and for the same reasons.

The Jesuits and the Oratorians also shared many iconographic interests, as we will discover throughout this book. One of the most prominent was martyr imagery. The two orders were the most active promoters of the iconography of early Christian martyrs as a symbol of the legitimacy of the Church and of the cult of the saints, although the Jesuits were the only ones to depict martyrs from their own order – a reference to a worldwide missionary enterprise the Oratorians lacked. Another interest was the use of classical-inspired allegory and emblematica, in an attempt to revive Graeco-Roman imagery in a Christian key that became especially popular under Pope Clement VIII and in the first decades of the seventeenth century. Both orders also took part in the Palaeochristian Revival, a movement that also involved a Christian reclaiming of the classical past. The Jesuits and the Oratorians alike valued naturalism in painting, and equated detailed and accurate depictions of landscape and still-life with spiritual truth, a concern evident in the writings of both Baronio and Bellarmine, and that also accounts for the interest in Northern landscape painters such as Paul Brill in the commissions of both orders.[69] Unlike those of the Oratorians, however, the Jesuit painting cycles in Rome include flora and fauna from the New World and Asia, and thus reflect knowledge acquired on the missions. Both orders were also concerned with creating an iconography based on a rich range of textual sources, from scripture and patristics to the classics, although the Oratorians never incorporated in their decorative cycles as many inscriptions as the Jesuits did. This affinity can be seen in a comparison of the textually saturated interior of the Novitiate infirmary at S. Andrea al Quirinale (chapter 3) with the equally erudite treatise on the visual arts by the Oratorian Gabriele Paleotti entitled *Discorso intorno alle imagini sacre e profane* (1582).[70]

The Jesuits and the Oratorians also faced the same iconographic challenge. As new orders they had no saints of their own, until 1622, a date beyond the range of this book; that was a disadvantage from which their Franciscan and Dominican counterparts did not suffer.[71] Although images of their own saints would form the core of Jesuit iconography in the second quarter of the seventeenth century and later, the early Jesuits had to use existing imagery to celebrate their heroes and their ministries. Accordingly, Francis of Assisi stood in for Francis Xavier, Ignatius of Antioch for Ignatius of Loyola, and early Christian martyrs for the martyrs of the Society's ever-expanding missionary enterprise. Nevertheless, the Jesuits were not shy about painting portraits of Jesuits in their more private buildings such as the Novitiate, where by the beginning of the seventeenth century there were pictures of Ignatius and Francis and a whole range of present-day martyrs, including some whose blood had barely dried on their wounds. Life portraits of Ignatius of Loyola had also circulated in the Society by as early as the 1550s, and images of Francis made from his corpse were sent from Goa by Alessandro Valignano, the Jesuit Visitor to the Indies, in 1583. The Jesuit concern with having a true likeness, or 'vera effigies,' of their most celebrated members was echoed by the Oratorians, who had portraits of Filippo Neri done during his lifetime, and a death mask made.

The event that set off a whole series of depictions of Ignatius was his beatification in 1609, which was celebrated by a profusely illustrated life of Ignatius entitled *Vita beati P. Ignatii Loiolae Societatis Iesu* (Rome, 1609) (fig. 20).[72] These anonymous prints exerted a powerful influence on Jesuit hagiographic pictorial cycles all over Europe, particularly after the canonization edition of 1622, which featured an additional picture showing the ceremony in which sainthood was bestowed on Ignatius. Ursula König-Nordhoff has concluded that the engravings are by Jean Baptiste Barbé (1578–1649), and others have suggested the Galle workshop, but it is still unclear who is responsible for most of the original drawings. There are some noteworthy exceptions. The drawing for the image on page 64, which shows Ignatius founding the Collegio Romano, was done by the youthful Rubens (1577–1640), who spent much of the first decade of the seventeenth century in Italy, most notably under the patronage of the Gonzaga duke of Mantua, and came to Rome in 1605.[73] Julius Held maintains that at least ten and perhaps as many as nineteen of the *Vita beati P. Ignatii Loiolae* drawings can be attributed to Rubens, and suggests that since most of them fall at the end of the series, they were additions to a series already in preparation.[74] During his stay in Italy, Rubens executed two large-scale commissions for the Jesuits in 1604–6, one a *Circumcision* in the Jesuit church in Genoa and another a trio of canvases for the Jesuit church of SS. Trinità in Mantua, including the severely mutilated *Holy Trinity Adored by Duke Vincenzo Gonzaga and His Family* (1604–5), now in the Palazzo Ducale.[75] Rubens was given the latter commission through the Gonzaga family, which had close ties with the Jesuits, thanks to their kinsman St Aloysius Gonzaga. The *Vita beati P. Ignatii Loiolae* inspired a very similar Oratorian series published on the occasion of the canonization of Filippo Neri, P.G. Bacci's *Vita di S. Filippo Neri fiorentino* (Rome, 1622), with a set of engravings by Luca Ciamberlano that the artist had begun to design the year after the appearance of the illustrated life of Ignatius.[76] Despite the similar straits in which the two orders found themselves in their early decades, the Oratorians never dared to depict as many of their unbeatified members as the Jesuits did in their iconographic cycles, printed or painted.

The art of the Jesuits spoke to many audiences beyond the Society itself. From noble students to poor labourers, from rich widows to prostitutes, the people addressed by Jesuit paintings represented the widest spectrum of society in one of the most heterogeneous cities on earth. The Jesuits were highly conscious of this diversity. Their experience in cosmopolitan Rome, together with their work elsewhere in Europe and in Asia, Africa, and the Americas, gave the Jesuits a uniquely global approach to iconography. Consequently, the Jesuits were one of the first patrons in Renaissance Italy to seek an art that could approach a universal audience.[77] Nevertheless, while some paintings were designed to be understood by all, others were calibrated in iconography and style to appeal to specific audiences, whether young novices of the order, future missionaries, lay students belonging to the nobility, or the families of the sick. The close attention to differences in audience, which related to the paintings' locations and the kinds of building they adorned, reflected contemporary theories about religious art by clerics like Gilio or Paleotti, who had a hierarchical conception of the audience for painting that has recently been considered by Pamela Jones.[78] In chapter 8 I will ask how successful this approach to audience actually was, and how it differs from the solution achieved by early Baroque painters such as Annibale Carracci.

In this book I will survey the first phase of Jesuit paintings (as well as the much rarer stuccoes and sculpture) in Rome, between 1565, when the Jesuits commissioned their first painting cycle at the collegiate church of SS. Annunziata, and 1610, the approximate completion date of the Novitiate paintings, which were described the next year by Louis Richêome in his *La peinture spirituelle* (Lyon, 1611), one of the longest and most fascinating ruminations on religious art of the late Renaissance and a central focus of this book. This period happens to take us from the death of Michelangelo to the death of Caravaggio. The paintings considered here adorned some of the key monuments of late Renaissance architecture, such as the Church of the Gesù and the Collegio Romano, as well as important early Christian churches renovated by the Society, such as the collegiate churches of S. Stefano Rotondo and S. Vitale. I will compare these decorative cycles to contemporary Jesuit painting commissions elsewhere in Italy, in cities such as Florence, Forlì, Perugia, and Ferrara, although the Roman cycles form a unified body of work and stand on their own. Jesuit architecture of the period has been treated extensively elsewhere.[79]

The Jesuit foundations will be discussed in roughly chronological order, according to when their decoration was begun. In chapters 2 and 3 I will consider the first decorations at the Novitiate of S. Andrea al Quirinale, which were begun in the 1560s, although most date from the late 1590s and first years of the 1600s. These include the paintings of the Novitiate infirmary, the subject of chapter 3, which date from 1594 to 1608 and represent not only the most complex iconography of any Jesuit foundation but the most extensive and original hospital decoration of the late Renaissance. In chapter 4 I will look at the first collegiate foundations, beginning with the Collegio Romano and Seminario Romano in the 1560s and 1570s and ending with the various chapels belonging to the German-Hungarian College, a Jesuit-run residence for diocesan seminarians from Central and Eastern Europe; their decorations include the first Jesuit martyrdom cycle (1582), an iconography invented by the Society that had a powerful impact on Italian sacred art in general. In chapter 5 I will turn to two later martyrdom cycles commissioned by the Jesuits in Rome, those of S. Tommaso di Canterbury (the Venerable English College) and S. Vitale (the new church of the Novitiate) in the 1580s and late 1590s. In chapters 6 and 7 I will focus on the most celebrated Jesuit paintings of this period, the original decorations of the mother church in Rome, the Gesù, which were executed between the mid-1580s and the early 1600s and are among the last undertaken before the hiatus in Jesuit art patronage that began in the early seventeenth century. For a combination of political and economic reasons, Jesuit painting commissions came to a halt after the first decade of the 1600s, and very little was executed until after mid-century, when the Society, like everyone else, promoted the new styles and ideals of the High Baroque.[80]

Few of the paintings considered in this book can lay claim to being 'Baroque' in style. Even though the last decade and a half coincided with the Roman innovations of Annibale Carracci and Caravaggio, only a few of the paintings reflected those changes. Several of the solutions made by the painters who worked for the Society, however, were similar in spirit to those of the early Baroque, and I will return to this theme in chapter 8. The Jesuits' involvement in the Baroque, especially the architecture of Bernini in the 1660s and the great frescoed ceilings of Baciccio and Andrea Pozzo in the last decades of the seventeenth century, have been treated extensively elsewhere, although we could still benefit from a comprehensive study even of the Roman monuments alone. There is another reason for leaving out the great contributions made by the Society to later seventeenth-century art. Our concentration in the past on the Jesuits' relationship with the Baroque has added to the persistent misconception that the styles of that period are the definitive expression of Jesuit identity.[81] Yet the Society of Jesus had been in existence for more than a hundred years before Bernini began the new church of S. Andrea al Quirinale in 1658, and we can learn about their original aesthetic ambitions only by looking at the art they commissioned during that period – not by projecting back onto it the more familiar images produced in the later years.

Throughout this book I will also look at non-Jesuit paintings that influenced Jesuit cycles, whether in style and composition or in iconography, and will in turn consider the impact of the Jesuit cycles on non-Jesuit painting in Italy. I will highlight the close relationship between these paintings and print culture, especially the products of the engravers and publishing houses of Antwerp, who were pivotal promoters of Jesuit iconography throughout Europe. This print culture played an intimate role in early Jesuit art commissions. Manuals for meditation published in Antwerp and Rome were reproducing entire painting cycles from places such as S. Tommaso and S. Stefano Rotondo within a year of their conception. Engravings of some of the paintings just completed in the Gesù or the Collegio Romano would be commissioned from leading Antwerp printmakers such as the Sadelers and Wierixes, with the result that soon they were familiar to people around the world. Some print projects even influenced the paintings themselves. The most important of these – and the crux around which much early painting activity of the Jesuits revolved – was Nadal's *Evangelicae historiae imagines*; as we have seen, images belonging to the volume circulated in the form of drawings for decades before it was printed in 1593.

Just under half the paintings discussed in this book no longer exist, and many of the others today find themselves in company very different from the company they enjoyed in 1600. This loss has been a major obstacle. However, thanks to the Jesuits' well-established habit of keeping records, we can get a glimpse of these forgotten decorations. By going back to archival documents, from account books, artists' contracts, and personnel records to letters, obituaries, diaries, and visitation reports from archives in Rome, Parma, and Florence, I have been able to reconstruct much of the original subject matter, chronology, and authorship of the paintings. My job has also been made easier by Richêome's description of the Novitiate paintings and especially by illustrated meditation manuals based on the martyrdom cycles at the Jesuit collegiate churches. I am not the first person to study many of these painting cycles, although no one has ever looked at them together, and the Novitiate and S. Tommaso remain virtually untouched in the literature. This lacuna is understandable, since so many of the original paintings have been lost and the consequent lack of visual evidence is not easy to overcome. Scholars such as Howard Hibbard, Leif Holm Monssen, Alessandro Zuccari, and Alexandra Herz have taken pioneering steps, especially for the decorations at the Gesù and S. Stefano Rotondo, and I am much indebted to their work.[82] But by returning to the archives I have been able to solve some mysteries and flesh out a fuller picture of the process, result, and legacy of Jesuit painting and stucco cycles.

The loss of so many of the Jesuits' first generation of paintings has necessarily had an effect on the character of this book. Chapters 2 and 3 draw on virtually no extant visual material and so make any discussion of style an approximation. They focus instead on iconography, reception, and function. The paintings in chapters 4 and 5 either still exist or have been preserved in prints, thereby allowing a more detailed discussion of style, although colour and detail can be given only a cursory treatment because the surviving frescoes at S. Stefano and S. Vitale have come down to us in what is best described as a ghostly state. Only in chapters 6 and 7, on the Gesù, can a consideration of iconography and function be united with a full analysis of style, since most of the paintings there survive intact and in relatively good shape. Nevertheless, in spite of the lacunae in our knowledge of early Jesuit painting projects, the surviving records are sufficient for us to appreciate once again the extraordinary unity of purpose and stylistic awareness that formed the basis of the first phase of Jesuit painting commissions.

The Debate over 'Mannerism,' and Art in Rome before the Jesuits

Before looking at the earliest Jesuit art, I will situate it within the major developments in Roman sacred painting at the time. But first I will tackle the issue of stylistic labels. Sacred painting in Central Italy after 1560 is plagued by an abundance of labels developed by twentieth-century art scholars in an attempt to make sense of its confusing variety of stylistic approaches. Since several of these new approaches bear trifling resemblances to what scholars now generally call 'Mannerist' painting (that is, the painting of Florence and Rome from ca. 1520 to ca. 1530–40) and especially 'Maniera' (or courtly late Mannerism, from ca. 1530–40 to the 1560s), most of the labels contain one or the other of these words in some form (e.g., 'anti-Maniera,' 'Counter-Maniera,' 'mannered Mannerism,' etc.). To my mind, these received terms serve only to make an already confusing situation even more so, and tend to emphasize the relatively trivial aspects of the paintings at the expense of their deeper meaning and purpose. I will therefore use neither term to refer to the art of the first Jesuits. The term 'Mannerism' is a convenient label at best, and has come to refer only to a very specific art movement in the third and fourth decades of the century that had no direct bearing on the earliest Jesuit painting cycles. 'Maniera' is an equally ahistorical term, and although certain features identified by scholars as belonging to 'Maniera' did appear in some Jesuit works (e.g., a sinuous line, or relief-like composition), they did so only on a superficial level. For want of a better label – and this may well be a period for which the fewer labels the better – I will refer simply to 'sacred painting,' or 'devotional painting,' because that is what the people of the time called it, and because these terms also emphasize the importance of the meditative and spiritual function.

It is nevertheless important to review exactly what scholars mean by the terms 'Mannerism' and 'Maniera,' because they are regularly used to describe the early paintings of the Jesuits. Even though these labels are often carelessly applied to any Italian art executed between 1520 and 1600, the twentieth-century debate over 'Mannerism,' along with its methodical cataloguing of stylistic features, has defined the parameters of that art quite specifically. The label 'Mannerism,' like 'Baroque,' is a modern invention. It is based on the commonplace but vague word *maniera*, which sixteenth-century Italians used to mean anything from 'manner' as an aspect of behaviour, to 'method.' Although sixteenth-century writers such as Giorgio Vasari and Ludovico Dolce used *maniera* to denote what we would mean by artistic 'style,' they never used the term to designate a period style distinguishing the art of their own era.[83] Some scholars have maintained that the most widespread application of the word to the visual arts interpreted it along the lines of 'technique,' 'workshop method,' or 'routine.'[84] Seventeenth-century art critics such as Giovanni Pietro Bellori (quoted at the head of this chapter) and his contemporary Giulio Mancini were the first to use *maniera* to describe painting after 1520 – and they did so in a decidedly pejorative sense – but they too never used it as an overarching stylistic label. Deriving from *maniera*, the term 'Mannerism' (*manierismo*) was not coined until 1792, when the Italian archaeologist and antiquarian Luigi Lanzi used it as a label for the sixteenth-century painters attacked by Bellori for their lack of taste.[85] Despite the vigorous efforts of twentieth-century scholars to justify their use of 'Mannerism' or 'Maniera' by turning to the word *maniera* in sixteenth-century Italian literature, there is no compelling evidence that the word ever had the meaning they give it. As Jeroen Stumpel has recently observed, 'The sixteenth-century literature in the visual arts does not allow for such a special absolute, or central meaning of maniera – we simply will not find a touchstone for our modern terminology there.'[86]

For nineteenth- and early twentieth-century scholars, 'Mannerist' art was anathema, and it became a convenient foil for the art of the High Renaissance, which Heinrich Wölfflin first labelled 'classic art' in 1898 in an attempt to define what he felt to be Italy's artistic apogee.[87] 'Mannerism' became anything that departed from these norms, a 'decline' and 'distortion' of classical ideals that would be saved, in Wölfflin's patriotic view, only by 'the Germanic North of Italy' and the art of Caravaggio at the end of the century. This dualism between High Renaissance and 'Mannerism' remains implicit in most of the literature today. 'Mannerist' artists included those of the first generation, such as Rosso Fiorentino (1495–1540), Jacopo Pontormo (1494–1557), and Giulio Romano (ca. 1499–1546), as well as later artists such as Giorgio Vasari (1511–74), Bronzino (1503–72), Francesco Salviati (1510–63), and Jacopino del Conte (fig. 1). Craig Hugh Smyth summarized the stylistic characteristics of 'Mannerist' art as defined by nineteenth-century scholars, most of which were meant to contrast with the ideals of 'classic art':

Repetition of formulae and eccentricities based largely on the imitated style, sameness from work to work and artist to artist, neglect of nature (except in prosaic details); also arbitrariness, affectation, capricious imaginativeness, and art for art's sake instead of a higher purpose; hence emptiness coupled with mere decorativeness, extravagant display in which form and object are not sufficiently merged, over-accentuation of grace and refinement, and over-emphasis on Michelangelesque muscular nudes multiplied in exaggerated, meaningless poses; at the same time crowding, lack of space, confusion, incorrect drawing, careless speed, hardness, lifelessness, and feeble color.[88]

Whether or not these characteristics actually reflect Italian painting styles between ca. 1520 and ca. 1560 is a subject beyond the scope of this book. More pertinent here is the truism that the art of this period was lacking in spirituality and deeper purpose, and that it served only art itself, an opinion that glossed over the enormous role played by sacred painting. Scholars all along have looked much more closely at the art of the secular courts than at art executed for the Church.

The conception of 'Mannerism' as 'anti-classic' was given a positive character in the early twentieth century, most systematically by Walter Friedländer in 1925, who applied it to a specific body of painting in Central Italy from 1520 to 1550.[89] Friedländer recognized the greatness in the art of Pontormo, Rosso, and Parmagianino (1503–40), especially its idealism and abstraction, and moved the decline ahead to the period after 1550, that is, to the second generation of painters after Raphael. A more dogmatic approach was taken by Max Dvořák, also in the 1920s, who championed 'Mannerism' *because* it was anti-classical, and saw it as the expression of a spiritual crisis very similar to that faced by Modernists at the beginning of the twentieth century; and this approach was echoed as recently as the 1960s by Arnold Hauser, who saw 'Mannerism' as a revolutionary first conscious divergence from the imitation of nature.[90] As Ernst Gombrich commented about critics such as Dvořák, 'What wonder that they saw in the rejected alternative of Mannerism the predecessor of an anti-realistic and anti-idealistic modern art that had been maligned as their friends were maligned?'[91] As Gombrich noted, Dvořák and his followers were more fascinated with the abstract idea of 'Mannerism' than with its historical reality.

An important debate also took place at about this time between Werner Weisbach and Nikolaus Pevsner, both of whom emphasized the link between art and the historical and intellectual aspects of the 'Counter-Reformation,' but who disagreed completely about the period of art concerned.[92] Weisbach, who saw the effect of the 'Counter-Reformation' on art as a positive thing, viewed the Baroque as its most characteristic style. He was leading the way for the revival of interest in the Baroque (eventually to be defined as art produced between the 1590s and ca. 1750) that began with Denis Mahon in 1947 and would culminate in the 1980s and 1990s.[93] He also helped promote the idea, so prevalent in later twentieth-century literature, that the Baroque was the most characteristic style of the Society of Jesus since, following Ranke, he saw the Jesuits as the right arm of the 'Counter-Reformation.' Pevsner, on the other hand, saw the 'Counter-Reformation' as a negative force, and, redrawing the boundaries of its aesthetic expression as between 1520 and 1620, declared that 'Mannerism' was the style that best represents the spirit of the era (for Pevsner, 'Mannerism' had the pejorative sense it held for nineteenth-century scholars). He also depicted the Society of Jesus as the quintessential expression of this 'Counter-Reformation' spirituality, a piety that suppressed human individuality and renounced free will. Therefore, although the two scholars disagreed as to whether 'Mannerism' or 'Baroque' best reflected the spirit of the age, they agreed that the Jesuits played a leading role in its artistic expression.

The next big debate over the definition of 'Mannerism' took place in the 1960s between John Shearman and Craig Hugh Smyth, in a pair of articles published in 1963 and also in monographs in 1962 and 1967.[94] Both Smyth and Shearman aimed for a more precise definition of 'Mannerism' by returning to contemporary literature and, especially in Smyth's case, by offering a systematic evaluation of style. In a masterful study of cultural context, Shearman looked at what he called 'Mannerism' (in Italy, 1520–70) not only in painting but in sculpture, architecture, metalwork, and poetry. He defined 'Mannerism' as a 'stylish style' emphasizing virtuosity and grace and relying on the High Renaissance as a precedent. As eloquent as Shearman's arguments are, critics such as Pevsner, Zerner, and Cropper have pointed out that his study really deals with only one aspect of the culture of the time, and that its focus is courtly and so largely avoids issues more pertinent to sacred art.[95] Like Friedländer, Smyth differentiated between the painting of the first and that of the second generation after Raphael, and termed the art of the period 1530–50 'Maniera' (with a capital M), after the word found in contemporary writings. Smyth was exceptionally rigorous in defining the stylistic parameters of 'Maniera,' such as the tendency to flatten figures against the picture plane, the use of a 'flat light' giving uniformity to the painting, the preponderance of twisted and foreshortened limbs and torsos to 'exploit the strain between two and three dimensions,' the propensity to juxtapose figures, and the inclusion of a notable angularity of forms.[96] Recognizing 'Maniera' as an art of figures, he isolated the crucial role played by antique relief sculpture as a model, a point recently emphasized also by Marcia Hall. Smyth moved the period of decadence further ahead than Friedländer, to the period after 1560: 'In this way Smyth not only defined a style, but also created for it a history that separated *its* own decline from the notion of post-classical decline in general.'[97] Thus, over the course of forty years of scholarship, the 'decline' of Italian painting moved forward the equivalent of forty years, from ca. 1520 to ca. 1560, where it remains today.

Friedländer's and Smyth's style periodizations were more thoroughly elaborated by Sydney Freedberg in his 1971 *Painting in Italy*, which is still the standard English text on Italian painting in the Cinquecento.[98] Through a detailed study of a wide range of artists of the period, including many who were all but unknown in their own day, Freedberg made extraordinary contributions to our understanding of stylistic development in the period. Many others have followed in his path, with the result that the works of Salviati, Vasari, the Zuccari, and others from the second half of the sixteenth century are almost as well known as those of Pontormo and Rosso.[99] He also reiterated the early understanding that the mid-Cinquecento was an anxious age facing a spiritual crisis, a belief he shared with Henri Zerner and Arnold Hauser.[100] This recognition of a spiritual side to 'Maniera' helped scholars move away from the 'art for art's sake' cliché. Freedberg made the crucial observation that the primary spirit of post-1560 sacred painting was profoundly antithetic to 'Maniera' style, with its courtly artifice.[101] Nevertheless, while Freedberg enhanced our understanding of the first three-quarters of the century, he only added to the confusion surrounding the post-Tridentine era by coining a new series of stylistic labels. We have Freedberg to thank for terms such as 'Counter-Maniera,' which he used to refer to what he saw as the deleterious effect of the 'Counter-Reformation' on painting at mid-century, and 'anti-Maniera,' for the 'witless' style that took hold in the 1590s with Scipione Pulzone, Giuseppe Valierano, Giovanni de' Vecchi, and others.[102] I have discussed his use of the Jesuits as a scapegoat for artistic decadence earlier in this chapter; and in general his work is marred by a heavy-handed anticlerical bias.

The debate over the definition of 'Mannerism' and 'Maniera' is now largely moribund, with a new generation of scholars generally avoiding larger historical studies – and their labels – and concentrating on individual artists or patrons. Many contemporary scholars are also moving away from the anticlerical attitudes of their forebears. As Elizabeth Cropper comments in an excellent recent survey of the literature (1992), the scholarship now faces a 'methodological stalemate' between the decades-old debate over 'Mannerism' and more recent work that has stepped aside from such definitions.[103] One new book that treads this ground again is Marcia Hall's *After Raphael* (1999), the first English-language survey of post-1520 Cinquecento painting since Freedberg. While her study is extremely thoughtful and illuminating, particularly in its characterization of the various stylistic movements of later Cinquecento sacred art and its situation of artistic developments within their historical context, she falls victim to the familiar craze for labelling and even coins such new terms as 'Transitional-Relieflike.' Things get especially confusing in the later part of the century, where Hall deals with the religious crisis of the Tridentine era, since she not only uses Freedberg's 'Counter-Maniera' but adds three neologisms of her own – 'Counter-Reformation' (the art, not the religious movement), 'Late Maniera,' and 'chastened Maniera.'[104] While 'Mannerism' and 'Maniera' are clearly here to stay, alongside their equally unscientific cousins 'Baroque' and 'Gothic,' we do the art of the period a disservice by creating ever more subdivisions of these already problematic terms.

One of Hall's greatest contributions is her careful stylistic analysis of the three main trends in Roman reformist sacred painting in the second half of the Cinquecento. I will briefly sketch these trends, the latter two of which appear in Jesuit painting, as well as two more from outside Rome. When the Jesuits commissioned their first painting cycle, in the mid-1560s, painting in Italy was more eclectic than at any point in its previous history. It was a transitional period, with no style yet emerging as the most progressive, or presenting a clear solution to the conceptual and aesthetic challenges being grappled with. Nevertheless, three principal reformist currents emerged in Rome, all of which sought an answer in the simplicity, rationalism, and sobriety of High Renaissance painters, particularly Raphael, Sebastiano del Piombo, and the early Michelangelo.

There was the style of the Lazio painter Girolamo Siciolante da Sermoneta (1521–75), which toned down the ornateness and complexity of the mid-century

'Maniera' style and returned to a High Renaissance monumentality and a rational concept of space, and also to Raphael's classically proportioned figure type. Like many painters of his generation, Siciolante also fell under the influence of Sebastiano del Piombo, one of the first artists to respond to the climate of Catholic reform after the Sack of Rome, as we have seen (fig. 3).[105] In works such as his *Pietà* (ca. 1542–4) (fig. 2), directly inspired by Sebastiano, Siciolante went back to the clear and simple expression of sincere devotion meant to appeal to the emotions of the viewer. There is a solemnity and weightiness to his figures, which avoid the capricious, twisting poses of those in much mid-century painting, and a deepening of the shading, even though he combines these features with the burnished, metallic surfaces and elongated figures of 'Maniera' painting. Siciolante's deepening of the shading, which offered a powerful contrast to the 'flat light' of mid-century painting, would characterize all three trends in Roman devotional painting in the late Cinquecento.

The second strain in Roman sacred art was the style of the *marchegiano* painter Taddeo Zuccaro (1529–66).[106] Like Siciolante, Taddeo sought a clearer form of narrative expression by eliminating some of the extreme artificiality and ostentation of courtly 'Maniera' painting, and there are hints of a High Renaissance conception of space and of classicizing, balanced colours, both deriving especially from Raphael. Taddeo also shared Siciolante's enthusiasm for the directness and deep shading of Sebastiano del Piombo. However, unlike Siciolante, Taddeo demonstrated a new interest in naturalism derived from Northern painting, especially in landscape and still-life details, an interest we will encounter frequently in Jesuit painting commissions. Despite his reformist tendencies, Zuccaro never abandoned the aristocratic grace, fluidity, or calligraphic line of mid-century painting, and his compositions are crowded with a pageantry of figures. His *Conversion of St Paul* (ca. 1563) (fig. 4) in S. Marcello returns to the structural clarity of Raphael, with its symmetrical composition and the basically pyramidal structure of the central figures, and his God the Father recalls Michelangelo's Sistine Ceiling. Nevertheless, he combines with these ingredients the complexity of detail and the elegance of the courtly 'Maniera' style. Especially telling is his juxtaposition of cruder, more expressive faces in the lower figures with idealized angelic faces above, the refinement of which recalls Bronzino.

Federico Zuccaro, who worked with Taddeo and absorbed his brother's style, would be a key contributor to the Gesù decorations in the 1590s, and I will return to him in much greater detail. The *principe*, or president, of the artists' academy called the Accademia di San Luca from 1593, Zuccaro was a literary man of aristocratic pretensions who combined an interest in spirituality with a commitment to urbane culture.[107] The greatest monument to his style was the Oratorio del Gonfalone in Rome (1565–75), which brought together Federico and others with similar tastes, such as Livio Agresti and Cesare Nebbia (1536–1614) (fig. 5).[108] The lavish decorations of this confraternity chapel recall the elegance and complexity of 'Maniera' painting, yet they heighten the *chiaroscuro*, simplify the composition, and make clear appeals to the viewer's senses in a way that heralded new directions in sacred painting. Federico's fresco of the *Flagellation of Christ* has the palatial setting of mid-century court painting, and follows 'Maniera' conventions by placing the main action in the middle ground, yet the central figures have been reduced to an almost iconic simplicity, and they are set against a brooding darkness. Other painters working in Rome at the time who absorbed something of Zuccaro's reform but never abandoned a courtly complexity of composition or artificiality of pose were Giovanni de' Vecchi (1536–1615) and Niccolò Circignani (1530/5–96), both of whom made important contributions to Jesuit painting cycles. De' Vecchi brought more warmth of colour and feeling to his painting, and Circignani, by contrast, moved toward cool abstraction, so that the gruesome scenes of martyrdom for which he is most famous (see chapter 4) are almost entirely lacking in emotion.

The third principal style in sacred painting is that of Girolamo Muziano (1532–92), a Brescian trained in Padua who was active in Rome from 1549, and who, like Siciolante and the Zuccari, revived the sombre directness of Sebastiano.[109] Muziano and Sebastiano shared northern origins, and Muziano was outside the 'Maniera' tradition of Central Italy. One significant ingredient in Muziano's style was the painting of Venice, especially Titian, and his work is often dominated by expansive landscapes with a Venetian-inspired atmospheric use of light. His fame as a landscape painter was sealed in 1570, when Cornelis Cort published a series of engravings of Muziano's paintings of penitent saints set in landscapes.[110] While working on a commission at the cathedral in Orvieto in the late 1560s, Muziano developed a kind of large altarpiece that would become standard with many of his contemporaries and that was one of the most successful artistic responses to the climate of spiritual reform. Characteristic were large, solid figures with normal proportions and natural poses, direct gestures that avoided theatricality, and a restrained emotion frequently tinted by melancholy, as in his *Raising of Lazarus* (1555) for the Duomo at Orvieto (fig. 6).[111] This Muziano canon, which set the figures against a background of simple classicizing architecture and an atmospheric landscape hinting at Venetian painting, was recently formulated by Hall: 'Christ appears standing at the center, surrounded by attentive onlookers. The setting is usually provided by some classical columns, a landscape perhaps dotted with a few ruins, and an interesting but not distracting sky. With a modest but dignified gesture Christ heals the cripple or the man born blind, or consigns the keys to the kneeling Peter ... As he conceived it, it emphasized the simplicity and humanity of the apostles and of Christ, recalling the spiritual vocation of the papacy rather than its claim to temporal power.'[112] The Muziano canon would inspire a new generation of painters, beginning with Cesare Nebbia, who in addition to his partnership with Federico Zuccaro worked with Muziano at Orvieto and went on to become one of the most popular painters of Sixtus V's Rome, and including other Northern Italians such as Marcello Venusti (1512/15–79) and Giovanni Battista Ricci (1545–1620). Muziano would paint the high altar of the Gesù, the most important picture in the church (see chapters 6 and 7).

The tendency toward increased solemnity, darker tones, an appeal to the emotions, and stable, centralized compositions continued through the decades during which the Jesuits commissioned their painting cycles in Rome. In addition to the three trends in Roman painting just mentioned, two major developments from outside Rome had an impact on painters who worked for the Jesuits. In the 1570s,

Santi di Tito led a group of painters, whom Freedberg has called 'the Florentine reformers,' in a more consistent return to Raphael's clarity and directness of communication and especially in a quest for descriptive naturalism.[113] Exposed in his twenties to the styles of Siciolante and Taddeo Zuccaro during a commission in Rome, Santi brought their reform back to Florence, the capital of courtly 'Maniera.' While his naturalism reaches almost photographic heights, as in his *Vision of St Thomas Aquinas* (1593) (fig. 7) at S. Marco, and his deepened shading betrays his contact with Roman painters, he avoids strong emotions and never abandons the idealism and polish of Bronzino. On the opposite end of the scale was the powerfully emotive style of Federico Barocci from Urbino, who like Santi came to Rome at a crucial time in his early career but worked mainly in his native region.[114] As a fellow *marchegiano*, Barocci befriended Taddeo Zuccaro while in Rome, and shared with him a reformist spirit. Although like the Zuccari he returned to the classical idealism of Raphael, Barocci more specifically revived the affective style of Correggio, as can be seen in his Perugia *Deposition* (1569) (fig. 8). No other painter of the time made such a strong appeal to the viewer's emotions, using a rhetorical mode that proved highly effective in an era when the Church wanted to get back in touch with the people. His paintings often approach sentimentality with their representation of liquid eyes and languid gestures, their bright, shimmering colours – saturated violets, vermilions, pinks, and golds – and their soft light, which the painter combines with elements of intense realism, especially still-life details. His is a very different approach from the solemnity of Sebastiano. Barocci made a decisive impression on later artists – we have seen his warm reception by Filippo Neri and the Oratorians – and scholars recognize him as a pioneer of the affective style that would flourish in the early Baroque.

Barocci was one of the master manipulators of colour of his age. The colour mode he employed, which he borrowed from Correggio (who in turn adopted it from Leonardo), is often called *sfumato* (smoky), a soft evanescence in which the outlines and the volumes of the forms seem to vanish in almost imperceptible shifts from light to dark and before a complex differentiation of often brilliant and artificial colours, especially in the drapery. The effect is like the flickering of the flame on a candle. *Sfumato* was one of three major colour modes, all Florentine in origin, that dominated Roman painting in the later Cinquecento and had a profound impact on Jesuit painting cycles (Venetian colourism, by contrast, had limited effect on Jesuit painting cycles).[115] They include *cangiantismo* (changeable colour) and Raphael's more harmonious, classicizing use of colour, which in his later works changed to a dramatic *chiaroscuro*. *Cangiantismo* is an effect of luminous iridescence achieved in the drapery of the figures by juxtaposing a variety of often brilliant and artificial hues. The name comes from the term *seta cangiante*, or 'shot silk,' a kind of shimmering textile in which the warp is one colour and the weft another, so that the cloth looks one colour from one angle and another from a different angle. Deriving originally from Trecento and early Quattrocento painting in Central Italy, *cangiantismo* was championed most notably by Michelangelo, and in the Cinquecento many artists used it in self-conscious reference to Michelangelo or Florentine courtly style. Raphael's colour mode aims at a harmony of colours that gives the effect of objective reality but is sufficiently idealized (reds balanced by blues, purples by greens) to remain detached. Santi di Tito led one of the most important revivals of Raphael's idealized balance of colours in the later Cinquecento. In his later work Raphael created a more dramatic effect with a heightening of the shading (*chiaroscuro*), as in his *Transfiguration* (1517–20), which uses sudden juxtapositions of light and dark and deeper, more saturated colours, a mode we have seen in the work of Sebastiano. *Chiaroscuro* appealed to viewers by highlighting key areas, figures, or actions of the painting and distinguishing them from the rest of the scene, a technique that increased the drama of the picture and gave the picture a warmth and sense of intimacy.

A final feature of Roman painting of the later Cinquecento worth pointing out here is a new sense of decorum – the idea that different painting styles are appropriate for different locations and functions, whether devotional, dynastic, or didactic.[116] Attention to decorum was first tried out on a grand scale under Pope Sixtus V (1585–90), during an extraordinarily active period in Roman painting, when fresco cycles in S. Maria Maggiore, the Scala Santa, the Lateran Palace, and the Vatican Library were executed with remarkable speed by huge teams under the direction of Giovanni Guerra and Cesare Nebbia. The style of the paintings varied not only between buildings, from the stuccoed opulence of the Lateran to the more sober style of the Vatican, but between paintings, so that the full spectrum of current painting trends was represented. The artists' choice of style and iconography was dictated by the people the paintings were meant to address: in some places it was devotional in emphasis, in others it was dynastic; sometimes it was easy to comprehend, sometimes it was intellectual and complex. Eclecticism was a necessary result of this approach to decoration. As we will see, this sensitivity to audience and occasion had already been anticipated by the Jesuits in the years leading up to Sixtus's reign, and the pope and his cardinals may have been following their lead.

The Directors of the Jesuit Painting Programs

Like most religious orders of the time, the Society of Jesus preferred to use in-house artists for their less showy commissions, not so as to promote a secret 'Jesuit style' but primarily as a cost-cutting measure.[117] However, since the Society was not only new but growing at lightning speed, there were not enough Jesuit artists to go round. Some of the most skilful Italian Jesuit artists, such as Bernardino Bitti (1548–1610) and Giovanni Niccolò (1563–1626), were sent to the overseas missions, and the few who were active in Italy were sent on projects not only all over the peninsula but also to Spain, Portugal, and the North of Europe. Most Jesuit artists were brothers, or *fratelli coadiutori*, men who joined the Society but did not aspire to the priesthood. Usually from working class or artisanal backgrounds and therefore not trained in an academic tradition, Jesuit brothers provided the backbone of the organization, acting as carpenters, masons, and stucco-workers, as well as cooks and gardeners. Among the brother artists active in Rome in the last decades of the Cinquecento were Rutilio Clemente, Giovanni di Benedetti, Giulio Cesare Fioravante, Bernardo Melcetti, and Michele and Gisberto Gisbert, men who never signed their work but whose names are preserved in Jesuit personnel catalogues.

We will meet them all soon. Perhaps we should be grateful that Jesuit artists were in such short supply, since very few Jesuit artists possessed more than a modicum of talent. Instead, the Society was compelled to hire professional artists for most of their projects, the same men who were working for the pope and for Rome's eminent private patrons, and comparably little was done in house. If there had been more Jesuit painters, probably we would not be very interested in looking at Jesuit painting.

The iconographic programs of Jesuit painting projects in Rome were closely monitored, and they were often planned well in advance of the paintings themselves. This supervision was partly to guarantee what the Jesuits called 'noster modus procedendi' (our way of proceeding); elsewhere I have discussed this rather vague term and related it to the Jesuits' notion of what was appropriate for their buildings.[118] More important, the supervision allowed them to maintain a certain thematic unity in their decorative cycles and to calibrate each to the specific audience it was meant to address. It is well known that the Jesuits had tried on several occasions to homogenize the architecture of the Society. In the Second General Congregation of the Society of Jesus in 1565, it was decreed, 'It seems good that the style and plans for any building proposed for construction by Ours should be submitted to Reverend Father General so that ... he may decide what he deems proper in the Lord.'[119] Although none of the more elaborate ideas for standardization materialized, the Jesuits did practise the formality of sending architectural plans to be reviewed in Rome before beginning construction.[120] While there was no similar attempt for the visual arts, designs of painting projects in Rome had to be submitted to a *consulta*, or internal review, before being approved. The two most important Jesuit artists on this board were Giuseppe Valeriano (1542–96) and Giovanni Battista Fiammeri (1550–1617), who themselves drew sketches and occasionally painted for these same commissions.

Neither Valeriano nor Fiammeri ranked among the best painters of their day, but they were both capable professionals and extremely skilled managers. In their zeal to accuse the Jesuits of a monolithic approach to art, art historians have tended to exaggerate the amount of personal intervention undertaken by these consultants. Valeriano in particular has achieved something of a cult status as the embodiment of 'Counter-Reformation' intolerance; Calì has recently called him 'the most authentic interpreter of the Counter-Reformation in the specific sense of the Society.'[121] Both artists were far too busy to have worked on more than a fraction of the paintings commissioned by the Society in Rome. Valeriano was in Spain between 1573 and 1580, later travelled to Bavaria (1591–2), and divided his time in Italy among Rome, Naples, Florence, Recanati, and various other towns where the Jesuits were building churches; he finally died of exhaustion in 1596. Fiammeri travelled just as widely in Italy, most notably during the years 1586–8, when he divided his time between projects in Florence and in Rome. Nevertheless, the presence of both artists was significant, since they were able to monitor the progress of the Roman Jesuit commissions and, more important, to conceive the basic plans and some of the designs of the Roman decorative cycles.

Giuseppe Valeriano is best known as an architect, and as such has been the subject of several studies in the past fifty years.[122] Born in Acquila in 1542, two years after the foundation of the Society of Jesus, Valeriano may have studied with his compatriot the painter Pompeo Cesura, a follower of Michelangelo, and Michelangelo's monumental figural style was an important early influence on the young artist.[123] At the beginning of his career as a professional painter, he worked in 'Maniera' circles, beginning with that of Perino del Vaga (1501–47), and he also had contacts with Salviati and Daniele da Volterra (ca. 1509–66). Through Perino and Daniele he was further imbued with the exaggerated musculature, giant figures, and twisting poses of Michelangelo, and through Salviati he developed a taste for the cold, polished world of Florentine 'Maniera.' Valeriano's first attributable painting is in the church of S. Spirito in Sassia (before 1572), near the Vatican and attached to an important hospital of the same name. Valeriano shared the commission for the interior decoration of this church with Pompeo and Livio Agresti da Forlì (ca. 1508–79), an artist who would prepare the first series of drawings for Nadal's illustrated Gospels.[124] S. Spirito was one of the first churches to be rebuilt after the Sack of Rome, and its decorations, begun in the 1540s, came to include both the courtly 'Maniera' represented by Agresti and the more reformist styles represented by Valeriano.[125] Valeriano was probably hired for the job by Bernardo Cirillo, the *commendatore* of S. Spirito and a fellow *aquilano*.

Valeriano's *Ascension* at S. Spirito (fig. 9) shows a strong tendency toward the vocabulary of Michelangelo – large, blocklike figures (Zeri calls them 'cubist') and twisted poses, though sometimes awkwardly executed.[126] But from the very beginning Valeriano also shows a sympathy for the darker tones and murky, atmospheric landscape of Sebastiano del Piombo, a legacy already noted by the biographer Giovanni Baglione.[127] The Christ figure in the painting follows very closely that of Sebastiano's own *Ascension* at S. Pietro in Montorio, a work Valeriano would certainly have known. More obviously, the painting is a homage to Raphael's *Transfiguration*, the supreme expression of the heightened *chiaroscuro* of his later years. A clarity of symmetry and simplicity in the drapery and setting, as well as the naive, wide-eyed faces of Raphael, made Valeriano's canvas accessible to ordinary people. His painting is also enlivened by a visionary fervour, especially through the weightlessness achieved by his figures despite their volume, and the elongation and abstraction of their forms, particularly the Christ figure. These affective qualities are enhanced by his use of rosy tones and incandescent colours such as the green and blue highlights of some of the garments; he shares with Barocci a consciousness of the power of glowing, shimmering hues. All these features would become more evident in his work for the Jesuits.

Scholars have blamed Valeriano's shortcomings as a painter on his identity as a Jesuit. Noting a separation of forms and a flatness in Valeriano's early work, Calì characteristically equates it with an absence of true religious sentiment: 'We have also seen how the breaking up of forms, which in the late work of Michelangelo was the result of a unique human experience ... in these artists [has] become an exterior pretext that relates to the opposite experience: the progressive loss of the capacity personally to live one's religious feelings and principles.'[128] She concludes that the flaws in Valeriano's style made him the perfect Jesuit painter: 'Small wonder that Valeriano, having moved to Spain, entered the Society of Jesus ... where, in the mystical rationalism of St Ignatius and in the iron rule of the Order, he was able to find the perfect ambience in which to pursue the method, the rigour, and the extremely controlled domination over the senses toward which he was already so clearly headed.'[129] Prejudices such as these, levelled against anyone who had ties with the Jesuits, have given rise to the popular notion of the Society as a kind of infectious disease that destroyed painting on contact. Valeriano is not in the same class as an artist like Barocci. But nor does the provincial quality of his art reflect either a lack of genuine religious sentiment or a monolithic Jesuit orthodoxy.

Valeriano indeed soon joined the Society, not long after he left for Spain around 1572. Although he was mostly occupied with architecture while in Spain and Portugal, where he fell under the influence of the sober style of Juan de Herrera (ca. 1530–97), he painted several pictures of the Madonna, some of which may have been sent to the world missions. At one point Valeriano almost got sent to Asia or the Americas himself, thanks to the efforts of the Italian Jesuit Alessandro Vallareggio, who in a letter to Father General Everard Mercurian (1514–80) added that while Valeriano was waiting in Lisbon for the ship he could paint altarpieces for the missions in Brazil.[130] In 1579, Valeriano was sent on a tour of Jesuit establishments in Spain to report on the state of their architecture, a laborious process that had the architect looking at clogged gutters, warping roofs, and bad masonry. After his return to Italy in 1580, possibly at the instigation of the new Father General, Claudio Acquaviva, Valeriano was also kept busy directing architectural projects, since these were more urgently needed by the rapidly expanding Society than paintings. Pietro Pirri notes how little time he had for painting between 1580 and his death, in Naples, in 1596: 'These [building projects] accumulated ever more each year, and Valeriano was reduced in the end only to making sketches, which other artists would paint.'[131] He was also plagued by ill health, as letters from as early as 1580 and 1581 attest.[132] Nevertheless, Valeriano made the decision to become a priest, in 1582, even though it meant he could work only on painting 'for two or three hours in the morning' while he was studying.[133] Valeriano thus became something of a rarity – a Jesuit artist with the title 'Padre.'[134]

The other artist who helped conceive the first Jesuit painting cycles in Rome, and who lent a hand to several of them, was the Florentine sculptor and painter Giovanni Battista Fiammeri, known during his youthful career as a sculptor as 'Battista di Benedetto.' Often mistaken for Valeriano in the literature, Fiammeri's name has been almost entirely lost to posterity. Milton Lewine even refers to a painter called 'G.B. Valeriano called Il Fiammeri,' and Michael Keine recently has made the same mistake, claiming that Giovanni Battista di Benedetto Fiammeri is not to be mistaken with 'the painter and architect Giovanni Battista Fiammeri (l'Aquila 1530–Roma 1606), later a Jesuit with the name of Giuseppe Valeriano.'[135] Yet Fiammeri was well known in his day. Giorgio Vasari mentions him in his *Lives of the Artists* as one of the more promising young pupils of Bartolommeo Ammannati, whose sculpture is 'in nowise inferior ... to [that of] any other of the young sculptors who are Academicians, whether in genius or judgment.'[136] Baglione also included an entry on this 'lively flame' (*viva fiamma*) in his *Lives of the Painters*, praising him for 'reducing the superfluous from the stone, reducing the form of the bodies to the idea of artifice, conforming to and using measurement,' and adding that 'accompanied by the judgment of his eye, he gives proportion and grace to ornaments and figures; and he was a fine sculptor.'[137]

We know virtually nothing about Fiammeri's parentage, although he seems to have been of Florentine ancestry. He was not the only artist in the family, as Giulio Parigi (1571–1675) appears to have been his cousin, at least by marriage.[138] A painter and architect, Parigi would collaborate with Fiammeri on the Jesuit college of S. Giovannino in Florence in the mid 1580s, and in the early seventeenth century he became well known as a set designer and landscape painter at the Medici court.[139] A certain 'Lisabetta Fiameri,' who was a widow in 1592 and had a daughter of marrying age, may have been Fiammeri's sister-in-law or stepmother, and the artist may also have had a younger brother, since a Lorenzo Fiammeri made his final vows as a Jesuit eight years after Giovanni Battista.[140] Even the Jesuit documents regarding Fiammeri are uncharacteristically inconsistent. His date of birth varies wildly in the catalogues of the Society, but the most likely candidate is 1543 or 1546. Fiammeri was apprenticed at a very young age: he was already present in Ammannati's shop in 1557, when he was in his early teens.[141]

Fiammeri was a member of the Florentine Accademia del Disegno from its very beginning in 1563, and for eight years he played an active role in the Academy, serving in its government as *consol, consigliere, accademico, camarlingo,* and *infermiere.*[142] Upon Michelangelo's death in 1564, Fiammeri executed a colossal artificial marble allegorical statue of the Arno to adorn his funeral bier at S. Lorenzo in Florence, part of an elaborate decorative funerary cycle created by thirty-six junior artists who were selected by the Academy and given the opportunity to test their mettle and gain the title of *accademico.*[143] Fiammeri also assisted Ammannati on his Neptune fountain in the Piazza della Signoria (begun 1575), executed designs with Ammannati for the Villa Medici in Rome in 1576, and was chosen to carve one of the three statues that adorn Vasari's Tomb of Michelangelo at S. Croce, although Ammannati in the end did not consent to the arrangement, stating that 'this said youth [Fiammeri] could be employed in other tasks he was working on, which are also numerous and important.'[144] Although none of this early sculptural work of Fiammeri survives, there are a couple of delightful sketches in sanguine at the Uffizi of projects for fountains, one of which echoes the lower structure of Ammannati's Neptune fountain (fig. 10). Typical products of a young sculptor working in the Ammannati circle, the drawings use shading at the expense of line, and they adopt an elongated form of Michelangelo's body type.[145] Fiammeri left the world of the Florentine Academy behind him between May and August 1575, when he stepped down from his position as *infermiere* to take holy orders, although when he left he paid his dues to the Academy in advance through May 1577.[146]

Fiammeri joined the Society of Jesus on 3 March 1576, entering the Novitiate of S. Andrea al Quirinale in Rome.[147] He was usually resident at the Collegio Romano, except for 1586–8 (and again in 1591), when he was working in Florence on the college of S. Giovannino. Although Fiammeri's true calling was that of a sculptor, he turned almost exclusively to painting after entering the Society, since the Jesuits needed this less expensive medium to cover their ever-expanding wall space. The catalogues list him variously as a 'quite talented painter' and a 'painter and sculptor of statues,' and in one case as being 'skilled at painting and engraving images.'[148] Baglione remarks that he painted 'many things' for the Jesuits after joining the Society, and 'was especially praiseworthy in making *cartelle* with various sorts of shading and with various caprices, and beautiful eccentricities, as indeed one can see throughout the college, and in the House of the Gesù, and in other places of that Society.'[149]

At the Florence college Fiammeri once again worked with his old *maestro*, Ammannati – there seem to have been no hard feelings about Ammannati's decision to remove him from the Michelangelo tomb project – and probably painted the panels depicting the Passion above the entablature of the nave, although not the false marble statues of the apostles traditionally attributed to him, which are eighteenth-century works by Giuseppe Cateni.[150] Ammannati, who had become very close to the Society of Jesus, was not only the architect of the building (begun 1579) but the donor, and he designated the altar of St Bartholomew as the location of his own tomb.[151] As would be the case at the Roman Gesù, the side chapels were paid for by well-to-do local families, who in the early 1590s hired professional artists, many of them part of the Florentine reform movement and followers of Santi di Tito, to execute the altarpieces and lateral frescoes. These men included some of the finest painters of Florence, such as Alessandro Allori (1535–1607), Il Passignano (ca. 1558–1638), Jacopo Ligozzi (1547–1627), Michele Tosini (1503–77), Bernardino Poccetti (1548–1612), and Francesco Curradi (1570–1661), as well as the Venetian Francesco Bassano (1549–92), who would also paint an altarpiece for the Gesù (see chapters 6 and 7).[152] The church interior had been finished in the early 1580s, with the last work of the stucco workers and carpenters dating from 1584.[153]

The rest of the decorations, begun earlier, in 1586, were largely the work of Jesuit artists, including – in addition to Fiammeri – the Perugian painter Rutilio Clemente, the Perugian sculptor Bartolommeo Tronchi, and various stucco workers and carpenters who also worked on the Jesuits' Roman projects.[154] Although there is no mention of it in past scholarship, Giuseppe Valeriano also briefly assisted with the paintings in S. Giovannino, for an intense period between November 1586 and early January 1587, and again in August and September 1588.[155] Ammannati seems to have taken a personal interest as early as 1582 in the subjects of the 'historie' that would be painted in the new church, but in a letter to the architect Acquaviva asked him to devote his attention to finishing the church instead.[156] Fiammeri is first mentioned as working on the church in October 1586, when he purchased pigments for the paintings.[157] Contrary to the understanding we have been given in the scholarship, Fiammeri did not stay in Florence the whole time but made a number of trips back to Rome, among them trips in February 1586 and April–May 1587, as well as another in late 1591, probably after he had moved there again permanently.[158] In his correspondence with Ammannati, Father General Claudio Acquaviva made it clear that he was eager to have the talented artist brother back in Rome, thereby demonstrating a great respect for Fiammeri.[159]

Fiammeri pronounced his final vows in the Casa Professa of the Gesù, during one of his brief sojourns in Rome while working on the Florence college, on 15 August 1587.[160] Although biographers and art historians tend to refer to him as 'Padre Fiammeri,' in fact he was never ordained, being a more traditional *fratello coadiutore* (the same is true of the late seventeenth-century painter Andrea Pozzo, who is still regularly – and incorrectly – referred to as 'Padre Pozzo'). In the later years of his life the Jesuits kept Fiammeri busy with diverse design projects, as Baglione tells us: 'And always for the Society he was working now on one thing and then on another, because he was skilled in everything to do with the profession of *disegno*.'[161] Fiammeri died on 23 August 1617 in Rome, three years before Lorenzo Fiammeri, who died at Viterbo.[162]

We can get an idea of Fiammeri's style not only from the paintings, which I will consider in chapters 4 and 7, but from his numerous drawings, which survive at the Uffizi, at Windsor Castle, and at the Louvre (fig. 11).[163] Fiammeri never abandoned his affinity with the sculptural figure type of Michelangelo, although his religious drawings have a dark sobriety typical of the reformist trends in painting at the time and in sharp contrast to the lively secular drawings from his Florentine period. Fiammeri's forms are still very three-dimensional, and he goes in for a heavy kind of drapery. He avoids outlining wherever possible, setting his figures instead against a background of shading or crosshatching. His treatment of faces is particuarly characteristic, with the bright, wide eyes favoured by Raphael, here bulging slightly, and thin, arched eyebrows that meet the curve of the nose. His noses are thin and aquiline, and he has a tendency toward small and pouty mouths.[164]

Fiammeri's most important contributions to the art of the late Cinquecento were his sketches for Nadal's *Evangelicae historiae imagines* of 1593 (figs 12, 13). The first series of preparatory drawings for Nadal's volume, by Livio Agresti, were circulated among Jesuit institutions in Rome as early as the 1550s or 1560s, but it was the second series, radically reworked by Fiammeri between about 1579 and 1582, that would have such a notable impact on the painting cycles of the Society. Although the images were made print-ready by Bernardino Passeri and Marten de Vos in the later eighties, these artists made only very minor changes to Fiammeri's creations. Maj-Brit Wadell recently attributed a group of preparatory drawings for the series in Windsor Castle to Fiammeri, proposing that they were the original series of sketches.[165] Fiammeri's restructuring of Agresti's images gave them a more vertical composition, a greater sense of unity, and the grand stagelike settings for which they are famous.[166] These drawings, to which I will return often, enjoyed an active dialogue with the first Jesuit painting cycles in Rome, influencing them in composition and figure and perhaps being influenced by them in the use of key letters.[167]

Whether or not the Florentine Fiammeri had anything to do with it, many of the key painters who worked for the Jesuits in Rome were Tuscans, and that 'nation' would make a crucial mark on the appearance of Jesuit painting. Niccolò Circignani, Agostino Ciampelli, and Andrea Commodi worked on multiple buildings, and Giovanni de' Vecchi, Ventura Salimbeni, Antiveduto Grammatica, Antonio Tempesta, Matteo da Siena, and others worked on single commissions. This preponderance of Tuscan painters was not limited to the Jesuits, and has recently been recognized as a phenomenon in Roman painting in the last decades of the Cinquecento, especially under Pope Clement VIII (1592–1605) and particularly among the religious orders.[168] Yet, typically of this eclectic period, the dominance of the Tuscan 'nation' in Rome did not guarantee stylistic unity, for the Jesuits or anyone else.

Another thing several of the artists who worked for the Jesuits had in common was membership in the Accademia di San Luca, the Roman art academy re-founded by Federico Zuccaro in 1593, which met every year and tried to set new standards for painting. Based on the Florentine Accademia del Disegno, which had been founded by Vasari in 1563 in imitation of humanist academies, the Academy hoped to foster intellectualizing and theorizing about art. Although the short-lived Academy had no palpable effect on artistic practice, and even failed, as Mahon has shown, to present a unified theory of art, its first years were active and zealous.[169]

The minutes of the earliest meetings were published in 1604 by Romano Alberti in his *Origine, et progresso dell'Accademia del Dissegno de' pittori, scultori, e architetti di Roma*. Aside from Zuccaro himself, the academicians who attended the first meetings in the 1590s and also worked for the Jesuits included Giovanni de' Vecchi, Durante Alberti, Cristofano Roncalli, Flaminio Vacca, the Cavaliere d'Arpino, Agostino Ciampelli, and the architect Giacomo della Porta; and Niccolò Circignani was scheduled to lecture there in 1594.[170] Durante Alberti, who painted several key altarpieces for the Jesuits beginning in the early 1580s, brought the Academy and the Society of Jesus even closer when, in 1598, he invited a Jesuit 'father' to speak at the Academy's fifth annual meeting.[171] This Jesuit, whose name does not come down to us but who may have been Fiammeri (most people were ignorant of the distinction between brothers and fathers), uttered a few platitudes essentially parroting the decree on painting of the last session of the Council of Trent. The Jesuit guest lecturer advised the *fratelli* of the Accademia 'to be careful to paint honest things, and on that matter he turned to a letter about a certain *Cleopatra*, who was shown as depicted with little honesty, and in criticizing it he gave many reasons, and warnings, which were a very pleasing thing. From this, he gave the hope that he would do something. But in resolution this was as much as he did, and the rest of the year went by without any other thing of notice.'[172] This appearance by the Jesuit guest speaker demonstrates two things. It shows, first, that as late as the 1590s artists were still paying lip service to the Tridentine decrees on art, but that, although these rules heightened artists' and patrons' awareness of key issues and iconographic problems, they were never brought to the practical level and could have only the most limited effect on the practice of art. It shows, second, that the artists of the Academy – and by extension those working for the Jesuits – were making a heartfelt attempt to arrive at a new kind of devotional art, one that could answer the needs of the reformed Catholic church. Since the reform of Catholic art did not occur in the realm of theory, let us look in the coming chapters at how it played out in practice.

2

The Novitiate of S. Andrea al Quirinale

The Jesuit Novitiate of S. Andrea al Quirinale in Rome is famous around the world as the site of one of Gianlorenzo Bernini's greatest architectural legacies, a chapel (built 1658–70) that is one of the premier monuments of the Roman Baroque. The principal training centre for the entire Jesuit order and the last resting place of St Stanislas Kostka, one of the most popular saints of the Catholic reform era, the Novitiate on the Quirinal Hill was a focus of intense patronage by the Jesuits and their supporters in the seventeenth century and later. Yet the church and its outbuildings were there long before the renovations in which Bernini participated, and in the later sixteenth century they were the site of another remarkable artistic phenomenon, one that itself would exert a powerful influence on artistic projects in the city. Unlike their Baroque successors, the earliest buildings at S. Andrea made their mark in the realm not of architecture but of painting.

Unfortunately, the painting cycle at S. Andrea is not only the most fascinating and original ever produced by the Jesuits but also one of the least well preserved. Not a single painting from the pre-1610 campaign survives, and only a handful of those are reproduced in engravings – and very poor quality ones at that. We are left guessing about how these works really looked, and especially about the role of colour – a crucial element that church theorists such as Gabriele Paleotti believed afforded one of the most potent means of arousing sensual delight in the viewer.[1] This chapter can therefore offer the reader only an imaginary tour of these remarkable paintings. Nevertheless, archival records and printed books allow us to reconstruct the location and iconography of virtually every painting with remarkable detail, and the descriptions that survive are so vivid and comprehensive that they can transport us into the past. The complex, as it appeared in 1610, is illustrated in figure 14. At the top of the picture, facing onto present-day Via di Quirinale (behind the buildings), were the main Novitiate structures, including the church of S. Andrea (A) and the residential wing (B, C). The Novitiate, centred around an interior courtyard, included a dormitory, refectory, lavatory, recreation room, and infirmary, all of which contained painted decorative cycles. The only part of the original Novitiate complex to survive today are some interior rooms indicated by the letters B and C, which were lovingly preserved inside the present structure as the death rooms of St Stanislas. Behind the main Novitiate complex was a formal garden with a fountain (D) that received water from the Acqua Felice down the road, and, below that, two more levels of garden, including the herb garden and another formal garden, now taken up by the Palazzo delle Esposizioni. At the bottom right, fronting present-day Via Nazionale, is the early Christian church of S. Vitale, given to the Jesuit Novitiate in the 1590s and discussed separately in chapter 5.

S. Andrea was one of the earliest Jesuit painting commissions in Rome to be undertaken, yet one of the last to be finished. The decorations were carried out in many stages, beginning possibly as early as the 1560s and certainly by the early 1570s, with piecemeal additions in the 1580s, and, finally, an extensive painting campaign between about 1597 and 1610. This once comprehensive series of frescoes, canvases, and relief panels was specifically programmed for the use of the Jesuit novices. Although most scholars are familiar with the martyrdom paintings that adorned the recreation room, there has been little mention of the panoply of painting cycles that originally adorned the interior of the entire complex. A combination of biblical scenes, stories from the lives of the saints, images of Jesuit heroism past and present, tales of antiquity, allegories, geographical vistas, and visual pharmacopia, this tightly controlled and interrelated series was calibrated to allow the novices to meditate on their vocation and prepare for their work as professed Jesuits. It gave them hope in times of doubt, warned them against transgressions, instructed them concerning their duties, provided recreation for their weary eyes, comforted or cured them when sick, and provided a visual punctuation of their day. More significantly, it was closely tied to the themes and sequence of Ignatius of Loyola's *Spiritual Exercises*, with its emphasis on self-examination, personal choice, and step-by-step pilgrimage toward union with God. Martyrdom was another crucial theme found in these cycles, one intimately related to mission work and to interest in the revival of the early Church. Martyrological imagery was first tested out in the Jesuit collegiate chapels, where such imagery was developed in the early 1580s, probably about a decade earlier than that at the Novitiate (see chapters 4 and 5).

These complex and original paintings were also characterized by a particularly Jesuit emphasis on geography, which we will see also in other Jesuit painting cycles in Rome. Through their depiction of exotic landscapes and flora and fauna, they brought the lands of the Jesuit missions and the biblical and Ptolomaic past into the living quarters of the young novices, many of whom were preparing to venture to somewhere else in Europe or to the Indies. Although the depiction of mission territories was entirely new, the Jesuits were not the first to promote the mystical journey or pilgrimage by means of paintings or other art works. The Observant Franciscans in particular promoted the interior pilgrimage as a devotion, beginning in Italy in the later fifteenth century, by constructing replicas of the pilgrimage sites of the Holy Land for those who could not make the journey to the Levant. Since the Franciscans were the guardians of the pilgrimage sites in Jerusalem, they were zealous in bringing the dramatic potential of the sites to viewers in Italy. The first replica of the Holy Land in Italy was the famous Sacro Monte (Sacred Mountain) at Varallo in Piedmont, founded in 1491, a three-dimensional re-creation of scenes of the Passion and the pilgrimage sites of Jerusalem in sculpture and painting set in chapels in a parklike setting.[2] These dioramas were meant to be experienced sequentially, beginning with the church of S. Maria delle Grazie below and progressing to each of the stations on the hill – a step-by-step presentation very close to that of the Jesuits' first painting cycles in Rome.

The Sacro Monte's affinity with Jesuit cycles is even closer than first appears. Alessandro Nova has identified a guidebook to the Sacro Monte from 1514, based on sermons delivered by Observant friars and liberally scattered with quotations from Pseudo-Bonaventure's *Meditationes*, which contains prototypes of the Ignatian 'composition of place.'[3] Nova shows that the friars carefully manipulated the experience of the visitor in a manner that would stimulate his or her imagination, and then exhorted the visitor to participate in the scenes. This Franciscan emphasis on the affective capabilities of art – and the sculptures at Varallo are emphatically affective, with their realistic hair and eyes, and dramatic poses and expressions – has been traced by scholars far beyond the Tridentine era to the time of Francis of Assisi and to the emergence of realistic tendencies in early Renaissance painting.[4] Particularly fascinating for the Jesuit context is the section in the 1514 tract that makes it clear visitors were meant to visit the church first and purge themselves of past sins before embarking on the mystical journey – precisely the method followed by someone making the Exercises, in which the First Week focuses on penitence and confession of the sins of one's past life, and is followed by a mystical pilgrimage through the events of Christ's life.

Randi Klebanoff recently has shown that the era of the Sacro Monte marked a change from the medieval culture of relics and pilgrimage: the goal was no longer the attainment of the sacred from a holy object but a mystical or interior pilgrimage, a kind of armchair travel: 'The activation of the sacred was embodied in the process of the experience and interiorization of the sacred narrative.'[5] *Sacri monti* began to proliferate, especially in Northern Italy, where Carlo Borromeo and his collaborators promoted the genre. The sites occasionally took different forms, such as that of the Sette Chiese in Monselice (near Padua), built under the supervision of Vincenzo Scamozzi (1552–1616) for Pietro Duodo after 1605, in which the seven basilicas in Rome are re-created in miniature on a hill, complete with paintings of the patron saints by Jacopo Palma il Giovane (1544–1628).[6] It is no coincidence that the Franciscans and the Jesuits shared an interest in geography. In addition to their patronage of the Holy Land sites, the Franciscans were the Jesuits' main rival in the overseas mission field, and the first Jesuit missionaries in Asia and the Americas owed a great deal to Franciscan methods.[7]

The Foundation and Construction of the Novitiate

S. Andrea, also known as S. Andrea a Monte Cavallo and S. Andrea de Caballo, was the first permanent novitiate for the Roman province of the Jesuits, and it took its name from a small church on the site that had been assigned to the Society of Jesus by Monsignor Giovanni Andrea Croce, bishop of Tivoli, on 20 May 1565.[8] The site was not arbitrary. Although in one of the least densely populated quarters of Rome, Monte Cavallo (the Quirinal Hill) was where the most important aristocratic families of Rome had their *vigne* and gardens, and the Jesuits were therefore quite literally in a position to exert influence over them.[9] These dignitaries included some of the most powerful churchmen of Rome, as well as the pope himself, who had his summer residence in the nearby Palazzo del Quirinale (now the presidential palace) from 1592. The original church of S. Andrea is mentioned as early as the eleventh century, but it was never very important and at times did not even have a resident priest.[10] By 1561 it was being described as 'desolate and deserted.'[11] The Jesuits' taking over of S. Andrea fit a pattern we will see in many of their Roman foundations: they would acquire a decrepit church in a good neighbourhood and restore it or rebuild it from the ground up, usually with funds provided by a generous private donor, and thereby insert themselves at minimal expense into a strategic neighbourhood of the city. Thomas Lucas has recently remarked on this intimate relationship between the Society and the city: 'Ignatius was the first founder of a major religious order in the history of the Church to locate his headquarters in Rome and the first to opt deliberately for complete insertion of a religious order's works and residences in the center of the urban fabric.'[12] The Novitiate of S. Andrea was endowed on 30 November 1566 by a Neapolitan noblewoman with strong Spanish connections, Duchess Giovanna d'Aragona Colonna (ca. 1500–77), who gave her land, a portion of her house, and an endowment of 6,000 scudi (1,000 of it in jewels) to the fledgling Society.[13] Giovanna was celebrated in her day as the mother of Marc'Antonio Colonna, the victor at the Battle of Lepanto of 1571.

At the Second General Congregation in 1563, with Father General Francis Borgia presiding, the Society of Jesus decided to house novices in a separate building during their initial two-year training. Correspondingly, it was decreed that it would 'be expedient to establish in each province a house of probation, either one connected with a college but in a distinct building or an entirely separate one.'[14] Although the training program for novices was standardized only in 1608 under Claudio Acquaviva, after the Novitiate painting cycles had been completed, it likely codified existing practice. The regimen involved two initial years of residence at the Novitiate, seven years of philosophy and theology at the Collegio Romano, and a third and final year at the Novitiate under the close supervision of the novice master.[15] The Roman Novitiate came under the responsibility of the Casa Professa (Professed House, or principal Jesuit residence, next to the Church of the Gesù) and was governed by a master of novices.

Most of what we know about the original decorations of the Roman Novitiate comes from manuscript histories in the Jesuit Roman archives, beginning with Ottavio Navarola's *Memorie della Casa di S. Andrea a Monte Cavallo della Compagnia di Gesù* (ca. 1609), which was revised by Alessandro Sisti (?) and entitled *Notizie istoriche appartenenti alle Cappellette di S. Stanislao Kostka* (1733) and is a historical guide to the death rooms and shrine of St Stanislas Kostka.[16] These descriptions are exceptionally detailed, the later ones even including step-by-step plans and elevations, because exact knowledge of the appearance of the original residence was an essential part of the cult of St Stanislas, and Jesuit historians demonstrated a concern for accuracy that verged on obsession.

The Jesuits began by building a larger but economical new church between 1567 and 1569, in such a way that 'a part of the wall of the old [church] served for the new church, and on the other side served a wall of the Duchess's palace' (fig. 15).[17]

The work was carried out under the direction of Giovanni Tristano (active 1558–75), the Society of Jesus' most prominent architect in its first quarter century.[18] The 'narrow and damp' church had three full altars and, after 1605, a gilt stucco altar over the tomb of Blessed (now St) Stanislas Kostka, and it was built very quickly, a matter of 'pochi giorni.'[19] According to existing plans and a manuscript description by Giovanni Antonio Brutio (ca. 1667), the church had a single nave, with the main altar in an apsidal tribune separated from the nave by four piers or columns, the two side altars on the flanking walls, and the tomb also on the right wall. Brutio describes the church as

> not very large ... and completely roofed in wood with coffering ... with various angels, and in the middle the arms of the Society. The high altar is under a vault that is completely stuccoed, gilt, and painted. There is the painting representing the crucifixion of St Andrew the Apostle, by the very famous Durante Alberti ... The said painting is framed with two wooden columns in the Ionic order, with a gilt open pediment. To either side of the altar are ... two [altars?] that are like two side chapels ... with the altar of the Most Holy Trinity ... framed with a similar ornament of two wooden columns of the Corinthian order. [Across from] this altar, and having the same proportions, is another chapel, of the Adoration of the Holy Magi, with its similar frame ... a painting by Durante Alberti ... Close to ... the main altar is the altar of Blessed Caetano [*sic*: he means Stanislas], under which his body rests, and which has a painting with his portrait and the apparition of the Most Blessed Virgin and a beautiful frame of gilt wood, and is enclosed by two balustrades. Over the main entrance at the foot of the church is the choir, made of wood, for the musicians.[20]

According to a 1593 aerial view in the *Pianta di Roma* by Antonio Tempesta, the facade was very similar in basic structure to Tristano's own facade at SS. Annunziata al Collegio Romano (completed 1567), as well as to the facade of the Roman church of S. Antonio Abbate (1572–5), both of which are now lost.[21] A tripartite facade of two storeys of superimposed pilasters crowned entirely by a triangular pediment, the facade featured niches in the side bays, and a circular oculus above, framed by strapwork, the so-called Serlian motif. The church of S. Andrea presented a suitably simple, classical spectacle to the passerby on the street.

In early 1569 the high altar, presumably with at least a provisional painting depicting St Andrew already in place, was solemnly consecrated and bestowed with relics by the archbishop of Taranto, who was a Colonna, at a ceremony also attended by his kinswoman, the duchess.[22] The high altar contained relics of the apostles St Peter and St Andrew, as well as of St Blaise, St Mauritius, the 11,000 Virgins, and other saints.[23] The history of S. Andrea notes that the church became much frequented by the nobility, who heard mass there especially in the summer and autumn, when the noble *vigne* that dotted the Quirinal Hill were inhabited by people trying to escape the unhealthy summer heat.

In 1569, under Francis Borgia, construction began on some of the Novitiate buildings, and the Jesuits would continue to enlarge them almost without a break until 1622, thanks to the growing number of novices needing accommodation. By the seventeenth century the building housed some hundred novices.[24] This initial expansion was aided by a gift, in the spring of 1569, of an additional 1,000 scudi by Dr Francesco della Torre.[25] First they built a two-storey building behind the old and new churches, where by the first decade of the seventeenth century there was a chapel for those making the Exercises. The lower floor included a room where family and friends could meet and talk with the novices, and the upper floor had various rooms, including the recreation room, where the novices would gather together, and the dormitory, all of which cost 500 scudi to erect, between January and June.[26] A building next to the old church was transformed into the refectory and kitchen. The choir mentioned in Brutio's description was built over the front door of the new church with a balustrade and shutters, and was reached by a corridor built over the old church on the right side and along the back, to connect with the dormitory.

Between 1570 and 1574 the old church was deconsecrated and converted into a two-storey building, with the dispensary below and the second storey as additional space for the dormitory, at a cost of more than 700 scudi. Over the sacristy behind the new church was a dormitory annex that was so poorly lit it earned the nickname 'le catacumbe.'[27] The entire complex was built by the novices themselves, under the guidance of one *maestro* and a youth (*garzone fratello*) who was probably a Jesuit temporal coadjutor.[28] At the same time a new refectory, lavatory (a place for washing the hands before eating, not the location of the toilets), and kitchen were added at the back of the residence complex, the end farthest from the street, as well as six rooms near the dormitory.[29]

The next major expansion of the Novitiate began under Father General Claudio Acquaviva, who made the renovation of the complex one of his first publicly stated goals following his election in 1580.[30] This renovation may have been assisted by a 1577 gift of an additional 1,150 scudi by Cardinal Alessandro Farnese, the patron of the Church of the Gesù (see chapters 6 and 7).[31] Between 1581 and 1587, Acquaviva charged the rector, Marcello Pallavicino, with applying 3,000 scudi to an annex to the Novitiate buildings, which included a three-storey wing behind the old church over the wine cellar known later as the Stanze de' Prelati.[32] On the ground floor were a portico and a passage leading to the garden at the back, and three rooms at the front; the middle floor was taken up by a grand *salone*; and the top floor had a large hall with a vaulted ceiling that served as the granary, as well as two other rooms.[33] The late 1580s were taken up with renovating the recently purchased garden, which was furnished with new walls, a surrounding pergola with a brick colonnade on one side, a gardener's cottage, a stairway, and a fountain fed by a pipe donated by Sixtus V that led from the nearby Acqua Felice.[34] Between 1592 and 1596 construction work was supervised by another Jesuit architect, Giuseppe Valeriano, who ran into trouble with the Capuchin nuns on the Quirinal Hill because they were afraid the new buildings would be so tall that the Jesuits could see into their convent.[35] It took papal intervention from Clement VIII to allow Valeriano to proceed with the construction of the Novitiate.

Under the new rector, Niccolò Della Fonte, in 1594 Valeriano converted the upper two storeys of Pallavicino's wing into the infirmary, a complex of 15, 17, or 18 rooms in the north wing of the Novitiate, with 9 rooms upstairs (plus a tiny *stanzino* of unspecified use near the stairs) and 9 plus a convalescent refectory downstairs (fig. 16).[36] Each floor was divided in the middle by a corridor, with half the rooms facing north and half facing south, and each room was capable of accommodating four or five people.[37] Della Fonte's principal legacy, however, was a new wing extending outward from the old Novitiate building at the back toward the wall of the Bandini property to the east, and containing a corridor to lead to the garden, the refectory itself, a lavatory and kitchen with running water, and a dispensary on the lower floor; and several rooms, halls, and corridors above. The refectory was large enough to hold more than a hundred people, and the lavatory acted as a vestibule for it.[38] Except for the infirmary, most of this construction was already finished by 1593, a few months after Valeriano had moved to Naples, and the total cost came to just over 9,727 scudi.[39] In 1605 this new wing was joined to the 1580s wing and Della Fonte's infirmary to create a courtyard at a cost of just over 3,282 scudi with the financial assistance of Francesco Maria Ciarpi.[40] First, an additional wing of four storeys of three rooms each was extended from north to south, and then the two corridors of the infirmary building were lengthened to meet it, an extension that added two more rooms on each of its floors. The construction undertaken in these years may also have been assisted by a princely gift from King Philip II of Spain, who donated 12,000 scudi to the Novitiate in five annual instalments.[41]

The Chronology and Authorship of the Novitiate Decorations

There is little information in the archival sources about the myriad paintings and stuccoes that once adorned the rooms of the Novitiate. The first paintings mentioned were executed in the chapel choir in 1570 and 1571.[42] References in the account books of S. Andrea show that money was spent on painting supplies as early as 1569, and especially between October and December 1574.[43] One payment makes specific reference to a painting of Jesus, perhaps the *Adoration of the Magi* in the main chapel. The first phase of the decoration of the Novitiate buildings may have ended before 1581, when Pope Gregory XIII made an official visit to the newly renovated rooms with an entourage of cardinals – although he seems to have been more interested in the living 'servants of God' than the painted ones.[44] The Acquaviva campaign began with a second phase of painting in 1582–3 and especially 1593–4, according to payments for pigments, gesso, gold leaf, and designs for window and door decorations listed in the account books, and it eventually extended over most of the new construction.[45] The recreation room paintings must have been among the last to be finished, since they included scenes of martyrdoms from as late as 1606, but it is very likely they were begun in the later 1580s. These paintings seem not to have formed a single campaign, since the recreation room served as a sort of trophy case for Jesuit martyrs, and new paintings may have been added as new martyrs joined their ranks. The final campaign of painting at the Novitiate probably coincided with the acquisition in 1595 of the early Christian basilica of S. Vitale (see chapter 5), a church that abutted the Novitiate at the bottom of the garden and was itself extensively painted in 1597–9.

Since the Novitiate was built by Jesuit brothers and there are very few references in the accounts to payments to artists, it is most likely that artists from within the order planned and executed most of its painting and stucco cycles. Those mentioned by name as having worked on the S. Andrea complex include Rutilio Clemente and Michele and Gisberto Gisbert. The *perugino* Rutilio Clemente (1558–1643) had the kind of peripatetic career typical of the early artists of the Society, in that he divided his time among several of the Jesuit complexes, in Rome, Florence, and Perugia.[46] He entered the order at S. Andrea in 1579, moved to the Collegio Romano in 1584, worked with Giovanni Battista Fiammeri on S. Giovannino in Florence in 1586–8, and then returned to Rome to reside at the Collegio Germanico in 1590.[47] Except for a brief sojourn at the Jesuit house in nearby Tivoli in 1595, Clemente was back at S. Andrea during Valeriano's renovations in 1594–7, and again in 1599–1600, after a stay at the Collegio Romano. Between December 1593 and April 1594 he purchased painting supplies to decorate Valeriano's additions to the Novitiate, and, as we will see in chapter 5, he assisted in the decoration of the Novitiate's new church of S. Vitale between 1597 and 1599.[48] Clemente left for Perugia in 1606 and returned to Rome only years later, and died there in 1643. Among his better-known works were the tribune arch in the Gesù in Perugia with the scene *Christ in Benediction among Angels*, and two tondos in *chiaroscuro*, *Joseph's Dream* and the *Adoration of the Child*.[49] He is also responsible for much of the interior decoration of the Jesuit church at Tivoli, which was finished in 1599 and praised by Acquaviva in a letter.[50] Although primarily a painter, Clemente was listed in the Jesuit catalogues as a sculptor, *stuccatore*, architect, and gilder as well; the list demonstrates that the early Jesuit artists were often required to be jacks of all trades.[51]

The only reference to an artist working on a specific part of the complex is found in a passage in which Navarola describes the devotion of the Flemish Jesuit painter Michele Gisbert, in another example of the common Jesuit topos whereby a conversion is enacted through imagery.[52] According to this source Gisbert was raised to have anti-Jesuit sentiments, and these were fostered by his friends in Antwerp, who spoke maliciously about an order dominated by a spirit of melancholy and anguish. But Gisbert undertook an art commission at the Novitiate in 1604, and while painting the decorations of the recreation room had a life-altering experience: 'It pleased the Lord that this man happened to be here in this house having occasion to paint some things from the life of Our Blessed Father [Ignatius] and other blessed and martyrs of the Society and to adorn with these the hall of the Novitiate, which was done at considerable expense. Where, being occupied for some months, and paying perhaps special attention to how things went on [in the Novitiate], he found everything to be the opposite to what he had imagined it to be ... and [saw] in particular that the novices were always so happy.'[53] The Jesuit archives provide little information about this elusive painter apart from this pious tale. We know that he was born in 1584 and that he joined the order with his older brother Gisberto, who was born in 1576 and may also have been an artist. Michele left the Novitiate in 1606, was living at Ancona in 1610 and 1622, and died in Tivoli in 1623.[54] The only other known artistic commission by Gisbert is at the Gesù in Perugia, where in 1620 he collaborated on an unidentified altarpiece with the Jesuit sculptor Francesco Brunelli (ca. 1572–1635).[55] Pio Pecchiai also maintains that the Gisberts are the anonymous Flemish brothers credited by Celio with painting the fresco over the main portal of the Roman Gesù (see chapter 6).[56]

Other Jesuit painter brothers also probably lent a hand with the Novitiate decorations, especially those who were in residence while the renovations were going on. They included men who would contribute to later Jesuit art projects in Rome and around the world. Chief among them was Fiammeri, who lived at the Novitiate in 1576 and is known much later (1597–9) to have painted the interior of S. Vitale (see chapter 5). Fiammeri frequently collaborated with Clemente, as at S. Vitale and S. Giovannino in Florence. As we will see in chapter 3, many of the images in the Novitiate infirmary were stucco panels, a technique in which Fiammeri specialized. An early resident of S. Andrea who may have worked on the original chapel decorations was the famed painter Democrito Bernardino Bitti from Camerino, later the founder of the colonial school of painting in Peru, who lived at the Novitiate between 1568 and 1573.[57] The first Jesuit painter to go to the missions, Bitti arrived in Lima in 1574 and was extraordinarily active in Peru until his death in 1610.[58] He had studied painting since the age of about 15, and had had five or six years of formal training before entering the Society, after which he painted occasionally for European patrons.[59] His contemporaries praised his 'great talent in his role as painter,' which served the Jesuits well in Lima, Cuzco, Arequipa, and elsewhere in the Viceroyalty of Peru.[60]

Other young artists living at the Novitiate in the early years included the 29-year-old Swedish sculptor Jan Redellux from Uppsala and the Bolognese painter Giovanni di Benedetti, both of whom were in residence in 1579, as well as Giulio Cesare Fioravante or Francischetti, a 23-year-old from Perugia, and the 20-year-old Bernardo Melcetti or Miletti from Faenza, who entered the Novitiate in 1586.[61] Two other Jesuit artists in Rome in the 1570s and 1580s combined their artistic skills with those of a pharmacologist and even a surgeon. Vincenzo Maria di Massa from Naples, who was at the Casa Professa in 1574, could boast of 'adequate' skills as a painter but was also a *dispensiero*, perhaps a supplier of household and even medical goods.[62] Giuseppe Roncalli, a Tuscan painter born in 1567 who was at the Novitiate from 1584, was also skilled in surgery and pharmacology, and may have been related to the much more famous artist Cristofano Roncalli from Pomarance (1551/2–1626), who painted an altarpiece for Clement VIII's campaign at St Peter's and contributed to the painting cycle of the Collegio Romano in the same year that Giuseppe entered the Society (see chapter 4).[63] Another kinsman of a famous artist at the Novitiate was Orazio Zuccaro (1584–1619), the son of the celebrated painter Federico Zuccaro, who worked for the Jesuits at the Gesù and the Collegio Romano and much more extensively for Alessandro Farnese at Caprarola.[64] The younger Zuccaro, who entered the Novitiate at the same time as the Gisbert brothers, in October 1605, quite likely had at least rudimentary training as a painter.

In summary, it is possible that the work in the earliest phase of painting – that of the church – was done by Bitti and Fiammeri in the late 1560s and early 1570s; that the work of the Acquaviva-era phases of the 1580s and 1590s, including the refectory and infirmary, was done largely by Clemente (probably working under Fiammeri), with contributions from a variety of other resident brothers such as

Benedetti; that the paintings executed together with the S. Vitale renovations in 1597–9 were done by Fiammeri and Clemente again; and that the work in the latest phase, that of the recreation room, was done by Gisbert and perhaps Orazio Zuccaro under the supervision of a senior Jesuit, either Clemente or Fiammeri, between 1604 and 1606. The architect of the expanded Novitiate, Giuseppe Valeriano, was himself a painter, but he was so busy working on the structural parts of the complex – not to mention major architectural projects in other parts of Italy – that it is unlikely he had the time to paint.[65]

It is fitting that the Novitiate was the only building decorated by the Jesuits in the sixteenth century in which the decoration was done primarily by Jesuit brothers. The decision almost certainly relates to the intended audience of the Novitiate decorations. Since the areas under consideration were private ones, to be used only by Jesuits, it follows that the Society should have been satisfied with the work of its own artists and not have spent money on professionals. By contrast, the public commissions described in chapters 4 to 7 show that the Jesuits tended to hire well-known professional artists when they wanted to make an impression on the outside world.

Only one, and at most two, professional artists contributed to the Novitiate decorations. Brutio tells us that two of the altarpieces in the 1569 chapel of S. Andrea (*Martyrdom of St Andrew* and *Adoration of the Magi*) can be attributed to the Tuscan painter Durante Alberti (1538–1616), a man who worked on almost every early Jesuit commission in Rome. Alberti was later hired to paint the main altarpiece in the Jesuit collegiate chapel of S. Tommaso di Canterbury in 1581 (fig. 64), a depiction of St Stephen Protomartyr for S. Stefano Rotondo in 1582–3, an altarpiece of St Apollinarius and other saints for S. Apollinare in the same years, and the *Transfiguration* in the Trinity Chapel of the Gesù in 1589 (see chapters 4, 5, 6, and 7).[66] From Borgo Sansepolcro, Durante was already in Rome in 1568, where he worked at the Vatican on the Casino of Pius IV and the Belvedere Palace with his reformist compatriots Santi di Tito and Giovanni de' Vecchi, and he also directed a crew of fresco painters at the Villa d'Este in Tivoli in 1570 and 1571.[67] Alberti painted several commissions for the Jesuits outside Rome as well, including a canvas of the *Circumcision* for the Gesù in Perugia (1575, now in S. Maria in Case Bruciate), and another *Martyrdom of St Andrew* for the Jesuit patron G.M. Lambertini in S. Domenico in Bologna (later 1580s).

Giovanni Baglione describes Durante as a very devout man, and he must have used his reputation to his advantage since he enjoyed the patronage of a number of religious orders. In addition to Jesuit commissions he painted frequently for the Capuchins and executed an altarpiece of the *Madonna della Vallicella Venerated by the Seven Angels*, for the Oratorian church of SS. Nereo ed Achilleo. We saw in chapter 1 that Durante helped found the Accademia di San Luca and served there as a sort of spokesman for the Society of Jesus.[68] His paintings have a clarity and naturalism unusual in the period, and show the influence of the nascent style of Santi di Tito. Like so many reformist painters of the period, Durante returns to a Raphael-inspired model with larger figures and centralized, simplified compositions, and also adopts something of Sebastiano's deeper shading. His concern for honesty and intelligibility is evident in a lecture he gave in 1594 to the Accademia on the subject 'the true imitation of truth, and that good painting consists in real substance.'[69] Although Durante's S. Andrea paintings are not dated, they may have been painted around the time the choir was painted in 1571, or possibly during the painting campaign of late 1574. They may also have been executed around 1581–2, when Alberti was working on the Jesuit collegiate chapel commissions of S. Apollinare, S. Stefano Rotondo, and S. Tommaso.[70]

The Novitiate records also make an intriguing reference to another professional artist who worked with the Jesuits on several projects. The Roman painter Gaspare Celio (1571–1640), a close friend of Valeriano's, made some of the most extraordinary contributions to the Gesù decorations, painted a chapel at the Jesuit church at Tivoli and perhaps part of S. Vitale, had an intimate relationship with Netherlands printmakers who worked for the Society, and worked with the Spanish Jesuit Juan Bautista Villalpando on his Temple of Jerusalem project (see chapters 5, 6, and 7).[71] Celio was a true Renaissance man, being not only a successful artist but a celebrated mathematician and astrologer; he is best known to art historians as the author of a valuable treatise on art, *Memoria fatta dal Signor Gaspare Celio dell'habito di Christo* (Naples, 1638).

The account books for S. Andrea note that Celio paid 300 scudi to the Novitiate on 6 June 1595, to help make up the 3,650 scudi needed for construction and planting of the new garden, an amount (termed a *censo*) the Jesuits appear to have repaid him by 1598.[72] It is not entirely clear what this amount is, but it looks like some sort of loan, and, curiously, it was lent a year before he was paid almost the same amount for painting the Passion Chapel in the Gesù, for which he may also have served as a kind of bursar (see chapter 6). Whatever the amount represents, it shows that Celio had a connection with S. Andrea during this period, and seems to confirm Baglione's reference to the painter's affinity for the Society: 'Gasparo Celio was at the service of the Jesuit Fathers, and they employed him in various works; and at the same time he gave them some indication of an intention of joining that Society. Instead, he put aside for them some money, which he had saved up from his labours, thereby demonstrating that his whole will was united with them.'[73] In the Gesù, Celio used his expertise as a fresco painter to execute Fiammeri's designs. Perhaps his work at S. Andrea also involved painting from sketches made by a Jesuit brother painter.

Louis Richeôme's Guide to the Novitiate Paintings

Almost everything we know about the subjects and appearance of the painting cycle at the Novitiate of S. Andrea comes from a single book, Louis Richeôme's *La peinture spirituelle* (Lyon, 1611), one of the most remarkable and entertaining treatises written about art after Trent.[74] Louis Richeôme was a skilled rhetorician and avid iconophile, and his wide-ranging manuals on images and their role in meditation place him with Possevino and Bellarmine among the most important Jesuit writers on the visual arts. His works include the earlier *Trois discours pour la religion catholique, des miracles, des saincts, & des images* (Bordeaux, 1597) and *Tableaux sacrez des figures mystiques du très-auguste sacrement et sacrifice de l'Eucharistie* (Paris, 1601), the former dedicated to Henri IV and read by Nicholas Poussin and Peter Paul Rubens.[75]

Richeôme went back to Sacred Scripture to justify the use of pictures in meditation and worship, maintaining that God the Father himself, in his act of Creation, was the world's first 'painter.' In Richeôme's opinion, representations of the saints, Jesus, God the Father, and the Trinity were all legitimate, provided that they were based closely on descriptions from holy texts – a concern with textual accuracy echoing that of Possevino and the Oratorian Cesare Baronio. Richeôme also conceived of visions as a kind of painting, a performance art produced by God's invisible brush. Like many other Early Modern Catholic theorists including Paleotti, Richeôme firmly believed that pictures, with their appeal to the senses, were more effective in addressing ordinary people than was reason. In his *Trois discours* he wrote, 'Painting is more suitable to an ordinary person ... because he is moved by the senses rather than the spirit, and would not see the profiles and colours of a well-woven argument as well as the lines and features of an image.'[76] As we will see, he also believed that images could speak more directly to the soul than mere words. The sequenced meditations on individual images found in Richeôme's writings, together with his interest in the use of the senses, echoes the *Spiritual Exercises*, not only in their general stucture but in their constant evocation of Ignatius's 'composition of place.'

Known as the 'French Cicero' for his mastery of ancient rhetoric, Richeôme had served as the Jesuit provincial of Gaul (1586–92), Aquitaine (1592–8), and Lyon (1605–8), and among other duties had taught rhetoric at the Jesuit college at Pont-à-Mousson.[77] His rhetorical approach was to combine objective descriptions of biblical events or scenes from the lives of the saints with emotionally charged and highly subjective exhortations and contemplations. A committed humanist, Richeôme quotes frequently from a wide variety of classical writers, and his understanding of images as visual oratory has been shown by Marc Fumaroli to derive from a book of descriptions of real or imaginary mythological paintings in Naples called *Imagines*, by the Greek writer Philostratus (b. ca. 190 AD).[78] As Fumaroli has indicated, Richeôme's manual owes a profound debt to Philostratus's sophistic style of rhetoric called *ekphrasis* (description), a form of description in which an object of art or nature is used as a springboard for a variety of modes of narrative and explanation that act as 'mirrors' of its various aspects.[79] On a more basic level, Richeôme's manual can be read as an elaborate Imitation of Christ, in which the saints, blessed, martyrs, confessors, and other figures in the paintings live lives that parallel the life and passion of Christ – 'a veritable palace of mirrors where, from reflection to reflection, from variation to variation, the example of Christ is repeated under different colours, in different circumstances and landscapes, inviting the reader-viewer to repeat it in turn, in the style and circumstances appropriate to him.'[80]

Richeôme's rhetorical acumen, knowledge of the classics, and love of images prompted Claudio Acquaviva to invite him to Rome in 1608; it was that year that the Father General standardized the training of novices. The purpose of the handbook was to help the young men make a spiritual journey like that of the *Exercises*, but based entirely on the S. Andrea paintings and gardens. As we saw in chapter 1, Acquaviva was one of the most active supporters of the visual arts in the early Society. Archival sources show that he closely supervised the decorative program at the Novitiate's second church, that of S. Vitale (see chapter 5), and he very likely oversaw the final master scheme for the remaining Novitiate decorations. Richeôme may also have contributed to the program from afar before he left France in 1608, especially by providing source material from antiquity. The freshness and enthusiasm with which Richeôme writes, together with his evident familiarity with a wide range of sources, seem to support this hypothesis.

Richeôme's enormous volume, dedicated to Acquaviva, is divided into three series of meditations, the first based on the paintings in the chapel and residence, the second on the plants and birds of the garden, and the third on the paintings in the early Christian basilica of S. Vitale.[81] In his discussion of the Novitiate paintings Richeôme describes an extensive series of frescoes, canvases, and relief carvings, adorning what seems to be every square foot of wall space in the chapel, dormitory, refectory, lavatory, infirmary, and corridors. Despite their diverse subject matter and sources, these cycles clearly all submit to a master plan, since they not only are linked iconographically with each other but also relate to themes appropriate to the rooms they adorn. Richeôme's manual was clearly meant to be used with the actual paintings before the eyes of the reader, since it reproduces only a small handful of engravings but constantly exhorts the reader to look at the paintings. Incidentally, the engravings are most likely by the German printmaker Matthäus Greuter (1564–1638), who signed the frontispiece and who did other work for the Jesuits.[82] Not only does Richeôme's manual tell us what the paintings looked like, but his detailed instructions to the reader give us insight into the way in which the Jesuit novices used the paintings. He discusses each painting separately, usually beginning with a detailed description and following with a meditation on the image and, often, parables and stories related to the scene and taken from cited sources. Remarkably, with the exception of the descriptions of the chapel, recreation room, gardens, and adjacent church of S. Vitale, art historians have virtually ignored Richeôme's richly informative and evocative text.[83]

Richeôme derives the very act of seeing and perceiving from the will of the Creator, and then turns it into a metaphor for Christ's transubstantiation, a theme he takes up in an extensive meditation toward the beginning of his book and returns to frequently. I will briefly paraphrase his argument, which he traces to the 'Philosophes,' and which is based essentially on Aristotle. He begins by describing the miracle by which a picture transmits its image through the air to the eye of the viewer: 'Who can explain how that image reaches the eye? It does not carry itself through the air – look how it stays fixed on the picture plane where it is painted: the images which you see in this room are exactly where they were when you entered, and they will not budge when you look at them again; how, therefore, do they arrive at your eyes, when that is what they perceive?'[84] He explains that it is not the image itself that travels, but the image of the image, just as the sound of a voice travels to the ears, or scents to the nose, taste to the tongue, or tangible things to the hand. But how, he asks, does this 'frail thing that quickly vanishes' travel through space, separately from the picture itself, to reach the viewer's eyes? How can it replicate with every glance, and give a different view from every angle? And how can the tiny pupil of the eye, which is 'no larger than a lentil,' immediately perceive a large and complicated painting in an instant, 'whether it be a giant, a house, or half of heaven'? 'Where,' he asks, 'is the hand, the paintbrush, and the instrument, which draws it in this tiny space?' It is only through the actions of the Creator, he concludes, that these miracles are possible. Then, as often in the book, Richeôme directly addresses the novices: It is time to open your eyes, 'my beloved brothers, you who are of a spiritual nature, and contemplate the power and capability of this powerful work.' Extending this concept into a metaphor for Christ's transubstantiation, Richeôme introduces an image of the Quarant'ore, or Forty Hours devotion: 'You have seen set up on the high altar of your church two large names of Jesus and his glorious Mother, lit by many hundreds of brilliant lamps, and two or three thousand candles, placed on and around this altar, and each one glowing and distinct in the same place in your eyes? Do you not perceive it all at once? Can you not describe these just as you can describe the multiplicity of images in these pictures?'[85] Richeôme concludes that all the paintings he has been discussing fit easily into the pupils of our eyes in the same way that the transubstantiated body of Christ, with all its abundance, fits into the small wafer of the Sacred Host, as displayed during the Quarant'ore. Incidentally, the Quarant'ore, a ceremony at which the bread of the Eucharist is exposed to clergy and laity for forty hours in the presence of candles, oil lamps, reliquaries, and elaborate stage sets called *apparati*, was one of the most important liturgical events of the sixteenth and seventeenth centuries. Derived from medieval vigil of Good Friday ceremonies, the Quarant'ore was revived in Milan in 1527 and introduced by Filippo Neri in Rome in 1550. The Jesuits held a sumptuous Quarant'ore every year at the Gesù, beginning in 1595, when the host was framed by damask and other hangings, reliquaries, silver vases filled with flowers, and many candles; later expositions included music and sermons as well.[86]

Richeôme's argument is a christianized version of the Aristotelian notion that the five senses perceive objects by means of 'forms without their matter.' This idea derives from a famous passage in Aristotle's *De anima* (II.5), a text that formed a central part of the third-year arts program in Jesuit colleges throughout Europe and beyond.[87] According to the Aristotelian theory of cognition, there are three categories of cognitive faculties, including the 'external senses' (vision and the other four senses), the 'internal senses' (such as common sense, imagination, and memory), and the 'intellect' (including the active or agent intellect and the passive or patient/possible intellect). When we look at an object, our external senses perceive it by means of a sub-material copy of that object, an invisible proxy that Aristotelians call a 'species' – Richeôme's 'frail thing that quickly vanishes.' Richeôme christianizes this idea by saying that the species can exist only by the will of the Creator and is therefore proof of his existence. In addition to this concept and to his using the 'species' as a metaphor for transubstantiation, Richeôme brings a third Christian dimension to Aristotelian cognition theory. Alison Simmons has recently shown that the Jesuits promoted a particular aspect of this theory whereby the mind of the viewer was altered by contact with an exterior form via the senses and even became assimilated to it.[88] In looking at a painting the mind shares in its essence, and by observing pictures of Christ and the saints we become joined to them. Richeôme gives us an Aristotelian legitimization of the medieval devotional practice of the Imitation of Christ.

Richeôme's frequent plea to readers to employ all five senses in their medita-

tions on sacred themes also had a more recent source in the *Spiritual Exercises*.
Here are Ignatius's instructions for using the senses in the Fifth Contemplation of
the First Day of the Second Week:

> After the preparatory prayer and three preludes, it will be profitable with the aid of
> the imagination to apply the five senses to the subject matter of the First and Second
> Contemplation in the following manner: First Point. This consists in seeing in imagi-
> nation the persons, and in contemplating and meditating in detail the circumstances
> in which they are, and then in drawing some fruit from what has been seen. Second
> Point. This is to hear what they are saying, or what they might say, and then by
> reflecting on oneself to draw some profit from what has been heard. Third Point. This
> is to smell the infinite fragrance, and taste the infinite sweetness of the divinity.
> Likewise to apply these senses to the soul and its virtues, and to all according to the
> person we are contemplating, and to draw fruit from this. Fourth Point. This is to
> apply the sense of touch, for example, by embracing and kissing the place where the
> persons stand or are seated, always taking care to draw some fruit from this (pars
> 121–5).[89]

The basic structure of Richeôme's meditations likewise is similar to that of the
Spiritual Exercises. Like Ignatius, Richeôme begins his discussion of each painting
with a 'composition of place' (description) and then moves on to the meditation,
with its development of different points. He also raises themes that are reminiscent of Ignatius, especially in his emphasis on the diversity of humanity, which
reflects the Society's involvement in ministries throughout the world. I will point
out more of these affinities below.

The Novitiate Chapel of S. Andrea al Quirinale

The Novitiate chapel (fig. 14, 'A'; fig. 15, far right) contained three principal
altarpieces. The high altar, dedicated to St Andrew, was placed in the apse under a
niche enclosing the painting *God the Father Enthroned with Angels*. Its tabernacle
was made of gilt bronze and bore two images in relief from the life of Christ, both
of which represented 'births.' The first was *Nativity*, showing Christ's birth into
this world, and the second *Resurrection*, showing his birth into the next.[90] In
Alberti's *Martyrdom of St Andrew* (fig. 17), reproduced in one of Greuter's engravings, Andrew was shown being martyred – but not yet dead – in front of crowds of
onlookers representing every walk of life – 'almost all the world saddened.'[91]
Pieter-Matthijs Gijsbers points out that the painting is the first depiction of this
particular episode in the passion of St Andrew, a subject that would recur many
times in the seventeenth century, even in this very church.[92] But not everyone
agrees with Gijsbers as to which scene is depicted. Gijsbers maintains that the
painting focuses specifically on St Andrew's love for God and shows the moment
when he beseeches his executioners to let him die Christ's death, a theme stressed
in a sermon by Acquaviva, and also in a 1575 sermon delivered under Mercurian's
generalate by the Jesuit Francisco de Toledo in the same chapel.[93] Giovanni Careri,
however, believes it is the moment described in the *Golden Legend* when Egeas's

servants are miraculously paralysed and so prevented from untying the saint after he has been pardoned, whereby he is likewise allowed to die a death in imitation of Christ.[94] In either case Alberti's painting typifies the christological emphasis found in many Jesuit martyrological cycles of the period, both printed and painted.[95] The painting remained *in situ* until 1670, when Bernini's church was finished, and it was replaced by a painting of the same episode by Pietro da Cortona's pupil Guglielmo Cortese.

Like the martydom scenes in the Jesuit collegiate chapels of S. Stefano Rotondo and S. Tommaso as well as in the illustrations to Nadal's Gospels, Alberti's *Martyrdom of St Andrew* includes a multitude of people, one of whom wears an exotic turban. Yet Durante never allows this crowd to become a distraction. The background shows a generic hilly landscape and cityscape that do not withdraw attention from the action in front. The use of a nonspecific, ahistorical landscape, which we will see increasingly in both the collegiate chapels and the Gesù, recalls the deliberately vague and non-specific guidelines for the 'composition of place' in the *Exercises*, whereby the exercitant must fill in the blanks left in the text. St Andrew is crucified at dead centre, with the X of his cross saltire forming the axis of the painting, and his tormentors flank him on the foreground stage. Durante's painting gives us restrained and conventional poses, and his focus on the main action in the centre and the large figures of his protagonists recall the emphasis on legibility and the classicizing compositions of reformist painters such as Santi di Tito and Taddeo Zuccaro. Durante also arouses the viewer's emotions. Andrew's followers, who are all shown frontally or in three-quarters view to reveal their facial expressions, exhibit a variety of emotions out of which the viewer can find a match for his own response.

This subject also appears later in the main altarpiece by Agostino Ciampelli in the St Andrew (Martyrs') Chapel in the Gesù (ca. 1588–90), a painting the iconography of which would already have been chosen when Durante was working at S. Andrea (fig. 95). But the Gesù version is very different, as the saint is shown kneeling in prayer before being crucified rather than in the iconic crucifixion as at S. Andrea; and, as Gijsbers points out, the grieving followers of Andrew are 'conspicuously absent' in the Gesù version.[96] In both cases the dedication to St Andrew was made necessary by the similar dedication of an earlier church on the site, but in both the necessity was turned to advantage by the creation of a site focused on martyrdom and the apostolate. The St Andrew Chapel in the Gesù becomes a celebration of martyrdom, with other early martyrs represented in the frescoes and wall canvases. Similarly, by making the martyrdom of St Andrew the principal image of the entire Novitiate, the Jesuits immediately proclaimed that martyrdom and ministry (especially missionary work) would be major themes of the painting cycles throughout the buildings. The S. Andrea altar also recalls some of the illustrations of early Christian martyrdoms by Adrian Collaert in the Jesuit martyrological manual by Bartolommeo Ricci entitled *Triumphis Iesu Christi crucifixi* (Antwerp, 1608), which has the same crowds, the same compositional divisions, and the same neutral landscape. Some illustrations even include figures crucified on a cross saltire, in one case upside down.[97] Ricci's book is one of the strongest statements ever made of the Jesuits' commitment to dying a death in Christ.

The impact of Durante's *Martyrdom of St Andrew* reverberated beyond Jesuit circles. The canvas was probably the model for an anonymous fresco in Cesare Baronio's titular church of SS. Nereo ed Achilleo (1596–7), the most important Oratorian monument of the Palaeochristian Revival movement, which includes Andrew's crucifixion among those of other apostles on the walls of the side aisles.[98] The SS. Nereo ed Achilleo version (fig. 18) has a virtually identical composition, with Andrew's crucifixion in the centre of the painting, his tormentors flanking him, and his followers at the rear. As in the S. Andrea altarpiece, the protagonists are seen from the front and in three-quarters view, allowing the viewers to share their reactions. The two paintings also share the same figure of a helmeted soldier and a similar group of elders. However, the Oratorian painting has the antagonists physically restraining Andrew's supporters while the Jesuit altarpiece keeps the two groups separate, with the result that the supporters seem to be looking on from another time and place – a more contemplative attitude that echoes the devotion of the viewers. The Oratorian crucifixion is depicted against a background of classical architecture rather than against the landscape of the Jesuit image. I will return to this series in chapter 4.

Angels also appeared prominently in the Novitiate decorations, reflecting a general Jesuit penchant for the cult of angels that we will see also in the Gesù. In addition to the angels painted on the coffered ceiling mentioned in Brutio's description, the chapel of S. Andrea contained a stucco or relief carving of an attendant angel on the right of the high altar, below *Martyrdom of St Andrew*. The angel was shown holding a candlestick while floating on a cloud and appearing to assist at the Eucharist. This figure inspired Richeôme to digress on the role of angels: 'This angel, my dear ones, is placed there to teach you that invisible angels are present, and ready to combat those who bring temptations to valiant men ... and when you serve at the mass, you are accompanied by the office of angels.'[99] Catholic doctrine maintained that angels assisted at the mass, and this tradition was enthusiastically revived in the years after Trent by clerics such as Francis de Sales (1567–1622), who wrote about it in his *Introduction à la vie dévote*.[100] According to sources such as these, angels attend the mass in adoration (a point that Richeôme mentions in his text) and can distribute the bread of the Eucharist outside mass, but cannot consecrate the bread, something that can be done only by the priest. Many of the most popular saints from the early Christian period and the Middle Ages, including St John Chrysostom and St Basil, saw angels at mass, but the most important one for S. Andrea was Stanislas Kostka, the Jesuit novice buried in this chapel, who was often shown present at a miraculous mass attended by angels. Stanislas (1550–68) was born in Rostków, Poland, and was the son of a senator.[101] His father prepared him for a diplomatic career and sent him to the Jesuit college in Vienna for his education, but after a serious illness in 1565 he began seeing visions in which the Virgin Mary called him to join the Society, and he eventually ended up in the Novitiate in Rome, where he died at the age of 18. Stanislas was beatified in 1605 and was the first Jesuit *beatus*; he was canonized in 1726. He became the favourite patron of Jesuit novices.

Ignatius himself was greatly interested in angelic intercession, and the Jesuits were great supporters of the cult of the Holy Guardian Angels. Although their cult was officially reflected in the liturgical calendar for the first time in 1608, it had found ardent supporters since the mid-fifteenth century, and was linked with the campaign for the canonization of St Francesca Romana.[102] The greatest Jesuit follower of the cult was Robert Bellarmine, who signed the appropriate office of the Breviary when the feast was approved in 1608, and who wrote a *Meditazione sopra gli Angeli Santi* (see also chapter 1). When his fellow Jesuit Francesco Albertini wrote his influential *Trattato dell'angelo custode* in 1612, a particularly vivid and colourful treatise that had a wide readership, he dedicated it to Bellarmine.[103] Albertini saw the Holy Guardian Angels as a sign of God's grace and love, and believed the angels had many purposes: they offer our prayers to God, for example, enlighten our intellects, and ignite our wills; they protect and guide us in life and invariably are present at our deaths. Claudio Acquaviva was a great devotee of the cult of angels, as his biographer demonstrates in this passage of his obituary:

> As soon as the office of the Guardian Angel was approved by Pope Paul V, [Acquaviva] embraced it with great happiness, and he said it every year with equal devotion, reciting every part of the prayer that is included for that angel. One time when visiting in Tivoli a parish church of St Michael the Archangel in that city, he saw that there was no other image of that Glorious Prince than a crude and ancient figure on paper, just stuck onto the wall. Moved by this sight, as soon as he returned to Rome he had made by one of our brother painters a large picture on good canvas, and donated it to the church, where today it is revered.[104]

Small wonder that we find references to angels throughout the Novitiate, where Acquaviva oversaw most of the decoration. Perhaps the Jesuit painter he hired to paint the Tivoli *St Michael* was also one who worked on the complex.

In the visual arts this type of attending angel became common in the fifteenth and early sixteenth centuries, the most famous example being Michelangelo's Angel Candelabrum in the church of S. Domenico in Bologna (1494). Another celebrated example, later than that at S. Andrea, can be found on the magnificent Tabernacle of the Sacrament in the Sixtine Chapel at S. Maria Maggiore by Bastiano Torrigiano and Lodovico del Duca, begun in 1587. Commissioned by Sixtus V for his chapel, this giant gilt bronze tabernacle consists of a nearly two-metre-tall octagonal tempietto with a dome.[105] Although the faces of the tempietto have relief panels of angels bearing a monstrance, the most relevant features are the four sculptures of angels who serve as bearers, each of them about two metres tall. With one hand and shoulder each supports a corner of the tabernacle, and with the other each holds a cornucopia that serves as a candelabrum, as in the S. Andrea chapel. Cherubino Alberti's frescoes for the Cappella Aldobrandini in S. Maria sopra Minerva (completed 1605) also include examples of this type of angel, holding torches in the spandrels.[106] Attendant angels appear in the Gesù as well. The marble angels by Flaminio Vacca from the 1590s in the Angels' Chapel closely match the description of the Novitiate chapel angel, except that they join their hands in prayer rather than holding candles (see chapters 6 and 7). The same goes for the rank of angels kneeling on either side of the tabernacle in Agostino Ciampelli's ceiling fresco in the Gesù sacristy (fig. 115).

The left altarpiece at the Novitiate chapel of S. Andrea was *Holy Trinity*, a crowded and triumphal image of great pageantry. Again, the subject was shared with a chapel in the Gesù (the Trinity Chapel), which featured as altarpiece Francesco Bassano's *Holy Trinity Adored by Saints* (before 1591); the painting also echoed the main altarpiece, by Durante Alberti (1581), of the English College chapel of S. Tommaso (figs 90, 64). Both these later altarpieces have similarities to S. Andrea's as described by Richeôme. In the S. Andrea painting, the Trinity is suspended above a multitude of souls representing all walks of life – 'in the millions, arranged in the depths of the clouds in ranks of innumerable heads ... admired by all the saints of heaven and earth: Prophets, Patriarchs, Apostles, Martyrs, Confessors, Doctors, and Virgins; Kings, Princes, the great and the small.'[107] This crowded empyrean is precisely what is depicted in Bassano's version, with its throngs of people in ancient, contemporary, Oriental, ecclesiastical, and military dress, including martyrs, virgins, patriarchs, and every conceivable kind of saint. In Durante's S. Tommaso version the number of figures is reduced and the Trinity itself enlarged, but the same universality is communicated by the expansive landscape in the distance and the map of England onto which Christ's blood drips.

Once more the theme of this painting has special relevance for its context in the Novitiate. The Trinity would have been pertinent in the formation of a young novice, since it was featured in the *Spiritual Exercises* as part of the First Contemplation of the First Day of the Second Week: 'I will see and consider the Three Divine Persons seated on the royal dais or throne of the Divine Majesty. They look down upon the whole surface of the earth, and behold all nations in great blindness' (par. 106).[108] Ignatius emphasizes the salvific power of the Trinity, through the Second Person (Christ), who comes to earth and pulls the souls of sinners from the jaws of hell. Like the S. Andrea altarpiece, Ignatius stresses the diversity of humanity in his image of the Trinity. He exhorts his reader to 'see the great extent of the surface of the earth, inhabited by so many different peoples ... in such great diversity in dress and in manner of acting. Some are white, some black; some at peace, and some at war; some weeping and some laughing; some well, and some sick; some coming into the world, and some dying' (pars 103–6).[109] This image of cultural and ethnic diversity went beyond reference to the *Exercises*, however, to refer to the themes of worldwide mission and the universality of the Church that are echoed throughout the Novitiate decorations.

The right altarpiece, opposite the *Holy Trinity*, was the *Adoration of the Magi*. The subject was not a coincidence, since the earthly triad of the Magi echoes the heavenly Trinity on the other side. The Holy Family also commonly served as a parallel for the Holy Trinity in the Tridentine era.[110] There was a similar juxtaposition in the Gesù, for example, where the Nativity Chapel was positioned adjacent to the Trinity Chapel, although not across from it as at S. Andrea. Like the other two paintings in the Novitiate chapel, the *Adoration* overflowed with crowds of onlookers, described by Richeôme as a 'numerous multitude.'[111] He stresses the triumphal aspect of the scene, likening Christ's authority over the Magi to a military victory without blood: 'A small child submits the wisdom of the wisest sages to his rule without debate, and the power of the kings without shedding blood, and he overwhelms the mightiest powers without arms.'[112] The triumphal message of the *Adoration* is reinforced for Richeôme by its depiction of Jerusalem in the background: 'this town ennobled by so many beautiful towers, pyramids [*sic*], and palaces' is a passage that refers not only to the historical but to the heavenly Jerusalem.

The focus in this painting and in Richeôme's meditation was not so much on Christ himself as on the devotion of the Magi, who served as a model for the novices. I mentioned in chapter 1 that the Nativity forms an important part of the Second Week of the *Spiritual Exercises*. The Adoration of the Magi is not given special emphasis, but the Magi are discussed in connection with the Mysteries of the Life of Our Lord (par. 267).[113] The passage in the *Exercises* can also be understood to refer to the universality of the Church and to the world missions, since the Magi traditionally served as symbols of Africa, Asia, and Europe as well as of youth, maturity, and old age, and to echo an interest in the reception of the Jesuits around the world by pagan princes of exotic lands.[114] As we will soon see, Richeôme makes an oblique reference to this theme in his discussion of a recreation room painting showing Francis Xavier being received by the Daimyo of Bungo in Japan, where he glories in the miracle of an Oriental prince bowing in obeisance before Christian men.

The last painting in the Novitiate chapel of S. Andrea, also on the right wall directly across from the sacristy door, was over the tomb of Stanislas Kostka. The *Miraculous Mass of Stanislas Kostka* depicted the former novice of S. Andrea receiving the Eucharist in a Lutheran chapel at the hands of an angel accompanied by other angels, the Virgin Mary, and St Barbara.[115] This divine communion, one of the principal miracles attributed to the young saint, supposedly took place in Vienna in 1566. Stanislas's death at S. Andrea gave him a special connection with the Novitiate, which felt honoured to have been blessed by such a saintly youth in the first year of its existence, and he was seen as an auspicious omen for the early Society. To this day Stanislas's death chamber, which now contains an unsettlingly realistic polychrome marble sculpture of the dying saint by Pierre Legros (1702–3), is preserved intact as a pilgrimage site; the room is the only part of the sixteenth-century structure to survive. Stanislas's original tomb and the painting of his miraculous mass were executed in 1605 as a commission by a group of Polish nobles.[116] The dedication was an extravagant affair attended by members of the Polish nobility and by influential Roman figures, and the Jesuits published two thousand printed images of the young blessed to distribute to visitors, a stock that lasted only a couple of days.[117] In later years Polish aristocrats continued to honour the tomb with gifts, such as the painting *Crucifixion with Stanislas Kostka and an Angel*, which was presented to the Novitiate by the duchess of Ostronia in 1611.[118]

Navarola provides a fairly detailed description of Stanislas's tomb, emphasizing its grandiose appearance and costly materials:

The sepulchre was adorned with two curtains (*portieri*) of Cardinal Montalto valued at 1,600 scudi. A most beautiful baldacchino was placed above the image, and under it was the tomb of the saint [*sic*], a frontal of white satin, all richly adorned with gold cloth, with the image of Stanislas above in the act of receiving communion from the angels in the company of St Barbara ... Above it were many beautiful flowers, and at the bottom around the predella in front of the tomb were six medium-size silver candles, and two large ones of the height of a man, with the lighted candles alternating with other flowers.[119]

Thanks to a passage in which he eschews the luxuries of the material world, Richeôme gives us more details about what the tomb looked like. He describes a richly adorned classical aedicule-like structure made of alabaster and gilding, and covered with relief carvings of angels and garlands:

I do not want to talk to you about the structure of the tomb, or its drapery, passing over the whiteness of the alabaster, which is like snow, nor to recount the manner of its pilasters, cornices, architraves, friezes, and finials, embellished and enriched by gold leaf, or the ornaments of its festoons, angels, and other figures worked in precious materials and with the most exquisite artifice: your eye can see all that without the ear. All this work is a present of the devout affection and liberality of the Polish nobility made in memory of their compatriots: but none of this touches an atom of your devotion or of mine, which beholds a much higher design.[120]

Francis Haskell, incidentally, cites this passage as an example of the prudishness and austerity of early Jesuit taste in the arts, which he contrasts sharply with the more luxurious and refined taste of the Barberini pope: 'a last, lonely voice from the harsher days of the Counter Reformation, valid more because it justified an unwanted simplicity than because it proclaimed a doctrine that was at all likely to be followed in the more prosperous and relaxed age of Urban VIII.'[121] In fact, nowhere does Richeôme actually disparage these rich adornments, with which, in Haskell's paraphrase, the Jesuits 'had pathetically tried to enrich their churches.' Rather, he praises the patrons of the tomb for its lavishness, which he believes quite appropriate, and merely points out that we do not need these riches in order to see the loftier wealth of God.

The painting of Stanislas itself raises once more the theme of angelic intercession and assistance at the mass. Stanislas not only receives the Eucharist from the hands of an angel, but is surrounded by angels. In his meditation on this image Richeôme emphasizes the young man's own angelic countenance: 'Would you not think this a portrait of an angel dressed as a human being?'[122] The painting was dominated by an expansive landscape, which Richeôme exhorted his readers to populate with the characters of the story in a 'composition of place.' It was replaced in Bernini's church by another *Miraculous Mass of Stanislas Kostka*, by Carlo Maratta (1687), a project for which Ciro Ferri also competed around 1679.[123] In typical High Baroque manner, these later images depict Stanislas in a swoon, an interpretation clearly absent from earlier depictions such as the engraving by Schelte à Bolswert (1586–1659), which shows the young *beatus* actively participating in the liturgy.[124]

The Refectory

Richeôme moves from the chapel to the refectory, from spiritual to bodily refresh-
ment. The refectory, housed in a wing at the back of the courtyard facing the
garden, rose to a height of two storeys and had a high vaulted ceiling and
clerestory windows (figs 14, 19). It was adorned with large framed paintings
between the lower windows and clerestory windows, and had frescoes in the
vaults. As had been traditional in refectories since medieval times, the dominant
painting was a *Last Supper*, a framed work much larger than the others and hung
directly over the high table at the end of the hall without clerestory windows. The
paintings in the refectory reflect Jerónimo Nadal's instructions for the design of
Jesuit houses: Nadal specifically recommended that Jesuit dining rooms have
paintings 'of the highest quality' (*optimae imagines*) on the four walls, and that one
of them be a *Last Supper*.[125] The subjects of the paintings in the Novitiate refectory
were chosen to relate to the room's function, and accordingly depict famous meals
from the Bible and the lives of the saints. They include the *Wedding at Cana*, the
Miracle of the Loaves and Fishes, *Christ Succoured by Angels in the Desert*, the *Parable of
the King's Feast for His Son* (from Matt. 22:1–14), *Christ in the House of Simon the
Pharisee*, and an allegorical fresco of the Eucharist placed directly above the *Last
Supper* in which the nine orders of angels are ranged over a table attended by
Abraham, Isaac, and Jacob and the apostles, patriarchs, prophets, martyrs, confessors, and virgins.[126] Richeôme calls on readers to use three senses in their
'composition of place,' since the activity in the refectory involves taste, sight, and
hearing (meals were accompanied by spiritual readings).

In the meagre engraving that begins this section of Richeôme's manual (fig. 19),
it is just possible to make out the two paintings above the high table. The *Last
Supper* is a crowded, bustling scene featuring a large, dramatically foreshortened
U-shaped table with Christ seated at the head and the apostles around the sides. A
smaller service table is placed at the front and is used by servants to carve a roast
lamb. The crowds of figures recall those found in the chapel paintings, and the
compositions reflect recent Venetian versions of the scene. The U-shaped table
brings to mind Veronese's *Marriage of Cana* (1562–3), painted about twenty years
earlier, and the sharp diagonals of the side tables are reminiscent of Tintoretto,
particularly his *Last Supper* at the Sala Grande in the Scuola di S. Rocco (1577–81),
painted just before the S. Andrea version. The arrangement of the S. Andrea *Last
Supper* also nicely echoes the actual arrangement of the novices' tables, also in a U,
directly below it. In fact, if we read the painting as reflecting the refectory, we see
that Christ is depicted at the head table directly above the seat of the master of
novices. The fresco scene above *Last Supper*, painted against a background depicting the heavenly firmament, mirrors the *Last Supper* below it, only this time with a
long horizontal table and crowned figures seated around it on all sides. In front of
the table a band of angel musicians plays a heavenly divertimento on viola da
gamba, organ, and other instruments in a way that recalls the lavish musical
entertainment at the foot of the table in Veronese's picture.

Although the composition of the *Last Supper* is quite different from that chosen for the same scene in Nadal's Gospel, which uses a rectangular table (Nadal plates 102, 103), there is a significant link between the subjects chosen for the refectory paintings and Nadal's meditations. Every scene depicted in the refectory is illustrated in Nadal, including *Christ Succoured by Angels in the Desert* (plate 14), *Wedding at Cana* (plate 15), *Christ in the House of Simon the Pharisee* (plate 34), *Miracle of the Loaves and Fishes* (plate 43), and even the unusual *Parable of the King's Feast for His Son* (plate 93). Since the primary aim of Nadal's book was to provide novices with an illustrated guide to meditation through the liturgical year, the paintings' affinity with the engraved series underscores the meditative function of the paintings and shows that the Jesuits' iconographic programs, whether printed or painted, were thematically integrated. Also, as we have seen, Giovanni Battista Fiammeri may have worked on both projects, since he prepared the principal sketches for the Nadal series and was possibly involved in the refectory decoration.

The refectory paintings made specific reference to the novices' vocation. Richeôme points out that the *Last Supper* repesents the moment when Christ made his apostles into priests, and symbolizes the role the novices will play after ordination.[127] The same Eucharistic message underlies the *Wedding at Cana*, in which Christ turns water into wine; it is also his first miracle and the one that seals the faith of the apostles. The transubstantiation of the host is also the principal metaphor behind *Miracle of the Loaves and Fishes*, and Richeôme gives the story particular relevance for men contemplating ministry by exhorting his readers not to fear spiritual starvation in the desert of the world.[128] An allegorical reference to self-sacrifice dominates the next painting, *Christ Succoured by Angels in the Desert*, which shows the moment after Christ has been tempted by the devil for forty days in the wilderness and is rewarded by a sumptuous feast. Although this scene usually depicts only Christ and a trio of angels, Richeôme describes a much more princely affair, with pages and with servants carrying plates, cutting bread, carving a roast, and opening wine. The scene also ties in with the angel imagery elsewhere in the Novitiate buildings.

The painting *Christ in the House of Simon the Pharisee* might seem an unusual scene for the novitiate of a male religious order, since the principal subject of the story is the Magdalene, in Richeôme's words 'one of the rarest women in the world.'[129] In the Tridentine era the Magdalene was the primary image of female penitence, the equivalent of St Peter for men.[130] The Jesuits may have included the Magdalene in the refectory out of a concern to promote her cult in the face of both Protestant and Catholic attacks, beginning in the early sixteenth century, on her spiritual identity. She also served as a model for selfless contemplation of Christ's passion, owing to a tradition that she spent her post-biblical life in exile in Southern France. On a more literal level, her penitence involved a supper table, a basic setting that this scene has in common with those of the other paintings in the room. Nevertheless, it is curious that she was chosen instead of Peter, and that she turns up again twice in the infirmary (chapter 3). The positioning of this scene of the Magdalene formed a female axis for the entire room. It was hung over the main doorway to the residential areas of the Novitiate, and directly below it, painted in fresco in the vault of the doorway, was the only other painting featuring a woman, *Queen of Heaven*, representing the Virgin. Mary was shown borne aloft and revered by crowds of angels. These angels in turn recalled those painted on either side of the windows in the refectory, and gave Richeôme another opportunity to digress on the powers of God's winged attendants. As in the chapel, images of angels played a subtle counterpoint to the scenes depicted on the canvases and in the large-scale frescoes.

The Lavatory and Galleries

Even the lavatory, a vestibule to the refectory through which the novices would pass on their way to the recreation room, boasted a painting cycle. Appropriately, the small paintings (it is impossible to tell from the text whether they are frescoes or canvases) depicted scenes relating to water, taken from the lives of the saints. Such were *St Placidus Rescued from Drowning*, in which the young saint is rescued from the water by St Maurus in miraculous circumstances, and *St Francis of Paola Spreading His Cape over the Sicilian Sea*, in which Francis crosses the water on a woollen cloak after being told he cannot board the ferry without money.[131] Another saint whose water-related miracles were included in this aquatic hagiography was St Columban, the Irish evangelizer of parts of France, Southern Germany, and Lombardy, who served as a potent symbol of the missionary vocation. By means of this painting cycle, even the most menial tasks and activities of daily life became meditations. This spiritual saturation of the novices is reminiscent of the walking meditation performed by Zen Buddhist monks in Japan.

The galleries themselves, as passageways, were decorated with scenes of voyages and journeys both earthly and spiritual. The first image the novices faced when entering the gallery was *The Good Old Man and the Young Novice*, an allegorical representation of the spiritual journey the novices would undertake during their years at the Novitiate under the guidance of their superior and of God. On the other wall of the gallery was an image with a similar message of succour in time of need, showing St Aerius and his companions, their bag of grain miraculously replenished by God after having run dry.[132] The gallery also included scenes of endurance and of conquest over the sins of the flesh, featuring St Francis of Assisi, St Benedict, and others. One scene showed a chaste young man presenting a hot iron to a religious without burning himself, a sign that Our Lord had extinguished the carnal passions with his grace.

The Recreation Room

The gallery leads to the recreation room, the best-known room and virtually the only one apart from the chapel that is mentioned in the scholarship. The recreation room was a place where 'every day after supper you have a little time for honest recreation in which to reflect on what you listened to during the meal, whether histories, which are depicted on the paintings in the tableaux placed on the walls in great numbers, or on some other matter of edification, or honest pleasure.'[133] Novices would pray, listen to lectures, and discuss sacred matters with their confreres. Richeôme's book, incidentally, follows the daily routine of the novice, from chapel to supper, then via the lavatory and corridor to the recreation room, and finally, as we shall see, to the dormitories and infirmary. Scholars almost universally claim that the recreation room murals comprised the earliest martyrdom cycle commissioned by the Jesuits. [134] They repeatedly date these murals to the 1570s, even when the most cursory look at the dates of the martyrdoms depicted shows that the series must have been begun somewhere around the mid-1580s and cannot have been completed until shortly before Richeôme's volume was published in 1611. One of the principal narrative pictures depicted a martyrdom from May 1583 – already later than the 1581–2 martyrdom cycles at S. Stefano Rotondo and S. Tommaso di Canterbury. There was a depiction of Aloysius Gonzaga, whose death was in 1591, and the latest martyrdom depicted was from 1606.

Nor were the recreation room murals as 'bloody'[135] as most people claim, and they were therefore quite different in spirit from the ones we will see at S. Stefano and S. Tommaso in chapters 4 and 5. Apart from the two main narrative images, most of the Jesuit martyrs (a hundred in total) were shown standing placidly in a row with their palm branches and their guardian angels, like so many trophies in a case. This more triumphal depiction of the martyrs was also characteristic of the only other martyrdom cycle commissioned after the collegiate churches, that of S. Vitale (begun 1597), which trades in the gore of its predecessors for placid landscapes and an iconic stillness (see chapter 5). Even the majority of the narrative paintings in the recreation room were more optimistic scenes emphasizing Jesuit identity, esprit de corps, and missionary work. There were *Ignatius's Vision at La Storta*, *Madonna as Protectress of the Society of Jesus*, *Ignatius Evading a Danger at the College of St Barbara*, and *Francis Xavier's Arrival in Japan*.

Ignatius's Vision at La Storta is reproduced in Richeôme's volume. It shows a profile view of Ignatius in the lower left in an enclosed chapel, praying before a ruined altar (fig. 21). A cityscape of Rome can be seen in the distance through the open doorway. Above the altar is the vision itself, in which Christ takes up the cross and exhorts Ignatius to follow him; it also includes the figure of God the Father, and the whole is surrounded by a framework of clouds and cherub heads. The painting of La Storta is very similar to the image published in the volume commemorating Ignatius's beatification, the 1609 *Vita beati P. Ignatii Loiolae*, printed in Rome with seventy-four small engravings illustrating the life of Ignatius in chronological order (see fig. 20 for an example).[136] This similarity, however, does not indicate that the Novitiate painting dates from after 1609, since as with Nadal's Gospel these drawings circulated among the Jesuits in Rome prior to their publication – although many of them no earlier than 1604–5 – and may themselves have been based on earlier depictions. Conversely, it is also possible that the Novitiate painting was the model for the engraving. We will see other paintings that resemble engravings in the 1609 series in this room and the infirmary.

Ignatius's vision at La Storta took place at a small wayside chapel on the northern outskirts of Rome: Ignatius was left with Christ's message 'I shall be propitious to you in Rome' and with God the Father's declaration to Christ 'I want you to take this man [i.e., Ignatius] for your servant.'[137] The vision was an important one, since it confirmed for Ignatius the name of the Society of Jesus, the name his companions had earlier chosen for their *compagnia*.[138] It also confirmed Rome as the centre of Jesuit activity. And it taught that Jesuits should pattern their lives on Christ's and bear their crosses in his name, a message especially apt in a room brimming with martyrs.

The next canvas, *Madonna as Protectress of the Society of Jesus*, places the Virgin at the centre of Jesuit identity, a theme that will be taken up again in the dormitory rooms. Located directly opposite *Ignatius's Vision at La Storta*, it depicts another vision, this one experienced by the Jesuit Martín Gutiérrez, who beheld the Virgin Mary extending her cloak around the men of the Jesuit order. This rare piece of Jesuit imagery relates to an iconography very common in other orders. Perhaps the best known example is *St Augustine and His Spiritual Successors*, engraved by Schelte à Bolswert in 1624, which shows St Augustine protecting the leading figures of the Augustinian order under his voluminous cloak. According to Richeôme, the Jesuits standing below the Virgin's gown included Ignatius of Loyola, Francis Xavier, Aloysius Gonzaga, and Stanislas Kostka, among 'many other men representing the *corps* of the Society, placed under the robe, and the protection, of the Mother of God.'[139]

The next painting, *Ignatius Evading a Danger at the College of St Barbara*, represents another scene included in the *Vita beati P. Ignatii Loiolae* series of 1609 (illustration 38), showing an event that took place when Ignatius was studying at the University of Paris. Ignatius presents himself before the academic tribunal assembled to punish him for his proselytization, but the punishment is held off at the last minute by the Portuguese rector, Diogo de Gouveia.[140] Ignatius stands in the middle ground, embracing Gouveia, who has fallen on his knees, while the various regents and students stand around in academic gowns and foppish dress, preparing to enforce corporal punishment. The painting serves, in Richeôme's words, to help us 'discover the envy and malice of the devil' in his attempt to thwart good works. The foppish students demonstrate the vanity of the world, the evil of which is overcome by the virtue of Our Lord and his servants, strengthened in adversity. The painting is yet another image of endurance and of the victory of the spiritual over the material.[141]

The last of the non-martyrological scenes shows Francis Xavier being received by the Daimyo of Bungo in Japan in 1549. Although there were no published illustrated lives of Francis Xavier at this time as there were for Ignatius, a highly popular text of the life of the Jesuit 'Apostle to the Indies' by Orazio Torsellino appeared as early as 1596, and was well regarded as much for its spiritual content as for its swashbuckling adventures and Oriental settings. The earliest known painted cycle of the life of Francis Xavier, full of exotic costumes and settings from his missions, was executed by André Reinoso for the sacristy of São Roque, the principal Jesuit church in Lisbon, around 1619.[142] It served as a model for several Xavier cycles in Portugal, and quite possibly could have had an impact on Italian versions, given Portugal's role as gateway to the Asian missions. The Reinoso series, however, did not include the episode at the court of the Daimyo of Bungo, and instead had one at the court of Yamaguchi. The earliest surviving scenes of Francis at the court of Bungo appear in the mid-seventeenth century, the most celebrated being Anthony Van Dyck's *St Francis Xavier before Otomo Sorin, Daimyo of Bungo* of ca. 1641, now in Pommersfelden.[143] Van Dyck's canvas, like many images of Japan in the period, depicts Japanese figures with European facial features; the ruddy-faced Daimyo looks strikingly like a young Dutch burgher. I know, however, of no precedent for the Novitiate's depiction of this event.

Richeôme uses this scene as an excuse for a mediation on sumptuous clothing and jewellery, since it depicts an event at court, and since not only the Japanese but also Duarte Gama, the captain of the Portuguese trading ship from Macao, and even Francis himself, are well turned out. Elsewhere Richeôme uses the dazzling riches of this world as a metaphor for its ephemerality and superficiality, but here he permits them as an appropriate echo of the divine glory. He dwells at great length on every bauble and button worn by the captain and by Francis. The captain he describes as

> draped with a levantine cape of moroccan leather, black, cut into strips and bordered in gold, with six diamond buttons on a violet damask tunic, embellished with pearls; on his neck he wears a large chain of gold, and he has shoes of the same material as the tunic, cut into strips in the Portuguese manner, a black beaver hat, lined with velvet of the same colour, worked in gold on the edges, with a gold cord in three great branches, and a great feather plume of white; his sword has a golden hilt, adorned with many gold tassels, and a green velvet scabbard with a golden tip; his coat is scarlet, garnished with six rows of golden baubles, lined with coarse-grained red taffeta.[144]

We would expect Richeôme to contrast this splendour with the sobriety and poverty of Francis Xavier. Instead, he describes Xavier as equally well dressed, only in priestly garb: 'Contemplate this blessed father, in his precious clothes contrary to his habit ... He wears a black robe of fine cloth, above which he wears a cambric shirt embroidered at the borders; the stole that hangs from his neck is made of fine green satin with gold braid; finished with beautiful fringes of the same material.'[145] Richeôme hopes to surprise the reader with the splendour of Francis's clothing, so that he can go on to explain that when meeting kings even Jesuits should dress appropriately, in order to give credit to the Church and reflect the glory of their spiritual enterprise. After you focus on kings and princes, he instructs the young novices, you can then turn to the poor, and you will have all the time in the world 'to make the tests and trials of religious poverty.'[146] These directives to future missionaries echo Ignatius's own policy, which was followed on all corners of the globe. In his instructions to future Jesuit missionaries Ignatius exhorted them to win the good will of princes and other rich and influential potentates.[147] The idea was that if the members of the Society converted the prince, his subjects would naturally follow; they would win the souls of an entire nation all the more easily. Their presence among the prominent would also make their activities visible and serve as a kind of advertising. In addition Ignatius knew from personal experience in Rome how important it was to obtain the financial support of wealthy patrons, and he instructed his followers to make wise use of such potential benefits. This painting of Francis's reception at the court of Bungo can therefore be read on two levels: as a celebration of Jesuit spiritual victory among pagan peoples, and as an instruction to future missionaries to gain a foothold with local rulers before beginning their missions among the people.

Images of martyrs dominated the recreation room. Like the Bungo picture, they were directed primarily at future missionaries. There were two large narrative scenes, one depicting the thirty-nine Jesuit martyrs killed when their ship was attacked en route to Brazil in 1570, and the other showing the murder of the Mughal missionary Rodolfo Acquaviva and his four Jesuit companions in Goa in May 1583. These subjects were chosen for the larger history paintings not only because they involved groups of men, but because they conveniently provided an attack on Catholicism's two main enemies – Protestantism and paganism. The Brazil missionaries (fig. 22) were killed by French Huguenot pirates, who boarded their ship, the *Santiago*, near the Canary Islands and threw overboard the provincial, Inácio de Azevedo, and his thirty-nine companions.[148] Rodolfo Acquaviva, the nephew of Father General Claudio Acquaviva and a former inhabitant of the Novitiate of S. Andrea, was murdered with his companions at the town of Cuncolim, near Goa, by Hindu 'idolaters.' Since many later examples of group martyrdom could have provided equally fertile subjects for large-scale history paintings, we can be fairly certain that these paintings were executed within a decade and a half of 1583, and probably in the 1580s. The most noteworthy absence is the 1597 crucifixion of the Japanese martyrs, which immediately became the most commonly portrayed Jesuit group martyrdom and therefore can serve as a *terminus ante quem*. Perhaps the choice of Rodolfo Acquaviva as a subject came directly from his uncle Claudio, who supported the young martyr in his vocation and was a strong promoter of his beatification.[149]

Most of the martyrs in the recreation room were given completely non-narrative depiction. They were painted below the history paintings, in a frieze running around the walls that Richeôme likens to a belt. This frieze represented both the martyrs themselves and individual figures of angels, one for each of the martyrs below. The martyrs were lined up like bowling pins, 'one by one,' standing upright with a minimum of gesture, against a plain background. The angels each held a crown and a palm branch, which they lowered over the heads of the martyrs 'to honour their victory and martyrdom.'[150] This placement of the martyrs closely recalls the more famous martyr imagery in the apse vault of Cesare Baronio's titular church of SS. Nereo ed Achilleo, which formed part of his 1596–7 renovation. In the Palaeochristian spirit, the frescoes in SS. Nereo ed Achilleo adopt a style consciously reminiscent of Early Christian mosaic decorations in Rome. The apse fresco, showing male and female martyrs flanking a giant cross (fig. 23), has an arrangement very similar to that in the recreation room at S. Andrea, and is itself inspired by an actual Early Christian mosaic in the apse of the Jesuit chapel of S. Stefano Rotondo.[151] The martyrs stand erect in a frieze formation, expressing only the slightest degree of emotion, each holding a palm branch, against a plain background. The angel figures are also found in the church, although not in the apse but in the spandrels above the columns in the nave, where Baronio placed a series of victory angels, each holding aloft both a crown and a palm branch (fig. 24). As Alexandra Herz points out, these angels wear a costume that resembles the *peplos* and tunic of ancient figures of victory; indeed the entire image, including the crown and palm branch, comes from classical prototypes.[152] Similar angels, with olive branches and other symbols in their hands, were painted by Paris Nogari in the clerestory at S. Prassede to accompany a fresco cycle of

Christ's passion, part of the Palaeochristian renovation undertaken there by Cardinal Alessandro de' Medici in 1594–6. The martyrs and angels in the Novitiate recreation room may have been the earliest example of this kind of imagery in Rome.[153]

The recreation room martyr frieze represented every single Jesuit to die a martyr's death from the first martyr, Antonio Criminale, who was clubbed and beheaded in Cape Cormorin in 1549, to the English Jesuits put to the rack and hanged as a result of the Gunpowder Plot in 1606. Even the forty-five martyrs already depicted in the history paintings were included here as well, so as not to leave any gap in the roll-call, or 'liste' as Richeôme aptly calls it.[154] The hundred figures making up this martyrological pantheon of the Society of Jesus' first half century were divided into two groups, with fifty running along one wall and fifty along the other. The martyrs were placed in chronological order, according to the year of death. Despite their relentless symmetry, the march of deaths was uneven. Although every decade was represented, almost half the martyrs died in just two years – in the Azevedo sea disaster in 1570 and in a Huguenot attack on another ship in the same flotilla in 1571 – and there was a notable gap between 1583 and 1593, when the Society apparently suffered no martyrdoms whatsoever.

What was especially remarkable about the recreation room martyr cycle was that, in contrast to Cesare Baronio's and other non-Jesuit martyrological cycles in Rome, not a single one of its martyrs had been declared a saint at the time of painting. The Palaeochristian Revival movement favoured early Christian saints whose antiquity would lend legitimacy to their titular churches. Baronio, for example, adorned the side walls of SS. Nereo ed Achilleo with the martyrdoms of apostles, and, as we have just seen, his apse is filled with early Christian martyrs. This celebration by the Jesuits of men whose road to sainthood was by no means guaranteed was an act of remarkable audacity and a sign of spiritual confidence, and it echoes Claudio Acquaviva's veneration of the same figures in his rooms. The Jesuits would have to wait until 1622 before even Ignatius and Francis Xavier were canonized, despite the appearance of hagiographies and iconographies for both saints in the first decade of the seventeenth century. A Jesuit pantheon such as that in the recreation room was possible only because it was a private chamber reserved exclusively for the eyes of Jesuit novices. The more public buildings were not so forthright, and no other Jesuit painted cycles express such unabashed self-celebration. As we will see, the first Gesù paintings tiptoed around overt self-commemoration and relied on parallels and metaphors to do the job, and S. Tommaso di Canterbury took a more orthodox approach by integrating a small number of Jesuit martyrs into a much larger cycle of early Christian and medieval saints.

Since most of the men represented in the recreation room died on overseas missions, the series also served as a commemoration of the Society's mission enterprise, proudly displaying the Jesuit imprint on five continents: 'In [Christ's] name they gave their lives, and coloured both land and sea with their blood; so that the sun rises and looks upon the diverse places in the inhabitable world.'[155] This too was a favourite theme of the young order, which had achieved spectacular success in the world missions by 1600. By the end of the sixteenth century, nearly nine thousand Jesuits served in twenty-six provinces around the world, in

Africa, Asia, and the Americas.[156] The recreation room paintings depict Jesuit missionaries who fell in Brazil, Ceylon, Africa, Florida, Goa, and Japan, among other exotic locales, and also in England, Transylvania, Portugal, and Sicily. Non-European Jesuits are proudly included: two Japanese crucified in 1597 are noted by Richeôme for their 'faces of olive colour and tiny eyes.'[157] These figures would have resonated particularly strongly with the residents of S. Andrea since the four young Japanese 'ambassadors' from a Jesuit-sponsored mock diplomatic mission had actually stayed there during their sojourn in Rome in 1586.[158] Richeôme especially rejoices in the conversions of non-Europeans, whose Christianity he contrasts with the disposition of heretics who 'carry the name of a Christian' but who are cruel sinners. This same irony was raised in a 1582 publication by the English Jesuit Robert Parsons when comparing the Protestants in England to the Daimyo of Bungo in Japan, although he acknowledged the practical reasons behind the Daimyo's generosity. In an open letter to English Protestants, he wrote: 'The kinge of Bungo in Iapan beinge a heathen hathe permitted & protected the catholique religion in his countries thes 28. yeres onlye for the commoditie he feelethe his commonwealthe to receave thereof ... The like dothe the great Turcke and other Princes of Mahometes secte at this daye.'[159] Richeôme notes with excitement that someone in the recreation room can experience virtual travel to the Orient, 'without leaving the harbour of this room,' and that 'in an instant we are transported to the West [i.e., the Americas].'[160] The paintings allow the viewer to engage in long-distance armchair travel in much the same way as Matthias Tanner's much later martyrological encyclopaedia, *Societas Iesu usque ad sanguinis et vitae profusium militans* (Prague, 1675), a giant compendium of Jesuit deaths on the missions that divides its martyrs by continent.[161] The notion recalls the Observant Franciscans and their virtual pilgrimages to the Holy Land.

In a fascinating passage Richeome makes quite explicit the purpose of the paintings in the recreation room, using traditional military language to rally his young soldiers of Christ. The pictures are meant to recall for the novices the 'victories and laurels' of their brother Jesuits and to serve as a model for the young men in their future ministry – not only to honour their memory, but to serve as an example for you, and an inspiration to follow the path of their spirit, and their faith, and their love, and their zeal toward God, for the glory and the salvation of humanity. These are just like lessons or sermons that speak to your eyes, and to your hearts without a word, to demonstrate to you and push you softly toward your duty and toward virtue.'[162] He draws a parallel with classical tradition, recalling that the brave young men of antiquity also used images of valiant men of the past to inspire them: 'The ancient Romans, possessing a natural prudence, placed in their homes statues of the valiant men of their race, and arranged them according to rank in rooms in niches, with paintings and epilogues of their accomplishments, with the purpose of inspiring those who look upon them to imitate the valour of those whose portraits they observe.'[163] This use of the portraits of great men to inspire later generations recalls the popularity in the later sixteenth century of history books punctuated with illustrations of warriors, church leaders, literary figures, and reformers from the past, all depicted as though the likenesses were taken from ancient coins. One of the most popular was by a Jesuit: Orazio

Torsellino's *Ristretto dell'historie del mondo* (1598), a history of great men and women from the time of Adam, was republished many times into the seventeenth century and was very popular among artists and patrons alike.[164] Richeôme also uses martial imagery when suggesting how the paintings can serve as a kind of visual boot camp: 'You are in the premier academy of this Society, where one learns how to handle arms, to stab and subdue the body, to give the death blow to vice, and vanquish the passions'; he fortifies his readers with a further exhortation: 'You will do well to grasp the particularities of these images, my little brothers, so that you will learn the lesson of enduring and fighting for our Saviour according to the example of your brothers.'[165] The role of the pictures as presenting a model for behaviour is especially effective since many of the martyrs, like Rodolfo Acquaviva, were themselves novices at S. Andrea.

In a typically Jesuit way Richeôme turns the tragedy of martyrdom into a victory, encouraging his readers not to dwell on the death of the flesh but to think of the attainment of paradise. He stresses the joyful and optimistic aspect of the deaths in serving as the road to salvation, an emphasis Herz has already noted in connection with the Gesù and the collegiate chapels.[166] As in these other cycles the recreation room martyrs and martyrdoms also have a christological basis: the cycle focuses on an image of Christ bearing the cross at La Storta and exhorting the faithful to take up their own crosses and follow him. This rejection of the vanity of the world and the superficiality of luxury and worldly pleasure, which we have already seen in the chapel, is a theme that runs throughout Richeôme's book.

The Dormitory

The next section of Richeôme's manual deals with the paintings that adorn the dormitory rooms. Since the dormitory was the literal abode of the novices, its paintings depicted the heavenly abode and its manifold inhabitants. Six large, crowded empyreans featured the Madonna and Child reigning over different groups of dwellers in heaven, including angels, patriarchs and prophets, apostles, martyrs, virgins, confessors, and, finally, departed Jesuits. The first painting, which is reproduced in one of Greuter's engravings, was *Madonna and Child Adored by Angels* (fig. 25). We have already encountered the Jesuit predilection for angels in the chapel and refectory, not to mention in the figures of the guardian angels assigned to each of the hundred martyrs depicted in the recreation room. This painting, however, introduces a more controversial aspect of the Jesuit interest in angels, one evident also in the Gesù's Angels' Chapel – the cult of the Seven Archangels. Although there are numerous cherub heads included in the sunburst around the Madonna and Child, there are only seven full-length angels depicted below, a highly significant number.

Sixteenth-century Italy witnessed a surge of interest in the Seven Archangels (Michael, Gabriel, Raphael, and four apocryphal angels by the name of Uriel, Sealchiel, Jehudiel, and Barachiel), whose cult is tied to the apocryphal Book of Enoch, cabbalistic texts, and the writings of the Church Fathers.[167] In 1516, amid great jubilation, a medieval fresco of the Seven Archangels (now destroyed) was 'discovered' in the church of S. Angelo Carmelitano in Palermo, igniting a fervour for the cult that quickly fuelled the dynastic pretensions not only of great families such as the Farnese in Rome but also of the Spanish imperial government, which ruled Sicily. Emperor Charles V wasted no time in founding a church devoted to the cult in Sicily, in 1523, and the Seven Archangels quickly took on imperial overtones, with the Spanish eventually commissioning works of art depicting the apocryphal angels in Spain and the Americas in order to glorify their regime in a spirit of Christian triumphalism.[168] The Farnese pope Paul III founded a monastery dedicated to the Seven Archangels in Sicily in 1542, which was later administered by Cardinal Alessandro until his death in 1589, and the Farnese were major supporters of the cult in Rome.[169] These Sicilian foundations, together with the inauguration of the Imperial Confraternity of the Seven Archangels in the same year, led to the consecration in their honour of the Roman basilica of S. Maria degli Angeli (St Mary of the Angels) on the site of the Baths of Diocletian in 1550; shortly afterward, in 1561 under Pope Pius IV (1559–65), it was transformed by Michelangelo into one of the largest churches in Rome.[170] For the high altar Domenico da Modena painted a canvas depicting the Seven Archangels on their knees adoring the infant Christ as the embodiment of the Divine Word (1575), and that depiction became a model for subsequent Seven Archangels imagery in Italy.[171]

The devotion of the Seven Archangels had been brought to Rome first by the Sicilian prelate Antonio Lo Duca, who wrote the illuministic bestseller *Messa dei sette angeli* (Mass of the Seven Angels, 1543) expounding upon the iconography and theology of the painting in Palermo and printed under the patronage of Cardinal Antonio Del Monte.[172] Lo Duca had close connections with the Jesuits: not only was he a personal friend of Ignatius of Loyola, but he ran an orphanage in Rome founded by Ignatius beginning in the year after the publication of his book. In his writings and preaching Lo Duca also drew on the angelic visions of the Portuguese mystic Beato Amadeo (Joannes Menesius da Silva, 1431–82), a Franciscan who had come to Italy and there became not only confessor to Sixtus IV but something of an agent for the Spanish crown.[173] Amadeo was based at S. Pietro in Montorio, which was lavishly restored by Ferdinand and Isabella in a renovation that included the construction of Bramante's Tempietto, and he founded a branch of Observant Franciscans. The so-called Amadeists would have a Jesuit connection as well, since the Amadeist father Teodosio da Lodi, also based at S. Pietro, became Ignatius of Loyola's confessor. Amadeo's angelic revelations were published in his immensely popular *Apocalipsis nova*, in which the Angel Gabriel reveals to him the names of the apocryphal angels.

From the time of Ignatius, several Jesuits promoted the cult of the Seven Archangels, although there was always a sense even within the order that it was dangerous theology. Some Jesuits took the cult too far and paid for their mistake. Guillaume Postel (1510–81), a wildly prophetic angelic visionary and a follower of Amadeo, was allowed to join the Society in 1543, but asked to leave in 1545 when his prophecies became an embarrasment. Although neither Ignatius nor Francis Borgia was entirely free of illusionistic tendencies, in 1549 Ignatius called Amadeo's *Apocalipsis nova* a dangerous book on the ground that it could lead to false prophecy. Later on, Robert Bellarmine joined forces with the Oratorian Cesare Baronio in prohibiting the use of the four apocryphal names, a decision adopted as Church policy in the later 1590s, although neither of those two men objected to the depiction of seven nameless angels. Nevertheless, the cult continued to be supported by several prominent Jesuits after the prohibition, and it went on to have a long afterlife in the seventeenth and eighteenth centuries, especially in the Spanish Empire, where the Church promoted apocryphal angel imagery – complete with the names – as a symbol for the triumph of Christianity. One of the most celebrated examples is the series of paintings of apocryphal angels in the parish church of Calamarca, in present-day Bolivia (seventeenth–eighteenth century). In Italy, Lo Duca's *Messa* was reprinted in 1604 (in Naples), and the cause of cabbalistic, apocryphal illuminism was taken up by mystically inclined Jesuits such as Athanasius Kircher (1602–80) well into the following century.[174]

The imagery of the Seven Archangels flourished along with the cult itself. Engravings of the Palermo fresco circulated from the 1540s, and paintings of the iconography appeared two decades earlier, when Vincenzo da Pavia executed a canvas showing the Seven Archangels for the *cappella maggiore* of the Palermo church.[175] Two paintings of the Seven Archangels also graced the temporary wooden altars set up at the original church of S. Maria degli Angeli during the church's consecration in 1550.[176] A highly influential engraved series of apocryphal angels identified by name and attribute was published in the later sixteenth century by the Antwerp printmakers Peter de Jode, Phillip Galle, and Crispijn de Passe the Elder.[177] In the second half of the century Italian and Flemish painters took several different approaches to the depiction of the Seven Archangels, showing them venerating either the Trinity, the Coronation of the Virgin, or the Madonna and Child, but most positioned the angels in the lower register and evoked the rigid medieval or Byzantine-inspired style of the Sicilian original. Some showed the angels in a contemplative pose, as in Domenico da Modena's altarpiece, which has them kneeling in a semicircle in prayer.[178] Other paintings, including Vincenzo da Pavia's lost version, are much more triumphalist, showing the angels marching in full battle regalia and lined up in a frieze. The cult of the Seven Archangels was also popular in Oratorian circles (Filippo Neri was a friend of Lo Duca), and Durante Alberti combined the Oratorian iconography of S. Maria in Vallicella with the Seven Archangels in his *Madonna della Vallicella Venerated by the Seven Archangels* (ca. 1599) for the church of SS. Nereo ed Achilleo.[179] Alberti's painting, possibly designed by Baronio himself, chooses the contemplative, introspective pose with the angels on their knees, although it avoids any overt references to the apocryphal names or attributes.

The most famous – and notorious – Seven Archangels picture is Scipione Pulzone's altarpiece for the Angels' Chapel in the Gesù. It may be the image immortalized in a popular print by Hieronymus Wierix of Antwerp (ca. 1600), which chooses the triumphalist iconography of the standing angels (see chapter 7) (fig. 26). The Pulzone picture was criticized for its indecency and ordered covered over by Clement VIII in 1594, although for an unknown reason the order was not carried out until 1600, by Federico Zuccaro (see chapters 6 and 7).[180] Zuccaro's version, still visible today under a heavy-handed seventeenth- and eighteenth-century restoration, includes all seven angels, but like Alberti's image in SS. Nereo ed Achilleo it has eradicated any reference to their names or their attributes (fig. 104). By the early seventeenth century this would become the norm; although artists still often grouped angels in sevens, in Italy (unlike Bolivia) they did not dare to inscribe the names of any more than the three orthodox angels.

Although the *Madonna and Child Adored by Angels* in the Novitiate dormitory is only superficially similar to Pulzone's Gesù version (if that is indeed what is depicted in the Wierix print), it does favour the 'battle-ready' appearance of the angels over the more contemplative model of Durante. Richeôme stresses the triumphalist and military qualities of the phalanx of archangels in the engraving. He calls the angels the 'hosts of the dormitory of God ... noble couriers of his Majesty, Generals of his army ... who especially guard this place, as they do all holy locations, protecting one and all, as your assistants and safeguards.'[181] The dormitory painting is closest in composition to a painting by the Neapolitan Giovan Filippo Criscuolo (1500–70/85?) now in the Duomo in Gaeta, which similarly features an iconic Madonna and Child in the upper portion of the canvas surrounded by cherubs, while the lower half is filled with a frieze of elegant, elongated angel figures, with Michael holding the banner as the pivot.[182] Here, the artist has arranged the angels asymmetrically, four on the left and three on the right, as a way of having Michael anchor the group at the centre. Since Richeôme's book postdates the Church's prohibition of the cult, his engraving of the Novitiate painting does not supply names for the angels (unlike the Wierix print). Nevertheless, given the number and odd arrangement of the angels, it is tempting to suggest that the original painting may well have identified both the orthodox and the apocryphal angels by name. Why else would the angels be separated into three (orthodox) and four (apocryphal)? There are more clues in the text.

Richeôme's book makes clear that the number seven is no mere coincidence. Using a dense tangle of scriptural sources, including Revelation and the Church Fathers, he states that there are seven angels, 'four on one side and three on the other, who represent the Seven Spirit Princes assisting God, as the scripture teaches us. And this mysterious number of seven denotes the general and universal court of celestial spirits.'[183] While his references are all orthodox, the division into two groups of angels remains unexplained. Another hint that the painting originally depicted the apocryphal angels is provided by his references to their attributes. Richeôme mentions that one of the angels is holding a crown, the attribute of the apocryphal angel Jehudiel (curiously, it does not appear in the picture itself), and the engraving shows another angel, the farthest to the left, holding a censer, the universal symbol of Sealchiel. There may be another apocryphal attribute as well. Two of the angels appear to be holding lilies, the symbol of Gabriel, as we can see in the third angel from the right. The other 'lily,' however, held by the second angel to the left, is much smaller and less defined – it looks more like a bouquet of mixed flowers, such as morning glories and roses. Bouquets of roses or morning glories are the symbol of the apocryphal angel Barachiel.

The rest of the paintings in the dormitory show the Madonna and Child reigning over the human inhabitants of heaven. The first is *Madonna and Child as Queen of Patriarchs and Prophets*. The Virgin's crown, made of brilliant stars and cherub heads, 'is the sign of the light of the virtues and glory with which the soul of this Woman is illuminated and ennobled above the angelic creatures.'[184] Below is a row of elders, of 'princes, patriarchs, prophets, and the oldest people of God,' including Abraham, Isaac, Moses, David, and St John the Baptist. The next picture, *Madonna and Child as Queen of the Apostles*, Richeome uses as an excuse to refer once more to the Jesuits' world missions. The apostles, after all, were the first missionaries, and the Jesuits believed that some of them travelled beyond Europe to the farthest reaches of Asia and even the Americas. Richeôme recounts how Thomas 'afterwards preached the faith in barbarian lands in India and Peru,' and emphasizes other apostles' work in Asia Minor, Ethiopia, Mesopotamia, and Persia, all regions where the Jesuits were active in the seventeenth century.[185]

The third picture, *Madonna and Child as Queen of Martyrs and Virgins*, also focuses on subjects dear to Jesuit hearts and related to other imagery in the Novitiate. The Virgin, who as Richeôme explains suffered her martyrdom at the foot of the cross, reigns over a microcosm of male and female martyrs, including ecclesiastics, popes, bishops, religious, kings, princes, gentlemen, magistrates, police, artisans, and workers – both young and old. The sexes are divided, with the men on the right and the women on the left. Martyrdom and virginity are related, Richeôme explains, since they are two prerogatives of the law of grace, and since both require endurance. At the bottom of the painting are the Holy Innocents, also illustrated in other Jesuit foundations, most notably at S. Stefano Rotondo and the Gesù. Richeôme ends his description of this painting with what can only be described as a battle cry: 'Oh, you happy ones, my little brothers – to be called ... to this house of innocence, of childhood, of combat, of victory, of triumph, in order to become small innocents, small children, great men, and grand captains, to learn there to endure and suffer, to fight and win, to triumph to the end, the palm of victory in their hand, and on their head the crown of laurels, and the immortal verdure of happiness!'[186] This painting is one of the very few in the Novitiate featuring women (other than the Madonna) among its principal subjects.

The next painting, *Madonna as Queen of Confessors*, continues the saintly catalogue of the dormitory, this time focusing on men who confessed and honoured God unto death. Here the division is not between the sexes but between the sacred and secular worlds. On one side (he does not indicate whether right or left) we find popes, Doctors of the Church, religious, hermits, cardinals, patriarchs, archbishops, abbots, and priests, and on the other side emperors, kings, princes, gentlemen, soldiers, judges, artisans, and labourers. Here Richeôme takes advantage of the diversity of the crowd to make a highly Ignatian statement: No two of us are alike, and everyone serves God in his own way, yet we are all men of common nature and essence. This theme of variety in unity echoes the flexibility in the *Spiritual Exercises*, which stresses that the Exercises 'must be adapted to the condition of the one who is to engage in them, that is, to his age, education, and talent' (par. 18).[187]

The final painting in the dormitory, *Madonna as Queen of the Blessed of the Society*, recapitulates the themes of the other five in a specifically Jesuit key. Here, in pre-1622 Rome, are depicted the closest thing the Jesuits had to saints – their heroes Ignatius of Loyola, 'the General Chief of this little spiritual army'; Francis Xavier, 'another great Captain'; Stanislas Kostka; and a multitude of fathers and brothers. Making a direct link with the Jesuits depicted in the recreation room and also with the young Jesuit viewers themselves, this painting represents the kind of saint-hood treated in the other dormitory paintings and gives it a Jesuit identity. Richeôme points out that there are both confessors and martyrs among these Jesuits, and explains that everyone can become a saint of one of the kinds depicted in the six paintings of the dormitory: if you are a father of an order (like Ignatius), you are patriarch; if you predict the future by divine inspiration (as did both Ignatius and Francis Xavier), you are a prophet; if you are sent to ignorant people to bring them news of the law and faith of Christ (like Francis Xavier and the multitude of missionaries), you are an apostle; if you shed blood for the faith, you are a martyr; if you are a practitioner of holy works, you are a confessor; and finally, if you guard your virginity, you are a virgin.[188] As we have seen, virginity is a theme Richeôme stresses throughout this section of the book, using mar-tyrological, missionary, and triumphalist imagery.

The list of categories of saints provided in the dormitory related directly to devotional practice. On a basic level, the categories corresponded with those in the Litany of the Saints, a solemn series of invocations to the Trinity that called upon the intercession of the Virgin Mary and of the angels, apostles, patriarchs, martyrs, confessors, and virgins, both individually and as a group. By this time every Jesuit community likely gathered once a day to recite together the Litany of the Saints, and it was the only communal prayer.[189] Like the students of the German-Hungarian College, the Jesuit novices probably also practised a weekly devotional cycle honouring different categories of saints on the different days of the week except for feast days. Monday was the angels, sometimes together with the patri-archs; Tuesday, the apostles; Wednesday, the martyrs; Thursday, the Doctors of the Church and the bishops; Friday, the confessors, religious, and hermits, or sometimes the cross; Saturday, the virgins; and Sunday, the Virgin Mary.[190] Each week thereby became a miniature All Saints cycle within the larger annual cycle of the liturgical calendar. The dormitory paintings at the Novitiate, representing similar categories of saints and all subject to the Virgin Mary, again recall the close relationship between imagery and the practice of devotion in Jesuit institutions.

3

The Novitiate Infirmary

None of the rooms we have seen so far in the Novitiate of S. Andrea al Quirinale prepares us for the iconographic complexity of the infirmary, the subject of Book Five of Richeôme's treatise and of almost two hundred pages of text. Decorated with one of the most extraordinary fresco cycles of the late Renaissance, this building has never been studied before – a remarkable omission, given the unusual iconography of the cycle and what it tells us about Early Modern medicine. The infirmary is also the only part of the Novitiate, as far as we know, in which inscriptions are incorporated into the decorations, in a kind of 'captioning' that will also appear in the collegiate chapels and the Gesù. An erudite and eclectic blend of biblical scenes, stories from the lives of the saints, images of the early Jesuits, ingenious allegorical tableaux, and what can only be described as the Early Modern equivalent of illustrations from a medical journal, the imagery was meticulously programmed to lead the sick on a spiritual journey by taking advantage of their maladies to teach lessons about moral choice, endurance, and salvation. The narratives and allegories are based on biblical, patristic, medieval, and modern sources, as well as on the writings of a wide range of classical authors such as Pliny, Aesop, Plutarch, Galen, Horace, Seneca, Virgil, and – appropriately – Hippocrates; the blend attests to the Jesuits' commitment to Christian humanism. It is like no other hospital decoration anywhere else in Italy.

One of the most fascinating things about the infirmary decorations is that the inscriptions have a different tenor depending on their location. Those on the lintel over the door outside the room address the visitor, exhorting him to walk in and visit the patient inside. The inscriptions over the head of the beds (each room could hold four patients, each of whom would have had his own bed)[1] are written as though issuing from the mouths of the patients. These passages are taken in many cases from Psalm 37, the third pentitential psalm and a prayer for remission of sin; Psalm 101, the fifth penitential psalm and a prayer for one in affliction; and Psalm 102, a psalm of thanksgiving. They are highly personal and often visceral expressions of pain and suffering.[2] The inscriptions on the wall between the beds and the side wall are addressed to the patient and speak of endurance and patience, sometimes quoting from the Book of Job. Finally, the inscriptions behind the door, to be read as the visitor leaves the room, are meant to symbolize the doctor's diagnosis. Taken exclusively from Hippocrates' *Aphorisms*, they universalize the personal suffering alluded to in the rest of the inscriptions. The effect when the rooms were in use must have been that of a three-dimensional emblem, with the people and paintings as the devices and the inscriptions as the epigrams.

No other part of the Novitiate is as carefully scripted, and nowhere – except perhaps in the recreation room – do we find the same iconographic density. The complex cluster of iconic and narrative imagery in each of the infirmary's thirteen bedrooms (there is also a small refectory) is given thematic unity not only by the four Latin inscriptions but by an allegorical 'keystone' image in the ceiling vault.[3] In addition, the iconography of each room is linked to that of adjacent rooms in the infirmary so that the entire complex resonates with the same overall themes. What emerges from an examination of these fascinating rooms is not only a clearer sense of the Jesuits' own self-image as manifest in the formation of their novices, but an enthralling glimpse at medical practices and beliefs during the late Renaissance.

The pride of place given in Richeôme's manual to the infirmary reflects a general concern within the Society of Jesus for physical health. Diseases and their cures were a major preoccupation of even the earliest Jesuits. Although they saw disease as having natural causes, they also shared a common belief that God had created sickness as a punishment for sin, and that the faithful could accept their diseases as a test and a purgation designed to perplex God's enemies.[4] Caring for the sick and visiting hospitals in the city ranked among the most important 'exercises of humility' listed in Jesuit accounts of the Novitiate and the colleges, as in this passage concerning the year 1596 in Navarola's history of S. Andrea: 'Many [young men] perform this exercise with great results, not only Ours but also the students of the German, English, and Greek Colleges, as well as other noble externs, some of them with the resolve to leave the world and enter into the religious life.'[5] Visiting the sick was also one of the corporal works of mercy. Disease wreaked havoc especially in religious houses, owing to the communal way of life therein, and the Jesuits were particularly concerned about the health of their members.[6] From at least 1562, directives for Jesuit colleges called for the segregation of the sick in special wings.[7] Ignatius of Loyola devotes an entire chapter of the *Constitutions* to 'The Preservation of the Body,' and comments that 'a proper concern about the preservation of one's health and bodily strength for the divine service is praiseworthy, and all should exercise it.'[8] Ignatius also charged Jesuit superiors with the task of promoting the health of their subordinates and caring for them when they became sick. Ignatius felt he had ruined his own health through severe penances and did not want his followers to repeat the mistake.[9] The Jesuits' letters of the sixteenth century frequently discuss illnesses in their own communities and in their congregations; the descriptions are so detailed that A. Lynn Martin has recently completed a major study of epidemics in Early Modern Europe based almost entirely on Jesuit letters.[10]

Richeôme prefaces his discussion of the infirmary with a brief meditation on how the pictures work on their viewers. The images we have looked at so far, he writes, are there to assist you when you are hale and healthy; these ones, on the other hand, are there to serve you in times of sickness.[11] The infirmary paintings are meant to help dispose you toward death if that is God's will; to make you patient, humble, and obedient in your pain and afflictions; and to encourage you to be indifferent as to living or dying. But above all they are meant to be studied closely, as visual lessons and meditations. Some of them, as we will see, are even meant quite literally to cure the patient. The paintings also have the same thematic relationship to function that we have seen elsewhere in the Novitiate. Almost all the frescoes and altarpieces in the infirmary depict either scenes of illness or death, or scenes of cures, both spiritual and corporal. There are famous episodes from the Bible, such as the illnesses of the prophets Ezekiel and Elisha and of Lazarus; a depiction of the death of Stanislas Kostka; and depictions of medicines and curative waters.[12]

The infirmary was a complex of small vaulted rooms carefully designed to provide a healthy circulation of air and sunshine in both summer and winter. As mentioned in chapter 2, the rooms were arranged on two floors along a corridor running east to west, so that half received more sun in the winter and the other half in the summer (fig. 16). The infirmary was located behind the old and new churches, in the north wing of the courtyard; it was built in 1594 and added to in 1605. Most of the paintings probably date from the mid- to late 1590s. Although the rooms were no more than some ten or twelve feet square, each had its own altar, with a small relief stucco altarpiece, and about eight narrative frescoes on the four walls, an allegorical fresco or image of a saint in the vault, and the four inscriptions. The account book also shows that the entrance to each room was flanked by thin columns (*colonelle*).[13] There were about a hundred novices by the early seventeenth century, but the rooms could hold over fifty patients, and its capacity suggests that the complex served as an infirmary not only for the novices but for the entire Jesuit community in Rome. That would have made sense, since the building had a healthier setting, on a well-ventilated hill, than the Jesuits' other foundations, which were in low-lying areas.

Each room was dedicated to a biblical figure, saint, or beatified Jesuit, and each altarpiece depicted a consecutive episode in the lives of the Virgin and Christ, beginning with the presentation of the Virgin at the Temple and ending with Christ's resurrection (Room Twelve) and the triumph of St Michael (Room Thirteen). I would like very much to be able to determine where each of these painted rooms used to be. Unfortunately, the room numbers given in Richeôme's text do not correspond to the numbers in figure 14, and – to make matters even more confusing – even the *number* of rooms does not correspond to the number represented in existing plans or diary descriptions. Richeôme does not even indicate which rooms are on the upper floor and which on the lower. For consistency, the room numbers used in this book are those listed in Richeôme's text.

Rooms One to Five

Room One was dedicated to Ignatius of Loyola, and included Old and New Testament scenes in addition to episodes from Ignatius's life.[14] The caption-like inscriptions found in the room created a model for the other rooms in the infirmary in combining material from the New Testament, the Old Testament, the Psalms, and classical antiquity. The inscription one saw over the door upon entering quoted Christ's words describing the Last Judgment and telling how the Son of Man will reward those who helped him in adversity: INFIRMUS ERAM & VISITASTIS ME (I was sick, and you visited me [Matt. 25:36]). The quotation could be read as an exhortation to the person visiting the patient inside the room. On the head of the beds were words from Psalm 101, a prayer of the afflicted: DIES MEI SICUT UMBRA DECLINAVERUNT, & EGO SICUT FOENUM ARUI (For my days are vanished like smoke, and I am smitten as grass [Ps. 101:3–4]). The inscription in the space between the beds and the wall was a cautionary reminder from the Book of Job, whose patience and endurance were a major theme throughout the infirmary rooms: HOMO NATUS DE MULIERE, BREVI VIVENS TEMPORE, REPLETUR MULTIS MISERIIS (Man, born of a woman, living for a short time, is filled with many miseries [Job 14:1]). Thus was the patient encouraged not to place importance in this life and to make his peace with God.

The theme of the brevity of life was taken up in the inscription behind the door, this time from a classical author, the Greek physician Hippocrates (ca. 460–ca. 377): VITA BREVIS, ARS LONGA OCCASIO PRAECEPS (Life is short, and art long; the occasion fleeting [*Aphorisms* I.1]).[15] Hippocrates' *Aphorisms* and Galen's *Tegni* were the two principal texts used in the examination of the College of Medicine and Arts of Bologna as early as the late fourteenth century; they had formed part of the curriculum in Italian medical schools since medicine became an autonomous discipline by about 1300.[16] The works of both Hippocrates and Galen (129–ca. 199 AD), another Greek physician who was the doctor of the Roman emperor Marcus Aurelius, were also found in Jesuit college libraries, such as that of S. Giovannino in Florence, where they are listed in an inventory of 1579.[17] The two men were the most influential physicians of antiquity, and their theories formed the basis of medieval and Early Modern medicine before the seventeenth century. It is remarkable that the Jesuits gave so much room to Hippocrates in the infirmary murals, since the Greek physician was a staunch opponent of the belief that diseases had divine causes. His ideas and writings, emphasizing the natural causes of disease, therefore served as a foil for the spiritual illnesses described in other frescoes and inscriptions.

The entire Jesuit outlook on matters of health struck a balance between belief in the spiritual and belief in the natural causes of illness. The Jesuits held to what they called 'primary' and 'secondary' causes and remedies for disease, the former being supernatural and the latter natural.[18] Primary causes had to do with the visiting of disease as a punishment for sin and as a test of the individual directed towards the purgation of sin. Diseases with spiritual origins called for spiritual remedies, such as penitence, confession, communion, processions, and prayers to protective saints. Secondary causes of disease were divided into 'natural' (including celestial influences, contagion, the corruption of the air) and 'unnatural' (such as intentional poisoning). Antonio Possevino wrote about primary causes in a pamphlet called *Causes and Remedies of the Pest and Other Diseases* (Florence, 1577), which attributed most disease to sin and recommended penitence as an 'adequate summary of the remedies,' but also acknowledged secondary causes such as 'bad quality of the humors, or ... corruption of the air, or ... contagion.'[19] In a 1562 set of directives for Jesuit colleges, Jerónimo Nadal encouraged such secondary remedies as fumigating rooms, purchasing medicine, consulting physicians, segregating the sick, striving to avoid infection, and keeping a supply of new clothes on hand.[20] Air quality was emphasized by the early Jesuits and is one reason why the S. Andrea infirmary rooms were arranged so that a draught could pass through them from north to south. When combating epidemic disease, the Jesuits promoted three therapeutic programs, all of which focused on secondary remedies: 'The first was the development of the healthy body through a healthy diet, regular exercise, and the promotion of moderation. The second was the restoration of balance within the body and the strengthening of the body's constitution through proper medication. The third was the expulsion of poisons or toxins through purging, bloodletting, and sweating.'[21] This regimen was based on the ancient theory of the four humours, to which I will return in more detail.[22]

The small altarpiece in Room One was the *Presentation of the Virgin at the Temple*, the first in the series of episodes from the lives of the Virgin and Christ, whose example was to serve as a model for the novice. In most of the rooms there was a direct link between the bas-relief altarpiece and the fresco behind it, an anticipation of the Baroque 'spatial involvement' noted by Hibbard in the early chapels of the Gesù; I will return to these in chapter 7.[23] In this case the Virgin was meant to be contemplating the heavens in anticipation of her giving birth to the Son of God. Consequently, the fresco on the wall behind this altar was the *Creation of the World*, in the form of a map of the celestial and earthly realms. At the top was a golden roundel containing the Holy Trinity, and below it another roundel containing the heavens and the stars. Below the celestial sphere were the elements, in the middle of them a representation of Earth with its multitude of beasts. Separate from the animals was humankind, in the form of Adam and Eve in the Garden of Eden. The theme of Adam was taken up in the fresco on the opposite side of the room, a complicated multiple image called the *Moral Causes of Maladies*.

Like many frescoes in the infirmary, this painting (it is reproduced in Richeôme's volume) had a rare and unusual iconography. Divided into *quadri riportati*, the painting contained seven separate images of illness, banishment, and redemption, with the overall message that bodily sickness can elicit spiritual cures (fig. 27). At the top was *Adam and Eve Expelled from the Garden*, and the sins of their progeny were personified by the plague-stricken mortals lying in the central section, entitled *The Probatic Pool*. This central image showed the curative pool in Jerusalem mentioned in John 5:2 into which those afflicted with every kind of illness immersed themselves in order to be cured during the periodic visits of an angel, who here was shown in the centre. Christ met a man there too weak to place himself in the waters, cured him on the spot, and later told him: 'Behold thou art made whole: sin no more, lest a worse thing come unto thee' (John 5:14). In the context of this painting, therefore, the pool filled with sick men and women represented the world of mortal sin, and Christ's words warned the viewer that he too might achieve spiritual healing through his sickness but must not take his second chance lightly.

Also known as the Pool of Bethesda, the Probatic Pool was a relatively rare subject for a painting and was usually incorporated in hospital decoration. An early example by Iacopo del Sellaio (1446–93) for the church of S. Agostino in

Castiglion Fiorentino (Tuscany) on a horizontal format is similar to the Novitiate version in that it depicts a hexagonal pool and shows the angel above; but Iacopo's version, with only a single figure at prayer in the pool, becomes a metaphor for baptism. Versions from the same period as the Novitiate painting include the circular pool featured in the version by the Bolognese painter Lucio Massari (1569–1633), which is set in front of an open portico crowned with narrow pyramid finials, with the people dispersed around the side in classically inspired poses.[24] A version with a square pool was painted by the Genoese painter Giovan Battista Paggi (1554–1627) for the chapel of S. Egidio in the Florentine hospital of S. Maria Nuova (1592); a bozzetto survives in the Villa Guinigi in Lucca, and an autograph copy made for S. Maria a Petrognano in Castiglion Fiorentino substitutes a group portrait (of doctors?) for some of the male bystanders on the right (fig. 28).[25] Paggi's version is so overwhelmed by the principal figures that the pool itself is relegated to the background, although the upper part of the picture is dominated by a Bramante-like dome and the grand columns of the foreground portico.

The tableaux that flanked the image of the Pool of Bethesda in the Novitiate fresco underscored the metaphor for sin and redemption by showing that God sends illness to men not only to punish them for their sins but also to test and prove their virtue. Clockwise from the upper left they included *Plague of the Israelites*, *Plague of the Philistines*, *Job upon the Ashes*, and *Tobias Stricken*. At the bottom of the fresco was a scene of Christ healing a leper (Matt. 8:3). The moral of this painting was that afflictions are sent to test and purify, that a corporal illness can cure spiritual sin, and that Christ can cure all maladies (Matt. 4:23). Affliction, Richeôme reminds us, can be just as profitable as health.

The next three images in Room One, appropriately enough, were from the life of Ignatius of Loyola. The first scene, painted on the wall opposite the door, was *Ignatius Putting a Nest of Vipers to Chase*. Set in a forest, where the hero is travelling as a pilgrim, the picture showed the Jesuit founder making the sign of the cross and repelling a group of snakes poised for attack. Richeôme compares Ignatius to biblical figures threatened by snakes, as well as to a plethora of saints including Pachomius, Hilary, Julian, Marcian the Syrian, Donatus, and Amand, and concludes with the remark that all these episodes show the saints as having the power to defeat both real and spiritual serpents. He also mentions the missions again, pointing out that snakes are commonly encountered in Brazil. The theme of serpents as a metaphor for evil, and of Satan's attempts to divert the faithful from their spiritual pilgrimage, will reappear throughout the infirmary. The last two frescoes also showed other scenes from the life of Ignatius, including *Ignatius Preaching*, painted over the door, and *Transfiguration of Blessed Ignatius*, in which Ignatius is surrounded by a multitude of triumphant angels playing musical instruments – a scene that gives Richeôme another excuse for a diatribe on guardian angels and prompts him to remark that angels rejoice at the penitence of sinners (Luke 16:10). The Ignatian theme of the room was taken up in the 'keystone' image on the vault, the monogram of Christ's name and symbol of the Society of Jesus, IHS.

Since Room One was devoted to Ignatius, it should come as little surprise that Room Two was named after Francis Xavier, the most important of his first companions and the founder of the Jesuit world missions.[26] Here the inscription on the lintel of the door resounded with a rebuke from the Book of Sirach (or Ecclesiasticus, from the deuterocanonical or apocryphal books) appropriate for someone who might be hesitating to enter and visit his companion: NON TE PIGEAT VISITARE INFIRMUM (Never disdain to visit those who are sick [Ecclus. 7:35]). Over the beds, a quotation from Psalm 37 created a more mournful atmosphere, as if the patient himself were speaking: AFFLICTUS SUM & HUMILITATUS SUM NIMIS (I am afflicted and humbled exceedingly [Ps. 37:9]). The greater theme of redemption through malady was taken up by the inscription in the space between the beds and the wall, from St Augustine's commentary on Psalm 102, MAGNI SUNT DOLORES TUI, SED MAIOR MEDICUS TUUS (Your pain is great, but your Doctor is greater).[27] Behind the door, as one left the room, an inscription from the same line of Hippocrates as in Room One gave a warning to physician, patient, and attendant alike: EXPERIMENTUM PERICULOSUM, IUDICIUM DIFFICILE (Experience [is] risky, and judgment difficult [*Aphorisms* I.1]).[28]

The altarpiece of Room Two was an *Annunciation*, the second episode in the life of the Virgin. Behind it, on the wall, was the first of the 'medical journal' illustrations, an elaborate diagram *Natural Causes of Maladies*, balancing *Moral Causes of Maladies* in Room One. The subjects of the painting were the four humours and the four elements, represented by a 'hieroglyph' of four men of different colours locked in combat, each grabbing and trying to throw the other, like the antagonists in Pollaiuolo's *Battle of the Nude Men* (ca. 1465). The red man with a mantle of flames was Fire and Choler; the man with wings of a violet blue was Air and Blood; the man completely covered in scales of a turquoise colour was Water and Phlegm; and the man wearing a cuirasse of bricks was Earth and Melancholy.

This painting illustrated one of the key principles of medieval and Early Modern medicine. The theory of the four humours began in antiquity, became widespread in medieval Europe when ancient texts were recovered from Islamic Spain, and was given an additional boost by the Aristotelian revival of the thirteenth century.[29] By the time the infirmary frescoes were painted the concept enjoyed wide popular appeal and was familiar not only to physicians but to laypersons. The four humours, according to the theory, are the bodily counterpart of Aristotle's four elements (fire, air, water, and earth). They take the form of fluids – blood, yellow bile, black bile, and phlegm – each of which is connected with one of four personality traits – sanguine, choleric, melancholy, and phlegmatic; the words are still used today. The four humours were also often linked with the four seasons, with the properties hot, cold, dry, and wet, with the signs of the zodiac, with the Four Ages of Mankind, and even with the four evangelists. The theory of the four humours was first formulated by Hippocrates and Galen.

According to Hippocrates, disease was not something that happened locally but a disturbance affecting the whole body, and it was created by an imbalance in the humours. In a healthy body the humours were kept in a delicate balance in the body's microcosm with the four elements of the macrocosm – earth, air, fire, and water – although all people had a slight imbalance even when healthy, and the imbalance accounted for difference in personality. Disease was caused when an excess of one humour resulted in a *dyscrasia* (abnormal mixture). The Hippocratic manual *The Nature of Man* notes: 'The human body contains blood, phlegm, yellow bile, and black bile. These are the things that make up its constitution and cause its pains and health. Health is primarily the state in which these constituent substances are in the correct proportions to each other. Pain occurs when one of these substances presents either a deficiency or an excess.'[30] This simple pathology conveniently derived all mental and physical diseases from the same natural causes. Galen also taught the importance of maintaining a balance among the four humours. If the body possesses an excess of one humour, the physician can effect a cure by introducing the opposite humour into the body in compensation. The procedure could be carried out by means of diet, medicine, and phlebotomy (bloodletting). Food and plants were believed to have hot, cold, wet, or dry properties that could be used in curing bodily imbalances, but phlebotomy was especially effective since blood was believed to contain aspects of all four humours. Although as late as the mid-seventeenth century Galen's four humours theory still formed the basis of many medical treatises, such as Robert Burton's *The Anatomy of Melancholy* (London, 1652), it had already begun to fall out of favour at the time the infirmary paintings were being executed. The German alchemist and physician Paracelsus (1493–1541), though with a limited following, had been an especially vocal opponent of Galenic theory, and with the publication of Francis Bacon's *The Proficiencie and Advancement of Learning* (1605) and René Descartes's *Discourse on Method* (1637), empirical method and experimentation changed the way physicians approached disease.

The next four frescoes in Room Two featured scenes of illness and redemption from the Old and New Testaments. On the wall across from *Natural Causes of Maladies* was *The Sickness of King Hezekiah*, an episode from the life of Hezekiah, King of Judah, who was stricken with a fatal illness (2 Kings 20:1). In the story, the prophet Isaiah prays for him, and the Lord tells Isaiah: 'Behold, I will heal thee ... And I will add unto thy days fifteen years; and I will deliver thee and this city out of the hand of the king of Assyria' (2 Kings 20:5–6). The second scene was *Christ Healing the Centurion's Servant*, showing Christ curing the servant, stricken with palsy, of a centurion in Capernaum (Matt. 8:5; Luke 7:2). The next two frescoes showed the beggar Lazarus. In the first he was covered with sores and lying at the gate of the rich man, who was dressed in fancy clothes (Luke 16:20). The second was *Lazarus Carried to the Breast of Abraham and the Bad Rich Man in Hell*, showing angels lifting the beggar's soul into heaven while the rich man writhes in agony in the inferno below (Luke 16:22). In all these biblical episodes, physical cures are followed by good works or redemption.

The seventh painting, a curious example of the 'medical journal' category, was *Miraculous Rainfalls*. The rainfalls in question were taken from the annals of history written by the ancients, including Pliny's *Natural History* (II:57).[31] They are not mere torrents of rain, but showers of snakes and toads, blood, iron, flesh, fire, sulphur, bricks, and pebbles. Only some of these phenomena are mentioned in Pliny, whose text reads:

It is entered in the records that in the consulship of Manius Acilius and Gaius Porcius [114 BC] it rained milk and blood, and that frequently on other occasions there it has rained flesh, for instance in the consulship of Publius Volumnis and Servius Sulpicius [461 BC], and that none of the flesh left unplundered by the birds of prey went bad; and similarly that it rained iron in the district of Lucania the year before Marcus Crassus was killed [53 BC] by the Parthians ... The shape of the iron that fell resembled sponges ... But in the consulship of Lucius Paullus and Gaius Marcellus [49 BC] it rained wool in the vicinity of Compsa Castle ... It is recorded in the annals of that year that while Milo was pleading a case in court it rained bricks.[32]

For those unlucky enough to have been outside during the downpours described in this passage, the message is very simple, as Richeôme reminds us: all sickness comes from heaven, whether produced by natural or by supernatural means, and, like disease, it is sent to chastise and instruct mortals. Pliny was widely read in the Jesuit colleges; editions of his *Natural History* could be found in the college libraries.[33]

Unlike all the other infirmary rooms except the convalescent refectory, Room Two had further frescoes in the spandrels of the vaults, including a monogram of the names of Jesus and Mary, a lily representing chastity, and a rose signifying charity – the latter two virtues were celebrated here in connection with Francis Xavier, to whom the room was dedicated. Additional pictures were *Francis Xavier Visiting Victims of the Plague* (an iconography that, according to a recent scholar, equates plague with heresy),[34] *Francis Xavier Saying Mass*, and an Indian scene, *Francis Xavier Encountering Demons upon Reaching the Church at Meliapur*, all of their subjects taken from the life of Xavier by Torsellino. Ever eager to draw connections between the early Jesuits and biblical figures, Richeôme here compares Xavier to Job. Xavier's role as a healer later earned him the honour of being one of the patron saints of the plague, especially in Naples in the mid-seventeenth century.[35] The last painting in the room was the wall fresco *Death of Francis Xavier*, showing the Apostle to the Indies dying on a beach on Sancian Island, within view of China, in 1552. Francis was shown here lying on the beach beneath a rude shack made of reeds, and the painting and Richeôme alike stress that he died in poverty, in imitation of Christ. This painting may have been the earliest example of what became the ubiquitous image of Francis's death. Made famous later by Carlo Maratta (1625–1713) and Baciccio (1639–1709), the *Death of St Francis Xavier* appeared in Rome only toward mid-century, and the earliest known surviving example is from Reinoso's 1619 cycle in Lisbon (fig. 29).[36]

The 'keystone' image in Room Two was an allegorical figure of Faith in the form of a young woman wearing a blindfold of black crepe and having a sun on her breast and a cube under her feet. This sort of emblem, which combined Renaissance-style pagan allegory with a Christian message, was especially popular in France, for example in G. de Montenay's illustrated *Emblèmes et dévises chrestiennes* (Lyon, 1571), and in the extraordinary engravings for the Jesuit Jan David's *Veridicus christianus* (Antwerp, 1601) and *Pancarpium marianum* (Antwerp, 1607). However, such devices are best known in late Cinquecento Italy from Cesare Ripa's celebrated *Iconologia* (Rome, 1593); they were most spectacularly transformed into a large-scale painting by Giovanni and Cherubino Alberti at the Sala Clementina in the Vatican (1595–1600) (fig. 30).[37] Ripa's *Iconologia* was created as a handbook of symbols and allegories, and was the fruit of his life-long study of classical mythology, Egyptian hieroglyphics, and Christian allegory. The infirmary allegory of Faith had some similarities with Ripa's allegory *Fede christiana*, in which the figure also stands on a cube-shaped stone, although in other respects the two were different.[38] Emblems or devices were especially popular among Jesuits, including Antonio Possevino (see chapter 1), David, and Richeôme himself, and would later find their ultimate expression in the Jesuit centenary volume *Imago primi saeculi Societatis Iesu* (Antwerp, 1640).[39]

Room Three was dedicated to another early Jesuit blessed, Aloysius Gonzaga.[40] Like Stanislas Kostka, Gonzaga (1568–91) was a young Jesuit scholastic whose life was taken before he professed his vows. The son of Don Ferrante Gonzaga, *marchese* of Castliglione delle Stiviere and a close confident of King Philip II of Spain, Aloysius was raised by his father to be a soldier.[41] But after witnessing the violence and corruption of noble society he became a missionary at the age of 16, over the strenous objections of his father, and he entered the Novitiate in 1585. He was felt to have a special relationship with the sick, since he had died, at the age of 23, tending plague victims in Rome. Over the lintel of the door was another quotation from Sirach: NON DESIS PLORANTIBUS IN CONSOLATIONE (Be not wanting in comforting them that weep [Ecclus. 7:38]). On the head of the beds was a humble cry from Psalm 37, the source of the quotation above the bed in Room Two: NON EST SANITAS IN CARNE MEA A FACIE IRAE TUE (There is no health in my flesh, because of thy wrath [Ps. 37:4]). Between the beds and the wall was another quotation from St Augustine's commentary on Psalm 103: OMNIPOTENTI MEDICO NULLUS MORBUS INCURABILIS (No sickness is incurable for the Omnipotent Doctor).[42] The inscription behind the door, once again, was from that great corporal doctor Hippocrates: QUE MULTO TEMPORE ATTENUANTUR CORPORA, LENTE REFICERE OPORTET (Those bodies which have been slowly weakened should be allowed slowly to recuperate [*Aphorisms* II.7]).[43]

In Room Three the altarpiece began the life of Christ cycle with a bas-relief *Nativity*, showing the infant Jesus resting at the feet of Mary and Joseph. On the wall behind it was another child, this time Aloysius Gonzaga at the age of 7, shown with rays of divine light extending from his body. Richeôme explains that Aloysius is shown at the same age as John the Baptist when he went out into the desert, so the entire ensemble becomes a Jesuit *Holy Family with St John the Baptist* in which Aloysius takes the place of St John. The painting on the wall opposite the altar wall, *The Prophet Elisha Falls Sick* (2 Kings 13:14), depicted the Old Testament story in which Elijah's successor is taken ill and dies. On another wall was a New Testament image, *The Sickness and Death of Lazarus*. Lazarus of Bethany was thought to be Mary Magdalene's brother, and Richeôme takes the opportunity to remind us of the humility and service of the Magdalene, who has already appeared in the refectory. *The Raising of Lazarus* was the next fresco depicting not only the scene of Christ bringing Lazarus to life but also one from Matthew (9:24) in which Christ raises from the dead a 12-year-old girl. Richeôme explains that these two scenes are provided not only because they represent the first two resurrections of sinners in the Bible, but because they can be read on a metaphorical level as representing two different kinds of sin, interior and exterior.

The allegorical 'keystone' figure in the vault was a representation of Charity. She was depicted as a noblewoman, crowned by an azure veil embroidered with golden stars and wearing a purple robe, with many young children at her feet whom she looks after and nourishes. This allegory is reminiscent of Ripa's *Charity*, which was interpreted by Cherubino and Giovanni Alberti in the Sala Clementina, as well as of Montenay's *Charity* of 1571; all these show a woman in pseudo-classical garb surrounded by small children (fig. 30).[44]

Since Room Three was devoted to Aloysius Gonzaga, it stands to reason that Room Four was given over to his counterpart in the Novitiate, Stanislas Kostka.[45] The inscriptions here followed the usual pattern. The quotation from Sirach in the lintel over the door addressed the visitor: CUM LUGENTIBUS AMBULA (Walk with them that mourn [Ecclus. 37:7]). On the head of the beds was written a cry of personal anguish from the patient, CIRCUMDEDERUNT ME DOLORES MORTIS (The sorrows of death surrounded me [Ps. 17:5]), which was answered from between the beds and the wall by a stern message from St Augustine's commentary on Psalm 103: NON TANTUM DELECTERIS DUM FECAT, ODIT REPELLENTEM MANUS SUAS (Do not only rejoice when God treats you sweetly, [but also endure it when he uses the knife] ... he detests those who reject his hand).[46] The doctor's advice behind the door asserted the practical with an equally stern word from Hippocrates: EXTREMIS MORBIS EXTREMA REMEDIA OPTIMA SUNT (For extreme diseases, extreme methods of cure ... are most suitable [*Aphorisms* I.6]).[47]

The bas-relief altarpiece in Room Four was a *Holy Family*, the next in the life of Christ series. But taken together with the wall behind it – which included an orchestra of musician angels and a group of shepherds in adoration – the altarpiece formed part of a single composition, *Adoration of the Shepherds*. On the opposite side of the room was *The Saviour Preaching and Healing* (Matt. 4:23), a significant scene for a young novice because it stressed Christ's ministry, and in particular the activities for which the novice was preparing.

The next two frescoes, more 'medical journal' illustrations, focused on types of sickness and illustrated the Jesuit notion of 'primary' and 'secondary' causes of and remedies for disease. The first was an allegorical figure, *Multitude of Maladies*, in which a man lying on his sickbed was shot through with a thousand arrows and darts raining down upon him from all sides. The arrows were meant to be piercing the five senses as well as the various parts of the body. Richeôme points out that there are many more maladies than there are parts of the body – three hundred in total if we follow Pliny.[48] The theme of the painting was the weakness of nature and of the body, and it stressed once again the ephemerality of life and the importance of spiritual health.

The next fresco, *Malady of Old Age*, featured a more specific kind of malady and was meant to teach the viewer that the sicknesses of the soul are far more dangerous than those of the body. The imagery of this painting was unusually contrived. In the upper part was an old man, speaking the words 'It is for nothing!' and rejecting the assistance of a doctor trying to lay hands upon him. Next to the old man and the doctor was a young man standing between a leopard and a fox and surrounded by surgeons ready with scalpels and razors to cut him open for an anatomy lesson. The old man, according to Richeôme, represents old age, which is incurable and stronger than the capabilities of humankind, and his rejection of the doctor follows a dictum by the Roman emperor Tiberius (14–37 AD) as recorded by Plutarch – who was also popular in Jesuit libraries – in his *Moralia* (136): 'It is not fitting for a sexagenarian to hold out his hand to doctors.'[49] Richeôme, who was no longer young himself, hastens to point out that not all elderly men have to follow this advice, but that everyone nevertheless should seek the advice of the good Doctor, Christ our Saviour. The figure of the young man signifies that just as the soul has faculties that correspond to the parts of the body, so also does it have spiritual maladies that correspond to corporal ones. These maladies, including vice, passion, and bad inclinations, are worse than any physical sickness. The fox recalls the fables of Aesop, who remarks, 'not in the language of the beasts but as a sage philosopher,' that the number of the fox's tricks is greater than the number of spots on the leopard's skin, meaning that the spots of the soul are far more numerous than those of the body.[50] Richeôme quotes in the same vein from Seneca's *Epistles* (LIII): 'A slight ague deceives us; but when it has increased and a genuine fever has begun to burn, it forces even a hardy man, who can endure much suffering, to admit that he is ill ... The opposite holds true of diseases of the soul; the worse one is, the less one perceives it.'[51] The work of Seneca, too, was included in Jesuit college libraries.[52]

Adjoining the last picture was the fresco *Diverse Remedies for Sickness*. On one side the artist painted two men dressed as doctors and on the other side two angels. These figures, in Richeôme's description, represent natural and supernatural doctors, who tend to our corporal and spiritual illness; the further division between the two men indicates that they represent lay and clerical doctors (one is a theologian). The most interesting element was in the lower half of the painting, below these figures – a panoply of stones, plants, birds, fish, and animals, laid out as if at a market. This cornucopia, taken from Pliny's *Natural History* (VIII:40–1), represented natural medicine.[53] More specifically, says Richeôme, the minerals and herbs are those that cure disease, and the animals, birds, and fish are those that have taught us through their behaviour how to use them. Pliny introduced the Romans to most of the pharmacopia of Greek medicine by collecting recipes from a variety of ancient sources; he did little, if any, of his own research.[54] These recipes promoted his idea of 'antipathy and sympathy' as the mysterious qualities that were the active principles in any cure.[55] For Pliny, animals have both a great sympathy with and a sharp antipathy to humans since they are close to them, and accordingly we can learn 'remedies [that] derive from plants and shrubs ... obtained from the very living creatures that themselves are healed.'[56] The hippopotamus, for example, taught us phlebotomy as a means of removing corrupt humours from the body: 'The hippopotamus stands out as an actual master in one department of medicine; for when its unceasing voracity has caused it to overeat itself it comes ashore to reconnoitre places where rushes have recently been cut, and where it sees an extremely sharp stalk it squeezes its body down onto it and makes a wound in a certain vein in its leg, and by thus letting blood unburdens its body, which would otherwise be liable to disease, and plasters up the wound again with mud' (VIII:40).[57] The infirmary painting included the hippopotamus along with several other animals and birds mentioned in ancient texts. One is the Egyptian ibis, which also practises bloodletting to relieve its gluttony and which, according to Pliny (VIII:41), 'makes use of the curve of its beak to purge itself through the part by which it is most conducive to health for the heavy residue of foodstuffs to be excreted.'[58] From the stag we have learned how to use the herb dittany (*Mentha pulegium*) to remove spears or arrows from the body, a medical fact noted not only by Pliny (VIII:41) but by Virgil in his *Aeneid* (Book XII), an epic that would have been very familiar to students of Jesuit colleges.[59] Similarly, the weasel has shown us the antidote to snake venom (in Pliny the antidote is to mouse bites). Ravens eat bay leaves to protect themselves from the poison excreted by the chameleons they kill; the humble swallow applies the herb great celandine (*Chelidonium majus*) to the eyes of its young when they are irritated; and the bear sticks his long tongue deep into an anthill to lick up the ants as a cure for the poison of mandrakes.[60] As a model for these botanical specimens the artist probably used an illustrated herbal of the sort that had its origins in antiquity and that became common in Europe in the late thirteenth century; it depicted individual medicinal plants together with descriptions of their properties and uses.[61] Dittany, for example, is common in late medieval and early Renaissance Italian herbals, such as a fifteenth-century illustrated herbal from Fermo, in the Marches, where it is touted as a cure for arrow wounds and snake venom.[62]

The last two paintings juxtaposed an Old Testament scene of sickness and succour with one from Jesuit history. *Elijah Cures the Son of the Widow* (1 Kings 17:17) depicted the widow of Zarephath taking care of Elijah, who in turn has God restore her afflicted son to life. The corresponding painting, devoted to the dedicatee of the room, was *Blessed Stanislas Kostka Is Sick and Visited by the Virgin*. Here, this 'grand captain ... and first soldier of his novitiate'[63] was shown as comforted in his illness by the Virgin. In another scene he was shown warding off the devil in the form of a cur by making the sign of the cross, and in another corner his soul was lifted gently into heaven by a group of beautiful young angels. The 'keynote' image in Room Four was an allegorical figure of Hope, in the form of a woman of noble bearing with a pair of wings, gesturing to the sky with her right hand and holding an anchor in her left. Although different in other respects, Cesare Ripa's Hope also holds an anchor in her left hand.[64]

Room Five was dedicated to Christ as Salvator Mundi, the first room so far not dedicated to a Jesuit.[65] Over the lintel another stern quotation from the Book of Sirach greeted the person visiting the sick novices resting inside: MELIUS EST IRE IN DOMUM LUCTUS QUAM CONVIVII (It is better to go into a house of sorrow than to banquets), a paraphrase of 'Better is the poor man's fare under a roof of boards then sumptuous cheer abroad in another man's house' [Ecclus. 29:28]. Above the beds, the patient metaphorically cried out with a quotation from the Book of Jeremiah: SANA ME DOMINE, & SANABOR. SALVA ME, & SALVUS ERO, QUIA LAUS MEA TU ES (Heal me, O Lord, and I shall be healed; save me, and I shall be saved: for thou art my praise [Jer. 17:14]). Between the wall and the beds, to instruct the sick, was another line from St Augustine's commentary on Psalm 101: SANAT OMNEM LANGUIDUM DOMINUS SED NON SANAT INVITUM, OPUS EST UT VELIS SANET (God cures all sick people, but not against their will; you must want to be cured to be cured).[66] Again, the captions stress the power of individual will. The exit quotation, behind the door, was a line from Hippocrates taking up the theme of fasting from the first quotation: CUM MORBI VIS EST MAXIMA, TENUISSIMO CIBO UTENDUM (When the disease is at its height, it will then be necessary to use the most slender diet [*Aphorisms* I.8]).[67]

The paintings in Room Five were restricted to stories from the Bible and the lives of the saints, with an overall theme of patience. The altarpiece, *Salvator Mundi*, depicted the child Jesus giving a benediction, orb in hand, and his prophecy was fulfilled on the wall behind the altar in the fresco *Resurrection*. On the wall on the opposite side was the fresco *Patience of Job* (Job 2:1–13), depicting the temptation of the patriarch by Satan in being covered from head to toe with sores. God the Father and his angels were shown watching Job's endurance from above. The next fresco, *Tobit's Blindness Is Cured*, showed a scene from the deuterocanonical Book of Tobit in which Tobias's father is cured by medicine made by Tobias from the heart, liver, and gall bladder of a miraculous fish he has caught with the assistance of the Angel Raphael (6:1–8). This story was depicted frequently in the late sixteenth and early seventeenth century, for example in the versions now in St Petersburg and the Metropolitan Museum of Art by Bernardo Strozzi (1581/2–1644).[68] In Strozzi's version, set inside a palace, the old man sits in a chair with his head thrown back, while Tobias, the angel, and the old man's wife attend him. To identify the scene, Strozzi has also included the fish, lying on its back exposing its ferocious teeth, on the lower right hand corner. The Novitiate version combined this episode with that of the discovery of the fish and the healing of Tobias's future wife's sickness by means of the same medicine, an act that culminated in their wedding (7:1–10). On another wall was the fresco *The Son of the Nobleman Cured* (John 4:46), showing the New Testament scene in which Christ cures the man's son on faith alone and does not allow the man to see the proof until he believes. This emphasis on faith reflected the thrust of the inscriptions in the room.

The next three frescoes in Room Five showed scenes of endurance from the lives of the saints that equated the physical pain of sickness with the human-inflicted tortures of martyrdom, and resonated with the martyr imagery of the recreation room. The first was *St Eligius Shot Through with an Arrow*, depicting the saint quietly suffering his agony like St Sebastian. The next two paintings showed female saints who bore terrible diseases with patience. The first, *The Illness of St Allegonde*, depicted the daughter of the king of France (d. 630) quietly enduring a terrible disease late in her life. The other, *The Illness of St Liduuine*, depicted a Dutch virgin (1395–1433) who for the whole of her brief life suffered continuous sickness throughout her body. Richeôme reminds us that this living embodiment of patience ate no more bread in all her life than a healthy man would eat in three days, and had only three nights' sleep. Like Christ in the wilderness and Stanislas Kostka, Liduuine was assisted by angels. The 'keystone' image in Room Five was not an allegory in the manner of Ripa but a picture of Moses with his tablets: Richeôme compares his act of leading the Hebrews out of Egypt to the way in which our faith leads us out of illness.

Rooms Six to Ten

Room Six was dedicated to Jesus and John the Baptist as children.[69] The lintel inscription, from Matthew, was an entreaty reminding the visitor that caring for even the most insignificant brother in Christ is tantamount to caring for Christ himself: QUOD VOS EX MINIMIS HIS FECISTIS MIHI FECISTIS (As long as you did it to one of these my least brethren, you did it to me [Matt. 25:40]). The bedhead inscription drew a metaphorical parallel between physical and spiritual illness: CIRCUMDEDERUNT ME MALA QUORUM NON EST NUMERUS (For evils without number have surrounded me [Ps. 39:13]). An instruction from St Augustine's commentary on Psalm 102 was offered in the inscription between the beds and the wall; it asked the patient to reflect on his miserable state as expressed in the bedhead inscription and offered him spiritual comfort: QUOD PATERIS MALUM UNDE PLANGIS MEDICINA EST & NON POENA, CASTIGATIO, & NON CONDEMNATIO (The evils which you endure, and which make you moan, are medicine and not punishment; chastisement and not condemnation).[70] The inscription behind the door, again from Hippocrates, read like a doctor's commentary and once again stressed the role of disharmony and imbalance in the Hippocratic notion of disease: QUI DOLOR VEHEMENTIOR EST IN UNA PARTE CORPORIS ALTERIUS SENSUM OBSCURAT (Of two pains occurring together, not in the same part of the body, the stronger weakens the other [*Aphorisms* II.46]).[71] The meaning here, however, was a Christian one; the reader was warned that a physical ailment can blind us to the much more dangerous illnesses of the soul.

The altarpiece in Room Six showed the two infants, Jesus and John the Baptist, playing with the lamb of sacrifice. Behind them, on the wall, was *Ascension of Christ*, showing the fruit of that sacrifice. On the opposite wall was the first of a series of frescoes devoted to temptation and patience, *Eulogius and the Cripple*, showing a tale related by the Greek prelate and writer Palladius (ca. 363–before 431). Here the painter depicted a quadriplegic taken in by the saintly Eulogius. After many years the crippled man was possessed by the devil and cursed his benefactor. At his wit's end, Eulogius finally took him to visit St Anthony at his hermitage near Alexandria. Anthony rebuked Eulogius for losing his patience and the quadriplegic for his ingratitude, but cured them both and sent them home to live in peace. Richeôme compares the patience of Eulogius until his visit to Anthony with the stoicism of the ancient Spartan youths whose sobriety kept their souls pure.[72] The theme of patience in *Eulogius and the Cripple* contrasted with the theme of desperation in the next picture, a scene from the deuterocanonical Books of Maccabees, *King Antiochus Stricken with His Malady*. Here the despairing Persian tyrant Antiochus IV lay in bed with an illness that befell him upon hearing of the Jewish victory over his armies and their refusal to worship the idol he had set up in their temple (2 Macc. 6:1–15). The afflicted king could not regain his strength and died as a direct result of his sins against the chosen people. Here the rich embroidery and pearls of his bed curtains serve as a foil for his wretched state, which, Richeôme explains, derives from his evil nature and cannot be cured by the legions of doctors who attend him.

An equally miserable fate befell the subjects of the next two paintings. The first, *Herod Eaten of Worms*, showed the Angel of God smiting King Herod on his throne and causing his body to be consumed by maggots after liberating his captive, St Peter, from prison (Acts 12:21–3). The next, illustrating a parable told by St Gregory (*Dialogues* IV:40), depicted the wicked novice Theodore, 'a very restless young man' in the words of Gregory, who entered a monastery against his will and as a result of his ingratitude was stricken with the plague.[73] The picture showed the boy lying in bed crying out in desperation like King Antiochus, with the devil in the form of a dragon waiting to consume him from above, while around the bed good novices huddle and pray for his salvation. Through their efforts the young man sees the errors of his ways, makes the sign of the cross, destroys the dragon, and is saved. This scene of redemption was particularly appropriate, since it not only had a connection with the themes of patience and temptation but depicted a novice and therefore was especially relevant to its audience. The 'keystone' image in Room Six, an unusually generic symbol, showed musician angels proclaiming God's glory.

Room Seven, dedicated to Mary Magdalene, was the first devoted to a woman; its inscriptions dealt with penitence.[74] But the other paintings in the room took up a new theme altogether, that of the curative power of music – a subject heralded in the musician angels in the ceiling vault of Room Six. The lintel and bedhead inscriptions were from the New Testament letters. The first resumed the theme of spiritual health in physical ailment: VIRTUS IN INFIRMITATE PERFICITUR (Power is made perfect in infirmity [2 Cor. 12:9]), a verse of which the visitor would have known the continuation, 'Most gladly therefore will I rather glory in my infirmities, that the power of Christ may rest upon me.' Unlike those in the other rooms, this inscription, it seems, was not directed at the visitor but meant to come from the mouth of the patient. Nor did the bedhead inscription conform to the others, since it read more like a general proclamation than a personal declaration: FLAGELLAT OMNEM QUEM RECIPIT (And he scourgeth every son whom he receiveth [Heb. 12:6]). Heroic endurance was emphasized also in the inscription between the bed and the wall, taken once again from St Augustine's commentary on Psalm 102: NOLI FLAGELLUM REPELLERE, SI NON VIS REPELLI AB HOEREDITATE (Never reject the lash, if you do not wish to be kept from your inheritance).[75] The inscription behind the door offered the usual doctor's advice from Hippocrates: IN OMNI MORBO VALERE MENTE, & BENE SE HABERE AD EA QUAE EXHIBENTUR, BONUM EST (In every disease it is a good sign when the patient's intellect is sound, and he is disposed to take whatever food is offered to him [*Aphorisms* II.33]).[76]

The Penitent Magdalene, the altarpiece, continued the theme of penitence, which was reflected also in a fresco on the wall behind, the *Last Judgment*. The *Last Judgment* had prophets, saints, angels, and souls rising from their graves, and Richeôme's description suggests that it was full of visual splendour and pageantry. It was also the first in the room to refer to music, since it featured an orchestra of musician angels. The opposite wall featured a musical subject from the Old Testament: *David Plays the Harp to the Sick Saul* showed the future King David curing the ailing Saul of his illness with the prayer of his music (1 Sam. 16:23).

Music also appeared as a remedy for illness in the next remarkable fresco, *Dancing the Tarantella*, a 'medical journal' illustration. Here, a young man was shown curing himself of snakebite by dancing furiously to the accompaniment of a flute. The tarantella, a folk melody from Apulia the harmonies of which were believed to aid in the extraction of poison from the bite of a tarantula through the phenomenon of sympathetic attraction, was later the topic of much reflection by the great Jesuit scientist and professor of mathematics at the Collegio Romano, Athanasius Kircher (1602–80). Kircher wrote extensively on music, most notably in his *Musurgia universalis* (Rome, 1650), a compendium on music and harmony, in which he sought to merge the ancient Pythagorean belief in world harmonies with the Christian belief in a creator God, and in his *Phonurgia* (Kempten, 1673), a book on sound production.[77] The tarantella itself features prominently in his earlier work on magnets, *Magnes, sive de arte magnetica* (Cologne, 1643), which catalogues a number of phenomena in which 'attractive virtues' were thought to play a part, the tarantella being one of the most memorable. These attractions were said to rely on occult qualities, or qualities that lay below the threshold of sensory perception; they aroused considerable interest in Early Modern Europe. In referring to this painting Richeôme makes his clearest statement yet of the curative function of the frescoes themselves, by saying that this picture and several that follow were chosen by 'our doctor' to provide instruction to look at as well as recreation for the patient.[78]

This nameless doctor is mentioned often in Richeôme's description of the infirmary paintings, and he seems to have been responsible for writing the program at least of the 'medical journal' type of illustrations. The doctor could not have been a Jesuit himself, since canon law at the time prohibited physicians from being ordained as priests, and since Jesuit brothers tended not to have the university education necessary for the practice of medicine. It was traditional in the Renaissance for doctors to contract with religious institutions, usually at a low salary as an act of charity, for the treatment of the brothers and priests of the order and sometimes the lay employees as well.[79] Ignatius specified in his rules for the rectors of Jesuit colleges that they should retain a doctor for both students and faculty on an annual contract.[80] In some cases a single doctor would have the work of both physician and surgeon; in others the work was divided between two doctors. The doctor who suggested the subjects of the Jesuit infirmary paintings would have been a physician, since the paintings illustrate concepts of 'physic' (learned medicine, originally referring to the whole field of natural philosophy), which was divided between *theorica*, the study of physiology and general principles of medicine, and *practica*, the study of specific diseases.[81] Surgery was a lowlier profession that did not require a university education.

The only doctor working at the Novitiate whose name I have been able to find in the archives is Marsilio Cagnati, a man who served also as the doctor of the English College. Cagnati began his tenure at the Novitiate in November 1587 and was still working for the Jesuits in 1595 – the year after the first series of infirmary buildings was finished – when he wrote up a report comparing the air quality of the Novitiate, the Collegio Romano, the German-Hungarian College, and the English College.[82] Cagnati was paid 20 scudi a year for his services, and the amount was raised to 25 scudi a year in 1588. If Cagnati is the doctor referred to by Richeôme – and there is no reason to suppose he is not – then we have the name of at least one of the people behind the program of this extraordinary painting cycle.

Cagnati was also responsible for the next painting, *Maladies Cured by Music*. This fresco featured the ancient Greek philosopher and musician Pythagoras (ca. 582–500 BC), so favoured by Kircher; he was shown here surrounded by men stricken with different diseases, many of them deriving from snakebite. Like the frantic dancer of the tarantella, Pythagoras and his academy use the sympathetic attraction of their music to cure the invalids. Richeôme refers to the four humours in his explanation of how music goes beyond sensory perception to cure the soul: 'Are not maladies caused by nothing more than an extreme disproportion and intemperance of the affections of the soul and of the humours of the body?'[83] He concludes his analysis of this painting with the message that music, with its curative powers, can serve as a symbol of the Word and Law of God.

The last picture in Room Seven, *Naaman the Syrian Stricken with Leprosy*, took its subject from the Book of Kings (2 Kings 5). A story of healing through faith and of conversion, it told how Naaman, the general of the king of Syria, was cured of leprosy after following the advice of the prophet Elisha, even though at first he ridiculed the latter's cure. The number of scenes featuring the conversion of kings and princes in the infirmary murals suggests that the Jesuits wanted to stress the importance of converting rulers and members of the nobility in their missionary work. The 'keystone' image in Room Seven was of the prophet Daniel, who foretold the coming of Christ, and whose presence here emphasized his message of salvation after penitence: 'to finish the transgression, and to make an end of sins, and to make reconciliation for iniquity, and to bring in everlasting righteousness, and to seal up the vision and prophecy, and to anoint the Most Holy' (Dan. 9:24).

Room Eight was dedicated to the Baptism of Christ.[84] The lintel inscription, from Psalm 15, presented the visitor with a dire warning equating sickness with punishment: MULTIPLICATE SUNT INFIRMITATES EORUM: POSTEA ACCELERAVERUNT (Their infirmities were multiplied: afterwards they made haste [Ps. 15:4]). The patient metaphorically cried out with Job's anguish from the head of the beds: MISEREMINI MEI SALTEM VOS AMICI MEI QUIA MANUS DOMINI TETIGIT ME (Have pity on me, at least you my friends, because the hand of the Lord hath touched me [Job 19:21]).[85] The inscription between the beds and the wall, taken again from St Augustine's commentary on Psalm 102, advised the young invalid to pay more attention to his spiritual state than to his physical pain: NOLI ATTENDERE QUAM POENAM SUSTINEAS IN FLAGELLO: SED QUEM LOCUM HABEAS IN TESTAMENTO (Pay no heed to the pain which you feel from the whip, but to the place which you have in the testament).[86] This quotation from the Church Father echoed that of his pagan counterpart Hippocrates behind the door: QUI ALIQUA PARTE CORPORIS DOLENTES, DOLOREM NON SENTIUNT, HIS AEGRA MENS EST (Persons who have a painful affection in any part of the body, and are in a great measure insensible of the pain, are disordered in intellect [*Aphorisms* II.6]).[87]

The altarpiece of Room Eight was of course a *Baptism of Christ*; it was, appropriately, set in front of the *Descent of the Holy Spirit*, a fresco in which the Holy Spirit was sent down from heaven in the form of tongues of flame. On the opposite wall was depicted another scene involving baptism, this time with a particularly Roman resonance, *Constantine the Great Cured of Leprosy*. In the story of this miracle, cited in Dante's *Inferno* and the subject of a medieval fresco cycle in SS. Quattro Coronati in Rome, the still pagan emperor of Rome was stricken with leprosy and could not be cured by any of the doctors who attended upon the terrified monarch in his imperial pavilion.[88] But the emperor was converted by a vision of Sts Peter and Paul, baptized by Pope Sylvester, and then miraculously cured, after which he made Christianity the state religion. The various episodes of the story, culminating in the baptism in front of cheering crowds, were combined in one painting here.

The next few frescoes were more examples of Cagnati's 'medical journal' type, this time extending the theme of baptism by depicting famous curative spas and waters in various parts of Europe and throughout history. These representations of healing waters were meant not only to provide moral instruction but actually to cure the patient. Leon Battista Alberti wrote on the subject in his *De re aedificatoria*, in which he described how looking at paintings of fountains and rivers could relax the mind and relieve the spirit, just as imagining them during insomnia could induce sleep to come; contemporary churchmen such as Cardinal Federico Borromeo of Milan had similar views on the benefits of contemplating painted landscapes.[89] The first depiction of curative waters in Room Eight was *The Waters of Baiae in the Campagna of Italy*, showing an ancient Roman spa a description of which can be found in Pliny (*Natural History* XXXI:2), who died there during the eruption of Vesuvius in 79 AD. Pliny writes, 'Nowhere ... is water more bountiful than in the Bay of Baiae, or with more variety of relief: some has the virtue of sulphur, some of alum, some of salt, some of soda, some of bitumen, some are even acid and salt in combination.'[90] The painting showed multitudes bathing in the restorative waters. The next painting, *Spa of Tungre in Flanders*, was a crowded scene showing a contemporary spa with curative waters at a small town near Liège. The third and fourth spa pictures reverted to the New Testament. The first, *Pool of Bethesda*, depicted the pool already featured in Room One. As before, the sick men and women in the pool represented the world of mortal sin, and the waters God's ability to cure – but the patient, Richeôme warns, must have the will to be cured. The second showed the pool in Emmaus in which Christ washed his feet and which afterwards cured all kinds of maladies. Richeôme brings up the theme of the Magdalene's penitence once more, by comparing Christ's washing of his feet in this fountain with Mary Magdalene's washing of his feet with the tears of her penitence, 'the fountains of her two eyes.'[91] The 'keystone' image in Room Eight, placed like the rest in the vault of the ceiling, was a symbol of the Church in the form of a walled city with three gates. This image also related to baptism, the prevailing theme of the room, since the water that flows from the city is the fountain of Holy Baptism prophesied by David.

Room Nine took the viewer to Jesus' adulthood; it was dedicated to his first sermon, or the first act of his manhood.[92] It also served to promote meditation on the vocation to priesthood, appropriate not only for the novices but for the other Jesuits who probably recuperated in these rooms. The lintel inscription was a quotation from the Book of Hosea that introduced two other major themes in this room, sin and penitence. God expressed his anger at a world living without knowledge of him: INFIRMANTUR HOMINES, & BESTIA AGRI, & VOLVERES COELI AB PECCATO IN HABITENTIUM, IN TERRA (Men and the beasts of the field and the fowls of heaven become sick by the sin of those who live on the earth); the words are a paraphrase of 'Therefore shall the land mourn, and every one that dwelleth therein shall languish, with the beasts of the field, and with the fowls of heaven'

(Hos. 4:3). The patient metaphorically responded with the bedhead quotation, a heartfelt cry of penitence: QUONIAM IN FLAGELLA PARATUS SUM, & DOLOR MEUS IN CONSPECTU MEO SEMPER (For I am ready for scourges: and my sorrow is continually before me [Ps. 37:18]). Between the bed and the wall was a stern warning to the patient from St Augustine's commentary on Psalm 141, reminding him not to lose sight of the remedy that is God: NIHIL EST SUPERBIUS AEGRO, QUI RIDET MEDICAMENTUM (Nothing is more arrogant for a sick person than to mock one's medicine).[93] The exit line, quoted as always from Hippocrates, had a similarly monitory tone: SPONTANEA LASSITUDINES PRAETENDUNT MORBOS (Spontaneous lassitude indicates disease [*Aphorisms* II.5]).[94]

The altarpiece in Room Nine continued the subject to which the room was dedicated; it was *Christ Preaching*, or perhaps *Christ Preaching the Sermon on the Mount* – and Richeôme refers to Christ metaphorically as the 'sovereign Doctor of our souls.'[95] Behind the altar on the wall was an *Allegory of Penitence*, showing a noble matron in widow's garb, her black dress sprinkled with tears, kneeling and imploring the mercy of God. She was surrounded by priests, and a group of small children knelt beside her, also confessing and receiving the virtue of the lamb. These figures were all renouncing the spiritual maladies of the soul, which Richeôme describes in military terms as a 'garrison.'[96] The message was that the patient must be more vigilant against sin than the healthy man, since sickness makes one prone to spiritual ills. Like the quotation between the bed and wall, this allegory exhorted the patient not to let his illness cause him to lose sight of his 'sovereign Doctor.' Richeôme illustrates the warning with a classical reference, to the life of Philotimus, the Greek physician (ca. 300 BC) in Plutarch's *Moralia* (43). Philotimus gave stern advice to a patient dying of consumption: 'When he had addressed the physician, asking him for something to cure a sore finger, Philotimus, perceiving his condition from his color and respiration, said, "My dear sir, your concern is not about a sore finger." And so for you, young man, it is not the time to be inquiring about such questions, but how you may be rid of self-opinion and pretension, love affairs and nonsense, and settle down to a modest and wholesome mode of living.'[97] Richeôme concludes with the appropriate warning that there is no need to worry about bodily sickness as long as it is not accompanied by an illness of the spiritual kind.[98]

The other three paintings were standard New Testament scenes of curing, the first being *Christ Cures the Man with Palsy* (Matt. 9:2). Here Christ was shown healing in spite of the jeers and disbelief of the scribes, a miracle used to emphasize his power to forgive sins. The second was *Christ Cures the Man with Dropsy* (Luke 14: 2–4), showing an act that led Christ (and leads Richeôme) into a reflection on humility and charity. The last painting was *Sicknesses Cured by the Apostles*. It began with the story of the shadow of St Peter (Acts 5:15–16), whose miraculous ability to heal the multitudes is immortalized most famously in Masaccio's fresco in the Brancacci Chapel at S. Maria del Carmine in Florence (1425). Like many of the paintings in the Novitiate, this scene featured crowds of people, this time representing a plethora of diseases both spiritual and corporal. At the top of the same painting was a depiction of a crowd of sick and maimed people who grab hold of pieces of cloth associated with St Paul and having curative properties (Acts

19:12). Peter and Paul also featured in the 'keystone' image in Room Nine, perhaps more as spiritual doctors than as apostles, where they stood holding their symbols of the crossed keys and the book and sword.

Room Ten was dedicated to Christ in Meditation, a theme appropriately directed to the patient's use of his time.[99] The lintel inscription quoted Christ's words when he had healed a man sick with palsy and sat down to eat with publicans and sinners: SANI NON EGENT MEDICO, SED QUI MALE HABENT (They that are well have no need of a physician, but they that are sick [Mark 2:17]). As in Room Nine, the message here was that the patient should be wary of spiritual sickness and follow Christ's guidance. The patient symbolically let out a moan of utter despair from the bedhead: PARCE MIHI DOMINE. NIHIL ENIM SUNT DIES MEI, QUID EST HOMO QUIA MAGNIFICAS EUM? (Spare me, for my days are nothing. What is a man that thou shouldst magnify him? [Job 7:16–17]). He was rebuked with severity by the inscription between the beds and the wall, from the chapter on medicine in the Book of Sirach: INFIRMITATE TUA NE DESPICIAS TE IPSUM, SED ORA DEUM, & IPSE CURABIT TE (In thy sickness, neglect not thyself: but pray to the Lord and he shall heal thee [Ecclus. 38:9]). The exit line, behind the door, from Hippocrates warned the patient and his visitors that they as well as the doctor were responsible for helping toward a cure: NON SOLUM MEDICUS DEBET OFFICIO FUNGI, SED AEGER, & QUI ILLI ASSISTUNT (The physician must not only be prepared to do what is right himself, but the patient and those who assist him [*Aphorisms* I.1]).[100]

The little altarpiece, *Christ Standing in Meditation*, was set in front of the *Sermon on the Mount*, a fresco that apparently was the second depiction of the subject. Richeôme uses the examples of the attentive apostles to encourage the novice likewise to abandon the vanities of the world and give ear to the Beatitudes pronounced by Christ. He stresses in particular the first, 'Blessed are the poor in spirit: for theirs is the kingdom of heaven.' The next painting, *Nebuchadnezzar's Dream* [Dan. 4:11], showed a story in Daniel in which the king of Babylon has a dream of a great tree and so is led to conversion and praise of the True God. Richeôme takes the opportunity to meditate once again on the vanity of the world and the miserable state of humankind.

The last two paintings in Room Ten were of the 'medical journal' variety, once more prepared by 'our doctor' Cagnati from a variety of classical sources; they illustrated various kinds of mental illness and insanity as a metaphor for different sins. Mental illness, like physical illness, was derived from the four humours, as Burton remarks in his *Anatomy of Melancholy*: 'As the body works upon the mind by his bad humours, troubling the spirits, sending gross fumes into the brain.'[101] In the Novitiate infirmary paintings, insanity became a metaphor for vanity. The first painting was entitled *Maladies of the Imagination*; it represented illnesses 'neither entirely corporal nor entirely of the spirit, but a part of one and a part of the other.'[102] At the bottom was a symbol of vanity. Below it was a solemn procession of men holding sceptres and wearing crowns on their heads. Richeôme explains that despite their royal appearance these men are nothing more than farmers operating under the illusion that they are royalty. Next to them was another crowd of people amusing themselves by attending upon these 'kings' and feeding their regal fantasies. Which group, Richeôme asks, is the greater sinner? In another part of the painting was a group of men shackled together in chains; they represented cruelty. These lunatics, Richeôme says, believe they are different animals, such as a bear, a leopard, and a lion, and must be restrained so as not to attack others. In another corner was a man, 'more fit for compassion and less dangerous than the others,'[103] scurrying away from some chickens and their rooster as if his very life depended on it. This poor fellow, we are told, believes he is a grain of millet and lives in fear of being snapped up by their beaks. Even the rooster is not really a rooster but a man who thinks he is a rooster. This figure is from the life of Pythagoras of Samos (ca. 530 BC) as recorded by Galen.[104] The painter looked to an ancient source for the next lunatic in his collection, the historian Pisander of Alexandria, who believed he had no soul because it had left his body in a rage and lodged itself in his shadow. This story is recorded by the Roman encyclopaedist Aulus Cornelius Celsus (ca. 14–37 AD), whose treatise on medicine *De re medicina* was one of the first to be printed (1478), and was represented in Jesuit collegiate libraries.[105] Pisander feared that if he encountered his shadow again he would anger his soul, and therefore spent the rest of his life avoiding it. All the sinners in this painting are preoccupied by their fantasies; they pay no heed to the transitoriness of this world and ignore the world that awaits.

The last picture, *Maladies of the Imagination and Others Cured by Passion*, had a similar theme. The first image, from Plutarch's *Moralia* (249), was a cityscape in which women could be seen everywhere trying to starve and strangle themselves, take poison, throw themselves out of windows, and jump off city walls. Richeôme explains that they are Milesian women in the sudden grip of self-hatred attempting to kill themselves in spite of the protestations of their families and friends. In the corner was shown the figure of a wise old man, who in Plutarch's story comes up with the cure for this insanity. He tells the women that if they kill themselves he will strip their bodies naked, and drag them through the city, and leave them for all to see in the town square. The women's sense of shame respecting their bodies is stronger then their desire to kill themselves, so they refrain. The story is slightly different from Plutarch's version, where the women all hang themselves, but it shares Plutarch's moral: 'Plainly a high testimony to natural goodness and to virtue is the desire to guard against ill repute.'[106] Richeôme explains that shame is given to 'the weaker sex' to preserve their chastity. Elsewhere in the painting was a dishevelled man jumping for joy in the middle of a street. He had appeared to be paralysed beyond cure, but his fear of fire was so great that when his house happened to be set alight he jumped from his bed and ran into the street. Both the illnesses in this painting – one mental, the other corporal – are cured by human passions, shame and fear. The 'keystone' image in the ceiling vault of Room Ten was the IHS borne aloft by angels, the symbol of the Society of Jesus and the monogram of the name of Christ, 'sovereign remedy of all imaginations and vicious fears.'[107]

Rooms Eleven to Thirteen, and the Infirmary Refectory

Room Eleven passed over Christ's passion to the *Pietà*, and the theme of penitence dominated once again. The room welcomed the visitor with a line from St Gregory of Nyssa (ca. 335–ca. 395) warning him to turn away from worldly things: SOLET

ANIMUS FLORERE QUANDO VOLUPTATES UNA CUM CORPORE MARCESCUNT (The soul flourishes when delight in the body wanes).[108] Richeôme provides neither the Latin text nor the source for the rest of the inscriptions in this room, but the bedhead inscription is recognizable as a line from Psalm 118; once again it seemed to represent an exclamation from the patient himself: 'It is good for me that I have been afflicted; that I might learn thy statutes (Ps. 118:71).' From the space between the beds and the wall the doctor intoned a similar message: 'A strong illness creates a sober soul.' The same asceticism greeted the visitor upon leaving the room, in a line from Hippocrates based on the theory of the four humours: 'Diseases which arise from repletion are cured by depletion [*Aphorisms* II.22].'[109] Richeôme is quick to elucidate the spiritual meaning, that people who spend their lives in pleasure must correct themselves through acts of penitence.[110]

Behind the altar, with its *Pietà*, was the painting *Peter Healing the Lame Man*, a subject from Acts (3:2–11), the first miracle performed by Peter after the Resurrection. Repentance once again was the message, as Peter exhorted his audience to cleanse their souls before coming into the presence of the Lord. The next painting, on the wall opposite, was *Doctor Cured of Incurable Gout through Baptism*, depicting a story from St Augustine's *De civitate Dei* (XXII:8).[111] A doctor of Carthage was shown lying in bed stricken with gout and surrounded by deformed and hideous 'Ethiopian' children representing evil spirits. These demons had appeared to the man in his dreams to prevent him from receiving baptism. The doctor goes ahead and receives baptism anyway, is cured forever, and at the bottom of the picture gives thanks to God. St Augustine was also the source of the next painting, on the third wall of the room, *Two Adolescents Cured by a Miracle* (*De civitate Dei* XXII:8).[112] The picture showed two young men, one cured of his blindness and the other exorcized of the devil and cured of a mortal wound, which was also to his eye. This was one of the few paintings in the Novitiate (along with *Sicknesses Cured by the Apostles* in Room Nine) that focused on the cult of relics: both boys were cured through contact with the relics of the Milanese saints Gervasius and Protasius. The first miracle took place in Milan under the supervision of Emperor Theodosius and St Ambrose, and the second during vespers at an African shrine to Sts Gervasius and Protasius in the episcopal see of St Augustine. Gervasius and Protasius will feature prominently in the frescoes of the Novitiate church of S. Vitale (see chapter 5).

The painting on the fourth wall, also from St Augustine's *De civitate Dei* (XXII:8) and also related to the cult of relics, showed a young man and woman who have been revived by the relics of St Stephen.[113] The woman, the daughter of Bassus of Syria, was brought to life when her father touched her with her own dress after it was blessed at St Stephen's shrine, a miracle that recalled the reference to the garments of St Paul in Room Nine. The young man was resucitated by holy oil blessed by the relics of the same martyr. At the bottom of the painting was a bishop carrying the relics in a solemn procession, followed by a joyful woman who has been cured of her blindness by their means and an unhappy woman who can see perfectly well but is so embarrassed by her ugly face that she smashes her mirror on the ground. The message was that those are blind who can see only the fleeting beauties and vanities of this world and who have no thought for the kingdom of heaven. The 'keystone' image in the ceiling vault of Room Eleven was of St John the Evangelist, with an eagle at his feet and a chalice in his left hand that he blesses with his right, 'with this sign mortifying the poison that was in it' – a symbol of the curative power of the Eucharist.[114]

Room Twelve was dedicated to the Risen Christ.[115] The lintel inscription once again reminded the reader to be vigilant in his righteousness, and like so many of the infirmary's lintel quotations it had to do with arriving and entering: BEATUS ILLE SERVUS QUEM CUM VENERIT DOMINUS EIUS INVENERIT VIGILANTEM (Blessed is that servant whom when his lord shall come he shall find so doing [Matt. 24:46]).[116] As usual, the bedhead inscription seemed to be a reply coming from the mouth of the patient himself, and it picked up the idea of vigilance: VIGILAVI, & FACTUS SUM SICUT PASSER SOLITARIUS IN TECTO (I have watched, and am become as a sparrow all alone on the house-top [Ps. 101:8]).[117] The inscription between the beds and wall, the source and Latin original of which are omitted by Richeôme, contrasted vigilance with sleep: 'The sleep of health in a man extends until morning, and his soul will be alleviated with him.' Both sleep and wakefulness were echoed in the final inscriptions, behind the door, from Hippocrates, which stressed his theory of balance in everything: SOMNUS, & VIGILANTIA MODUM EXCEDENTIA, MALUM (Both sleep and insomnolency, when immoderate, are bad [*Aphorisms* II.3]).[118]

The theme of awakening from sleep fit perfectly with that of the room's dedication and its first two paintings. In the altarpiece, *Risen Christ*, in bas relief, the adult Christ was shown wielding the banner of the cross as Salvator Mundi. Behind him, on the wall, was *Resurrection*, showing Roman soldiers and angels peering into the open tomb as Christ rises triumphantly above. The third painting, on the opposite wall, featured another image of mental illness prepared by Cagnati to give the viewer 'fruit and pleasure.'[119] *The Earthenware Pots* depicted a story taken again from Galen.[120] In this unusual composition was a group of soldiers armed not with cuirasses and firearms but with clay pots and sticks. These men, afflicted with a mental disorder that makes them think they are clay pots, walk in constant fear of smashing against a wall or tree trunk. Richeôme explains that they deserve our compassion because they serve as a metaphor for the folly of the worldly and so make us the wiser. Their folly consists not in fearing the trees and walls but in failing to fear God, who should be dreaded above all things. They may be lunatics, but they are not so far off the mark since we mortals are all vessels of earth.

The next picture, also drawn from Cagnati's library, was *The Three Maladies of the Imagination*. In this scene the painter presented three men from antiquity possessed by insane delusions. The first, taken from Galen's *On the Differences of Diseases*, was Dr Theophilus, who imagines that there are minstrels in the corner of his bedchamber, playing night and day and interrupting his sleep.[121] He shouts to his valets and chamberlains to stop the racket, but the noise goes on relentlessly because it comes from inside his head. This man is typical of those who blame their harassment on external factors instead of looking to the vanity within as the true cause of their troubles. The next man shown had the opposite problem. A prominent Greek citizen of Argos, mentioned by Horace in his *Epistles* (II:128–40), he is depicted standing in front of a theatre full of actors and musicians.[122] The theatre is empty, however, and the players merely figments of his imagination. In Horace's story the man is finally cured of his delusion by family and friends, but he is unhappy with the cure: 'You call it rescue, my friends, but what you have done is to murder me! You have destroyed my delight and forcibly swept from my mind the most gloriously sweet of illusions!'[123] Richeôme points out that he is doubly blind and deaf, since he attends to the beautiful but vain sights and sounds of his imagination yet ignores the ugliness and clamour of his own soul's sickness. The last figure shown, Trasyllas, represented the sickness of avarice and ambition. This Athenian from Piraeus has persuaded himself that all the ships coming and going in the busy harbour before him belong to him. He becomes obsessed with their routes, schedules, and cargoes, and the sailors play along with his delusion because they find it amusing.

The next painting was lent to the Novitiate by 'one of our good Sicilian friends,' a phrase suggesting that it was not a fresco but a framed canvas. It depicted a scene of mental lunacy on the Sicilian coast and was entitled *Maladies of the Galley*. Taken from an unnamed Greek source, the painting showed a scene in the sunny port town of Agrigento, in which hundreds of young men were running around desperately trying to escape from a building on the main square as though it were on fire. The building is not on fire, of course. Thanks to the 'sweet waves of their stomachs' and the 'smoke and vapours' in their brains, the men believe that the house is a galley caught in storm at sea and that the astonished crowd gathered in the square below is a school of fish.[124] The 'keystone' image in Room Twelve was a figure of Truth; it contrasted the eternal truth of God with the fleeting vanities of this life, which the entire room equated with mental insanity. A female allegory sitting atop a rock, she wore a gold blindfold and was dressed in a blue damask robe encrusted with diamonds. Her right hand pointed to heaven and her other hand to what was below. Under her head hung a banderole with an inscription from Psalm 116, VERITAS DOMINI MANET IN AETERNAM (The truth of the Lord remaineth for ever [Ps. 116:2]); and another banderole bore an inscription quoting from Ecclesiastes: VANITAS VANITATUM (Vanity of vanities [Eccles. 1:2]). She was quite different from the images of Truth listed in Ripa, almost all of which are nudes.[125]

Room Thirteen had some of the most complex imagery in the entire infirmary.[126] A practical metaphor for the culmination of a spiritual journey, this last room made a powerful statement of the triumph of Good over Evil, and of the nature of the Church itself. Appropriately, it was dedicated to St Michael the Archangel, and it was saturated with military imagery. Angels were everywhere, and their presence echoed the central role played by angels in the chapel and refectory. Quoting from the story of Lazarus of Bethany, the lintel affirmed God's love for the patient inside: ECCE QUEM AMAS INFIRMATUR ([Lord, behold], he whom thou lovest is sick [John 11:3]). The bedhead inscription was a cry for help from the afflicted: MISERERE MEI DOMINE QUONIAM INFIRMUS SUM: SANA ME DOMINE QUONIAM CONTURBATA SUNT OSSA MEA (Have mercy on me, O Lord, for I am weak: heal me, O Lord, for my bones are troubled [Ps. 6:3]). Stern advice from the Book of Sirach followed in the inscription between the beds and wall, stressing once again that physical ailments can help purify the soul: IN INFIRMITATE TUA AB OMNI DELICTO MUNDA COR TUUM (In your infirmity, clean your heart of every sin [Ecclus. 38:9–

10]). In the exit quotation, behind the door, Hippocrates reminded the visitor that if the soul is not clean no amount of medicine can help: IMPURA CORPORA QUO MAGIS NUTRIS, EO MAGIS LAEDIS (Bodies not properly cleansed, the more you nourish the more you injure [*Aphorisms* II.10]).[127]

The military imagery began with the altarpiece, the relief *St Michael Vanquishing the Dragon*. On the wall behind it was the large painting *The Church Triumphant*, portraying the armies of God arrayed on a plain and preparing to attack the forces of Evil. Angels and martyred saints with palm leaves were assembled in phalanxes under the Holy Trinity, which was bathed in brilliant light. The scene recalled the 'Two Standards' meditation from the Fourth Day of the Second Week of the *Spiritual Exercises* (pars 136–48), meant to harden the reader toward the temptations of Satan: 'It will be here to see a great plain, comprising the whole region about Jerusalem, where the sovereign Commander-in-Chief of all the good is Christ our Lord; and another plain about the region of Babylon, where the chief of the enemy is Lucifer' (par. 138).[128] The forces of God being assembled, the painting cycle moved on to the forces of Lucifer. The painting on the opposite wall was the first of a series depicting the sicknesses of the soul and their cures, spiritual enemies and their foes. These were given the form of the Seven Capital Sins, each personified by a monster and each countered by a corresponding angel.

The first sin was Pride, shown as a knight riding on the back of a seven-headed dragon with the wings of a bat, sprinkled with eyes and covered in flames. Each of the frightening female heads of the dragon represented one of the sub-categories of Pride, the most heinous of all sins and the mother of all spiritual maladies – Disobedience, Conceit, Hypocrisy, Contention, Obstinacy, Discord, and Presumption. These same vices were represented on the knight in the form of seven horns extending from his head. This demonic knight and his mount were met on the opposite side of the painting by the Angel of Humility, accompanied by a small child and holding a shield in his left hand and a flaming sword in his right. The angel was shown striking the knight on his head and feet, and thereby upending him and revealing his worthlessness and sin. He also cuts the horns off his head and replaces the maladies of the seven horns with their opposites – Obedience, Silence, Candour, Repose, Flexibility, Accord, and Modesty. The angel makes the knight as humble in his soul as the 2-year-old child standing by his side.

The fourth painting represented Avarice and Lust, both in the form of monsters. The first was a beast with eight heads and the body of a wolf, being followed by a hydropic man. Together these two stand for Avarice, since the first cannot satisfy his hunger and the second cannot quench his thirst. The eight heads represented Betrayal, Fraud, Deception, False Witness, Anxiety, Violence, Inhumanity, and Hardness of Heart. This miserable pair was confronted on the other side by the Angel of Mercy, reminding them from Acts (20:35) that it is more blessed to give than to receive. Armed with the spirit of God, this angel transforms the eight vices into the opposing eight virtues – Fidelity, Frank and Good Faith, Truth, Elation, Tranquillity of Spirit, Sweetness, Humanity, and Tenderness of Heart. The other sin, Lust, was depicted as a monstrous billy goat accompanied by a leper. The billy goat had nine horns on his head representing Blindness of Spirit, Thoughtlessness, Fickleness, Haste, Narcissism, Hatred for God, Excessive Desire for the Present Life, Horror of Death and the Judgment of God, and Despair of Eternal Life. This demonic duo were stopped dead in their tracks by the Angel of Chastity, holding a lily in his left hand and wearing a gold and green silk sash encrusted with jewels about his loins. Wielding a scimitar in his right hand, the angel hacks off the nine horns on the goat's head and so replaces the vices with the corresponding virtues – Light of Understanding, Good Counsel, Constancy in Doing Good, Patience, Laudable Hatred of the Self, Love of God, Magnanimous Contempt for the Mortal Life, Confidence against Death, and Hope for Divine Mercy and Heaven.

The last four of the Seven Capital Sins were featured in the next painting, in which each was represented by an animal emblem and a human counterpart. Envy was given the form of a sightless asp biting its own tail and a man suffering from inflammation of the eyes, devices that emphasized the self-destructiveness and blindness of envy. Gluttony was represented, appropriately, by a pig, who appeared in tandem with a human figure seated at a table laden with meats and wines and eating with the insatiable appetite of his animal companion. The third sin, Anger, was signified by a ferocious tiger and an equally violent man. The painter looked to the missions for an emblem for the last of the sins. Sloth was represented by the beast that bears its name, an 'animal of Peru ... of two feet in length, about the size of a large cat, with the face of a woman [, which] is so slow moving that it takes a quarter hour for every step.'[129] This exotic visitor from South America was attended by three human exemplars of the vice in question, a paralytic, a lethargic, and an apoplectic. As in the previous two pictures, all four vices here were counterbalanced by angels. The first, in opposition to Envy, carried the olive branch of peace in his left hand and eye lotion in the other (collyrium). This spirit of Gentleness was shown striking the asp on the head and rubbing the lotion into the inflamed eyes of the sick man. The next angel was the Spirit of Sobriety, opposing Gluttony. He carried a crystal dish full of manna from heaven in his left hand and a golden bridle in his right; with the one he fed the man and with the other he restrained the pig. The third angel, the Spirit of Sweetness, had a chain of fire in his right hand and a balm-yielding plant in his left; with those he restrained the tiger and calmed the man. The last angel, the Spirit of Diligence, was shown striking out against Sloth with a javelin in his right hand and a torch in his left.

The triumphalist themes of the room were summarized by the 'keystone' device, which depicted the jewelled crown of triumph placed over a cross tied with two palm branches, together with a banderole bearing the motto 'The end crowns the work' (the Latin is not given). This emblem is of Early Christian origin and appears with some variations in Palaeochristian epitaphs.[130] More important, it was introduced by Cesare Baronio into his *Annales ecclesiastici* (1588–1607) and appears above the main entrance of his titular church, SS. Nereo ed Achilleo, on the inside of the door frame. By combining the crown with the palm branches, the image reiterates the martyrological theme of the other parts of the Novitiate, a theme on which the infirmary paintings are largely, and curiously, silent.

Opposite Room One, dedicated to St Ignatius, was the last room in the infirmary complex described by Richeôme, the refectory for the convalescents. The only room that can be definitively identified on the 1733 plan, this small dining space was the last on the northern side of the corridor (fig. 16). It featured a fireplace over the mantle of which was painted the monogram of the names of Jesus and Mary, 'names that light the celestial flame and fire in our soul,' as well as an emblem of the pelican in her piety.[131] As was traditional in monastic dining rooms, including the Novitiate's own main refectory, the principal painting here was a *Last Supper*. The rest of the paintings were frescoes in the four spandrels. The only other room in the complex with spandrel paintings, as we have seen, was Room Two (Francis Xavier), which adorned the spandrels with scenes from the life of the future saint. The spandrel paintings in this refectory balanced those with additional scenes from the life of Ignatius of Loyola. The four scenes were *Ignatius Cured of His Illness by St Peter, Ignatius at Manresa, Ignatius Contemplates the Soul of Blessed Osius,* and *Ignatius Gives Help to Those Who Seek His Intercession.* All these scenes were later depicted in the *Vita beati P. Ignatii Loiolae* (see chapters 1 and 2).

Richeôme finishes his description of the paintings of the infirmary, and by extension of the entire Novitiate, with a lengthy meditation on a painting the location of which is not clear, but which may also have been in the convalescents' refectory (fig. 31). Called *Sleep and Death*, the work showed two children asleep in two beds in a belvedere overlooking a military encampment.[132] Above the roof of the belvedere the souls of the dead rose from the ground, and in the sky Christ ruled as Salvator Mundi surrounded by choirs of angels. In his discussion of this painting Richeôme refers to several ancient writers, including 'Filon' (Philo Byblius, first–second century AD?), Alexander the Great, Aeschines (389–ca. 314 BC), Epaminondas of Thebes (ca. 430–362 BC), and Homer, as well as to Sacred Scripture. Perhaps the armies doing exercises in the background were a reference to Epaminondas, a general who defeated the Spartan army at Leuctra in 371 using innovative tactics. The first child shown in the picture is dead, a corpse without a soul, a condition Richeôme refers to as the 'Iron Sleep.' The other child is merely sleeping, the so-called little death, or 'Bronze Sleep.' The beds were coloured accordingly, with the sleeping child lying in a bronze bed. The message was that the two states of existence are similar and that we are as senseless in sleep as in death. Sleep therefore should be a *memento mori*, and we must be wary in our sleep not to lag in our love for God. The picture equated waking with resurrection, represented by the figures of souls rising from the ground. *Sleep and Death* was an appropriate conclusion to a complex cycle of images adorning rooms occupied by the bedridden.

Despite the complexity and originality of the subject matter, the infirmary cycle can be read on a basic level as having offered an extended meditation on the 'Two Standards' section of the *Spiritual Exercises*, in which Christ and Lucifer line up their armies and battle for the soul of the exercitant.[133] The infirmary frescoes, reliefs, and canvases exhorted the sick novice to make choices between Good and Evil, between the path of Christ and the path of Satan, and led him step by step toward the right choice in a closely controlled sequence. The cycle encouraged a spiritual pilgrimage, the end result of which would be either healing or death, either salvation or damnation. The dual path was summed up in the final picture, with its two seemingly identical images of children asleep in bed. The message of the infirmary rooms can also be found in contemporary printed manuals published by the Jesuits, such as that of Antoine Sucquet's *Path of Eternal Life* (Antwerp, 1630), in which plate 4, by Boetius Bolswert, shows a pilgrim on a spiritual journey waylaid at every step by the temptations of the devil. Bolswert's engraving is labelled, with each letter referring to Capital Sins – Voluptuousness of the World, Vanity, Sin, Gluttony, Avarice, and Vainglory – in a fashion that recalls the imagery of Room Thirteen.

What Sucquet, the *Spiritual Exercises*, and the Novitiate paintings have in common is a recognition that the human soul faces constant threats to its faith, and, most important, that the individual is ultimately responsible for the choice between succumbing to or rejecting these temptations. The Jesuits emphasized that free will is a gift from God and that humanity is endowed by God's grace with the powers of thought and action. This emphasis had a tremendous effect on their artistic programs, where it provided a distinctly personal, meditative element. Jeffrey Chipps Smith has recently noted: 'This stress upon the individual and his or her conscious action (or inaction) shapes the Society's artistic programs. These are designed with the specific goal of aiding the individual worshipper.'[134] Seen in this light, the infirmary paintings present nothing less than an elaborate and erudite voyage of spiritual discovery, a pilgrim's progress, often passionate yet with touches of humour, drawing upon scripture and also upon antiquity, and cognizant of both the spiritual and the natural sources of illness and curing, life and death.

**The Novitiate Infirmary Cycle in Context:
Hospital Decoration in Renaissance Italy**

The paintings just surveyed may represent the most complex and original hospital imagery of the Italian Renaissance. Unfortunately, the scholarship deals only with the hospital decoration of early and High Renaissance Italy (ca. 1430–1520), and very few paintings from hospitals survive from the late Cinquecento. Little comparison, therefore, can be made. Although Italian hospitals were adorned with painted decorations from at least the first decades of the fourteenth century, more substantial painting cycles became common only in the fifteenth century with the monumental Sala del Pellegrinaio in the hospital of S. Maria della Scala in Siena (1437–44) and the giant Corsia Sistina in the Roman hospital of S. Spirito (begun 1476). By the end of the fifteenth century most hospitals in Central and Northern Italy had at least some basic painted or terracotta imagery on their facades or interiors, and these had certain narrative and iconic subjects in common. A number also included inscriptions, either explanations of the action depicted or commentaries on the action provided by biblical or patristic passages. Nowhere, however, is found the range of classical and pharmacological subjects and sources, or the complicated interweaving of Christian and pagan attitudes toward medicine and health, that cover every wall in the infirmary of the S. Andrea Novitiate.

Hospitals in medieval and Renaissance Italy were usually built to house pilgrims, the poor, the elderly, and, especially, foundlings, who were known by various names, such as *gettatelli* (castaways) in Siena, *trovatelli* (foundlings) in Pisa, *innocenti* (innocents) in Florence, and *bastardini* (bastards) in Bologna. The first large urban hospitals had been founded by the late medieval period. Some were specialized, such as the Spedale degli Innocenti in Florence (founded 1445), which administered solely to orphans, and S. Onofrio in the same city, devoted to poor dyers; but many, like the Scala in Siena or S. Spirito in Rome served different groups and social classes in a single building.[135] Hospitals were traditionally attached to religious institutions, although beginning in 1400 lay powers began to take over hospital hierarchies as secular political forces in general became more influential. Hospitals became symbols of civic virtue and the object of intense patronage on the part of powerful families keen to be associated with public welfare, perhaps most famously at the Ospedale Maggiore in Milan (early 1460s), which was founded with great public ceremony by Duke Francesco and Duchess Bianca Maria Sforza. By the mid-fourteenth century there were twenty-five hospitals in Rome itself.[136]

The decoration of medieval and early Renaissance hospitals, very little of which survives, was similar to that of churches, in featuring frescoes and altarpieces depicting stories from the Bible and personages from the calendar of saints, distributed often haphazardly around the interior of the chapel and the hospital. While many of these images were generic, such as *Annunciation* and *Nativity*, others related more specifically to the building's function as a hospital – scenes from the stories of Tobias and Job, for example, both of which were featured prominently in the Jesuit infirmary. One of the earliest recorded examples, at the Roman hospital of S. Giacomo al Colosseo, which was associated with St John Lateran, had facade decoration with eleven scenes from the story of Tobias and nine from that of Job (ca. 1430–50).[137] Beginning in the early fifteenth century, hospitals began to feature large narrative scenes relating to their founding and their donors, a reflection of the increasingly significant role played by secular powers in hospital administration and patronage, and some hospitals had scenes of contemporary hospital life.

The Scala hospital in Siena has the most famous fresco cycle from this period. In a prototypical instance of the shift from religious to lay authority, the administration of this hospital for pilgrims and foundlings was taken over by secular officials in 1404.[138] Although there were frescoes and other paintings in the chapel, reliquary room, and certain other areas of the hospital, the Sala del Pelligrinaio had the largest and most important cycle. Finished in 1444, this convalescent ward featured prophets, saints, and Doctors of the Church in niches in the ceiling, and the walls were to be painted with scenes from the life of Tobias. However, in a bold and innovative move, the rector, Giovanni di Francesco Buzzichelli, had the long walls decorated with secular images relating to the founding of the hospital and to its charitable activities, several of them chosen specifically to underscore the institution's independence from ecclesiastical authority. Some of the most remarkable scenes are those showing hospital activity, such as Domenico di Bartolo's *Care and Governance of the Sick*, which illustrates surgery and bedside care (fig. 32), and *Reception and Marriage of Trovatelli*, which illustrates the various stages in the life of a foundling. Two other panels, painted in the later 1500s by Giovanni Navesi or

Pietro Crogi when the hall was extended (and therefore close to the Jesuit Novitiate in date), are fascinating images of the practical aspects of midwifery, *Wetnurses Are Paid Their Salary in Grain* and *Wetnurses Suckling and Paid in Cash*.

Buzzichelli's decision to decorate the Pellegrinaio was made after his return from Florence, where he had served on the advisory board of the hospital of S. Maria Nuova.[139] Florence was not only Siena's greatest cultural rival but a city that lavished generous patronage on hospital buildings. At the time of Buzzichelli's sojourn in Florence, Domenico Veneziano was beginning to fresco the chapel of S. Egidio, at S. Maria Nuova hospital, with scenes from the life of the saint; his work would be carried on after his death in 1461 by Andrea del Castagno (the frescoes were later destroyed). Egidius, like St Roch and many other saints popular in hospital decoration, was associated with healing. The facade of the hospital also featured a fresco by Bicci di Lorenzo (either 1420 or ca. 1440–3), still extant in a hospital lecture room, of the consecration of the hospital chapel by Pope Martin V in 1420; it is a lively painting full of contemporary figures including members of the hospital order and the papal retinue and prominent citizens of Florence. Another fresco painted to commemorate the hospital's founding showed the granting of papal privileges to the members of the hospital order in 1474.[140] The later decoration in S. Egidio included another typical hospital image, Giovan Battista Paggi's *The Probatic Pool* (1592), mentioned earlier in this chapter (fig. 28); and Niccolò Circignani executed the grand fresco *Annunciation* for the hospital portico.[141]

No less eminent were the decorations of Brunelleschi's Spedale degli Innocenti, although their subjects were more traditional.[142] Some of the city's finest artists executed works for this hospital, especially under the patronage of the energetic prior Francesco Tesori (from 1483). The most notable was Domenico Ghirlandaio, who painted an *Adoration of the Magi* (1488) with two Holy Innocents in the foreground, a scene of the building of the hospital in the background, and a predella featuring the consecration of the Innocenti chapel by St Antoninus. It was also in this period that Andrea Della Robbia's famous roundels with babies in swaddling clothes were added to Brunelleschi's loggia (these became the symbol of the hospital), as well as a magnificent *Annunciation* in the cortile, and Piero di Cosimo painted a *Madonna and Child with Saints* (1493) for the chapel. One of the most interesting paintings is a much later fresco (1610–12) by Bernardino Poccetti in the refectory, *Massacre of the Innocents*, depicting a very common subject for orphanages, together with scenes from the life of the orphanage, including wetnurses suckling infants, young girls at prayer, and boys at supper and at school.[143] The nearby S. Matteo hospital, now the Accademia delle Belle Arti, also has religious subjects by the Della Robbia workshop under its portico facing the Via de' Ricasoli, and once had narrative frescoes inside the wards. A rare survivor is a detached fresco fragment in grisaille by Jacopo Pontormo (1494–1557), *The Women's Ward at S. Matteo Hospital*, a delightful depiction of contemporary hospital life, now housed incongruously in the hall of the plaster casts.[144] Second only to the Innocenti in its fame as a monument of Renaissance hospital architecture, thanks to its publication in his *Trattato di architettura* (1464), Filarete's gargantuan Ospedale Maggiore in Milan was based on these Tuscan models.[145] Along the facade, under its portico, was an extensive cycle of historical frescoes, probably executed by Vincenzo Foppa before 1465, illustrating the founding ceremonies directed by the Sforza duke and duchess and ending with the laying of the foundation stone.

One of the most prominent Roman hospitals at the time the Jesuit Novitiate infirmary was being built was the Spedale di S. Spirito in Sassia, along the Tiber on the Vatican side of the river. I mentioned the decorations of the church in chapter 1. The most notable feature of S. Spirito is a 120-metre-long sick ward called the Corsia Sistina, which resembles a basilica with a dome in the middle. The hospital was founded in the late twelfth century by Innocent III as a foundling hospital, but it was reconstructed by Sixtus IV as a monument to his own fame in 1478, and cared for pilgrims and the urban poor as well as the sick nobility. In a conscious attempt to distinguish it from the secularized hospitals in Milan, Florence, and Siena, Sixtus had the Corsia Sistina painted with two long series of frescoes celebrating the role of the papacy in the hospital's founding and works. Possibly painted by Antonio da Viterbo, Antoniazzo Romano, and others, the cycle also included a series of biographical episodes in Sixtus's life, from his childhood to the present – proof that a pope could be just as self-congratulatory as a Sforza duke.[146] The series also included scenes of infanticide and of wetnurses suckling infants.

The S. Spirito narrative frescoes are the only substantial hospital cycle to survive with inscriptions. They are arranged in a straight line in the clerestory level of the hall, with, in panels below them, giant Latin captions that explain the action above and also occasionally cite scripture. Above the windows are images of prophets holding scrolls with passages from the Old and New Testaments and the deuterocanonical books. These texts emphasize the need to care for the sick, and also make theological statements about the patronage of the hospital. One of them (not all survive) is the quotation from the Book of Sirach that appears in Room Two of the S. Andrea infirmary: NON TE PIGEAT VISITARE INFIRMUM.[147] Two of the pendentives in the dome have paintings of angels who also hold banderoles with inscriptions, including another that appears in the Jesuit infirmary, in Room Thirteen (John 11:3): DOMINI ECCE QUEM AMAS INFIRMATUR.

The hospitals just surveyed, along with many others in the cities and towns of Central and Northern Italy, had relatively little variety in their decoration. Imagery also tended to be located in certain key places. All hospitals had imagery in their chapels. Paintings or terracottas were concentrated also on the facade of the hospital, either in lunettes under the portico, as at S. Maria Nuova and S. Matteo in Florence, the Ospedale Maggiore in Milan, and smaller institutions like the Spedale Serristori in Figline Val d'Arno, or above the arcade, as at the Ceppo in Pistoia.[148] Others were found in the sick wards, as at S. Matteo in Florence, the Scala hospital in Siena, and the Ospedale di S. Spirito in Rome. The subjects fell within a limited number of categories. The more standard religious imagery ranged from images of saints associated with health and curing and protective Madonnas (such as the Madonna di Misericordia or the Madonna degli Innocenti) to biblical stories related to illness such as those of Tobias, Job, and the Probatic Pool. Allegorical representations were also common, such as in the personification entitled *Faith* by Poccetti at the Innocenti and, especially, in the magnificent seven Della Robbian terracotta panels at the Ceppo in Pistoia, *Seven Acts of Corporal Mercy* (1525–8).

Founding scenes also became fairly standard, from Milan to Rome, as did scenes of hospital life, most notably in Siena.

The Jesuit infirmary murals are all the more spectacular against this background. Although they depict some of the same biblical themes as earlier hospitals and have a similar self-referential quality, their range of scriptural and patristic citation is unprecedented. There is also nothing like the infirmary's 'medical journal' illustrations – Cagnati's depictions of mental maladies, miraculous rainfalls, botanical simples, animals, and curative spas – or its elaborate allegories of the battle between Good and Evil. Although some earlier hospitals had captions below their paintings (as at S. Spirito), none used textual quotation to create a three-dimensional emblem, a kind of imagery that recalls the erudite world of Jesuit colleges. Furthermore, no other hospital imagery is so clearly pedagogical or so specifically designed to encourage meditation. But the most extraordinary feature is the use of a wide range of classical references from Plutarch to Galen, combining the best of Greek and Roman medicine and pharmacology, a feature notably absent from the Italian tradition of hospital decoration. This balancing of Christian and pagan sources in such a way that neither dominates is the clearest possible statement of the Jesuits' commitment to humanistic learning, one far from the oppressive, 'Counter-Reformation' attitude with which the Jesuits are so often charged in the scholarship.

4

The Jesuit Collegiate Foundations of the Collegio Romano, the Seminario Romano, and the German-Hungarian College

Although the pictorial cycles at the Novitiate of S. Andrea al Quirinale were among the most innovative and original of the entire Jesuit enterprise in Rome, the fresco programs of the Jesuit collegiate institutions, painted between 1565 and 1608, were the most influential. Scholars have long recognized the debt owed by post-Tridentine iconography to the paintings that adorned the walls of the collegiate chapels of S. Apollinare, S. Stefano Rotondo, S. Tommaso di Canterbury, the Collegio Romano, and the Seminario Romano, including the first large-scale martyrdom cycles in Italy. These painted cycles had their most powerful impact on the Palaeochristian Revival movement, especially the commissions of the Oratorian Cesare Baronio and of Pope Clement VIII; and they were echoed in anti-Protestant illustrated books of the late sixteenth and of the first half of the seventeenth century, printed primarily under Jesuit auspices in Antwerp and Rome, some of which reproduced entire collegiate fresco cycles within a year or two of their completion. But contrary to what most scholars have maintained, the struggle against heresy was not the only inspiration behind these frescoes, and in most cases not even the greatest. It is true that some of the cycles, especially at S. Tommaso, spoke of the urgency of the spiritual battle that had engulfed Northern Europe and England, since they were directed specifically at men training to join the front lines in the North. But unlike the Novitiate frescoes, the collegiate cycles were directed not primarily at young Jesuits ready to commit their lives for the faith, but at non-Jesuits. The colleges were not Jesuit seminaries, but schools for laymen and diocesan priests. Even the Jesuit-run Seminario Romano was a diocesan training ground. Few recognize this important distinction.

The scholarship has treated the collegiate chapel paintings, especially at S. Stefano and S. Tommaso, as the paradigm for 'Counter-Reformation' imagery and therefore has exaggerated not only their anti-Protestantism, but their role as 'propaganda,' with all that term's sinister twentieth-century associations.[1] Just as the Catholic reform movement in general was not as fixated on the Reformation as is popularly maintained, neither were the Jesuit collegiate murals exclusively promoting an anti-heretical message.[2] More important was the desire to link present-day Catholicism with the early Church; the frescoes were concerned with celebrating the role of Rome and the papacy as the legitimate and historical centre of Catholicism, and the inheritor of the glory of antiquity. This Roman message, boosted by references to Roman triumphal processions and victories, is mostly glossed over in studies of the frescoes' connection with heresy. Even though the Protestants may have inspired the idea of the martyrdom cycle, as we will see in chapter 5, the theme of martyrdom itself was extraordinarily popular in Palaeochristian times; it was its connection with the early Church that gave it such appeal for sixteenth-century churchmen, not its usefulness in the campaign against Protestantism. The frescoes also identify emphatically with the landscape of the classical and medieval world, including places as distant as Africa and Asia, and exhibit an interest in geography that recalls the interest in the worldwide mission of the Novitiate frescoes. In addition, although the collegiate frescoes are well known for featuring some of the most gruesome scenes of torture and death ever achieved in Italian art – John Paoletti and Gary Radke call them 'almost journalistic' – they share with the Novitiate cycles an unmistakable message of Christian triumph.[3] Their central idea, as Alexandra Herz has indicated, was to depict martyrdom and death not for their own sakes but as the means to salvation.[4] Together with this theme is the christological emphasis as at S. Andrea: the martyrdoms echo the passion of Christ and model the taking up of one's cross to follow the Saviour into spiritual battle – whether literal or metaphorical.

Many of the collegiate fresco cycles also share the Novitiate paintings' link with Jerónimo Nadal's *Evangelicae historiae imagines*, but the connection here is more direct (see figs 12, 13).[5] The basic architectural and landscape setting, the division of the scene into three or more separate fields, and the composition of the figures are very close to those of the illustrations in Nadal – at least in the frescoes that survive. So is the generic classicism of the scenery and costume and the universal sense of place. The most important link, however, is in the key letters. As we will see, the collegiate church murals were among the first in Italy to feature letters in the image that were keyed to explanatory text below. This emphatically didactic method of presentation, so akin to the Jesuits' program of education and meditation in the colleges, either inspired or was inspired by Nadal's manual. In either case, when the Nadal illustrations were published in 1593 they exposed that method to the widest possible audience, and it reappeared frequently in later Jesuit publications such as emblem books.

The collegiate frescoes were also similar to the Novitiate paintings in that they were meant to be used. They were pitched toward a specific program of liturgy, study, and meditation that was related to the students' course of studies and to their future pastoral or charitable work. Scholars have drawn connections between the paintings and the *Spiritual Exercises*, the Roman Breviary, and the Litany of the Saints, as well as hymns, psalms, and scripture. The imagery also has links with the learning methods of the *Ratio Studiorum*, the program of study used in the Jesuit colleges (see chapter 1), and was meant to function as a memory aid for meditation, based on classical artificial memory techniques. The collegiate chapel frescoes also shared themes and iconographies with the paintings in the Novitiate. Such an affinity is not surprising given that Jesuits lived at the colleges and students from the colleges often went to the Novitiate to make the Exercises. Some of the collegiate frescoes also shared artists with the Novitiate, including Fiammeri and Clemente. But the main difference between the collegiate paintings and those of the Novitiate is that the former were meant for a wider, more public audience and were therefore mostly the work of professional painters.[6]

The collegiate institutions in this chapter include the Collegio Romano, the original buildings of which still stand on the Piazza Collegio Romano, and the Seminario Romano, which was housed in several different locations in the sixteenth century and was moved in 1608 to its home on the Via del Seminario Romano. Nothing survives of their sixteenth-century decoration except textual descriptions. The bulk of this chapter will be concerned with the various properties belonging to the German-Hungarian College, including the college buildings and the church of S. Apollinare, located just north of the Piazza Navona on the Piazza S. Apollinare. This structure was razed and rebuilt in the seventeenth and eighteenth centuries, although the painting cycle of S. Apollinare survives completely in printed form. The chapter will also consider the German-Hungarian College's satellite churches, beginning with S. Saba on the Aventine Hill, the Palaeochristian Revival apse frescoes of which have been preserved to this day, and, most important, another early Christian church, S. Stefano Rotondo on the nearby Caelian Hill, the decorations of which are by far the most significant of all the Jesuits' collegiate commissions, and have fortunately survived not only in the original but in printed form as well.

Jesuit Teaching and a Brief History of the Roman Collegiate Institutions

Teaching was the central ministry of the Society of Jesus.[7] The first teaching order in the Catholic church, the Jesuits made the founding, management, and staffing of schools one of their most characteristic activities, even if they did not start out that way. Ignatius and his early followers, although students at the University of Paris, never intended to be anything more than an order of itinerant catechists and preachers, with an early interest in missionary work. It was only in the late 1540s that the Society began to take on teaching responsibilities, having seen 'the benefits of labors sustained with the same group of people over a long period of time.'[8] The Jesuits received their first college unexpectedly, when in 1547 the viceroy of Sicily through the citizens of Messina invited Ignatius to start a college in that city and staff it with Jesuits.[9] Other schools followed, in Sicily and then in Vienna and Rome, and by Ignatius's death in 1556 the Society was already running about thirty schools, a number that would increase to over eight hundred by 1773.[10] In the North, particularly Flanders and Germany, the schools played a special role as the vanguard against Protestantism, a goal emphasized by Ignatius himself, who wrote, 'The best means to help the Church in this distress would be to multiply the colleges and schools of the Society in many regions, especially where it is thought that there will be a concourse of students.'[11] This goal, however, did not keep the Jesuits from accepting Protestant students, whom they treated with remarkable equality. The earliest schools were secondary schools, but beginning with the Roman College, the Collegio Romano, many were raised to the status of universities. Jerónimo Nadal was particularly connected with Jesuit education from the start. The founder and first director of the Messina school, Nadal went on to supervise colleges in Greater Germany and elsewhere in Northern Europe, and he spent most of his adult life drafting curricula.

The curriculum of studies at Jesuit colleges was not standardized until the generalate of Claudio Acquaviva in 1599, when the *Ratio Studiorum*, the comprehensive guide John W. O'Malley calls the 'Magna Carta of Jesuit education,' was published by Antonio Possevino (1593).[12] Differing from the study guides of other orders in that it addressed lay as well as Jesuit students, the *Ratio* was infused with humanistic learning, so that subjects such as literature, history, and drama were added to the traditional subjects of philosophy and theology. The *Ratio* demonstrated an extraordinary commitment to 'secular' literature, the literature of antiquity, and it gave the students a knowledge of Latin and Greek writers such as Pliny, Virgil, and Cicero, a classical foundation evident in the erudite literary references embedded in the infirmary murals in the Novitiate. The *Ratio* was more structured than the mainstream Latin curriculum of the day and introduced a more systematic and chronological progression of classes according to ability and age, a sequential structure that is also reminiscent of the Novitiate paintings.[13]

By 1551 the basic program of the colleges had been established. Students were encouraged to go to confession either every month or every two weeks, assisted daily at the celebration of the mass, listened to homilies on Sundays and feast days as well as to other moral instruction, attended vespers on those same days, and practised a daily examination of conscience.[14] Before long, students were invited or even required to make part of the Spiritual Exercises, with the result that Ignatius's manual became a focal and familiar element in every young man's education. Students were also encouraged to take part in charitable works of mercy with the Jesuits, and after 1563 the Marian congregations, a kind of confraternity, were introduced in Jesuit schools. In the German-Hungarian College older students were assigned to instruct younger ones in matters of spirituality and to act as role models for their younger brethren. Jesuit colleges soon became the locus of more extravagant and public spectacles. In 1553 the Collegio Romano opened its academic year with disputations on philosophy, theology, and rhetoric that were attended by some of the most important churchmen and nobles of Rome.[15] By 1555 this spectacle had come to last eight days and to include subjects such as humane letters and the 'arts' (logic, ethics, physics, mathematics, metaphysics); it became 'a popular entertainment for the Roman intelligentsia.'[16]

Another tradition that gained wider audiences for the colleges was that of the so-called *affixiones*, public exhibitions of epigrams, letters, orations, emblems, and visual poems written by the students, which were displayed in the college courtyard, usually attached (hence the name) to drapery or tapestries.[17] These exhibitions formed part of the students' training in emblematics, a pedagogical method widely employed by the Jesuits in their colleges, and a hint of which appears in the Novitiate infirmary paintings with their allegories and captioning.[18] One of the earliest took place in 1561, when Philip II's ambassador Francesco Varga and Carlo Borromeo visited the Collegio Romano and were 'greeted by an extraordinary number of poetical compositions in various languages which, written on large folios, were affixed to the walls.'[19] A similar display greeted the Father

General when he visited in 1581 and encountered 'so many verses and emblems adorning the upper and lower corridors.'[20] Paulette Choné has recently published a manuscript emblem book of 1585 from the college of Verdun in France that features brightly-coloured emblems with Latin and Greek inscriptions of the sort that would have been made at the Roman colleges, and elsewhere I have discussed similar exhibitions at the Jesuit colleges in Japan in the 1590s.[21] Jesuit emblems were works of art in themselves, and related to similar images in Jesuit printed emblem books.

One aspect of Jesuit college life that has received new attention in the work of Louise Rice is the thesis defence, an elaborate production paid for by the defending student's family or patron and involving not just his formal rhetorical speech but also music, illustrated broadsheets or booklets, and other embellishments such as expensive floral arrangements.[22] Some of the earliest publications of the Collegio Romano press, in 1556, were thesis booklets.[23] Illustrated thesis prints became popular from the early seventeenth century, and Jesuit teachers were responsible for many of their designs, which also manifested a love for erudite emblematica based on ancient texts and on Sacred Scripture. Especially at the Collegio Romano, these events were designed as a way of attracting rich and influential patrons, and they became major public events. Such exhibitions show that the visual arts had an intimate place in the Jesuit curriculum from the very beginning.

The education of lay students was the Jesuits' first concern, but not their only one. After the Council of Trent decreed the establishment of seminaries for the formation of clergy, the Jesuits played a leading role in educating a new generation of priests – not only their own, but diocesan priests as well.[24] It was the need to serve laymen and clergy alike that led Ignatius to found the two first Roman collegiate foundations of the Society of Jesus, the Collegio Romano (1551) and the German College (soon to be the German-Hungarian College, 1552).[25]

The Collegio Romano opened very humbly, with an inscription over the door summing up its simple purpose: 'School of Grammar, Humanities, and Christian Doctrine, free.'[26] Owing to that last word, it was plagued by financial troubles in the early years, and moved several times, once because it was flooded out by the Tiber, before finding its permanent home on what is now called the Piazza di Collegio Romano.[27] Its final site was granted to the Collegio by Signora Vittoria della Tolfa, the Marchesa della Valle, who gave her family *isola* in 1560, a property she had intended to donate to another religious order to found a small monastery.[28] The move was ratified by Pius IV. In O'Malley's words the 'apple of Ignatius's eye,' the Collegio Romano was intended from the beginning to be an international institution and the pre-eminent college of the Society.[29] Paul IV (1555–9) granted the college the right to grant higher degrees in philosophy and theology in 1556, thereby raising the college to the status of a university.[30] Under Father General Everard Mercurian (1573–80) the Collegio Romano started holding regular classes in controversial theology, in order to train students through debate how to counter the arguments of Protestants and non-Christians.[31]

Although Jesuits and Jesuit scholastics were housed there with their teachers in a residence building, the Collegio was never limited to members of the order; it was designed primarily for lay students, and also took in students training for the diocesan priesthood. Enrolment grew at an extraordinary rate. In 1555 there were 130 professors and students in the college, and by 1556 there were 70 Jesuit scholastics alone.[32] By 1563 the number of Jesuits at the Collegio Romano had risen to 218. Yet the college was straining under severe financial burdens: in a series of letters to the pope, the Jesuits wrote alarmingly of the 'strettezza' of the buildings, which were in urgent need of amplification so that together with the Seminario Romano the Collegio could provide enough manpower to carry out the pope's command, both in Rome and in 'the missions in countries beyond the Northern regions' and 'the Indies.'[33]

The Collegio was set back on its feet by Gregory XIII (1573–85), a pope for whom education was a primary concern and who had founded colleges for the Jesuits in places as far away as Japan.[34] Gregory gave it an annual allowance of 4,000 scudi, as well as the income of the Abbey of Chiaravalle di Fiastra (Marches), which amounted to 6,000 scudi per year.[35] He reluctantly agreed to be called 'founder' of the college, a title offered in acknowledgment of his generosity, even though he thought it more properly belonged to the Marchesa della Valle. Nevertheless, Gregory and his supporters envisioned the college as a powerful symbol of the pope's benevolent rule and his role as defender of the faith against heresy and paganism; its goal was, through education, 'to uphold the Holy Catholic Faith, and to extirpate heresy.'[36] In his rhapsodic celebration of Gregory's papacy, Marc'Antonio Ciappi had this to say about the Collegio Romano:

> But what can we say about the most sumptuous buildings of the Collegio Romano, erected by the fathers of the Society of Jesus, built in the tenth year of his pontificate, with such marvellous architecture, and at such a cost, with many very spacious lecture halls, and such departments, [including] sciences, and diverse languages, with no end but to serve all of the poor, whether youths or children, not only from Rome but all of Italy, and beyond, to make them learned in the languages, sciences, and in every knowledge, and to teach them as well the ways of a Christian with the catechism and penitence of those fathers, who every day show themselves to be more useful and fruitful for the Church of God, and the Christian Republic.[37]

This glowing description, adorned with an engraving of the facade of the Collegio Romano, shows clearly that the school was regarded as a papal institution and that its identification with the Jesuits was secondary to its identification with Gregory XIII.

The German College was the only other Roman college founded by Ignatius. Initially, he had intended to create an institution to house a hundred German seminarians ranging in age from 16 to 21, under the leadership of a handful of resident Jesuit supervisors.[38] Unlike the Collegio Romano, the German College would be little more than a residence, since these students would attend their classes in humanities, philosophy, and theology at the Collegio Romano.[39] The college was officially founded in 1552 by Pope Julius III, whose bull of foundation, *Dum sollicita*, indicates that the original intention was primarily to combat Protestantism, to 'search out the hidden venom of heretical doctrine, to refute it, and then to replant the uprooted trunk of the tree of faith.'[40] The institution began with a mere 19 students, a number that increased to about 60 in 1554. Like the Collegio Romano, the German College was beset with financial troubles, and the Society applied regularly to major donors such as Cardinal Alessandro Farnese for a subvention, writing that 'since our Society has not taken on the task of assisting this holy work temporally, but only spiritually ... our debts have built up.'[41] The situation reached such a desperate pass under the generalate of Diego Laínez (1558–65) – he wrote of 'dire need' (*stretto bisogno*) – that paying lay boarders, mostly Italian noble children under the age of 15, were admitted.[42] By 1573 the number of students had risen to about 200, with a ratio of about one German seminarian to ten Italian boys. Aside from the fact that the boys were unruly and the relationship between the national groups was far from optimal, many Jesuits felt that the original mission of the college had been contaminated. An exception was the minister and future rector Michele Di Loreto, to whom we will return.

The answer to the Jesuits' dreams came in 1573, when Gregory XIII made the institution a pontifical college directly under the jurisdiction of the Holy See and assigned it cardinal protectors.[43] It still belonged to the Jesuits, but they no longer had to assume full responsibility for its maintenance. With the bull *Postquam Deo placuit* and an extremely generous endowment of 10,000 ducats annually, Pope Gregory refounded the German College, evicted the non-German students, and restored it to its original function as a seminary. Gregory also reaffirmed the college's anti-Protestant character. Students were required to take an oath of obedience to the pope after six months, and to swear that they would receive holy orders and then return to Greater Germany to strike out against heresy. Another change was that some courses began to be taught at the college to supplement the students' education at the Collegio Romano. These classes were tailored specifically to the situation in their homeland and focused on controversial theology and on Sacred Scripture. Now, in addition to their daily instruction at the Collegio Romano, they had one hour in the morning and a half hour in the afternoon of instruction at the German College aimed at combating Protestant arguments. Even scriptural studies were moulded to fit the German situation, as Cesareo explains: 'This entailed an explanation of Scripture within the context of the errors then present in Germany. Thus, the study of Scripture became oriented toward the particular circumstances in Germany, which gave rise to a dogmatic and polemical approach to scriptural interpretation aimed at refuting the errors of the Protestants.'[44] The final change in the makeup of the college took place in 1580. The year before, Gregory XIII had founded the Hungarian College, with the bull *Apostolici muneris sollicitudo*, but the enrolment was so small that it was merged with the German College in 1580 to become the German-Hungarian College.[45] The German-Hungarian allegedly became Pope Gregory's favourite college.[46]

The Jesuits also took the helm at other national colleges in the city, such as the Venerable English College, which I will discuss in chapter 5, and the Collegio Greco, or Greek College. Although the Greek College was a Catholic institution, it used the Greek rite. It had been founded as early as 1576 by Gregory XIII as part of a plan to exert influence over the Eastern Church, and a distinguished church was built for it, S. Atanasio on present-day Via Babuino, by Giacomo della Porta (1583), the architect of the facade of the Gesù.[47] The college was handed over to the Jesuits in 1591. Nevertheless, owing to problems with other religious orders resident in the college the Jesuits did not actually take it over until 1621, and the college was founded as a Jesuit entity under the patronage of Urban VIII only in 1623. Its history and its paintings, therefore, are beyond the focus of this book.

Although a Jesuit institution, the Seminario Romano was a direct papal response to the need for seminaries proclaimed in canon XVIII of the Twenty-third Session of the Council of Trent ('Method of Establishing Seminaries for Clerics, and of Educating the Same Therein'). Recognizing the urgent need for a standardized regimen for the formation of diocesan clergy, the council concluded in this detailed decree:

> Whereas the age of youth, unless it be rightly trained, is prone to follow after the pleasures of the world; and unless it be formed, from its tender years, unto piety and religion, before habits of vice have taken possession of the whole man, it never will perfectly, and without the greatest, and well-nigh special, help of Almighty God, persevere in ecclesiastical discipline; the holy Synod ordains, that all cathedral, metropolitan, and other churches greater than these, shall be bound, each according to its means and the extent of the diocese, to maintain, to educate religiously, and to train in ecclesiastical discipline, a certain number of youths of their city and diocese ... Into this college shall be received such as are at least twelve years old, born in lawful wedlock, and who know how to read and write competently, and whose character and inclination afford a hope that they will always serve in the ecclesiastical ministry ... And that the youths may be the more advantageously trained in the aforesaid ecclesiastical discipline, they shall always at once wear the tonsure and the clerical dress; they shall learn grammar, singing, ecclesiastical computation, and the other liberal arts; they shall be instructed in sacred Scripture; ecclesiastical works; the homilies of the saints; the manner of administering the sacraments, especially those things which shall seem adapted to enable them to hear confessions; and the forms of the rites and ceremonies.[48]

Pope Pius IV founded the Seminario Romano in 1564 for the archdiocese of Rome as a Tridentine seminary, that is, an independent and self-sufficient institution reserved exclusively for the education of future diocesan clergy under the direct jurisdiction of the local bishop.[49] The pope assigned the seminary to the Society of Jesus, even though he was displeased with them at the time and they were far from enthusiastic about taking on the responsibility. It opened with an enrolment of eighty students, and it caused no end of resentment among diocesan clergy against the Society, since their future ranks were being trained by the Jesuits and they were being taxed to support the new foundation.[50] The first doctorate at the Seminario was received by Pompeo Ugonio, the author of the guidebook to Rome, who matriculated in 1569 and published one of the earliest extant thesis broadsides.[51]

Like the German and Venerable English colleges, the Seminario Romano functioned essentially as a residence for students who took classes at the Collegio Romano. These students caused the Jesuits much trouble since the Society was without jurisdiction over admissions and dismissals. O'Malley, paraphrasing Jesuit sources, characterizes this disorderly bunch: 'Although they came from the lowest rungs of Roman society, they were nonetheless filled with an overweening pride. They were liars, cheats, ingrates, utterly untrustworthy, corruptors of the few good among them, devoid of any pastoral or religious motivation, intent only upon gaining fat benefices with no pastoral duties attached. They called the seminary a "prison" and the Jesuits "spies and hypocrites," their "jailers and executioners." In the rector's opinion, the Germanico was in comparison a "paradise."'[52] The Jesuits made formal remonstrations to the pope (by now Pius V) to be relieved of their stewardship of the Seminario, but to no avail. The experience left such a bitter taste in their mouths that it was officially decreed in the Second General Congregation of the Society of Jesus (1565) that 'it did not seem proper to accept [seminaries of clerics].'[53] The Jesuits were rightly worried that if they allowed themselves to run these episcopal foundations they would lose their independence, and they also believed, to quote Juan Alfonso de Polanco, that their own colleges already sufficed as 'true and excellent seminaries.'[54]

The Paintings of the Collegio Romano and the Church of SS. Annunziata

The first recorded Jesuit painting commission in Rome, begun around 1565, adorned a hopelessly undersized church dedicated to the SS. Annunziata in the Collegio Romano, a church meant 'for the convenience of those young men from our Society who, having finished their novitiate, were invited to do their studies in this Collegio Romano.'[55] A small three-aisled church with five altars, it was built between 1562 and 1567 on the foundations of what had been intended to be the church of a minor nunnery of the Order of the Poor Clares called S. Maria della Nunziata.[56] The Marchesa della Valle, the original founder of the Collegio Romano, was then persuaded to leave the *isola* and its existing buildings to the Society in memory of her late husband, Signor Camillo Orsini, the Marchese della Guardia. Since the earlier church had already been built to the height of the ground floor in 1555, there was no way for the Jesuits to expand the structure to hold the increasing number of students who were flocking to the Collegio.[57] The chapel was located halfway in the middle of present-day Via di S. Ignazio, on the site of the right transept of today's church of S. Ignazio.

Although the Jesuits got the Marchesa's land, they did not get any money from her for completing the church, and budgetary restraints compelled them to hire their own architect.[58] Construction of the Jesuit chapel was taken over immediately by the Jesuit architect Giovanni Tristano, who sent the elevation and facade plans from Perugia, where he was working on the church of the Gesù in that city. Although he later came to Rome to inspect the site, he was already back in Perugia when the chapel was completed. Construction began rapidly, so that the church could be described as 'già quasi fatta' in 1563; however, work then lagged on until 1567, when it was first used for worship.[59] SS. Annunziata was built entirely by Jesuit labour, a matter of no small consolation and pride to members of the order. We know something about the appearance of this church from engravings and drawings, and from contemporary descriptions.

The church of SS. Annunziata was basically rectangular, in the Doric order, with a rounded and vaulted apse and four very shallow side chapels on each side. Hardly a grand structure, it was approximately 74¼ feet long and 41½ feet wide, not counting the side chapels, which were originally a mere 5¼ feet in depth.[60] Girolamo Francini writes in his *Le cose maravigliose dell'alma città di Roma* (Rome, 1580) that there were five altars, 'of which the main [altar] has a vaulted tribune where there are painted the Annunciation, some Prophets, Choirs of Angels, God the Father above, with great variety and artifice, made according to the design and work of Federico Zuccaro, excellent painter; the other [altars] have their paintings made by different masters, namely the Crucifixion, the Madonna, St Sebastian, and St Francis.'[61] From a letter from Tristano dated 1563 we also know that the church had 'rooms above, where there are lattices,' which Milton Lewine surmises were used by students to look in during services without being seen or having to enter the church.[62] These were likely on the college side of the chapel, whereas the other side had open clerestory windows, allowing in light from the street. The facade was very similar to that of the contemporary chapel of S. Andrea al Quirinale (1567–9), which was also designed by Tristano (see chapter 2), and was of a type used elsewhere in the city, for example in S. Caterina dei Funari (1565) and S. Spirito in Sassia (1585). Like the interior of the church, the facade was of two storeys, and was divided into three bays by pilasters, Doric below and Ionic above. The entire facade was crowned by a large triangular pediment with small obelisks on the corners. On the lower floor the door was flanked by niches, whereas there were three windows above, the central one being a Serlian window. In accordance with the wishes of the Marchesa, the facade also proudly displayed the Orsini arms.[63] SS. Annunziata was enlarged in 1580 when Gregory XIII expanded the college itself, especially the side chapels.[64] The church was then demolished in 1650 to make way for the gigantic church of S. Ignazio, which was begun in 1626 by Orazio Grassi and finished only at the end of the century.[65] In striking contrast to SS. Annunziata, which occupied only a small section of the Collegio, S. Ignazio took up a quarter of the entire block when it was completed.

The sources do not indicate whether the Jesuits or the Marchesa della Valle paid for the paintings in the church or the gilding of the tabernacle, but the Jesuits employed professional artists. The tribune vault fresco by Federico Zuccaro has fortunately survived in the form of an engraving by Cornelis Cort dated 1571 (fig. 33), as well as a description by Giorgio Vasari: '[Zuccaro] made a choir of many angels and various splendours, with God the Father who sends the Holy Spirit above the Madonna, while she is given the annunciation by the Angel Gabriel, and placed in the middle of six prophets, larger than life and very beautiful.'[66] A heavenly cloudburst of angels, prophets, and patriarchs, the painting is divided horizontally into two main sections, the celestial and earthly realms. The upper portion, culminating in an image of God the Father and the Holy Spirit, is flanked by rows of musician angels and winged cherubs, immersed in clouds. The lower section centres on the Annunciation scene itself, placed so that the central axis of the painting from top to bottom can be read as a symbol of the Trinity (Father, Holy Spirit, Christ in the womb of the Virgin). On each side of the Annunciation scene are three prophets and patriarchs, holding tablets with inscriptions from the Old Testament that foretell the coming of Christ. In the background, set in a generic landscape, are various symbols of the Virgin, including the *hortus clausus*, the tower, and the well.[67]

Cristina Acidini Luchinat has identified two preparatory drawings for the apse fresco.[68] Giovanni Baglione, who mentions Federico Zuccaro's participation in this chapel, also attributes two additional 'frescoes' in the church to his hand, including a *Nativity* and a *Circumcision*.[69] Either Francini or Baglione must be mistaken about the subjects of the other paintings, which were either a *Circumcision* or a *Crucifixion*, and we are left wondering whether the 'Madonna' mentioned by Francini is the *Nativity* mentioned by Baglione. Since the painting of St Francis was an oil painting, it seems unlikely that two of the other side chapel paintings would be in fresco. If one of the side chapels indeed showed a *Circumcision*, it would have had the same link with the naming of Jesus and hence the Society of Jesus that the high altar of the Gesù would later evoke.[70] It would also have meant that three of the paintings dealt with scenes of Christ's conception and childhood, the theme of the entire church.

On the spandrels on either side of the tribune arch Federico's brother Taddeo Zuccaro painted images of Adam and Eve (fig. 33), the former of which recalls in its pose Michelangelo's *Dawn* from the Tomb of Lorenzo de' Medici at S. Lorenzo in Florence (designed 1521).[71] It is remarkable that the Jesuits could hire a man of Taddeo's stature, since not only was he in high demand in Rome itself, but from 1561 he was working at a very favourable salary for Cardinal Alessandro Farnese on the interior of his villa at Caprarola.[72] Taddeo's large shop included his younger brother Federico, who participated in the execution of the Caprarola paintings from the beginning and eventually took the helm upon his brother's untimely death in 1566. Possibly Farnese's role as a major patron of the Society of Jesus helped secure these artists for the Jesuits. In addition to his work at SS. Annunziata, Federico would later work on the Angels' Chapel in the Gesù. Taddeo's contributions to SS. Annunziata of course date from before 1566.

The side chapel paintings survive in title alone (and, as we have seen, even the names are not consistent). According to Giovanni Baglione, the canvas *St Francis Receiving the Stigmata* was by the post-Tridentine painter *par excellence*, Girolamo Muziano (1582–92), a favourite painter of Gregory XIII whom even Alessandro Farnese could not obtain for Caprarola, but who worked for his arch-rival Ippolito d'Este at the Villa d'Este in Tivoli from 1560 to 1566.[73] Muziano later painted two versions of the same scene, one of them for a Capuchin church at Frascati (later 1570s) (fig. 34), both of which survive today. Both canvases show the saint in a rich landscape setting, the Roman version a sombre image in a dark grotto and the Frascati version a brightly lit scene in an open area. The paintings are enlivened by their natural setting, the mysticism and atmospheric effect of which recall Titian, yet their attention to botanical detail also shows the influence of Northern paintings and engravings.[74] Alessandro Farnese eventually did secure Muziano's services in 1588–9 for the *Circumcision* at the high altar of the Gesù, but the elderly cardinal died before it was completed (see chapter 6). There was also a painting cycle of St Francis in the Gesù, placed there partly because Francis Borgia (general 1560–72) was especially devoted to him but also because Francis of Assisi served as a precursor of Francis Xavier, who died in 1552 and was not canonized until

1622. Since Francis Borgia was general at the time of the construction of SS. Annunziata, it seems likely that he was responsible for the choice of St Francis for this chapel as well. Francis of Assisi also served as a model for living one's life in Christ, since he became a second Christ through his reception of the stigmata.

One final item of great importance in the original church of SS. Annunziata was the tomb of Aloysius Gonzaga. Like that between Stanislas and the Novitiate, there was a close link between Aloysius and the site of his tomb, since he had been enrolled in the Collegio Romano at the time of his death. Within a year his body was placed under the pavement of SS. Annunziata in the Cappella del Crocifisso, and in 1598 it was moved to the wall of the church. Aloysius's cult was given a boost by his beatification in 1605, and in that year (the same year in which Stanislas's tomb was commissioned by members of the Polish nobility) the Marchese Tiberio Lancellotti erected a chapel in his honour and built a rich altar of polychrome marble that still exists in the sacristy of S. Ignazio.[75] Robert Bellarmine, who wrote affectionately of Aloysius as his 'spiritual son,' asked in his will, dated 23 January 1611, that he be buried at the foot of the young man's tomb.[76]

The fresco cycles in the lecture halls of the Collegio Romano were not painted until nearly two decades after those in SS. Annunziata. The Jesuits had wanted to rebuild the existing college buildings from the moment they took over the Marchesa's bequest. The structures already there were far from adequate given the number of students enrolled, and the Society had its eyes on the block adjacent to the south, facing the present-day Piazza del Collegio Romano. With this new parcel of land in place, the Jesuits laid the first stone of the new buildings in 1581, under the patronage of Pope Gregory XIII, the new 'founder' of the college.[77] The college buildings were also a pet project of another superior general, Claudio Acquaviva, who, as we have seen, was responsible for most of the renovations and almost all the painting cycles at the Novitiate. Although the buildings, which included classrooms to the south of SS. Annunziata and a Jesuit residence to the north, have traditionally been assigned to Bartolommeo Ammannati, Pietro Pirri has pointed out that there is no evidence for this attribution and that the buildings were almost certainly the work of the Jesuit architect Giuseppe Valeriano.[78] In the early stages of the project Valeriano was assisted as a consultant by Giacomo della Porta, who would design the facade of the churches of the Collegio Greco and the Gesù, and who was the architect of St Peter's. Like Tristano before him, Valeriano also contributed extensively to the Novitiate buildings. In a sombre but monumental style, which answered the Jesuits' need for austerity in their residences but allowed the pope to proclaim his patronage, the new buildings of the Collegio Romano became one of the grandest and most recognizable educational institutions in Italy. The building was finished quickly, and opened for classes as early as 1584. It had eleven classrooms, in addition to the grand Aula Magna and two other halls for the Marian congregations.

Unfortunately, there is no Richeôme to tell us what was depicted in the original decorations of the 1581–4 college buildings. According to the account books, first published in their entirety by Pirri, the painting campaign was very fast; it began in January 1584 and ended a few months later.[79] Most of the painters were virtual unknowns, with two notable exceptions. The first is the Fleming Paul Brill (1554–

1626), one of the most popular landscape artists of late Cinquecento Rome, who contributed to the papal apartments of Gregory XIII as well as executing important commissions for Sixtus V (1585–90) and Clement VIII (1592–1605).[80] Another well-known painter working on this commission was Cristofano Roncalli (Il Pomarancio, 1551/2–1626), whose supposed teacher Circignani – confusingly, also called 'Il Pomarancio' – worked a couple of years earlier on the frescoes in the church of the German-Hungarian College, S. Stefano Rotondo, and that of the English College, S. Tommaso di Canterbury.[81] A certain Giuseppe Roncalli, perhaps his kinsman, entered the Society in the Roman Novitiate in the same year that Cristofano contributed to the Collegio Romano (see chapter 2). Roncalli later collaborated with Paul Brill and others on the Nave Clementina of Clement VIII at the church of St John Lateran, and was commissioned to paint a canvas of the *Punishment of Sapphira* for St Peter's, also under Clement VIII.[82] The other painters included Bartolomeo Sogliani (possibly a relative of the Florentine painter Antonio Sogliani, 1492–1544), who was responsible for most of the work and painted a large fresco *Christ the Saviour* in the Theology Aula; Andrea Aretino; Matteo Neroni (perhaps a relation of the Sienese painter Bartolomeo Neroni, 1505/10–1571); Cesare Rossetto; Antonio de' Monti; the Milanese sculptor Ambrogio Buonvicino; and the calligrapher Alessandro de Magistris (Il Caldarola). Another artist working on the project, who seems to have had a hand in nearly every commission covered in this book, was Giovanni Battista Fiammeri, who is mentioned as purchasing paints on 18 August 1584; so too did his assistant Rutilio Clemente.

Paintings adorned the Aula Magna, the Theology Aula, and the head of the grand staircase, as well as other public areas of the college. They included fourteen landscape paintings by Brill and Neroni of the colleges founded by Gregory XIII, with Latin epigrams in labels by Alessandro de Magistris below; figure paintings; and simple friezes and adornments. Andrea Aretino, for example, painted a series of six false doors. The only painting mentioned by name is a *quadro* of the *Madonna della Congregazione de Piccoli*, the work of Rutilio Clemente.[83] Antonio de' Monti, who specialized in portraits of popes, executed a portrait of Gregory XIII, and Buonvicino made a stucco papal coat of arms that dominated the head of the staircase. They are described in some detail in the Annual Letter of 1584:

At the back of the hall, the eyes of the visitor are attracted right away by the portrait of Gregory XIII seated in a throne, surrounded by a large crowd of cardinals, [and] a large number of our colleagues prostrated at his feet in the act of benediction, together with a group of the most distinguished alumni representing the respective colleges. If we turn our gaze inside onto the walls of the *aula*, we will see the most beautiful images of buildings depicted on all sides. They are the Gregorian colleges founded by the zealous pontiff in various parts of the world for the propagation of the Faith, six on the right and seven on the left. On the right one sees the colleges of Vilnius in Lithuania and Claudiopolis in Transylvania, and three others in Japan, along with the seminary at Fulda. On the left are the colleges of Vienna in Austria, the Illirico in Piceno, and, finally, the five Roman ones, namely, in addition to the three already exant, the seminary of Greek neophytes and, last, that of the Maronites. The facing wall has at the front a view of the Collegio Romano, larger than all the others, and in front of this, on the entrance wall, can be seen another five colleges, smaller in proportion and in works, namely, Pont-à-Mousson [Richeôme's former college] in Lorraine, Braunsberg in Prussia, Olmütz in Moravia, Graz in Styria, and, finally, Prague in Bohemia. All these various images are represented inside the room as if unfolded on a large tapestry, and to enliven them a brief and elegant Latin epigram is placed on each, indicating their characteristics in a few words.[84]

What is striking about the paintings in the Collegio Romano is that the iconography is not so much Jesuit as papal. Although the vistas of Jesuit colleges the world over celebrate the Jesuit educational and missionary enterprise and the emphasis on landscape echoes painting cycles in other Jesuit foundations in the city, the overriding theme is one of papal prerogative and the glorification of Gregory XIII. The images of the colleges immediately recall a contemporary publication meant as a panegyric ode to Gregory: Marc'Antonio Ciappi's *Compendio delle heroiche et gloriose attione, et santa vita di Papa Gregorio XIII* (Rome, 1596), quoted earlier in this chapter, which includes woodcut illustrations of colleges founded by Gregory, such as the Japanese colleges of Usuki, Funai, Arima, and Azuchi (fig. 35).[85] It is likely that these images, which show blocklike structures in a severe mid-sixteenth-century Roman style, were based on the now lost paintings of the Collegio. They also recall fresco cycles commissioned by later popes to celebrate papal foundations, such as those in the Salone Sistino in Sixtus V's Villa Montalto, which included obelisks, fountains, and public architecture funded by the pope, and similar imagery at the Salone Sistino at the Vatican Palace, both from the later 1580s.[86] Paul Brill himself contributed frescoes showing papal properties in a landscape setting in Clement VIII's Sala del Concistoro in the Vatican in the 1590s.[87] Two paintings traditionally assigned to the Collegio Romano campaign, canvases showing Gregory founding the Collegio Romano and the international Jesuit colleges, have recently been dated to 1655.[88]

Pope Gregory wasted no time in making an official visit to his newest foundation, which he dedicated on 28 October 1584. Naturally, the event was used as an excuse for *affixiones*:

> There was a most beautiful exhibition of pictures and compositions throughout the courtyard and in all the stairways. The pope came, saw, and was much pleased with everything: he was brought to the *salone* already painted with pictures representing the buildings of various colleges founded by His Holiness. At the end of the *salone* had been painted the same Pope Gregory with many cardinals on the sides and many young men at his feet with many emblems [*devise*] according to the dress of their colleges, in the act of blessing them, as still can be seen today. The Pope's throne with its baldacchino was set up facing this painting. The Pope departed completely satisfied and encouraged the fathers to begin classes.[89]

Girolamo Nappi mentions the event in his *Diario del Seminario Romano* (1640s): the passageways in the college are draped with luxurious textiles and emblems, and in them Gregory stands and contemplates the picture of himself facing the throne he sat upon.[90] The elaborate emblems, inscriptions, and temporary papal arms hung for this occasion are also mentioned in the account book, which lists payments for various supplies such as walnut oil, white lead, and ground gold for the emblems, as well as payments to the sculptor Flaminio Vacca for two papal arms to go above the staircase in the school courtyard, and to Bernardino Passero and Bartolommeo Argentires da Torino for creating the commemorative medallions minted to celebrate Gregory's patronage.[91]

The grand public rooms were not the only places adorned with paintings. Like those of early Jesuits such as Ignatius and Francis Borgia, as well as that of Claudio Acquaviva, the bedrooms of the Jesuits at the Collegio Romano contained sacred images, one near the bed where the resident said his prayers, and the other over his desk. This practice even predates Gregory's new construction, as a reference to the year 1574 from the manuscript *Historia del Collegio Romano* attests.[92] As in all the Jesuit foundations in Rome, art served both a public and a private function. One final decorative campaign at the Collegio Romano took place not at the college itself but at one of its properties. In 1586 and 1587, Fiammeri and Clemente also painted decorations at the Abbey of Chiaravalle di Fiastra, the college's holding in the Marches, at a time when both of them were working on the Florence college of S. Giovannino. Fiammeri made the trip twice, in January 1586 and 1587, when he purchased pigments for the abbey.[93] Rutilio Clemente travelled there in September 1587, bringing colours he had purchased for the abbey.[94]

The Paintings of the Seminario Romano

We have an even more detailed description of how images were used in college buildings for the Seminario Romano. It took some time for the Seminario to find a final home. In the first year after its foundation, in 1564, it was located in the Palazzo Rospigliosi Pallavicini in Campo Marzio, and within the year it moved to the Palazzo Madama so that it could be near the Collegio Romano.[95] Housing the institution was always a problem on account of the sheer number of seminarians: as early as 1567 there were 150 people in residence, 130 seminarians and 20 Jesuits.[96] Over the next four decades the Seminario moved to four other locations, including a part of the Palazzo Colonna near the church of the SS. Apostoli, the Palazzo Valle near the church of S. Eustachio, and the Palazzo Nardini in Rione Parione, and the account books show especially extensive building activity among woodworkers and stonemasons in 1575. It was not until 1608 that the Seminario was finally lodged permanently in the Palazzo Gabrielli Borromeo and a neighbouring house on present-day Via del Seminario Romano, between the Collegio Romano and the Pantheon.[97] The three-storey palazzo had been built earlier in the sixteenth century and included a garden for the use of the seminarians. An anonymous description written after 1622 gives detailed insight into the use of the different rooms of the Seminario, uses that match those mentioned in a more piecemeal fashion in letters from as early as the late 1560s.[98] There were a grand hall, which served for public functions such as debates on philosophy or theology, commencement exercises, public speeches and recitations of poems, performances of tragedies and other plays customary during Carnival; rooms for class meetings of seminarians; and, finally, a chapel in which the seminarians heard mass every morning with music, or attended services on feast days.[99] Music was important in the life at the Seminario. As early as 1565, singing lessons formed part of the curriculum, and in 1567 the composer and musician Giovanni Pierluigi da Palestrina (ca. 1525–94) served as music master.[100]

Every month the seminarians were required to receive communion, and every fifteen days they were obliged to gather for special prayers, according to their class, in four different oratories located on the ground floor and cortile level. The first oratory was dedicated to the Visitation of the Most Holy Virgin, and was for the middle classmen. The second, named for the Nativity, was for the upper classmen. The third, also dedicated to the Nativity, was for the youngest class. The fourth oratory was named for the Immaculate Conception and was for the clerics. These oratories undoubtedly featured paintings of the mysteries to which they were dedicated, and the paintings would have served as the focus of prayer and other devotions. The Seminario also gathered for prayer to the Virgin Mary during feast days, for special indulgences.[101] Opposite the oratory of the clerics and under the grand hall was the refectory, which had a capacity of more than two hundred and thus was twice the size of Acquaviva's refectory at the Novitiate of S. Andrea. A grand affair, the dining room was hung with paintings and had an elaborate gilt stucco vault with frescoes.[102] In this refectory the seminarians would dine while hearing readings given by clerics, who spoke from a *pulpitino*.

The rest of the Seminario was divided between the offices and rooms of the fathers, and ten study halls (*scrittori*), eight for the seminarians and two for the clerics. Each of these was named for a saint, and on the wall of each was likely also a painting of the saint. The rooms for the seminarians were named for the Madonna, St John the Baptist, St Bartholomew, St Andrew, St Paul, St Michael, St John the Evangelist, and St Francis Xavier, the last possibly having originally been dedicated to Blessed Francis Xavier, before his canonization in 1622. The clerics' study halls were devoted to St Gregory (the older clerics) and St Peter (the younger ones).[103] The seminary had communal dormitory rooms, each of which had a Father Prefect who maintained discipline and a servant charged with making the beds, fetching water, and performing other domestic tasks. Each bedroom had a patron saint, whose image hung on the wall (as at the Collegio Romano), and every morning the Father Prefect would lead the seminarians in prayer to the Immaculate Conception; then, on their knees in rows, they would pray to the patron saint of their bedroom, facing the image on the wall.[104] Although this information comes from at least the second decade of the seventeenth century, it provides a rare glimpse into the daily regimen of one of the key Roman foundations of the Society of Jesus, and demonstrates how images of saints punctuated the lives and devotions of the young men who lived there. It also indicates that the iconography on the walls was more mainstream and ordinary than the imagery at S. Andrea, as befit its primarily non-Jesuit audience – no martyrdoms, no Jesuits other than Francis Xavier, and no emblematic allegories.

The Paintings of the German-Hungarian College and the Palaeochristian Revival Movement

The German-Hungarian College was the site of some of the most influential artistic contributions of the Society of Jesus, particularly in its three churches, S.

Apollinare, S. Saba, and S. Stefano Rotondo. The S. Stefano Rotondo paintings (begun 1582) have been examined more thoroughly than any other pre-Baroque Jesuit paintings in Italy, and studies of this supposed paragon of 'Counter-Reformation' iconography are still so popular that they form something of a cottage industry.[105] Having fascinated and appalled visitors long before Charles Dickens characterized them in 1846 as 'such a panorama of horror and butchery no man could imagine in his sleep, though he were to eat a whole pig raw, for supper,' the images of martyrdoms that encircle the visitor to this early Christian church are among the most visceral and gruesome in the history of painting.[106] Over thirty full-sized vistas on the interior walls of the church depict more than four hundred years of martyrdoms, beginning with the Holy Innocents, with unblushing candour, all set against an incongruously placid setting of verdant landscape and classical architecture. Since the church is round and can be taken in all at once, the frescoes present a vast panorama of torture in a single glance. These frescoes depict every imaginable method and instrument of torture, and they catalogue these atrocities with capital letters keyed to text panels below in Latin and Italian. Dickens summed it up best:

> Grey-bearded men being boiled, fried, grilled, crimped, singed, eaten by wild beasts, worried by dogs, buried alive, torn asunder by horses, chopped up small with hatchets: women having their breasts torn with iron pincers, their tongues cut out, their ears screwed off, their jaws broken, their bodies stretched upon the rack, or skinned upon the stake, or crackled up and melted in the fire: these are among the mildest subjects. So insisted on, and laboured at, besides, that every sufferer gives you the same occasion for wonder as poor old Duncan awoke, in Lady Macbeth, when she marvelled at his having so much blood in him.[107]

Even the Marquis de Sade (1740–1814) called it 'one of the most frightening collections of horrors that it is possible to gather together.'[108] Such a relentless catalogue of suffering was bound to leave an indelible impression on the viewer, and the Jesuits, fully aware of the power of these paintings, wrote proudly of their effects not just on their young collegiate audience but on the great churchmen of Rome and Europe. Capitalizing on their visual potency, the Society published an illustrated manual based on the paintings within a year of their execution, and the book was so popular that it was reprinted two years later, in 1585. The paintings have left a comparable impression on scholars today, who have treated them as a prototypically Jesuit kind of imagery, a paradigm for an anti-aesthetic, didactic style of painting aimed at the widest possible audience, one that has even been compared to the visual propaganda of the Nazis.[109]

The paintings of the three churches of the German-Hungarian College are key manifestations of the Palaeochristian Revival, a movement that was given its first major impetus under Gregory XIII and gained special momentum under Clement VIII in preparation for the 1600 Jubilee – despite some scholars' reluctance to draw the connection.[110] An ideological restoration of the era of the Church of late antiquity, the movement aimed to return to the perceived purity of Christianity's first centuries in the wake of Catholic reform. In Rome it was marked by the restoration and renovation – often heavy-handed – of the most ancient of its basilicas and churches, and by a concomitant revival of the late antique and early medieval styles of painting and stucco decoration found in these monuments. Cardinal patrons were especially active in restoring their titular churches, such as Cardinal Rusticucci's titular church of S. Susanna, Cardinal Giustiniani's S. Prisca, and Cardinal Sfondrato's S. Cecilia in Trastevere. Some of the most active of these cardinals were the Oratorian Cesare Baronio, whose history of the Church entitled the *Annales ecclesiastici* (1588–1607), begun at the request of Filippo Neri, became the classic text of the Palaeochristian Revival, and the equally learned Alessandro de' Medici, the author of the program of restoration at St John Lateran and at his titular church of S. Prassede.[111] Baronio's early Christian titular church of SS. Nereo ed Achilleo, which he began restoring in 1596, underwent one of the most scholarly restorations of the Palaeochristian Revival movement (figs 18, 23, 24). Baronio filled in lacunae in the damaged apsidal mosaic with painted stucco in a careful attempt to be consistent in style and theme, and even brought in Palaeochristian furnishings and works of art from other sites. He also imposed a precise iconographical program on the facade and interior, including Early Christian motifs such as the jewelled cross and *strumenti di martirio* (instruments of martyrdom) inspired by his fellow Oratorian Antonio Gallonio's *Trattato degli istrumenti di martirio* (1591), with engravings by Antonio Tempesta.[112] Some aspects of this restoration show the unmistakable influence of Jesuit projects, as we saw in chapter 2 and will see again.

Many supporters of the Palaeochristian Revival movement, like Baronio and Medici, were also amateur archaeologists, philologists, and collectors of antiquities who combined an erudite interest in the ancient world with a reformed Christianity, 'in which the values of humanistic culture and the needs of tridentine "reform" co-existed, or were still placed in dialectical mode.'[113] The movement favoured the cult of the early Christian martyrs, such as Cecilia and Susanna, whose martyrdoms were treated as symbols of Christian triumph, and it revered their relics. These triumphal overtones were often quite overt, as when in 1597 Baronio staged a spectacular Roman-style triumphal parade in which the recently discovered bodies of the early Christian martyrs Nereus, Achilleus, and Domitilla were carried in procession through the Roman triumphal arches in the Forum and brought to his titular church.[114] Baronio devoted the first volumes of his *Annales ecclesiastici* to the trials of the early Christian martyrs, the accounts of which were based on a series of nightly talks he gave on the history of the Church at the Roman Oratory; and in 1583 he revised the Church's official version of the lives of the saints, the *Martyrologium romanum*, at the behest of Pope Gregory XIII.[115]

In artistic terms the movement was animated by a desire to re-create the aura of naive sanctity and austerity belonging to the Early Christian and medieval mosaics, sculpted panels, and icons that originally adorned these ancient churches and that often survived only in fragmentary form. The attraction to the primitive style came from the belief that it was relatively unmediated and therefore made the religious message more intense and more iconographically correct than did art in a contemporary style.[116] One major impetus was the discovery, in 1578, of the Catacomb of Priscilla on the Via Salaria, the Early Christian imagery of which, linked to the years of the persecutions, made an enormous impression on intellectuals and artists in Rome.[117] Not only did they fuel enthusiasm for the early Christian martyrs, but they proved beyond a doubt that the first Christians used sacred images, and they provided Baronio with archaeological data for his writings on the early Church. Many of the Palaeochristian Revival restoration projects began by filling in lacunae, especially in the apses and tribune arches, where most of the Early Christian decoration had been centred. The first example of such artistic restoration was probably Taddeo Zuccaro's apse at S. Sabina, done for Cardinal Truchsess in 1559; it was a free interpretation in fresco of a mosaic panel, parts of which still survived *in situ*.[118]

Typically, commissions of this type would be done in fresco but in the style of Early Christian mosaics, with rigid, frontally posed figures of saints set against a plain blue or gold background. Early Christian symbols such as the jewelled cross, the empty throne, and, especially, the martyr's palm and crown proliferated, as did triumphal depictions of angels, based closely on classical victories, in which the angels carried the trophies of martyrdom and the Passion, such as the crown of thorns, the nails, the holy column, and the whip. Although the style of the figures does not abandon the shading and foreshortening of contemporary painting, or sometimes even the elongated bodies and exaggerated *contrapposto* of the post-Michelangelo era, artists do simplify their facial expressions and provide them with a minimum of interaction and movement so as to give the imagery an archaic and numinous appearance. The prototypical example is the apse of SS. Nereo ed Achilleo, with its martyr saints lined in a row against a blue-gold background in the apse and over the door, and its angels with instruments of martyrdom and the Passion over each column of the nave and recalling the Italo-Byzantine mosaics of Ravenna (figs 23, 24). Another inspiration for many Palaeochristian Revival painters that is rarely mentioned in the scholarship can be found in the Florentine and Umbrian painting styles of the Trecento and Quattrocento; their simplicity, still-ness, and bright colours appear in some of the Jesuit paintings. Popular with several reformist schools in sacred painting, this return to the 'devout style' was also one of the ingredients of the Carracci revolution at the dawn of Baroque painting, as has recently been elucidated by Charles Dempsey.[119]

Before the early 1580s, Palaeochristian Revival decoration in Rome focused almost exclusively on the apse and the altarpieces, as we will see at S. Saba. After this date, however, it became fashionable throughout the city to combine these relatively archaic images with narrative paintings in a more contemporary style along the side walls of the church or in the nave above the entablature; the productions usually depicted biblical scenes or episodes from the lives of early Christian saints, set in a self-consciously classical setting.[120] Many showed martyrdoms. Such are those in the side walls of SS. Nereo ed Achilleo (fig. 18), and the scenes of the Passion in the nave of Alessandro de' Medici's church of S. Prassede. Even in these paintings, however, there is a movement toward clarity, with more centralized action, a reduction of foreground repoussoir figures, and a movement forward of the background, all of which techniques indicate a rather didactic and archaizing goal.[121] The artists who most commonly worked on this kind of Palaeochristian imagery included Baldassare Croce, Agostino Ciampelli, Niccolò Circignani, Taddeo and Federico Zuccaro, Giuseppe Cesari (Cavaliere d'Arpino), Cesare Nebbia, Cristofano Roncalli, Giovanni Battista Ricci, Cherubino and Durante Alberti, Giovanni Battista Pozzo, Girolamo Massei, Giovanni de' Vecchi, Francesco Zucci, Domenico Passignano, Anastasio Fontebuoni, Marzio Ganassini, and Fabrizio Parmigiano. More than half these painters worked for the Jesuits, as did the Flemish expatriate Paul Brill, who contributed landscape paintings to a number of Palaeochristian Revival decorations.

The majority of the Palaeochristian restorations took place in the late 1590s, more than a decade after the German-Hungarian College's second phase of decoration (that of S. Apollinare and S. Stefano Rotondo) was completed. Scholars have long recognized the crucial contribution made by the earlier Jesuit examples to this flurry of activity in preparation for the 1600 Jubilee, but few recognize that S. Apollinare and S. Stefano Rotondo began the tradition of painting narrative scenes on the side walls or in the nave above the entablature. Milton Lewine proposes that such cycles began with the church of the Madonna dei Monti, the titular church of Cardinal Sirleto, which was built between 1580 and 1582 by Giacomo della Porta.[122] Nevertheless, as Lewine points out, sources show that only the building was complete in 1582, and the sole contracts he could find for the interior decoration (for the two left side chapels) indicate that it was begun in 1584.[123] S. Apollinare, the nave paintings of which were begun in 1582, was the first example of this new trend in Rome, a fact that accounts for the degree of attention its paintings and those of S. Stefano received throughout the city when they were unveiled.

The Church of S. Saba

A typical example of the first phase of Palaeochristian Revival decoration is the church of S. Saba, on the Piccolo Aventino in Testaccio, the first church belonging to the German-Hungarian College to be renovated. Dating from the late sixth or early seventh century, S. Saba had an illustrious history as one of the premier monasteries of Rome in early medieval times, and was traditionally associated with St Gregory the Great.[124] It also had a fountain on the premises that was believed to have miraculous curative properties and was especially helpful in aiding the flow of blood.[125] At first the home of a Greek order of monks, it was handed over to the Cluniacs in the twelfth century, and then again to canons regular in the sixteenth century. In 1573, Gregory XIII gave the church to the German-Hungarian College, and two years later – a Jubilee year – he paid out of his own resources for the restoration of the apse decoration, which included new fresco painting in the Palaeochristian style.[126] Outlying churches such as S. Saba and S. Stefano Rotondo, neither of them anywhere near the college itself, were given to the Jesuits because the churches had ancient pedigrees yet were orphans, without titular cardinals to take care of them. In some cases it made historical sense to attach them to the German-Hungarian College (S. Stefano had belonged to an order of Hungarian monks), but, more important, the pope assured their upkeep by placing them in Jesuit hands. The students of the college probably travelled out to S. Saba and S. Stefano Rotondo only on feast days and Sundays.[127]

S. Saba was a perfect candidate for Palaeochristian restoration, since it had an ancient heritage and contained the relics of early Christian saints such as St Saba and St Anastasia; and during excavations in 1575, workers discovered two lead coffins containing the bones of early Christian martyrs – just the sort of discovery that was typically made during such renovations, the most famous example being that of the body of St Cecilia made by Sfondrato in S. Cecilia in Trastevere in 1600.[128] The S. Saba restorations were almost certainly the work of the rector Michele Di Loreto (better known in the latinized form of his name as Lauretano), as is recorded in a mid-eighteenth-century reference by Terribilini that mentions Di Loreto's restoration of the lead coffins. Ciappi also mentions that 'the rectors' of the German-Hungarian College directed the restorations of S. Saba, S. Apollinare, and S. Stefano, under the guiding hand of Gregory XIII.[129] Although Di Loreto is not mentioned by name in the Jesuit records as directing the restoration of the church, the account books show that the college spent more than 886 scudi in 1575 on 'repairs of the church of S. Saba.'[130]

Born in 1537 at Recanati in the Marches, Michele Di Loreto was of Albanian descent, born of parents who were forced to flee Illyria after the Ottoman conquest.[131] He studied at the Jesuit school in Loreto, was minister for several years before he became rector (1573–87), and had taught the humanities at Forlì and theology at the University of Bologna, where he formed a close association with the Oratorian bishop Gabriele Paleotti (1522–97).[132] Paleotti, who saw the eye as the primary cognitive organ, was a great supporter of the use of images as a universal language and firmly believed in their didactic potential, especially as models for imitation. His ideas likely inspired the Jesuit rector, since his book was first published at the very time the S. Stefano frescoes were being executed, and since he himself visited S. Stefano on a number of occasions during that period.[133]

Di Loreto himself was a strong advocate of education as a means of furthering Catholic reform, and was especially convinced of the importance of training the laity; he went so far as to fight with other Jesuit administrators in an attempt to keep the college open to the Italian lay nobility.[134] He conceived of the German College not just as a seminary for clerics but as what he called a 'universal seminary,' directed at training 'all states of life; because of those youths who are trained within it, some will be persons involved in the government of their republics and cities, others fathers of families, others masters of vassals, others prelates, and others of different professions.'[135] Although Di Loreto lost the battle and the lay boarders were evicted in 1573, his concern for education can be seen in his painting commissions at the German-Hungarian College. These frescoes also demonstrate the importance for Di Loreto of role models. He wrote that it was essential for their learning that younger students have older students to observe, so that they can emulate their elders' behaviour and look to them for models of the spiritual life.[136] Similarly, the frescoes at the German-Hungarian College allowed students to fortify themselves for their future ministry with images of triumphant martyrdoms from the past.

The S. Saba apse paintings were executed in preparation for the 1575 Jubilee and are typical of the kind of restoration work carried out elsewhere in the city in preparation for that event. The apse had originally been decorated with mosaics and some medieval frescoes, which remained in a fragmentary state at the time of the restoration. An anonymous painter was called in to fill in the lacunae, and did so in a generically archaizing style, harmonizing with the fragments already there (fig. 36). The upper part of the apse is dominated by a medieval figure of a large Christ in a mandorla, flanked by standing figures of St Andrew and St Saba, all set against a plain background. Below is a row of twelve sheep, of the kind common in early Christian basilicas in Rome (e.g., S. Marco and S. Maria in Trastevere), who represent the twelve apostles and are shown departing from the gates of Jerusalem and Bethlehem and advancing toward a lamb, representing Christ, at the centre. Below these symbols are the newer frescoes, including images of the apostles themselves, shown in a typically rigid, frontal pose without interaction, flanking an enthroned Madonna and Child. Below this level the painter has inserted a row of illusionistic niches enclosing more standing figures, this time of Gregory XIII, St Andrew, St Michael the Archangel, St John the Baptist, St Augustine, and a female saint, perhaps St Barbara. Unlike the heavily decorated apse area, the nave remained unadorned, as was the practice at that time in church decoration in Rome. A tabernacle was added over the high altar in 1578.[137]

The Church of S. Apollinare

The scholarship is very confused about the exact circumstances of the second phase of painting at the German-Hungarian College, that of the churches of S. Apollinare and S. Stefano Rotondo and of the college itself. Nevertheless, two things are certain: they were the brainchild of Michele Di Loreto, and they have an intimate relationship with the sketches for Nadal's *Evangelicae historiae imagines*. Several contemporary reports, including Jesuit Annual Letters, Di Loreto's obituary, and his own diary, attest to the leading role played by the rector in creating both martyrological fresco cycles.[138] Di Loreto's commissions included the first two large-scale martyrdom cycles ever executed. It was a genre that may have been inspired by Protestant martyrdom books, as we will see in chapter 5, but that took on an emphatically Roman, Palaeochristian meaning in the German-Hungarian College. The cycles' use of key letters, their basic composition, and their generic, classicizing landscapes give them a close affinity with Nadal's cycle as conceived by Giovanni Battista Fiammeri.

It is a sign of these frescoes' importance that Jesuit sources, which are normally frustratingly reticent about artistic activity, discuss this project in glowing and loving detail. Gregory XIII himself paid for all the paintings, another sign of the Church's high hopes for the educational role of the pictures, and Ciappi's panegyric history of the pope's reign speaks with open praise especially of the S. Stefano paintings: 'S. Stefano in particular ... he had decorated completely with noble pictures of the most celebrated histories of the Holy Martyrs of Christ.'[139] One passage concerning the frescoes, from Michele Di Loreto's 1582 Annual Letter, is typical of Jesuit enthusiasm for the two commissions: 'And it is in this way that the great number of Martyrs, and infinite varieties of torments, which are depicted here – and since the painting is of a restrained beauty but very devout –

have given great edification to everyone, and renown to the College, and there are many who cannot look at them without tears. The Pope continually demonstrates great affection for this work, and is very satisfied with it.'[140] Cardinal Farnese, a frequent visitor to S. Stefano Rotondo, was 'very satisfied' with the paintings, and Pope Gregory 'continuously demonstrates great affection for this work, and is very content with it.'[141]

The unveiling of the fresco cycles of the German-Hungarian College was one of the greatest arts news items of the early 1580s. They were touted as an especially worthy example of Christian devotional art. Pompeo Ugonio wrote in his *Historia delle stationi di Roma* (Rome, 1588):

> And this church of S. Stefano was so magnificently adorned and illustrated, that there was perhaps no church in all of Rome that is more beautiful and pleasing to see. For all of the wall that encloses and encircles the church has been painted with the history of the Holy Martyrs, beginning with the Holy Innocents, the first of them, and then on to Christ, becoming the glorious King of the same Martyrs. Then it is through St Stephen that all the others continue in the path of imitating Christ, following according to the order of their time and the various persecutions of the Christian name right up to our times.[142]

Other sources report that the frescoes of S. Apollinare and S. Stefano directly inspired the martyrdom cycle in S. Tommaso di Canterbury (see chapter 5), and a cycle of the martyrdom of St Lawrence at S. Lorenzo in Damaso in the Palazzo Cancelleria (1587), financed by Cardinal Alessandro Farnese, as well as the choir of S. Cecilia in Trastevere (1599–1600), the titular church of Cardinal Paolo Camillo Sfondrato.[143] These reports are confirmed by another written by 'one of the students in the college,' which also connects the S. Apollinare and S. Stefano murals with those at S. Lorenzo and S. Cecilia.[144] To this list of martyrdom cycles inspired by those of the German-Hungarian College, I would add the series of martyrdoms of apostles executed for the Oratory of the Confraternity of SS. Annunziata in Florence by Bernardino Poccetti, Andrea Boscoli, and others (1585–90), now in the Società Dante Alighieri, as well as some of the martyrdom paintings at S. Susanna in Rome (1591–1600).[145] Another, better-known source in Italian provides few details about the trajectory of influence of Di Loreto's commissions, but is unequivocal that they are the first such cycles ever executed.[146] The manuscript sources also claim that the S. Stefano martyrdom cycle was influential in France and Germany, for example that it inspired a martyrdom cycle painted on the nave walls of the cathedral in Hildesheim – proof that Di Loreto's cycle was successful in hitting one of its target audiences, Northern Europeans.[147]

The first of the fresco cycles to be painted was S. Apollinare, another early Christian church, located across from the Palazzo Altemps, just north of the Piazza Navona.[148] Founded under Pope Onuphrius I (625–38), S. Apollinare was revered like S. Saba because it contained the relics of martyrs, this time St Aussentius, St Eustace, St Mandarius, St Eugenius, St Orestes, and St Massentius.[149] The church went through various incarnations during its early history, including stints as a parish church and as a *collegio de' canonici*. In 1575, two years after S. Saba, Gregory

XIII handed the church over to the German-Hungarian College, just in time for the 1575 Jubilee. The church became celebrated for its services and music, and was frequented by such luminaries as Filippo Neri, the founder of the Congregation of the Oratory, and his disciple Cardinal Cesare Baronio.[150] It was especially renowned for its Quarant'ore displays, which the Jesuits set up twice in 1583 and which attracted 'almost all of Rome' to the little church, according to the hyperbolic Annual Letter of that year.[151]

Unlike that at S. Stefano, the painting cycle has been destroyed. The original church was severely damaged by a flood in 1598 that also nearly destroyed the Casa Professa, and what was left of the church was finally razed in 1740, when a new church was commissioned from Ferdinando Fuga. A plan drawn in 1632 shows that the original was a three-aisled rectangular structure with a small apse at the end and two small, transept-like side chapels, one on either side.[152] The church also had a large narthex, and could be entered by two doorways, one at the front and the other off the Via dei Pianellari. This plan is confirmed by a description by Ugonio (1588):

> This church has three naves supported by columns, ... pilasters, and walls ... The floor was all done in beautiful inlay work with much variety in the stones employed, a good part of which is still there ... Under the pontificate of Gregory XIII ... the Church of S. Apollinare was very well restored by the Fathers of the Gesù, and brought to that beauty and splendor that is seen today ... The ceiling has been painted and gilded, and the tribune, with the middle nave beautifully painted with the history of St Apollinarius, and the choir above and below, and the organ, and the altars, the high altar as well as the others, all has been renovated with admirable order and ornament. So that whereas before this church was hardly even known, at the present it is visited by many, and honored.[153]

It had a flat, wooden roof, and a very modest exterior, judging by Tempesta's map of Rome and a perspective drawing of the later seventeenth century, fronted by a marble cornice.[154] The altar painting, a scene of unidentified saints but almost certainly including the titular saint Apollinarius, was painted by Durante Alberti, whom we have already seen at S. Andrea.[155] The sources are not clear about the dedications of the six side chapels, but Giulio Mancini has identified three: one was dedicated to the Crucifixion, another to St Anthony or the Confessors, and the third to St John the Baptist or the Patriarchs. Without specifying the names of the saints to whom these altars were dedicated, Di Loreto's diary shows that each of the seven altars was assigned to a saint of one of the different categories venerated on the different days of the week. This arrangement perfectly suited the devotional practice of the students at the college, who on the different days of the week would attend mass at the different altars, of the angels and patriarchs (Monday), of the apostles (Tuesday), of the martyrs, or the high altar (Wednesday), of the Doctors and bishops (Thursday), of the confessors and hermits (Friday), of the virgins (Saturday), and of the Virgin Mary (Sunday).[156] We have already seen this arrangement in the dormitory of the Novitiate of S. Andrea al Quirinale (see chapter 2).

As Ugonio and the archival descriptions tell us, the S. Apollinare paintings were executed in the tribune area, which was begun first, and also on the nave wall above the entablature.[157] The twelve panels of the principal narrative cycle were not so much an illustration of the life of the saint as a meditation on his imprisonment, slow torture, and death, rendered in excruciating detail. It was, accordingly, a true martyrdom cycle. The panels survive today in a series of engravings entitled *Beati Apollinaris martyris primi ravennatum epi res gestae* (fig. 37), printed in Rome in 1586 and bound together with illustrations from S. Stefano in the second edition of Giovanni Battista Cavallieri's *Ecclesiae militantis triumphi ... in Ecclesia S. Stephani Rotundi Romae Nicolai Circiniani pictoris manu visuntur*.[158] Also included in the series are four allegorical scenes of Life, Death, Sin, and Grace that were probably not part of the fresco cycle but added in the printed version to enhance the book's function as a meditation manual.[159] Judging from the engravings – even though they are of poor quality – the frescoes were similar in style to those at S. Stefano and S. Tommaso. The tortures are presented in all their variety, so that the saint is shown hanging upside down by his feet, beaten with canes, hung from a rack, and stoned. They are set against the same kind of generic, classicizing landscapes as those in the Novitiate and that will become even more prominent at S. Stefano and S. Tommaso. Nevertheless, the S. Apollinare images are more direct than the later series since there are fewer figures per frame and since they are much larger, generally taking up two-thirds of the scene or more.

A single painter was responsible not only for S. Apollinare and the main series at S. Stefano Rotondo, but also for the cycle at S. Tommaso di Canterbury – Niccolò Circignani (1517/24–1597), a Tuscan from Pomarance (near Volterra) best known by his nickname Il Pomarancio. Circignani was assisted at S. Apollinare by another painter known only as Orazio, possibly the young Orazio Gentileschi, a fellow Tuscan who was already active as a fresco painter in Rome in the later 1570s.[160] Circignani may be more responsible than any other single artist for formulating a Jesuit iconography in the Cinquecento. One of the most sought-after and best employed fresco painters of Gregory XIII's Rome, he studied in Florence with Santi di Tito, and his first work in Rome was with Giovanni de' Vecchi on the Vatican Belvedere in 1562–3.[161] In 1564 he moved to Città della Pieve, in Umbria, where he executed many commissions in Perugia, Orvieto, and Città di Castello. The most important is his extensive fresco cycle for the Palazzo Corgna in Castiglion del Lago (begun 1575), which includes scenes of the battles of the Corgna family and of antiquity, as well as mythological subjects; its townscapes, compositions, and even taste for blood anticipate his frescoes for the Jesuits. Circignani's most extensive cycle of devotional paintings outside Rome, shared with the Flemish painter Arrigo Fiammingo, is at the shrine of the Madonna di Mongiovino, south of Lake Trasimeno (ca. 1569), where he demonstrated a fondness for brilliant colours, courtly elegance, and naturalistic detail.[162] His most important Roman commissions include the Torre de' Venti at the Vatican Palace (1581), the *History of the True Cross* in the Oratorio del SS. Crocifisso (1582), the cupola of S. Pudenziana (1587), and the Cappella di S. Francesco in S. Giovanni de' Fiorentini (1586–7). Incidentally, Circignani's paintings at the Torre de' Venti also included martyrdoms.[163]

Circignani's work for the Jesuits in the 1580s may have been the most critical development in his career, since after he finished the three Jesuit series he went on to direct similar cycles for non-Jesuit patrons at S. Lorenzo in Damaso and S.

Cecilia in Trastevere, and he was also one of the principal painters of the Gesù (see chapters 6 and 7).[164] Even his son benefited from his father's connections with the Society. Antonio Circignani, an artist whose work survives in places like the Volterra Duomo, painted frescoes for a *vigna* owned by the Society near the Baths of Diocletian, not far from S. Andrea al Quirinale.[165]

Baglione called Niccolò Circignani a 'practical' painter who worked quickly and cheaply, and Mancini reported that the Tuscan painter could finish one panel a day when he was working at S. Stefano.[166] Mancini added that Circignani worked in two modes, that of a *maestro ordinario*, as seen in his frescoes at S. Tommaso, S. Apollinare, and S. Stefano, and that of a *buon e pratico maestro*, as exhibited by his work at the Gesù and S. Lorenzo in Damaso. These distinctions presumably referred at least in part to the speed and care with which he executed the scenes, and I will return to them later. Circignani's reputation as a fast but workmanlike artist has led scholars to dismiss the Jesuits' decision to hire him as another sign that they were more driven by poverty than other patrons of late Cinquecento Rome and had no interest in aesthetics. Yet the Jesuits paid him relatively handsomely for his work (at the Gesù he was one of the better-paid artists, and he was also well compensated in the college chapels), even when they could get plenty of free labour from their own brothers or from other, more charitably inclined artists. Brill, for example, worked for a paltry single scudo on a panel at the Collegio Romano in 1584. Undoubtedly Circignani's speed added to his attraction, yet he was no faster than many of his contemporaries working on the voluminous papal cycles, such as Sixtus V's mercurial team of Giovanni Guerra and Cesare Nebbia. Speed was the rule of the day in 1580s Rome. I think the Jesuits went out of their way to hire Circignani for another, equally simple reason: they liked his style.

Circignani's style seems a strange choice at first for images of martyrdom. His paintings are dominated by a feeling of weightlessness and a mystical abstraction from emotion or earthly care. Although full of circumstantial detail, they have a disjointed quality, and they tend to lack the strong focus on the central figures that was so typical of many reformist painters (such as Durante Alberti).[167] Circignani takes the elongated figure type of Florentine 'Maniera' painting and stretches it to such a degree, with long limbs and torsos and tiny heads, that it becomes almost ghostlike (this is especially evident at the Palazzo Corgna and at S. Giovanni de' Fiorentini). There is also a strongly generic look about Circignani's scenes, especially in the faces and poses, which become impersonal through repetition and are almost totally lacking in emotion. Yet it was precisely these generic, universal features that attracted Circignani to the Jesuits, as we will soon see. Another source of Circignani's appeal may have been his association with papal commissions, which gave his work an added prestige.

Work began on the frescoes of S. Apollinare in 1580, when the *muratori* finished repairing and plastering the walls and the painter Orazio was paid for frescoing the upper part of the apse.[168] Circignani is first mentioned in July 1581, when he was paid 60 scudi to paint the lower level of the tribune, below the section frescoed by Orazio, which must have been like a dado.[169] Circignani's final payment for frescoing the tribune area was an additional 20 scudi, received the next month.[170]

There follows a hiatus, and he does not return to S. Apollinare until May 1582, when he presumably started work on the nave cycle. The account books show that Circignani executed the ten nave paintings at exactly the same time he was working on the S. Stefano cycle, since his first payment, for 130 scudi, was for both S. Apollinare and S. Stefano.[171] He seems to have finished frescoing the nave with characteristic speed, since his last payment for that work was 100 scudi, received at the end of August 1582, the same month in which he received another 10 scudi to paint a banner (*stendardo*) of S. Apollinare for the newly decorated church.[172]

The sources do not indicate whether there were painting cycles in the residence quarters of the German-Hungarian College, which were located in the palace adjacent to S. Apollinare and in its outbuildings across the street, which could be reached by an arched passageway.[173] Originally the palace of the titular cardinal of the church, the college buildings were razed and rebuilt in stages in 1631, 1742, and 1773, and completed only after the suppression of the Society. Nothing remains of the original structure today. There were almost certainly paintings in the refectory and lecture halls, and perhaps in the stairwells, as at the Collegio Romano and the Seminario Romano. There were also paintings in a kind of room called a *camera* or *camerata*, a hall dedicated to a saint in which a group of ten students would meet under the direction of a prefect and assistants to honour the saints of the particular liturgical month, who had been divided up among the students.[174] The congregations and their *camerate* were named after one or more saints – the Camera of Sts Peter and Paul, the Camera of St James, the Camera of the Angels, and so on – and each had an altarpiece at the end of the room with a painting of the dedicatory saint(s). This passage from Michele Di Loreto's *Diario* gives us a look at the feast day celebrations of the dedicatory saint: 'The rooms are all dedicated to some saint, and during [the saint's] feast day they adorn very beautifully his or her altar, which they have in the room, with verses and other ornaments, and in addition, after fasting and other forms of devotion, they call [upon] the other congregations, and after having sung some motet, all those in that room together make penitence in some nearby place.'[175] After the celebrations in the *camerate*, in which they may have recited the Litany of the Saints, the students of the particular congregation would make a pilgrimage to a church dedicated to the saint, and especially to the altar that contained his or her relics. The Jesuits also encouraged their students' devotion to images through elaborate *affixiones* displaying verses and probably pictures drawn or painted by the students, as at the Collegio Romano. Ciappi records such a tradition in the church of S. Apollinare, where during the Quaran'tore the students of the German-Hungarian College set up elaborate temporary triumphal arches and adorned the *apparato* with inscriptions, verses, and other texts in Greek and Latin.[176]

The Church of S. Stefano Rotondo: Paintings by Niccolò Circignani and Matteo da Siena

The third and most prominent church building belonging to the German-Hungarian College was the spacious round church of S. Stefano Rotondo on the Caelian Hill. Erected in the late fifth century under Pope Simplicius, S. Stefano was probably built not as a regular house of worship but as a martyrium, as is suggested by its round shape, traditional for martyrs' burial places.[177] One of the most celebrated features of the church was a seventh-century apse mosaic showing Sts Primus and Felicianus flanking a triumphant jewelled cross against a gold background, which I have already mentioned as an inspiration for Baronio's apse restoration at SS. Nereo ed Achilleo (see chapter 2). S. Stefano became a regular church under Leo IV in the ninth century, and by the twelfth century it had gained collegiate status and property at Tusculum. Neverthess, despite being under the care of a canon of the nearby basilica of St John Lateran, the building was abandoned in the early fifteenth century and allowed to fall into ruin. Throughout the Middle Ages and into the Renaissance, the neighbourhood of S. Stefano was undeveloped and surrounded by countryside, so the building had the aspect of a country church even though it was within the walls of ancient Rome. In 1545, Pope Nicholas V handed the church over to a convent of Hungarian hermits who lived on the same hill, and they held it in name into the 1570s, even though the Ottoman invasion of Hungary by then had reduced their numbers drastically (there was only one Hungarian hermit there at the end).[178]

S. Stefano was renovated during the Hungarian hermits' ownership, although apparently not in the archaizing style of the Palaeochristian Revival movement. A series of frescoes, discovered only in the 1990s and now almost entirely destroyed, appears on the facade of the church, under the front portico, and may have formed part of a more extensive cycle.[179] Depicting the lives of St Paul the Hermit and St Stephen, it is composed of grisaille narrative panels showing the miracles and martyrdoms of the two saints, with small panels above showing divine approbation from Christ and God the Father. This kind of grisaille facade decoration was quite common at the time, but used mainly for secular buildings such as urban palaces. The S. Stefano facade frescoes were known to early writers, including Mancini, who attributes them with some hesitation to a certain 'Baldassare,' and Pompeo Ugonio and Giovanni Antonio Bruzio, who do not identify the artist of the series.[180] Veronica Biermann has recently been able to date these paintings precisely to April and May 1546, the year after the church was handed over to the hermits.[181] Although the scenes of the lives of the two saints are not martyrdom cycles, they include a scene of the martyrdom of St Stephen that may have influenced Circignani's version of the same episode in his later fresco cycle in the church.

In 1573, in view of S. Stefano's association with Hungarians, Pope Gregory XIII assigned the convent to the newly formed Hungarian College, and in 1579 the Jesuits established a seminary there. With the unification of the Hungarian and German colleges in 1580, the seminary closed and its Hungarian students moved across town to the German College buildings at S. Apollinare. But the church only gained in importance after the adjacent seminary was shut down. S. Stefano was already a major pilgrimage site since it had the relics of many early Christian martyrs, including St Stephen Protomartyr, St Lawrence, the Holy Innocents, Sts Primus and Felicianus, St Catherine of Alexandria, St Brigid, St Cornelius, and St Domitilla.[182] Under the tutelage of Michele Di Loreto and the German-Hungarian College, the church's popularity increased, especially on feast days such as St

Stephen on 26 December, when thick crowds, including the most important church-men of the age, flocked there to watch the students assist at mass and recite the Liturgy of the Hours.[183]

Yet people from all over Rome as well as from Germany and beyond thronged to S. Stefano on feast days in the early 1580s for more than just to hear the German seminarians' oratorical skills. The church was soon famous as the site of some of the most horrifying and moving pictures of the age, paintings the vivid imagery and authoritative textual keys of which transported devout Christians into the past to share the pain and benefit from the miracles of the beloved first martyrs of Christianity. It was this opportunity to take part in a pious exercise using imagery that brought popes and paupers alike to marvel, weep, and pray in the church of S. Stefano.

The principal martyrdom cycle of thirty-one panels was the work of Circignani, who painted them in 1582 while working on the decorations at S. Apollinare.[184] Circignani was also working at that time on a fresco in the cycle *History of the True Cross* at the Oratorio del SS. Crocifisso and a commission for Gregory XIII in the Vatican.[185] According to the biographer Giovanni Baglione, Circignani was as-sisted at S. Stefano, probably with the perspectives and landscapes, by Matteo da Siena (1553–88), a landscape painter specializing in fantasy *paesetti* who worked for Gregory XIII at the Vatican and at the Villa d'Este in Tivoli.[186] Monssen proposes that Matteo was also responsible for the landscapes in S. Apollinare, although only 'Orazio' is mentioned in the sources.[187] In addition to the principal martyrdom series, Circignani probably also painted twenty-four small grisaille panels of the life and veneration of St Stephen on a balustrade surrounding the altar of Pope Nicholas V (dedicated to St Stephen) in the centre of the church, in 1583.[188]

In 1583 or 1584, Antonio Tempesta (1555–1630), a third Tuscan artist who like Matteo was known for his skills as a landscape painter, executed an additional fresco program in the church. The paintings included two scenes in the ambula-tory, *Massacre of the Innocents* and *Madonna of the Seven Sorrows*, in addition to a fresco cycle in the first chapel to the left (high altar) of the martyrdoms of Sts Primus and Felicianus and of St Stephen, and a painting in the lower part of the apse showing Christ flanked by the apostles.[189] Tempesta was a student of the Flemish painter Giovanni Stradano (Jan van der Straat, ca. 1523–1605) and also worked with other landscape painters for Gregory XIII in the Vatican in the early 1580s (including the Terze Loggie, Galleria delle Carte Geografiche, and Sala Vecchia degli Svizzeri).[190] He also worked on secular commissions, such as his scenes of hunting and fishing at the Palazzina Gambara at Bagnaia (1582–3) and at the Villa Farnese at Caprarola, and he is responsible for the vast ceiling with *decorazioni a grottesca* in the East Corridor at the Uffizi in Florence (1579–80). Tempesta made a name for himself especially as an engraver, having produced about fifteen hundred prints during his lifetime – including his famous map of Rome of 1593 – but he continued throughout his career to receive important public painting commissions such as the Cappella Benozzi in S. Giovanni de' Fiorentini (1597). Tempesta was no stranger to martyrdoms: as mentioned earlier, he later illustrated a manual of martyrological torture instruments by the Oratorian Antonio

Gallonio entitled *Trattato degli instrumenti di martirio e delle varie maniere di martoriare usate dai gentili contro christiani* (Rome, 1591).[191]

The chronology of the painting cycles at S. Stefano can be reconstructed from the documents, although there has been considerable confusion in the scholarship. As at S. Apollinare, Circignani's first payment, for 50 scudi, dates from 1581, although slightly later, at the end of October.[192] Circignani is mentioned again in December as purchasing nine barrels of wine from the college. Then, as at S. Apollinare, there is a hiatus before he begins work again on the frescoes, in 1582.[193] The entire cycle was completed between March and August 1582, and Circignani received 10 scudi for each of the 32 panels, adding up to 320 scudi plus extra payments for retouching earlier pictures and other work in the church.[194] Scholars disagree about the number of panels painted by Circignani. Leif Holm Monssen insists that there were only the 31 panels mentioned in Di Loreto's *Diario* and included in the engraved series by Cavallieri, and that the 32 mentioned by Baglione included the two panels by Antonio Tempesta (one of which replaced one of the original 31).[195] Mara Nimmo discovered the source just cited, however, which states unequivocally that Circignani was paid for 32 panels; she surmises that the two missing ones (only 30 survive today) were replaced in the late eighteenth century by the two contiguous panels, *Martyrdom of St Margaret* and *Martyrdom of St Polycarp*, at least one of which (the latter) has the same subject as the picture it replaces.[196] Only one preparatory drawing for Circignani's cycle has been published, a *Martyrdom of St Stephen* in the Gabinetto Nazionale delle Stampe in Rome, and it shows that he did not depart significantly from his original design when executing the fresco.[197] It is also quite possible that this drawing was made for Cavallieri's engraving and not for the actual fresco.

After the nave frescoes were finished, Circignani probably returned to S. Stefano to paint the twenty-four 'little histories' in *chiaroscuro* around the balustrade, for which he received 40 scudi. Nimmo has published two documents in the archives of the German-Hungarian College that prove the balustrade paintings were completed as late as 13 September 1583; one of the documents, she maintains, mentions Circignani by name.[198] Nevertheless, in checking the source, I found no direct reference to Circignani; the document (an account book) merely mentions the paintings, the date, and the amount of money paid, without naming the artist.[199] I have no reason to doubt Circignani's authorship (Monssen also believes that the balustrade was painted by Circignani), but I could not find a source that credits him directly.

Monssen maintains in one article that Antonio Tempesta's contribution to the church decoration dates from 1580, the year Gregory XIII built the balustrade around the central altar; he does so on the basis of a inscription of that date underneath one of the pictures that commemorates Gregory XIII's renovations but does not mention the paintings.[200] Antonio Vannugli is more cautious, dating the frescoes to between 1580 and 1585, the date of Gregory's death; and elsewhere Monssen comments that a date between 1583 and 1584 is 'probabilissima,' a conclusion I too am inclined to accept.[201] One final artist who has not yet been mentioned in any of the literature is Durante Alberti, who received 22 scudi for a canvas 'in tela d'argento' of St Stephen between June and December 1582, at the same time that he was working at S. Andrea and S. Apollinare.[202] The amount paid to Durante is so low that the artist must have worked at a charitable cut rate, which seems also to have been the case at the Gesù (see chapter 6).

The painting cycles at S. Stefano have been the subject of several thorough studies, including complete catalogues by Leif Holm Monssen and Antonio Vannugli.[203] The main body of paintings is Circignani's cycle of thirty-two frescoes, now reduced to thirty (figs 38–52). They are essentially a catalogue of early Christian martyrdoms over the first 480 years after Christ, with each panel usually representing the reign of a single Roman emperor. The series starts in the southeast part of the ambulatory, in the first arcade to the right of the chapel of St Paul the Hermit and the Hungarian king St Stephen, and ends in the northeast arcade, directly to the left of the entrance vestibule. Each fresco is framed by two engaged columns or one engaged column and a brick pillar, and above each is a small oculus window. The fresco cycle is punctuated at the centre and the four cross-arms of the church by five altars, dedicated to St Stephen, Sts Primus and Felicianus (a chapel, not just an altar), the Holy Cross, St Clement or the Madonna, and St Francis. There is also a chapel off the cross-axis and next to the chapel of Sts Primus and Felicianus, dedicated to St Peter the Hermit and St Stephen, king of Hungary.

The panels of Circignani's cycle show not individual martyrdoms but several martyrdoms going on at once, so that the landscape and architecture divide the scene into sections, with each section enclosing a single action or group of actions. This combination of several narrative scenes in one picture is a deliberately archaizing format reminiscent of medieval and early Renaissance fresco cycles, such as Masaccio's and Masolino's cycle at the Carmine in Florence (1424–8), and it is in keeping with the spirit of the Palaeochristian Revival. The key letters help the viewer identify the episodes shown, and they are explained in bilingual inscriptions below, in a kind of 'captioning' similar to that which appears in the Novitiate (although there only in Latin). Each picture is also headed with a Latin inscription, above, that provides commentary on the scene.

The division of the frescoes into different narrative scenes and the use of key letters also links them with Nadal's *Evangelicae historiae imagines*, and like Nadal's manual they can be interpreted as a classical 'memory palace,' or mnemonic tool.[204] This connection is no coincidence. As we saw in chapter 1, Giovanni Battista Fiammeri was already executing his transformations of Livio Agresti's drawings in 1579–82, when he was still in Rome, and these drawings would have been available to upper-level Jesuits and, presumably, their artists. I believe it very likely that Fiammeri was consulted by Di Loreto and Circignani when the S. Apollinare and S. Stefano cycles were being planned, and may have been responsible for choosing their vertical format, the segmentation of the scenes, and the placement of the key letters. Some individual compositions are strikingly close, such as the background to fresco II (fig. 39), which divides two scenes with architecture in much the same way as Nadal's plate 2, but in reverse, as it is in Fiammeri's original sketch. Nadal's image cycle may also have influenced Di Loreto's decision to create a series of pictures related to various dates on the liturgical calendar.

Since these texts have already been published in their entirety, I will not reprint them here except to note that their sources vary, including Sacred Scripture, the

Psalms, hymns, and the Roman Breviary, with the result that the pictures 'acted as a visual counterpart to recitations of the Litany of Saints, readings of saints' lives, and the Roman Martyrology, providing Jesuit novices [*sic*] with appropriate Christian *exempla*.'[205] The appearance of Italian in the inscriptions is especially noteworthy, since it indicates that the images were directed at the general public, who would not have known Latin, and not exclusively at the students or Jesuits, who would have been well versed in the ancient language. These frescoes were meant to have a universal audience, as the enthusiastic early accounts of their unveilings also attest, and they were by no means intended exclusively for young missionaries contemplating a dangerous career of ministry in the Protestant North.

The inscriptions probably also served as punctuation for a procession that accompanied the recitation of the Litany by members of the college every Second Sunday of Lent, when the procession would advance slowly along the frescoes of the ambulatory wall in a clockwise fashion. Students could also honour the saints on an individual basis, privately or in groups, on their feast days according to the calendar of the Roman Church and guided by the inscriptions above. Monssen relates the pictures to mnemonic methods sanctioned in the Jesuit *Ratio Studiorum* and related to classical oratory: 'Thus the martyrdom series displays to the *alumni* a Christian "archaeological theater" to be memorized by natural memory and strengthened by memory.'[206] He also connects the paintings with the 'composition of place' in the *Spiritual Exercises*.[207]

The paintings were ideal for the 'composition of place.' Both Monssen and Vannugli note that Circignani's and Tempesta's frescoes in S. Stefano are marked by a generic quality, and their simplified classicizing landscapes and almost complete lack of symbols or allegories allow viewers to fill in the gaps out of their own imaginations. For example, fresco IV (fig. 38) is set in a landscape of green valleys against distant mountains. The valleys are occupied by figures and classical buildings, particularly a large stadium on the left. Although this circular structure, formed of a double row of columns, broadly recalls a Roman circus, it does so only with the barest minimum of architectural features, providing a kind of visual shorthand for the viewer. Neither the mountains nor the foreground landscape offers further clues as to the geographical location of this picture, other than to suggest that it is somewhere in the classical world, and there is little evidence even of time of day or year.[208] Similarly, the figures throughout the cycle are neutral and almost emotionless, compelling the viewers to impose their own feelings on the scene. In the fresco just referred to, the figures possess an iconic stillness that seems to negate the horrors being portrayed. The two executioners are mirror images of each other, so that they look more like symbols of an action than real villains engaged in one. Their mechanical twisting on an axis and their nearly identical costume give them the appearance of puppets – they remind me of the metal players on a mechanical hockey table. The impassive martyrs and docile onlookers also demonstrate little feeling and look like stock characters or actors rehearsing a role. In fact, the scene looks like a drama acted out by college students, an effect made stronger by the stagelike architectural settings of some of the scenes. Like the S. Apollinare frescoes, these have an aura of piety proper to the archaizing style, which Buser and Leslie Korrick suggest might be what Mancini meant when he referred to Circignani's 'pennello ordinario.'[209] Perhaps the most startling feature of these frescoes is that with the single exception of fresco II (fig. 39) none has any overt representation of divine favour, such as an angel with a martyr's palm or crown – a motif that was a standard feature of mainstream depictions of martyrdoms.

The onus was on the viewer to bring the figures to life and provide the landscape with a geographical identity, as though flipping a switch and activating it with an electric current. In these paintings Di Loreto and Circignani step back from the specificity of time, place, and personal identity to allow the viewer the maximum freedom to re-create the scene in his or her own mind. The theoretical foundation of Circignani's style can be found in the *Exercises*, where Ignatius exhorts the reader to translate biblical scenes into the present and thereby turn what would otherwise be a remote episode of history into something alive and personally affecting. As we saw in chapter 1, the descriptions of these episodes in the *Exercises* are equally vague and provide only the most basic signposts for the reader. Through this kind of transformative meditation alone could the worshipper at S. Stefano Rotondo experience for himself or herself the sufferings experienced by the martyrs or the exhilaration of their spiritual salvation. It required the most active kind of looking.

Most of the paintings are divided so that the foreground takes up two-thirds of the picture, including the principal figures and narrative, and the one-third remaining is given over to landscapes and cityscapes *all'antica* dotted with additional smaller figures, sometimes mere stick men like those found in ancient *grotteschi*. Monssen assigns the lower zone of the paintings to Circignani and the upper zone to Matteo da Siena, except for the figures, which he also attributes to Circignani.[210] A few of the paintings divide more evenly in half, with a monumental architectural setting in the background that uses arches and columns to divide it into two more sections, each framing individual episodes like a stage set. Some of the frescoes, notably XVII (fig. 47) and XX (fig. 49), look as though set entirely on a stage, with a classical backdrop, angled wings flanking the scene upstage, and sometimes even a proscenium arch (as on the right in fresco II [fig. 39]) or spectators viewing from boxes (as in fresco VIII [fig. 42]). The viewer's eye level would be at the base of the stage, which sloped upward toward the back as would a real stage. In fact, fresco XX (fig. 49) is framed by a cityscape that recalls the woodcut of the Tragic Stage from Book II of Sebastiano Serlio's *Tutte l'opere d'architettura et prospetiva* (Paris, 1545), which was the first work to illustrate the design and construction of a court theatre. This theatrical ambience helped give the scene immediacy, in presenting the action as a moral or religious *exemplum* and encouraging a heightened emotional reaction in the viewer. Each scene includes the same stock characters – emperor, magistrate, soldiers, executioners, martyrs, disciples, spectators, and so on – who switch identity according to the particular saint's life being depicted.

The costume in Circignani's scenes is as generic as the landscape. Unless they are being skinned, cooked on a grill, shot through with arrows, or boiled in a pot –

in which case they are shown naked with a loincloth – most martyrs wear a mantle over a long tunic, and are shown either barefoot or wearing simple shoes. Occasionally, martyrs who happen to be popes or bishops wear a *triregnum* or a mitre and a *pluviale*.[211] Female martyrs are shown with plunging necklines so that their necks and chests are exposed, and most martyrs – understandably – are shown looking upward for their reward, often in a position of prayer, and not at their executioners. The executioners wear Roman military garb, usually including a thorax, a short-sleeved tunic, and sandal boots, and sometimes a helmet. Occasionally they also feature Orientalist details, such as the turbans worn by the executioners in fresco VI, *Martyrdom of St John the Evangelist and Pope Cletus*, or even contemporary dress, such as that of the magistrate and his witness in fresco XV, *Martyrdom of St Agatha*. Executioners tend also to be depicted with strongly twisted torsos and exaggerated musculature, and they are usually seen from behind with their faces hidden, a feature we have already seen in Durante Alberti's altarpiece for S. Andrea (see chapter 2). In fact, the exaggerated poses and gestures of the killers serve to underscore the passivity and docility of the martyrs. The horror of their actions, stressed by the preponderance of knives and the ruthless depiction of gore, also contrasts sharply with the inner peace of the martyrs, expressed by their loving gazes and relaxed, placid gestures.

The non-specific Roman architecture that dots the landscape includes exedrae, pyramids, rotundas, obelisks, bridges, and miniature colossea. This sort of classicizing landscape is similar to that in Nadal's Gospels. That is especially true of the frescoes showing small classical towns with rotunda buildings, or Renaissance street scenes ending in an open gateway, such as in the Nadal plate 119 and the Circignani fresco XXII. The large rotunda in the background of fresco XIII (fig. 44) recalls Nadal's plate 64. Even the pseudo-military formations of Circignani's background figures, as in frescoes XVIII and XXV (fig. 50), seem to follow Fiammeri's lead in Nadal's plates 42–5 and 62. In addition to this fantasy architecture there are occasional abbreviated references to actual buildings, such as the Pantheon, the Roman Forum, and the Colosseum, as well as to contemporary palace architecture in Rome. Scenes of gladiatorial battles between people and animals in the Circignani cycle resemble those in the anonymous frieze of the Sala delle Oche in the Palazzo dei Conservatori (1570s).[211] Many of the landscapes, like that of fresco XXII, *Martyrdom of St Erasmus*, recall the kind of ideal Renaissance cityscape that was popular at the end of the Quattrocento as well as Serlio's comic and tragic set designs and views of ancient Rome.[212] The exedra motif used in fresco V, *Martyrdom of Sts Gervasius and Protasius*, is found in Serlio as well. Other backgrounds have something of a Tuscan feel, like that of fresco XX, *Martyrdom of St Agapitus* (fig. 49), which recalls Giorgio Vasari's Palace of the Uffizi (1560–74) in Florence. Classical details also appear in the props of the main scene, such as the classical altar in fresco XXIII, *Martyrdom of Sts Primus and Felicanus*, or the Roman-style tub being used to boil the victim in fresco XXV, *Martyrdom of Sts Vitus, Modestus, and Crescentius* (fig. 50).

This classicizing architecture, along with the way in which the saints are depicted sequentially like trophies, gives Circignani's frescoes the flavour of a classical Roman triumph, whose christianized variant is the iconographic category known as *ecclesia triumphans* (the Church Triumphant). As Monssen has indicated, this triumphalist quality is made quite explicit in the text over the first image, which has the words TROPHAEA SACRA, and is also referred to in the title of Cavallieri's printed series of these frescoes, *Ecclesiae militantis triumphi*.[213] Christianized triumphal processions, like the one organized by Baronio at SS. Nereo ed Achilleo, were a favourite activity of the Palaeochristian Revival movement in Rome. Circignani's paintings also emphasize the importance of geography, since despite their non-specific appearance they act as a catalogue of the various regions of the Roman Empire, and in addition they have a local resonance, since many of them are set in the city of Rome.[214] Although for his figures Circignani uses the bright, artificial *cangiantismo* colours common among painters of the later Cinquecento, greens and other earth tones dominate, giving the entire series a pervasive sense of landscape that we will see also at S. Vitale.

One of the most frequently imitated features in Circignani's cycle is the pair of flanking executioners, as seen in his *Martyrdom of St Vitalis, St Thecla, and Others* (fresco IV) (fig. 38) and *Martyrdom of St Stephen* (fresco II) (fig. 39), and it also appeared at S. Apollinare (fig. 37). Although Circignani did not invent this motif, he was the first to apply it to images of martyrdom. Flanking executioners are frequently found in traditional Passion imagery, most recently in Federico Zuccaro's fresco *Flagellation* in the Oratorio del Gonfalone (1573) (fig. 5) as well as in Sebastiano del Piombo's versions in S. Pietro in Montorio (1516–21) and the Museo Civico in Viterbo (fig. 3).[215] The motif is common in Trecento and early Renaissance painting, as in the flagellation panel in the tabernacle doors painted by Agnolo Gaddi (1394–6) at the Capella del Crocifisso at S. Miniato al Monte in Florence, or the lunette in the *Madonna and Child with Saints* (1461–3) by Matteo di Giovanni in the Duomo in Pienza; occasionally it includes four flagellants, as in the version by Luca Signorelli (ca. 1445–1523) at the Museo Diocesano in Cortona. Circignani probably chose the motif because of its medieval roots, and he repeats the motif of the flanking executioners so often throughout the cycle that he transforms it from a narrative scene into an almost heraldic symbol of martyrdom. He first used it in an earlier *Martyrdom of St Stephen* in Città del Castello (1570) (fig. 55), which may have loosely inspired Santi di Tito's *Martyrdom of St Stephen* in SS. Gervasio e Protasio (1579).[216] The motif went on to become a stock feature of martyrdom scenes, in Italy and beyond, such as Tommaso Laureti's canvas of the *Martyrdom of St Susanna* at S. Susanna in Rome or the French painter Eustache Le Sueur's (1617–55) *Martyrdom of Sts Gervasius and Protasius*. Flanking executioner figures are also a notable feature of Domenico Cerroni's (?) martyrological cycle at SS. Nereo ed Achilleo (1599–1600) (fig. 18), where like Circignani's they are often seen from the back, have powerfully twisted torsos, and wear similar costume.[217]

The Subjects of Circignani's Paintings at S. Stefano

Circignani's S. Stefano scenes begin and end with two non-narrative images in which different kinds of martyrs are grouped together to symbolize the universal goal of all Christians: to give themselves for Christ. The first is a scene of the Crucifixion surrounded by male and female martyrs, along with two Holy Innocents at the base, a reference to the first martyrs, the victims of the Massacre of the Innocents.[218] This relatively rare iconography may link the blood of the first Innocents with the sacrament of the Eucharist at the altar. Although Ugonio treats Tempesta's narrative painting *Massacre of the Innocents* as the beginning of the series, that fresco was executed later and was not included in the printed set by Cavallieri. The final scene depicts another crowd of martyrs, representing both sexes and including popes, cardinals, bishops, and kings, against a background of martyrological carnage on a field in front of a massive city (fig. 52). This painting portrays the Golden Age of Christianity, brought about in part by the deaths of these martyrs, and brings the series to an appropriate close. Circignani's cycle therefore begins with the death of Christ, stressing the christological emphasis of the entire cycle, and ends with the Millennium, when Christians have 'abolished the cult of the demons,' in the words of the inscription below, and the martyrs reign in heaven, having 'acquired with their deaths peace for the Church of God.'[219] Alexandra Herz has noted that the role of the cross as a symbol of triumph is also echoed by the Early Christian mosaic in the apse.[220] These paintings have little directly to do with the struggle against heresy in the North and focus instead on antiquity as a way of legitimizing the Jesuits' activities – within and outside Rome – by linking them with those of the heroic first Christians. As Herz comments, 'The decorations ... are more correctly about the establishment of God's Kingdom by the saints.'[221] They are not, after all, scenes of German martyrdom equivalent to the scenes of English martyrdom in S. Tommaso.

The martyrdoms themselves begin with *Martyrdom of St Stephen* (fresco II) (fig. 39), Stephen being both the first (adult) martyr and the patron of the Church. It is set just outside the walls of Jerusalem, and so once again reminds the viewer of the christological emphasis of the series, made explicit in the inscription below. Federico Barocci may have borrowed the figure of the right executioner from Circignani's image in his final *Martyrdom of St Vitalis*, painted in 1583 for the Olivetian church of S. Vitale in Ravenna (fig. 57).[222] Fresco III (fig. 40), the first of three panels from the reign of Nero, is the *Martyrdom of Sts Peter and Paul*; it introduces the first apostles and also makes a reference through Peter to the papacy and the Church in general. As apostles, Peter and Paul can also be seen as the first missionaries, and so serve as appropriate role models for the young seminarians. As in many panels in Circignani's series, one saint is featured at the expense of the other. The entire foreground is taken up with Peter's martyrdom, while Paul is reduced to a mere detail in the background. The fresco recalls Michelangelo's *Crucifixion of St Peter* at the Pauline Chapel in the Vatican (1545–50) (fig. 53), although Circignani's main composition is much simpler, and Peter's head hangs more passively than in the Pauline Chapel fresco.[223] Circignani later painted a similar version of this subject in the Chapel of Sts Peter and Paul in the Gesù in 1585–7 (fig. 85) (see chapter 7).

Fresco IV, *Martyrdom of St Vitalis, St Thecla, and Others* (fig. 38), features Vitalis in the foreground flanked by two executioners very similar in pose to those of fresco II. Alessandro Zuccari has noted that Caravaggio's *Burial of St Lucy* in Syracuse (1608) (fig. 58) uses the same flanking shoveller figures as fresco IV.[224] In the background Christians are set aflame in a miniature representation of Nero's circus, which has been cut away so that we can see inside. Fresco V takes us into the circus, where five martyrs are shown dressed in animal fur and being devoured by dogs. In the background, among other martyrs are the dying Gervasius and Protasius, the Milanese saints whose posthumous miracles are depicted in the Novitiate infirmary and whose cult was promoted by St Ambrose. They will appear again at S. Vitale (see chapter 5).

The next two panels show martyrdoms during the reign of Emperor Domitian. Fresco VI is *Martyrdom of St John the Evangelist and Pope Cletus* (fig. 41), with the main protagonist boiled alive in a fiery cauldron between two Oriental executioners who are similar in pose to those in frescoes II and IV. The composition of this fresco closely echoes Battista Naldini's altarpiece of the same scene in S. Giovanni Decollato (before 1584) (fig. 54), especially in the pose of the saint and the tripod pot.[225] Fresco VI enjoyed a flourishing afterlife, inspiring the work of first-tier painters such as the Fleming Bartolomäus Spranger (1546–1611), whose *Martyrdom of St John the Evangelist* in the Lateran (originally from S. Giovanni a Porta Latina) pays homage to the S. Stefano original, as well as of second-tier artists in the provinces, such as the anonymous late sixteenth-century artist responsible for the martyrdom scene in the church at Settignano, near Florence, which combines Circignani's frescoes VI and XVII. Fresco VII, *Martyrdom of St Dionysius, St Domitilla, Sts Nereus and Achilleus, and Other Saints*, is unusual because the main scene is not the execution of Dionysius but a triumphant procession led by the saint after his death in which he holds his own head in his hands. Perhaps the most curious feature of fresco VII is the appearance of contemporaries in the crowds following Dionysius, one of whom Monssen thinks is Di Loreto.[226] The next panel, fresco VIII (fig. 42), focuses on the death of St Ignatius of Antioch, a saint of special significance to the Society of Jesus since he shared its founder's name, who is torn apart by six lions in the Colosseum in front of Emperor Trajan. Federico Zeri has suggested that the contemporary-looking palazzo in the background is the Villa Montalto or the Villa Mattei al Celio, both in Rome.[227] Fresco IX takes us to the reign of Emperor Hadrian to witness the deaths of a group of saints including St Eustace, who was very important to the college since his relics were deposited in S. Apollinare. There is a detailed rendering of the Castel Sant'Angelo in the upper left that is more clearly visible in Cavallieri's engraving of the same scene.

Fresco X, representing the reigns of Antoninus Pius and Marcus Aurelius, is the first in the series to feature a woman as the primary subject. St Felicity is shown bound to a tree and tortured while her seven sons are martyred in the background; once again, her body, nude except for a loincloth, is flanked by two executioners whose poses are mirror opposites. The figure of St Felicity is very close to that of St Agatha, similarly tied to a tree, in an engraving by Cornelis Cort after a drawing attributed to Giulio Clovio (1567), again in reverse.[228] The right executioner very closely resembles the left executioner in Correggio's *Martyrdom of St Placidus and St Flavia* (ca. 1526) in Parma. Another woman, St Blandina, is featured in the next scene, fresco XI, also during the reign of Marcus Aurelius. Again with the Colosseum as setting, the saint is bound in a net and attacked by a bull, while in the background

Sts Attalus and Ponticus meet their demise. Fresco XII (fig. 43), showing the reign of Septimus Severus and Caracalla, takes us once more into the stadium, where two men and two women have been fed to the leopards and lions in front of an exedra like that in fresco V. One of these women is again St Felicity, finally put to death after her torture, and the other is St Perpetua. In the background Popes Victor and Zephyrinus meet their end, along with Sts Leonides and Basilides and the Virgin from Alexandria, who are all shown in the upper zone. Fresco XIII (fig. 44), the first of two representing the persecutions under Alexander Severus, makes an emphatic reference to papal Rome. Its main protagonist is Pope Callistus, who is thrown from a balcony that closely resembles a benediction loggia into a well below. The architecture of the loggia dominates the middle ground and retreats into the picture along a dramatic diagonal like a stage wing. A placid townscape in the background, with a Pantheon-like rotunda building and another round structure, is the scene of further carnage, including the deaths of St Calepodius and St Martina.

The popular Roman saint Cecilia is the subject of fresco XIV (fig. 45); she is shown, a sensuous nude bust with a serpentine neck, being boiled alive in a tub. She is surrounded by the usual executioners, as well as other witnesses dressed *alla turca*. The composition of this fresco is quite similar to that of another boiling scene, fresco VI (fig. 41). The iconography of the female figure standing in a tripod pot in an attitude of prayer is quite old, and shows that Circignani looked at medieval and early Christian paintings when preparing his cycle. An early fourteenth-century English textile version, in which a female saint is shown with her arms outward in the traditional *orans* position, is preserved in an ecclesiastical garment belonging to Pius II Piccolomini in the diocesan museum in Pienza. The landscape in fresco XIV is unusually expansive, showing a seascape and a variety of ruins and towns as a setting for the beheading of Pope Urban, as well as St Maximus and his companions, while Pope Pontian travels to Sardinia in a boat in the background.

A prominent female saint is also the subject of fresco XV (fig. 46), the first of four depicting the reigns of Valerian and Gallienus. Here, St Agatha has her breasts cut off gruesomely while tied to a column that reflects her grace and purity in the way the column in Parmagianino's *Madonna of the Long Neck* (1534–40) reflects the Madonna's. Agatha stands in an elegant S-shaped pose with a beatific gaze, and her onlookers, a magistrate and a witness, are dressed in contemporary garb, including a very fashionable feather cap, which brings the scene into the viewers' present. In the mountainous landscape behind her can be glimpsed the beheadings of Pope Cornelius and Bishop Cyprian, St Triphon being torched as he hangs from a tree, and Sts Abdon and Sennen being attacked by lions. The same basic pose is repeated for the principal saint in fresco XVI, *Martyrdom of St Apollonia and Other Saints*. In this fresco the saint is bound to a tree and has her teeth ripped out by her executioners against a verdant landscape dotted with other butchery, including the deaths of Popes Stephen and Sixtus as well as of St Cointa and St Venantius.

St Lawrence is the subject of fresco XVII (fig. 47), stretched out on his grill in an elegant pose as if reclining in a triclinium. His muscular body is one of the best defined in the entire series, and he is also one of the most active of the martyrs, shown gesturing as if speaking to the judge behind him, who sits in a grand colonnade. In fact, the martyr and judge seem to be engaging in a theatrical dialogue of the sort that characterized religious dramas in Jesuit colleges. The half-recumbent figure of the saint is likely based on a print by Marcantonio Raimondi after the Florentine sculptor and painter Baccio Bandinelli from the mid-1520s, and the composition recalls earlier paintings of the same scene by Salviati and Girolamo Macchietti.[229] Behind him, in a field before a Roman city, St Hippolytus is dragged on the ground by four daintily prancing horses, while Sts Rufina and Secunda are thrown into the water and Sts Protus and Hyacinth have their necks run through with knives. *The Martyrdom of St Lawrence* by the Flemish painter Francesco da Castello (ca. 1589) at the abbey church of Casamari repeats the basic composition along with the positions of the key players and the figure of St Lawrence, and Cesare Nebbia's version of the scene in the Peretti Chapel at S. Susanna (1591–1600) also echoes Circignani's model, although he has altered the character of the painting by tightening up the composition to increase its diagonal thrust and by heightening its emotion (fig. 56).[230]

Fresco XVIII, *Thirty Christian Martyrs*, is one of the most crowded in the series. In the foreground a burning kiln devours the martyrs, one of whom, a nude, kneels with a forcefully twisted torso before the flames. Monssen has traced the kneeling nude in fresco XVIII to Michelangelo's *Battle of Cascina* (1504–6).[231] In the background 260 more Christians stand in military formation as they are annihilated by a shower of arrows from Roman soldiers. As if 290 martyrs were not enough, the painting also includes the deaths by fire and beheading of Sts Tertullian, Nemesius, Simpronian, Olympias, Theodolus, and Exuperia.

Fresco XIX (fig. 48) moves into the reign of Claudius, with a novel composition in the foreground of three sections resembling a triptych and thereby giving the whole much more of an iconic appearance. In the centre hangs the tortured body of St Marius, whose rack with its wooden supports forms the divisions among the three 'panels.' As Monssen indicates, the figure of Marius was copied from Circignani's own depiction of his martyrdom at S. Apollinare (fig. 37).[232] On either side are figures of almost the same size of his two sons and his wife, St Martha, shown in gory detail as they are flayed and her hands are cut off and hung around her neck. In composition the 'triptych' part of the scene recalls a Crucifixion, with the crucified Christ in the middle and St John the Evangelist and the Madonna on the wings. The landscape, a pastoral setting framed by two blocks of urban Renaissance architecture, features Sts Cyprian and Justina being boiled alive, St Valentine about to be decapitated, and the deaths of forty-six additional Christians. The gently rolling hills and non-specific architecture in this scene are especially characteristic of the neutrality of Circignani's and Matteo da Siena's frescoes.

Fresco XX (fig. 49) provides a clever counterpart for fresco XIX, since in that last fresco the main protagonist is hung from his arms while here the victim is hung upside down by his legs (compare figs 48 and 49). Again depicting the reigns of Valerian and Numerian, the scene features St Agapitus being hung from a crossbar and set aflame. The executioners' poses are exceptionally artificial here; the one on the right poses like a dancer in a ballet. In the background, enclosing the martyrdoms of Sts Christina, Columba, Chrysanthus, and Daria, is a Renaissance cityscape with a Vasari-like loggia in the centre, and, as seen earlier, it echoes Serlio's design for a tragic stage. Fresco XXI, the first of five panels commemorating the reigns of Diocletian and Maximian, is superficially similar in composition to frescoes XV (fig. 46) and XVI, in which a single female saint is shown standing in the centre between two principal executioner figures. Here, however, the protagonist St Agnes stands straight up with her hands aloft, in a gesture of prayer of Early Christian derivation that was popular in the Palaeochristian Revival movement.[233] The executioner figures, here almost mirror opposites, twist around in an especially exaggerated way. Behind her in a mountainous landscape is a circular fortress structure in a lake, the shores of which are bathed in a general bloodbath of martyrdoms of all descriptions, including those of Bishop Anthimus and his companions, Pope Caius, and St Emerentiana.

St Erasmus, whose martyrdom is usually one of the most revolting of the entire company of saints, is the principal player in fresco XXII. Curiously, Erasmus is not shown in his traditionally gory state, with his entrails being wound over a crank, as in *Martyrdom of St Erasmus* by the Roman painter Orazio Borgianni (1574–1616), for example; one would think Circignani would have jumped at the chance.[234] Instead, the saint lies in a box into which his executioners pour molten lead, establishing fire as the primary theme of the painting. Behind Erasmus, his very Ottoman-looking executioners, and Bishop Blaise tied to a tree trunk is another expansive Renaissance 'ideal city' stage setting like that of fresco XX (fig. 49).[235] In this dramatic space we witness the murders of St Barbara and St Eustratius and his companions. Fresco XXIII takes us out of the city again and into the countryside. In the centre of the foreground are two cheerful and healthy looking boys with curly blond hair who stand behind a classical altar and place their hands in the flames without appearing to feel any pain. The didactic message of this scene is underscored by the boy on the right, who lifts his right hand in a gesture used to make a point during a sermon as the executioners and witnesses on either side stare with almost comical expressions of confusion and wonder – a rare expression of emotion. The crowded background contains two saints very important for the church of S. Stefano – Primus and Felicianus, oddly relegated to the distance but directly behind the two boys in the foreground. They share the valley with St Boniface being boiled in pitch, St Vincent on his grill, and St Anastasia on her pyre, as well as the Four Crowned Martyrs (SS. Quattro Coronati) and Sts Peter, Marcellinus, Sisinnius, and their companions.

Fresco XXIV has two female protagonists, each given half the foreground, the one, St Euphemia, sunk in a pit of vipers, and the other, St Lucy, having her neck lanced by a soldier. St Lucy's demure expression as she lowers her head quietly to meet her fate is one of the most moving of the series. The powerful thrust of the executioner's body, with its concave form, contrasts sharply with her convex, passive stance. The landscape is one of the most pastoral in the series, yet instead of shepherds and nymphs there are Christians having their eyes gouged out and being encased in lead boxes, tossed into the sea, hung from trees, and otherwise mutilated. Finishing up the martyrdoms of Diocletian and Maximian, fresco XXV (fig. 50) substitutes these expansive valleys for an overcrowded martial encampment where the Theban legion is enclosed by the Roman legions and slaughtered wholesale in military formation. The gore continues in the middle ground, where St Sebastian is shot through with arrows, twelve Christians are fed to the lions and other carnivores, and, on the left, a pile of corpses includes the bodies of Sts Cosmas and Damian, Pantaleon, Tiburtius, Susanna, Gorgonius, Adrian, and their companions, among them a mother whose cadaver still holds the body of her dead child. The foreground presents the unappetizing spectacle of Sts Vitus, Modestus, and Crescentius being boiled alive in lead in a giant cauldron that resembles one of the tubs from the Baths of Caracalla now in front of the Palazzo Farnese. We can just make out the heads of these unfortuate souls, who are being stirred in a steaming brew that resembles a giant pot of stew.

The next few panels move into the Middle East and Africa. Fresco XXVI moves on to the reign of Maxentius and to one of the most beloved of the saints depicted in the series, St Catherine of Alexandria. She kneels at prayer, flanked by the two broken halves of her wheel and by five executioners who surround her on all sides with menacingly twisted poses. Behind them rises the city of Alexandria, with its pyramids, obelisks, and circular Vesta temple.[236] Within the walls of this Egyptian city the fifty philosophers she had converted are burned on a pyre, and Pope Marcellus and Sts Faustina and Porphyrus lie dead or dying in the streets. The next panel, fresco XXVII, depicting the reigns of Licinius and Maximinus, takes us from Egypt to Persia. The fresco shows a scene of general carnage so overwhelming that it recalls photographs of concentration camps at the end of the Second World War. Heaps of corpses fill the valleys from the furthest horizon to the foreground, including sixteen thousand martyrs together with Bishop Simeon and Bishop Peter of Alexandria, many of whom are dressed in Orientalist garb. In the foreground an anonymous Christian martyr is hacked to pieces by a powerful Asian figure wielding a machete. Perhaps the best known fresco of the S. Stefano Rotondo cycle is fresco XXVIII (fig. 51), which takes us to Antioch and the reign of Julian the Apostate and Valens. The panel features four mutilated corpses laid out in the foreground, the first two beheaded (Sts John and Paul, martyrs), the third with her throat gored (St Bibiana), and the fourth (St Artemius) being compressed between two slabs of stone, with blood oozing all over and his eyeballs hanging from his head by sinews. As if this were not enough slaughter, the classical city in the background serves as a setting for St Pigmenius being drowned, the bodies of unnamed dead Christians, and, most spectacularly, a ship filled with eighty Christians being set aflame on the high seas.

The penultimate panel, fresco XXIX, is the last narrative scene of the series, and takes us into Africa long after Christianity had been accepted by the Roman Empire, during the reign of Hunneric, king of the Vandals (477–84). What is interesting here is that the series has deliberately avoided showing the more celebrated and positive event of Constantine's conversion, a scene that appears in the S. Tommaso series, and instead has moved into the realm of a man who is clearly labelled in the text below as a 'heretic' (Valens too is called a heretic). It is also the first scene that labels the protagonists not as 'Christians' but as 'Catholics.' Although none of the scholarship has yet remarked on it, this is the only picture in the series with an explicitly anti-Protestant message. In the foreground we see two groups of martyrs, those on the left having their right hands hacked off and those on the right their tongues ripped out. The demure expression of the woman on the left submitting peacefully to her fate is very close to that of St Lucy in fresco XXIV. The executioner on the right throws himself into his task with gusto, as Monssen notes: 'There is a twinkle of amazement in his eyes as he performs his gruesome task.'[237] In the background the heretic African emperor and his armies attack thousands of Christians on the plain. The emperor on his horse closely resembles the statue of Marcus Aurelius on the Capitoline.[238] One of the two missing frescoes survives in Cavallieri's printed edition. Originally fresco XII in the series, representing the reign of Marcus Antonius Verus, it depicts the martyrdom of Sts Polycarp, Justin, Victor, and others. The main composition, showing Polycarp bound to a tree that has been set aflame, and flanked by his two tormentors, is very close to that of fresco X (fig. 43).

The Church of S. Stefano Rotondo: Paintings by Antonio Tempesta

Although the Circignani cycle at S. Stefano enjoyed a considerable legacy in Rome and beyond, its most immediate progeny was Antonio Tempesta's series in the chapel of Sts Primus and Felicianus in the same church. Executed only two or three years after the thirty-two panels in the main ambulatory, Tempesta's frescoes followed the lives and trials of two individual martyrs in greater detail than was devoted to any other saint in the church except for St Stephen himself. Tempesta's contribution also included two new panels in the ambulatory, *Massacre of the Innocents* (fig. 60) and *Madonna of the Seven Sorrows* (fig. 59), both of which were restricted in size to accommodate a door in the one case and a window grate in the other. The first of these subjects allowed the artist to indulge in a scene that traditionally was depicted with exceptional violence and horror.

The brutal tone of *Massacre of the Innocents* is set by a pair of sharp parallel knives at the centre, which are echoed by others behind, almost all of them pointed in the same direction. Antonio Vannugli traces the central foreground group to the Marcantonio Raimondi print of the subject after Raphael, and relates the architectural setting – which is far more monumental and dramatically foreshortened than those of Circignani – to a prototype diffused by Florentine artists of the circle of Vasari in the 1560s and 1570s.[239] Tempesta's panel also produced offspring, including two later versions of the scene by Circignani, one of which is in the Nativity Chapel of the Gesù (fig. 88) (see chapter 7). Another version very similar in its configuration is the one by Giovanni Battista Pozzo in the Sixtine Chapel at S. Maria Maggiore (1587) (fig. 61), which copies the central foreground figures of the mother and child and the left executioner almost exactly.[240] Even Guido Reni's celebrated version of the scene (1610) shares some noteworthy features with the Tempesta fresco, including the triangular empty space in the centre, which is similarly punctuated by knives, and the pose of the male executioner on the left. Antonio Tempesta may himself have painted another version of the *Massacre of the Innocents* in the later 1570s at the Vatican Loggia II; however, the composition and most of the figures in that work are quite different from those in his S. Stefano version.[241]

The purely iconic *Madonna of the Seven Sorrows* (fig. 59) creates a powerful contrast to the emphatically narrative *Innocents*. The subject is derived from the cult of the Fifteen Mysteries, at that time widely popular in Europe. The Virgin is shown pierced by swords and surrounded by medallions representing scenes from Christ's life and passion. A very similar version of the icon, popularized especially by Northern printmakers such as Hieronymus Wierix, was painted along with *Madonna of the Seven Joys* by the Flemish painter Bernart van Orley (ca. 1492–1541/2).[242] A Latin verse inscription under Tempesta's fresco indicates that the role of the icon in this church is to serve as a symbol of Mary as Queen of Martyrs (as in the St Andrew, or Martyrs', Chapel in the Gesù), and the inclusion of the medallions of scenes from the Passion underscores the christological basis of the martyrdom scenes elsewhere in the church.

The remaining paintings by Tempesta at S. Stefano are the series of the life and martyrdom of Sts Primus and Felicianus in their chapel, which is also the high altar and incorporates the Early Christian mosaic of the jewelled cross flanked by the figures of the two martyrs. The cycle of ten panels begins on the left with *Funeral Procession of Sts Primus and Felicianus* (fig. 62). This crowded scene features the bodies of the two saints being carried on a bier by men dressed as Roman soldiers and accompanied by acolytes holding tapers, while a parade of paired churchmen, also holding tapers, leads far into the valley beyond. The scene is dominated by a luxurious landscape framed by two wooded hills, and the ground is strewn with wildflowers. In general, Tempesta's landscapes are richer, darker, and more detailed than the sketchier settings by Matteo da Siena in Circignani's cycle. The direction of the procession and the prominence of the landscape recalls an earlier painting possibly by Tempesta at the Galleria delle Carte Geographiche in the Vatican, *Appearance of St Michael in Mount Garganus* (late 1570s), and also resembles other contemporary processional scenes, such as those relating to the Madonna della Quercia by Baldassare Croce in the Palazzo dei Priori in Viterbo (after 1581).[243] Monssen has pointed out how close Tempesta's integration of procession and landscape is to Nadal's plate 151, showing the burial of the Virgin Mary.[244]

Tempesta's depiction of the funeral procession ultimately recalls the triumphal parades of imperial Rome, a motif that was embraced by the Palaeochristian Revival movement and made part of the dedication and consecration ceremonies of churches, as well as of the Corpus Domini or Corpus Christi procession, which had been introduced in Italy in the fifteenth century.[245] One Jesuit image strikingly close to Tempesta's scene is the 1584 print *Translation of Sts Abundius and Abundantius to the Church of the Gesù*, published in a book on the lives of those early Christian martyrs, which shows the same configuration of paired ecclesiastics holding tapers and the remains of the saints being carried on a similar bier (see chapter 6).[246] As the first painting encountered by the visitor in the chapel of Sts Primus and Felicianus, the funeral scene leads the viewer on a mental procession through the fresco cycle, with the actual relics of the saints at the altar as its goal, together with the messianic image of the jewelled cross in the apse vault. This procession is especially appropriate for S. Stefano, since the translation of the relics of those two martyrs by Pope Theodore I (d. 649) to S. Stefano marked the first time in recorded history that the bones of martyrs were reburied within the walls of Rome.[247]

The next panel, perhaps the weakest of the series, shows Primus and Felicianus in the Colosseum, surrounded by lions. The composition, with the two kneeling saints in the pit and an exedra-like structure in the background, is derived from Circignani's frescoes V, VIII (fig. 42), XI, and XII, although the architecture is simplified to the extreme, and the lions, who according to the story did no harm to their prey, look more like pussy cats. Tempesta shares Circignani's fondness for crowd scenes, as in the mob thronging the top of the exedra. The next panel, *St Primus Tortured with Boiling Lead*, takes us back into the countryside, with a long vista of hills, a castle, herds of sheep, and a bay. The costumes of the figures, as well as the pose of the executioner on the right, also recall Circignani's prototypes. *Sts Primus and Felicanus Consoled by an Angel*, in which the two protagonists languish on the floor on the left and witness a brilliant backlit vision of an angel, evokes Raphael's *Liberation of St Peter from Prison* (1513) in the Stanza d'Eliodoro in the Vatican.

The next scene, *St Felicianus Nailed to a Tree for Three Days*, also follows Circignani closely, by reproducing the basic composition of fresco XIX (fig. 48), with its central figure of a man tied to a frame, and by showing a figure virtually identical to that in the earlier fresco. Circignani had used the same composition in his S. Apollinare series, as we have seen. Likewise, *Sts Primus and Felicianus Beaten with Rods*, the next narrative panel in the series, is very close to Circignani's fresco X, of St Felicity, in which there is also a central figure (Tempesta's has two) bound to a treetrunk while two flanking executioners strike her with branches. Tempesta somewhat incongruously has added the upper half of a repoussoir figure to the lower left corner of his panel.

Circignani's fresco XIX (fig. 48) is evoked once again in Tempesta's next panel, *St Primus Burned Alive*, which has the same central figure and wooden gibbet. *Beheading of Sts Primus and Felicianus* (fig. 63) is also in the Circignani mode, although the duality of his subject enables Tempesta cleverly to invert Circignani's standard motif and have a pair of victims flanking the executioner. The final narrative scene, *Sts Primus and Felicianus Thrown to the Bears*, repeats the formula of the second panel, in which they are thrown to the lions. Here the architecture, while still very simplified, is closer to a specific Circignani prototype – fresco V; but Tempesta lowers the line of vision and so makes the exedra more monumental, and it bears a closer resemblance to a real Colosseum than the miniature and out-of-scale structure in Circignani's painting. The scene is also very close to *Exposure to Dogs and Wild Animals*, Tempesta's own illustration for Gallonio's catalogue of martyrdoms.[248]

Aside from a handful of trompe l'oeil angel figures, the only other fresco by Tempesta is a long horizontal apse painting depicting standing martyrs flanking the figure of Christ as Salvator Mundi. Placed directly below the apse vault with its Early Christian jewelled cross, Tempesta's painting unites the main themes of the church: the triumph of the martyrs, their submission to Christ, and the Golden Age. The painting is done in the style of the early Gregory XIII–era Palaeochristian Revival, with iconic, stationary figures standing frontally before an empty background, and resembles the earlier saints' frieze at S. Saba. Herz has shown that this combination of jewelled cross and parade of martyr saints inspired the apse vault painting at SS. Nereo ed Achilleo (fig. 23) and may also have inspired a long fresco over the main doorway showing six martyrs crowned in heaven.[249] In keeping with the church's function as a chapel for an all-male college, the S. Stefano apse fresco is made up almost entirely of men, whereas the version at SS. Nereo ed Achilleo has an equal number of male and female martyrs, divided into the left and right halves of the panel.

The Church of S. Stefano Rotondo: The Balustrade

The final series of frescoes to be undertaken at S. Stefano was the set of twenty-four 'little histories' (1583) that adorned the octagonal balustrade around the central altar and are probably by Circignani.[250] In contrast to his large and colourful main cycle, the balustrade series takes the form of small horizontal panels painted in grisaille, or *chiaroscuro*. The action takes place primarily in the foreground, with figures lined up in the manner of a classical sculpture frieze, like the decoration of a Roman sarcophagus. The background scenes are reduced to a minimum and hardly resemble the expansive vistas provided by Matteo da Siena in the main series. The panels are enclosed in stucco frames and flanked by stucco relief carvings with twenty standing figures of individual saints, which Mara Nimmo attributes to Giovanni Jacopo de' Negri, a *stuccatore* who had worked with Circignani at S. Apollinare two years earlier.[251] Because of the size and technique of the frescoes, the figures are very sketchy, although lively in their simplicity. In Cinquecento Rome, rows of *chiaroscuro* panels framed by stucco or false stucco carvings and alternating with standing figures were typically found on the dado level of a wall – for example, Perino del Vaga's caryatids and battle scenes at the lower level of Raphael's frescoes in the Stanza della Segnatura in the Vatican, painted under Paul III (1534–49). The S. Stefano balustrade is adorned with two separate cycles, one on the outside and one on the inside, both of which run clockwise and have two scenes per wall.

Both the interior and the exterior cycles illustrate the life and death of the dedicatory saint, St Stephen, and identify each scene with text. As is typical of Jesuit painting cycles in Rome at the time, each has been calibrated to appeal to a different audience. The exterior side, seen by the congregation, shows more traditional scenes taken from the Acts of the Apostles (Acts 6:8–15; 7:54–60; 8:2), with quotations from scripture. These include Stephen's election to the diaconate, his miracles, the dispute in the synagogue, Stephen taken before the council, his confutation, the anger of the priests, the ecstasy of Stephen, the attack on him, the stoning of Stephen, his asking for clemency from God for his attackers, his death, and his entombment. By contrast, the interior cycle, seen only by the clergy, uses less orthodox sources that would have been appreciated by relatively learned viewers. The scenes depict Stephen's miracles after death, including the one involving Lucian, who had Stephen's grave indicated by the Jewish rabbi Gamaliel; the exhumation of his corpse; the healing of the sick through his intercession; the translation of his body to Jerusalem; the miracle of the temple saved from fire; the prediction of the birth of Stephen I of Hungary; and other miracles – the blind woman restored to sight, the dead man revived, Euchario brought back to life, a girl brought back to life, a boy restored to life after being killed by a cart, and Paul and Palladia cured of the tremors. The sources for these stories include Augustine's *De civitate Dei*, which we encounter in Room Eleven of the Novitiate infirmary, also meant for a clerical audience.

Monssen, who has published a study of the textual sources of the balustrade, comments that these more eclectic interior scenes 'are supplementary, and suitably accompany the celebration of the Mass and the distribution of the sacrament.'[252] Several of the scenes are unique in Italy, and one draws a connection between the martyr St Stephen and St Stephen, king of Hungary, an appropriate gesture given that the German-Hungarian College was assigned in part to students from that country. The stucco saints' panels include several of the saints illustrated in the main panels, such as St Stephen, Sts Primus and Felicianus, St Agnes, St Catherine of Alexandria, St Lawrence, St Cecilia, and St Erasmus. Their style is classical but very simplified and plain, in keeping with the generic quality of the main fresco series.

The S. Stefano frescoes of Circignani and Tempesta were soon made familiar to the widest spectrum of Catholics in Italy and abroad, thanks to the almost immediate publication of the printed copies, mentioned earlier, by the Roman engraver Giovanni Battista Cavallieri (1525–1601) and the book by the Oratorian scholar Antonio Gallonio.[253] These publications allowed artists around the world to use the Jesuit martyrdom cycles as copybooks for their own work, and we have already had a glimpse of some of their progeny. We can get an idea of how broadly these books were diffused when we realize that in the 1590s there was already a copy of one of Cavallieri's volumes in Northern India.[254] Finally, the Tempesta frescoes in the chapel of Sts Primus and Felicianus were published in *SS Martyrum certamina in templo S. Stephani in Caeli Monte visuntur expressa* (Rome, 1591), a work by Gallonio, with whom Tempesta also collaborated on the manual of martyrological instruments.

It was no accident that these books enjoyed such wide circulation. Unlike the frescoes themselves, they were meant to address a 'Counter-Reformation' audience in the strictest sense of the word. If the frescoes were more a statement of Catholic triumphalism, the books served primarily as anti-Protestant propaganda and were therefore distributed with particular zeal in the North. Kristin Noreen has shown that Cavallieri's first volume included four allegories that were not in the original frescoes – the S. Stefano paintings included little in the way of symbols or allegories.[255] She suggests that these allegories (of Life, Death, Sin, and Grace) were chosen because they substantiated religious ideology that was being attacked by Protestants, and concludes that the books were meant primarily for missionaries on the front lines, in the North of Europe. Another clue is provided by the long inscription that accompanies Cavallieri's print of fresco XXXI (fig. 52) but is absent in the S. Stefano original. The text is in Latin, the lingua franca of Catholicism, and does not include the Italian vernacular found in the fresco cycle. A long eulogy to martyrdom, it expressly mentions England, Germany, and Eastern Europe, whereas the S. Stefano inscriptions are entirely embedded in the classical past. It was only in the printed versions of these images – much better known than their painted models – that their message with respect to contemporary martyrdom in the face of heresy became explicit.

5

The Collegiate Church of
S. Tommaso di Canterbury and
the Novitiate Church of S. Vitale

This chapter deals with two more medieval or early Christian churches belonging to the first generation of Roman Jesuit foundations. In one the decorations survive only as engravings, while the other has lasted to this day almost intact. The Venerable English College chapel of S. Tommaso di Canterbury, near the Piazza Farnese on the Via Monserrato, was destroyed in the early nineteenth century and replaced with a neo-Romanesque structure in the 1860s. Like those of S. Apollinare and S. Stefano, the original painting cycle was published by Cavallieri in the form of engravings shortly after they were executed, and the engravings were detailed enough to allow an artist in the late nineteenth century to execute a painstaking replica of the images in fresco in the choir of the present church. Part of the original college buildings may still stand, but there is no trace of any sixteenth-century decoration – in fact the most prized artwork is an exuberant early eighteenth-century ceiling fresco by that epitome of Jesuit Baroque painting, Andrea Pozzo. The church of S. Vitale, on the Via Nazionale at the bottom of what was then the Jesuit Novitiate garden, was originally part of the Novitiate. An early Christian church like those of S. Apollinare, S. Stefano, and S. Saba, this church is not strictly speaking a collegiate building; nevertheless, it served a much more public function than the rest of the Novitiate buildings, and more attention was paid to quality in its original decoration. Fortunately, most of the decorations in this church have been preserved. A sombre structure, almost hidden from view because the level of its foundation is now so far below that of the street, S. Vitale is one of the most important monuments of the Palaeochristian Revival movement.

The Venerable English College and S. Tommaso di Canterbury

Unlike the German College, which had been the brainchild of Ignatius, the Venerable English College came about by accident.[1] Although England had been a concern of Ignatius, he had never intended to tax Jesuit resources further by founding a third college in Rome, and had hoped that English students could eventually live at the German College.[2] Under Elizabeth I (1558–1603) the persecutions of Catholics grew so severe that England became one of the most dangerous places for missionary work in the world. The English Catholic cardinal William Allen founded a college in Douai, France, to train English priests for the dangerous pastoral work they would face in their homeland. Owing to the extraordinary number of young Englishmen who were willing to send themselves to the gallows for Christ, the Douai college was soon overcrowded, and Allen tried to persuade someone to found a similar institution in Rome.[3] In 1560 the English community in Rome came up with the pragmatic idea of converting an already existing institution, the medieval English pilgrims' hospice near the present-day Piazza Farnese, which had been there since the fourteenth century.[4] The campaign gained momentum in 1578, owing largely to the efforts of Allen and Owen Lewis, a professor from Douai. In that year Gregory XIII had appointed the Welshman Maurice Clynnog as rector over a group of English and Welsh students who had come from Douai.

The earliest years of the new college revealed two contrasting aspects of the English character – a single-minded sense of duty that gained the students the nickname 'flowers of martyrdom' from Filippo Neri, and a boorish violence reminiscent of present-day football hooliganism. The main problem was that the English and the Welsh did not get along. The English students started the rumour that their rector and Lewis, also a Welshman, were favouring the students from their homeland by giving them warmer clothing and other privileges.[5] They also objected to the rector's statement that the goal of the college was to prepare them to return to England after the restoration of Catholicism there, rather than to train them as soldiers for the current fight against Protestantism.[6] In 1578, Gregory XIII and Cardinal Morone asked Father General Mercurian to appoint two Jesuits on a temporary basis to try to quell the dissent, although they were not to meddle in college affairs. But temporary measures were not enough. The 'sharp bickerment' between the two groups – to use the words of the future rector Father Robert Parsons – quite literally erupted into a bun-fight in 1579 at the college refectory: '[The rector] began at the table presently to revile some of our company with foul words, and [the Welshmen] preparing their knives in their hands to have strucken some of those that sat next to them ... Judge you, what time we had to look unto ourselves. But if it had not been for the common cause and for God's especially, we had been sure to have payed [them] for it.'[7] Things finally came to a head that year, when the English students banded together and threatened to leave the institution, taking their grievances directly to the pope. They demanded that the Society of Jesus take over the college, since they admired the Jesuits' reputation for missionary work, and Gregory acquiesced with the bull *Quoniam divinae bonitati*.[8] As in the German College, all students were compelled to take a 'missionary oath' after six months, promising to return to England and serve persecuted Catholics.[9] The college also offered its own courses in controversial theology directed toward an English context, and weekly disputations were held in which the students took both the Catholic and the Protestant sides in order to practise their debating skills. The college remained closely linked with Douai on the front lines; in the words of Cardinal Allen in his *Apologie and True Declaration*, there was 'no distinction between them as to aim or recruitment. There is a similar course of studies, the kinds of sermons preached, the exercises of religion and devotion, are the same.'[10] In 1583 the Sodality of the Blessed Virgin, one of the Marian congregations, was founded by the students, who met regularly for the Spiritual Exercises.[11] The first 'flowers of martyrdom' were sent to England in 1579, and by 1585 forty-two of them had made the perilous trip. Forty-four alumni were tortured or executed for their pastoral work in England, beginning with Ralph Sherwin (1550–81), who was hanged, drawn, and quartered along with the Jesuit Edmund Campion at Tyburn in 1581.[12]

If the S. Stefano murals took on their 'Counter-Reformation' aspect only after they were published, the frescoes of the Venerable English College chapel were anti-heresy from the beginning. In fact, the very idea behind the martyrdom cycle may have come from the English Protestants. In 1563 the Anglican John Foxe published a graphically illustrated devotional manual entitled *Acts and Monuments of These Latter and Perillous Days* (London, 1563), a history of the Church from the first millennium to the present, concentrating in particular on the martyrdom of Protestants under Queen Mary in the mid-1550s.[13] Foxe's enormous book had over fifty graphic woodcuts of torture and death, a number that increased to 150 in the 1570 edition. Cleverly designed to mimic a Catholic calendar of saints' days, Foxe's volume begins with a 'Kalendar' of Protestant martyrs, Protestant leaders (Luther is listed there as a 'confessor'), and others mistreated by the 'papists' over the centuries. In its dedication to Elizabeth it associates her with Constantine (who was born in England of an English mother) and Foxe himself with Bishop Eusebius, who drew up the early Christian calendar of martyrs; it states grandly that 'the goodes and ornaments of the Church chiefly ... consist, not in Donatives and patrimonies, but in the bloud, actes, and lyfe of Martyres, the seekyng and settynge foorthe whereof ought to occupie the studie of true Christian Byshoppes.'[14] The book was extremely well received among Protestants and enjoyed such a wide circulation that Robert Parsons wrote, '[The book] hath done more hurt alone to simple souls in our country by infecting and poisoning them unawares under the bait of pleasant histories, fair pictures, and painted pageants, than many other of the most pestilent books together.'[15] But the Catholics were just as skilled as the Protestants at this kind of media war.

In the same year that Foxe's book was reprinted again (1583), the English Catholics responded with several salvos of their own from Rome and Douai. The most heavily illustrated volume was written by Cardinal William Allen, the head of the English Catholic church in exile. It was *A Briefe Historie of the Glorious Martyrdom of Twelve Reverend Priests*, which he had translated into Italian and published under the patronage of the Venerable English College as *Historia del glorioso martirio di sedici sacerdoti* (Macerata, 1583) with six engravings, each with a Latin inscription. The illustrations themselves may have been cut one year earlier to illustrate a similiar tract written by Parsons himself entitled *An Epistle of the Persecution of Catholicks in Englande* (Douai, 1582).[16] In that tract Parsons made clear that his book was primarily a reaction to Foxe and other Tudor martyrologies, an attempt to counter slander against the Catholics, who were treated in these tracts as cruel tormentors. He wrote, 'If we compare the procedings of Catholiques to protestantes generallie, or of Englishe Catholiques towardes them of Calvin's parte in Queen Maries tyme, (for that is most of all brought and urged against us:) we shall finde that in all respectes, this far to surmounte and to ouer reach that, and to be bothe greater, and incomparablye more grevouse ... and as for tormenting and rackinge ... it is not practiced amongst us, vppon the greatest heretiques that ever were.'[17] A similar tract was compiled by John Gibbons and John Fenn in 1583 under the title *Concertatio ecclesiae catholicae in Anglia, adversus Calvinopapistas & Puritanos*. All three of these books deal in detail with the death of the Jesuit Edmund Campion, who had been executed under Elizabeth I in December 1581, and of various of his companions and followers. Allen's book counters Foxe by recounting the martyrdoms of twelve Catholic priests in England (the number twelve was no coincidence, with its echoes of the apostles), and Thomas Buser has shown that the illustrations follow those in Foxe very closely.[18]

William Allen's engravings also have similarities to the cycle of frescoes painted on the upper part of the nave walls in the chapel of the Venerable English College, the church of S. Tommaso di Canterbury. The only question is which came first. Like the churches of the German-Hungarian College, S. Tommaso was a medieval structure, having served the English hospice as its chapel for centuries before Gregory XIII handed it over to the Jesuits. The original church, dedicated to the Trinity, was built in the fourteenth century and reconstructed with an added dedication to St Thomas of Canterbury in 1445. It was not built from scratch in 1575, as Milton Lewine proposes.[19] Pope Gregory helped enhance the church's status as a pilgrimage site by donating a piece of St Thomas of Canterbury's forearm, a precious relic that formerly had belonged to S. Maria Maggiore, and in 1580 he granted a perpetual plenary indulgence to all who visit the church on St Thomas's feast day and Trinity Sunday.[20] Later he also made a present to the college of the Abbey of S. Saviano and the Priory of S. Vittoria near Piacenza, as well as a vineyard outside the Porta del Popolo for the recreation of the students. Like any church in Rome at the time, S. Tommaso owed its prestige to its relics, which also included a piece of the veil of the Madonna, a tooth of St Andrew the Apostle, another tooth from one of the Holy Innocents, hair from the Magdalene, a piece of bone from St Victor, relics of St Lucy, a fragment of bone from St Peter the Confessor, and a piece of the rib of St Philip, all in gilt wooden reliquaries.[21]

But the English College and Pope Gregory were both eager to make the church a pilgrimage site of a very different kind, one devoted to the living and recently deceased 'flowers of martyrdom' who had studied within its walls. The pope made a number of concessions to this effect between 1580 and 1585, among them that the relics of present-day English martyrs could be used in the consecration of altars, that the Te Deum should be sung upon hearing news of the martyrdom of an English missionary, and that pictures of these martyrs might be painted on the church walls.[22] S. Tommaso was therefore converted into something quite unique for Cinquecento Rome – a pilgrimage site devoted to present-day and future martyrs, so that even living students were revered as walking relics with the greeting 'Salvete Flores Martyrum.' This reverence for contemporary heroes recalls the paintings in the Novitiate recreation room, but here it was not exclusively Jesuit.

The church of S. Tommaso was an active place of worship for eminent foreigners as well as for bishops and other clerics, who were attracted there by the piety of these young students: 'The church and sacristy are maintained with such care and polish that many foreigners come every day to celebrate in our church, among whom are four, three of great importance, who celebrate every day here and on feast days take supper. Among others who come are bishops and prelates as well as simple priests. Furthermore, at vespers and on feast days so many people gather that often they cannot fit in the church.'[23] Since the church was located in the heart of the old city and was not remote like S. Stefano or S. Saba, it enjoyed more regular attendance. A report from 1585 describes the way in which the altarpieces were decked on feast days with church silver, brocades, candles, and flowers: 'The high altar is decently adorned with the relics, and above with gilding and flowers. On the altar of the Madonna are placed the church silver with its lamp, and four flowers on each of the other altars. On the high altar [is] the white frontal with a flower pattern.'[24] Each altar was the site of special prayers every day or week for the souls of the benefactors of the college. Every day the college prayed for the soul of Cardinal Reginald Pole, the former guardian of the English hospice, at the altar of St John, and every Sunday they prayed for the souls of their English benefactors at the altar of the Crucifixion, and also at the chapel of St Edmund (the high altar).[25] Musicians and the college choir participated in regular Sunday services, which were festive occasions that helped draw crowds into the little church. There were also two gilt wooden angels holding candles that were brought out to 'attend' at Mass on festive occasions, much like the stucco angel at S. Andrea.[26]

According to a plan that survives in the college archives, the church of S. Tommaso was a square, three-aisled structure with a main altar on a raised platform and two side altars in individual chapels.[27] There were also two small altars at the west end of the side aisles and a choir above. In 1630, Orazio Torriani described it as 'divided into three naves with pilasters and columns, with four small altars and one large altar ... The centre aisle has carvings on the roof and the small aisles have plain roofs, and in the centre aisle at the end is a choir for music.'[28] The church also had a sacristy, an organ, a bell tower with three bells, a clock, and two common tombs, in addition to private sepulchres.[29] The principal entrance was not at the west end but in the south wall, in the middle, and there was a corresponding doorway in the north wall that led into the college buildings. The main entrance to the college was to the right of the east wall of the church. The church was ravaged by Napoleon's troops, and when Cardinal Nicholas Wiseman visited it in 1818 as part of the first delegation of English students to return, he described a scene of desolation: 'The library with its books piled up in disorder, and the whole house bore evidence of not having been inhabited for nearly the space of a generation. The old Church of the Holy Trinity, which had formed part of the ancient Hospice, out of which the College had been formed, was still standing, although its roof was gone.'[30] The old church was allowed to collapse, largely owing to lack of funds, and finally it was razed and a new church built in its place in 1866.

The frescoes in S. Tommaso, by Niccolò Circignani, were paid for by one of the Venerable English College's greatest benefactors, the lay pensioner George Gilbert (d. 1583), who became a Jesuit at the end of his life.[31] A man of legendary devotion and a major supporter of English Catholicism, Gilbert was treated as a hero by his panegyrists for 'the assiduity of [his] prayers and meditations, whether by day or night, the desire to be in the presence of God ... the singular devotion he had for the Most Holy Sacrament of the Altar, the affection he had for the saints, the honour he brought to their relics, the reverence he had for their images.'[32] While still in England, Gilbert helped defray the costs of missionary work, assisted Catholic priests in enemy territory, and set up a printing press at his own cost for the Catholic mission.[33] After his properties were seized by Elizabethan officials, Gilbert left the country and went to France and Rome, where he continued to finance missionary activities with his now depleted funds. Upon his death in October 1583 he left the college a sum of money that was used in later years to assist young missionaries and the college in France.[34] Gilbert paid not only for the martyrdom cycle but also for the three altarpieces on the east wall of the church, a *Trinity*, a *St John the Evangelist*, and a *Crucifixion*.[35] There has been some debate about when he financed the martyrdom scenes in S. Tommaso. Lewine dates them as early as 1573 but prefers 1580, while Buser and Herz assume a date around 1583.[36] The account books, albeit scanty, suggest that most were painted in the summer of 1582 and a few in early 1583.

We know most about the altarpiece *Holy Trinity with St Edmund and St Thomas of Canterbury* by Durante Alberti (fig. 64), who painted the altarpiece at S. Andrea al Quirinale. Fortunately, the painting survives today, having withstood the Napoleonic siege, as recounted in this description by Cardinal Wiseman: 'The old altarpiece, a painting by Durante Alberti, representing the Holy Trinity and the two patrons of the college, St. Edmund the King and Martyr and St. Thomas of Canterbury, still occupied its place among the surrounding desolation.'[37] The account books show that Alberti was already working on the altarpiece in August 1581, when he was paid 20 scudi, roughly the sum he had received at S. Stefano.[38] The painting does not date from 1575, as Lewine and Herz suggest.[39] Durante's canvas is a remarkable and original example of reformist sacred painting, with large, weighty figures, deep shading, and a rational, focused composition based on an X. The Trinity is displayed in vertical format, taking up just over half the upper part of the canvas. The Father, an elderly man with a beard, holds up the dead body of his son before him, so that the limp body forms a cross, and the Holy Spirit as a dove floats between the head of the Father and that of the Son. Christ's body, with its well-defined muscles, hangs downward with a believable heaviness, its foreshortened knees jutting outward dramatically. The inscription, which reads IGNEM VENI MITTERE IN TERRAM (I have come to bring fire to the earth [Luke 12:49]) – still the motto of the college – served as a rallying-cry for the young English seminarians.

This manner of presenting the dead body is quite different from that of the traditional Trinity iconography, which shows the Father and Son as two living adults seated on either side of the globe of the world, or else shows the Father holding a crucifix with a much smaller, doll-like figure of Christ on it. The first of these iconographies can be found in the illusionistic dome at S. Girolamo degli Schiavone (1589) and in Francesco Bassano's crowded version in the Trinity Chapel at the Gesù (before 1591) (fig. 90), and the second in Circignani's *Trinity* in the apse vault of the Cappella Marzetti in S. Maria in Loreto, in which Christ looks more like the statue on a crucifix than a real person.[40] Durante's treatment of the subject, with the emphasis on the presentation of the dead body, looks more like a *pietà*, such as Michelangelo's Florence Pietà (1550–5), with its vertical format. Painted versions with a very similar format include the Pietà by Antonio Campi in the cathedral in Cremona (1566), Marco Pino's *Pietà with Saints* in the Mattei Chapel of S. Maria in Aracoeli (1568–70), and Antonio Viviani's Pietà at S. Maria dei Monti (1585).[41] A later version of the Trinity that is treated in the same way as Durante's canvas and may have been inspired by it (although the Christ figure is much closer to Michelangelo) is the fresco by Taddeo and Federico Zuccaro at the Cappella Pucci in SS. Trinità dei Monti (1589) (fig. 65); however, the Christ in this fresco looks crowded, and the angel figures also have a claustrophobic confusion very different from the spatial clarity of Durante's image. As Herz has noted about Durante's painting, the placement of the Trinity/Pietà at the core of a martyrdom cycle stresses that the English martyrs 'repeat, renew and complete Christ's victorious struggle for man, represented by the *Pietà* alone,' and thus provides the same christological emphasis we have seen in the Novitiate and other Jesuit collegiate cycles.[42]

In Baglione's opinion Durante's *Trinity* is one of the finest paintings he ever did, and the rational composition and dramatic lighting anticipate early Baroque painting, so that the altarpiece looks more like something from the 1590s or the early seventeenth century than a work of the early 1580s.[43] In fact, the two kneeling figures of St Thomas and St Edmund bear more than a passing resemblance to the lower half of Annibale Carracci's S. Ludovico altarpiece (1589–90) (fig. 66), with which Durante's canvas also shares its pyramidal, High Renaissance–inspired composition and the solemn, restrained gestures of the figures. Both paintings also share an intense realism in details such as costume and still-life elements.

It is more difficult to determine when work began on the Circignani cycle. The *scarpellini* were restoring the plaster of the walls between 1581 and 1583.[44] We also know that the *falegname* Mastro Ambrosio was working on the tabernacle as late as October 1584.[45] But the books do not tell much about the paintings. George Gilbert gave 1,184 scudi in July 1582 to the college, which may have included the 700 scudi he had raised to pay for the paintings.[46] Accordingly, the first payments for 'paintings' date from August of that year, the very next month, amounting to just over 100 scudi.[47] A list of the expenses of the English College for the years 1579–85 indicates that almost twice as much money was spent on the church in 1583 as in any other year (1235.35 scudi) – but, maddeningly, the entry for 1582 is missing altogether.[48] We know that the cycle was finished by 1583, since an Annual Letter for that year (the same year as Gilbert's death) describes the paintings as being already complete.[49] In addition Torriani's report from 1630 states unequivocally that the paintings were executed in 1583, although he may mean only that they were finished in that year.[50] The cycle cannot have been finished before 20 May 1583, since one of the martyrs depicted, Richard Thirkeld, died on that date. The next reference to artistic activity in the account books is for some small coats of arms and a baldacchino painted by a Mastro Simone, *pittore*, in 1591, and some carvings of religious images in 1592.[51]

Circignani probably worked on the cycle in two separate campaigns. The first began in August 1582, the very month he completed the S. Stefano cycle, and included thirty panels, taking us from the time of Christ's apostles to the beginning of the reign of Elizabeth, but before any Jesuit martyrdoms. The number thirty made sense given the architecture, since the nave was only five bays and thirty panels would have fit three to a bay, above the architrave of the colonnade as at S. Apollinare, S. Lorenzo in Damaso (1587), and the church of the Madonna dei Monti, frescoed at the same time in 1581–2.[52] Then Circignani was hired for a second campaign in 1583 to commemorate the deaths of Jesuit martyrs and of martyrs who were alumni of the Venerable English College, and William Allen's book, published that year, served as a model for these illustrations. This last campaign was finished sometime before Gilbert's death in October 1583, and the paintings perhaps fit three to a bay on either side of the last bay before the altar, or on the east wall over the door.

Circignani's fresco cycle (figs 67–71), which features no fewer than sixty-three English martyrs, as well as other English saints – so that the church was 'illuminated from floor to roof with the Saints of England' – made an enormous impression on Catholics in Rome at the time, and was heralded and praised with a fervour that exceeded even that for the S. Stefano paintings.[53] Pope Gregory XIII hastened to take credit for these paintings, even though everyone knew they had been commissioned by Gilbert.[54] In fact, Gilbert's project became one of the most widely circulated Jesuit devotional tales of the year. The most glowing report is found in Gilbert's obituary, written by Alfonso Agazzari, the rector of the Venerable English College, to Claudio Acquaviva in June 1583:

> Of all the saints, he had a great veneration for the martyrs, thanks to the ardent desire he had to become their companion in torture and death. Hence the holy man took great pains to note down all the English martyrs, both ancient and modern, and to have their martyrdoms painted on panels, with which he adorned the entire church of this college in the manner Your Paternity has seen, placing also those of the holy confessors between the pictures, above the capitals of the columns, on which he spent 700 scudi, having gathered together for this end some contributions from several of his English gentleman friends. He used to say that he did this not only for the honour of these most glorious martyrs, and to show the world the glory and splendour of the English church, but also so that when the students in this college should see the example of these predecessors of theirs they might also be stirred toward martyrdom. And, moreover, that with the images of our new martyrdoms the miserable state of his fatherland would be placed before the eyes of Rome and of all the world, and thus move the people to pray to God on its behalf.[55]

There could be no clearer statement of the didactic purpose of these paintings, and also of the renewed Catholic enthusiasm for the cult of images. The report continues with an interesting anecdote, through which we learn that Circignani's painting of St George was a portrait of his namesake George Gilbert. In an appropriately humble gesture, Gilbert tried to get Circignani to blot out his face with a visor since he felt it was inappropriate to substitute his own face for that of the saint. But, to the consolation of the college, Circignani – and the rector – refused:

> Among the pictures there was one of St George, Protector of England, in which his martyrdom was painted, and when he freed the daughter of the king by killing the dragon. Some people asked the painter if he would make the face of St George similar

to that of Signor George [Gilbert], since his virtue merited it and he was so similar to the saint in every way. When this man [Gilbert] learned about this, he stopped appearing in the presence of the painter while he was working on the picture so that the painter would not paint the saint to look like him, since he judged it much opposed to custom. But he was not able to prevent the painter from giving it a certain air of resemblance to him. When he looked at the St George, [Gilbert] said to him: 'How is it that you have painted a man in armour and in the act of combat without a visor? Do us the favour of giving him a visor.' The painter was opposed to this, and the matter was settled in the following way, with his placing a helmet on his head. But [Gilbert] was not satisfied, and in order to cover more of the face he desired him to paint two plates that would cover the ears and lace up below the chin. But the Father Minister was opposed to this, and desired him to do nothing of the sort, since he was satisfied with it. The result was that the portrait of this gentleman stayed in the college, to the consolation of everyone.[56]

And indeed, in Cavallieri's print of the subject, St George appears proudly without his visor. One is reminded of the possible portrait of Di Loreto, the patron of the S. Stefano murals, in Circignani's cycle there (see chapter 4). This tale of Gilbert's humility was repeated as a piece of edification in the Annual Letter of 1583, where Gilbert was praised for 'beautifully decorat[ing] the college chapel with the pictures of those from that nation who, from the very first conversion of England to the present day, had given their lives for the faith.'[57]

Everything we know about the cycle of frescoes at S. Tommaso comes from Cavallieri's *Ecclesiae anglicanae trophaea ... Romae in Collegio Anglico per Nicolaum Circinianum depictae* (Rome, 1584), which reproduces the thirty-six panels from Circignani's series, as well as Durante Alberti's altarpiece as the frontispiece. As Gilbert's obituary makes explicit – and contrary to the general scholarly perception of these paintings – the Circignani cycle did not consist only of martyrdoms. In fact, unlike the series at S. Stefano, it was punctuated by several more positive images relating to English Christianity, from the reputed voyages of the apostles Peter and Simon and Joseph of Arimathea to England (print III) to Gregory the Great's decision to evangelize the British Isles under St Augustine (print X). These scenes were chosen to stress the legitimacy of the Roman Church in England. No scene could be more symbolic of the papacy's role in England than the presence there of Peter himself, and this connection was strengthened by a reference to Gregory the Great, who began the mission to England, with the famous line attributed to him that a group of English boys he witnessed at a slave market were 'not Angles but angels' (*non Angli sed angeli*). The Joseph of Arimathea story, which reputedly took place during the reign of King Arthur and is associated with the Holy Grail and the town of Glastonbury, took England's Christianity even farther back and related it to the blood of Christ and the Eucharist.

The presence of other early saints subtly reinforces the message of papal legitimacy. There is Lucius (print IV), a legendary British king, who wrote to Pope Eleutherus in 156 asking for baptism, while the persecutions by the Roman Empire were still in full swing (if we compare it chronologically with the S. Stefano series, this painting would fit in during original fresco XII).[58] The ancient ties between

Britain and Rome are also embodied in the beloved St Alban (print V), a Roman Briton from Verulamium (St Alban's) who was persecuted in England by the Romans for his faith, and his baptizer, St Amphibalus (print VI).[59] Even Emperor Constantine (fig. 67), who ended the persecutions and founded a Christian empire, had an English connection, having been born in England; Circignani's images stress both his and his mother's (St Helen was the daughter of an English king) connection with the True Cross, and so incorporate a triumphalism.[60] Constantine is shown in print VII having his vision of the True Cross and also being cured of leprosy by Pope Sylvester, a story we saw depicted in the infirmary at S. Andrea (see chapter 3).

The saints depicted in the S. Tommaso series fall into virtually every category, from apostles and confessors to virgins, bishops, and hermits, thereby giving the series the flavour of a universal catalogue of sainthood and relating it to the weekly devotions of the students as at the Novitiate and the German-Hungarian College. The martyrdoms become more regular with print IX (fig. 68), which shows the murder of St Ursula and the 11,000 Virgins. Indulging in his taste for crowds, Circignani depicts this daughter of an English king and her followers succumbing to a rain of arrows. In print X we are introduced to the first attack on heresy, cloaked in early Christian garb. The saint in question is St Germanus of Auxerre (ca. 378–448), who was called to England twice to end the Pelagian heresy, which in Bede's words had 'seriously infected the health of the British Church.'[61] With the help of dramatic signs of God's approval such as the calming of a storm on the English Channel, Germanus asserted the truth of the Church of Rome. The tie with Rome is further stressed in print XI, which depicts King Edwin of Northumbria (d. 632), a just and righteous monarch who was baptized by St Paulinus of York, a member of the second papal mission to England, as well as his successor Oswald (d. 642), both of whom were killed in battle by the pagan Welsh and Mercians.[62] In view of the political state of the Venerable English College at the time, it is interesting that Circignani was not discouraged from depicting an English hero being killed by a Welshman. Elsewhere the series makes an effort to include Welsh figures such as St Winifred and St Beuno (print XXII, seventh century). Other Christian kings include St Ethelbert, king of East Anglia (print XVII), who was murdered at Sutton Walls, Herefordshire, in 794 and to whom the cathedral in Hereford is dedicated; St Edmund, another East Anglian king and martyr (print XIX, d. 869), who was shot through with arrows, St Sebastian–style, and beheaded by the Danes; and the nationalist hero St Edward the Confessor (print XXIII, ca. 1004–66).

Two archbishops of Canterbury are included, the archbishop and martyr Alphege (print XXIII, 952–1012), and the patron of the church, St Thomas of Canterbury (print XXV) (fig. 69), to whom an entire panel is dedicated. As elsewhere the connection with the papacy is emphasized, and Thomas is shown appealing to Pope Alexander III, the man who gave him almost instant canonization in 1173 and founded one of the greatest pilgrimage centres of medieval Europe. Several of the frescoes depict English missionaries who travelled to places such as Sweden and Germany to preach the gospel and met their demise, thereby providing a model for latter-day English missionaries. Such were St Sigfried (print XIII,

b. ca. 1045), St Boniface of Crediton (print XVII, ca. 675–755), St Henry of Uppsala (print XXIV, d. ca. 160), and St Eskil (print XXIV, d. 1080). St George of course makes an appearance (print XIV), with a helmet but no visor, and he is shown not only liberating the king's daughter but meeting his end through martyrdom. The composition of the St George panel closely resembles that of Raphael's version in Washington (1504–5), with the same position of the figures and diagonal thrust of the lance. One saint featured in the series, St Wulstan (print XV, ca. 1009–95), was a bishop and a champion of celibacy, an appropriate role model for the young men in the college. Two other saints are included in print XXVI probably because their youth made their cult resonate in the college. St William of Norwich (d. 1144) and Little St Hugh of Lincoln (d. 1255) were two boys popularly believed to have been killed by Jews, and their stories, especially that of St Hugh, prompted severe anti-Semitic persecutions in medieval England. Only a handful of women appear in this saintly cycle, at least in the early Christian and medieval two-thirds of the series (aside from the 11,000 Virgins). In addition to Helen and Ursula there are St Ebba and her nuns (print XVIII) and St Winifred (print XXII). Again, this lacuna can be accounted for by recalling the audience of the cycle, which would have been primarily the male students at the college and visiting male churchmen and nobility.

Suddenly, in print XXVII (fig. 70), there is a dramatic change. Time is telescoped forward from the thirteenth century to the generation before the present day. Rather generic costumes and settings are replaced by more specifically Northern architecture, contemporary costume, and, like a battle display, a series of large, prominent Tudor roses on the tunics of soldiers in the foreground. We are in the reign of Henry VIII (1509–47) and the beginning of the English Reformation, and the enemy is depicted with journalistic accuracy. The print illustrates the Act of Supremacy, whereby Henry declared himself head of the Church of England and severed the English Church from Rome. In the first scene we witness the deaths of two of the most important opponents of Henry VIII's marriage to Anne Boleyn, John Fisher (St John of Rochester, 1469–1535) and Thomas More (later saint, 1478–1535). The fruit of Henry's tyranny forms the subject of the next illustration, print XXVIII, which commemorates the Dissolution of the Monasteries, whereby Henry shut down all the religious houses in England, seized their property on trumped-up charges, and prohibited monastic life (1536–40). Circignani's image shows Observant Franciscans being burned alive, Augustinians being disembowelled, and Benedictines being hanged. The slaughter continues in print XXX, which shows mass executions of priests under Henry VIII and the arch-enemy herself, Elizabeth I (1558–1603) – a scene that conveniently passes over the wholesale slaughter of Protestants under the interim queen, Mary (1553–8), the very subject of John Foxe's tract.

After this introduction to the treachery of the Tudors, the cycle moves to the present day – and to Jesuit subjects (fig. 71). Edmund Campion, Ralph Sherwin, and Alexander Briant, who were martyred while the plaster was still wet on the first panels, in 1581, are the subjects of prints XXXI to XXXIII, contemporary depictions that recall the painted 'trophy case' in the recreation room at the Novitiate. The graphic depictions show them being disembowelled and broken on the rack and their body parts boiled in a large vat (fig. 71). Sherwin was the first student of the Venerable English College to lay down his life for Catholicism. Curiously, and in keeping with the classicizing spirit of the earlier scenes, the executioners revert in places to Roman dress. After a scene, print XXXIV, showing a variety of horrible deaths and tortures being inflicted on English Catholics, men and women, we arrive at the penultimate panel, print XXXV, a kind of school photograph showing four martyrs from the college (John Shert, Luke Kirby, William Lacey, and William Hart), as well as the Douai College students Robert and Lawrence Jonson, William Filby, Richard Thirkeld, Thomas Cottam, John Payn, Thomas Ford, and others. But this image does not mark the end of the series. The final scene, print XXXVI, allows it to end on a positive and militant note by representing the founding of the Venerable English College. It shows Gregory XIII kneeling before an altar together with a crowd of young English students, whom he is sending forth to defend the faith against heresy.

Stylistically, the S. Tommaso cycle is consistent with Circignani's series at S. Apollinare and S. Stefano, and especially recalls the latter, with its more crowded scenes and bigger vistas. The frescoes have the same generic, classicizing architecture – although with the addition of some Northern details such as pitched roofs – the same wide valleys dotted with crowds of people, and in some cases a very Nadal-like division into three sections using palace architecture. As in the frescoes of the German-Hungarian College, the figures have the exaggerated torsion and musculature of Michelangelo, including many recumbent nudes that resemble classical river-gods. The S. Tommaso cycle also uses key letters in the same way as the S. Stefano cycle, although we have no way of knowing whether the original texts were bilingual since the printed version is in Latin only. Some details in the prints are so close to details in the S. Stefano series that the artist evidently copied his own designs. Print XXI, for example, shows St Decamus the hermit holding his own head in his hands much as the figure does in fresco VII at S. Stefano. The poses of the executioners in print XXXIII look much like those in fresco XXIX. The entire composition of print IX, St Ursula and the 11,000 Virgins (fig. 68), is copied from that of fresco XXXI (fig. 52), showing the martyrs of the world, and the Renaissance cityscape in print XXIV is very close to that in fresco XXII. Curiously missing in most of the S. Tommaso pictures is the motif of the paired executioners, which became such a cliché at S. Stefano and was also present at S. Apollinare.

Now let us return to the Foxe and Allen pictures. Many scholars have noted the similarities between the S. Tommaso prints and some of the illustrations in John Foxe's and William Allen's books. In particular, prints XXXI and XXXII, showing the torture and execution of Edmund Campion and his companions, share their main subjects and poses with these other publications, although their style is quite different. Print XXXI (fig. 71), showing Campion on the rack, borrows the figure of the victim from Foxe's 1563 book (p. 505), although Circignani translates the stocky, heavily clothed Northern executioners into lithe and muscular Italianate ones. The artist also takes the scene out of the congestion of the Tower of London and sets it in a gracious hallway giving onto a courtyard reminiscent of that of the Palazzo Ducale in Urbino.

Circignani's scenes are also much more classicizing in spirit than those of the other series of prints that served as a link between the Foxe and Circignani versions – the illustrations for Allen's tract, which may have been cut a year earlier for Robert Parsons.[63] Like the Foxe print, Allen's illustration of the rack features more consistently Northern costume, complete with Shakespearean doublets. Although Allen's image includes the men at the table that appear in Circignani's version, the interior is a cramped English castle and not a Renaissance palazzo, and the print has none of Circignani's grace or careful perspective. The same goes for Allen's print of a victim being dragged on a straw mat behind a horse. Allen's version is almost entirely devoid of perspective, and crowds the figures together in a confusing jumble. Circignani's print XXXII, on the other hand, reduces the number of people and sets the whole in an expansive landscape; and, despite the heavy Northern woollens worn by some of the executioners, the painter cannot resist placing in the foreground a figure in classical Roman dress whose rippling torso twists into the *serpentinata* pose of Michelangelo so beloved by 'Maniera' painters. This same scene of a man being dragged by a horse inspired an engraving on a broadsheet published by Cavallieri in Rome in 1584 entitled *Crudelitas in Catholicis mactandis*. Other than this handful of similarities, Circignani made few references to Foxe's pictures, with the possible exception of the hanging figure 'A' in print XXIX, which may derive from Foxe's page 496, although the gibbet is reversed.

Only three drawings survive of Circignani's cycle at S. Tommaso, including a design in the Louvre for print XXXIII, showing the martyrdoms of Campion and his companions, and a more sketchy sheet in Göttingen of print XXV, the murder of St Thomas of Canterbury.[64] The Paris drawing is highly finished and even leaves an appropriate amount of space below for the text, suggesting, as with the single surviving S. Stefano drawing, that it was executed for the printmaker. The Göttingen drawing, however, is in an entirely different format and is less finished, which invites the suspicion that it was a preparatory drawing for the fresco itself. In addition to these two drawings, there is also a drawing in the British Museum of print XVIII, the martyrdom of St Ebba and her nuns, in which the figures are executed in some detail but only the outlines of the architecture are given.[65]

Like the S. Stefano and S. Apollinare series, Circignani's cycle at S. Tommaso was designed to inspire young men to follow in the footsteps of the martyrs in their defence of Christianity, and it celebrated the legitimacy of the Roman Church. But unlike the earlier series, the cycle in the Venerable English College was designed specifically to convey an anti-Protestant message, by countering Protestant accusations of Catholic cruelty in the reign of Queen Mary and by advertising to all the world the terrible state of the Catholic church in England. Whereas the geographical scope in the S. Stefano series was encyclopaedic, with an emphasis on Rome as the New Jerusalem, the sense of place in the S. Tommaso series is much narrower, focusing exclusively on England and especially on the themes of England's ties with Rome and papal legitimacy. If the earlier series can be seen as a celebration and a victory procession, the frescoes at the Venerable English College are nothing short of a battle cry, rousing the troops to action and shining the Roman spotlight on these flowers of martyrdom, both living and dead.

The Novitiate Church of S. Vitale

The decorations of the new Novitiate church of S. Vitale heralded a dramatic change in Jesuit martyrdom imagery at the beginning of the seventeenth century. Although the collegiate church cycles of the 1580s had already shown a marked interest in landscape and geography, these earlier paintings focused on the human figures and stressed human pain and suffering. At S. Vitale this figural emphasis gave way to a more symbolic and meditative treatment of martyrdom, in which most of the scenes were dominated by landscape. In fact the presence of landscape was so overpowering that the frescoes were mistaken for the work of the French landscape painter Gaspard Dughet (called Poussin, 1615–75) until the nineteenth century.[66] The omnipresence of landscape relates closely to Ignatius's own vision of connecting with the origins of the Church and the lives of the saints through their geography, as Alessandro Zuccari has recently noted.[67] On the facade, and in the gardens, the figural element disappears altogether, as the representation of martyrdom is carried to an emblematic, symbolic level. Even the apse paintings, which feature more traditional large figures, show the martyrs standing in noble *contrapposto* and emphasize their beauty and musculature instead of their suffering or emotion – not unlike those of the Novitiate recreation room, which are contemporary (see chapter 2). Yet the viewer is not lost in a world of cool abstraction. At the same time S. Vitale stresses the christological basis of martyrdom even more forcefully than does S. Stefano or S. Tommaso. The triumphant theme of following Christ was announced directly over the apse with Andrea Commodi's emotionally charged figure of Christ holding the cross and beckoning the multitudes to pick up their own crosses and follow him. As had now become typical of Jesuit interiors, the walls of S. Vitale are also enhanced by inscriptions done in a manner similar to that on the walls of the Novitiate infirmary and in S. Stefano Rotondo, from simple captions under the individual martyrdoms on the walls to more erudite scriptural quotations accompanying the larger narrative scenes and the figures of prophets.

When it was acquired by the Jesuits, S. Vitale became the largest and most public church associated with the Novitiate. As with the smaller S. Andrea, the acquisition and restoration of S. Vitale by the Jesuits was made possible only through the generosity of a noblewoman from Naples, this time Isabella della Rovere (b. 1552), the daughter of Guidobaldo II, the duke of Urbino, and Vittoria Farnese, and the wife of the Neapolitan nobleman Nicolò Bernardino di Sanseverino, the prince of Bisignano.[68] Isabella donated a huge fortune of 90,000 scudi to the church, of which just under half was in the form of jewels, considerably more than the rather modest 6,000 scudi that had been given by the Novitiate's first *fondatrice*, Giovanna d'Aragona – even with inflation.[69] A tragic figure, Isabella was physically deformed as the result of a botched operation that destroyed her nose, had lost her only son at 14, and had endured her husband's death in debtor's prison. As her misfortune increased, Isabella sought solace in the spiritual life and forged ever closer connections with the Society of Jesus, to which belonged her confessor, Vincenzo Maggio. The greatest proof of her affinity with the Jesuits was her endowment of the Gesù Nuovo in Naples, one of the grandest Jesuit foundations in Italy. A reliance on the patronage of rich matrons or widows became typical of the Society of Jesus and was responsible for their endowments not only at S. Andrea but also at the Collegio Romano and several of the Gesù side chapels. In fact, the Jesuits were so notorious in their targeting of matronly prospects that the practice of luring rich widows to donate side chapels was lampooned in anti-Jesuit tracts from the time of the *Monita secreta* (see chapter 1).[70] It is remarkable, as Maria Conelli points out, that the traditional scholarship has almost completely overlooked Isabella's role as founder; Francis Haskell, for example, focuses instead on Acquaviva's activities.[71]

As we saw in chapter 2, the shortage of space at the Novitiate had already reached the crisis level, particularly since the original founder, Giovanna d'Aragona, had given the adjacent property to the Capuchin nuns in 1575, thereby severely restricting the space available for new novices. Consequently, at the same time that the Jesuit enterprise enjoyed virtually untrammelled expansion throughout the world, new Jesuits could barely fit in their own Novitiate chapel in Rome. The answer was found in an early Christian basilica that happened to be at the foot of the Novitiate garden, on present-day Via Nazionale. Like S. Stefano, S. Vitale had excellent credentials as an early Christian basilica and martyrium. As early as the fourth century a modest oratory was built on the site in honour of the fourth-century Milanese martyr saints Gervasius and Protasius. This wayside chapel was expanded into a basilica in the same century and dedicated to the martyrs' father Vitalis, thanks to the generosity of a patroness named Vestina, who left her worldly goods to the church in the form of precious jewels bequeathed to the oratory.[72] This ancient connection with female patronage, and especially with the sale of jewels, was not lost on the Jesuits, who compared the devotion of their new *fondatrice* to that of her early Christian predecessor (Giovanna, incidentally, also gave part of her fortune in jewels, although her foundation was strictly limited to S. Andrea).[73] The new sanctuary was consecrated by Innocent I in 412, was largely reconstructed under Leo III in the eighth and ninth centuries, and was restored in the Middle Ages. S. Vitale originally had three aisles ending in a narthex, but the aisles were removed under Sixtus IV (Isabella's kinsman) in 1475, so that only a few bays were left at the end to form transepts. The church was officially handed over to the Jesuits, in a semi-ruined state, on 20 November 1595, and Isabella's foundation dates from 2 April 1598, when she and Giovanna d'Aragona were named as the dual founders of the entire Novitiate complex.[74]

The Jesuits finished what Pope Sixtus had begun by removing all traces of the aisles in favour of a single-naved church.[75] Under Acquaviva's direct leadership, five altars were constructed, one in the apse and two flanking altars on each side wall, and the entire inside and facade were painted with narrative and symbolic imagery.[76] The emblematic program of the complex was carried into the garden as well, where herbs and trees were planted in a deliberate program of martyrological symbolism, a subject that has been treated elsewhere.[77] Although Isabella della Rovere's donation financed the restoration and interior decoration of the church, work had already begun before her foundation, and there is no evidence that she had any influence whatever on the iconographic program or the choice of artist.[78] Acquaviva's obituary declares in no uncertain terms that the program derived from the Father General, and that 'he himself chose the majority of the mottoes, which are so very beautifully appended to [the paintings].'[79]

Acquaviva assigned two Jesuits to oversee the work on S. Vitale. The architect Giovanni de Rosis was responsible for all construction and repair work to the fabric of the church, and Giovanni Battista Fiammeri took charge of the iconographic program and decoration. Acquaviva's letters to Fiammeri indicate that he held the Jesuit artist in the highest esteem and believed him uniquely capable of carrying out his iconographic program in a manner consistent with the Jesuit *modus procedendi*, or way of proceeding. In a letter written at Frascati in August 1599, when work was already well under way on S. Vitale, Acquaviva demonstrates not only the crucial role played by Fiammeri as overseer of the project, but also the degree to which he valued the Jesuit brother's professional opinion:

> As far as the design goes, dearest Giovanni Battista, I say to you that it pleases me greatly; I will only make a suggestion to you (submitting myself entirely to your expertise): it might be better if the columns that support the cornice of the tribune might instead be pilasters with fluted surfaces, to give it a little variety, since all the other ones in the church are columns. Think about it and make your judgment. As for the figures in the tribune, I well understand that you did not want to use up space and [wanted] to make handsome divisions, but still I would be pleased if the Most Holy Madonna and the other Marys were together and if they would go in front of Our Lord, who would look at his mother, and she him, with affection. As for the rest, I am satisfied. As far as dealing with Paris [Nogari?] for the paintings, I am satisfied with the subject you mentioned about Christ Our Lord at the Column, and it seems to me that you could begin to negotiate with him; but do not decide anything else before we come to Rome, which will be soon.[80]

Fiammeri, it is clear, sent designs and iconographic ideas to Acquaviva for approval. The Father General's comments relate more to subject than to style, a matter he was confident he could leave in Fiammeri's hands.

Work began on the paintings in 1597 with the facade, portico, and ceiling, and in the same year the high altar canvas and other *ornamenti* were completed.[81] The interior wall frescoes were begun in 1598, when the first part of Isabella's bequest was made available, and in that year two of the new altarpieces were executed as well.[82] Alessandro Zuccari maintains that these were the ones belonging to the two side altars closest to the apse, *Agony in the Garden* and *Immaculate Conception*, both of which are traditionally attributed to Fiammeri but the first of which Stefania Macioce argues is by a different hand.[83] In 1598 the Jesuits spent 300 scudi on painting at S. Vitale, an amount large enough to suggest that the scenes from the life of St Vitalis in the tribune were already under way.[84] Giovanni Baglione and Filippo Titi credit Fiammeri with painting the entire facade and portico and the large-scale images *Holy Virgin Martyrs* (fig. 78) and, across from it, *Holy Confessors* (fig. 79), both of which were likely painted around the same time as the first two canvases and were certainly finished by 1600, when the altars were consecrated.[85] Fiammeri was probably assisted from the beginning by the *perugino* Annibale Priori, a specialist in perspective and *quadratura*, who executed the architectural frameworks of the interior walls and perhaps also of the facade.[86] Macioce challenges the attribution of *Holy Confessors* to Fiammeri, and assigns it instead to the Flemish painter Giuseppe Penitz (possibly Joseph Heintz the Elder; see chapter 6), on the basis of a figural treatment superficially similar to that in his image of St Francis at the Gesù.[87] On close inspection, however, it appears that Heintz uses a sharper and more angular kind of drapery, and not the flowing kind used in *Holy Confessors*, which is more consistent with Fiammeri's work at the Gesù; the figure types also betray Fiammeri's hand, as I will discuss below.

The year 1599 was exceptionally active, as attested by large payments for paintings and references in Acquaviva's correspondence.[88] That is also the first year that Rutilio Clemente's name appears in connection with S. Vitale, although he is not mentioned in any of the scholarship. As we have seen, Clemente had been Fiammeri's assistant before, not only at the Novitiate but at the Florentine college of S. Giovannino. In two letters dated January and February 1599, Acquaviva writes that he cannot spare Clemente any longer for work on the decoration of another chapel because he has his hands full at S. Vitale.[89] Annibale Priori's replacement as a perspective painter was Tarquinio Ligustri, who completed the framework for the interior side wall frescoes between May and November 1599, yet there is no mention in the sources about who was responsible for the landscape martyrdoms themselves.[90] Ligustri was paid 181 scudi to paint false pilasters and decoration around the stucco sculptures and a dado, as well as an 'augmentation of the ornamentation around the landscapes.' Ligustri's last contribution to the church probably included the false architectural framework of the apse and end wall, for which he received his final payment of 30 scudi on 8 July 1603.[91] Macioce suggests that these last paintings included the illusionistic backgrounds of the two stories of Samson and Gideon.[92]

According to Baglione, Filippo Baldinucci, and Filippo Titi, the Florentine painter Andrea Commodi (1560–1638) was responsible for the narrative paintings in the apse, probably around 1599–1600, including the main scene of Christ carrying the cross and the two flanking frescoes of martyrdoms.[93] Active in Rome in 1583 and then in 1592–1614, Commodi was a reformist painter and friend of the Florentine painter Cigoli (Ludovico Cardi), and he was likely exposed to the workshops of Alessandro Allori and Santi di Tito as a young man.[94] He shared Santi's vision of naturalistic painting with large, weighty figures and rational compositions, and he gave his scenes consistently realistic light effects and still-life details. There are several references to Commodi's activity in the archives of the Accademia del Disegno in Florence that show him active there between 1588 and 1591, at a time when Santi was also deeply involved with the institution.[95] After a brief sojourn in Cortona, where his works include *Consecration of the Church of SS. Salvatore*, now in the Duomo, he returned to Rome, where his most famous commission is for S. Carlo ai Catinari (1621–2).

Baglione and Titi assign the two tribune frescoes of the torture and death of St

Vitalis on either side of the altar to a fellow Florentine, Agostino Ciampelli (1565–1630), another product of the reformist circle of Santi di Tito, but who favoured more crowded compositions and lither figures than Commodi's.[96] Ciampelli executed several important works in Tuscany before going to Rome, including canvases in the Duomo and SS. Stefano e Nicola in Pescia, a *Nativity of the Virgin* in S. Michelino Visdomini in Florence, and a fresco cycle of Old Testament themes for the Palazzo Corsi. His name also appears in the records of the Florentine Academy between 1590 and 1594.[97] Alessandro de' Medici was Ciampelli's most important patron and protector, and it was he who in 1594 took him to Rome, where the artist would remain until 1630. Ciampelli's principal commissions in the city included work at Alessandro de' Medici's titular church of S. Prassede and at S. Agnese fuori le Mura, St John Lateran, and S. Maria in Trastevere. The attribution to Ciampelli at S. Vitale is borne out by two surviving drawings by Ciampelli for S. Vitale that Abromson maintains were executed between 1601 and 1603.[98] One of the drawings is a complete study for *Martyrdom of St Vitalis*, with a grid superimposed on it for transfer to a larger surface, and the other is a study of a pair of heraldic angels very close to those that appear in the tribune over the martyrdom scenes. The first drawing corresponds fairly closely to the final fresco, although the architectural setting is different and the angel above has been moved to the centre, and it bears an inscription (possibly autograph) describing the scene depicted.[99] Both Commodi and Ciampelli worked around the same time at the Gesù, where they collaborated on the crypt chapel of SS. Abbondio and Abbondanzio (1603), and where Commodi also painted scenes from the life of Ignatius to adorn his tomb there in 1605–8.

Federico Zeri has proposed that Gaspare Celio was also involved in the decoration of S. Vitale, on the basis of the curious reference we have already seen in the Novitiate account books to the extinction in June 1598 of a 'censo' that had been lent by Celio to the Jesuits in June 1595 (see chapter 2).[100] I have suggested that he may have had a hand in the Novitiate decorations, and it would not be surprising to find that he also contributed to S. Vitale, especially since he had already collaborated with Fiammeri at the Gesù. The reference in the letter of Acquaviva quoted earlier suggests that the Jesuits may have been negotiating with the Roman painter Paris Nogari to work at S. Vitale, but neither he nor the subject he was to paint (the Flagellation) was selected.[101]

One major lacuna remains regarding the authorship of the S. Vitale frescoes – the landscapes themselves. None of the scholarship to date has offered a convincing attribution for these pastoral scenes of martyrdom, and most scholars, like Federico Zeri and Macioce, assign them to Ligustri, even though it would have been highly unlikely in the specialized world of late Cinquecento Roman painting that a *quadratura* painter would be expected to paint landscapes.[102] Nowhere does the documentation say that Ligustri painted the landscapes; in fact, it says very clearly that he painted everything but. There is also no reason to suppose that either Commodi or Ciampelli contributed to anything outside the tribune. Fiammeri also did not do landscapes – he was primarily a figure painter – and we have seen how the Jesuits employed another specialist landscape painter, Matteo da Siena, at S. Stefano Rotondo. Since Matteo had been dead for a decade before the S. Vitale wall frescoes were begun, his participation is out of the question here.

I propose that another landscape specialist, possibly Paul Brill and certainly a close follower of that Flemish master, was responsible for the landscapes on the side walls. Brill himself had already worked for the Jesuits at the Collegio Romano in the early eighties, where he was mentioned a mere two times in the accounts and was paid for materials alone (he was paid 1 scudo per landscape in May 1584), and about the same time that the S. Vitale landscapes were being executed he was painting landscapes in the St Francis Chapel at the Gesù (ca. 1599–1600) in collaboration with a figure painter, possibly Joseph Heintz the Elder. As we will see below, the style of the S. Vitale landscapes is consistent with Brill's work elsewhere, such as at S. Cecilia in Trastevere and the Palazzo Rospigliosi Pallavicini, and the figures are not so large that Brill would have needed to collaborate with a figure painter. The choice of Brill and other Flemish and German artists to execute commissions at the Collegio Romano, S. Vitale, and the Gesù shows that the Jesuits particularly valued the expertise of Northern painters in naturalistic landscape painting. I will return to this point shortly.

Among the last works to be done at S. Vitale were the magnificent wooden doors, which took two years to carve and were completed just in time for the 1609 beatification of the two founders of the Jesuits.[103] These doors depict scenes from the martyrdom of St Vitalis as well as the life of Ignatius of Loyola. In addition to these narrative panels, there are small sculpted images of Vitalis, Valeria, Gervasius and Protasius, and Ignatius, and also Francis Xavier, the 'Apostle to the Indies' and protomissionary. The panels showing the torture and martyrdom of St Vitalis are copied directly from Ciampelli's apse paintings of the same subject, and even appear on the same sides as their models. Some of the other images are also taken from earlier sources. The scenes of Ignatius of Loyola as a pilgrim and during the vision at La Storta are directly inspired by the illustrations in the *Vita beati P. Ignatii Loiolae*, which was published only in 1609 but the drawings for which circulated earlier, and the depiction of St Francis tearing at his shirt comes from a common image of the saint circulated in engravings at the beginning of the century.[104] Golzio attributes these panels to Fiammeri, who was after all primarily a sculptor, while Pietro Pirri assigns them to Giacomo and Gian Paolo Taurino, two Jesuit brothers active at the turn of the century who were living at the Roman Novitiate at the time.[105] I see no reason to doubt Fiammeri's authorship, and even Pirri admits that the style is more like Fiammeri's than that of the Taurino brothers elsewhere: 'It is quite true that the door of S. Vitale, in the decorative areas, is executed with a sobriety and composure of line that distinguishes it notably from the baroque decorative forms of the Taurini.'[106]

Although damaged, and despite several missing frescoes, the interior decoration of S. Vitale has survived sufficiently to allow us to reconstruct its original appearance. The walls are divided in much the same way as in the description in the account books of May 1599, in two passages that delineate the different partitions of the wall decoration.[107] The frescoes are placed in a framework of fictive architecture, so that on the side walls each landscape panel is enclosed between a pair of feigned marble columns, which also enclose an image of a prophet in a false niche or an actual window above; the niche or window is itself framed in a false aedicule with a triangular pediment. The architecture is monumental and boldly three-dimensional, presenting a palatial spectacle with its brightly coloured false marbles and gilded capitals – although the walls are now darkened, and the paintings are destroyed at the bottom owing to an ill-advised rewiring job. The four altarpieces on the walls are *Holy Virgin Martyrs*, *Holy Confessors*, *Immaculate Conception*, and *Christ at Gesthemane* (now lost). At the high altar is *Sts Vitalis, Valeria, Gervasius, and Protasius*, with the altar flanked by scenes of their martyrdom, as is confirmed by a mid-seventeenth-century description: '[It is] all painted with the history of the life and death of St Vitalis, St Valeria his wife, and Sts Gervasius and Protasius their children.'[108] The apse is dominated by Commodi's painting of Christ with the cross surrounded by saints, and the tribune area is flanked by scenes of the triumphs of Samson and Gideon painted in the niches of the triumphal arch. In niches below Ciampelli's frescoes in the tribune stand four dramatic plaster statues of the Doctors of the Church.

The first painting to greet the early seventeenth-century visitor would have been the encyclopaedic panorama of torture instruments that covered the facade of the church over the Early Christian portico (fig. 72). This painting, preserved in an engraving by Greuter in Richeôme's manual, was an example of a recent surge of interest in the symbolic and didactic value of *strumenti di martirio*. The trend was especially favoured in Oratorian circles and was given its widest circulation by Antonio Gallonio's manual on martyrological instruments, *Trattato degli istrumenti di martirio* (1591), but it had already begun to appear in decorative *grotteschi* in church painting in the 1580s, as at the Scala Santa (ca. 1589), or possibly even at S. Spirito in Sassia in the 1570s.[109] Very similar facade frescoes had already been painted the year before (1596) at Cesare Baronio's titular church of SS. Nereo ed Achilleo; they are still visible today, and included bundles of lances, whips, clubs, and other instruments of torture arranged in compartments like heraldic devices. Originally derived from early Christian iconography, these symbols were given a triumphalist character by being bundled together like the weapons (*trofei*) that adorn Roman triumphal arches, in a secular symbolism that had been very popular during the Renaissance. Fiammeri's image is perhaps the most crowded of them all, in that it includes not only a panoply of instruments of torture ranging from wheels armed with razors to claws, pincers, cooking pots, and firebrands, but also seemingly innocuous items the functions of which have been perverted in the name of persecution, such as a drum used to imprison and suffocate Christians. While many of the instruments are generic, such as maces and clubs, others were used for a specific historical persecution, such as the bronze bull in which the tyrant Phalaris of Agrigentum stuffed his victims and which he then placed over a fire so that the sound of their cries would resemble the grunts of a bull, a torture described in canto XXVII of Dante's *Inferno*.[110]

Richeôme uses this fresco as an excuse for a diatribe against the power of Satan to transform every object in the universe into an instrument of cruelty: water and air can be used to suffocate; every kind of animal from lions and dogs to birds and fish can be set to devour the bodies of Christians; and metals, liquids, stones, and trees can similarly be made to serve the devil.[111] Yet despite these horrors Richeôme concludes on a victorious note. The instruments are here to remind us of the struggles we must overcome if we are to serve Christ, and to show us the essential weakness of our fear of death (here he quotes Aristotle), which will be vanquished by our faith.[112] This message concerning the taking up of one's cross and following Christ is also clearly conveyed in the painting itself. At the apex of the jumble of lances, spikes, and wheels, set apart from everything around it, is a cross, 'the cruellest, the most ignominious and abominable instrument of all, upon which Our Lord chose to endure and suffer so that we might live.'[113] The cross at the top of the facade becomes the leitmotif of all of the imagery in the church, and a direct link with the one in Commodi's painting in the apse (fig. 73), the first picture the visitor would see upon entering S. Vitale.

Commodi's fresco is painted in a grand manner and features a procession of figures, arranged as in a classical frieze, who surround and assist the central figure of Christ, fallen under the weight of a giant cross made of logs. The figures are powerful, with sculpted musculature, heroic poses, and splendid, brightly coloured costume. Like the work of Santi di Tito, Commodi's figures are remarkably naturalistic, and there is an attention to detail (especially in the costume) and a luminous light that points also to Northern painters. They are strongly modelled, too, and give a sense of weightiness. The figures are taken from all eras, from antiquity to the present. Particularly dramatic is the soldier on horseback, his mount charging as if to battle, with a flag unfurled. In the sky a rank of cheerful putti shower God's blessings on the crowds below. The fresco is generically inspired by the monumentality of Raphael's frescoes in the Stanza della Segnatura, but it also approaches the liveliness and celebratory tone of such early Baroque frescoes as Annibale's *Triumph of Bacchus* at the Palazzo Farnese (begun 1597), which was being painted at the same time that Commodi was working at S. Vitale, or Guido Reni's *Aurora* at the Palazzo Rospigliosi Pallavicini (1613–14).

The position of the cross itself, on a dramatic diagonal and in the centre of the scene, may have been inspired by Celio's version of the scene in the Passion Chapel in the Gesù (1596) (fig. 100), which also features a rearing horse; that version was itself inspired by Fiammeri's depiction of the same episode in Nadal's *Evangelicae historiae imagines* (1593) (fig. 12). The heavy cross of logs appears also in a version by the Faenza painter Ferraù Fenzoni (1562–1645) at the Galleria Pallavicini in Rome.[114] If S. Vitale's facade is a response to that of SS. Nereo ed Achilleo, Commodi's apse painting has considerably more vigour and energy than the corresponding tribune painting in the Oratorian church. The SS. Nereo ed Achilleo version, done in the iconic style of the Palaeochristian Revival movement, depicts a row of placid male and female martyrs, standing on either side of an empty cross but not engaged in any activity other than quiet devotion (fig. 23). Commodi has also moved far beyond the meek submission of the martyrs in Circignani's collegiate frescoes, with their humble and passive stances and expressions. Richeôme uses military imagery in referring to the angels in this painting: 'Raise your eyes to heaven and look at these immortal squadrons who sang the motet of Glory and Peace during the nativity of this Prince, who now sing a lamentation.'[115]

The narrative energy and triumphal tone are maintained in the frescoes on the tribune walls, beginning with Commodi's own *Decapitation of St Protasius* (fig. 75) and *Flagellation of St Gervasius* (fig. 74). Here, much more so than in Circignani's martyrdoms in the collegiate chapels, the figures are rendered with a sculptural monumentality and powerful torsion, and, in the case of Gervasius, the martyr himself looks out at the viewer with an expression of confrontation and reproach. This change is all the more startling when we realize that Commodi has relied on Circignani's model for the basic layout of the picture. From Circignani he has borrowed the palatial setting and composition, the twisting executioner seen from the back, the generic classical costume, and the judge figure on a throne. The executioner in *Flagellation of St Gervasius* is a more forceful version of the kind of executioner seen in the S. Stefano fresco, and the judge is in the same position as that in fresco XVII (fig. 47). Everywhere there is more emphatic modelling and perspective, with darker shading, so that Circignani's frescoes appear flat by comparison. Commodi's fresco also refers to traditional imagery associated with the flagellation of Christ developed by Sebastiano del Piombo (1525–6) and Federico Zuccaro (early 1570s) (figs 3, 5), with the noteworthy difference that the saint is moved to the right of the picture plane, so the executioners do not flank him but stand to one side. Commodi may have shifted the action to the side owing to the position of the fresco in the tribune, since the protagonist in *Decapitation of St Protasius* is correspondingly centred on the left (fig. 75).

The inscriptions from the sermons of St Bernard (Sermons 43, 47), below, underscore the militant tenor of these paintings. Under the picture of St Gervasius were written these words, recently destroyed when the apse was rewired: PUGNANTEM TE SPECTO, DOMINE, NON SOLUM CORONANTEM: SED UT CORONAM (I look to you in battle, O Lord, not only that you crown me but that you will be my crown); and under that of St Protasius, DOMINE IESU UTRUMQUE EST MIHI, & SPECULUM PATIENDI, & CORONA PATIENTIAE (You, Lord Jesus, are both my mirror of suffering and my crown of patience).

Commodi also painted the high altar, which depicts the family of saints to whom the church is dedicated and who serve as the protagonists of the entire tribune and apse area: Sts Vitalis and Valeria and their twin sons Gervasius and Protasius, dressed in classical costume. Here the saints are shown standing at attention in *contrapposto*, with the same sculptural massiveness found in the narrative frescoes surrounding them. Although there are clouds and angels above, showing God's approbation, the saints stand passively against a plain background in imitation of Early Christian or medieval mosaics or painting. This way of depicting the martyrs at ease but ready for action echoes Cristofano Roncalli's altarpiece at SS. Nereo ed Achilleo, which shows St Domitilla flanked by Nereus and Achilleus, and which would later inspire Rubens's more dramatic version of the same image at the Chiesa Nuova.

The spirit of victorious martyrdom extends into the transept area with the frescoes of Agostino Ciampelli, whose figures have a sculptural quality and energy similar to those in Commodi's scenes, even though the action is less forceful and the scenes more crowded (figs 76–7). The shading here is also less strong, and Ciampelli uses more pastel-like colours. Ciampelli's figures and facial features are more delicate and are without the solidity of his compatriot's, although they share an interest in naturalism with those of Commodi and of their mentor Santi di Tito (fig. 7). Figure 76 also has a rich and detailed landscape showing forests and castles that are lacking in Commodi's frescoes and that help it blend in with the principal landscape martyrdoms on the nave side walls. Like Commodi's narratives flanking the altar, Ciampelli's martyrdoms are inspired by Circignani's prototypes at S. Stefano, but here the artist expands the scenes into a horizontal format.

The two main panels on either side of the transept area are *Stoning of St Vitalis* (fig. 76), on the right, and *Torture of St Vitalis* (fig. 77), on the left. *Stoning of St Vitalis* borrows the figure of the saint in the pit flanked by two shovellers from Circignani's fresco IV (fig. 38), although the saint himself is much closer to the figure in fresco VI (fig. 41). Even the cityscape on the left is a more elaborate and convincingly perspectival version of the kind of background often found in the S. Stefano series. Although Ciampelli's sense of scale is not always convincing – the three men conversing in the middle ground and the men running behind them are somewhat awkward in their setting – the main group, anchored by the two figures with shovels and forming a pyramid with the man throwing the huge stone at the top, is well balanced, solid, and dramatic. This monumentality and energy, together with the prominent landscape setting, anticipates early Baroque painting. The inscription below the painting is not a quotation from scripture or the patristic writings but a simple explanation of the action: s. VITALIS IN FOVEA LAPIDIBUS OBRUITUR (St Vitalis is stoned in a pit).

Ciampelli's corresponding fresco on the left side, showing St Vitalis being put to death on the rack (fig. 77), owes an equally profound debt to Circignani, this time to a scene from S. Tommaso showing the torture of the Jesuits Campion, Sherwin, and Briant (print XXXI in Cavallieri's book), itself taken from William Allen's martyrology (fig. 71).[116] However, Ciampelli has given the figure of the saint greater prominence by raising the rack into the centre of the picture and has placed the scene in a splendid and airy palatial setting reminiscent of Veronese. This is the fresco for which the drawing survives in the Uffizi, and it is interesting to note the changes Ciampelli made when executing the final version of the scene. The drawing tilts the perspective so that there is more space on the left and the main action is concentrated more to the right, a direction stressed by the diagonal position of the rack. Ciampelli treated the perspective in this way for the same reason that Commodi moved his martyrdoms to either side of the frame: he wanted the picture to accommodate to the optical distortions of its setting on the left-hand side of the sanctuary, where the perspective would correct itself when viewed from the nave. Although a subtle shift to the left still exists in the final version of his fresco, Ciampelli has made his composition much more centralized, including the angel above, who is now directly in the centre. Another noteworthy change from the drawing is that Ciampelli has cut off the tops of the columns and eliminated the architrave of the palace loggia, so that the columns seem to be rising infinitely upward, a trick of perspective often used by Venetian painters to give their settings added monumentality. The executioner on the left adds energy to the scene, his body coiled tightly like a spring as he turns the massive wheel of the rack. Again, the inscription below is nothing more than a simple explanation of the action: s. VITALIS EQUULEO TORQUETUR (St Vitalis is tortured on the rack).

Each side fresco is surmounted by a pair of frescoed angels resting on false pediments, and another pair of painted angels rests on the real pediments of the doors below. Both sides of the tribune arch are also flanked by smaller narrative paintings by Ciampelli, *Triumph of Samson* and *Triumph of Gideon*, that bring the narrative of the entire tribune area to a victorious conclusion. These frescoes are smaller and therefore less dramatic than the large scenes on the side walls, and the figures are less prominent. The tableaux are enclosed in illusionistic frames, and each has an inscription above and below, the upper one from scripture. The Gideon scene is surmounted by a quotation from Judges 7:19 describing the troops of Gideon at the edge of the camp: CUM HYDRIAS CONFREGISSENT TENUERUNT SINISTRIS MANIBUS LAMPADES (They broke the pitchers and held the lamps in their left hands): underneath it is an inscription giving the scene a christological meaning: LACERATIS CORPORIBUS CHRISTI SPLENDOR EMICUIT ET SONUS EXIIT AD VICTORIAM (The splendour of Christ shines forth from their tortured bodies, and the sound to victory is heard). As Richeôme explains, Christ is Gideon and his apostles and martyrs are the hundred men who marched with Gideon, their lamps representing the light of their virtue.[117] Especially noteworthy is the scene of Samson, which shows him standing before the carcass of a lion that leaks honey and is surrounded by bees. This image is the answer to the riddle Samson asks the Philistines, which is inscribed above: DE COMEDENTE EXIVIT CIBUS, & DE SORTI EGRESSA EST DULCENDO (Out of the eater came forth food, and out of the strong came forth sweetness [Judg. 14:14]), but it also appears in Gallonio's *Emblematica sacra* (1589, emblem IV) as a symbol of martyrdom. The martyrological meaning is taken up by the inscription below: IN ORE MORTIS A CHRISTO INTEREMPTO MARTYRES MEL INVENIUNT (At the brink of death, met by Christ, martyrs find honey). Richeôme compares Christ to Samson, and Samson's killing of the lion is a metaphor for Christ's vanquishing of the devil.[118]

Flanking the two main panels by Ciampelli are stucco figures in niches representing the four Doctors of the Church, each with an inscription from a sermon that exhorts the viewer not to fear the pains of martyrdom. As Golzio and Macioce suggest, these are very likely the work of Fiammeri himself, since stucco sculpture was his forte.[119] Below *Torture of St Vitalis* are St Gregory on the right, with the words MARTYRES TOLERANT SCISSURAS VULNERUM & ALIIS PROFERUNT MEDICAMENTUM SANITATIS (Martyrs endure tearing of wounds and give to others medicine for health), and St Jerome on the left, with the words BASILICAS MARTYRUM DAEMONES FUGIUNT FORTITUDINEM & FLAGELLA SANCTI CINERIS NON FERENTES (Demons flee the churches of martyrs; they cannot endure the force and blows of their holy ashes).[120] Below *Stoning of St Vitalis* are St Ambrose on the left, with the words PRAEMIUM FECIT RELIGIO, QUOD PERFIDIA PUTABAT ESSE SUPPLICATUM (Religion makes its prize from what unbelief thought a punishment), and St Augustine on the right, with the words QUID ERIT CUM CORPORIS INCORRUPTIONE FONS VITAE QUANDO ROS EIUS INTER TORMENTA TAM DULCIS EST? (What will the font of life be like with an incorrupt body, since its dew is so sweet in the midst of torment?). These plaster figures are quite remarkable for their time, since they burst boldly from the confines of their niches and gaze outward in a way that would become typical in the work of High Baroque sculptors, as in Gianlorenzo Bernini's *St Longinus* at St Peter's (1629–38). What distinguishes them from Baroque sculpture is the drapery, which hangs somewhat stiffly and fails to cooperate with the sense of movement suggested by the poses of the figures. The head of the St Jerome figure resembles that of Michelangelo's *Moses* at S. Pietro in Vincoli.

The four side altarpieces present the viewer with a concise compendium of 'All Saints' such as we have seen at the Novitiate and in the collegiate churches, including Christ, the Virgin Mary, female saints, and male saints. At the two altars closest to the door are Fiammeri's triumphant canvases *Holy Virgin Martyrs* (fig. 78) on the right and *Holy Confessors* (fig. 79) on the left. Brilliantly coloured and with bold figures, these paintings carry the celebratory tone of the tribune and transept area into the main body of the church. Each shows a group of saints from all walks of life, including nobles, the poor, priests, monks, and a pope, gathered in a semicircle, illuminated with the golden light of divine approval from above, and accompanied by flying cherubs. The painting on the right side is the more militant, with the monumental figures of fourteen female martyrs standing in proud *contrapposto* and looking as if ready to march into battle.[121] In addition to the palm of martyrdom, each holds her emblem, so that we can identify Sts Catherine, Agatha, Martha, Margaret, Thecla, Lucy, Agnes, Barbara, Cecilia, Anastasia, Prisca, Emerentiana, and Bibiana. On the floor, rendered in a checkerboard pattern of red and white marble, are scattered broken instruments of torture and a pagan altar, as well as petals and blossoms representing divine grace. Typical of Fiammeri are the straight, classicizing noses, large eyes, and pouty lips of the faces, as well as the robustness and heavy drapery of the figures, all of which are found in his drawings and in his work at the Gesù.[122] Especially characteristic are the eyebrows, which link with the nose high above the eyes, forming a single line and making the already bulging eyes seem larger than they really are, as well as the outline invariably painted under the eyes.

The same stylistic features are found in the opposite picture, *Holy Confessors*, which Macioce puzzlingly attributes to Penitz (Heintz the Elder). This canvas shows eleven male saints, including Sts Silvester, Athanasius, John Chrysostom, Basil, Gregory Nazianzen, Ambrose, Augustine, Jerome, Gregory the Great, and Bernard. It is curious that the picture represents confessors rather than martyrs, since the corresponding female saints are martyrs and martyrdom is the principal theme of the church. Here the mood is less militant, as the men seem to be huddling together to hear the word of God instead of marching off to war like the women across from them. There is also no central figure like that of St Catherine to lead the way. Nevertheless, the triumphant spirit of the picture is loudly proclaimed by the golden light from above and the bright colours of the clothing, and the men come from a similar variety of backgrounds – as Richeôme reminds us, 'churchmen, laymen, nobles, the rich, the poor, captains, soldiers, judges, religious, hermits, and every sort of man.'[123] The facial features, especially the eyes and aquiline noses, attest to Fiammeri's hand. So does the figure of St Jerome, whose face is virtually identical to that of St Peter in a drawing by Fiammeri in the Louvre (fig. 11).[124] Both pictures are accompanied by quotations from scripture. The architrave of the altar of female saints bears a paraphrase from the Psalms: ADDUCENTUR REGI VIRGINES POST EAM (The virgins shall be brought to the king after her; derived from 'She shall be brought unto the king … the virgins her companions that follow her shall be brought unto thee' [Ps. 45:14]). Above the painting of the male saints are the words QUI SUNT CHRISTI CARNEM SUAM CRUCIFIXERUNT (And they that are Christ's have crucified their flesh [Gal. 5:24]).

The next pair of altarpieces (only one of which survives today) are also traditionally attributed to Fiammeri. On the right is *Immaculate Conception*, a subject that would become increasingly popular throughout the Catholic world and on the Jesuit missions (the Italian Jesuit painter Bernardino Bitti painted several versions in Peru in the 1580s and 1590s) but that was unusual in early Jesuit commissions in Italy. The painting can be related to Fiammeri's other work on stylistic grounds, despite Macioce's reluctance to accept the attribution. The cherub heads, with their exaggerated foreshortening, are particularly close to those of Fiammeri's *Holy Virgin Martyrs*, as is the face of the Virgin, which has the same stencilled eyebrows, elongated nose, and pouty mouth. The Virgin is shown in a garden with her mysterious symbols, an imagery that would soon be the focus of a tract by the Jesuit Jan David called *Pancarpium marianum* (Garden of Mary, Antwerp, 1607) and of another painting attributed to Fiammeri at the Istituto S. Maria in Aquiro.[125] These symbols are related to the extremely popular Litany of Loreto, which encouraged the worshipper to meditate on the Virgin Mary by meditating on symbols of her – Seat of Wisdom, Tower of David, Tower of Ivory, House of Gold, Ark of the Covenant, Gate of Heaven, Mystical Rose, Morning Star, Cedar of Lebanon, and so on – that come ultimately from the Song of Songs and from elsewhere in the Old Testament, such as the Books of Genesis, Numbers, and Kings.[126] The inscription appended to this altar is taken from the Book of Sirach, so favoured in the Novitiate infirmary, and names another of the Virgin's attributes: VAS ADMIRABILE & OPUS EXCELSI (An admirable instrument, the work of the Most High [Ecclus. 43:2]). The inscription over the lost painting *Agony in the Garden*, on the left side of the church, proclaimed a powerful millennialist message of healing and salvation, with a passage from Isaiah that is echoed almost verbatim in Luke: UT MEDERER CONTRITIS CORDE ([He hath sent me] to heal the contrite of heart [Isa. 61:1; Luke 4:18]). The painting itself was meant to remind the viewer that even Christ trembled before his own martyrdom.[127]

Above two of the altarpieces and some of the martyrdoms are figures of Old Testament prophets, an allegorical figure, and Jesus, all holding scrolls with commentary on the theme of martyrdom. Most of the texts come from the Old Testament and provide a counterpart to the quotations from the patristic works in the tribune area. These figures, which may be by Commodi, are set within Ligustri's illusionistic niches. Beginning above *Agony in the Garden* there is King David standing between two lions with the words PRECIOSA IN CONSPECTU DOMINI MORS SANCTORUM EIUS (Precious in the sight of the Lord is the death of his saints [Ps. 115:15]). Near *Holy Confessors* is Jesus with words from Matthew 10:32: QUI ME CONFESSUS FUERIT (Whosoever therefore shall confess me [before men, him will I confess also before my Father which is in heaven]). Near *Holy Virgin Martyrs* is a female allegory of the Church, holding a scroll that may have borne an inscription from Proverbs: MELIOR EST QUI DOMINATUR ANIMO SUO EXPUGNATORE URBIUM (He that ruleth his spirit [is better] than he that taketh cities [Prov. 16:32]).[128] Close to *Immaculate Conception* is a figure of Solomon with the words FORTITUDO, & DECOR INDUMENTUM EIUS (Strength and beauty are her clothing [Prov. 31:25]). Other prophets are found above some of the martyrdom scenes, alternating with the clerestory windows. These include Zechariah (13:9), with the words URAM EOS

SICUT URITUR ARGENTUM ([And I will bring the third part through the fire,] and will refine them as silver is refined, [and will try them as gold is tried]); the refinement of silver serves as a symbol not only of martyrdom but of the Novitiate itself, 'God's great house of probation, where all the children of his heritage must be formed, and where they must pass to perfection and to the possession of immortal glory.'[129] There are also triumphant words by Jeremiah: DOMINUS MECUM EST QUASI BELLATOR FORTIS (But the Lord is with me as a strong warrior [Jer. 20:11]); by Daniel: FULGEBUNT IUSTI (And they that be wise shall shine [as the brightness of the firmament] [Dan. 12:3]); by Micah: TRANSIBIT REX EORUM CORAM EIS & DOMINUS IN CAPITE EORUM (And their King shall pass before them, and the Lord at the head of them [Mich. 2:13]); and by Joel, who ends on an appropriately pastoral note: GERMINAVERUNT SPECIOSA DESERTI QUIA LIGNUM ATTULIT FRUCTUM SUUM ([Fear not, ye beasts of the fields:] for the beautiful places of the wilderness are sprung, for the tree hath brought forth its fruit [Joel 2:22]).

The rest of the nave and back wall are dominated by the landscape martyrdom scenes, the natural settings of which are so prominent that they give the visitor the sense of being in a forest instead of a church (figs 80, 81). In fact, the interior, with its combination of architecture and countryside, resembles a grand garden pergola. Like the S. Stefano cycle, the S. Vitale martyrdoms emphasize the universality of the Church by means of geography, with scenes representing every part of the ancient world from Rome to the Crimea, Armenia, Asia Minor, and Egypt. At the same time, through a careful choice of saints, they reinforce the primacy of Rome and the papacy, and like the earlier Jesuit martyrdom cycles they hold up the period of the early Church as an example for contemporary Christians. They also have a similar catalogue-like arrangement, since the martyrdoms are divided according to Roman imperial reigns, and the names of the relevant emperors are listed below each panel. As in the earlier cycles, the S. Vitale frescoes relate their subjects to the calendar of the Roman Church by listing the saint's feast day below the painting, although there are no key letters as in their earlier counterparts. The S. Vitale martyrdoms also use the same archaic device of presenting more than one episode in a single scene.

Stylistically, however, the S. Vitale landscapes are a world apart from the S. Apollinare, S. Stefano, and S. Tommaso frescoes. Whereas those used landscape merely as the setting for terrifying images of human suffering, here the suffering is diminished by making the tiny figures meld into the landscape. Trees and bushes, virtually absent in the Circignani cycles, overwhelm any buildings or man-made structures. Human beings are as small as mites, sketched with only the most summary of brushstrokes and often virtually devoid of facial features. They bear no weight, and flit about on the cliffs and in the woods like fairies. Even the instruments of torture, such an important aspect of the facade and tribune of this church itself, are minimized and can barely be made out in the copses and valleys of the landscape. The same impressionistic dotting and dabbing of the brush characterizes not only the figures but the trees, rocks, and grasses, with the result that the whole image is subordinated to a gentle, breezy sense of movement. In the S. Vitale landscape frescoes martyrdom looks almost like fun.

The subjects of the martyrdoms range from the familiar to the obscure. The first on the left wall of the church shows the martyrdom under Trajan of St Clement (fig. 80), who as Peter's third successor as pope and a champion of orthodoxy was a symbol of Roman authority. Although it is difficult to make out what the gossamer figures in this scene are actually doing, Clement is shown in his reputed exile in the Crimea, where he played the part of an apostle, baptizing the people, building churches, and destroying temples, before his martyrdom on the end of an anchor tossed into the sea – a scene that would resonate strongly with the young novices preparing for the overseas missions.

The dehumanization of the S. Vitale martyrdoms becomes apparent in a comparison of this martyrdom of St Clement with a contemporary fresco of the same subject by Agostino Ciampelli, the author of the S. Vitale transept paintings, in a lunette in the Sacrestia dei Canonici at St John Lateran (ca. 1600). The two paintings contain the same basic elements, in keeping with the iconography of the scene, and also probably because the two artists were in contact with each other during the execution of the paintings. These features include the crowds of people in the background, representing Clement's flock in exile, the rolling hills dotted with buildings and cities, and the protagonist being thrown off a promontory. But Ciampelli's figures are giants given the size of the lunette and the background, and they have the powerful musculature and dramatic gestures of his S. Vitale frescoes. The artist contrasts this feeling of oppressive weight with the perilous fragility of the ledge of rock that supports the figures. The anchor tied to St Clement is larger than he is, and the figure to the saint's left kicks him off the rock with believable force. Nothing could be further from the S. Vitale version, which is dominated not by the precipice from which the saint is cast – here it is reduced to a small ledge barely visible at the lower left – but by a huge and purely decorative rocky outcropping covered with trees that is balanced on the other side by an even larger hardwood tree in the foreground. Whereas Ciampelli positions the main action in the centre of the picture and adds a sense of drama by accenting the diagonal of the cliff, the S. Vitale painter leaves most of the centre open for a placid view of a valley. Although Ciampelli's picture is not entirely free of decorative elements (his waves are quite stylized), the S. Vitale image has an anecdotal quality and looks more like a conglomeration of details than a unified scene. The inscription below states plainly, S. CLEMENS ROM. IN INSULA LYCIA TRIANO IMP. DIE XXIII NOVEME (St Clement, Roman, on the island of Lycia under the Emperor Trajan, 23 November).

The next martyr shown is St Januarius, a great patron of Naples, who might have been chosen in honour of the church's Neapolitan patroness, Isabella della Rovere. Januarius is shown undergoing torture and decapitation with his six companions at Pozzuoli, near Naples. The inscription summarizes, S. IANUARIUS EP.US AD SULPHURARIUM PUTEOLANAM DIOCLET.A ET MAXIM.O IMP. DIE XIX SEPTEM (St Januarius, bishop, in the sulphur pit at Pozzuoli under Emperors Diocletian and Maximian, 19 September). The next scene transports us to Cappadocia, where forty Christian soldiers in the army of Constantine's brother Licinius are put to death for their beliefs by being stripped naked and made to stand in the middle of a frozen pond in Little Armenia. The inscription reads, S.S. QUADRAGINTA MILITES AD SEBASTEN ARMENIAE URBE REGE LICINIO DIE IX MARTII (Forty soldier saints in the city of Sebastea in Armenia, under King Licinius, 9 March). This scene, the protagonists of which are not even known by name, was obviously chosen because it served as a perfect symbol of Christians as soldiers of Christ, and fit into the generally militaristic imagery elsewhere in the church. The last fresco on the left wall depicts the martyrdoms of four more Christian soldiers, this time Sts Martinian, Saturian, and their two brothers in Egypt. These unfortunate men were beaten with rods and pierced with spikes, yet during their subsequent exile in the deserts of Africa they attracted crowds of Christian and pagan Moors, who serve in the picture here as a symbol of missionary work. After converting many pagans the saints were put to death by roasting. The entire fresco and its inscription have been destroyed.

The right wall begins with the martyrdom of St Ignatius, bishop of Antioch, one of the most celebrated victims of Trajan's persecution. Although clearly selected because he shared a name with the founder of the Society of Jesus, Ignatius was also the first person to adopt the name 'Christian' and is therefore an important symbol of Christian identity. Ignatius is shown being attacked by three lions in front of a ruined Colosseum, the largest architectural element in the landscape paintings; the whole composition recalls Circignani's and Tempesta's gladiatorial scenes at S. Stefano Rotondo (fig. 42). He is accompanied by the inscription s. IGNATIUS EPISCOPUS ROMAE TRAIANO IMP. DIE I FEBR (St Ignatius, bishop, at Rome under Emperor Trajan, 1 February). The next painting, now very heavily damaged, comes by its wooded setting naturally. It depicts the decapitations of Sts Marcellinus and Peter the priest in a forest near Rome known as the Black Forest, saints whose bodies would be buried on the Via Labicana in a place known as Two Laurels. The inscription reads, S.S. MARCELLINUS ET PETRUS ROMAEAN SYLVA NIGRA DIOCLETIANO IMP. DIE II JUNII (Sts Marcellinus and Peter, in the Roman Black Forest, under Emperor Diocletian, 2 June).

The next painting, which has survived in the best condition and features a pleasing rosy sunset, is one of the most frequently reproduced. The scene shows St Paphnutius the monk being murdered in Egypt under Diocletian (fig. 81). In a scene of crucifixion highly appropriate to a forest setting (although a forest like this could hardly be found in Egypt), Paphnutius is shown nailed hand and foot to a palm tree and left to die a slow death. Although the scene is superficially similar to that in Circignani's fresco of the martyrdom of St Felicity (fresco X), the body of poor Paphnutius is so inconsequential that it seems to blend into the very bark of the tree. The inscription reads, s. PAPHNUTIUS MONACHUS IN AEGYPTO DIOCLETIANO IMP. DIE XXIV SEPT. (St Paphnutius, monk, in Egypt under Emperor Diocletian, 24 September). The final fresco on the right wall brings the group to a resoundingly military conclusion. The painting shows St Andrew, not the apostle but the Roman tribune and captain, together with his troops, 'freshly massacred' by the troops of Antiochus, an Asian general and tyrant, looking like petals scattered on the forest floor.[130] The inscription reads, s.s. ANDREAS DUX EXERCITUS ET SOCII IN CILICIA MAXIMIANO IMP. DIE XIX AUG. (St Andrew the captain and his companions, in Cilicia, under Emperor Maximian, 19 August).

The last two martyrdom frescoes, now damaged and hard to see, are on the end wall. To the right of the door is the martyrdom of St Victor and St Corona. Victor was decapitated in Syria by a judge named Sebastian who had inflicted a litany of tortures upon the unfortunate man, using a surprising number of the instruments of martyrdom depicted on the facade. Corona was a soldier's wife, one of the few women martyrs depicted in the landscape martyrdoms, who converted upon watching Victor's death and who was – in an appropriately sylvan punishment – torn in four by having her arms and legs tied to four trees. The inscription reads, S.S. VICTOR ET CORONA IN SYRIA ANTONIO IMP. DIE XIV MAII (Sts Victor and Corona, in Syria, under Emperor Antoninus, 14 May). The final fresco, on the left side of the door, presents an especially nasty torture related closely to its wooded setting and in keeping with the military theme of the church. The first martyr depicted, whose name is not given, is a soldier in Thebes, who is stripped naked, covered with milk and honey, and tied to a tree. There, exposed to flies and hornets, not to mention the hot Egyptian sun, the miserable wretch dies a slow and exquisitely painful death. His companion, who is more a symbol of chastity than a martyr, is a man from the same region who bites off his own tongue rather than talk back to a courtesan whom his captors were trying to have seduce him. These dreadful scenes are placed against a setting of elegantly waving cypresses. The inscription summarizes, XPI MILES FUCIS EXPONINTUR IN AEGYP. DECIO ET VALERIANO IMPP DIE XXVII [...] (Christian soldiers sent into exile in Egypt, under Emperors Decius and Valerian, 27 [...]). It is probably no coincidence that the scene brings us back to the motif of honey as a symbol for martyrdom, a theme introduced in Ciampelli's fresco of Samson on the side of the tribune.

It was quite rare, at this early stage in the development of Italian landscape painting, for a major series of frescoes to give such emphasis to the natural element at the expense of the human. One early exception can be found in the work of Polidoro da Caravaggio (ca. 1500–43), who introduced the genre in Rome as early as the 1520s with his wall paintings (not frescoes, but oil), in the chapel of Fra Marino Fetti in S. Silvestro al Quirinale, of the lives of the Magdalene and of St Catherine of Siena (ca. 1525). In a remarkable innovation inspired by classical Roman landscape painting and enlivened by antiquity's typical impressionistic brushwork, Polidoro painted scenes that came close to pure landscape: 'Their subject matter becomes irrelevant, for not figures, but the mood of noble nature pervades the pictures.'[131] Yet Polidoro's series still paid considerable attention to architectural elements, such as *tempietti* and classical townscapes, features all but suppressed in the S. Vitale paintings. A classicizing setting also characterized the work of a group of Northerners and second-tier Italian painters active in Rome in the second half of the century, who painted the landscapes in the background of other peoples' paintings and whose reputations were also relegated to the background. One who rose above the rest was Matteo da Siena, the painter of the landscapes in the Jesuit collegiate chapels of the early 1580s – and therefore the pioneer of the Jesuit landscape genre – who, in the words of Richard Turner, was 'the first man to grasp the principles of Polidoro's art.'[132] Another was Paul Brill, who became the most sought-after landscape painter of the late sixteenth century and who, in Wittkower's words, 'held a key position in the process of assimilating Flemish landscape painting into Italy.'[133]

Brill made his debut in Rome at the Torre de' Venti in the Vatican, where in 1583 he worked under his brother Mattheus (d. 1584) on a large and important landscape cycle, heavily inspired by the Roman genre, featuring narrow, almost Chinese-looking rock outcroppings and tiny, toylike temples, bridges, and towns. After painting the Collegio Romano landscapes the next year as an act of charity for the Jesuits, Brill painted two cycles for Sixtus V that would rank among the most important of his career – a cycle at the Scala Santa (1588) including the story of Jonah and the whale, and a series of lunettes in the *piano nobile* of the nearby Lateran Palace (1588–9); he also worked for the same pope at the Sixtine Chapel in S. Maria Maggiore. Brill gave these landscapes the characteristic agitated brushstrokes and near pastel colours that would become typical of his work in fresco, dominated by light greens, yellows, blues, and greys. The abundance of surface detail gave them a certain flatness and decorative quality that was enhanced by the figures, which were so airy and weightless they seemed to float. In 1599–1600, Brill collaborated with Francesco Vanni, Giovanni Baglione, and Guido Reni on the decoration of Cardinal Paolo Emilio Sfondrato's titular church of S. Cecilia, one of the most important renovations of the Palaeochristian Revival.[134] There, Brill executed a series of landscape martyrdoms very like the ones at S. Vitale in the corridor leading to the Calidarium. The artist continued to enjoy success as a papal painter during this period; Clement VIII hired him in 1602 to paint a monumental seascape *Martyrdom of St Clement* at the Sala Clementina, as well as some *paesetti* of famous monasteries in the adjacent salotto, around the time that the S. Vitale frescoes were being painted.[135]

The S. Vitale cycle shares many features with these last two commissions, especially the S. Cecilia series, and if the anonymous artist was not Brill he was clearly a close follower, and probably a Northerner. The relative scale of the figures and the landscape in the S. Cecilia scenes is very close to that in the S. Vitale scenes, and even the Sala Clementina fresco, grander in keeping with its size and location in a papal audience hall, has much smaller figures than Ciampelli's version of the same episode at the Lateran. At S. Cecilia, the landscapes also have the emptiness in the centre typical of the S. Vitale series, and the same agitated, choppy treatment of the clouds, which is sometimes echoed in the leaves as well. Also very close is the treatment of the individual leaves of the hardwood trees, which are often reduced to oval dabs with a characteristic 'bite' taken out of one side. All the frescoes treat architectural elements in a decorative manner, constructing them of volutes, cartouches, and other fanciful details, a technique visible, for example, in the little tomb at the lower right in *Martyrdom of St Clement* at S. Vitale (fig. 80), and in the boat in the same scene at the Sala Clementina. The toylike *tempietti* in the upper left of the Sala Clementina fresco are also similar in spirit if not in detail to those of the S. Vitale scene. The S. Cecilia series has much more in common with the S. Vitale paintings than with the Sala Clementina fresco, since the two were done in a hurry in the artist's *pennello ordinario* instead of with the more careful and structured brush used in the papal commission, and have a loose and impressionistic feel. The S. Vitale series was begun while the paint was still wet at S. Cecilia; Brill received his final payment for that cycle on 16 December 1600.[136]

Pamela Jones has traced some of the paintings from Brill's S. Cecilia series to a series of engravings of hermits in landscapes by Jan Baptist Collaert I, after drawings by Marten de Vos, entitled *Solitudo, sive vitae foeminarum anachoretarum* (undated).[137] Brill, who was a printmaker himself and frequently used the engravings of his compatriots, also copied another pair of engravings by Jan and Raphael Sadeler in his *Landscape with Mutius* and *Landscape with Anub*, two hermit portraits executed for Federico Borromeo and now in the Pinacoteca Ambrosiana in Milan; and he used the same series as an inspiration for his *St Paul the Hermit*, a small copper painting in Arezzo. Perhaps prints also served as an inspiration for the S. Vitale series, although I have not been able to identify a source in the work of the Sadelers or Collaert.

The S. Vitale and S. Cecilia landscapes represent nothing less than a revolution in Roman painting – and one that has received little acknowledgment. Paintings in which human figures are hardly more than accents in the landscape were very rare after Polidoro, and even Polidoro and the earlier Brill and his followers pay more attention to classical architecture and human figures than we see here at the end of the century. The introduction into Italian painting of landscapes in which human figures played a role secondary to that of nature has traditionally been associated more with the early Baroque, especially with the first decades of the 1600s and Emilian painters such as Annibale and Domenichino, who were themselves inspired by the Northern tradition, but via Venice. Typical is this summary of late Cinquecento painting by Richard Turner, who sees a gap between Polidoro and Annibale: 'We close on a note of anticlimax, in Rome of the 1580's where landscape was valued as decoration but hardly as a serious genre of painting. Yet all of this was to change with the advent of Annibale Carracci, who brought the lessons of Venice to Rome, and developed a landscape art worthy of Polidoro's precocious suggestions.'[138] The idealized landscapes of a Domenichino have a much more tamed look than the work of Brill, and their careful construction has a specifically Italian and classicizing spirit, but that does not mean we should ignore the role played by Brill and his followers in the legitimization of self-contained landscape painting as a Roman genre immediately prior to the first of these Emilian contributions. It is characteristic of the lack of attention the scholarship has paid to this transitional period between Renaissance and Baroque that neither the S. Cecilia nor the S. Vitale cycle is reproduced in any of the major surveys of Cinquecento painting in Italy.[139]

This iconographic revolution was not merely stylistic, but went deeper, into the very heart of the Jesuit understanding of *ad maiorem Dei gloriam*, 'to the greater glory of God.' For the Jesuits, landscape represented the created world, the natural reflection of divine glory in which the meditative viewer could meet God in his least creation. This *Spiritual Exercises* exhort the reader to 'reflect how God dwells in creatures: in the elements giving them existence, in the plants giving them life, in the animals conferring upon them sensation, in man bestowing understanding' (par. 235).[140] Instead of seeing landscape as an agglomeration of symbolic plants and trees, as in the S. Vitale gardens discussed by Richeôme, or as an appropriate setting for biblical figures as in the 'composition of place,' the S. Vitale frescoes used the landscape itself to elevate the mind to celestial things. This approach to landscape was shared by Cardinal Federico Borromeo, archbishop of Milan in

1595–1631 and Brill's patron.[141] Borromeo made a practice of contemplating paintings of landscapes in his study at the archiepiscopal palace, and in treatises such as *De pictura sacra* (Milan, 1624) he wrote about landscape as allowing us to marvel at God's ability to create an orderly and harmonious universe.[142] This contemplation of birds and fish from another of his devotional works, *I tre libri delle laudi divine* (Milan, 1632), gives an idea of what might have been going through a Jesuit's mind as he looked at the S. Vitale frescoes: 'After which consideration [the habits of birds], entering thoughtfully into the most ample fields of the sea, then we will find schools of fish, which, in addition to their number, with enormous greatness of types, provides us testimony of the generosity of that Lord who produced them.'[143] Here Borromeo demonstrates a view he expressed elsewhere as well, that it was precisely by contemplating God's smallest and lowliest creations that we are reminded of his glory. The most important element of a landscape painting was the landscape itself, not the human subject, be it a hermit or a martyr. As Jones has commented, 'To Borromeo, the spiritual significance of landscape paintings was imbedded in the very creatures, objects, formations, and natural phenomena themselves rather than being dependent upon the work's containing religious figures or narratives.'[144] Herein, I believe, lies the key to the S. Vitale paintings. It is not the tiny, insect-like martyrs themselves who matter, but the awesome natural settings that reduce them and all humanity to comparative insignificance.

The church of S. Vitale exercised a very different pastoral role from that of any of the structures considered so far. The Novitiate paintings were directed at an exclusively Jesuit audience, and at a particular kind of Jesuit – a young novice beginning to contemplate life as a religious. The painting cycles in the colleges were directed both at young men contemplating life in the priesthood – yet few of them as Jesuits – and at laymen who were expected to serve Christ in the world, and they also interacted with the surrounding community, especially on certain feast days related to the churches' patron saints. S. Vitale was an even more public church. Although tied to the Novitiate like the smaller church of S. Andrea, S. Vitale was conceived primarily as a civic church, one that could advertise the good works of the Society of Jesus to the world at large. Its role was therefore similar to that of the Gesù, the chapel decoration of which was just being completed at the same time. But whereas the mother church was also a grand statement of Farnese glory, the humbler S. Vitale belonged more entirely to the Jesuits.

In his history and diary of life at the Novitiate, Ottavio Navarola shows how actively S. Vitale participated in the lives of the people of Rome, local residents and pilgrims alike. The church was especially busy on Wednesday mornings, when it was thronged with visitors eager to hear the novices preach or to take catechism lessons, in numbers that by 1610 often reached five hundred people at a time:[145]

> Every week on Wednesday morning in our church of S. Vitale, or on another morning if this one were perhaps impossible, Christian doctrine is taught to the poor, catechizing them every half hour, singing the litany of the Madonna, things to do with Christian doctrine, and spiritual matters ... and a continuous throng of about four hundred passed through it in good order ... from every nation and language, and

upon other occasions it has happened that some people have come who are completely ignorant of the articles of the faith, who do not even know perhaps the sign of
the Holy Cross, or the Paternoster or Ave Maria.[146]

It is this public aspect of S. Vitale that Richeôme chooses as the final theme of his
almost eight-hundred-page manual on imagery. It is depicted in the well-known
engraving in his book showing the full spectrum of Roman society in the church,
each group being addressed by a Jesuit novice or priest, and each representing one
of the Jesuits' works of spiritual mercy (such as instructing the ignorant) or
corporal mercy (such as feeding the hungry or visiting the sick), or else their
administering of one of the sacraments of the Church (such as confession) (fig. 82).

Richeôme's is a utopian vision, one that recalls a famous Franciscan engraving
by Fray Diego de Valadés, from his *Rhetorica christiana* (Perugia, 1579), showing an
ideal mission in early colonial Mexico, with a huge patio in which different groups
of Indians are ministered to by missionaries, each group symbolizing one of the
sacraments.[147] It is also an international vision, informed by the world missions in
which the Jesuits had already built their reputation, taking the mantle from their
Franciscan predecessors. Richeôme underscores this universal message. At the
end of his book he leaves us with a glowing description of S. Vitale's pastoral
activities that serves as an extended metaphor for Pentecost, that moment in Acts
when all Christ's people speak in one tongue, symbolizing the universal message
of Christianity: 'You will see Italians, Germans, Poles, Bohemians, Hungarians,
Flemings, Walloons, Irish, Scots, English, Greeks, Spanish, French, and other
nations of Christianity, and all are taught in their mother tongue, and each of you
have your separate group and your school in the same place, and without confusion.' He concludes, like St Peter, by exhorting his followers to acknowledge the
global range of their charitable works, and to let the message of S. Vitale reach 'not
only you, but also everyone who dresses like you, in other similar houses placed
on the five parts of the habitable world.'[148]

6

The Church of the Gesù in Rome: Documents

The Gesù is one of the most crucial buildings in late Renaissance Italy. Whether recognized as the last work of the Renaissance or the first work of the Baroque, this monumental church dominated the architectural life of Central Italy in the late sixteenth and early seventeenth centuries. Ever since the English traveller Grey Bridges (1620) marvelled at the 'gloriousness of their Altars, infinit number of images' the Jesuits used to 'catch men's affections, and ... ravish their understanding,' and long before the French critic and historian Hippolyte-Adolphe Taine (1828–93) compared the building to a 'magnificent banquet hall in a royal town house,' friends and enemies of the Jesuits have held up the Gesù as the embodiment of either Catholic reform or mundane sensuality.[1] In a less polemic way – although one by no means free of these earlier prejudices – the Gesù has also dominated Renaissance and Baroque architectural history. Book-length studies, innumerable articles, and a guaranteed reference in even the most basic art history surveys have earned the Gesù a permanent place in the canon. Scholars ranging from Carlo Galassi Paluzzi in the 1920s, Pio Pecchiai and Pietro Pirri in the 1950s and 1960s, and Rudolf Wittkower and James Ackerman in the 1970s to Klaus Schwager, Richard Bösel, and Clare Robertson in the 1980s and 1990s have deepened our understanding of the architectural significance of this most critical of monuments in the transition between the Renaissance and the Baroque era.[2] Yet comparably few – Pecchiai, Howard Hibbard, and Alessandro Zuccari are among them – have looked inside the walls of this imposing and palatial church to consider what the original decorations were like, especially those that predated the major revisions of the second half of the seventeenth century – the great ceiling painting by Baciccio, and the sumptuous altarpieces of the by-then canonized Ignatius of Loyola and Francis Xavier in the transepts, the first being by that master of perspective art, the Jesuit Andrea Pozzo.[3] It was the transformed interior, triumphantly Baroque in spirit and sumptuous in material, that captured the imagination of latter-day viewers, and not the interior that greeted visitors at the beginning of the seventeenth century, with its subtler opulence and its message of salvation and victory in the name of Jesus.

In this chapter, following a 'state of the question' review of contemporary scholarship of the Gesù interior and a brief biographical sketch of the artists who worked on the commission, I will present all the existing documentation relating to the conception, execution, and reception of the first decorations of the Gesù and the Casa Professa, from the 1580s through the first decade of the seventeenth century. The sources include manuscript contracts, account books, letters, legal documents, and diaries, as well as early printed sources, among them biographies of the artists and descriptions of Rome. Although about two-thirds of these sources have been cited in previous literature, they have never been treated in a systematic and unified way, and many lacunae and disagreements are to be found. The other third of these sources has never been published before. I have chosen to present this material in the form of a narrative instead of as a catalogue of appendices, because a narrative ties the account together more clearly and allows for a more vivid presentation of the chronology of the decorations. A narrative approach also permits me to make hypotheses, debate points, and analyse the data with the documents in hand. Using the sources, I will attempt to date and attribute the paintings, stucco work, and sculptures of the nave chapels, the transepts and apse area, the chapels flanking the apse, the west wall, and the sacristy. Owing to the great volume of material, I will leave most considerations of style, iconography, and audience to chapter 7, where I will focus on the interpretation of the paintings as a paradigm of Jesuit iconography and look at their function in Early Modern Rome in general.

Overview of the Scholarship of the Gesù

The first paintings of the Gesù have suffered much more than the architecture from scholarly polemics. The unenthusiastic scholarly reception of the first decorations of the Gesù interior owes something to the Jesuits' enduring reputation for being concerned with propaganda and didacticism at the expense of quality, or aesthetics. Typical is Sydney Freedberg's characterization of the Gesù paintings as 'intended for the delectation of the simple-minded ... propaganda for the faith directed primarily to an audience oppositely unliterate to that to which the religious painting of the Maniera was intended to appeal.'[4] Condemned as second-rate art with little stylistic coherence and even less impact on future stylistic trends, the original side chapel and tribune paintings tend to serve as a paradigm for everything that went wrong with Italian painting at the moment just before Caravaggio and Annibale saved the day. Yet the Gesù decorations used the same artists as many of the other major painting commissions of the late Cinquecento – including some of the busiest such as the Cavaliere d'Arpino and Paul Brill – and they share whatever faults they have with the contemporary fresco and canvas cycles of the popes, the cardinals, and the other religious orders.[5] More important, perhaps, the Gesù paintings would go on to exert profound influence over later art commissions in the city and beyond, and were seen regularly – even daily – by the artists who helped shape the coming era, men such as Caravaggio, Annibale Carracci, and Gianlorenzo Bernini. Even scholars in the anti-aesthetic school such as Howard Hibbard grudgingly acknowledge the immense legacy of these paintings: 'I think that this influence from lesser painters to greater ones is typical of the influence exerted by the Gesù decorations ... The influence of the painted decorations of the Gesù can hardly be overestimated, for this reason alone.'[6]

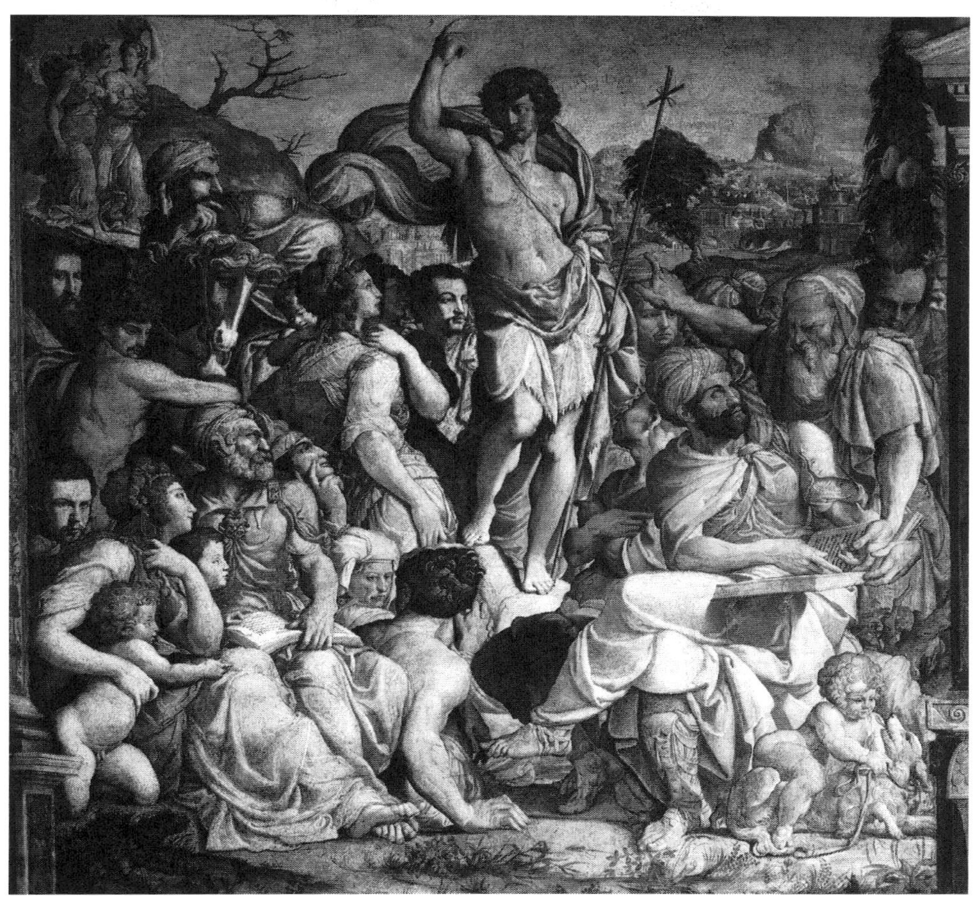

1. Jacopino del Conte, *St John the Baptist Preaching*. Fresco, Oratorio di S. Giovanni Decollato, Rome (1538). Photograph courtesy Art Resource, New York.

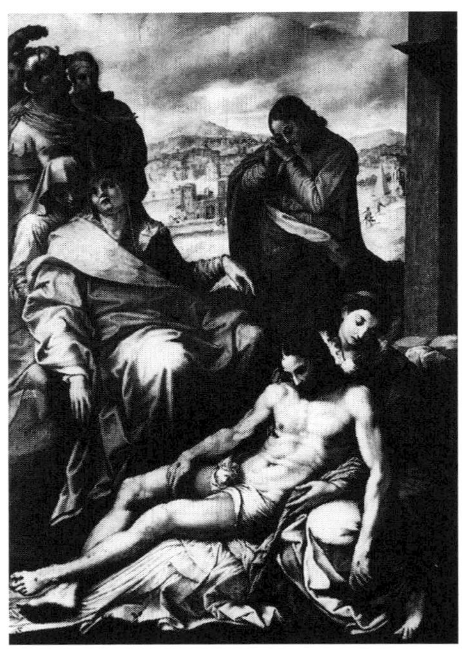

2. Siciolante da Sermoneta, *Pietà*. National Museum of Poznan (ca. 1542–4). Photograph courtesy of the Muzeum Narodow w Poznaniu, Raczyński Foundation.

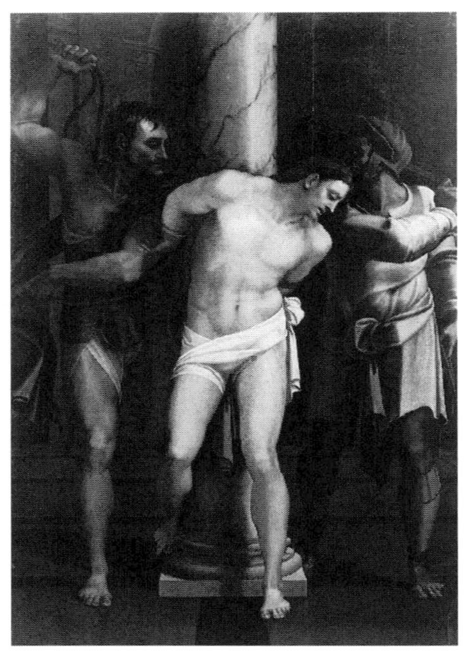

3. Sebastiano del Piombo, *Flagellation*. Panel, Museo Civico, Viterbo (1525–6). Photograph courtesy of the Istituto Centrale per il Catalogo e la Documentazione, Ministerio per i Beni Culturali e Ambientali, Rome.

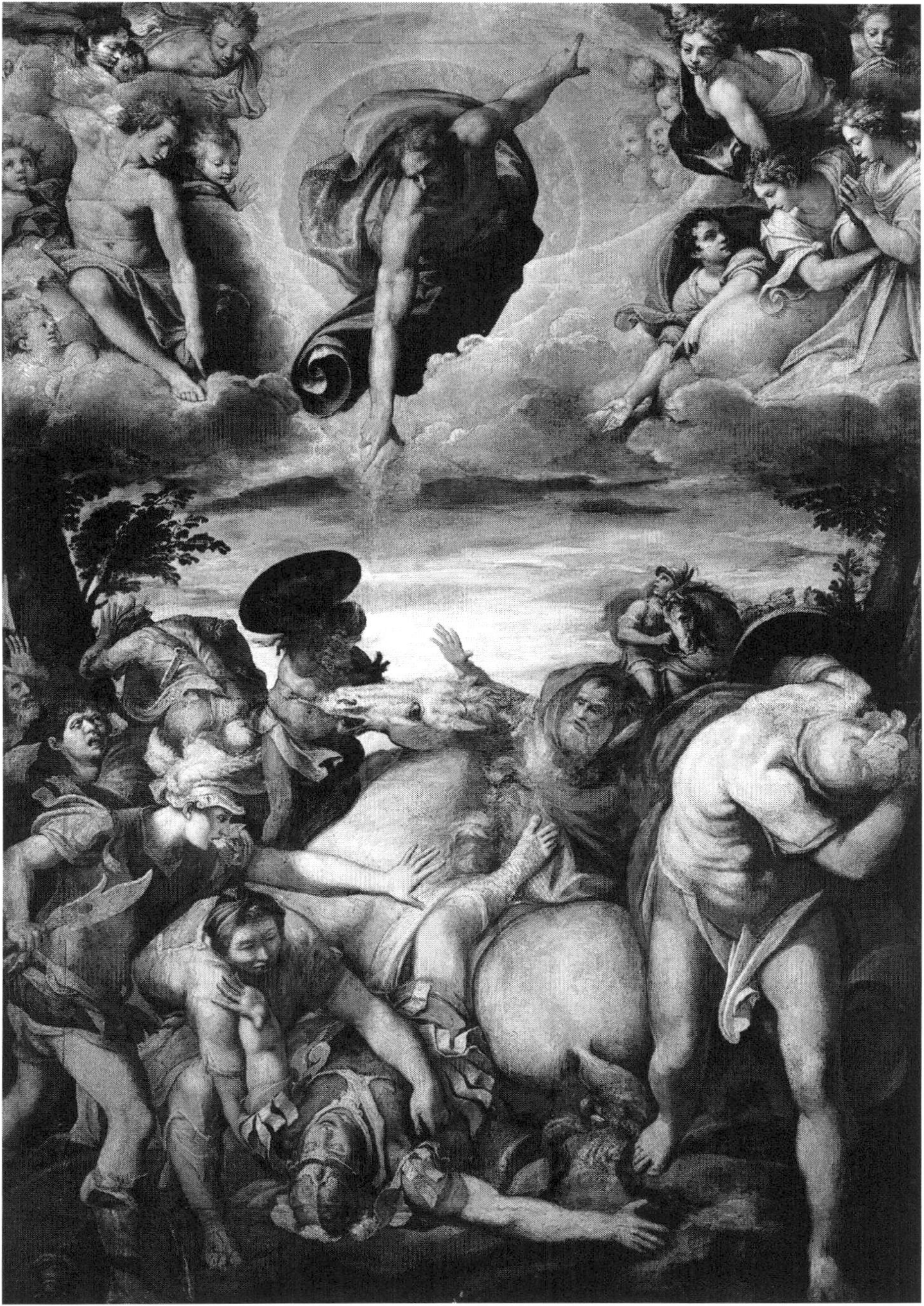

4. Taddeo Zuccaro, *Conversion of St Paul*. Fresco, S. Marcello al Corso, Rome (ca. 1563). Photograph courtesy of the Istituto Centrale per il Catalogo e la Documentazione, Ministerio per i Beni Culturali e Ambientali, Rome.

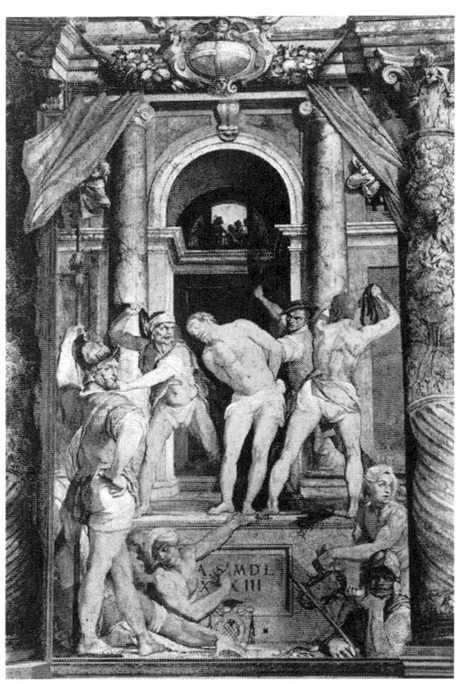

5. Federico Zuccaro, *Flagellation*. Fresco, Oratorio del Gonfalone, Rome (early 1570s). Photograph courtesy of the Istituto Centrale per il Catalogo e la Documentazione, Ministerio per i Beni Culturali e Ambientali, Rome.

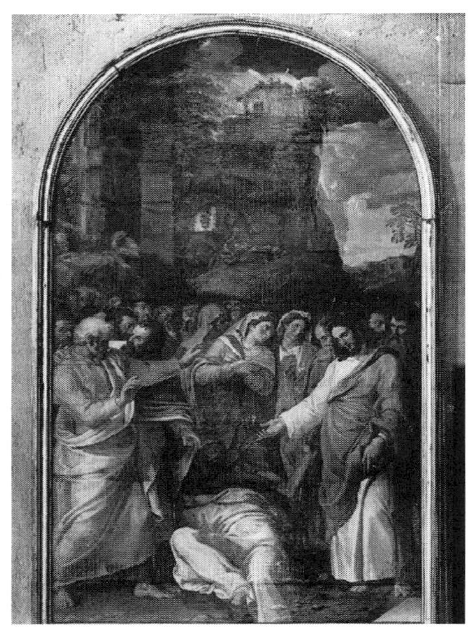

6. Girolamo Muziano, *Raising of Lazarus*. Panel, Museo del Opera del Duomo, Orvieto (1555). Photograph courtesy of the Istituto Centrale per il Catalogo e la Documentazione, Ministerio per i Beni Culturali e Ambientali, Rome.

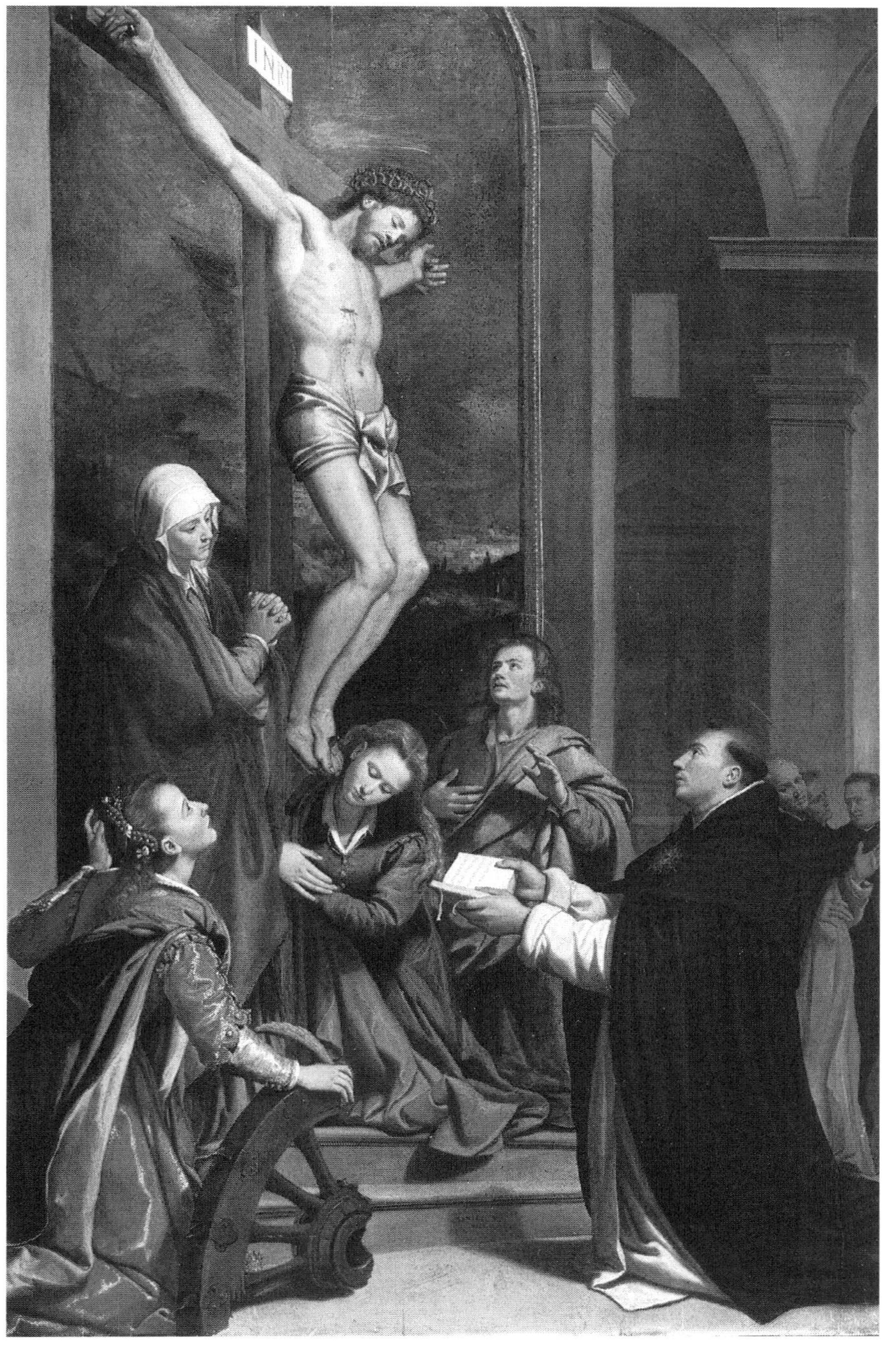

7. Santi di Tito, *Vision of St Thomas Aquinas*. Panel, S. Marco, Florence (1593).
Photograph courtesy Art Resource, New York.

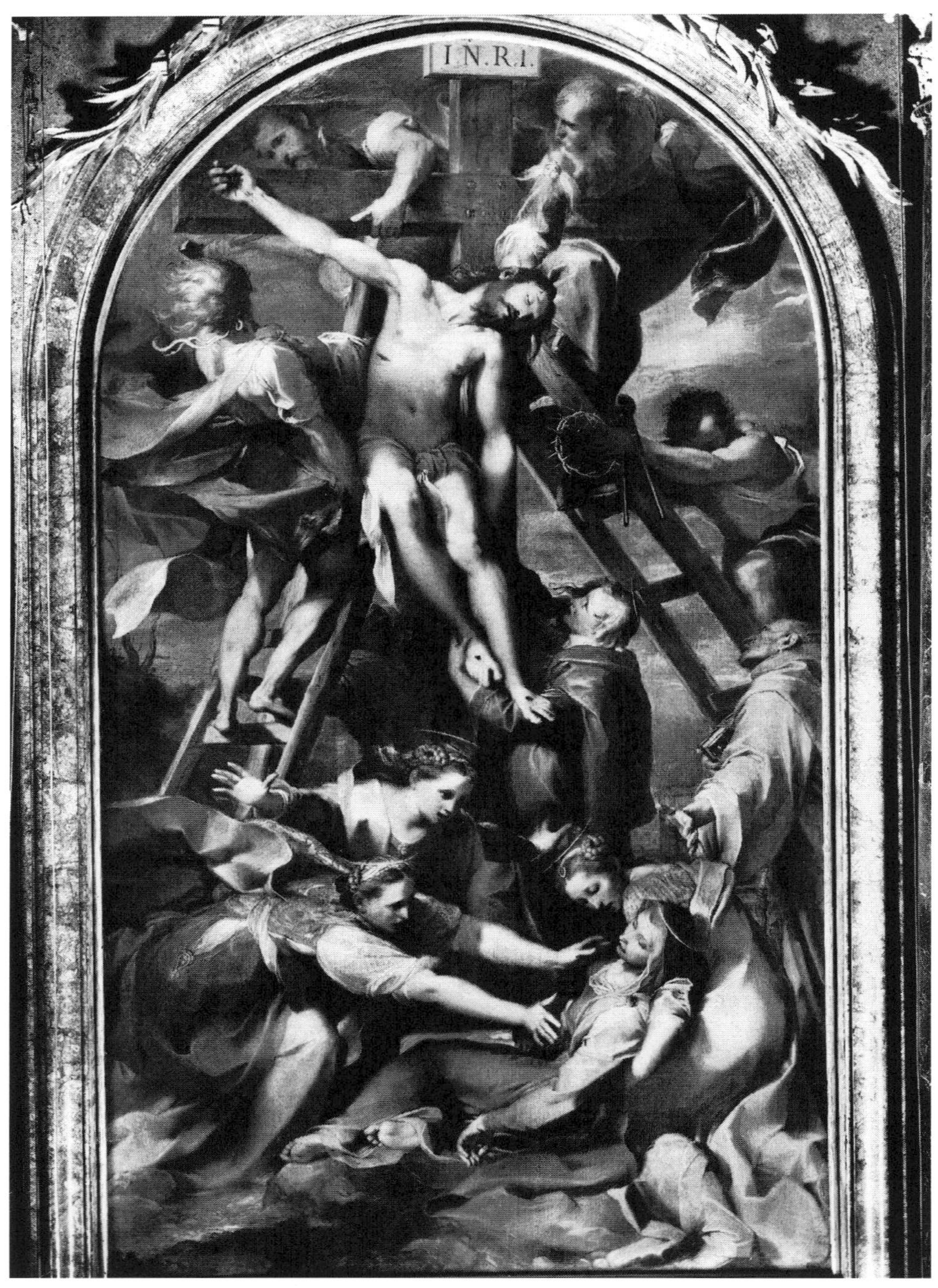

8. Federico Barocci, *Deposition*. Duomo, Perugia (1569). Photograph courtesy
Art Resource, New York.

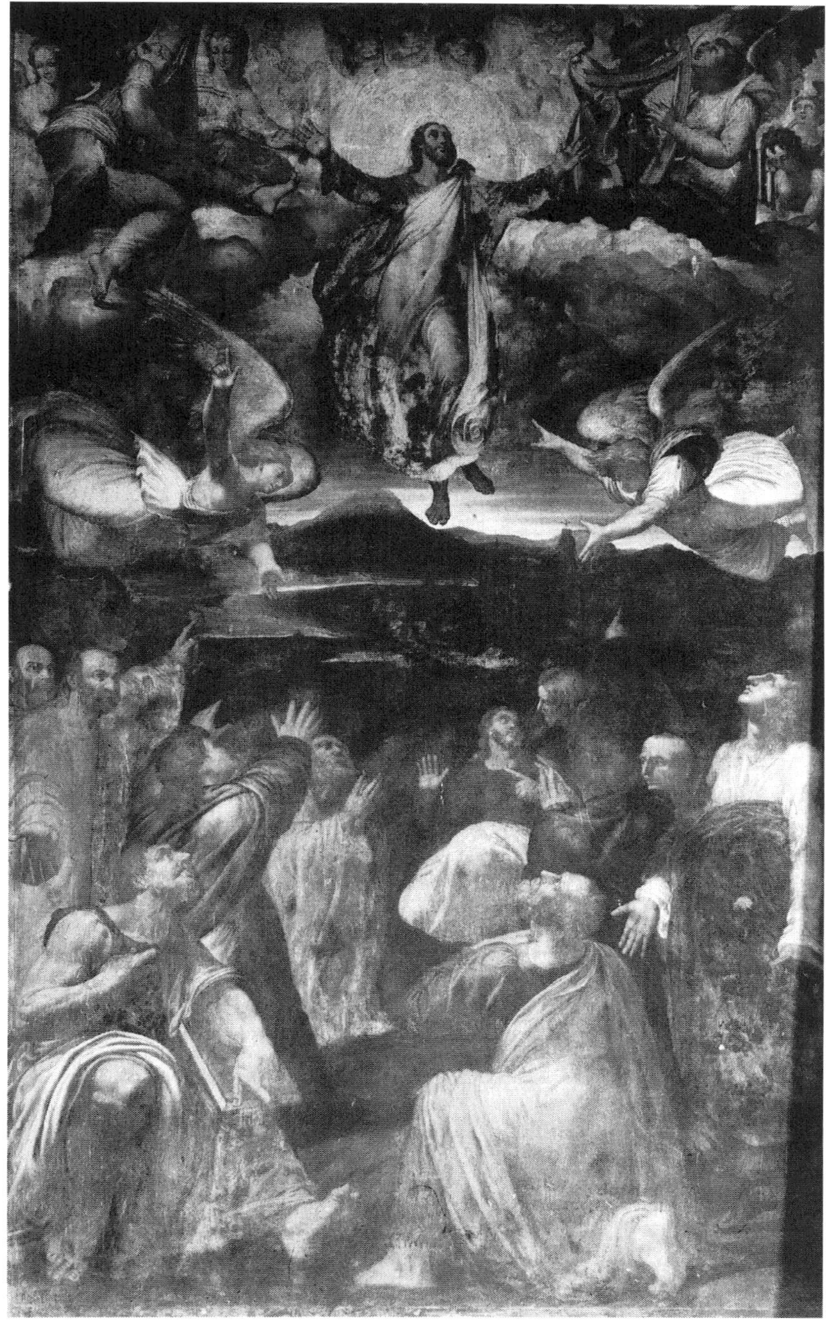

9. Giuseppe Valeriano, *Ascension*. Panel, S. Spirito in Sassia, Rome (before 1572). Photograph courtesy of the Istituto Centrale per il Catalogo e la Documentazione, Ministerio per i Beni Culturali e Ambientali, Rome.

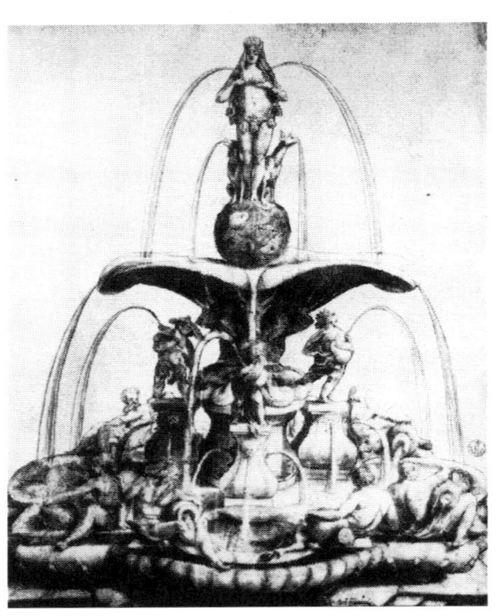

10. Giovanni Battista Fiammeri, *Study for a Fountain*. Uffizi, Florence (ca. 1575). Photograph courtesy of the Gabinetto Disegni e Stampe, Galleria degli Uffizi, Florence.

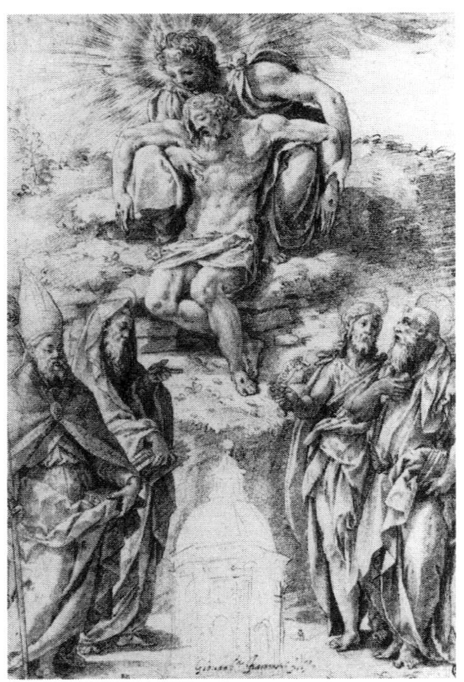

11. Giovanni Battista Fiammeri, *Dead Christ with Saints*. Louvre, Paris (ca. 1580s–90s). Photograph courtesy of the Musée du Louvre, Département des Arts Graphiques.

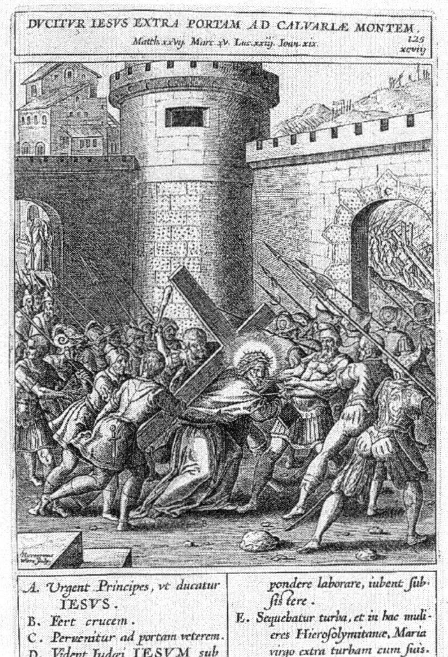

12. Livio Agresti, Giovanni Battista Fiammeri, and others, *Christ on the Road to Calvary*. From Nadal, *Evangelicae historiae imagines* (1593). Photograph courtesy of the John J. Burns Library, Boston College.

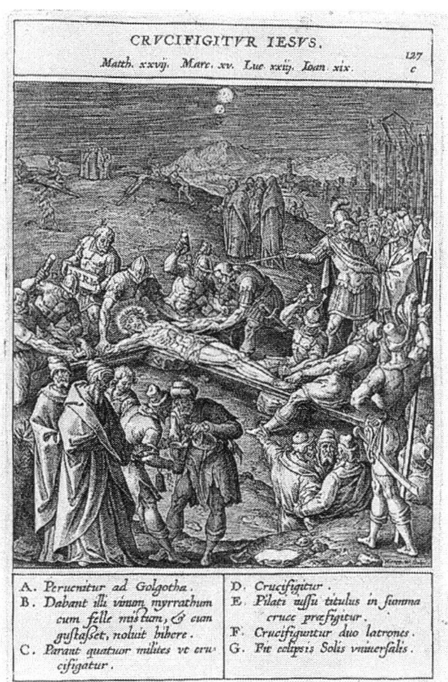

13. Livio Agresti, Giovanni Battista Fiammeri, and others, *Christ Nailed to the Cross*. From Nadal, *Evangelicae historiae imagines* (1593). Photograph courtesy of the John J. Burns Library, Boston College.

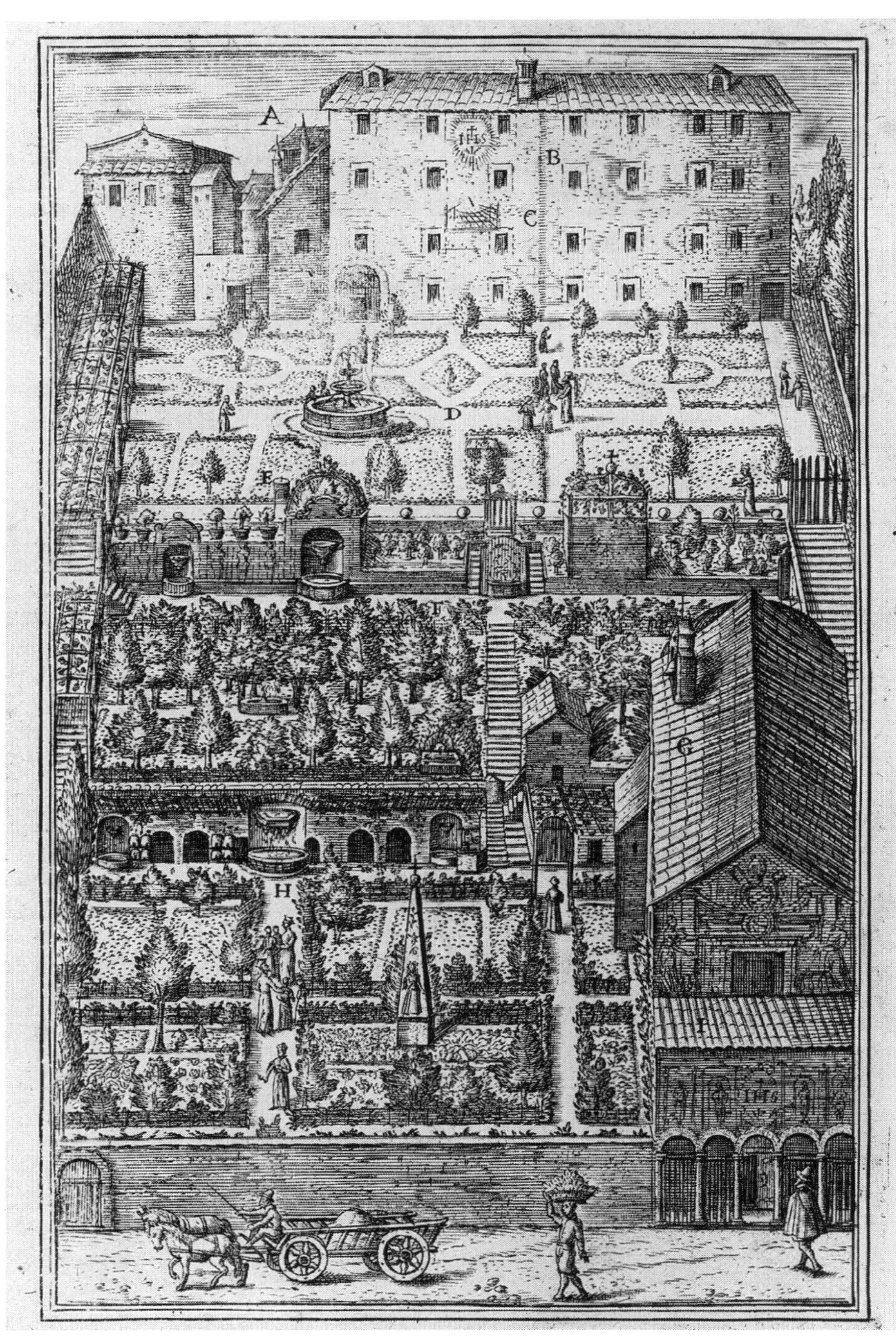

14. Matthäus Greuter, *The Novitiate of S. Andrea al Quirinale*. From Richeôme, *La peinture spirituelle* (1611). By permission of the Folger Shakespeare Library.

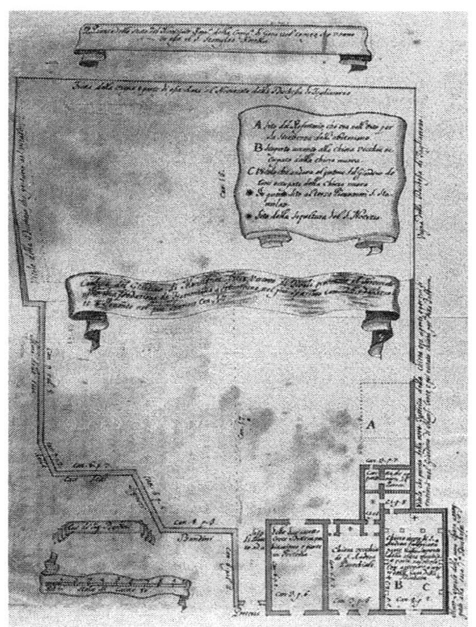

15. Anonymous, *Plan of the First Renovations of S. Andrea al Quirinale.* From Sisti, *Notizie istoriche appartenenti alle Cappellette di S. Stanislao Kostka* (1733). Gouache and ink on paper, ARSI, Rom. 167a. Photograph courtesy of the Archivum Romanum Societatis Iesu, Rome.

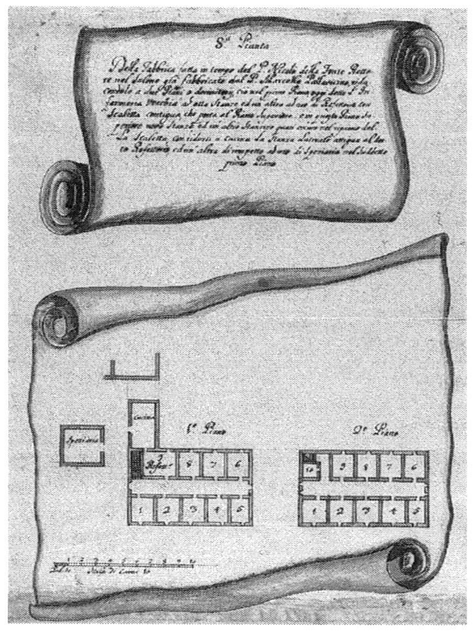

16. Anonymous, *Plan of the Novitiate Infirmary.* From Sisti, *Notizie istoriche appartenenti alle Cappellette di S. Stanislao Kostka* (1733). Gouache and ink on paper, ARSI, Rom. 167a. Photograph courtesy of the Archivum Romanum Societatis Iesu, Rome.

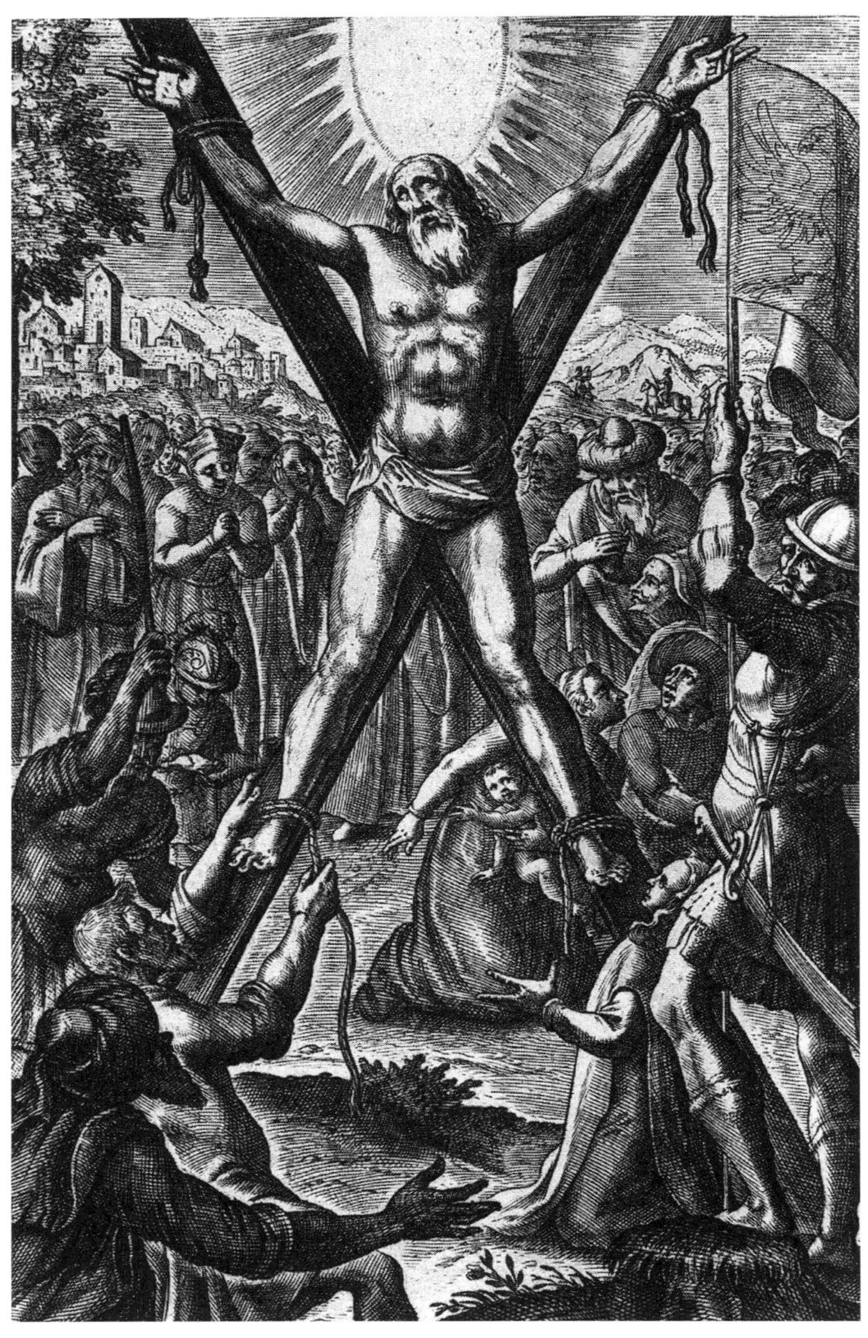

17. Matthäus Greuter after Durante Alberti, *Martyrdom of St Andrew*. Formerly in S. Andrea al Quirinale, Rome. From Richeôme, *La peinture spirituelle* (1611). By permission of the Folger Shakespeare Library.

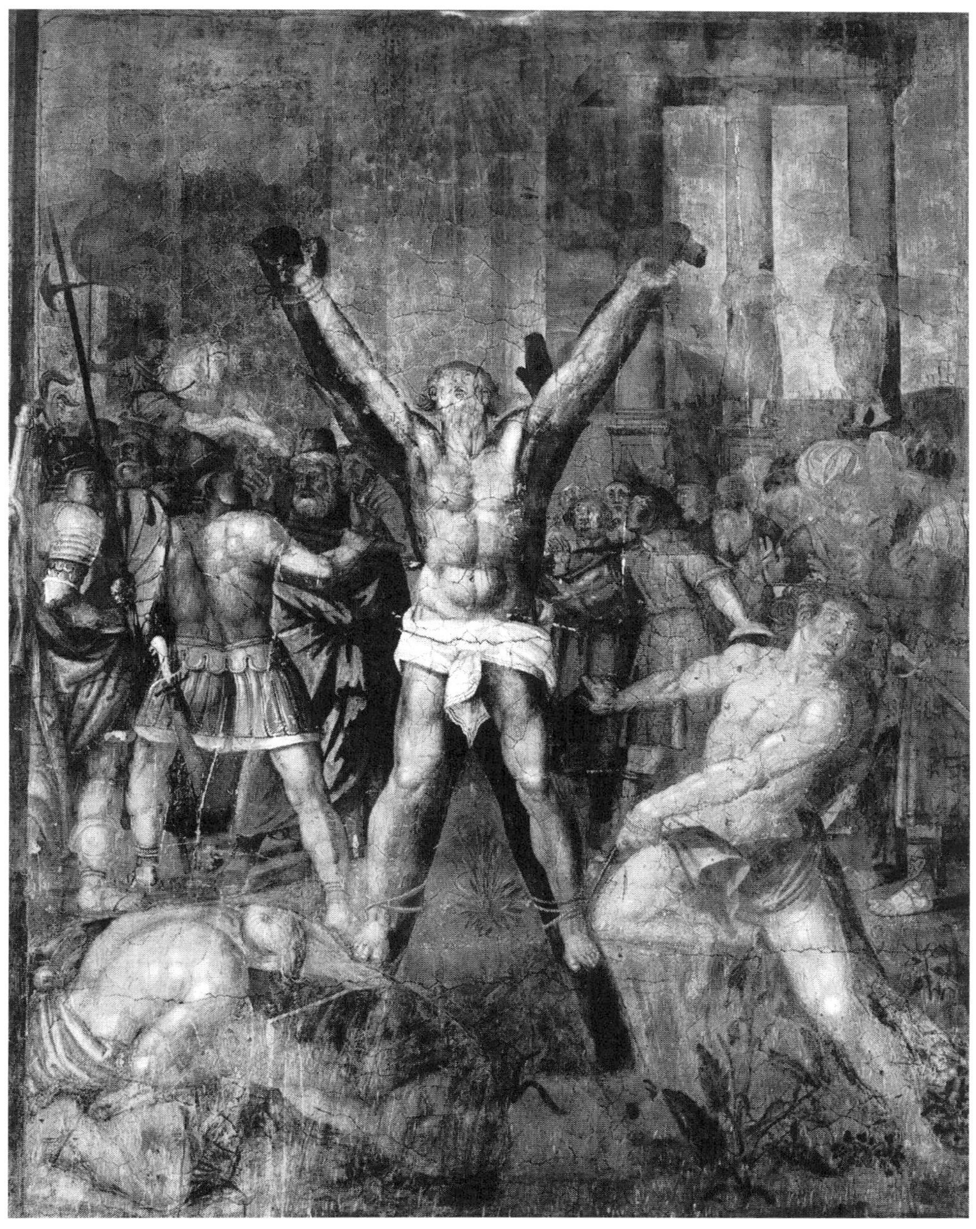

18. Attributed to Domenico Cerroni, *Martyrdom of S. Andrew*. Fresco, SS. Nereo ed Achilleo, Rome (1590s). Photograph courtesy of the Istituto Centrale per il Catalogo e la Documentazione, Ministerio per i Beni Culturali e Ambientali, Rome.

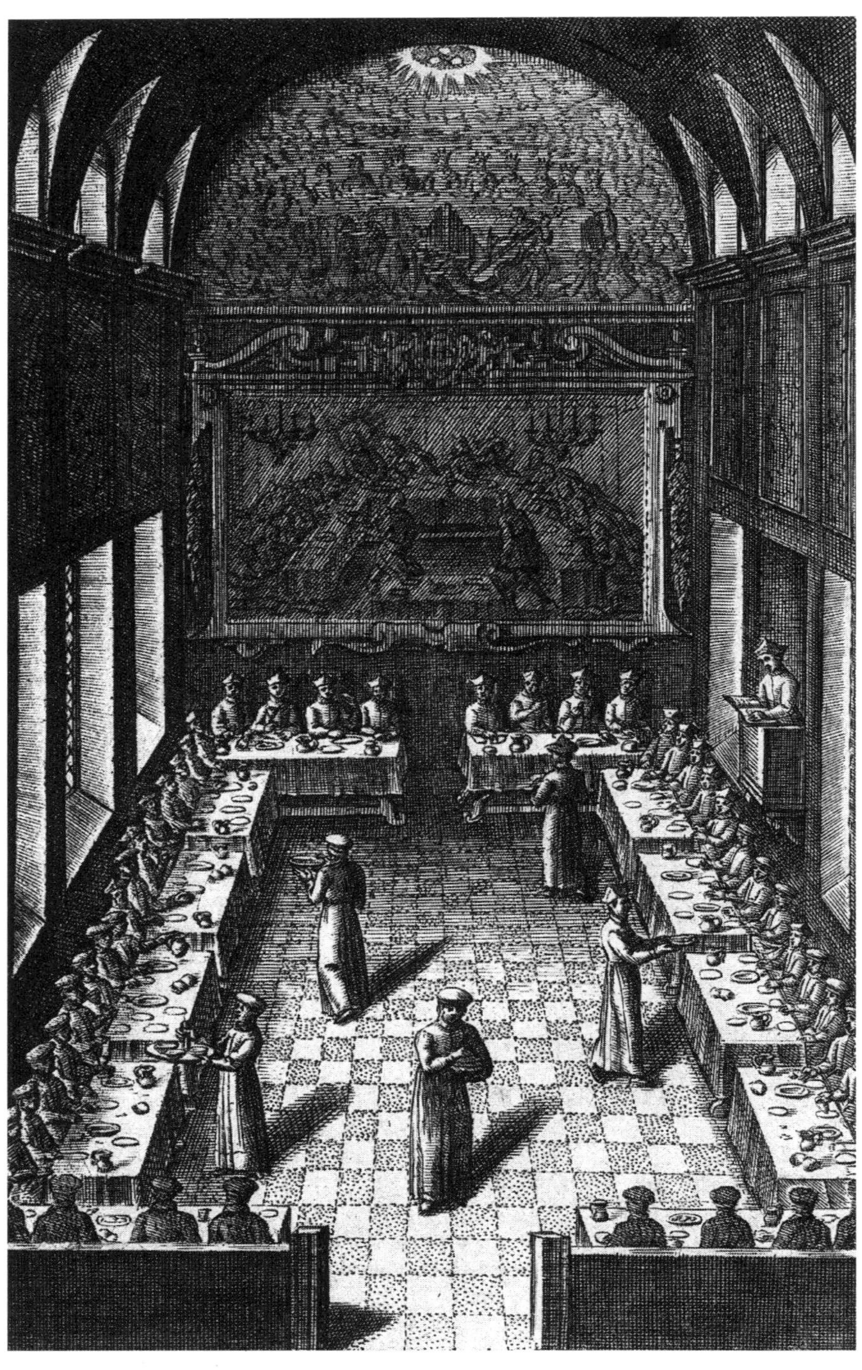

19. Matthäus Greuter, *The Novitiate Refectory*. From Richeôme, *La peinture spirituelle* (1611). By permission of the Folger Shakespeare Library.

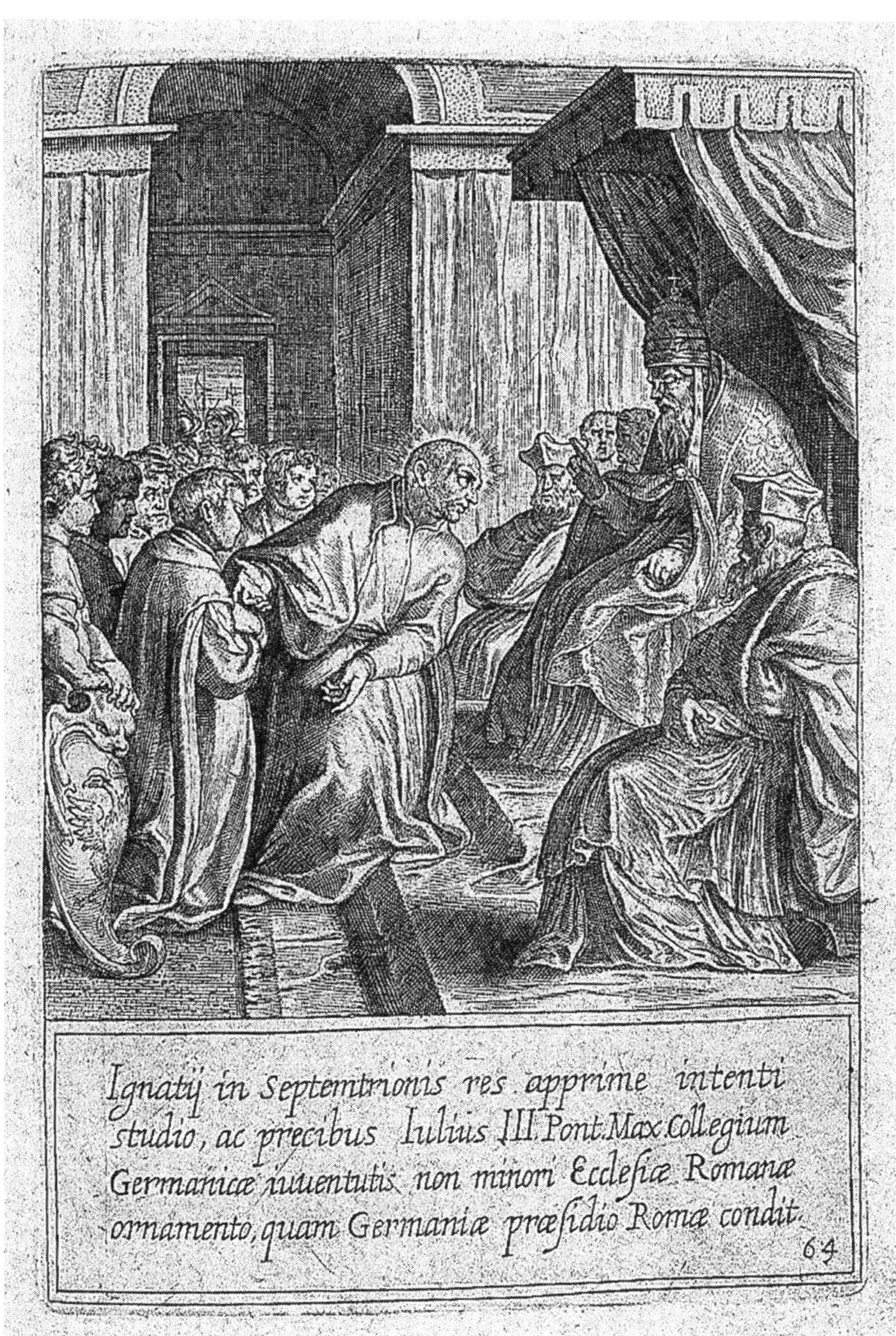

20. Galle Workshop, *The Foundation of the Collegio Germanico*. From *Vita beati P. Ignatii Loiolae* (1609). Photograph courtesy of the John J. Burns Library, Boston College.

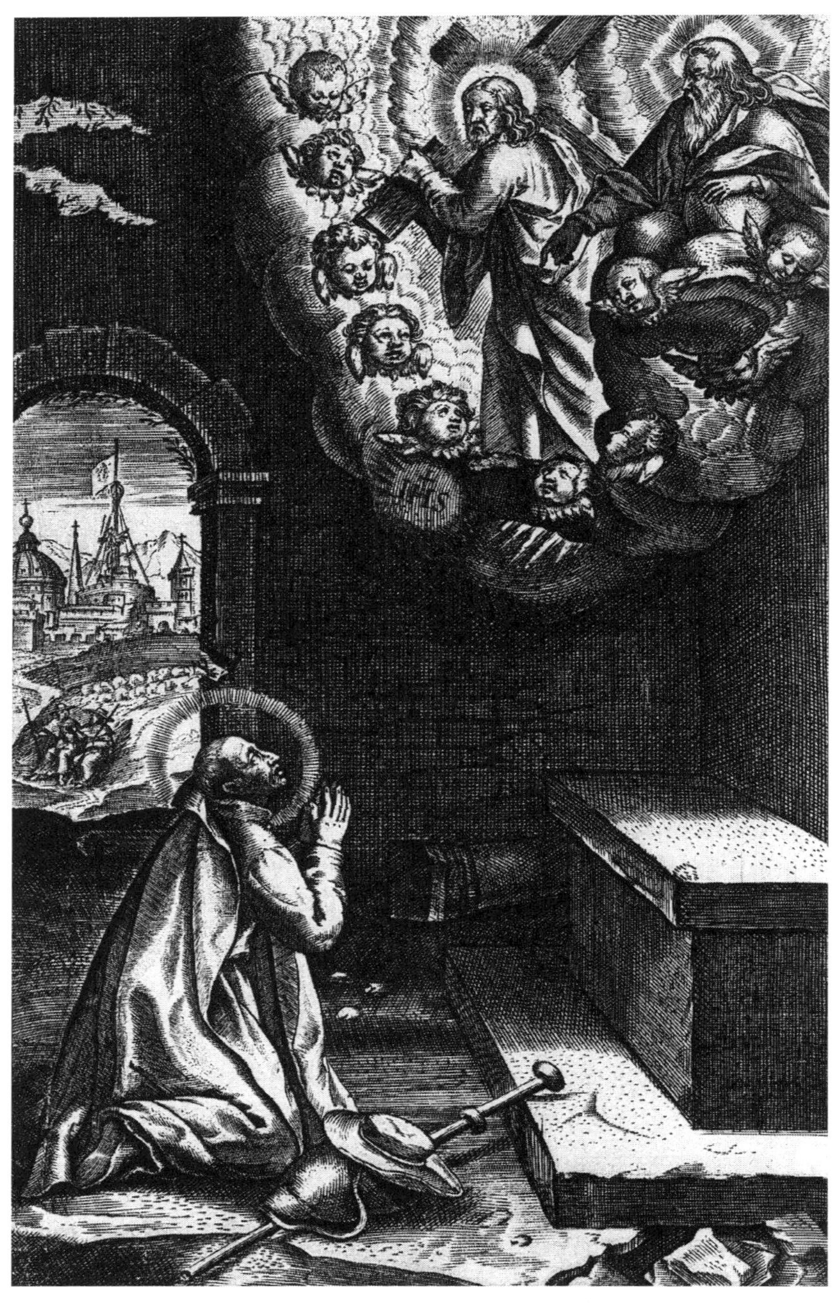

21. Matthäus Greuter, *Ignatius at La Storta*. From Richeôme, *La peinture spirituelle* (1611). By permission of the Folger Shakespeare Library.

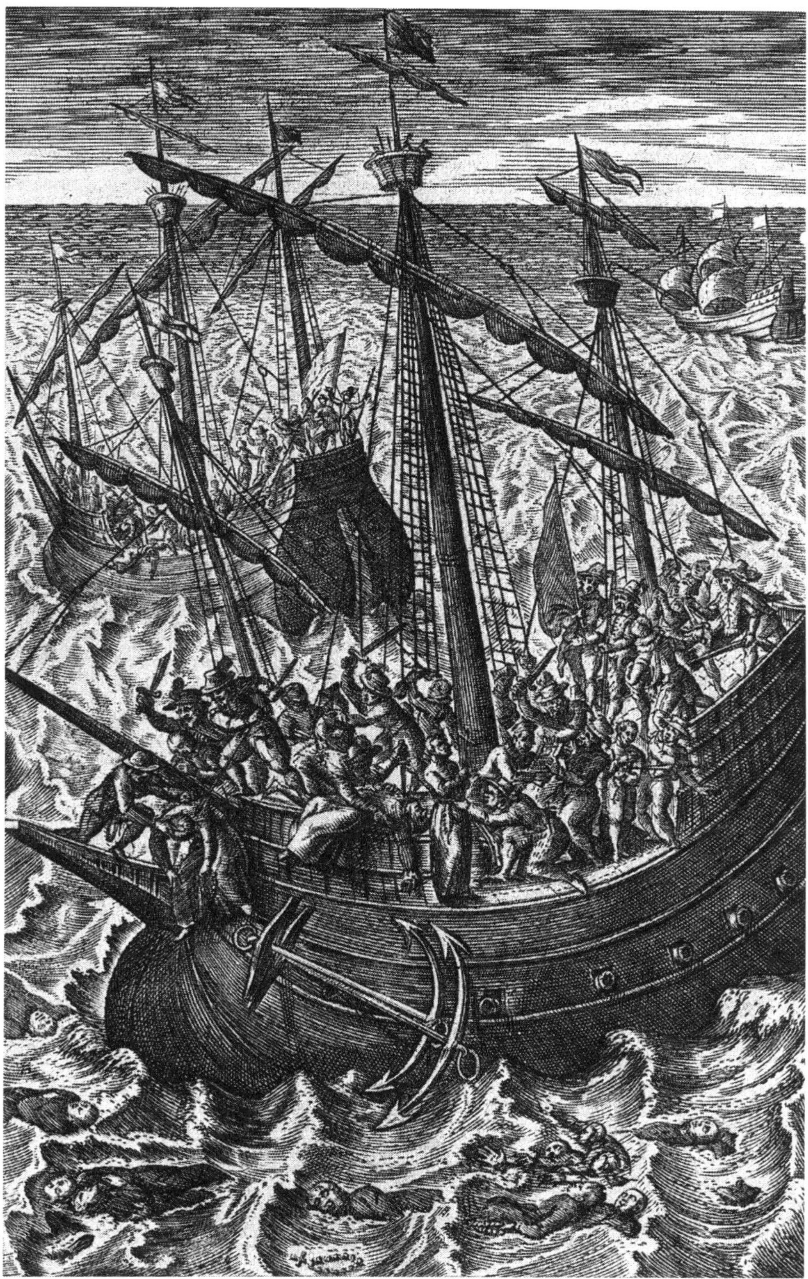

22. Matthäus Greuter, *Martyrdom of the Brazil Missionaries in 1570*. From Richeôme, *La peinture spirituelle* (1611). By permission of the Folger Shakespeare Library.

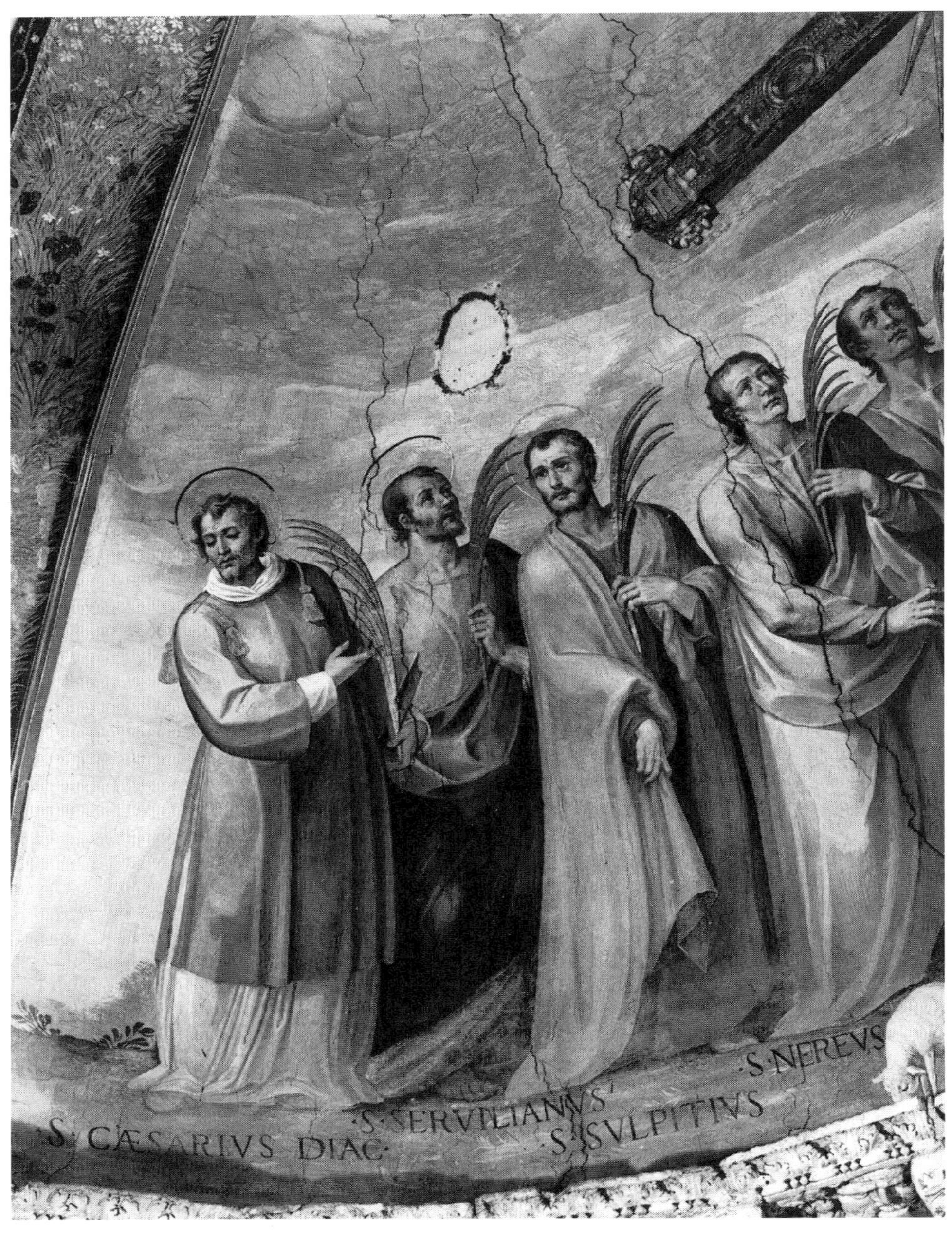

23. Attributed to Cristofano Roncalli, *Male and Female Martyrs*. Fresco, SS. Nereo ed Achilleo, Rome (1590s). Photograph courtesy of the Istituto Centrale per il Catalogo e la Documentazione, Ministerio per i Beni Culturali e Ambientali, Rome.

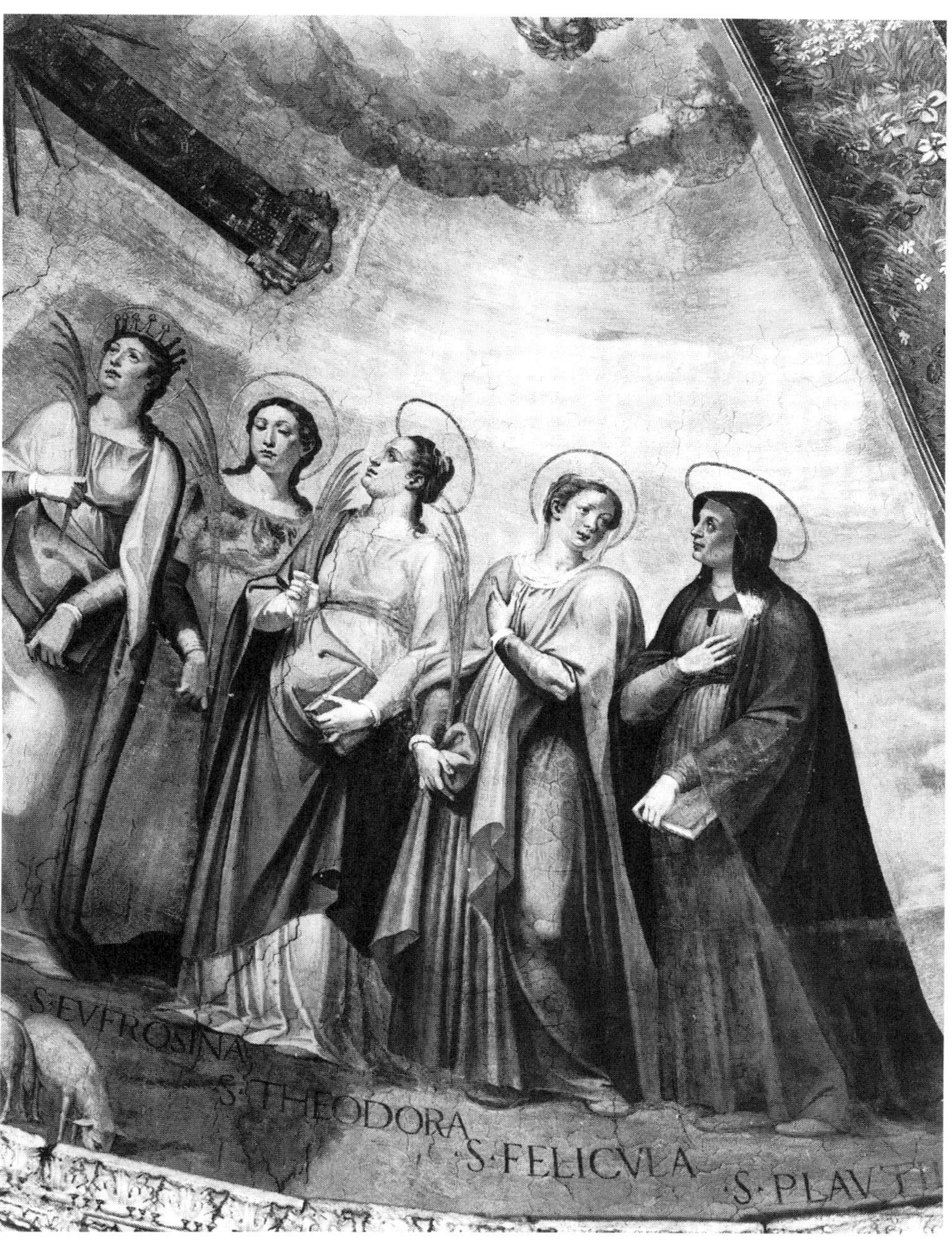

S·EVFROSINA
S·THEODORA
S·FELICVLA
S·PLAVTI

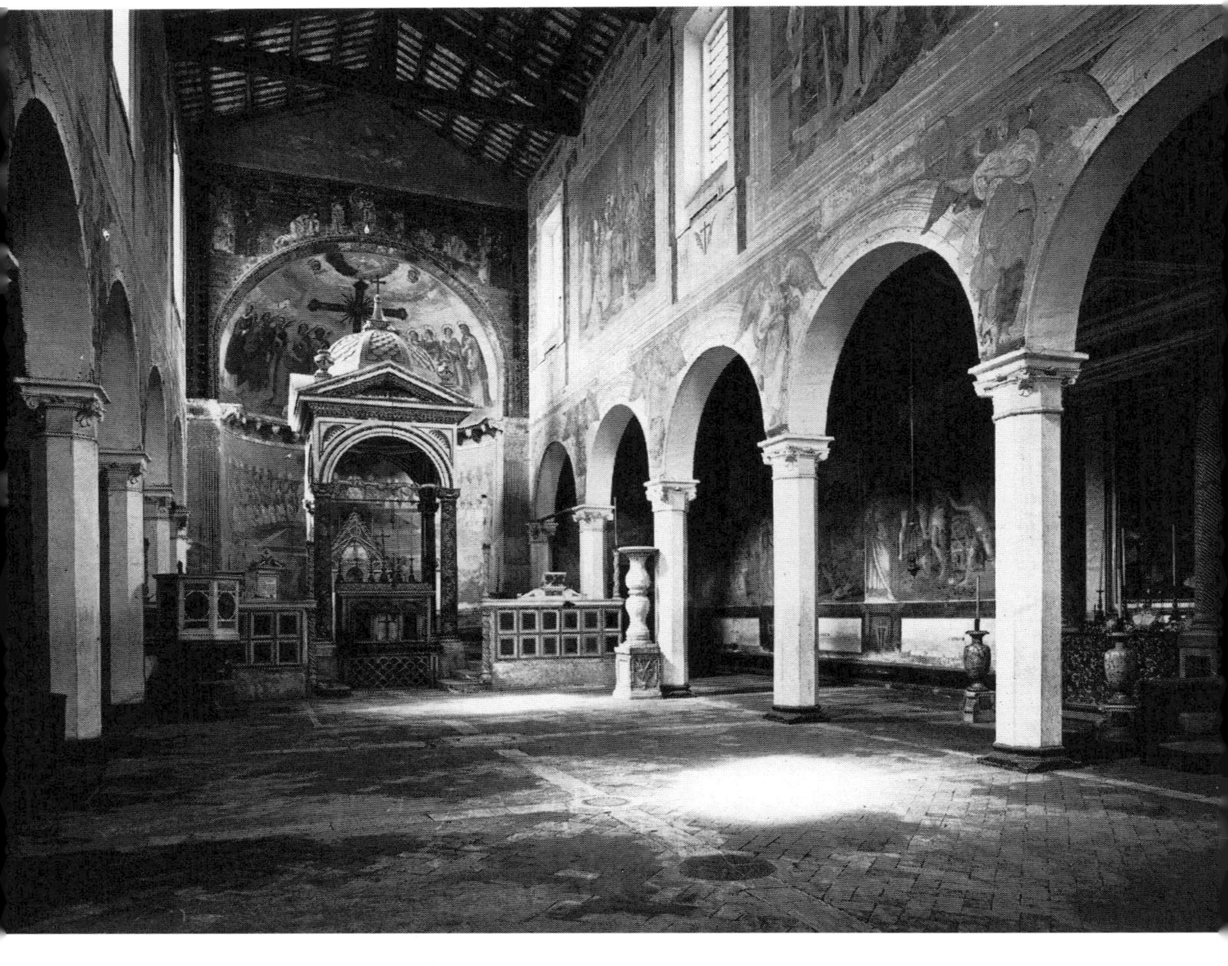

24. Anonymous, *Victory Angels*. Fresco, SS. Nereo ed Achilleo, Rome (1590s). Photograph courtesy of the Istituto Centrale per il Catalogo e la Documentazione, Ministerio per i Beni Culturali e Ambientali, Rome.

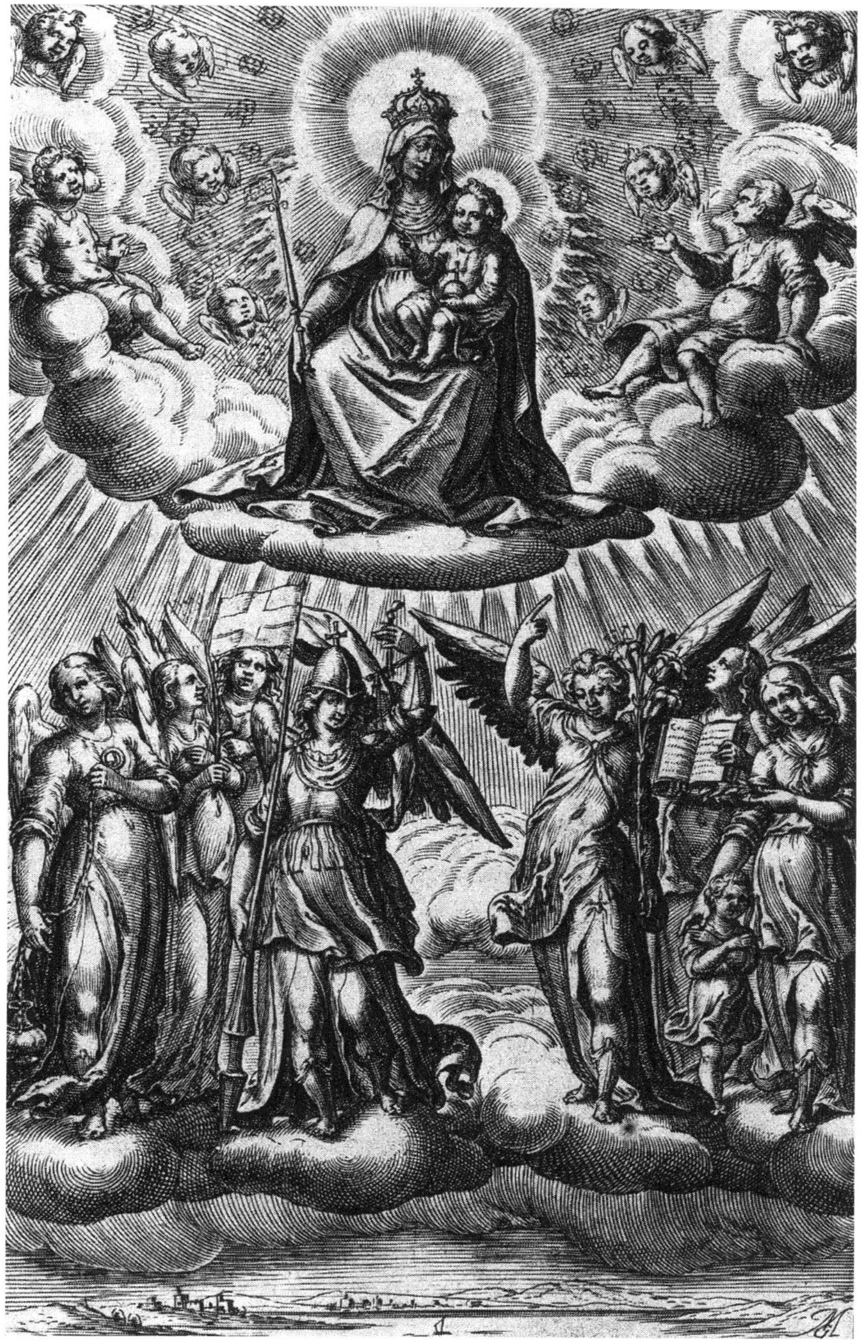

25. Matthäus Greuter, *Madonna and Child Adored by Angels*. From Richeôme, *La peinture spirituelle* (1611). By permission of the Folger Shakespeare Library.

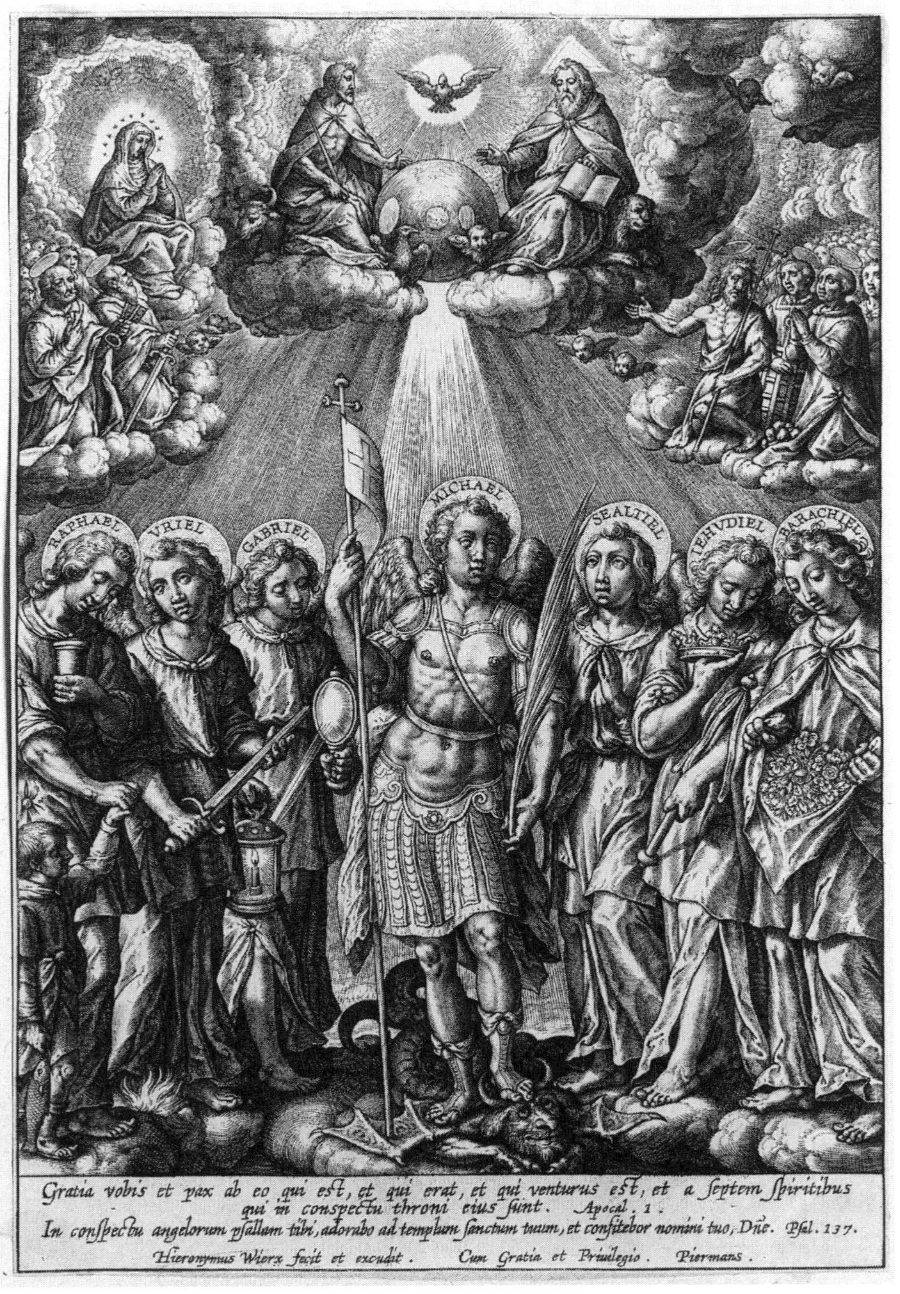

26. Hieronymus Wierix, *The Seven Archangels* (ca. 1600). Possibly after a painting by Scipione Pulzone formerly in the Gesù. The Metropolitan Museum of Art, The Elisha Whittelsey Collection, The Elisha Whittelsey Fund, 1951. Photograph © The Metropolitan Museum of Art (51.501.6402).

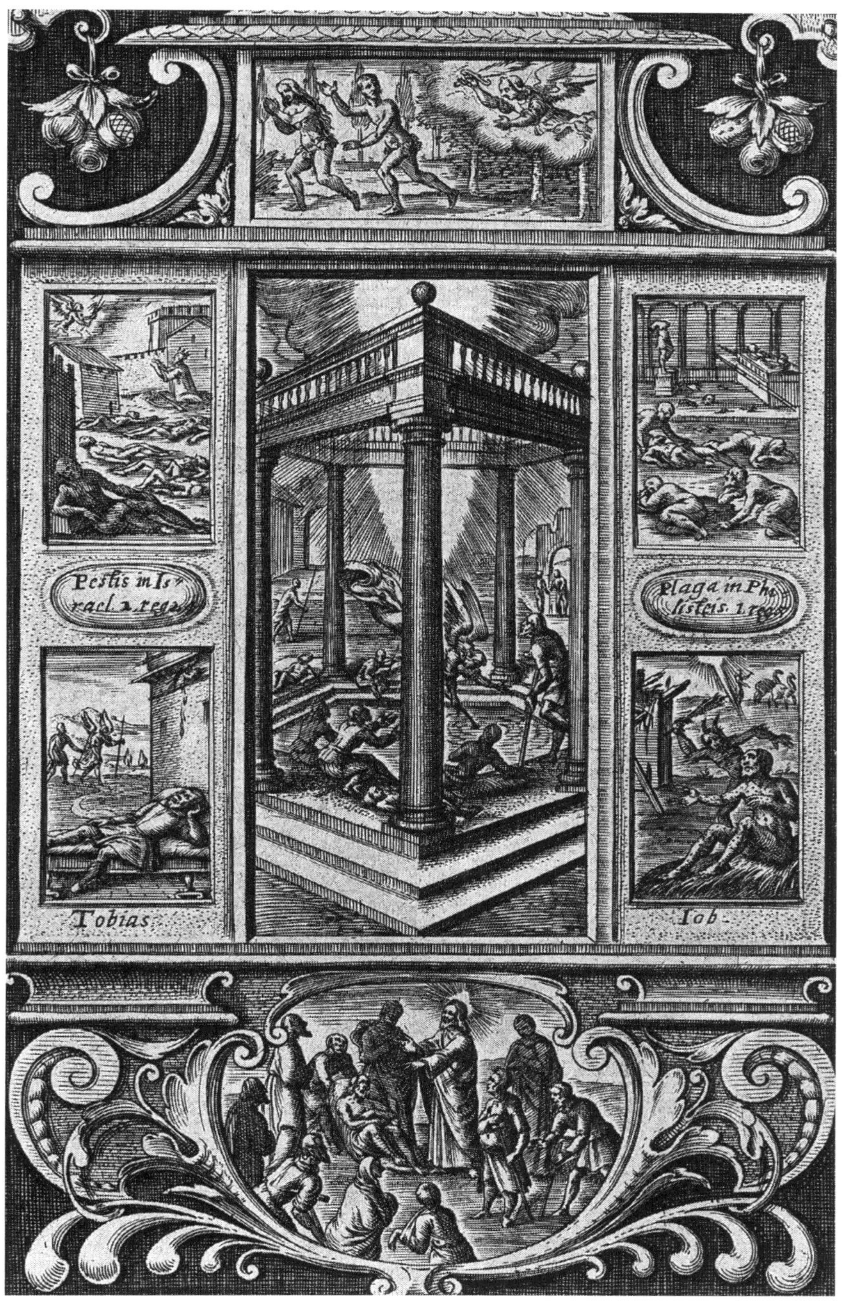

27. Matthäus Greuter, *Moral Causes of Maladies*. From Richeôme, *La peinture spirituelle* (1611). By permission of the Folger Shakespeare Library.

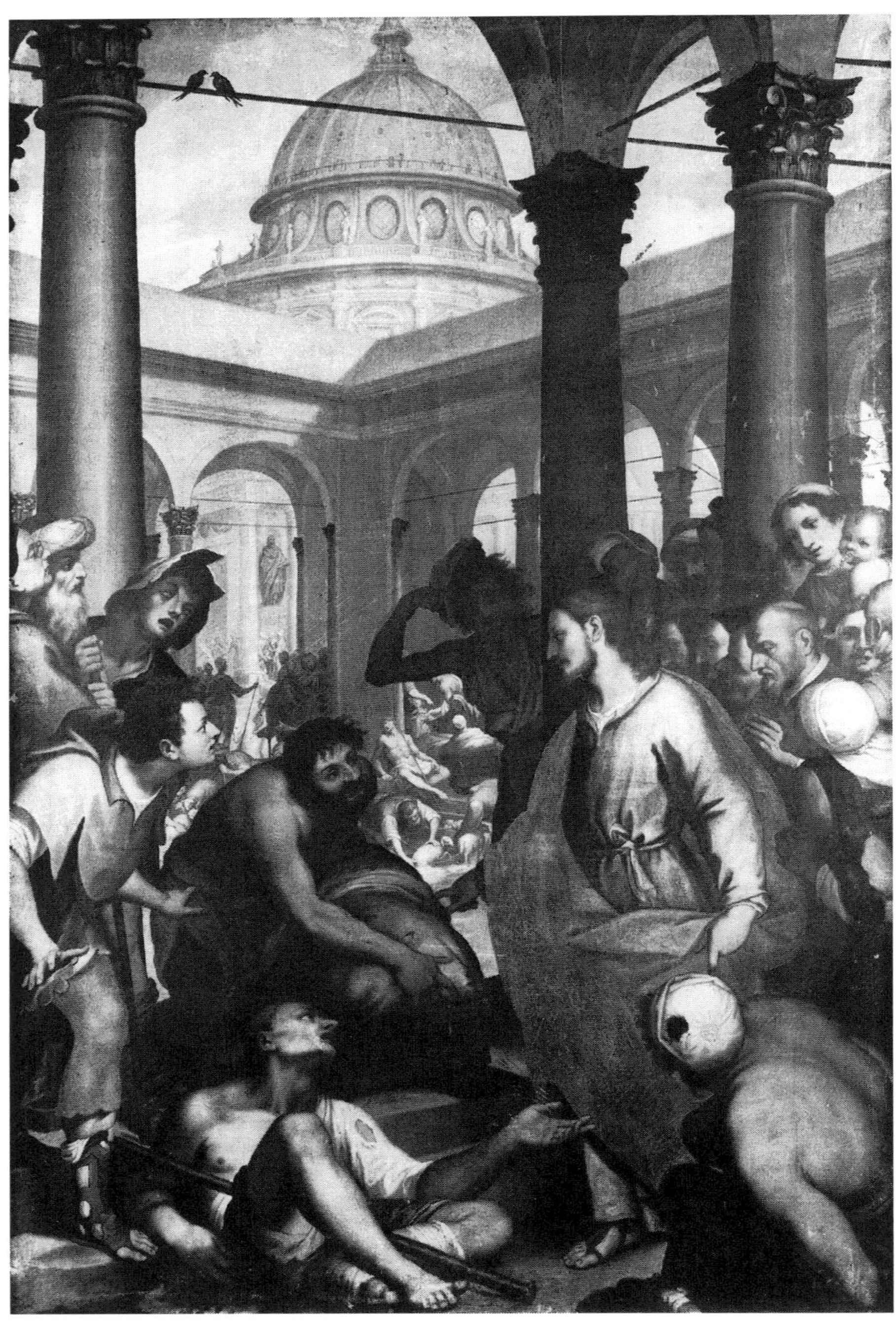

28. Giovan Battista Paggi, *The Probatic Pool*. Canvas, Museo Guinigi, Lucca (ca. 1592). Photograph courtesy of the Fototeca Soprintendenza di Pisa, Lucca, Livorno, Massa.

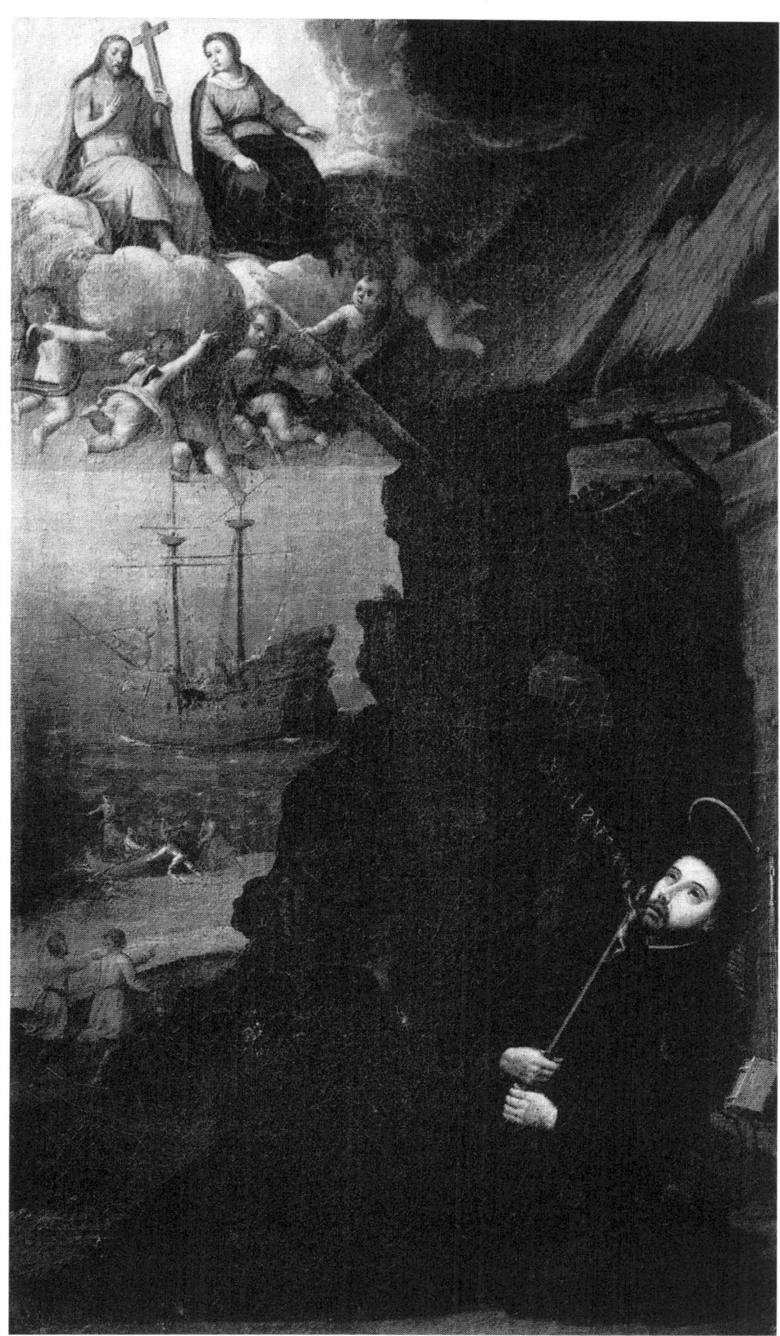

29. André Reinoso, *Death of St Francis Xavier*. Panel, São Roque, Lisbon (ca. 1619).
Photograph courtesy of the Museu de São Roque, Santa Casa da Misericórdia, Lisbon.

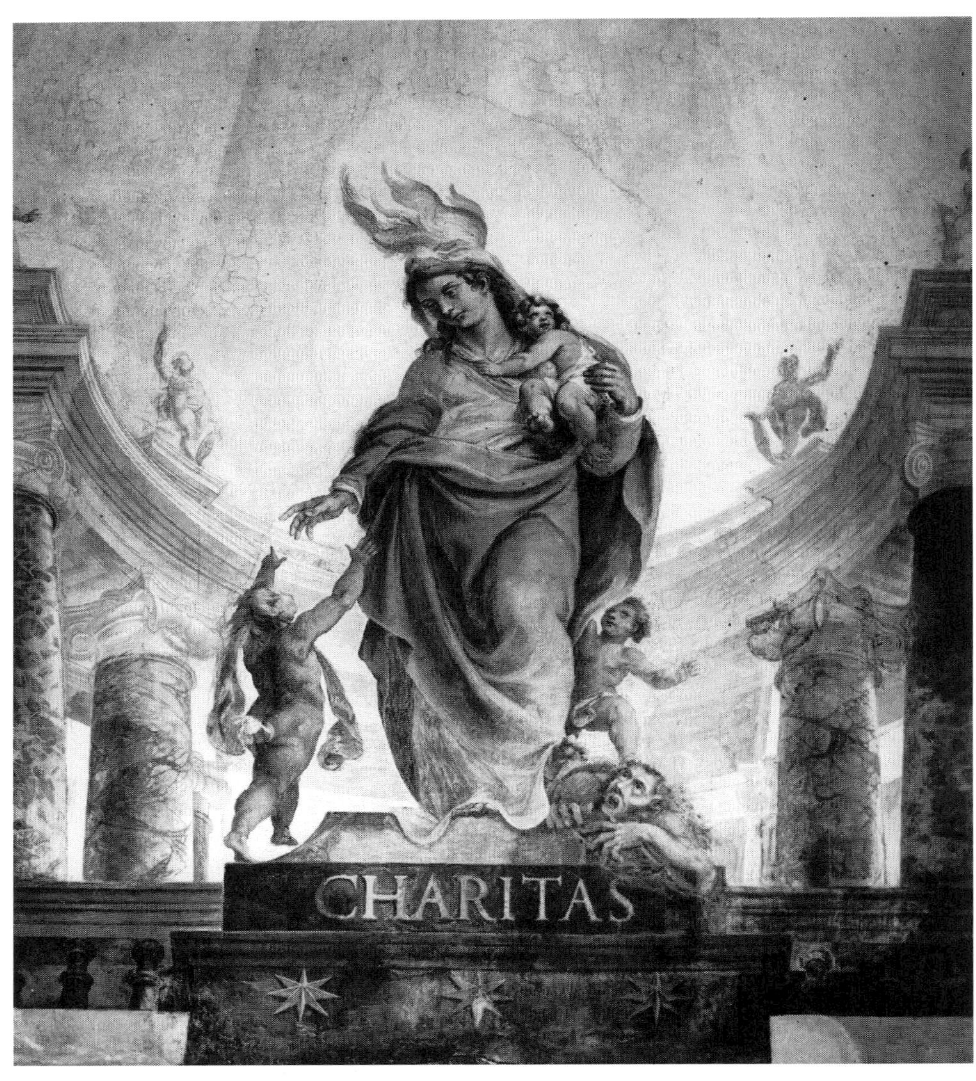

30. Giovanni and Cherubini Alberti, *Charitas*. Fresco, Sala Clementina, Vatican Palace (ca. 1600). Photograph courtesy of Monumenti, Musei e Gallerie Pontificie, Vatican.

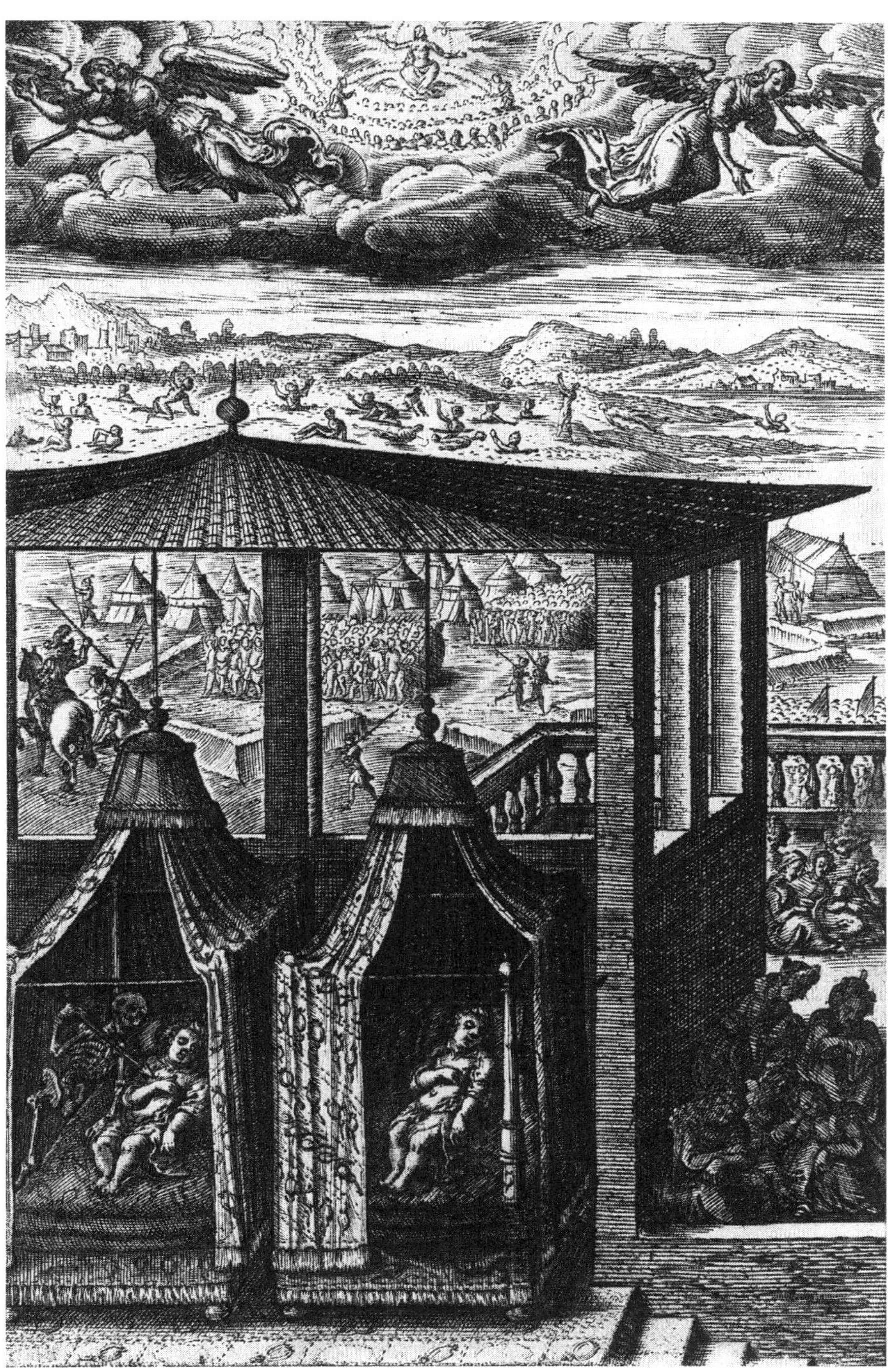

31. Matthäus Greuter, *Sleep and Death*. From Richeôme, *La peinture spirituelle* (1611). By permission of the Folger Shakespeare Library.

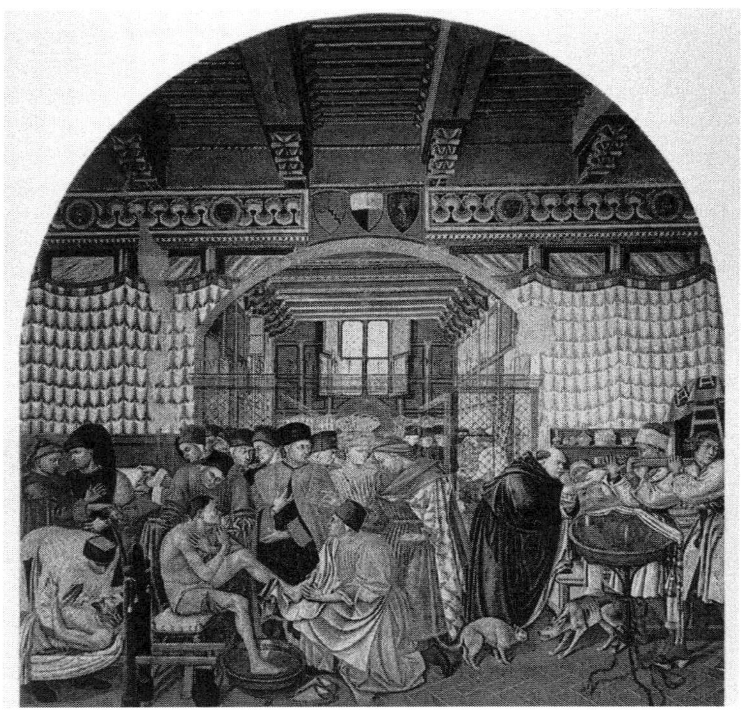

32. Domenico di Bartolo, *Care and Governance of the Sick*. Fresco, Pellegrinaio, Spedale della Madonna della Scala, Siena (after 1444). Photograph courtesy Fototeca Soprintendenza di Siena.

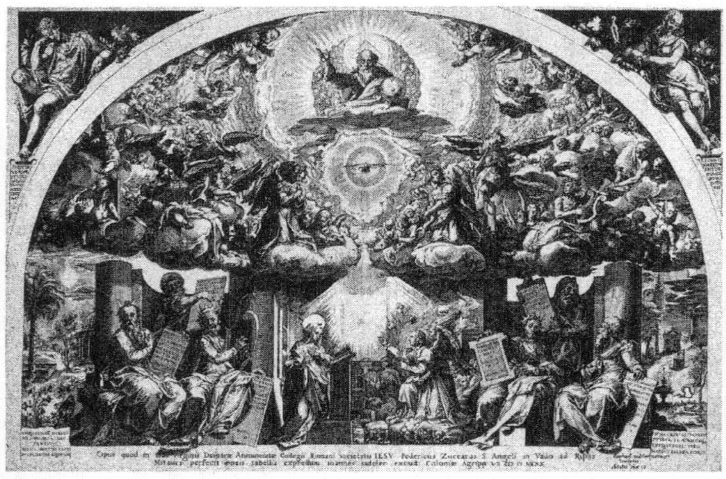

33. Raphael Sadeler I, *Annunciation (surrounded by six prophets), copy of the engraving by Cornelis Cort after the fresco by Federico Zuccaro in the now destroyed Church of SS. Annunziata in Rome* (1580). Fine Arts Museums of San Francisco, Achenbach Foundation for Graphic Arts, Mr and Mrs Marcus Sopher Collection, 1993.63.76.

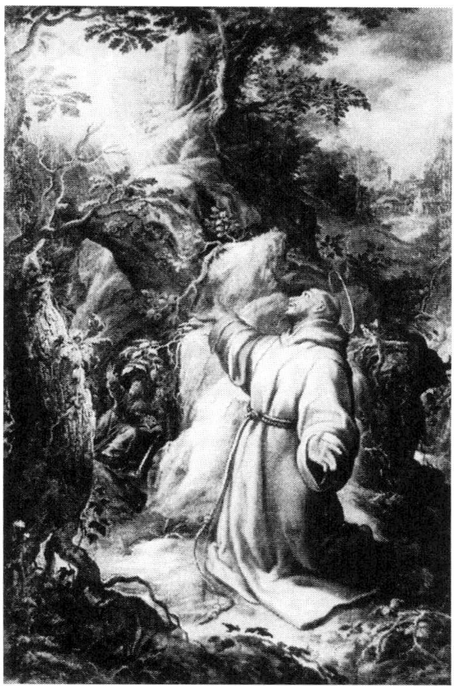

34. Girolamo Muziano, *St Francis Receiving the Stigmata*. Convento dei Cappuccini, Frascati (1570s). Photograph courtesy of the Istituto Centrale per il Catalogo e la Documentazione, Ministerio per i Beni Culturali e Ambientali, Rome.

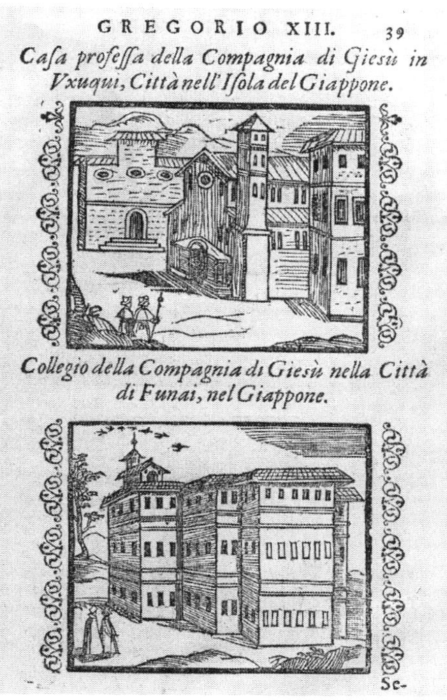

35. Anonymous, *The Jesuit Colleges in Japan* (*Casa professa della Compagnia di Giesù in Vxuqui, Città nell'Isola del Giappone* and *Collegio della Compagnia di Giesù nella Città di Funai, nel Giappone*) (1596). From Marc'Antonio Ciappi, *Compendio delle heroiche*. Typ 525 96.281, Department of Printing and Graphic Arts, Houghton Library, Harvard University Library.

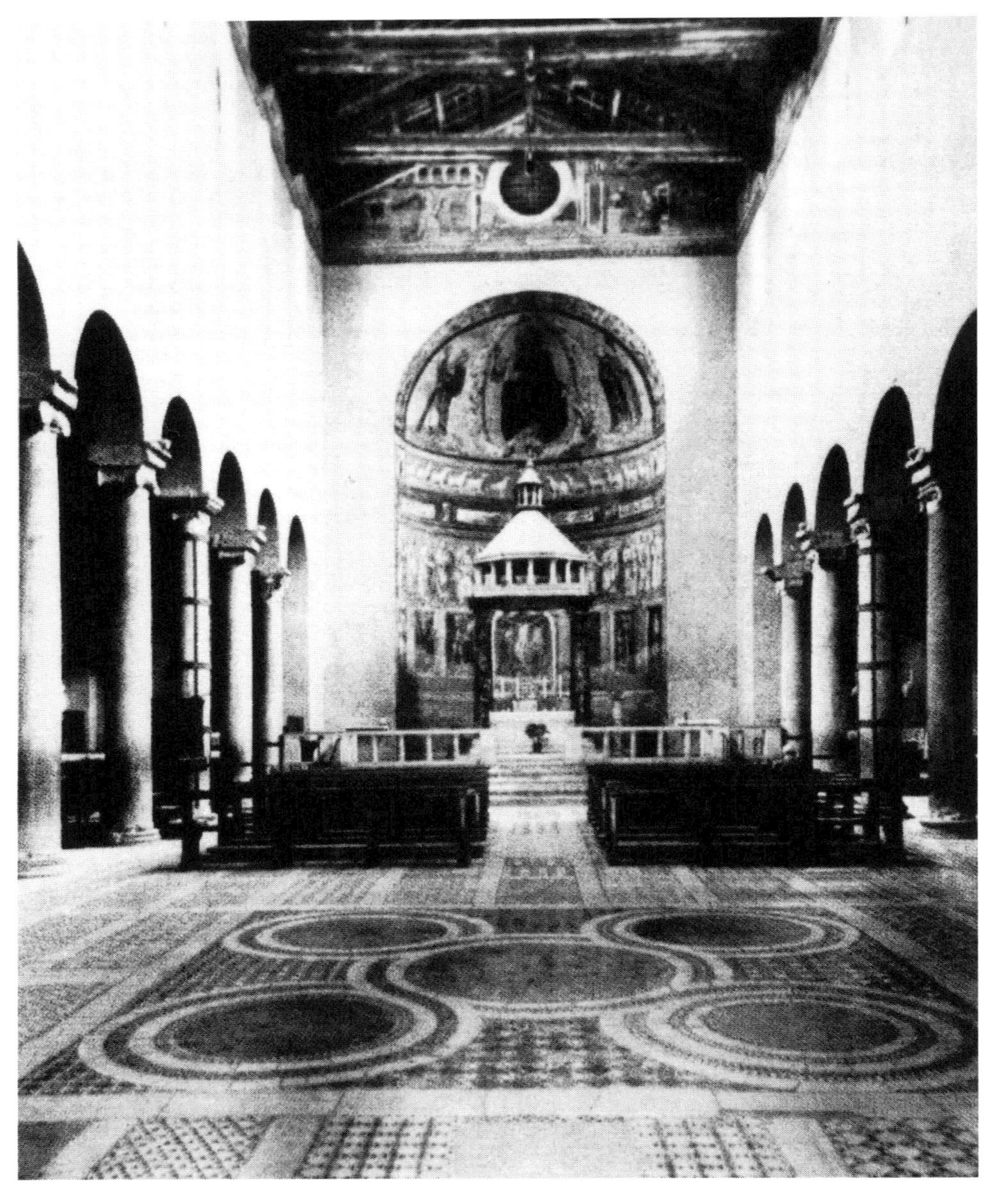

36. Anonymous, apse fresco. S. Saba, Rome (before 1575). Photograph
courtesy of Stuardt-Mikhail Clarke.

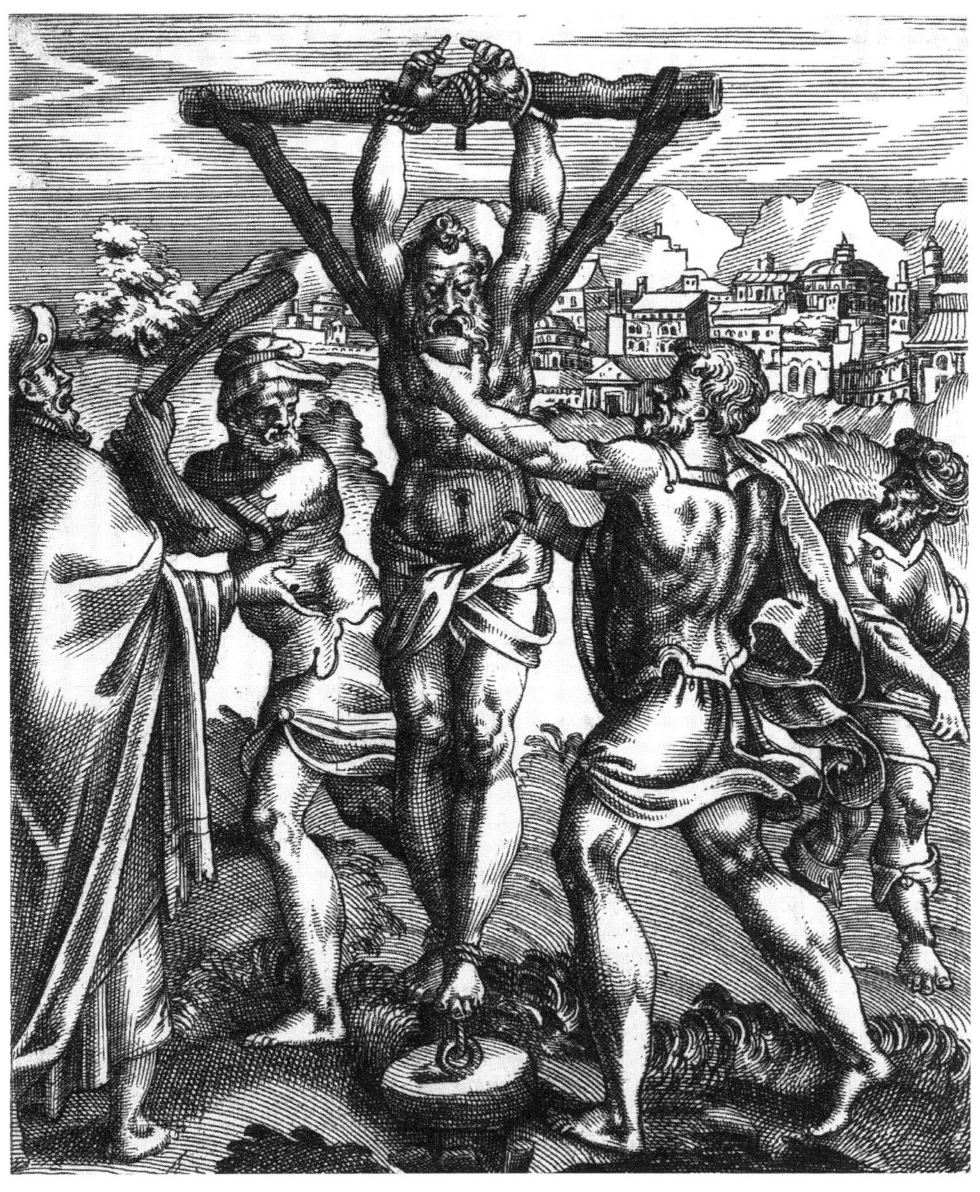

37. Giovanni Battista Cavallieri after Niccolò Circignani, *Martyrdom of St Apollinarius*. From *Beati Apollinaris martyris* (1586). Photograph courtesy of the Biblioteca Apostolica Vaticana.

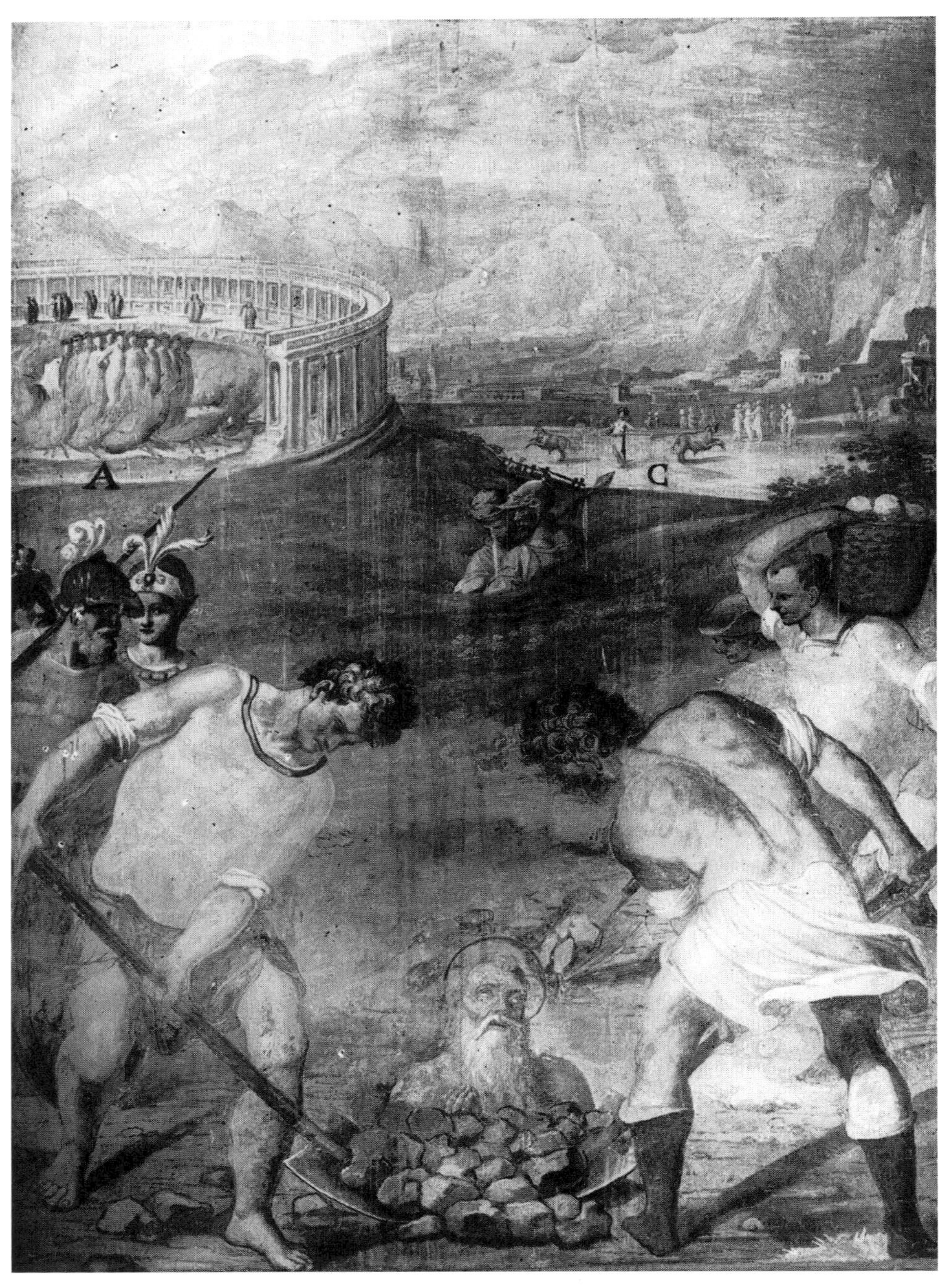

38. Niccolò Circignani, fresco IV: *Martyrdom of St Vitalis, St Thecla, and Others*. S. Stefano Rotondo, Rome (1582). Photograph courtesy of Monumenti, Musei e Gallerie Pontificie, Vatican.

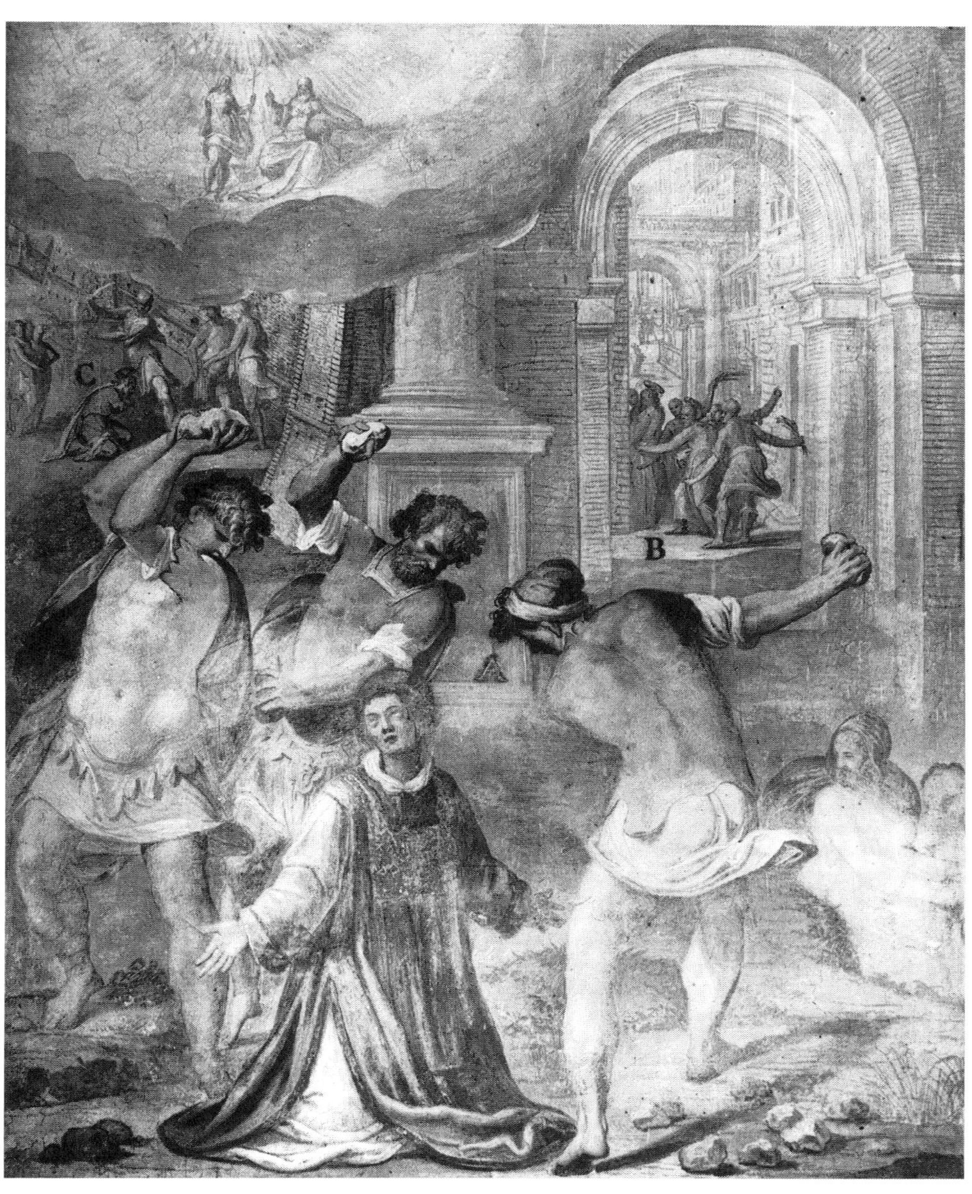

39. Niccolò Circignani, fresco II: *Martyrdom of St Stephen*. S. Stefano Rotondo, Rome (1582). Photograph courtesy of Monumenti, Musei e Gallerie Pontificie, Vatican.

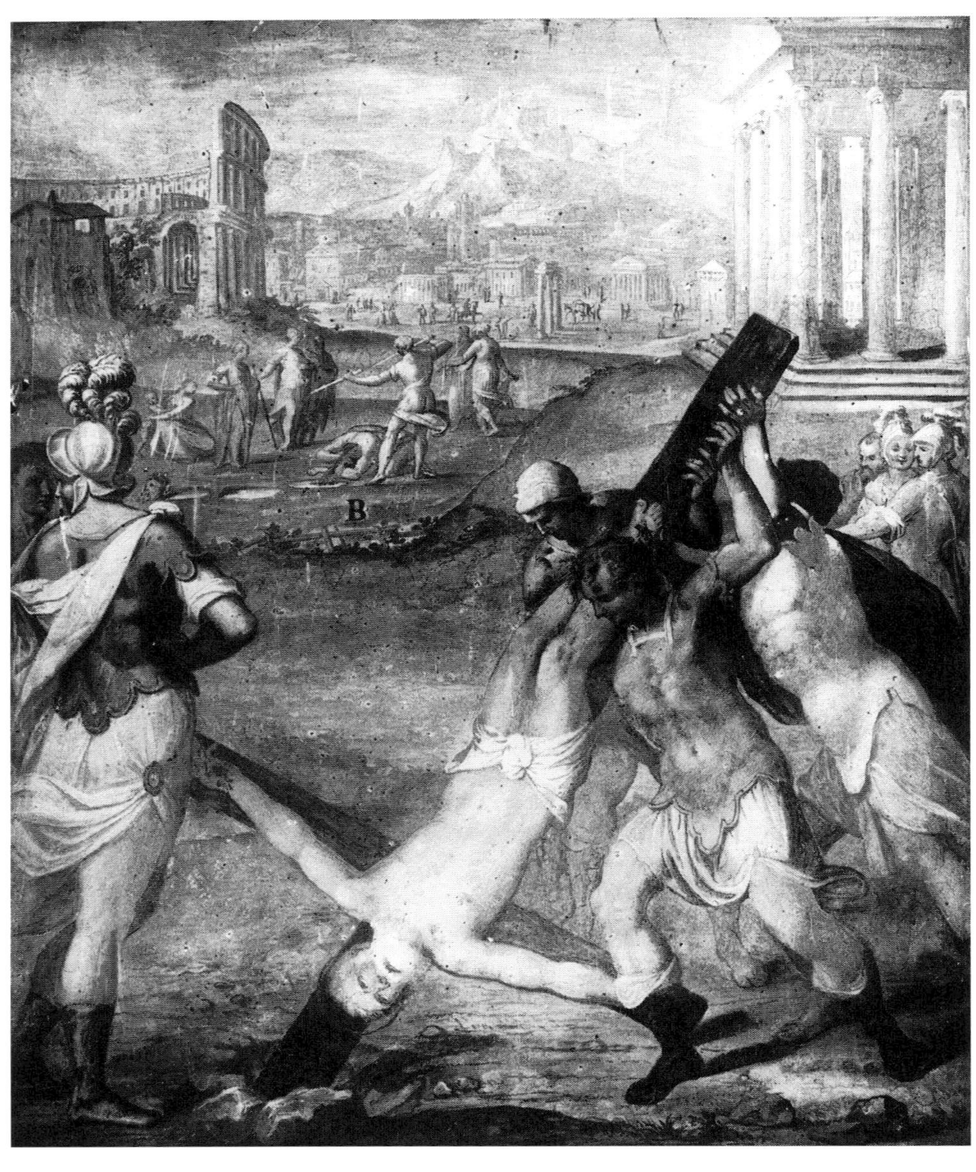

40. Niccolò Circignani, fresco III: *Martyrdom of Sts Peter and Paul*. S. Stefano Rotondo, Rome (1582). Photograph courtesy of Monumenti, Musei e Gallerie Pontificie, Vatican.

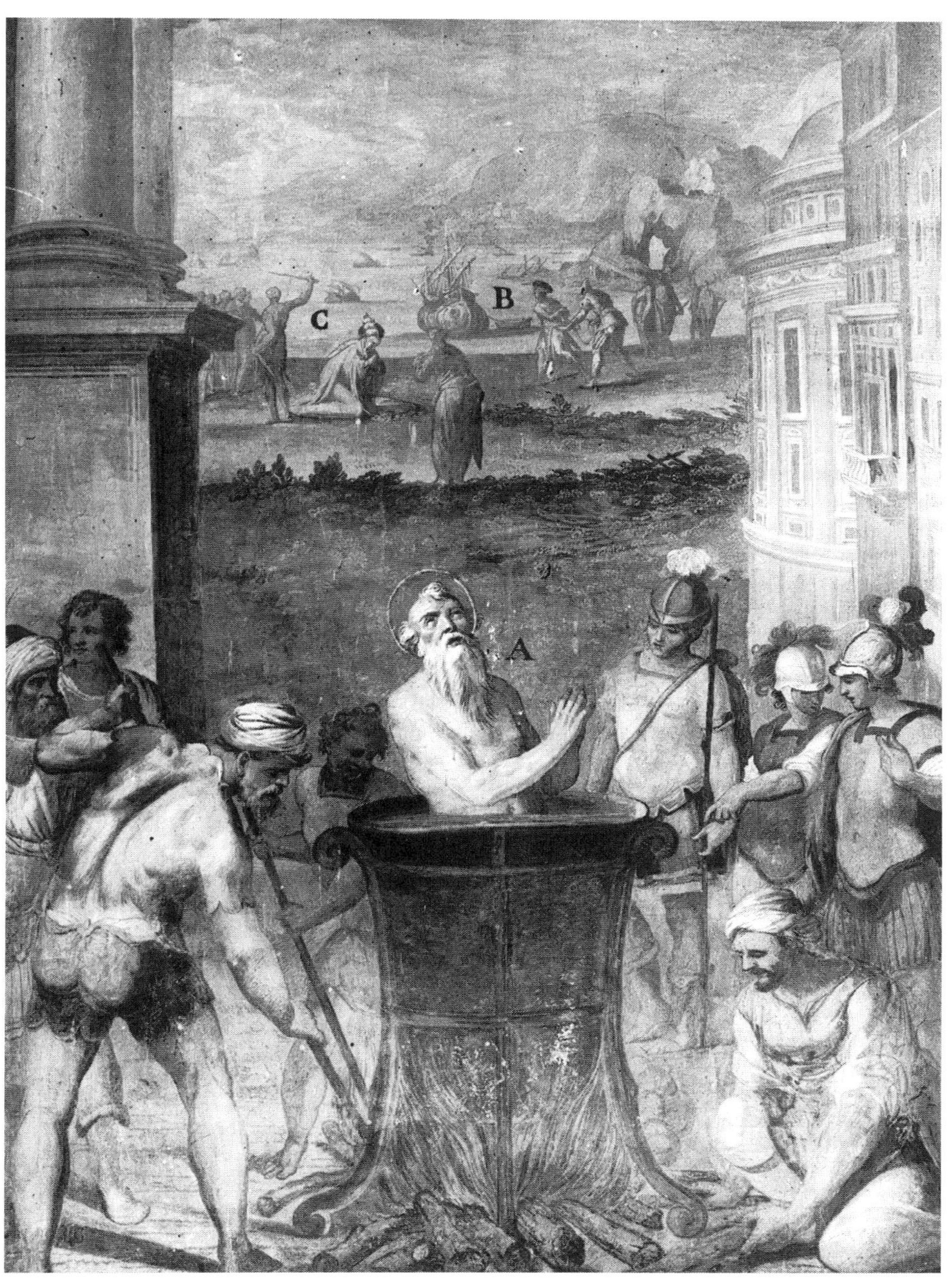

41. Niccolò Circignani, fresco VI: *Martyrdom of St John the Evangelist and Pope Cletus*. S. Stefano Rotondo, Rome (1582). Photograph courtesy of Monumenti, Musei e Gallerie Pontificie, Vatican.

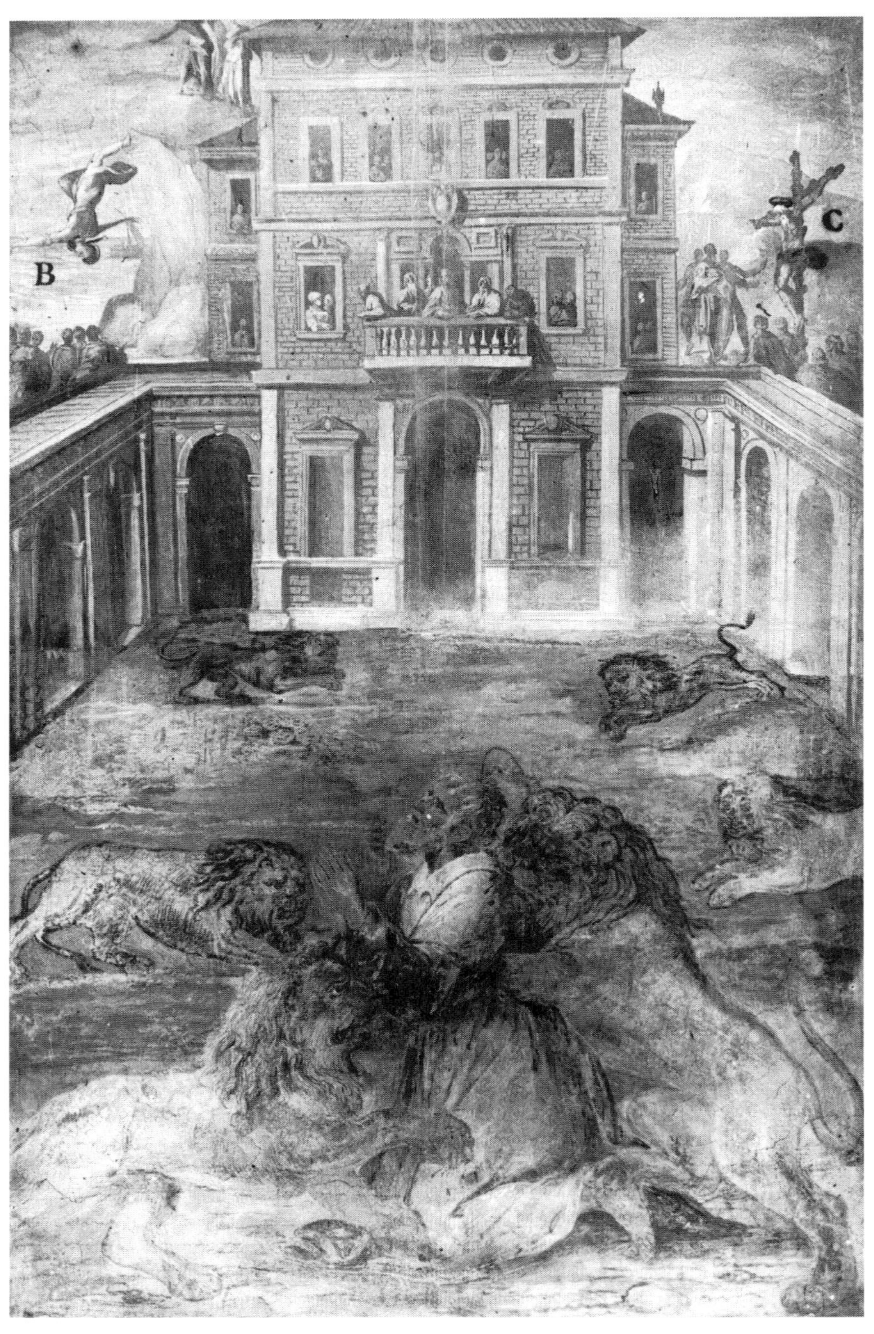

42. Niccolò Circignani, fresco VIII: *Martyrdom of St Ignatius of Antioch*. S. Stefano Rotondo, Rome (1582). Photograph courtesy of Monumenti, Musei e Gallerie Pontificie, Vatican.

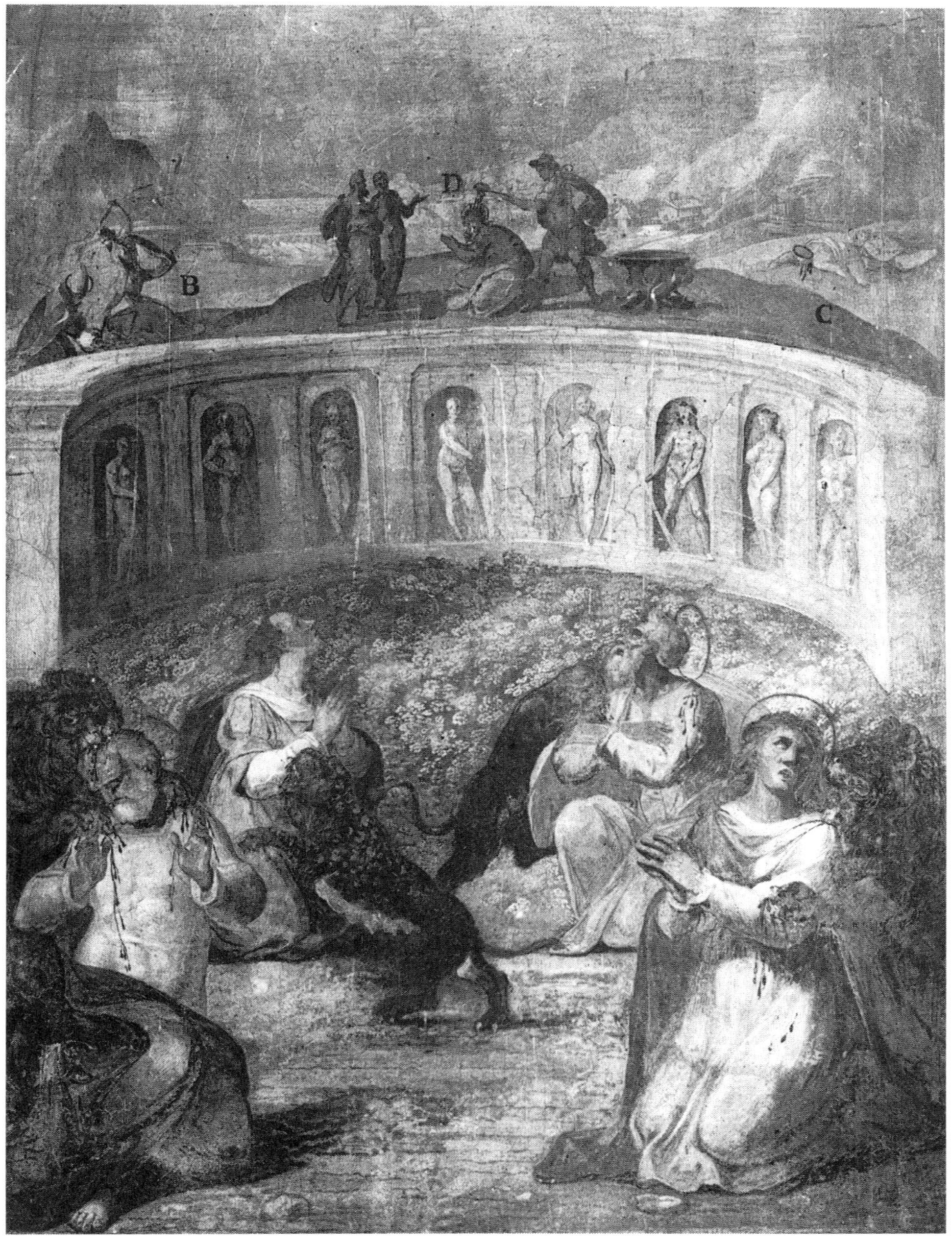

43. Niccolò Circignani, fresco XII: *Martyrdom of Sts Perpetua and Felicity*. S. Stefano Rotondo, Rome (1582). Photograph courtesy of Monumenti, Musei e Gallerie Pontificie, Vatican.

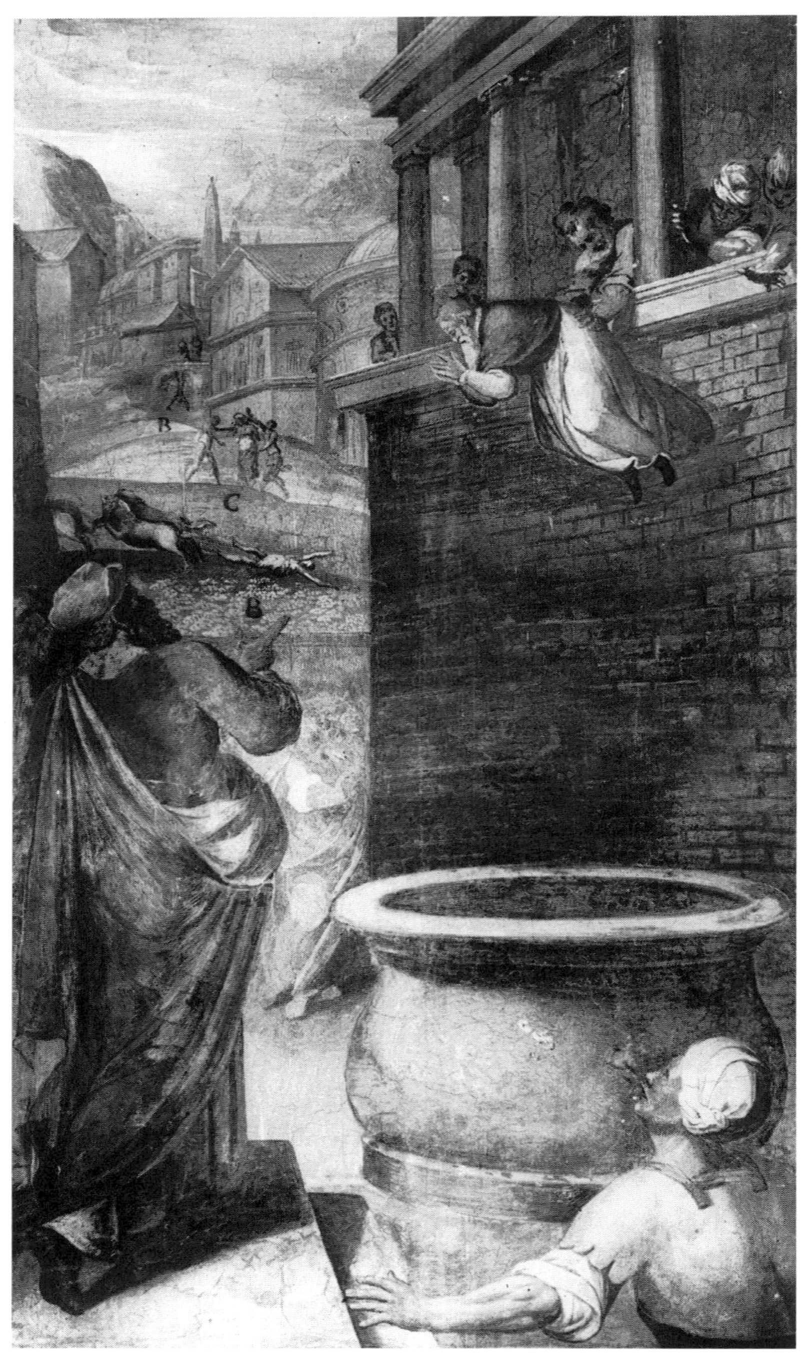

44. Niccolò Circignani, fresco XIII: *Martyrdom of Pope Callistus*. S. Stefano Rotondo, Rome (1582). Photograph courtesy of Monumenti, Musei e Gallerie Pontificie, Vatican.

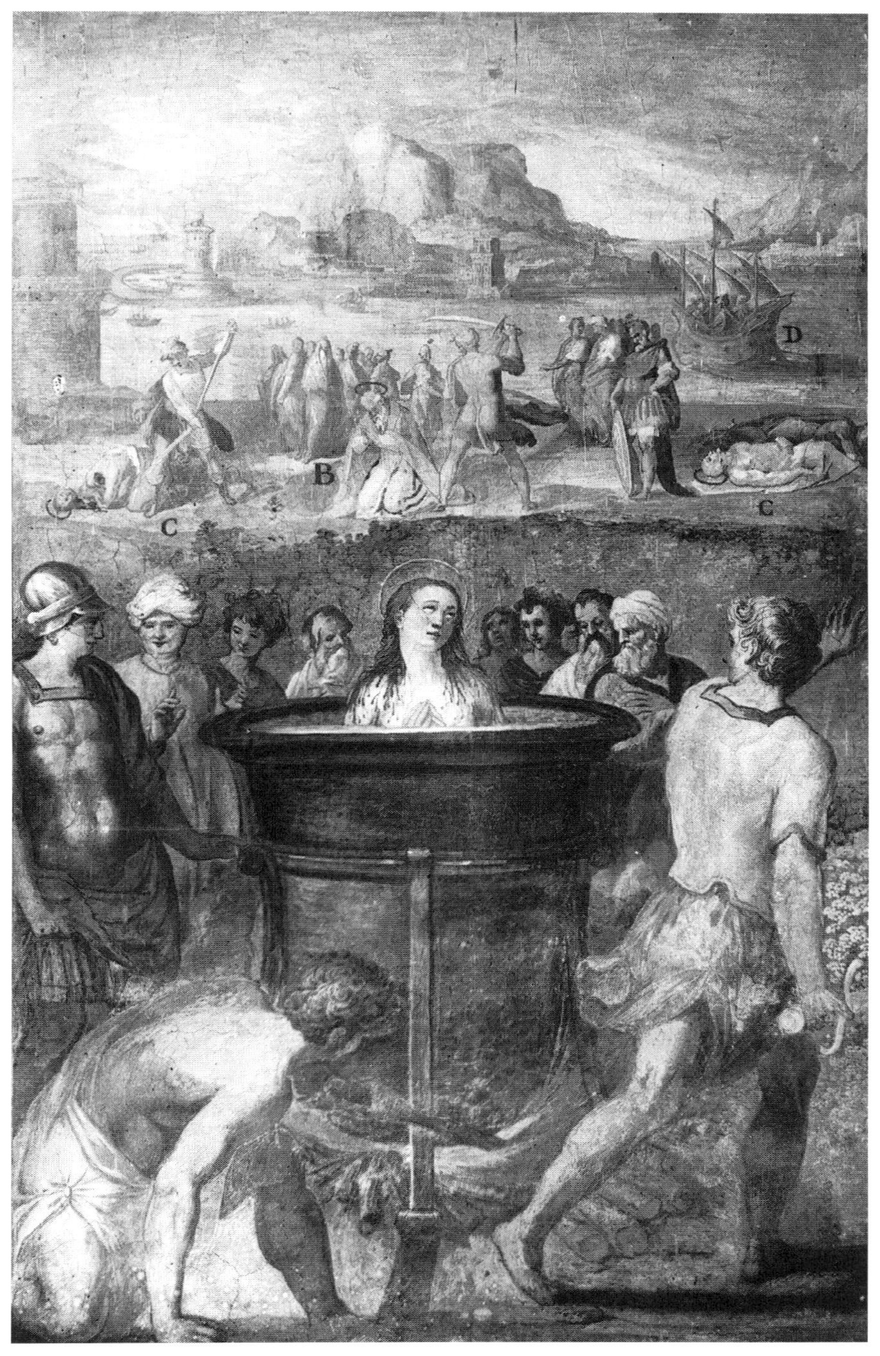

45. Niccolò Circignani, fresco XIV: *Martyrdom of St Cecilia*. S. Stefano Rotondo, Rome (1582). Photograph courtesy of Monumenti, Musei e Gallerie Pontificie, Vatican.

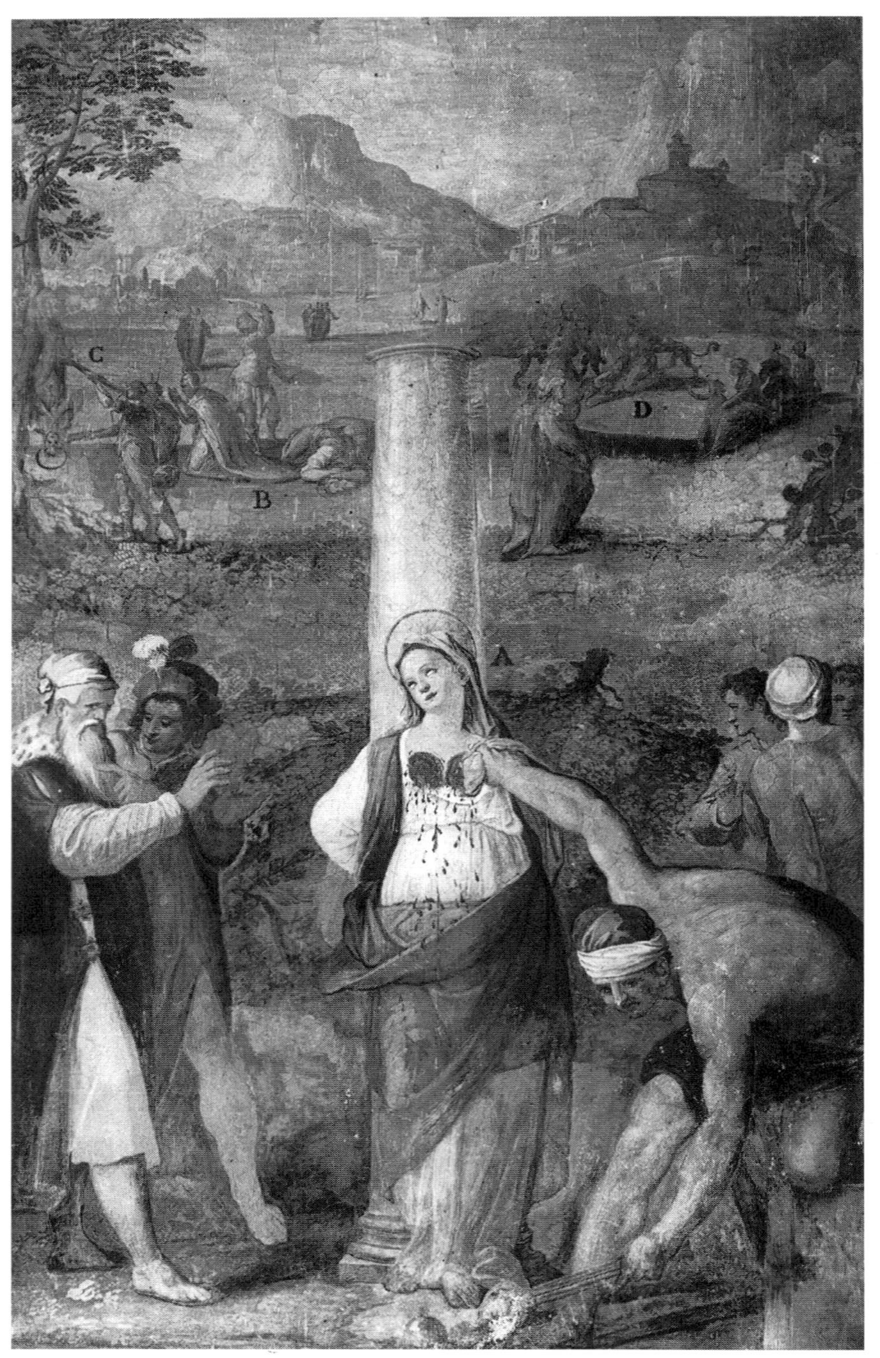

46. Niccolò Circignani, fresco XV: *Martyrdom of St Agatha*. S. Stefano Rotondo, Rome (1582). Photograph courtesy of Monumenti, Musei e Gallerie Pontificie, Vatican.

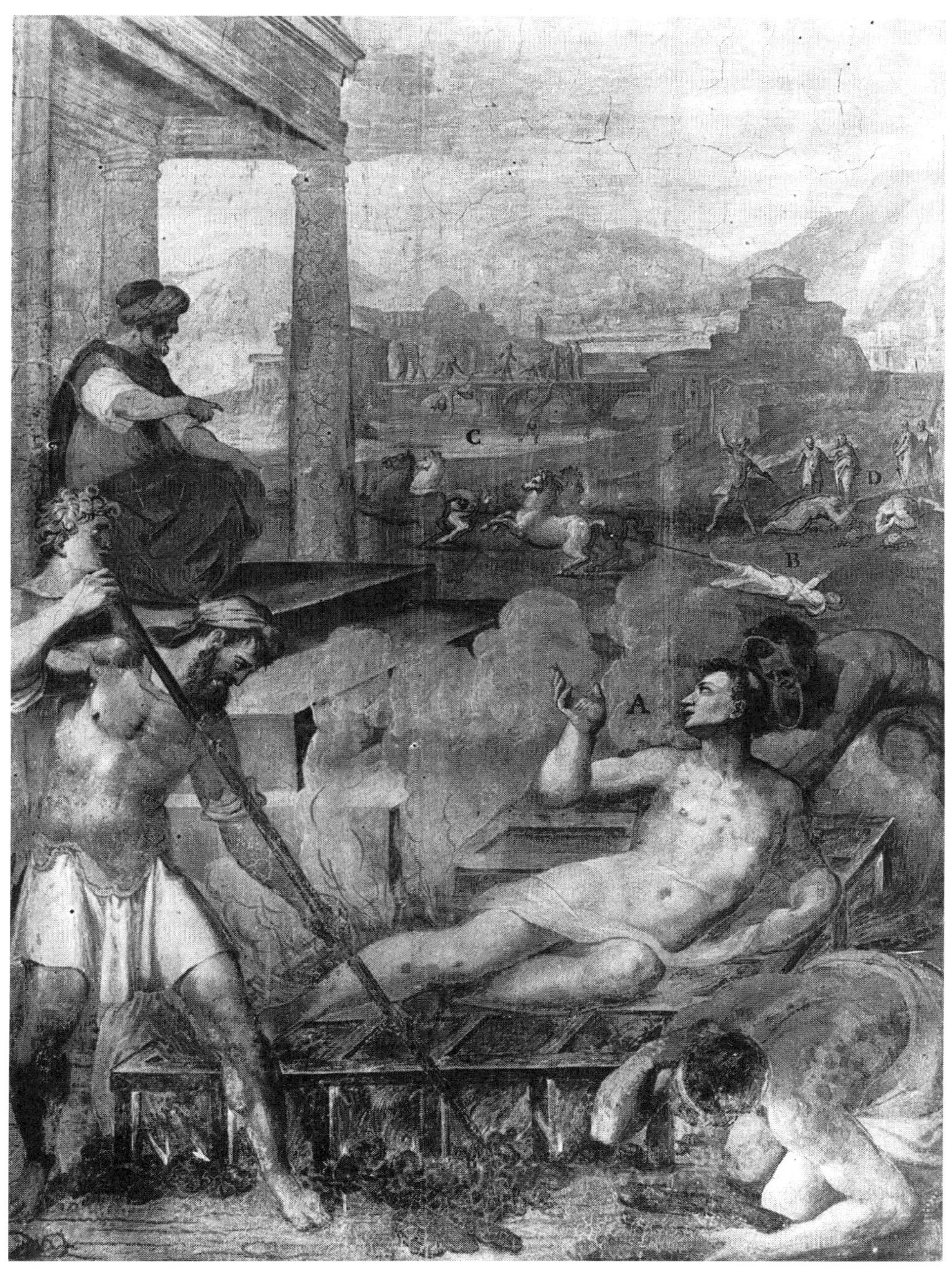

47. Niccolò Circignani, fresco XVII: *Martyrdom of St Lawrence*. S. Stefano Rotondo, Rome (1582). Photograph courtesy of Monumenti, Musei e Gallerie Pontificie, Vatican.

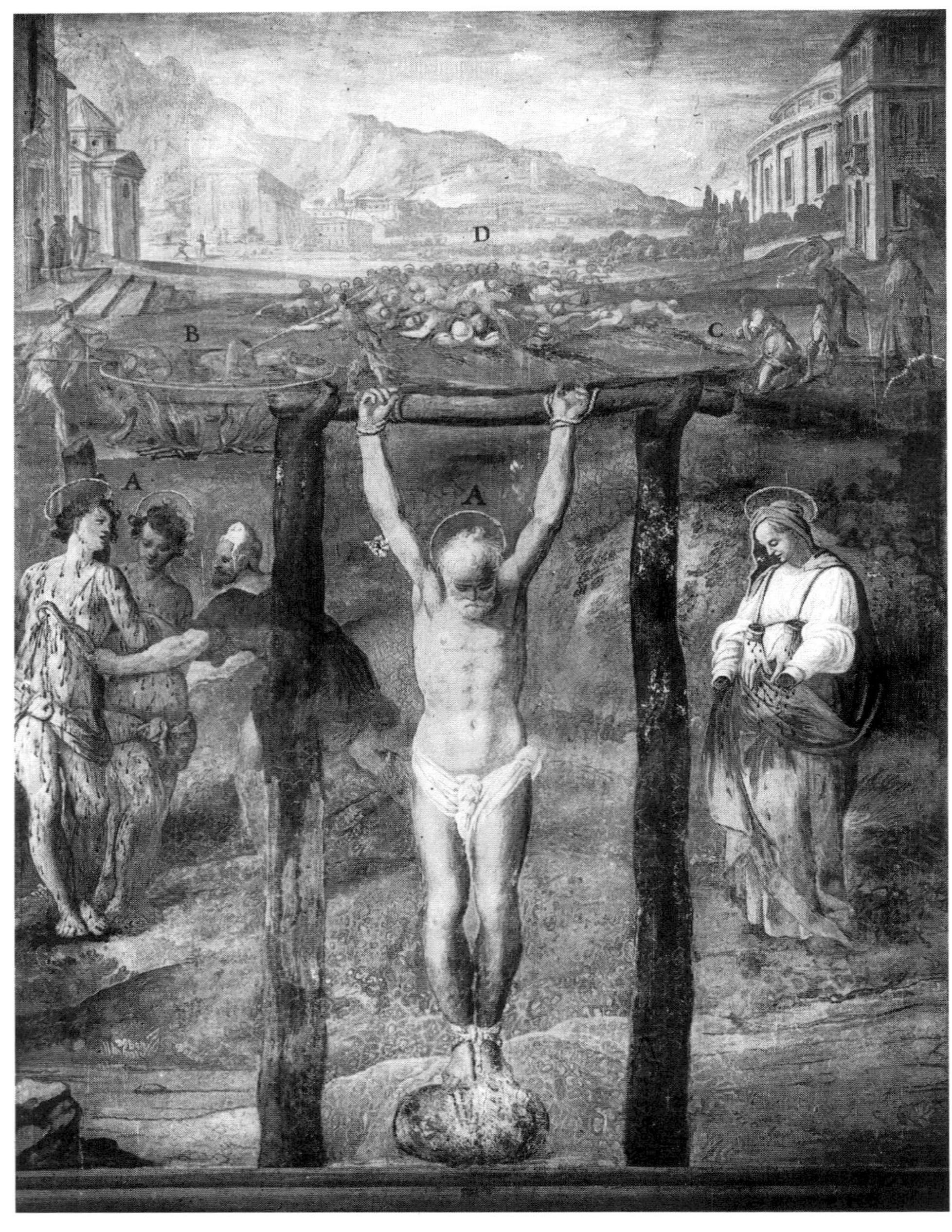

48. Niccolò Circignani, fresco XIX: *Martyrdom of Sts Marius, Martha, and Their Sons.*
S. Stefano Rotondo, Rome (1582). Photograph courtesy of Monumenti, Musei e Gallerie
Pontificie, Vatican.

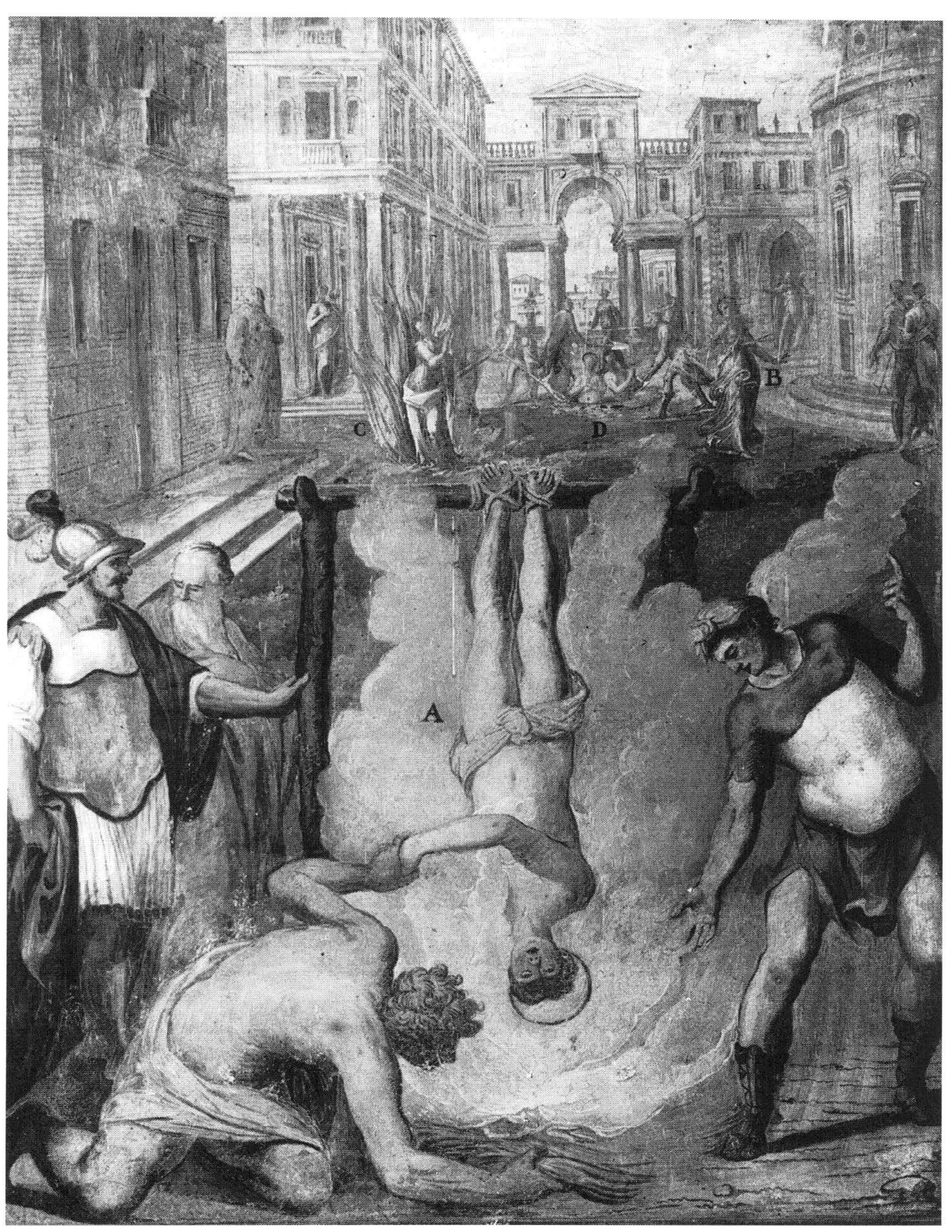

49. Niccolò Circignani, fresco XX: *Martyrdom of St Agapitus*. S. Stefano Rotondo, Rome (1582). Photograph courtesy of Monumenti, Musei e Gallerie Pontificie, Vatican.

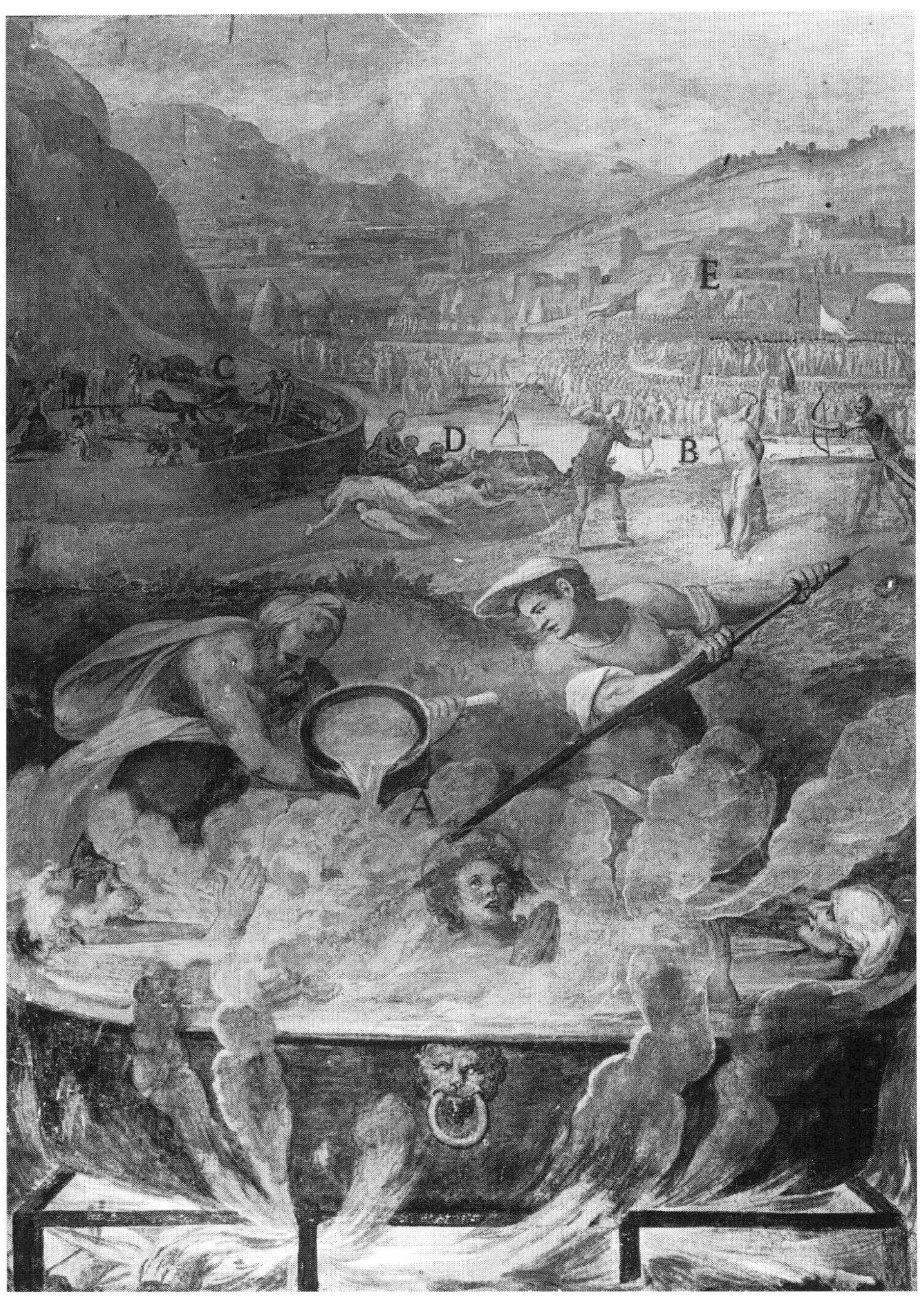

50. Niccolò Circignani, fresco XXV: *Martyrdom of Sts Vitus, Modestus, and Crescentius*. S. Stefano Rotondo, Rome (1582). Photograph courtesy of Monumenti, Musei e Gallerie Pontificie, Vatican.

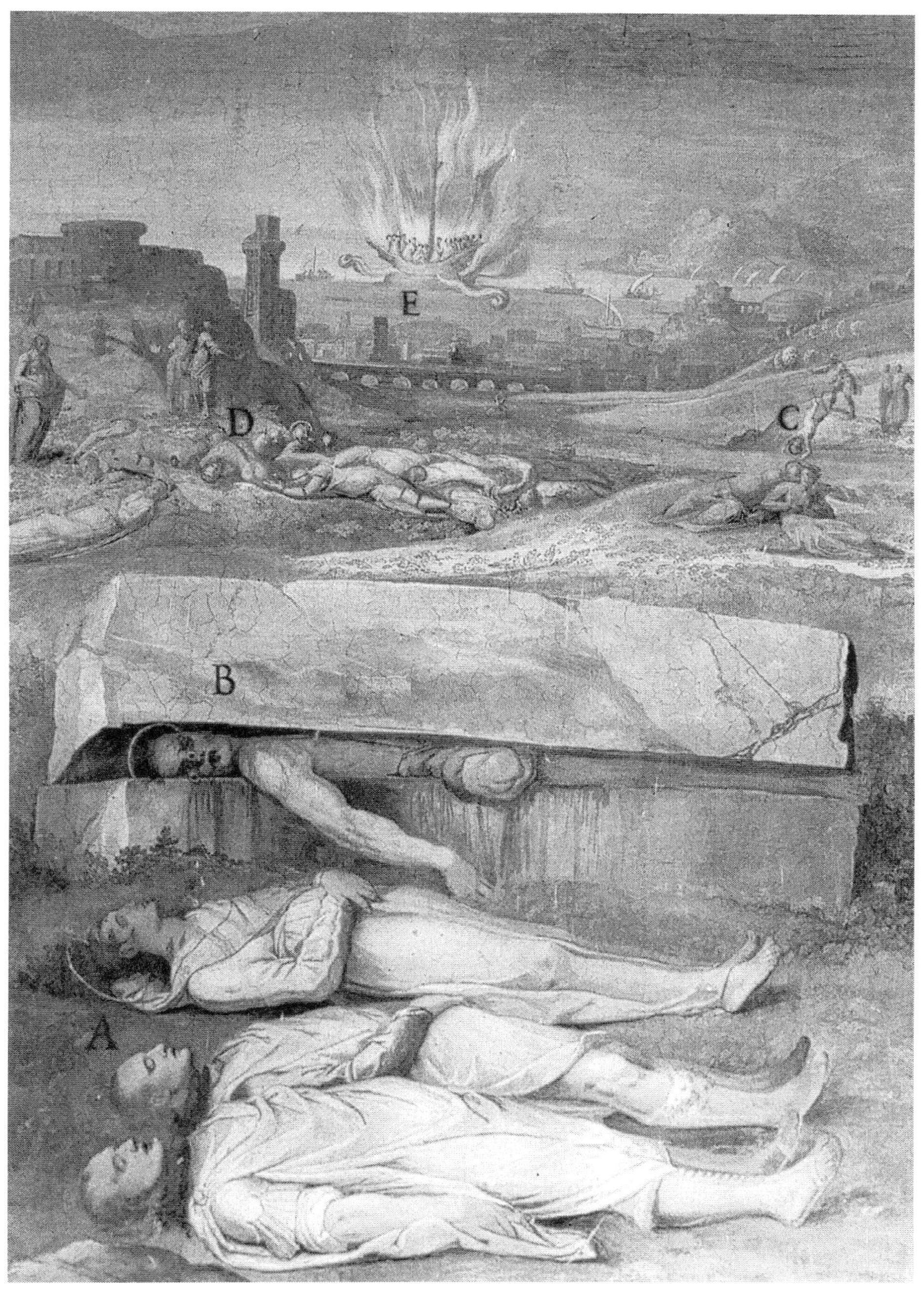

51. Niccolò Circignani, fresco XXVIII: *Martyrdom of Sts John, Paul, Bibiana, and Artemius.* S. Stefano Rotondo, Rome (1582). Published by permission of H. Brandenburg, photographer Daniela Gauss.

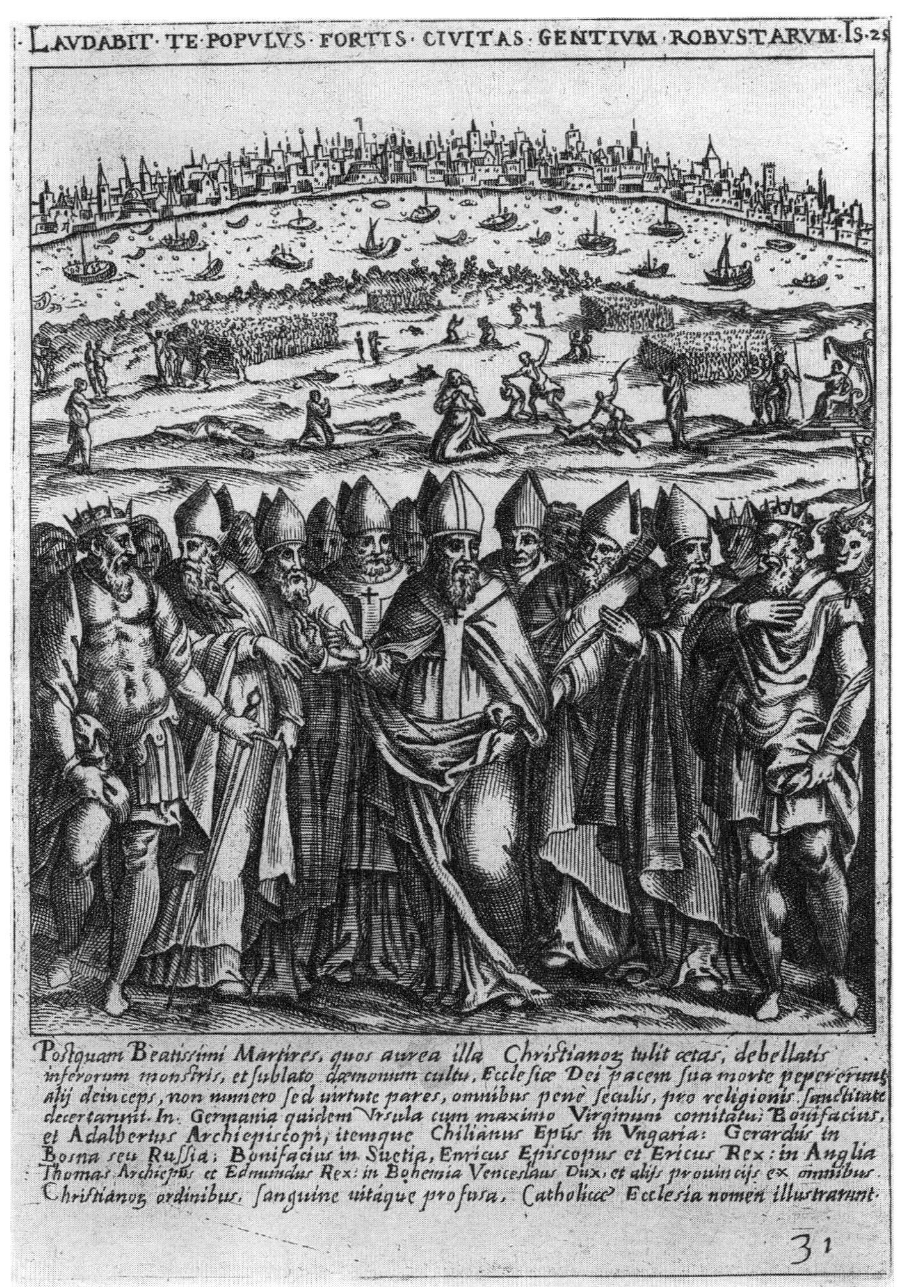

52. Giovanni Battista Cavallieri, *Laudabit te populus fortis civitas gentium robustarum*. Engraving after Niccolò Circignani, fresco XXXI: *Triumph of the Martyrs* from S. Stefano Rotondo, Rome (1585). Typ 525 85.285F, Department of Printing and Graphic Arts, Houghton Library, Harvard University Library.

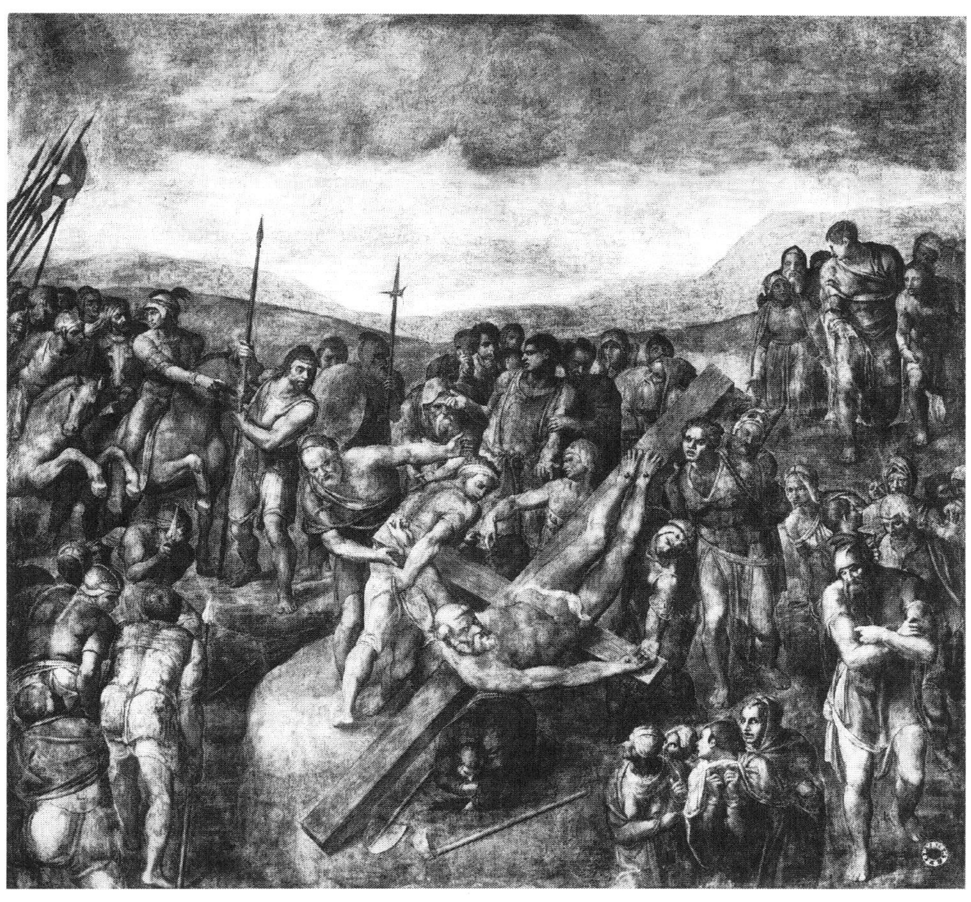

53. Michelangelo, *Crucifixion of St Peter*. Fresco, Cappella Paolina, Vatican (1545–50). Photograph courtesy Art Resource, New York.

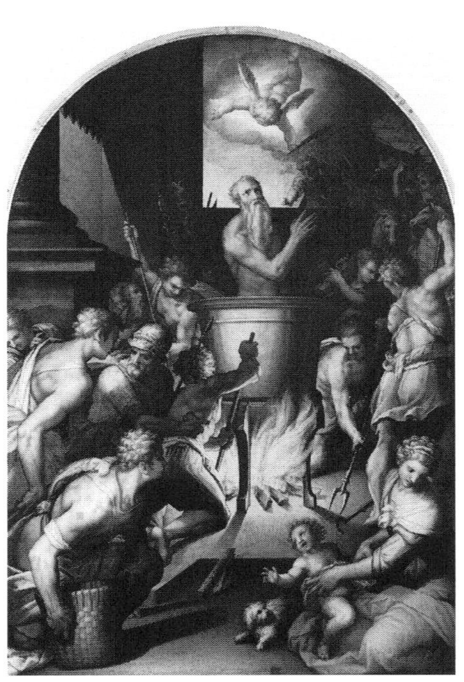

54. Battista Naldini, *Martyrdom of St John the Evangelist*. Fresco, S. Giovanni Decollato, Rome (before 1584). Photograph courtesy of the Istituto Centrale per il Catalogo e la Documentazione, Ministerio per i Beni Culturali e Ambientali, Rome.

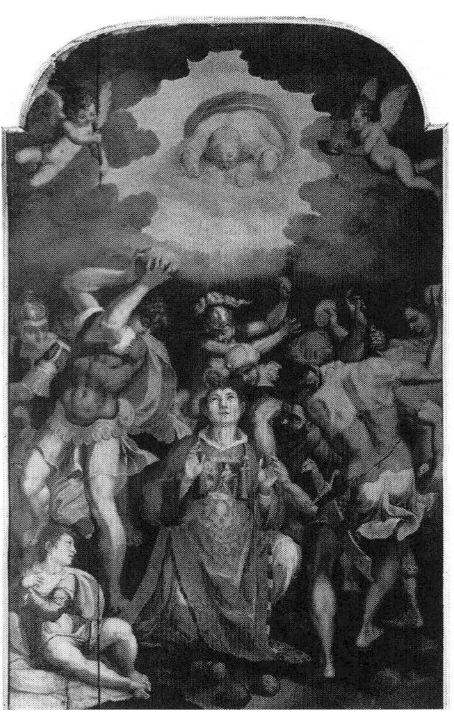

55. Niccolò Circignani, *Martyrdom of St Stephen*. Canvas, Pinacoteca, Città di Castello (1570). Photograph courtesy of the Comune di Città di Castello.

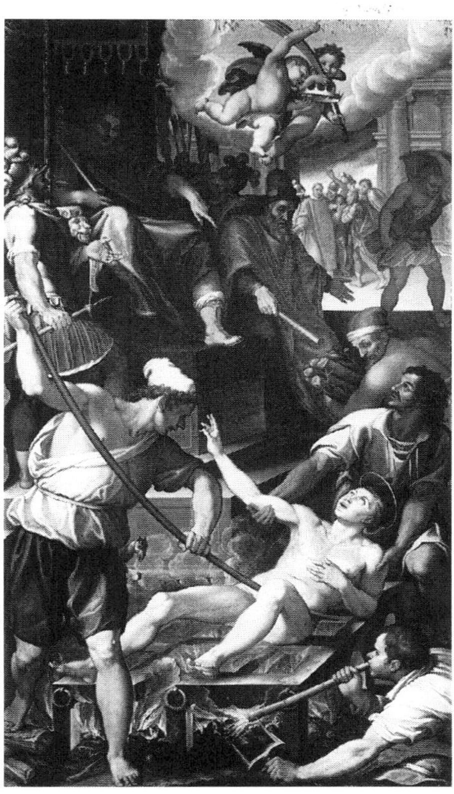

56. Cesare Nebbia, *Martyrdom of St Lawrence*. Fresco, Peretti Chapel, S. Susanna, Rome (1591–1600). Photograph courtesy of the Istituto Centrale per il Catalogo e la Documentazione, Ministerio per i Beni Culturali e Ambientali, Rome.

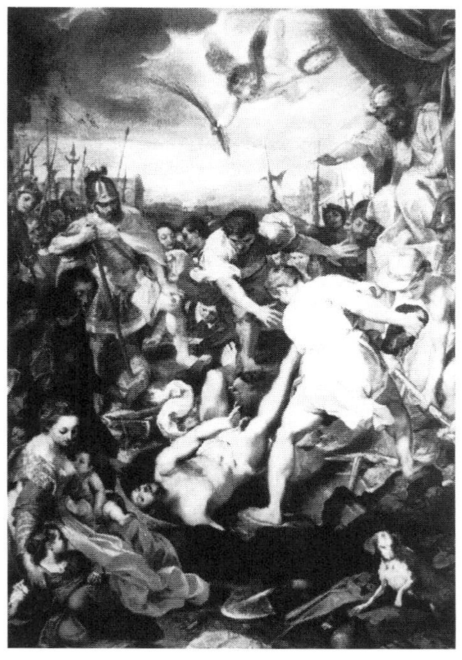

57. Federico Barocci, *Martyrdom of St Vitalis*. Canvas, Pinacoteca di Brera, Milan (1583). Under licence from the Italian Ministry for Cultural Goods and Activities.

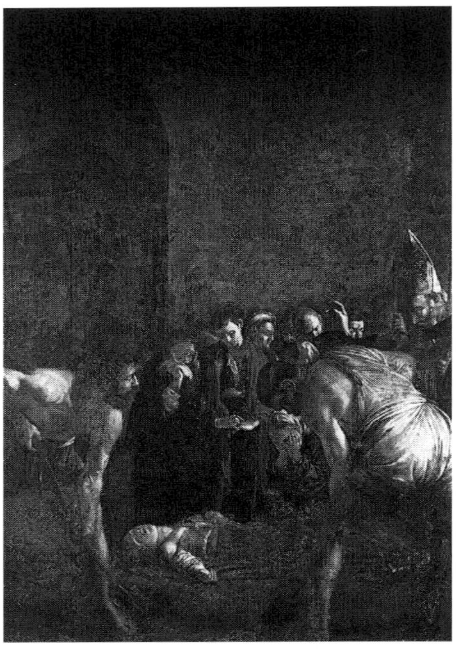

58. Caravaggio, *Burial of St Lucy*. Canvas, S. Lucia, Syracuse (1608). Photograph courtesy Art Resource, New York.

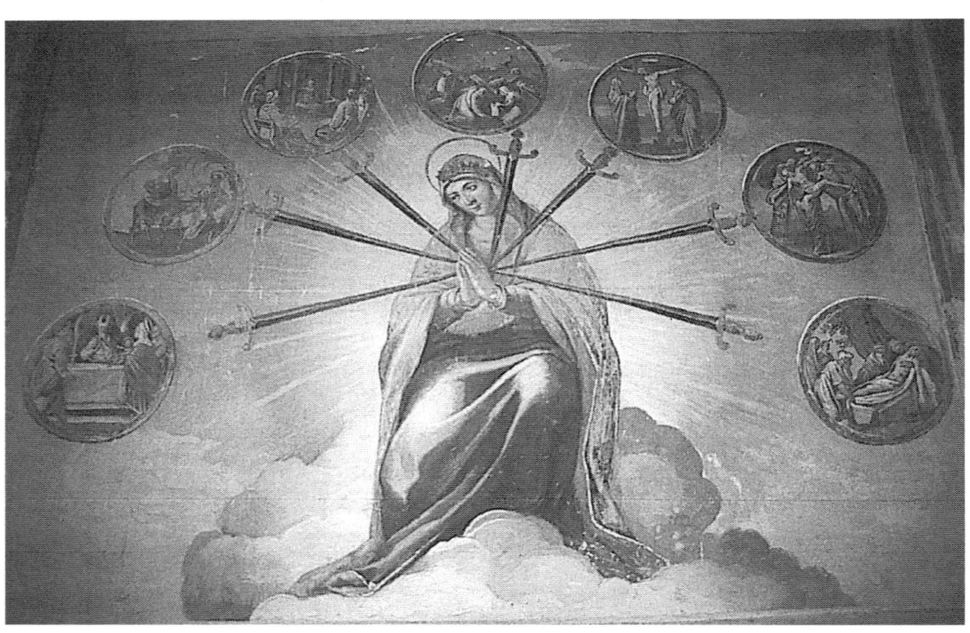

59. Antonio Tempesta, *Madonna of the Seven Sorrows*. Fresco, S. Stefano Rotondo, Rome (1583). Photograph by the author.

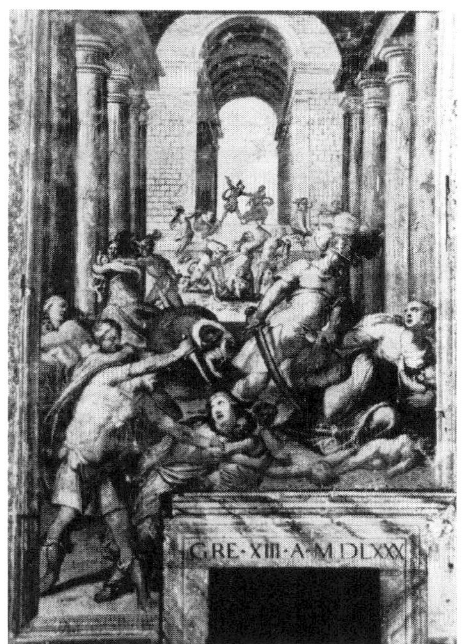

60. Antonio Tempesta, *Massacre of the Innocents*. Fresco, S. Stefano Rotondo, Rome (1583). Photograph courtesy of Monumenti, Musei e Gallerie Pontificie, Vatican.

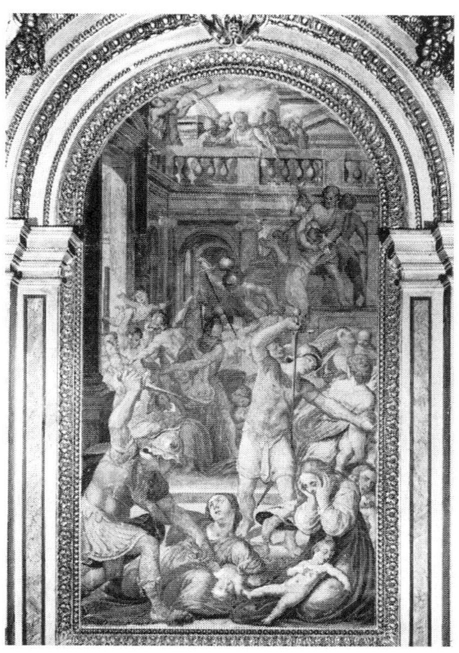

61. Giovanni Battista Pozzo, *Massacre of the Innocents*. Fresco, S. Maria Maggiore, Rome (1587). Photograph © Photo Vasari Rome.

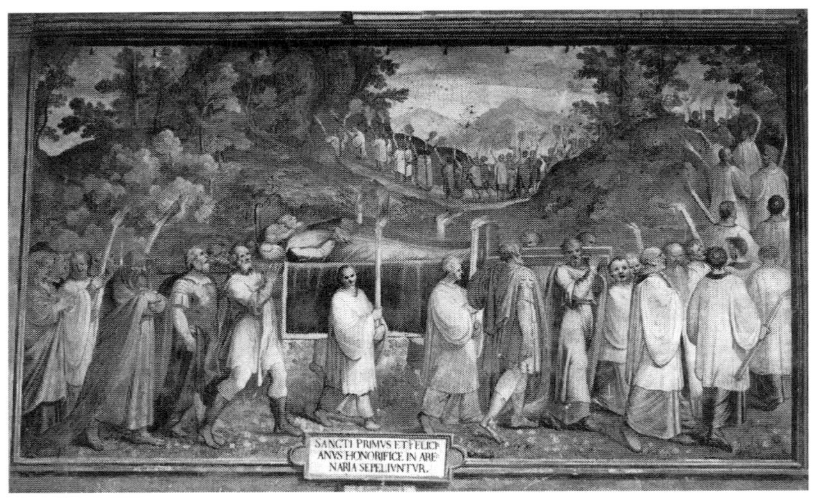

62. Antonio Tempesta, *Funeral Procession of Sts Primus and Felicianus*. Fresco, S. Stefano Rotondo, Rome (1583). Photograph courtesy of the Research Library, Getty Research Institute, Los Angeles (86.P.8).

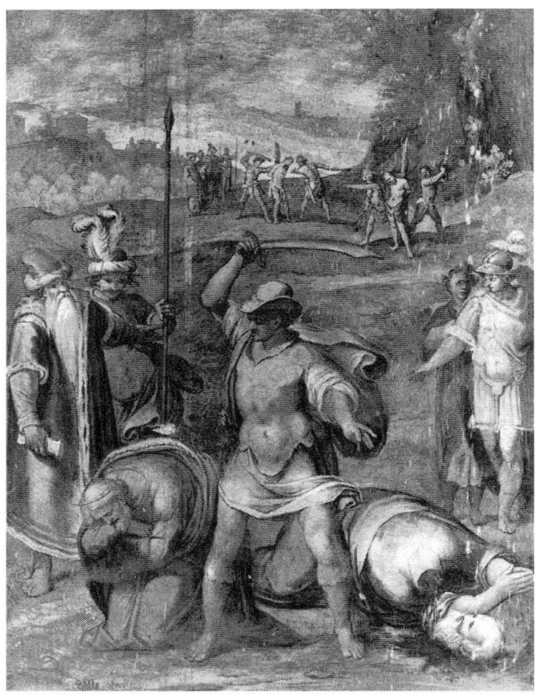

63. Antonio Tempesta, *Beheading of Sts Primus and Felicianus*. Fresco, S. Stefano Rotondo, Rome (1583). Photograph courtesy of the Research Library, Getty Research Institute, Los Angeles (86.P.8).

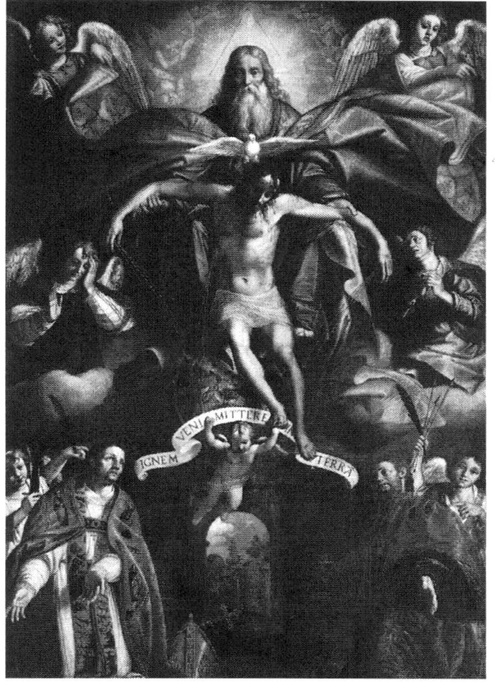

64. Durante Alberti, *Holy Trinity with St Edmund and St Thomas of Canterbury*. Canvas, S. Tommaso di Canterbury, Rome (ca. 1581). Photograph courtesy of the Istituto Centrale per il Catalogo e la Documentazione, Ministerio per i Beni Culturali e Ambientali, Rome.

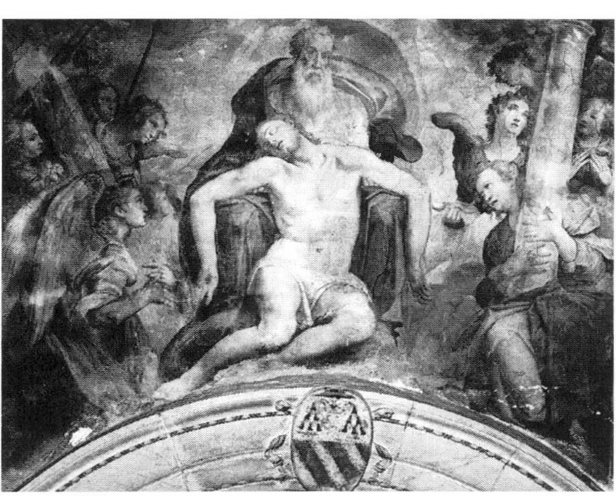

65. Taddeo and Federico Zuccaro, *Trinity Pietà*. Fresco, Cappella Pucci, SS. Trinità dei Monti, Rome (1589). Photograph courtesy of the Istituto Centrale per il Catalogo e la Documentazione, Ministerio per i Beni Culturali e Ambientali, Rome.

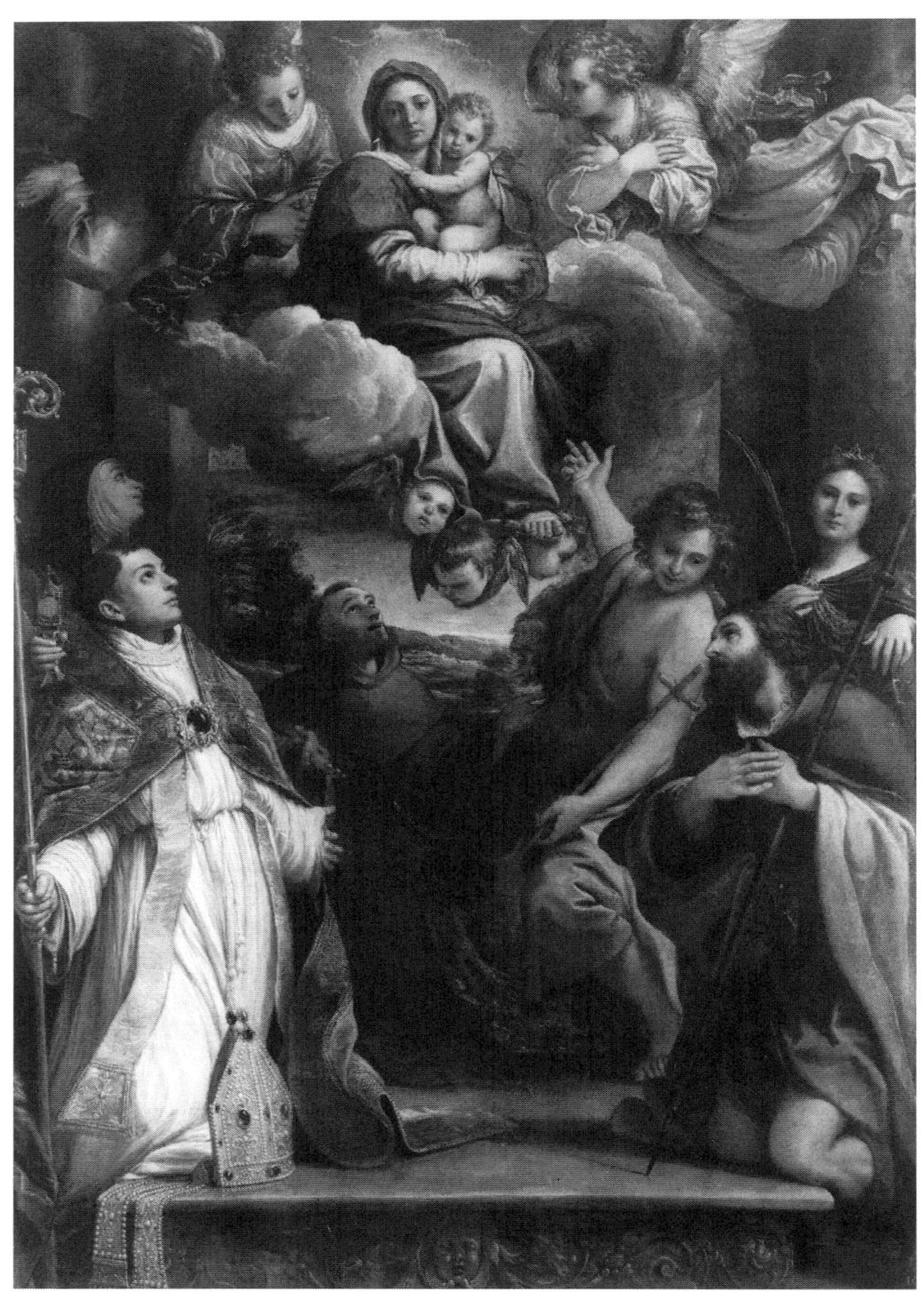

66. Annibale Carracci, S. Ludovico altarpiece. Canvas, Pinacoteca, Bologna (1589–90). Photograph courtesy of the Soprintendenza per il Patrimonio Storico Artistico e Demoetnoantropologico, Bologna.

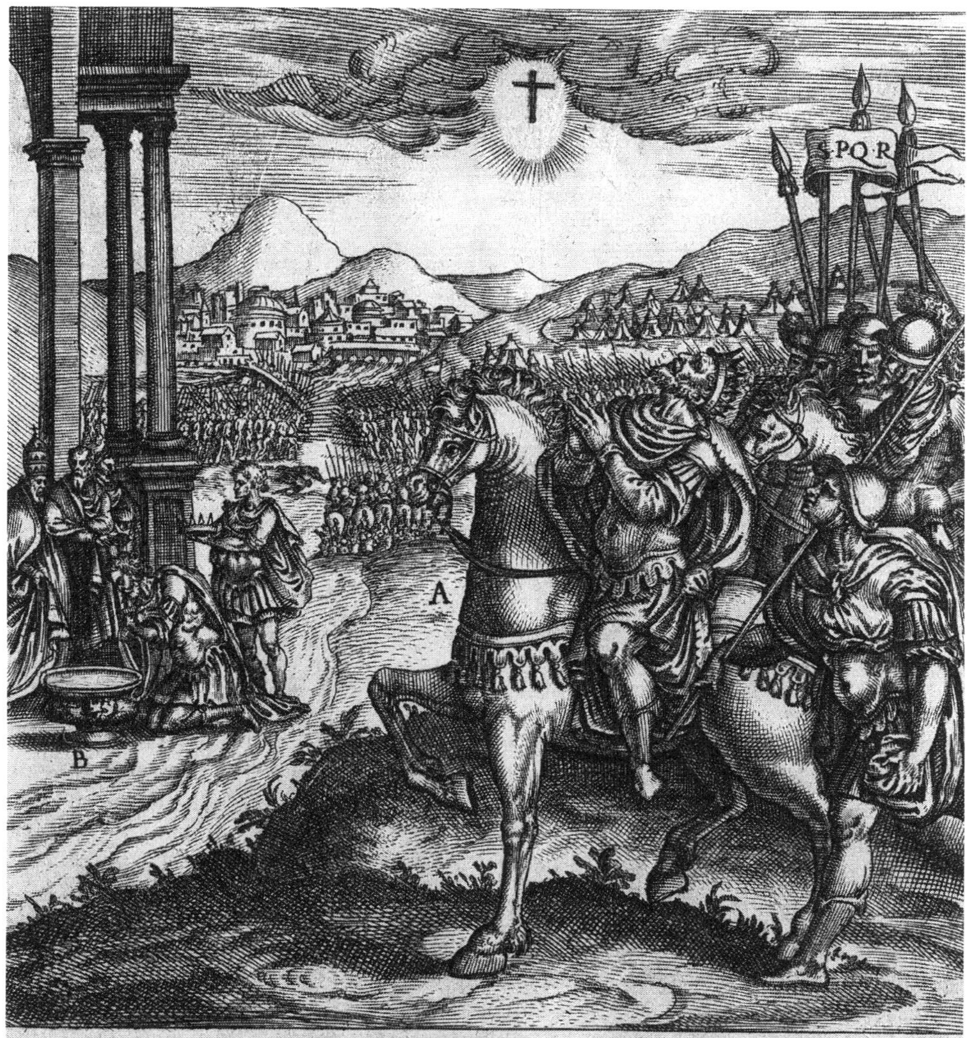

67. Giovanni Battista Cavallieri after Niccolò Circignani, *Conversion of Constantine the Great*. From *Ecclesiae anglicanae trophaea* (1584). Typ 525 85.285F, Department of Printing and Graphic Arts, Houghton Library, Harvard University Library.

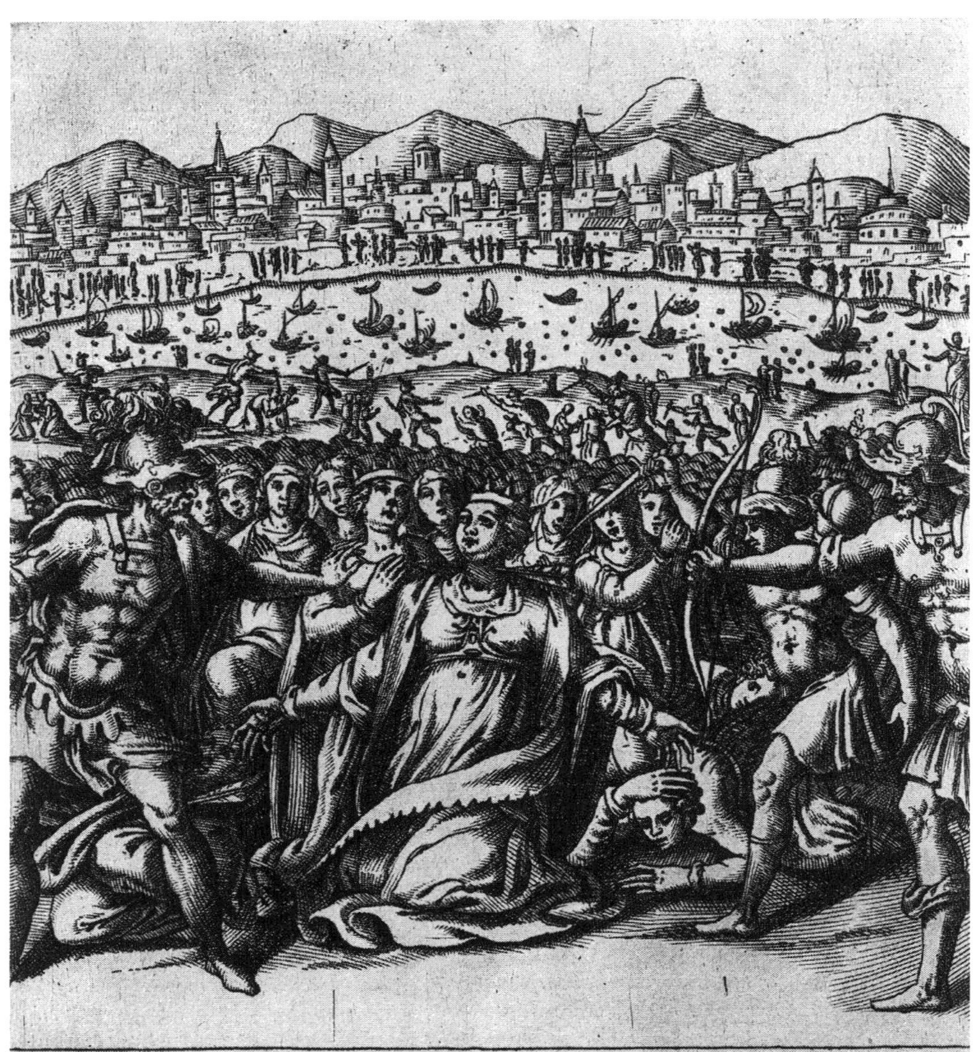

68. Giovanni Battista Cavallieri after Niccolò Circignani, *Martyrdom of St Ursula*. From *Ecclesiae anglicanae trophaea* (1584). Typ 525 85.285F, Department of Printing and Graphic Arts, Houghton Library, Harvard University Library.

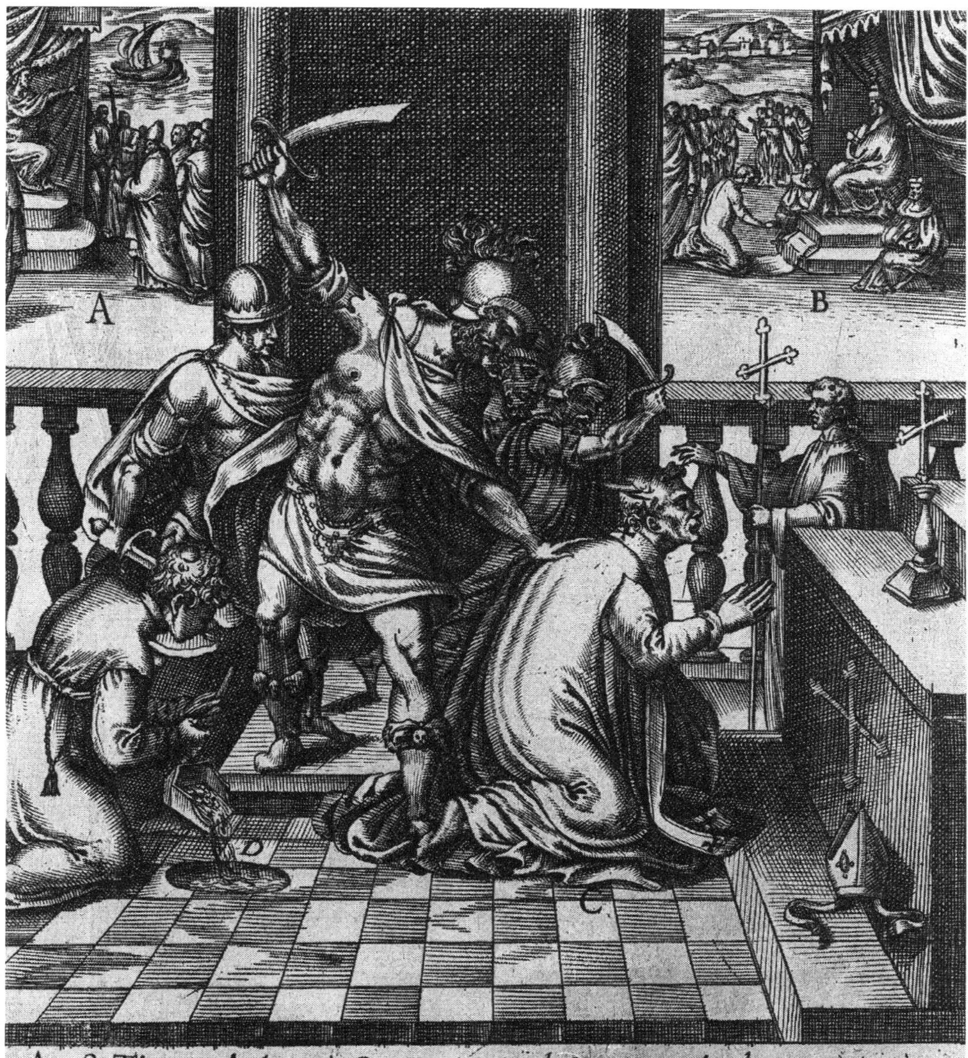

69. Giovanni Battista Cavallieri after Niccolò Circignani, *Martyrdom of St Thomas à Becket*.
From *Ecclesiae anglicanae trophae*a (1584). Typ 525 85.285F, Department of Printing
and Graphic Arts, Houghton Library, Harvard University Library.

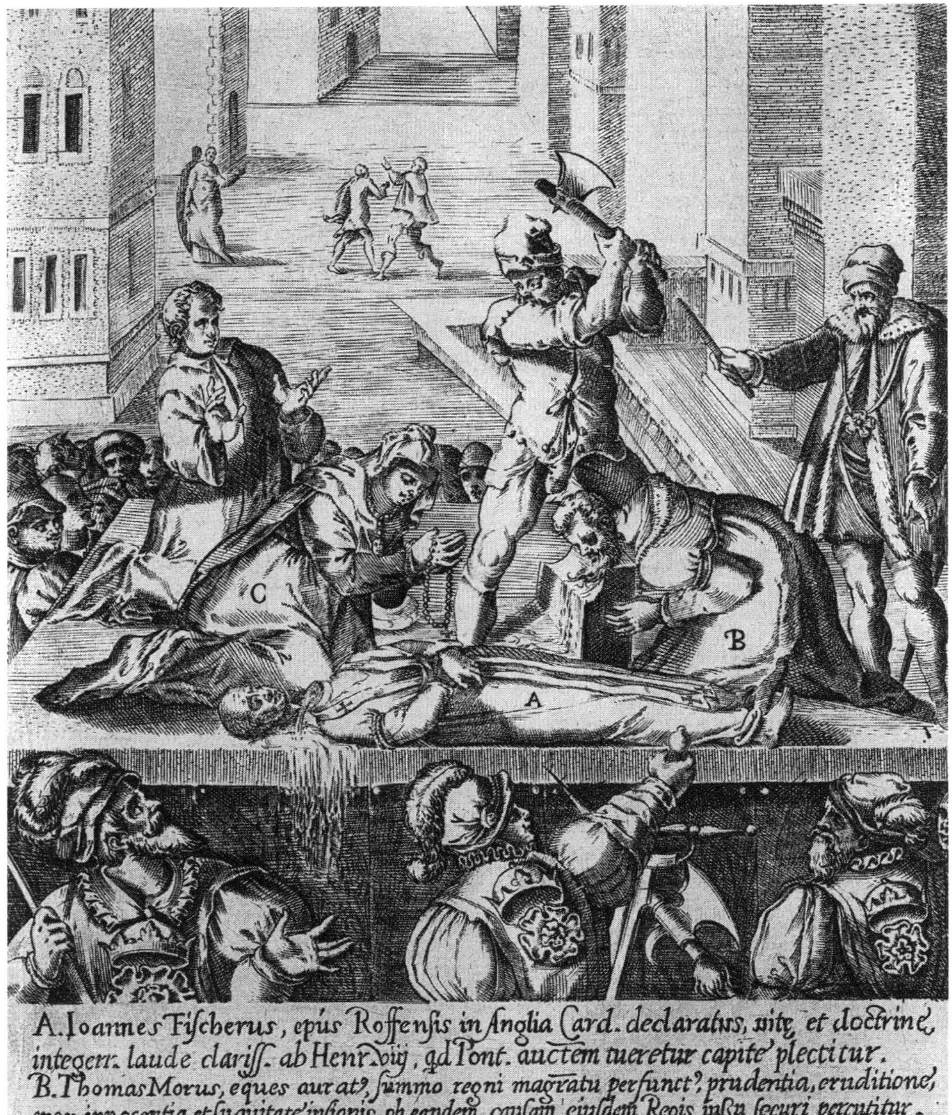

70. Giovanni Battista Cavallieri after Niccolò Circignani, *Martyrdom of John Fisher and Thomas More*. From *Ecclesiae anglicanae trophaea* (1584). Typ 525 85.285F, Department of Printing and Graphic Arts, Houghton Library, Harvard University Library.

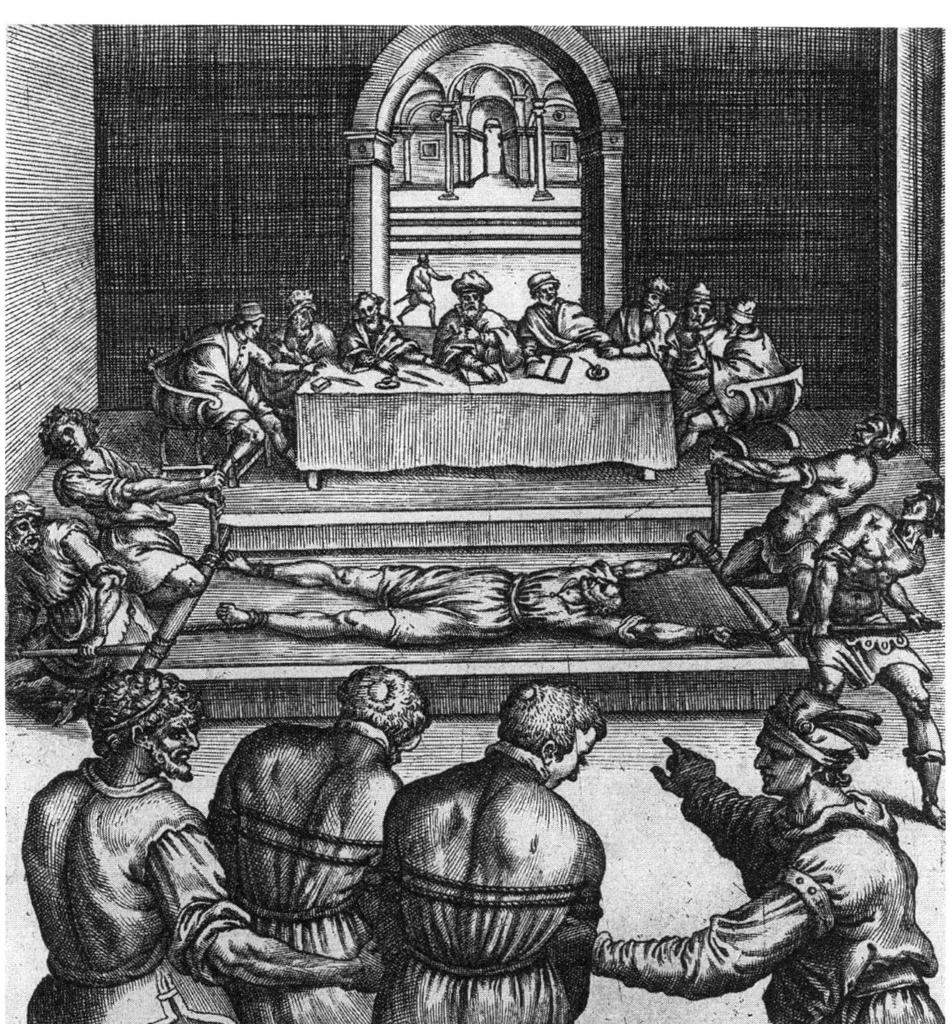

71. Giovanni Battista Cavallieri after Niccolò Circignani, *Martyrdom of Campion, Sherwin, and Briant*. From *Ecclesiae anglicanae trophaea* (1584). Typ 525 85.285F, Department of Printing and Graphic Arts, Houghton Library, Harvard University Library.

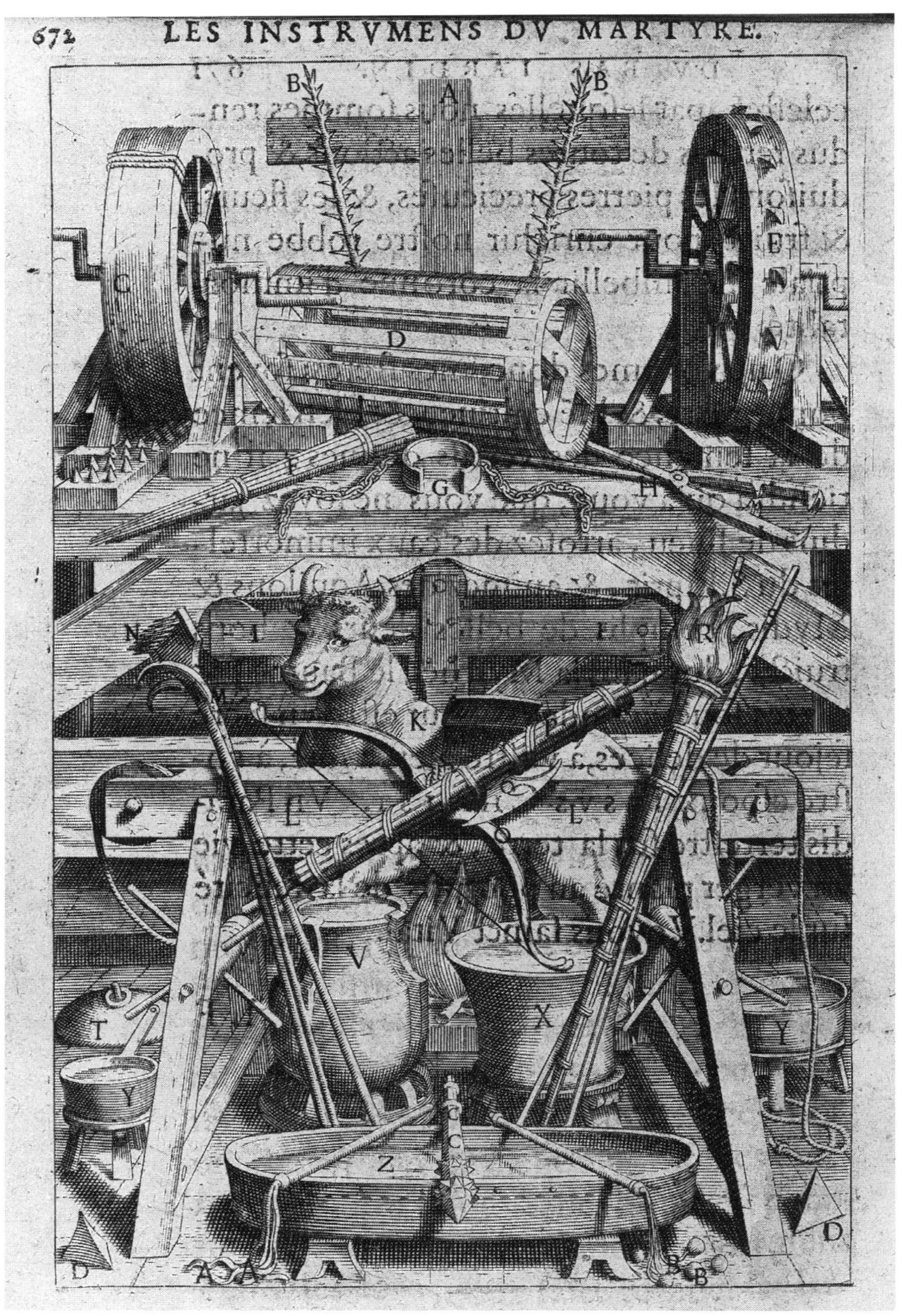

72. Matthäus Greuter after Giovanni Battista Fiammeri, *The Instruments of Martyrdom*. From Richeôme, *La peinture spirituelle* (1611). By permission of the Folger Shakespeare Library.

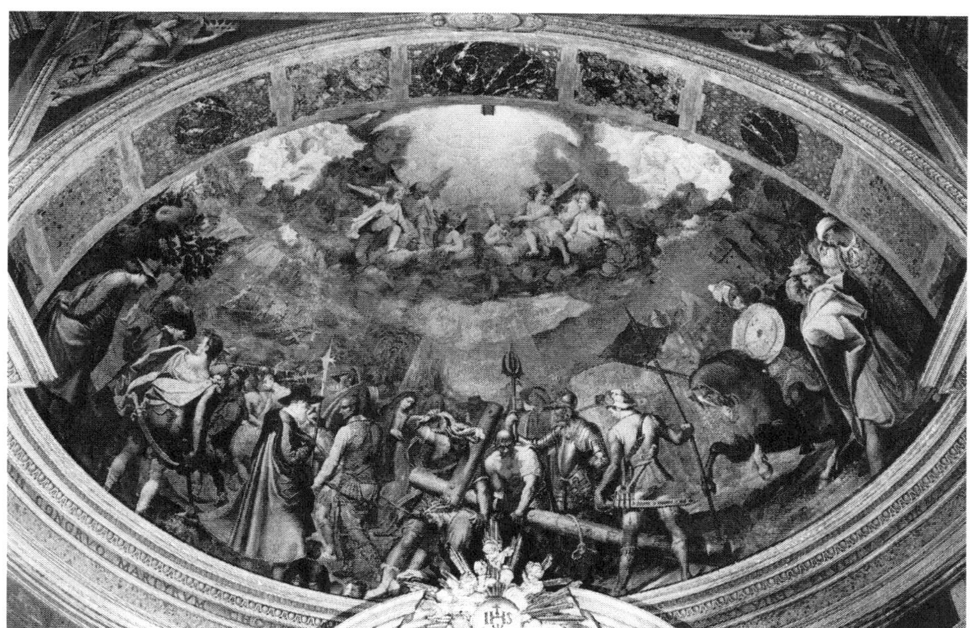

73. Andrea Commodi, *The Way to Calvary*. Fresco, S. Vitale, Rome (ca. 1599–1600). Photograph courtesy of the Archivio Fotografico Soprintendenza Speciale per il Polo Museale Romano.

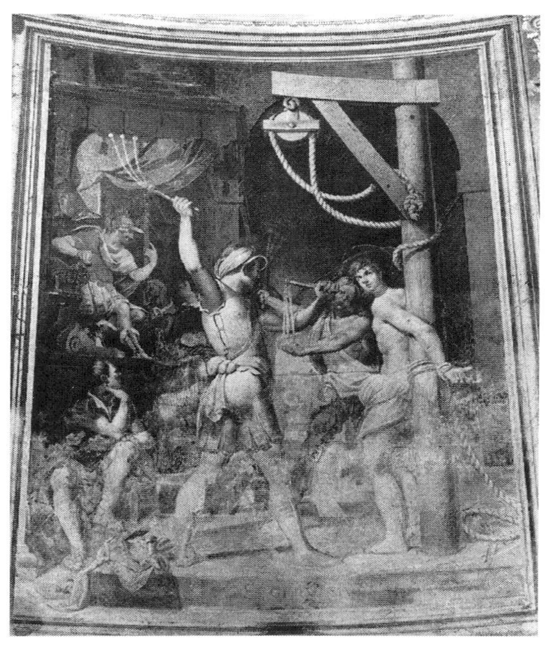

74. Andrea Commodi, *Flagellation of St Gervasius*. Fresco, S. Vitale, Rome (ca. 1599–1600). Photograph courtesy of the Archivio Fotografico Soprintendenza Speciale per il Polo Museale Romano.

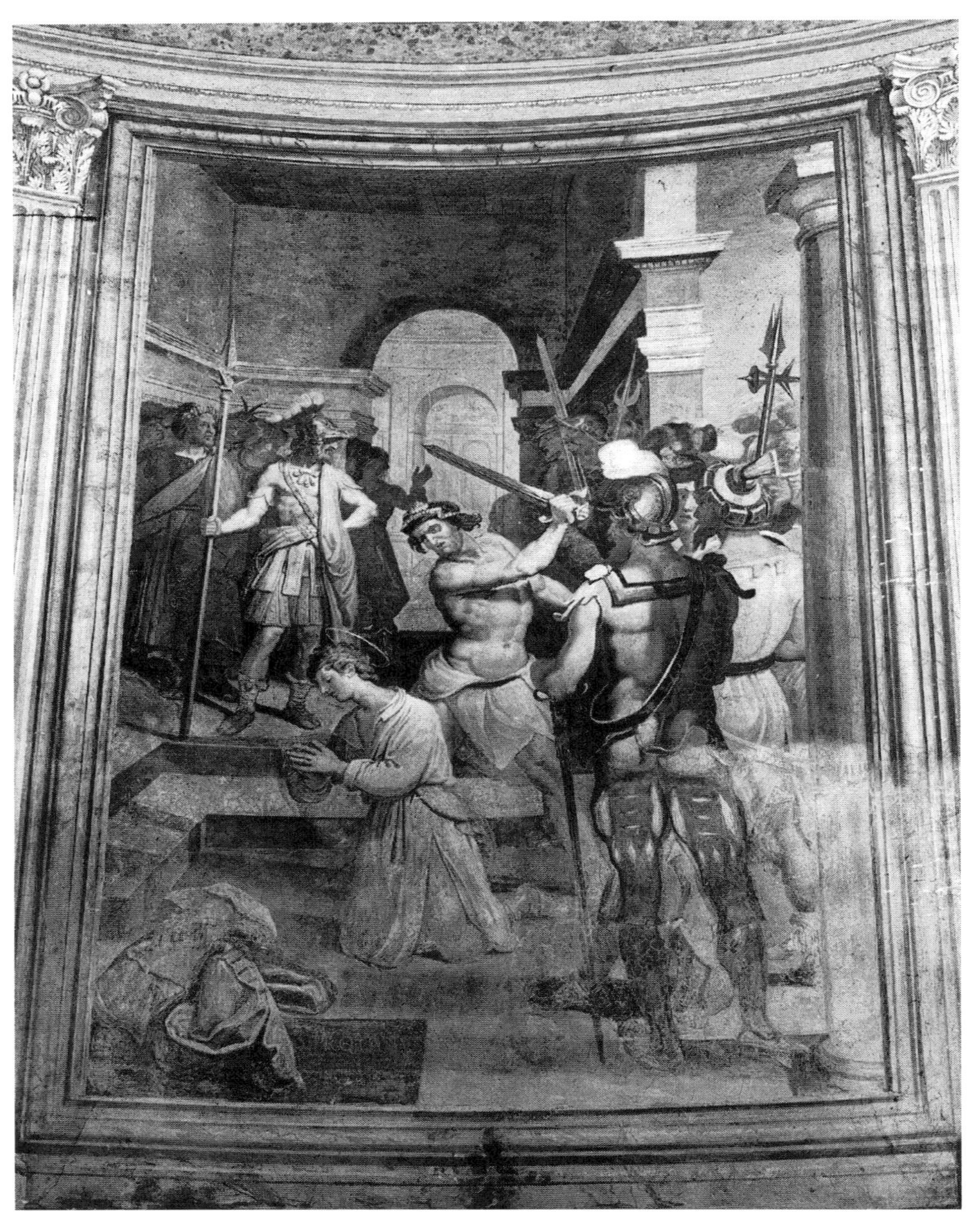

75. Andrea Commodi, *Decapitation of St Protasius*. Fresco, S. Vitale, Rome (ca. 1599–1600). Photograph courtesy of the Archivio Fotografico Soprintendenza Speciale per il Polo Museale Romano.

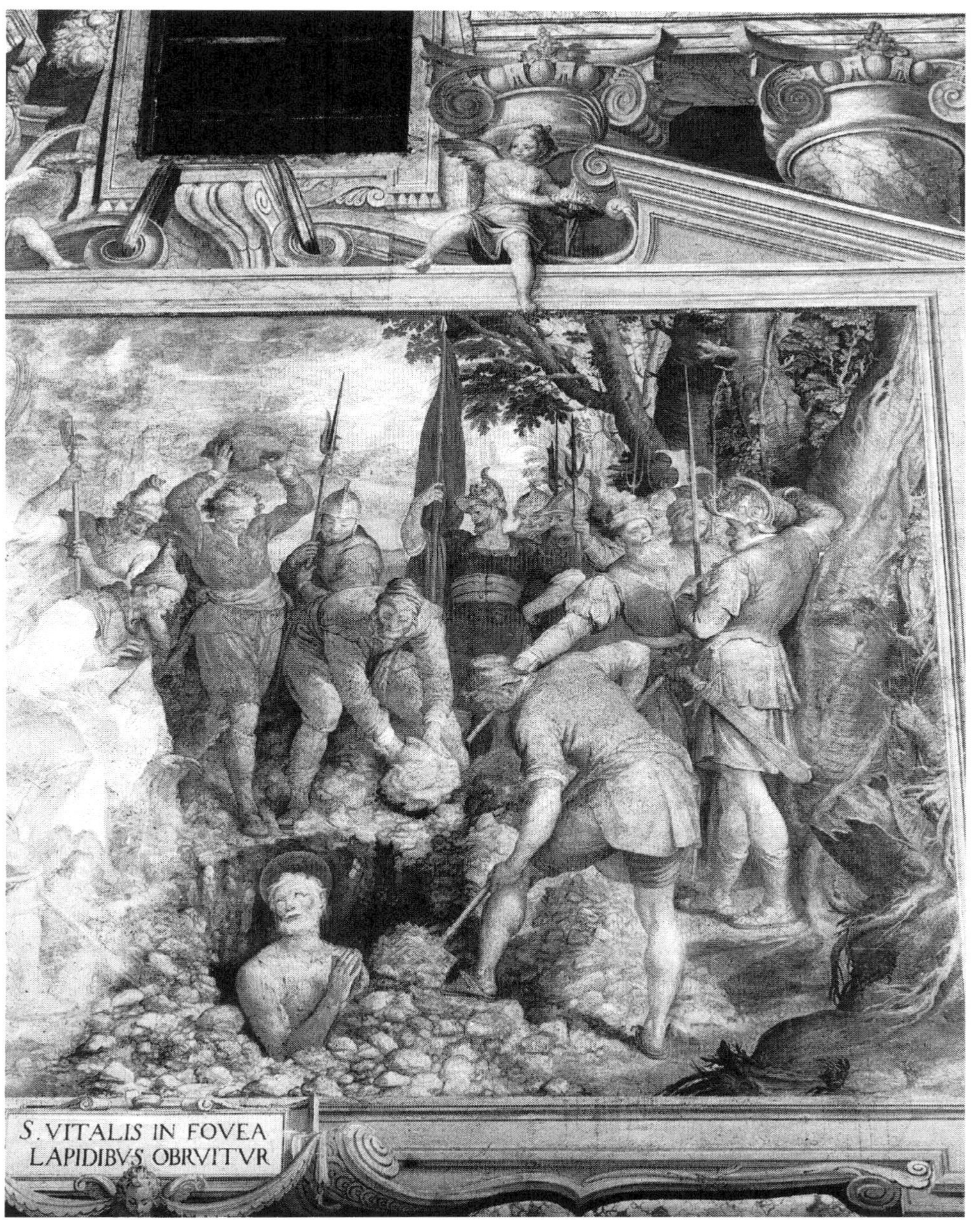

76. Agostino Ciampelli, *Stoning of St Vitalis* (detail). Fresco, S. Vitale, Rome (ca. 1601–3). Photograph courtesy of the Archivio Fotografico Soprintendenza Speciale per il Polo Museale Romano.

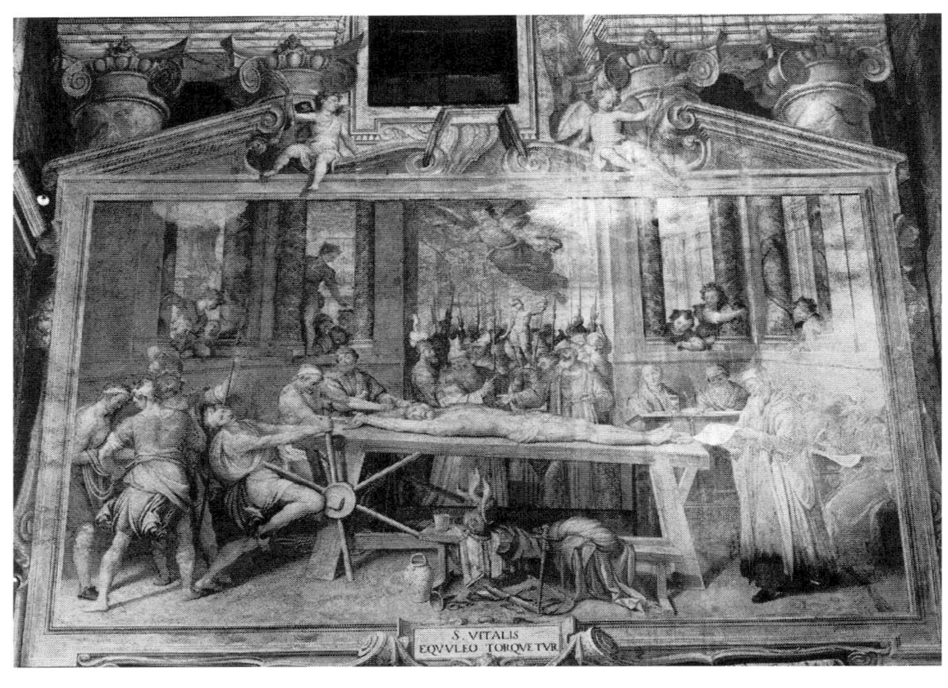

77. Agostino Ciampelli, *Torture of St Vitalis*. Fresco, S. Vitale, Rome (ca. 1601–3). Photograph courtesy of the Archivio Fotografico Soprintendenza Speciale per il Polo Museale Romano.

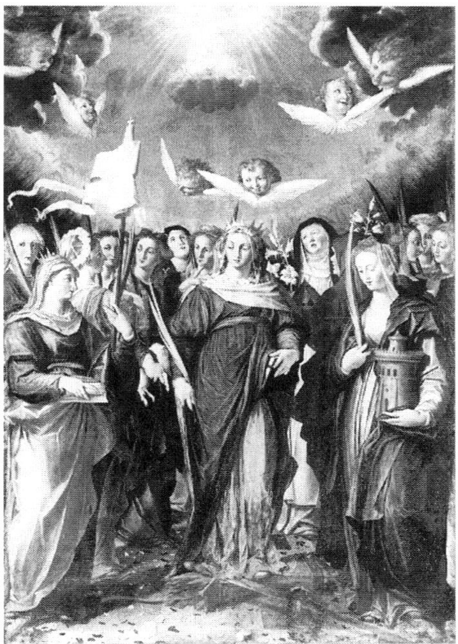

78. Giovanni Battista Fiammeri, *Holy Virgin Martyrs*. Canvas, S. Vitale, Rome (ca. 1598). Photograph courtesy of the Istituto Centrale per il Catalogo e la Documentazione, Ministerio per i Beni Culturali e Ambientali, Rome.

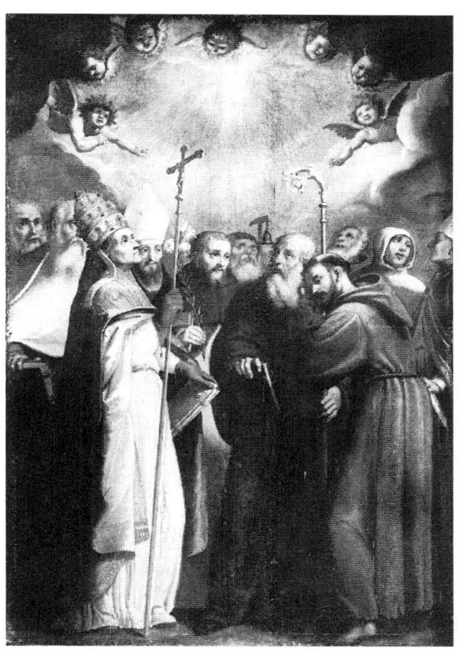

79. Giovanni Battista Fiammeri, *Holy Confessors*. Canvas, S. Vitale, Rome (ca. 1598). Photograph courtesy of the Istituto Centrale per il Catalogo e la Documentazione, Ministerio per i Beni Culturali e Ambientali, Rome.

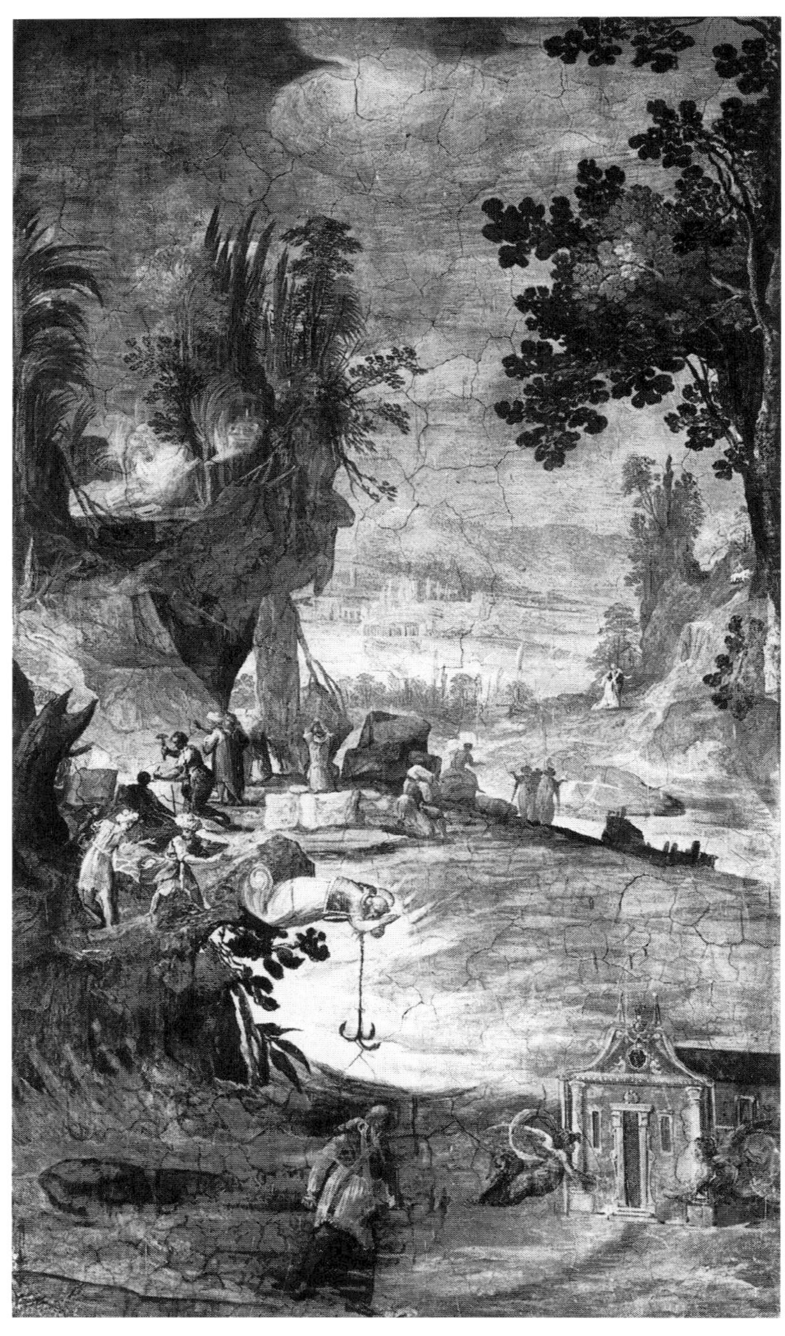

80. Follower of Paul Brill, *Martyrdom of St Clement*. Fresco, S. Vitale, Rome (ca. 1599). Photograph courtesy of the Istituto Centrale per il Catalogo e la Documentazione, Ministerio per i Beni Culturali e Ambientali, Rome.

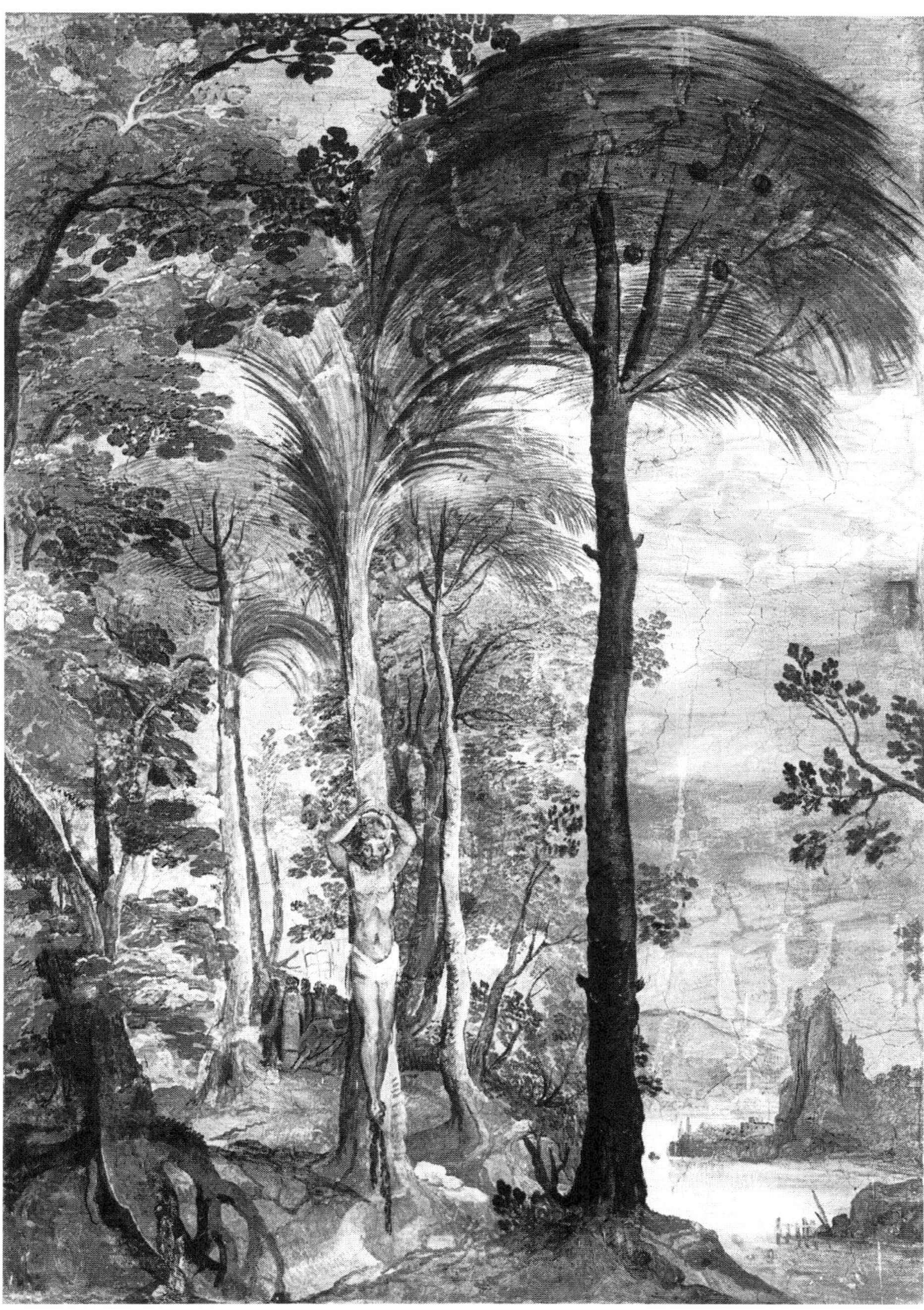

81. Follower of Paul Brill, *Martyrdom of St Paphnutius*. Fresco, S. Vitale, Rome (ca. 1599). Photograph courtesy of the Istituto Centrale per il Catalogo e la Documentazione, Ministerio per i Beni Culturali e Ambientali, Rome.

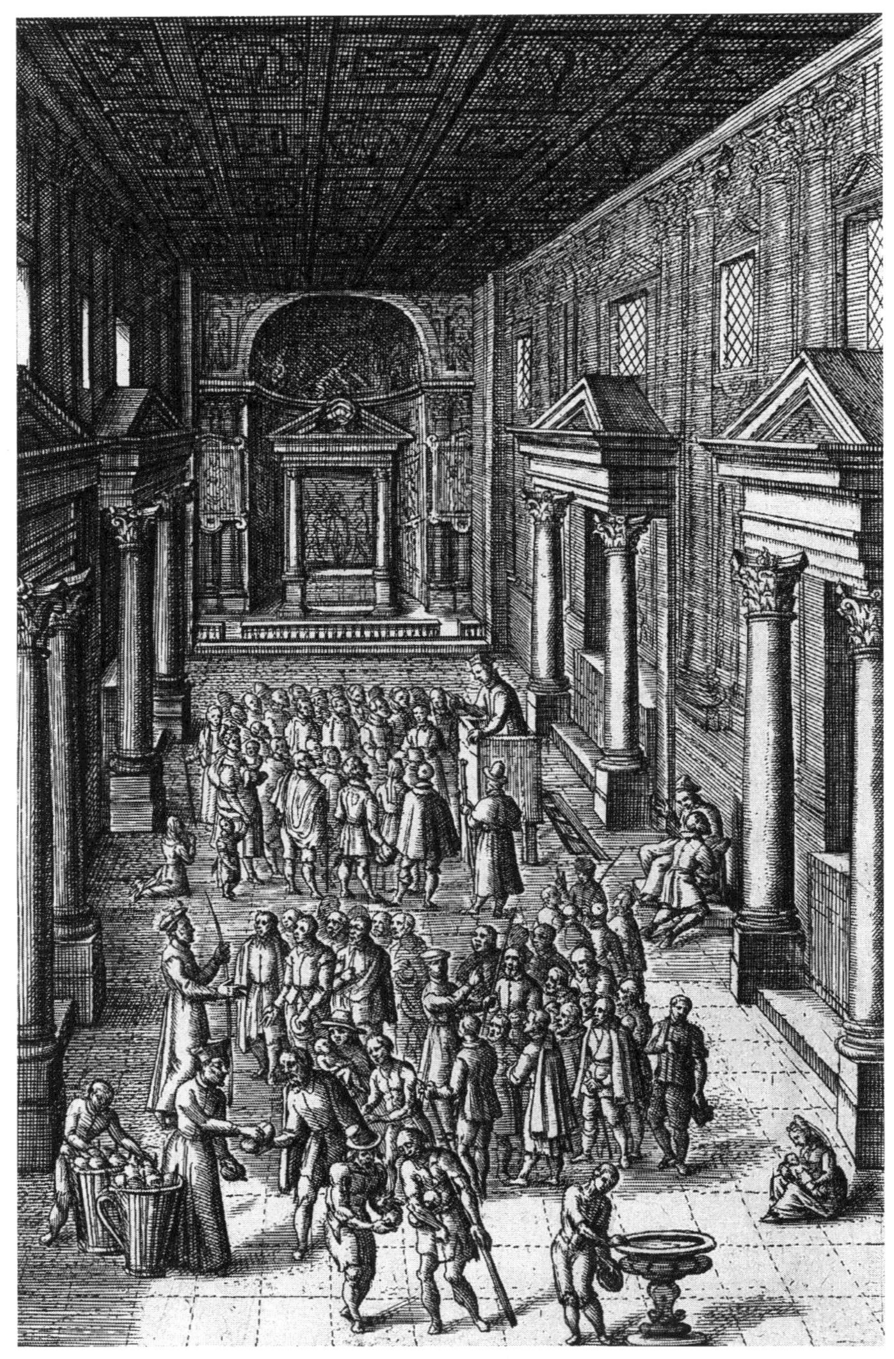

82. Matthäus Greuter, *The Community of S. Vitale*. From Richeôme, *La peinture spirituelle* (1611). By permission of the Folger Shakespeare Library.

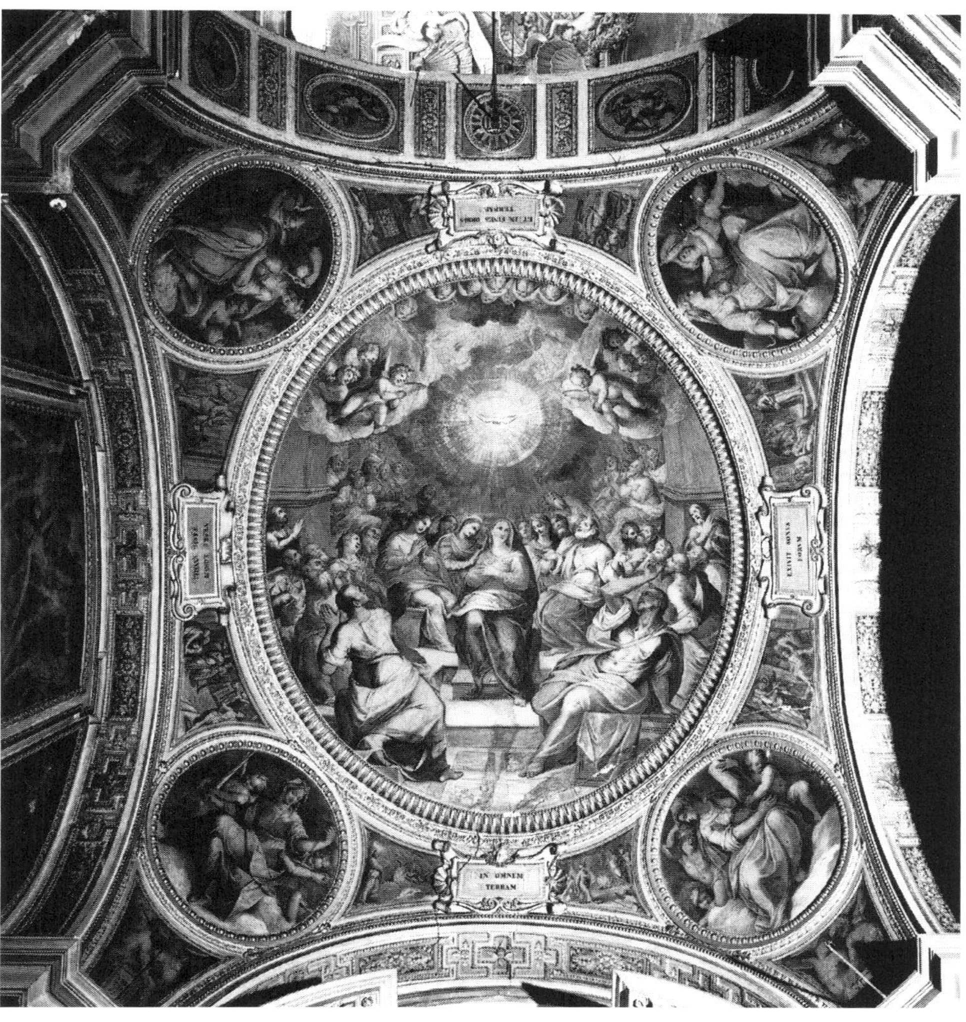

83. Niccolò Circignani, *Pentecost*. Fresco, Apostles' Chapel, Gesù, Rome (1585–7). Photograph courtesy of the Research Library, Getty Research Institute, Los Angeles (86.P.8).

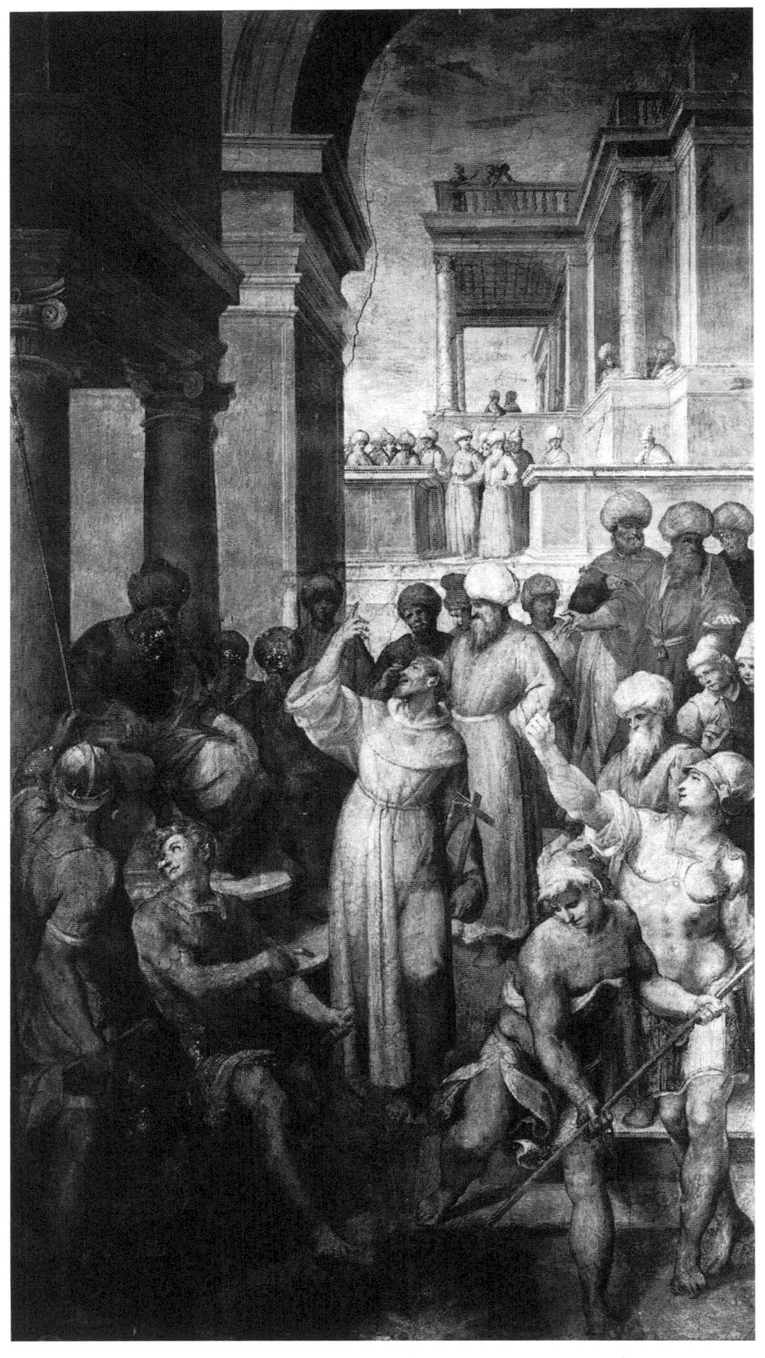

84. Niccolò Circignani, *St Francis in Front of the Sultan*. Fresco, S. Giovanni de' Fiorentini, Rome (1583–5). Photograph courtesy of the Istituto Centrale per il Catalogo e la Documentazione, Ministerio per i Beni Culturali e Ambientali, Rome.

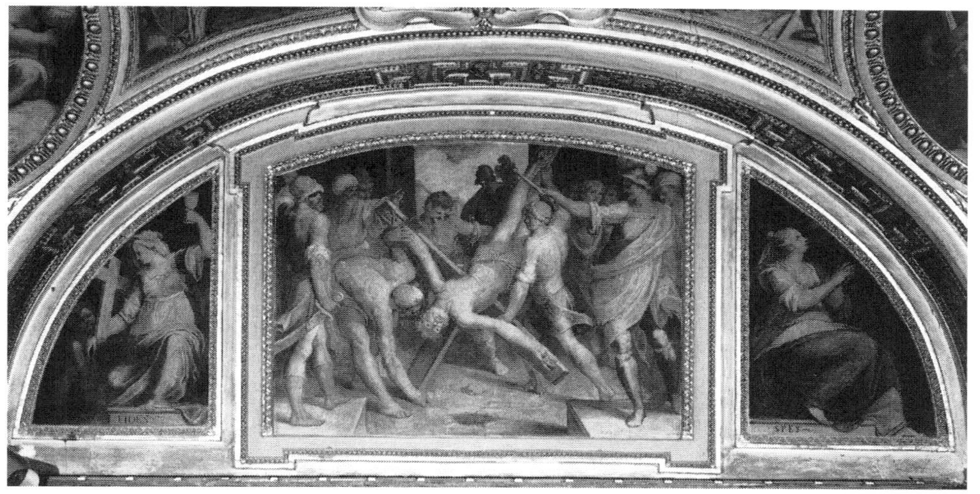

85. Niccolò Circignani, *Martyrdom of St Peter*. Fresco, Apostles' Chapel, Gesù, Rome (1585–7). Photograph courtesy of the Istituto Centrale per il Catalogo e la Documentazione, Ministerio per i Beni Culturali e Ambientali, Rome.

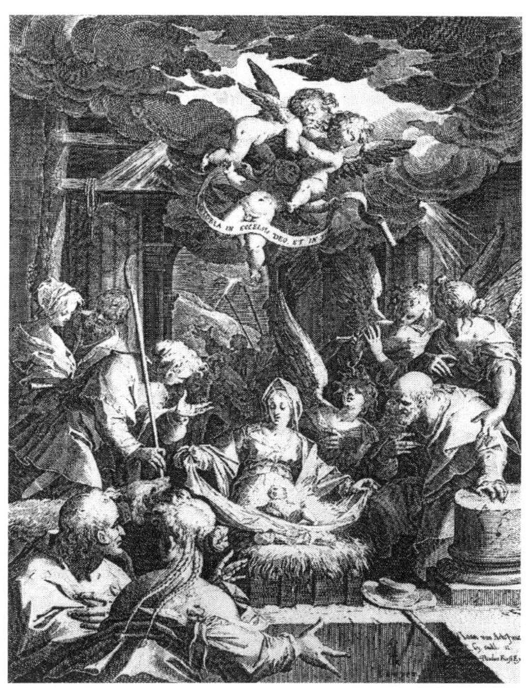

86. Aegidius Sadeler after Hans von Aachen, *Nativity*. Formerly in the Nativity Chapel, Gesù, Rome. The Metropolitan Museum of Art. The Elisha Whittelsey Collection, The Elisha Whittelsey Fund, 1951. Photograph © The Metropolitan Museum of Art (51.501.6496).

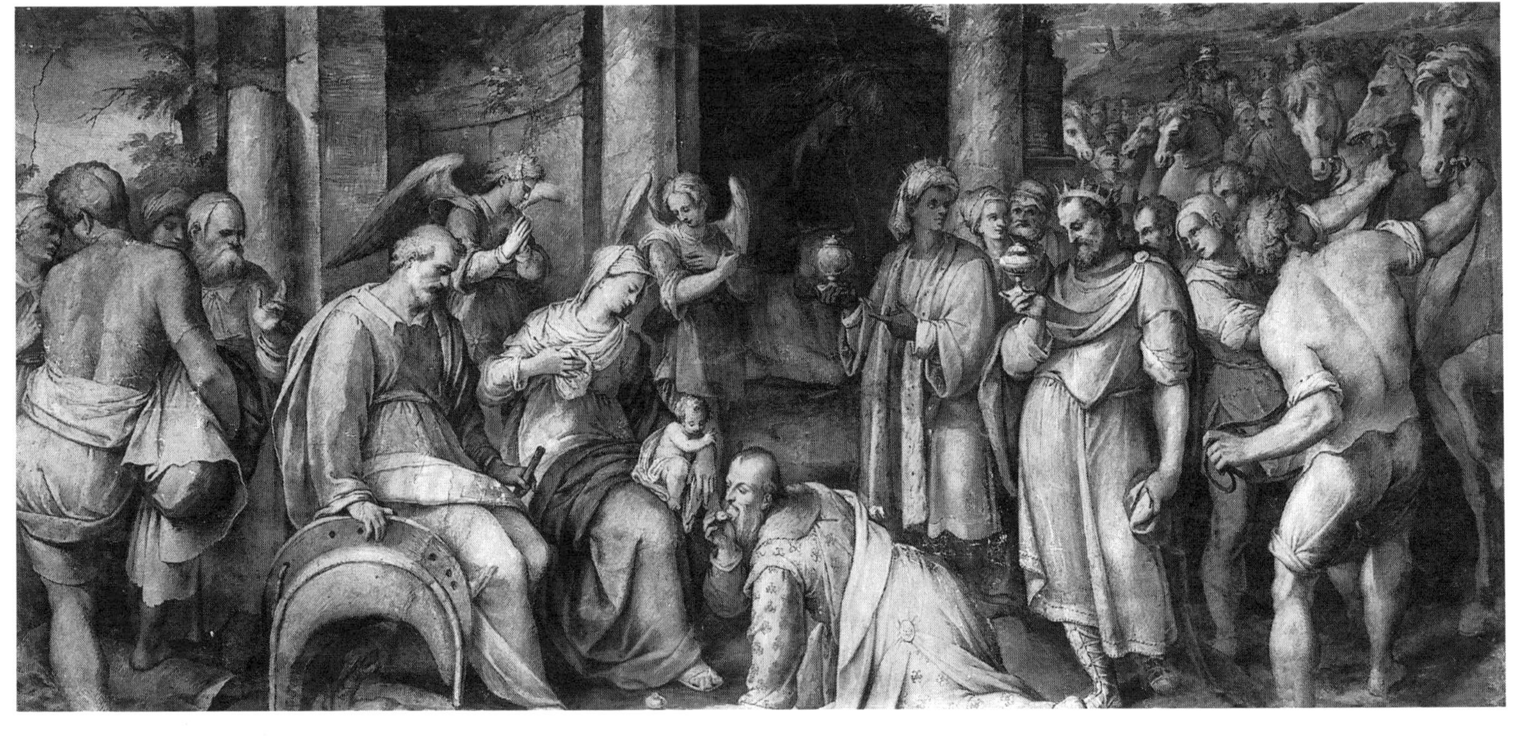

87. Niccolò Circignani, *Adoration of the Magi*. Fresco, Nativity Chapel, Gesù, Rome (1584). Photograph courtesy of the Istituto Centrale per il Catalogo e la Documentazione, Ministerio per i Beni Culturali e Ambientali, Rome.

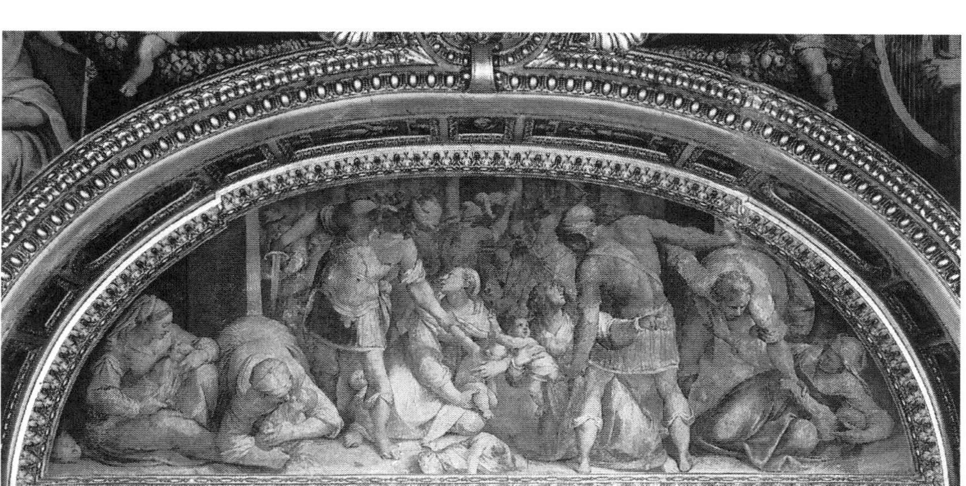

88. Niccolò Circignani, *Massacre of the Innocents. Fresco*, Nativity Chapel, Gesù, Rome (1584). Photograph courtesy of the Istituto Centrale per il Catalogo e la Documentazione, Ministerio per i Beni Culturali e Ambientali, Rome.

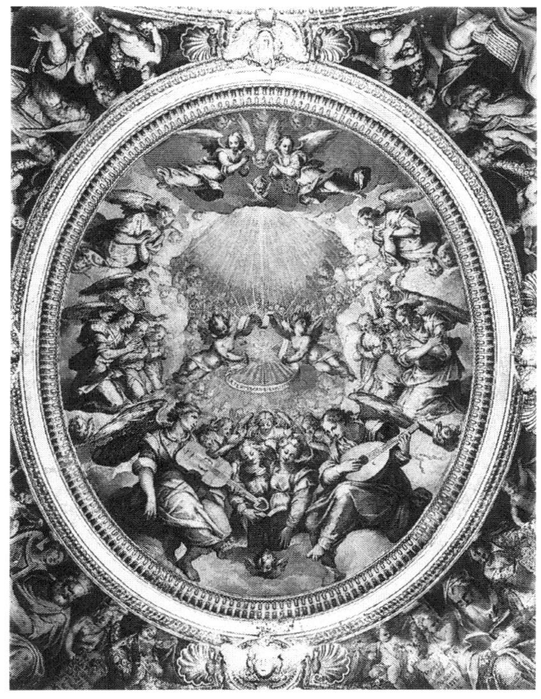

89. Niccolò Circignani, *Heavenly Celebration of the Birth of Christ*. Fresco, Nativity Chapel, Gesù, Rome (1584). Photograph courtesy of the Istituto Centrale per il Catalogo e la Documentazione, Ministerio per i Beni Culturali e Ambientali, Rome.

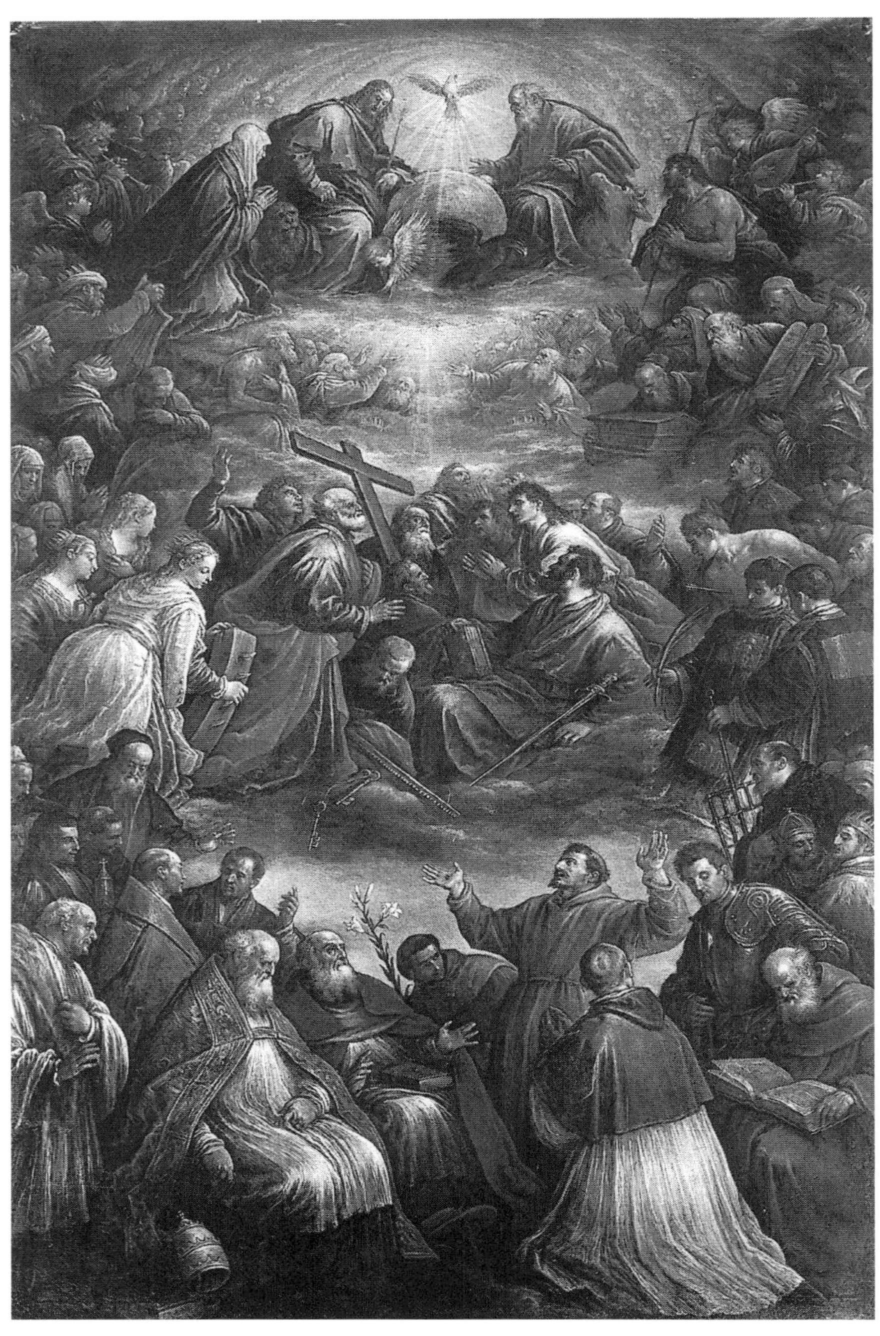

90. Francesco Bassano, *Holy Trinity Adored by Saints*. Canvas, Trinity Chapel, Gesù, Rome (before 1591). Photograph courtesy of the Istituto Centrale per il Catalogo e la Documentazione, Ministerio per i Beni Culturali e Ambientali, Rome.

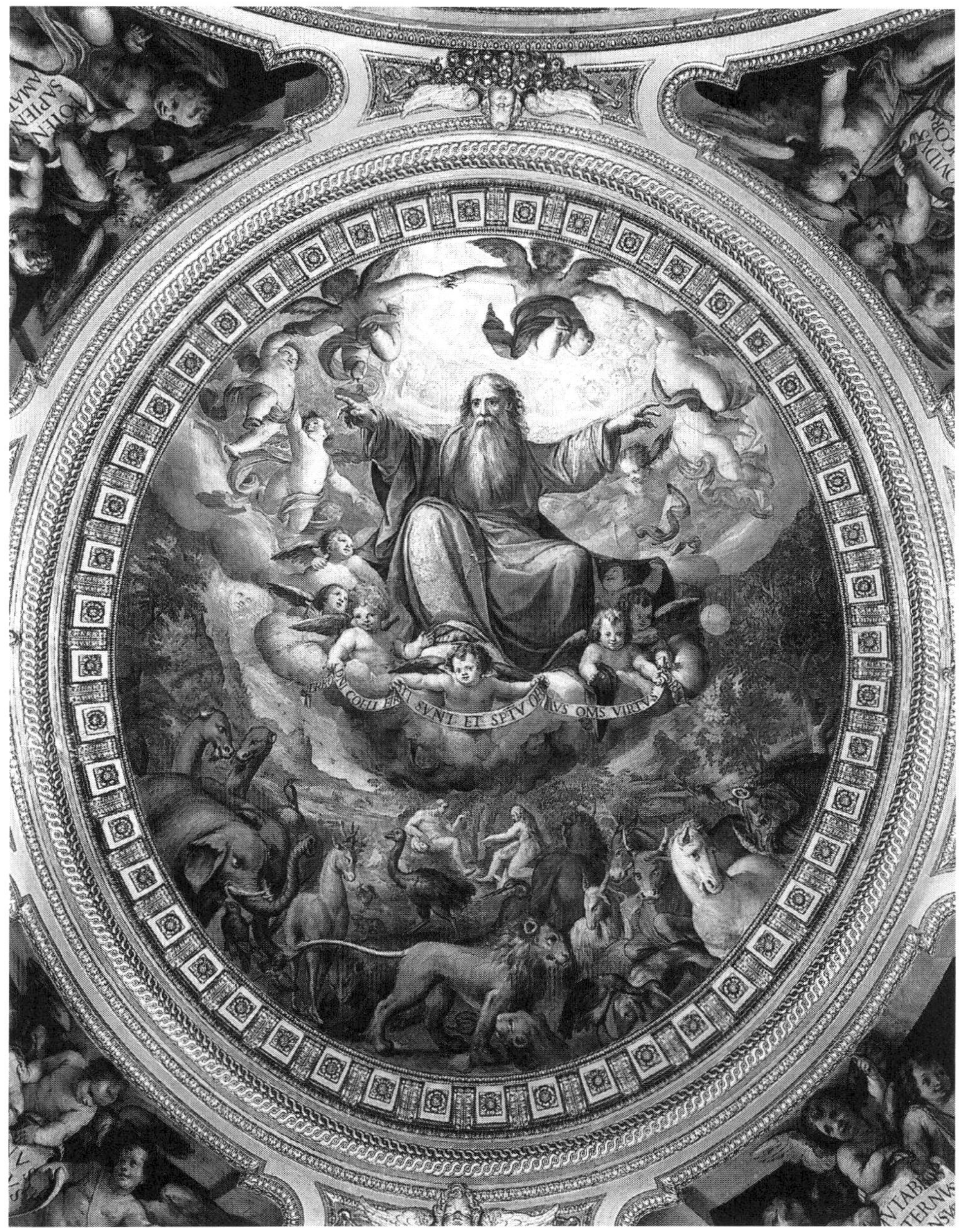

91. Giovanni Battista Fiammeri, *Creation*. Fresco, Trinity Chapel, Gesù, Rome (1588–9). Photograph courtesy of the Istituto Centrale per il Catalogo e la Documentazione, Ministerio per i Beni Culturali e Ambientali, Rome.

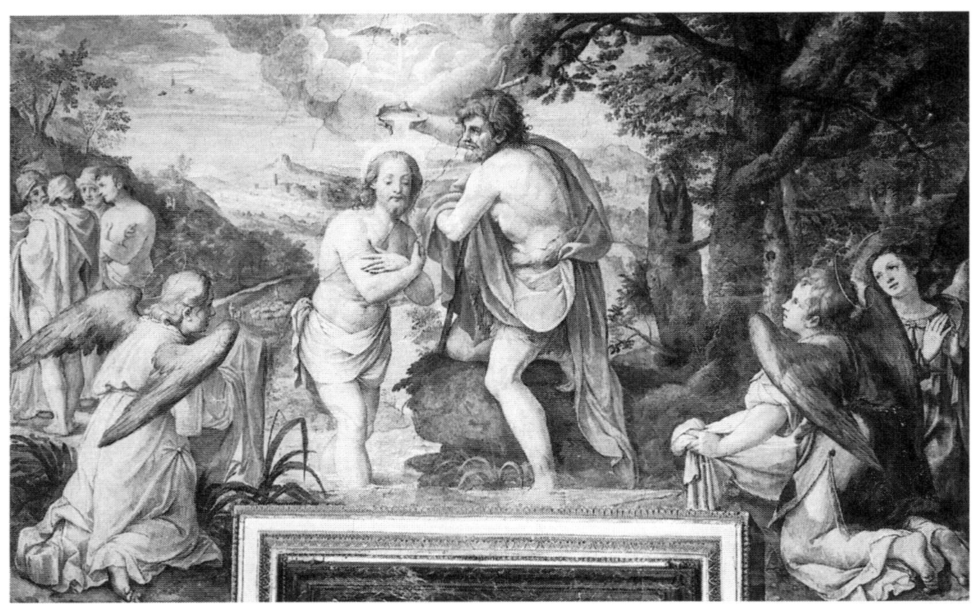

92. Maestro Bernardino and Ferraù Fenzoni, *Baptism of Christ*. Fresco, Trinity Chapel, Gesù, Rome (1588–9). Photograph courtesy of the Istituto Centrale per il Catalogo e la Documentazione, Ministerio per i Beni Culturali e Ambientali, Rome.

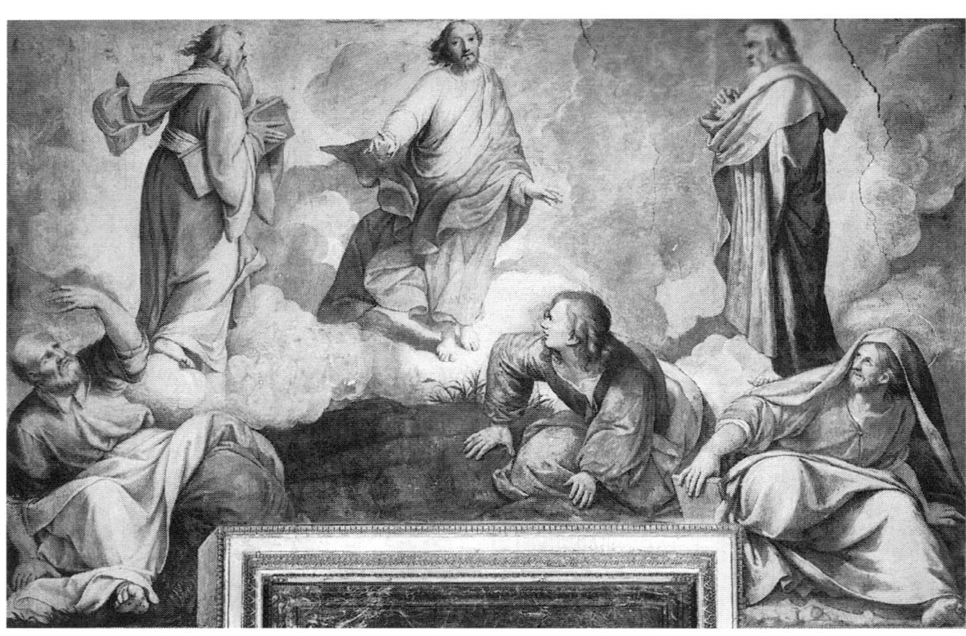

93. Durante Alberti, *Transfiguration*. Fresco, Trinity Chapel, Gesù, Rome (1588–9). Photograph courtesy of the Istituto Centrale per il Catalogo e la Documentazione, Ministerio per i Beni Culturali e Ambientali, Rome.

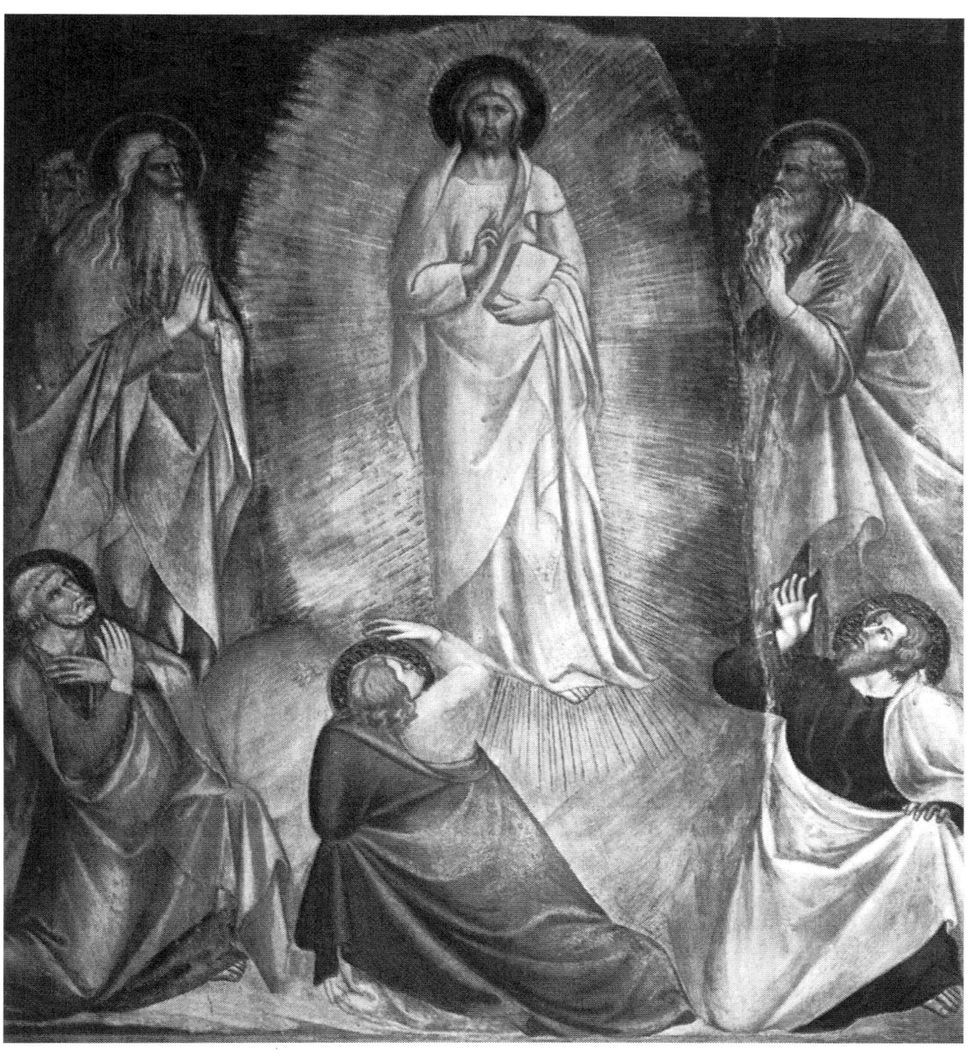

94. Anonymous, *Transfiguration*. Fresco, Collegiata, San Gimignano (ca. 1380).
Photograph © Umbriagraf, Terni.

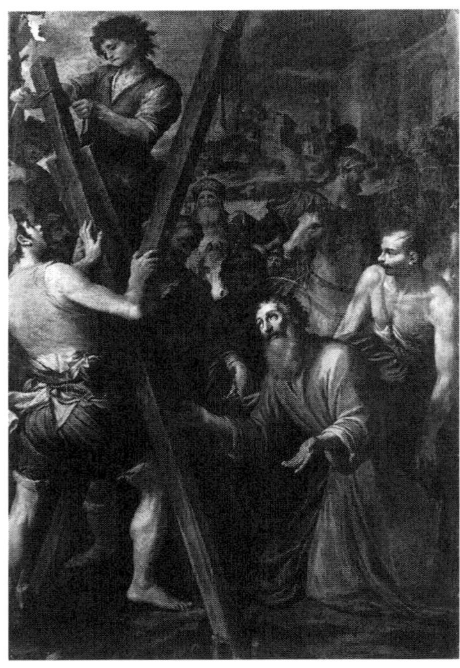

95. Agostino Ciampelli, *Martyrdom of St Andrew*. Canvas, Martyrs' Chapel, Gesù, Rome (ca. 1590). Photograph courtesy of the Istituto Centrale per il Catalogo e la Documentazione, Ministerio per i Beni Culturali e Ambientali, Rome.

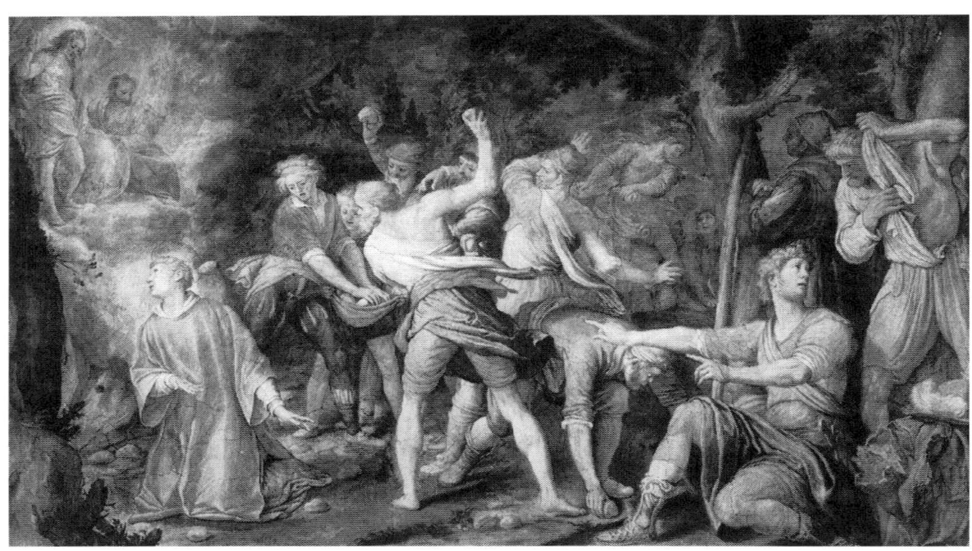

96. Agostino Ciampelli, *Martyrdom of St Stephen*. Fresco, Martyrs' Chapel, Gesù, Rome (ca. 1590). Photograph courtesy of the Istituto Centrale per il Catalogo e la Documentazione, Ministerio per i Beni Culturali e Ambientali, Rome.

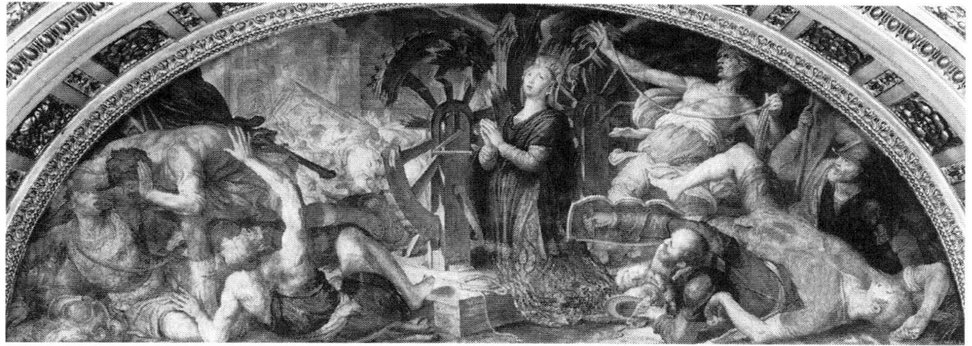

97. Agostino Ciampelli, *Martyrdom of St Catherine*. Fresco, Martyrs' Chapel, Gesù, Rome (ca. 1590). Photograph courtesy of the Istituto Centrale per il Catalogo e la Documentazione, Ministerio per i Beni Culturali e Ambientali, Rome.

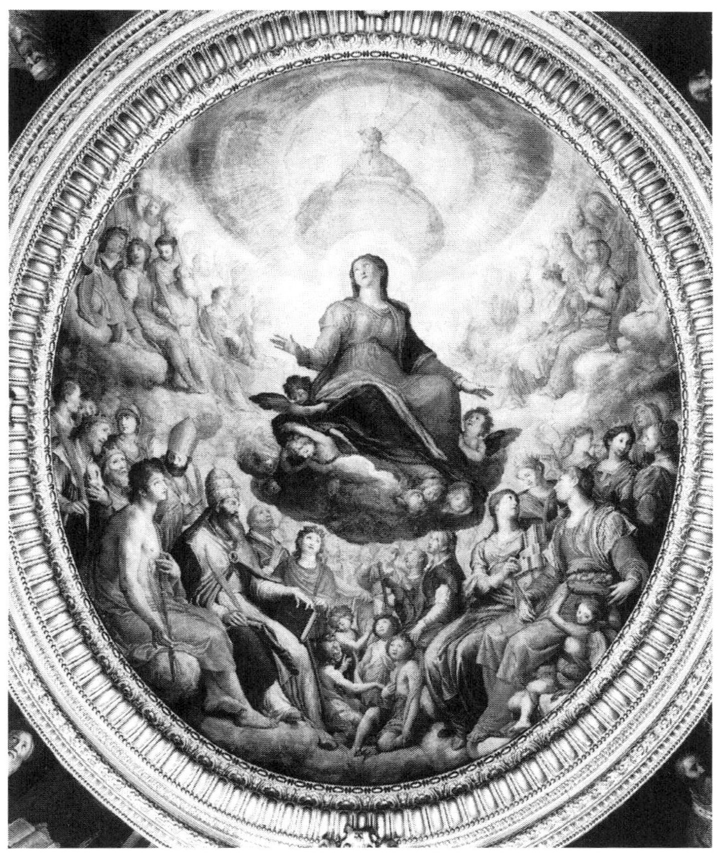

98. Agostino Ciampelli, *Mary, Queen of Martyrs*. Fresco, Martyrs' Chapel, Gesù, Rome (ca. 1590). Photograph courtesy of the Istituto Centrale per il Catalogo e la Documentazione, Ministerio per i Beni Culturali e Ambientali, Rome.

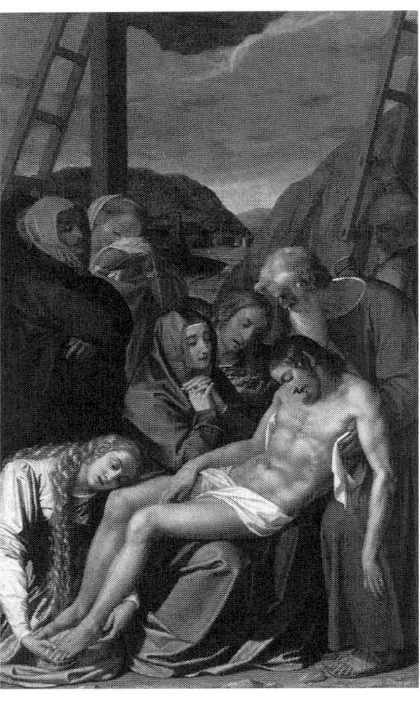

99. Scipione Pulzone, *Lamentation*. Canvas, formerly in the Passion Chapel, Gesù, Rome (1590). Metropolitan Museum of Art, New York. The Metropolitan Museum of Art, Purchase, Anonymous Gift, in memory of Terence Cardinal Cooke, 1984 (1984.74). Photograph © 1984 The Metropolitan Museum of Art.

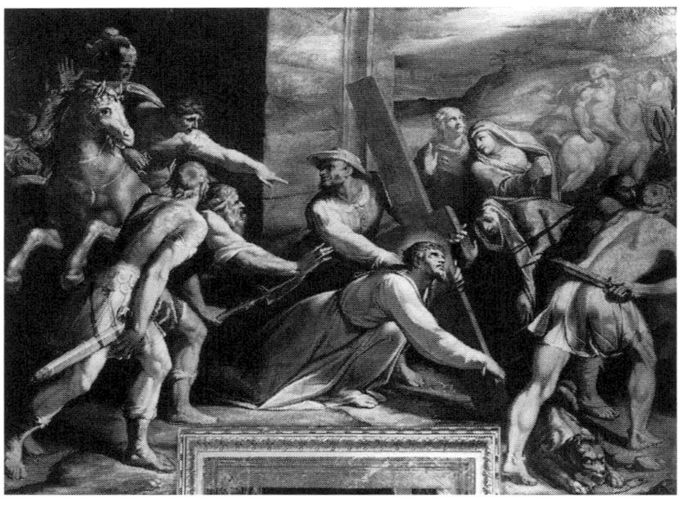

100. Gaspare Celio, *Christ on the Road to Calvary*. Canvas, Passion Chapel, Gesù, Rome (1596–7). Photograph courtesy of the Istituto Centrale per il Catalogo e la Documentazione, Ministerio per i Beni Culturali e Ambientali, Rome.

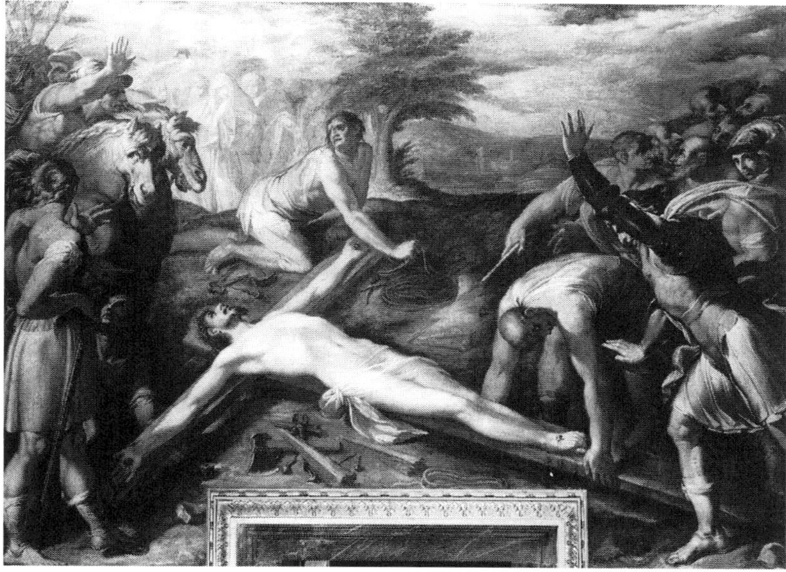

101. Gaspare Celio, *Christ Nailed to the Cross*. Canvas, Passion Chapel, Gesù, Rome (1596–7). Photograph courtesy of the Istituto Centrale per il Catalogo e la Documentazione, Ministerio per i Beni Culturali e Ambientali, Rome.

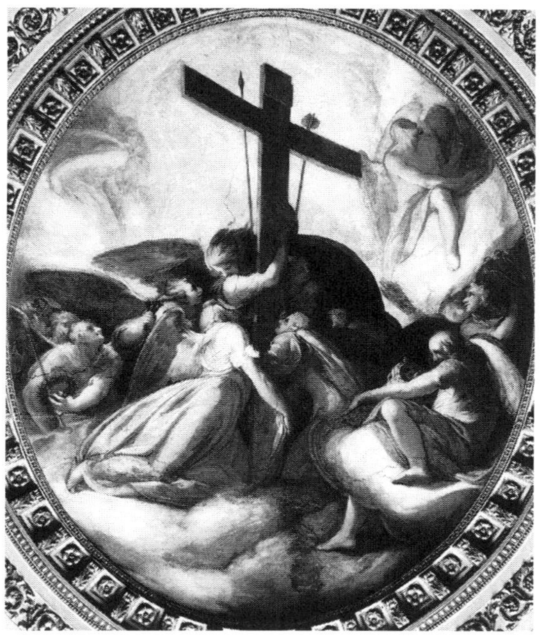

102. Gaspare Celio, *Apotheosis of the Instruments of the Passion*. Fresco, Passion Chapel, Gesù, Rome (1596–7). Photograph courtesy of the Istituto Centrale per il Catalogo e la Documentazione, Ministerio per i Beni Culturali e Ambientali, Rome.

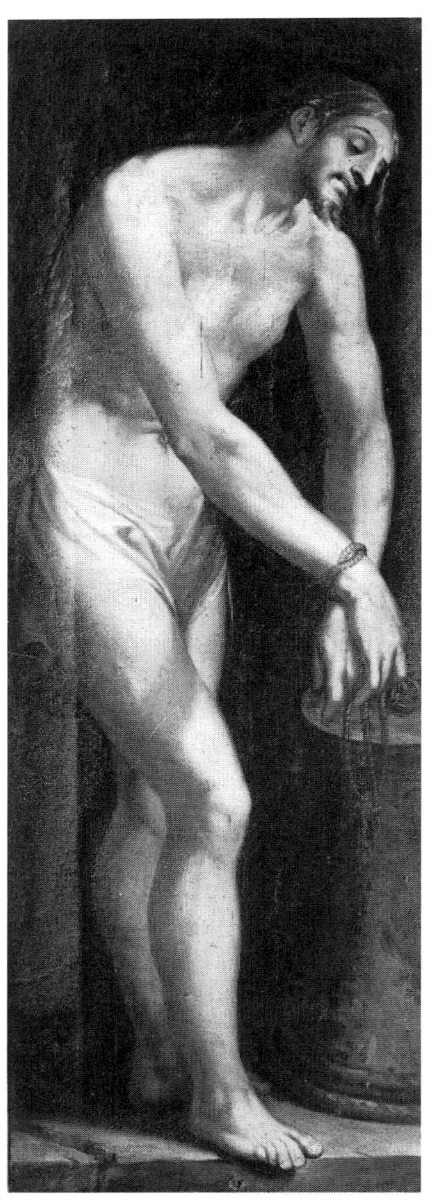

103. Gaspare Celio, *Christ at the Column*. Canvas, Passion Chapel, Gesù, Rome (1596–7). Photograph courtesy of the Istituto Centrale per il Catalogo e la Documentazione, Ministerio per i Beni Culturali e Ambientali, Rome.

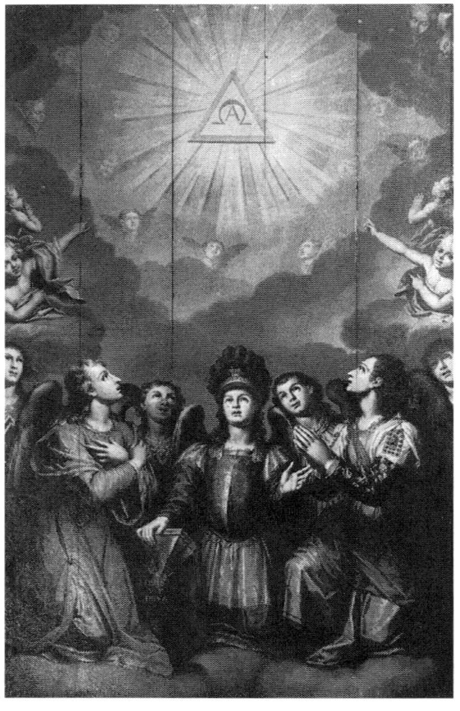

104. Federico Zuccaro with later overpainting, *Seven Archangels in Adoration of the Trinity*. Panel, Angels' Chapel, Gesù, Rome (1600). Photograph courtesy of the Istituto Centrale per il Catalogo e la Documentazione, Ministerio per i Beni Culturali e Ambientali, Rome.

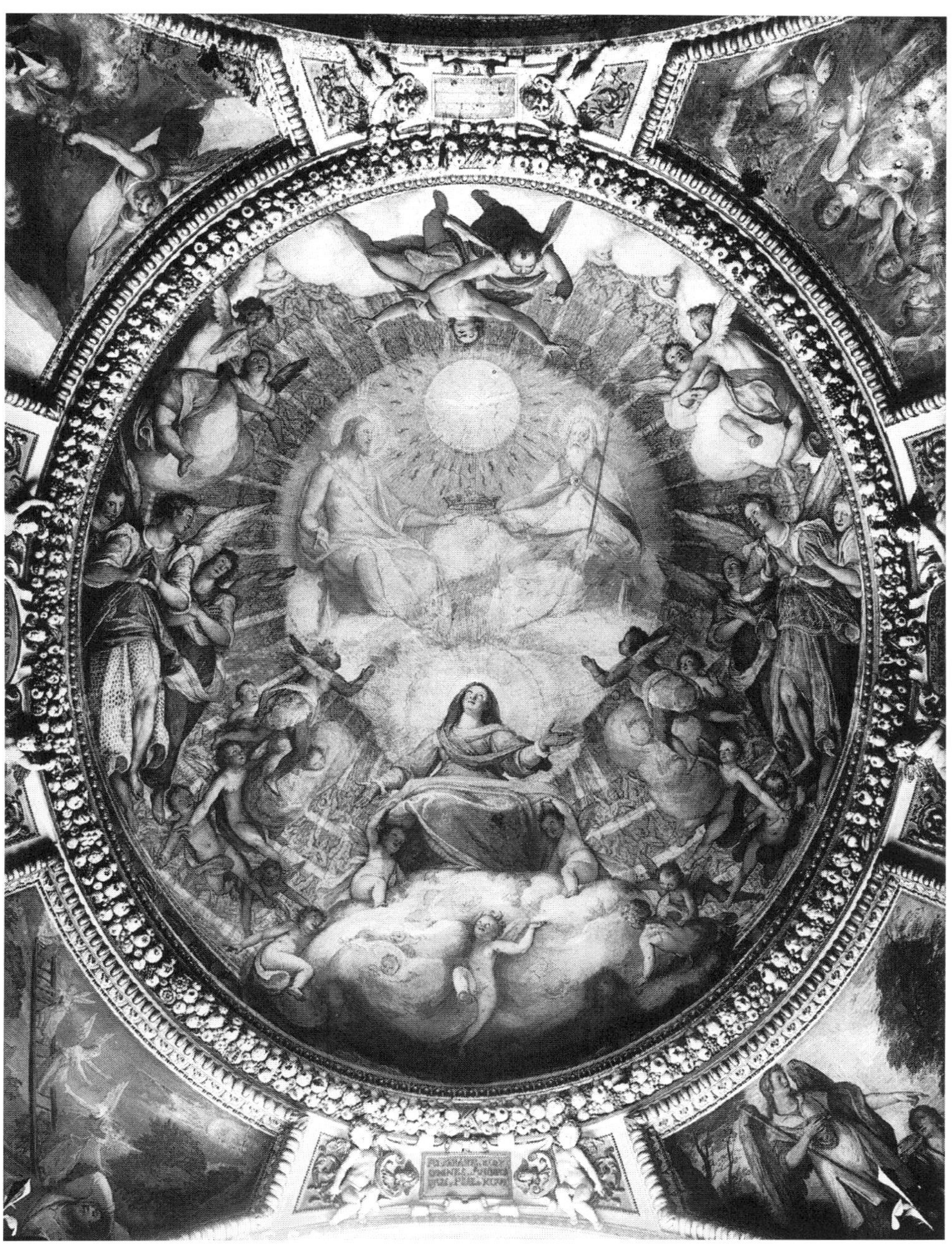

105. Federico Zuccaro, *Triumph of Mary*. Fresco, Angels' Chapel, Gesù, Rome (ca. 1600).
Photograph courtesy of the Istituto Centrale per il Catalogo e la Documentazione,
Ministerio per i Beni Culturali e Ambientali, Rome.

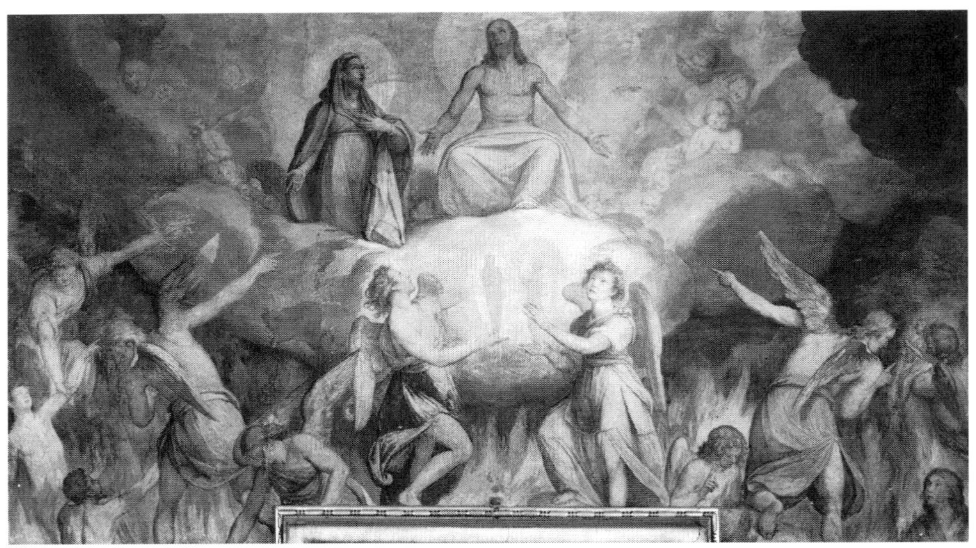

106. Federico Zuccaro, *Angels Freeing Souls from Purgatory*. Fresco, Angels' Chapel, Gesù, Rome (ca. 1600). Photograph courtesy of the Istituto Centrale per il Catalogo e la Documentazione, Ministerio per i Beni Culturali e Ambientali, Rome.

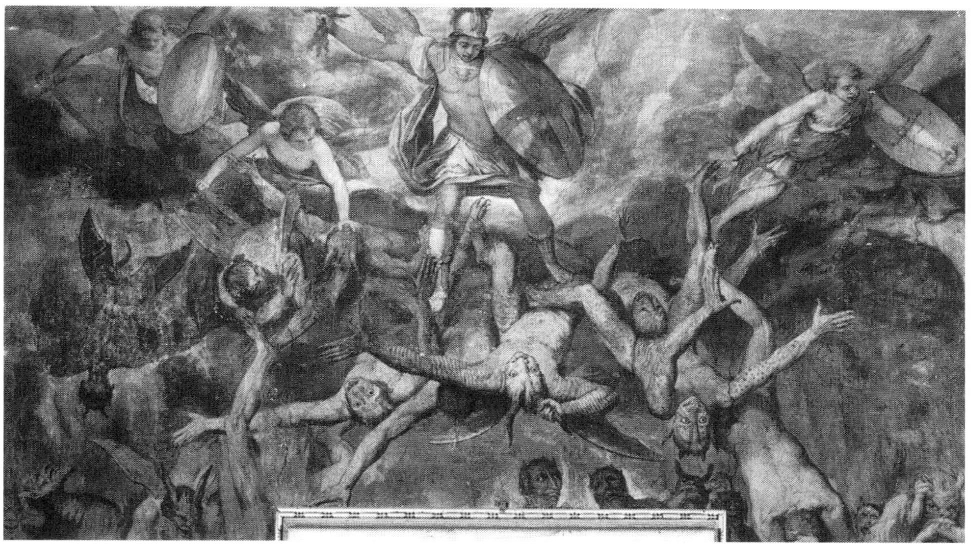

107. Federico Zuccaro, *Fall of the Rebel Angels*. Fresco, Angels' Chapel, Gesù, Rome (ca. 1600). Photograph courtesy of the Istituto Centrale per il Catalogo e la Documentazione, Ministerio per i Beni Culturali e Ambientali, Rome.

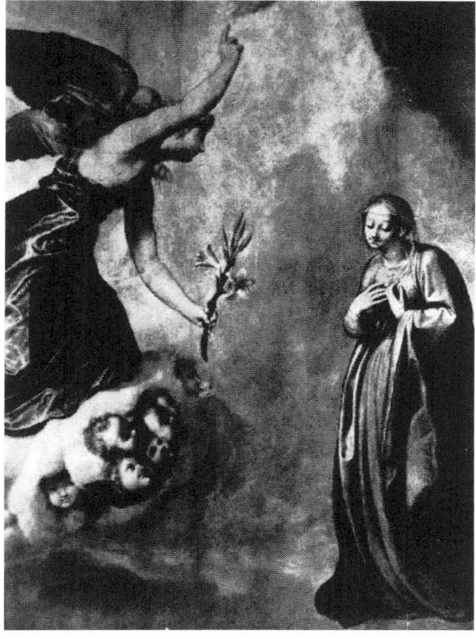

108. Giuseppe Valeriano, *Annunciation*. Panel, Chapel of the Madonna della Strada, Gesù, Rome (1586–8). Photograph courtesy of the Istituto Centrale per il Catalogo e la Documentazione, Ministerio per i Beni Culturali e Ambientali, Rome.

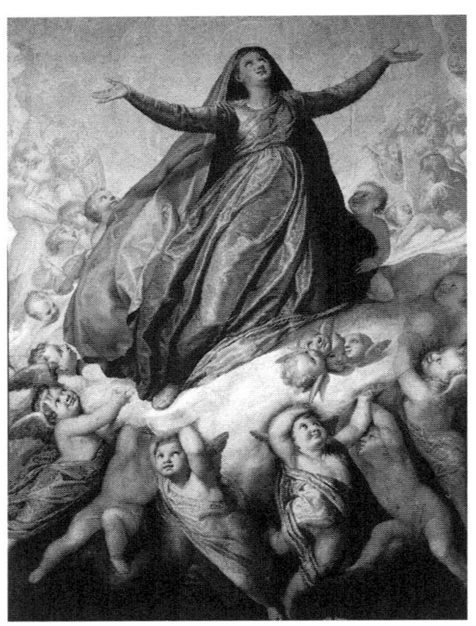

109. Giuseppe Valeriano, *Assumption of the Virgin*. Panel, Chapel of the Madonna della Strada, Gesù, Rome (1586–8). Photograph courtesy of the Istituto Centrale per il Catalogo e la Documentazione, Ministerio per i Beni Culturali e Ambientali, Rome.

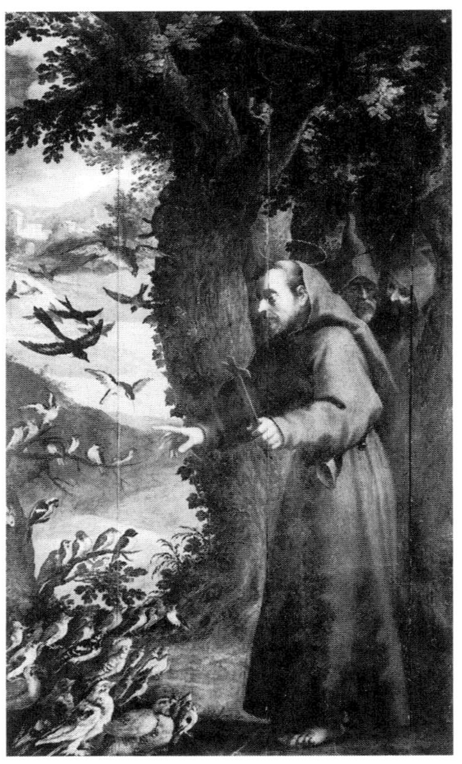

110. Joseph Heintz the Elder, *St Francis Preaching to the Birds*. Panel, St Francis Chapel, Gesù, Rome (ca. 1599). Photograph courtesy of the Istituto Centrale per il Catalogo e la Documentazione, Ministerio per i Beni Culturali e Ambientali, Rome.

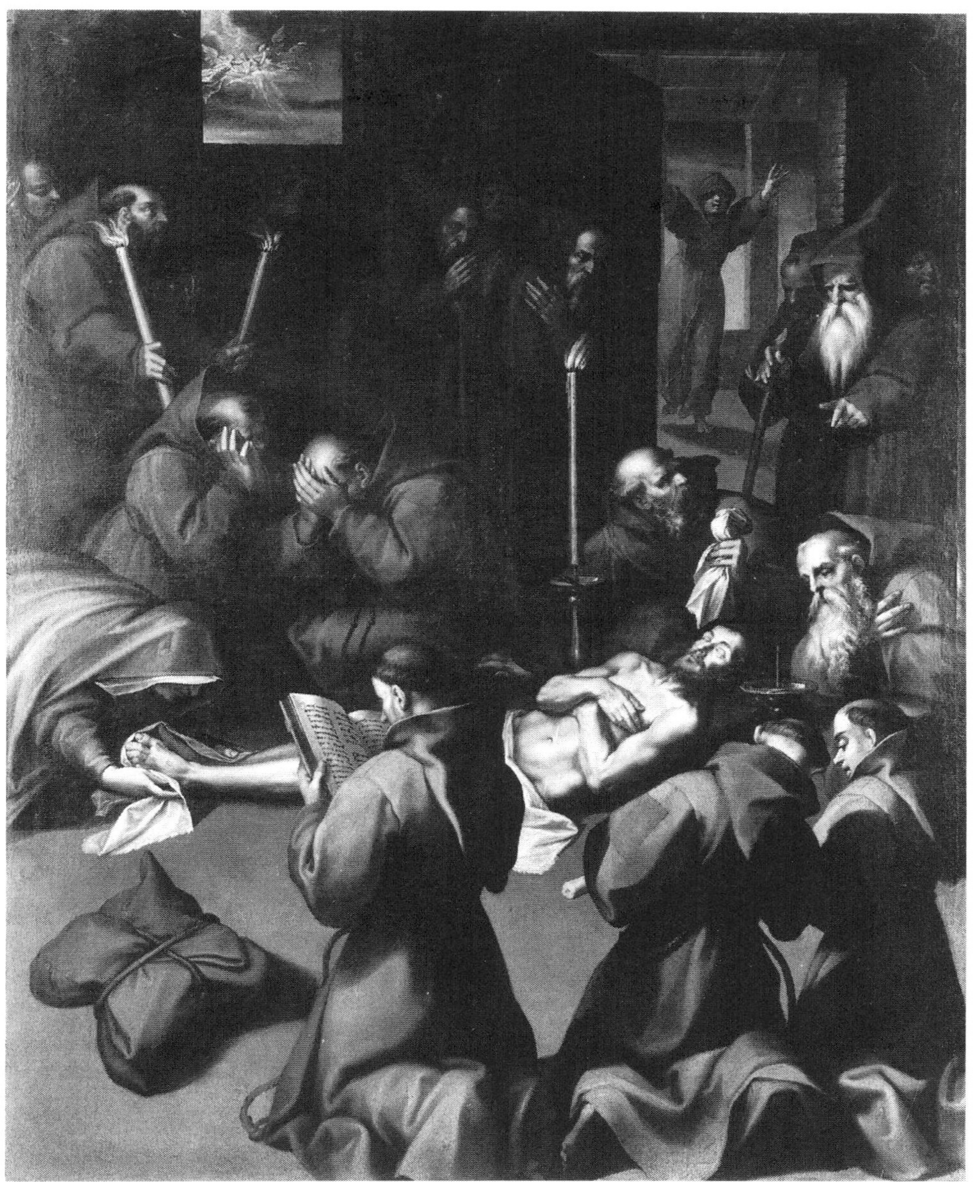

111. Joseph Heintz the Elder, *Death of St Francis*. Canvas, St Francis Chapel, Gesù, Rome (ca. 1599). Photograph courtesy of the Istituto Centrale per il Catalogo e la Documentazione, Ministerio per i Beni Culturali e Ambientali, Rome.

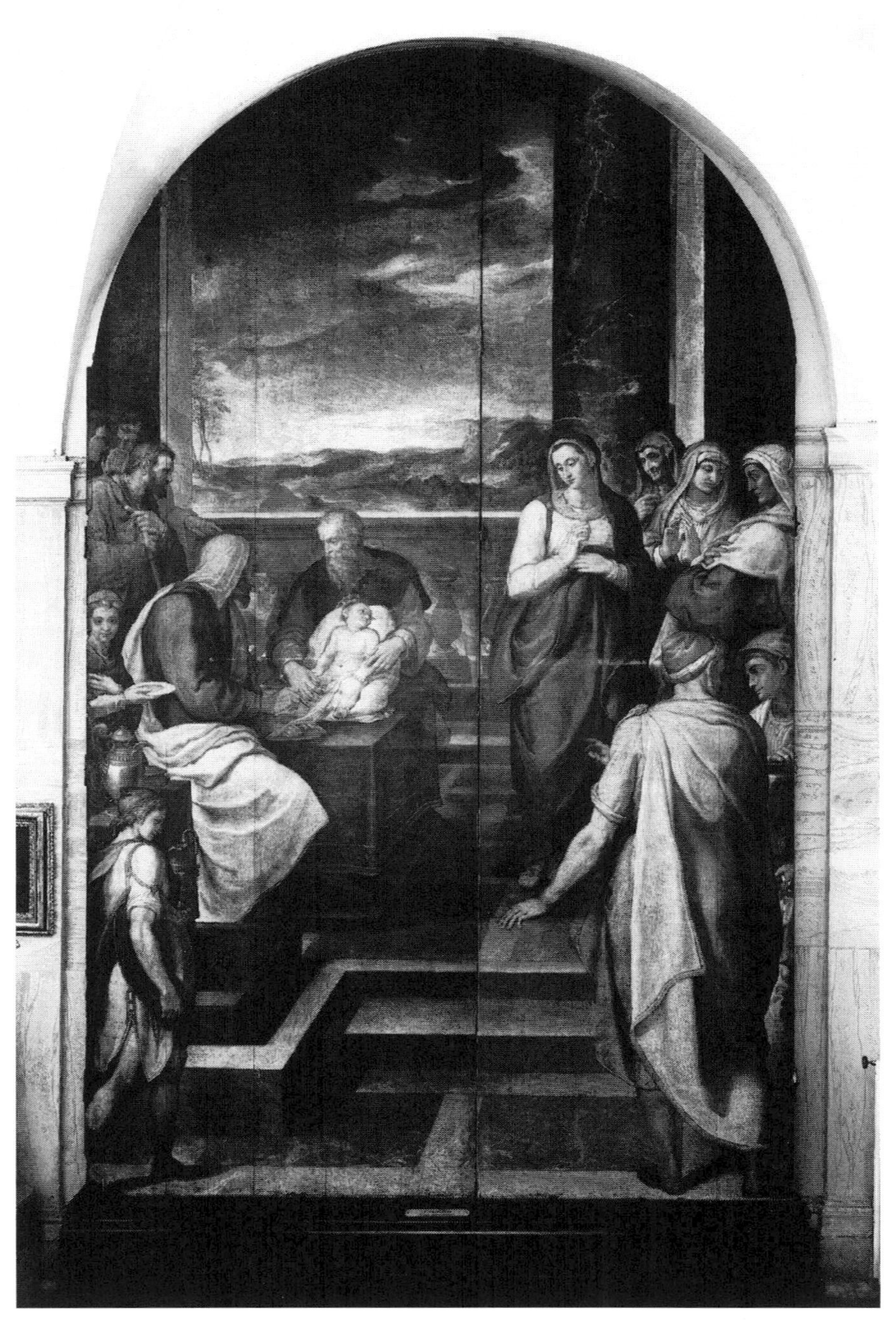

112. Girolamo Muziano, *Circumcision*. Panel, formerly at the high altar, Gesù, Rome (1587–98). Photograph courtesy of the Istituto Centrale per il Catalogo e la Documentazione, Ministerio per i Beni Culturali e Ambientali, Rome.

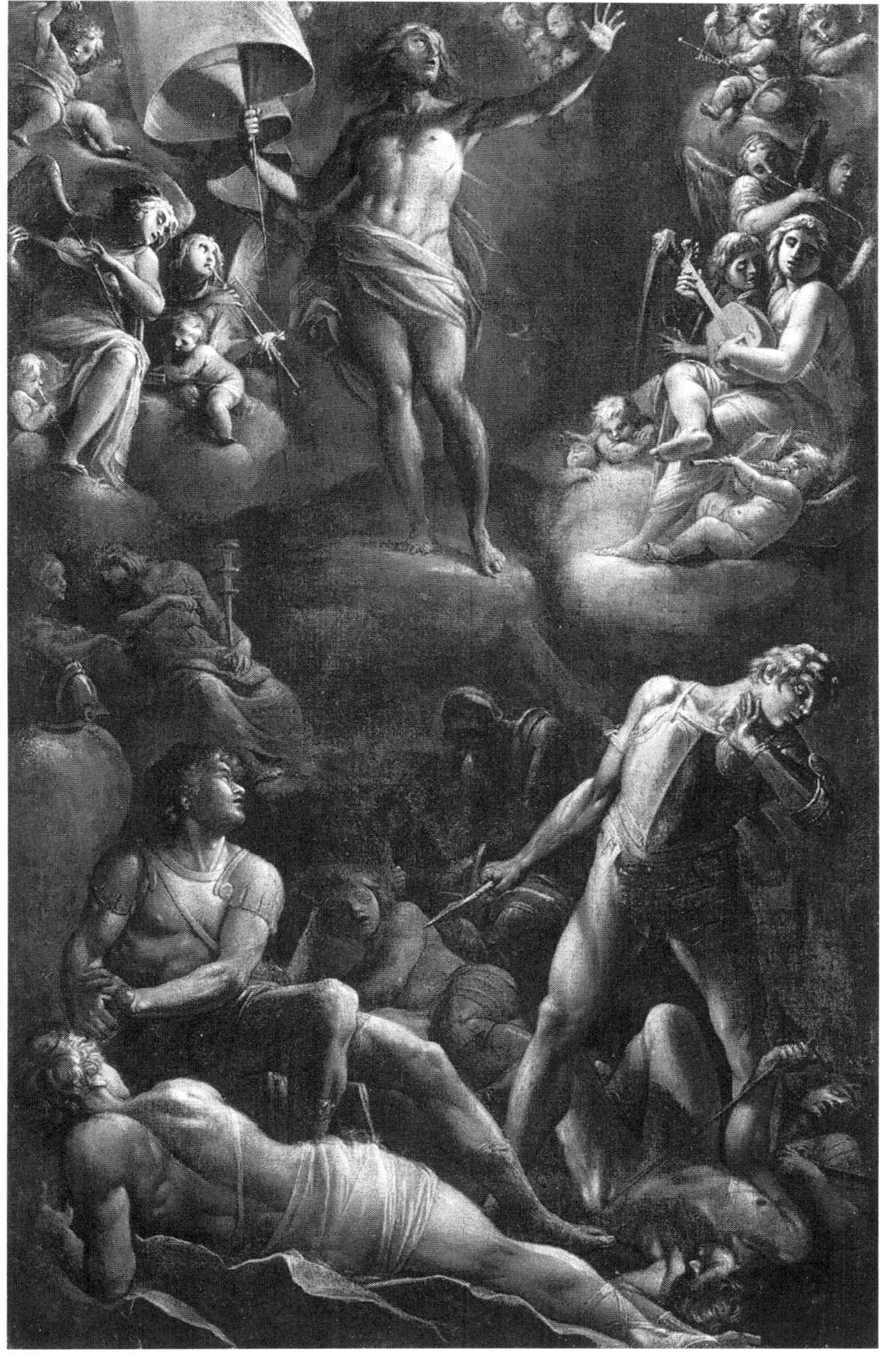

113. Giovanni Baglione, *Resurrection*. Bozzetto for the right transept altar project at the Gesù, oil on canvas (ca. 1602). Musée du Louvre, Paris. Photograph © Réunion des Musées Nationaux / Art Resource, New York.

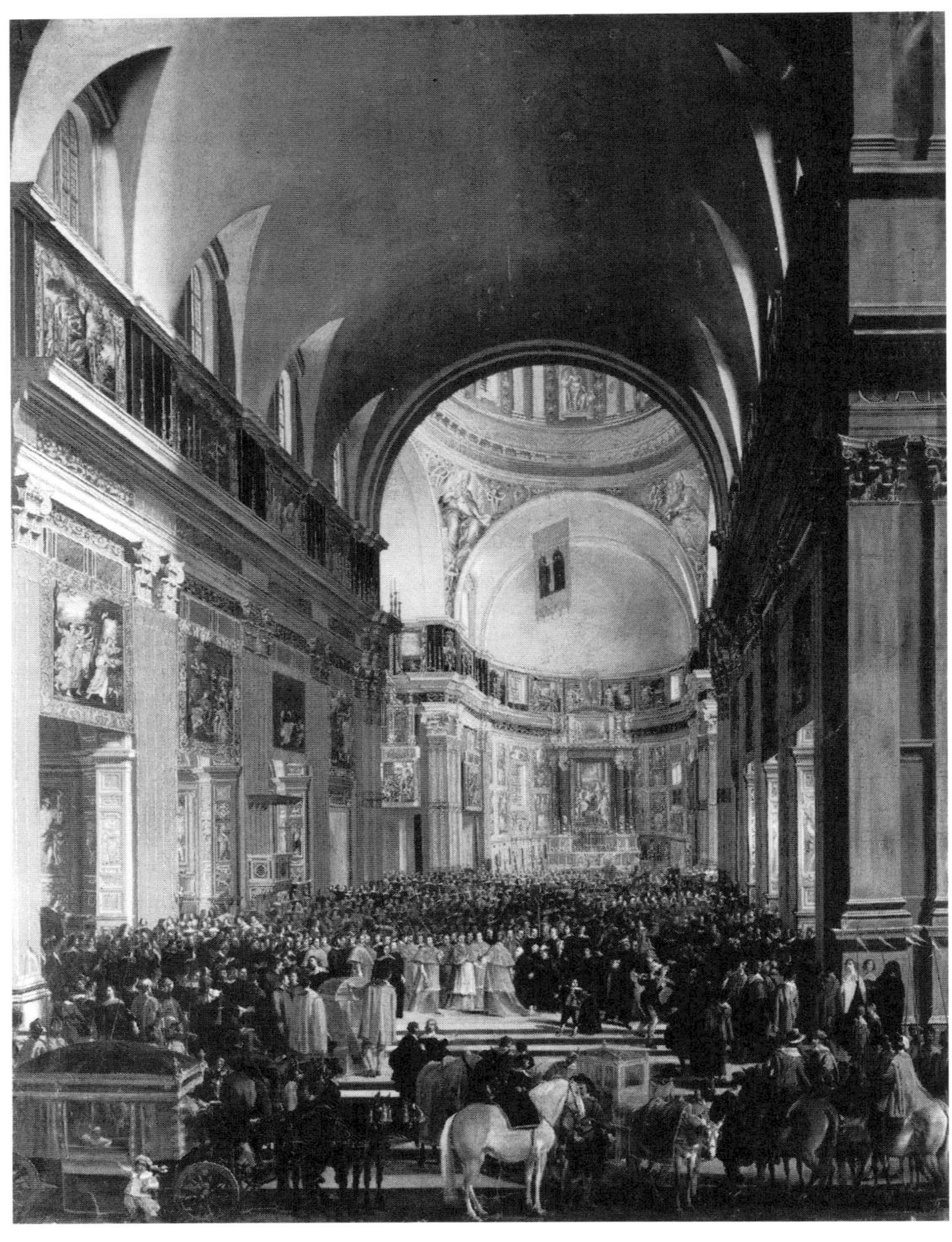

114. Andrea Sacchi, *Ceremony Celebrating the Centenary of the Society of Jesus* (detail, ca. 1640). Photograph © Photo Vasari Rome.

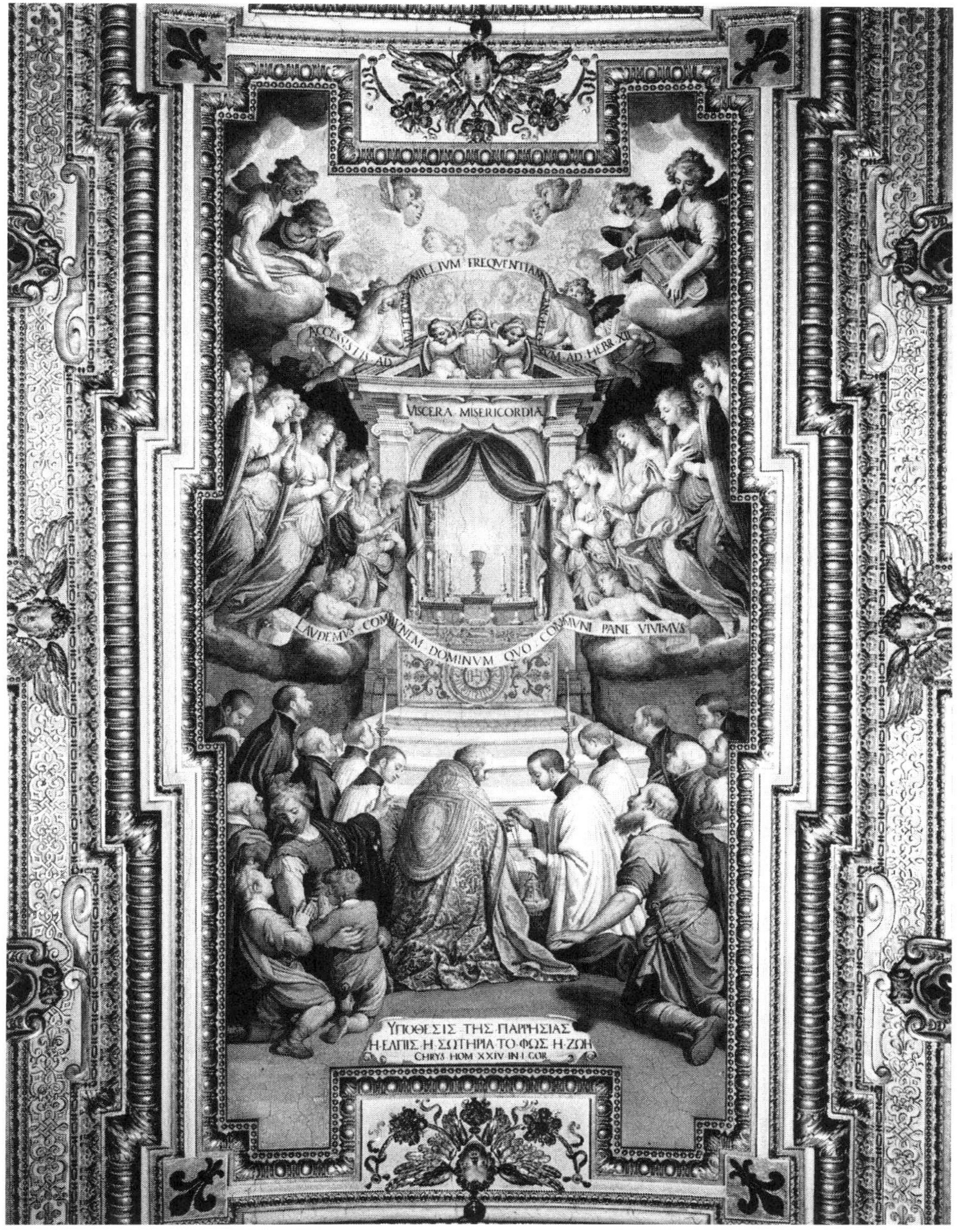

115. Agostino Ciampelli, *Angels Adoring the Blessed Sacrament*. Sacristy, Gesù, Rome (after 1599). Photograph courtesy of the Research Library, Getty Research Institute, Los Angeles (86.P.8).

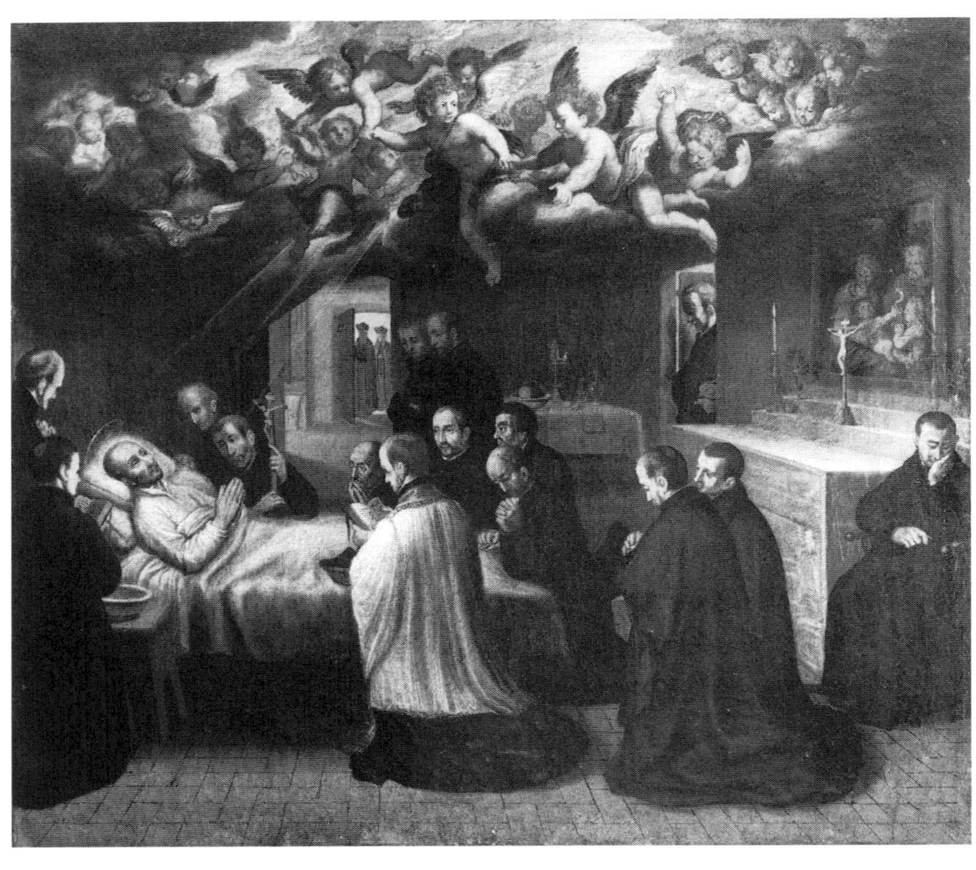

116. Andrea Commodi, *Death of Ignatius*. St Ignatius Chapel, Gesù, Rome (1605–8). Photograph © Photo Vasari Rome.

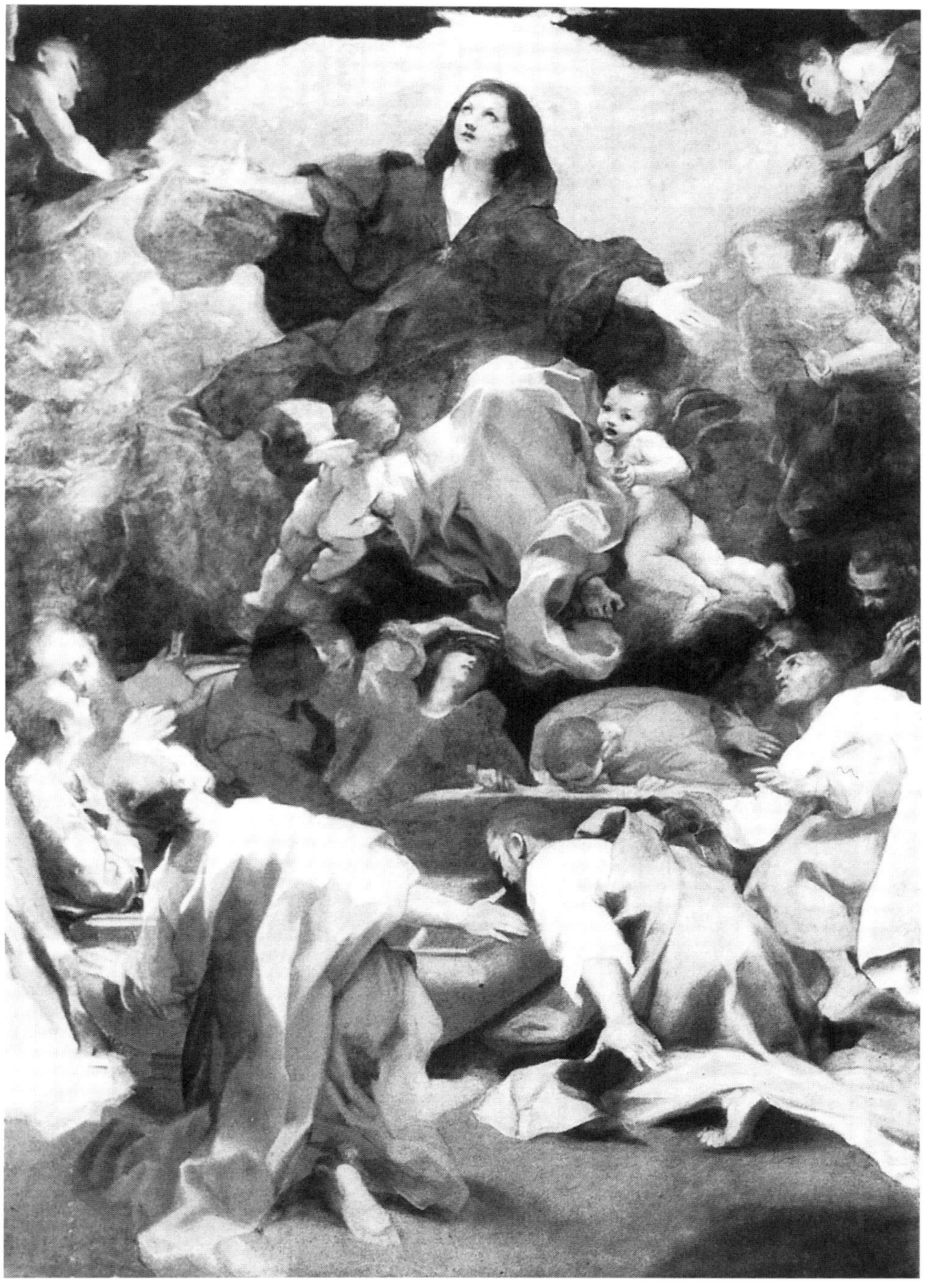

117. Federico Barocci, *Assumption*. Palazzo Ducale, Urbino (before 1612). Photograph courtesy of the Soprintendenza per il Patrimonio Storico Artistico e Demoetnoantropologico delle Marche, Urbino.

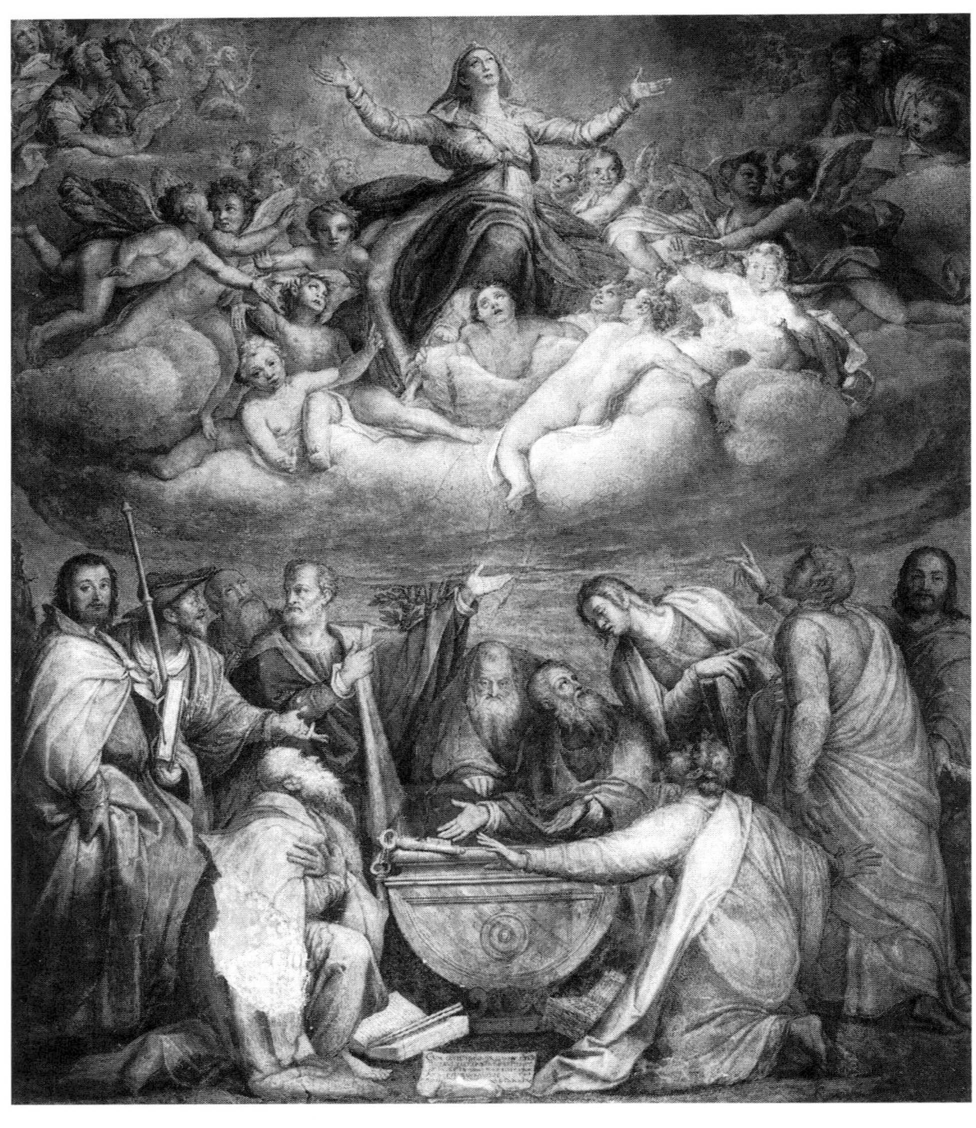

118. Taddeo and Federico Zuccaro, *Assumption*. Pucci Chapel, SS. Trinità dei Monti, Rome (finished late 1580s). Photograph courtesy of the Istituto Centrale per il Catalogo e la Documentazione, Ministerio per i Beni Culturali e Ambientali, Rome.

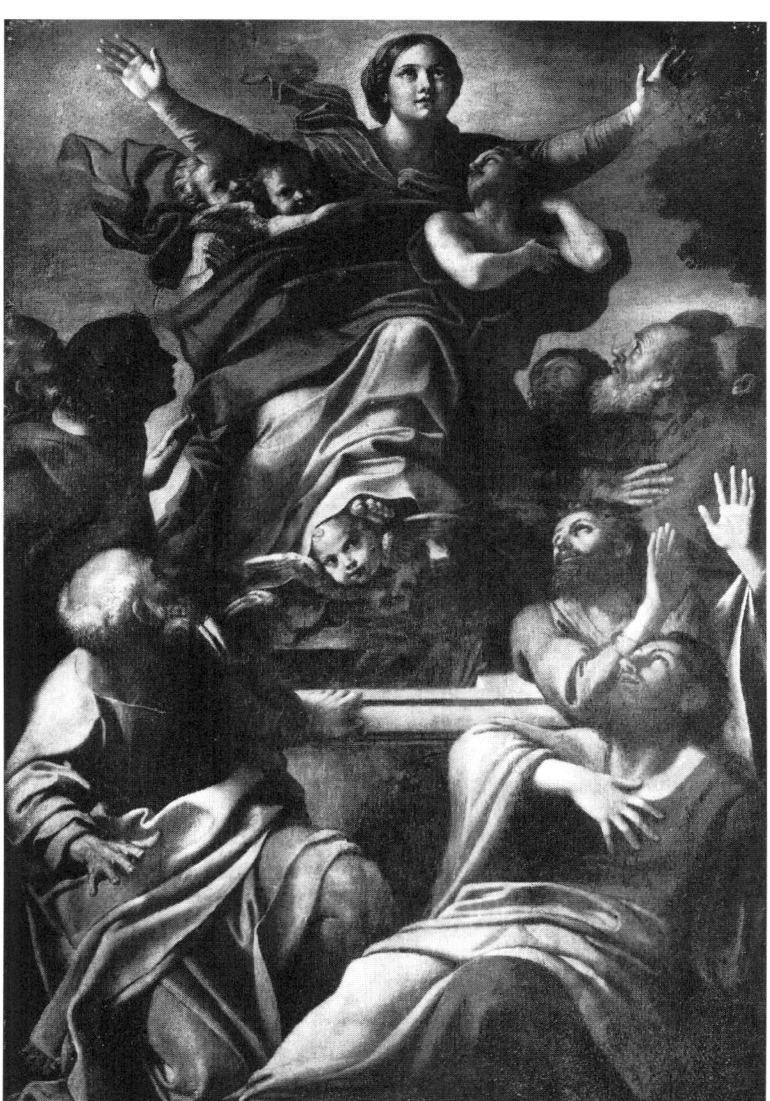

119. Annibale Carracci, *Assumption*. Cerasi Chapel, S. Maria del Popolo, Rome (1601). Photograph courtesy Art Resource, New York.

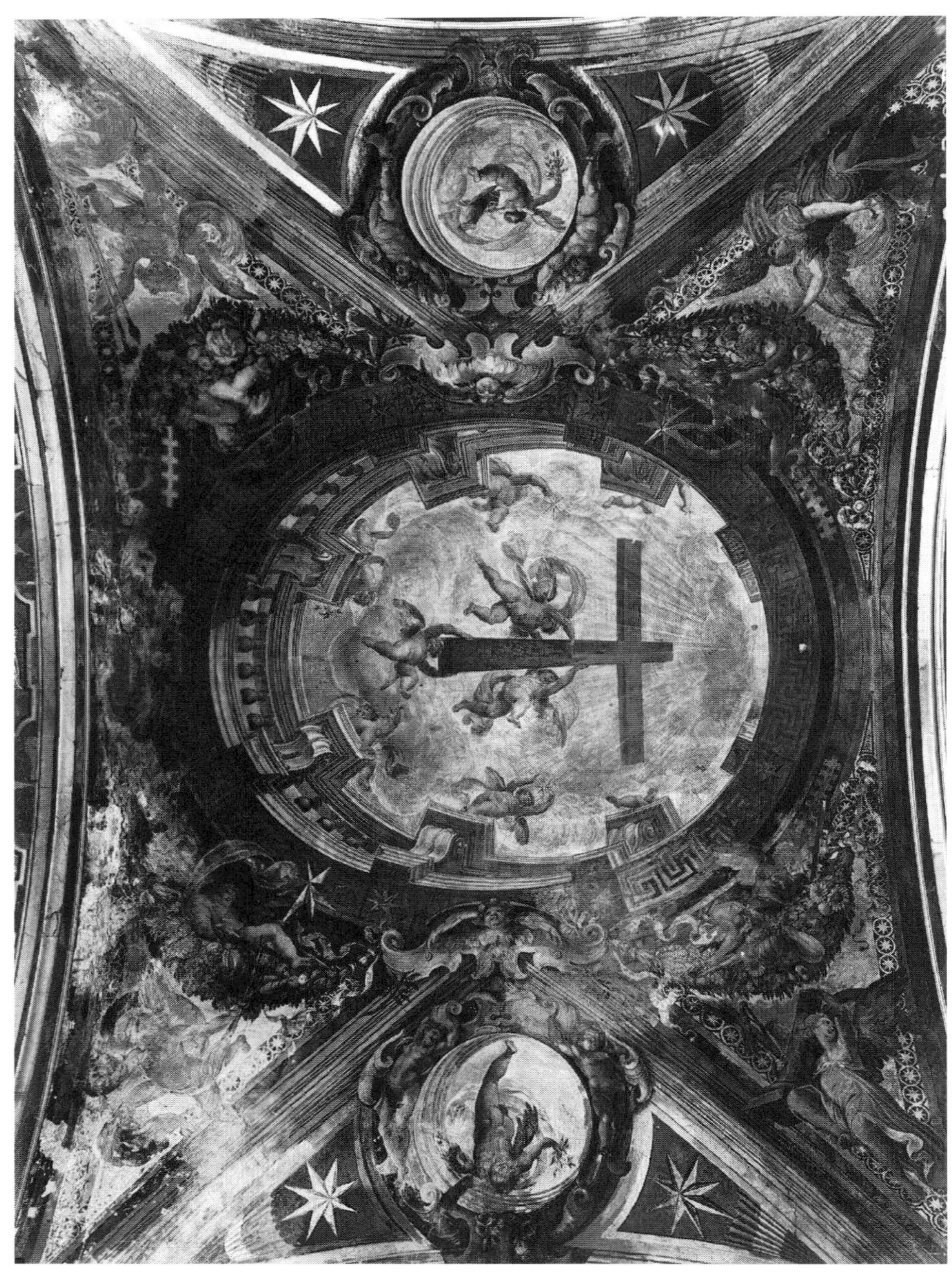

120. Cherubino Alberti, *Glory of the Cross*. Aldobrandini Chapel, S. Maria sopra Minerva, Rome. Photograph courtesy of the Istituto Centrale per il Catalogo e la Documentazione, Ministerio per i Beni Culturali e Ambientali, Rome.

Critics have traditionally disparaged the Gesù paintings by comparing them with those of the Oratorian mother church, the Chiesa Nuova, which featured altarpieces by Barocci, Caravaggio, and Rubens, as well as vault, apse, and dome decoration by Pietro da Cortona.[7] Francis Haskell put the matter very simply when he wrote, 'The contribution made to the artistic life of Rome by the Oratorians was very much more impressive than that of the Jesuits.'[8] Yet the difference between the Gesù and the Chiesa Nuova was more one of timing than of attitude. Most of the contracts for the Gesù side chapels and altarpieces were drawn up in the 1580s and early 1590s, when Rubens was still in Flanders and Pietro da Cortona had not yet been born. On the other hand, the patrons of the Chiesa Nuova were still hiring people to do several key altarpieces in the first two decades of the seventeenth century – Rubens painted three of them in 1606–8 – and they were also in a position to hire Cortona between 1647 and 1665 to paint their vault, apse, and dome, whereas the Jesuits for various practical reasons had to wait until 1674 – five years after Cortona's death – for Baciccio to do the same work at the Gesù. The Jesuits would probably have hired Rubens and Cortona for the Gesù had they been able. Rubens had a close affinity with the Society thanks to his Gonzaga connections, and he worked on smaller projects such as his sketches for the 1609 life of Ignatius, as well as large altarpieces for the Jesuits in Genoa and Mantua earlier in the same decade, as we have seen (see chapter 1). Later in his life, Cortona too collaborated with the Jesuits, in co-authoring a theoretical treatise on the arts with the Florentine Jesuit Giovanni Domenico Ottonelli in 1652; despite being hackneyed and of little impact, the volume demonstrates an affinity between the artist and the Jesuits. There is even evidence that he may have made designs for the altar and altarpiece of St Francis Xavier at the Gesù shortly before his death.[9]

As I pointed out in chapter 1, the first phase of the paintings at the Chiesa Nuova (in the 1570s and 1580s) was more similar to the Gesù decorations than different from them. Artists such as Scipione Pulzone, Girolamo Muziano, and the Cavaliere d'Arpino made significant contributions to both interiors.[10] Alessandro Farnese had hoped to hire Barocci for the Gesù and failed only because of the artist's notoriously slow working habits and tendency to overbook himself. There is no reason whatever to doubt that the Jesuits shared Neri's enthusiasm for Barocci's affective style, and their choice of Ventura Salimbeni and Andrea Lilio d'Ancona, two artists profoundly influenced by the *marchegiano* master, for the side chapels at the Gesù, reveals their enthusiasm for Barocci's flickering colours and sweet piety. It is true that the Jesuits could have had a Caravaggio, as the Oratorians did when they hired him to paint their *Deposition* altarpiece (1602–3). We have no idea why the Jesuits turned down Caravaggio in the competition for the right transept altarpiece in 1602, but we should be wary of attributing their decision to hire Giovanni Baglione instead as a sign of prudishness or a preference for mediocrity.[11] Since Baglione imitated Caravaggio's tenebrism so closely in his *Resurrection* (fig. 113) that it led to a libel case between the two artists, we can even assume that the Jesuits wanted someone who could paint a picture in his style. Even the Oratorians were guilty of the occasional lapse in taste. Cardinal Baronio's titular church of SS. Nereo ed Achilleo, the paintings of which were executed in

the 1590s and are therefore more contemporary with those of the Gesù, are dominated by frescoes on the side walls, derivative martyrdom scenes of appalling
quality by a justly anonymous painter (perhaps Domenico Cerroni) who makes
Circignani's S. Stefano frescoes look like paragons (fig. 18).[12]

The Chiesa Nuova is also said to have more stylistic unity than the Gesù.
Despite claims that the painters who worked for the Chiesa Nuova shared an
'underlying affectivity,' this supposed unity of style is extremely debatable: it is
something of a stretch to consider Arpino's *Presentation at the Temple* or Pulzone's
Crucifixion as having anything in common stylistically with Rubens's *St Domitilla
with Sts Nereus and Achilleus* or with Federico Barocci's *Presentation of the Virgin at
the Temple*, all originally in the same church – not to mention Cortona's much later
contributions.[13] The Chiesa Nuova paintings are instead the result of a more
pragmatic approach similar to that of the Jesuits, as Alessandro Zuccari recently
noted about Baronio: 'In the choice of artists, Baronio did not use a criterion of
formal homogeneity, but preferred to maintain a reasonable range of options, also
according to the opportunities that presented themselves.'[14] The Gesù was eclectic
not because the Jesuits were anti-aesthetic but because late Cinquecento painting
in general was eclectic. If stylistic unity was 'an ideal foreign to the Jesuits of the
1580s and '90s,' then the same must be said for most of the major decorative
projects of the era, including the Chiesa Nuova.[15]

Scholars also commonly maintain that the Jesuits had little control over the
artists chosen for the side chapels, and that such aesthetic concerns were firmly in
the hands of the families who patronized the chapels, an administrative factor that
contributed to the stylistic anarchy. Hibbard, for example, remarks that 'the
patrons ... surely had their choice of artists for the altarpieces,' and Marcia Hall
states that the Jesuits 'did not interfere in the patrons' choice of artist.'[16] As we will
see, with one or two exceptions there is no evidence whatever that the patrons
chose the artists employed in their chapels. Moreover, the artists who did most of
the work – from Circignani to Celio – were Jesuit regulars. The principal exception
was the tribune area, which should be seen more as a Farnese commission than a
Jesuit one. The evidence suggests that the Jesuits approached their patrons in
much the same way as did their Oratorian counterparts, who dictated everything
from the subject of the altarpiece to the design of the tabernacle and on at least one
occasion gave a patron a choice between two specific painters.[17]

It is also often remarked that the Jesuits hired only the cheapest artists.[18]
Although this statement is true for commissions such as the Novitiate – the Jesuits
were not rich, and they had a lot of walls to cover – few recognize that the Jesuits
insisted on hiring professional artists for their most important commissions, even
when cheaper brother artists were available from among their ranks. We have
seen this with Circignani and Tempesta at the collegiate frescoes and with Commodi,
Ciampelli, and others at S. Vitale. Nowhere was this concern with quality as
important as at the Gesù, the Society's showcase church. Yet in their desire to label
the Jesuits as anti-aesthetics, scholars have often claimed that the Jesuits relied
extensively on their own painter brothers even for the Gesù, 'draw[ing] many of
the artists they used from among their own ranks.'[19] Haskell wrote unkindly
about the artists who worked on the Gesù, 'Forced back on their own resources,

the Society cut down the expense by employing as principal painter one of their own members, Padre Valeriano, whose crudity and clumsiness can be benevolently interpreted as mystery and power.'[20] Yet, as we will soon see, the frenetically overworked Valeriano was far from being the principal painter of the Gesù, and instead filled a more supervisory role. The same goes for Giovanni Battista Fiammeri, whom Rudolf Wittkower saw as a paragon of mediocrity typical of the Jesuits' lack of aesthetic ambition.[21] Fiammeri designed the programs of several of the paintings but touched few with his brush. In fact, the Gesù campaign is remarkable for how *few* Jesuit artists were employed, especially when we consider how many brothers of adequate talent were available to the order at the time. It is true that many of the masons, carpenters, and *stuccatori* were Jesuit brothers. But when it came to public art, something that would reflect on the entire order, the Jesuits went to experts. The Gesù was overwhelmingly the work of professional painters, men who were good enough for the Oratorians, the pope, and the most influential cardinals in Rome. No religious order as concerned with the spiritual and didactic power of imagery as the Jesuits could afford not to care about quality.

The Foundation and Construction of the Gesù

The Gesù was not only the Jesuits' most significant building but also the chief ecclesiastical commission of Alessandro Farnese (1520–89), grandson of Paul III and one of the wealthiest and most influential men in Rome, and also the city's leading patron of the arts in the mid-sixteenth century.[22] A cardinal from the age of 14 thanks to his doting grandfather, Alessandro was so rich that he could afford every kind of patronage, from extensive fresco cycles in his palatial villa at Caprarola and in S. Lorenzo in Damaso to miniatures such as the magnificent Farnese Hours by Giulio Clovio (1538–46) and the Cassetta Farnese (1544), one of the most important examples of Renaissance metalwork. He was also rich enough to hire most of the leading artists active in Rome during his lifetime. Since Alessandro's grandfather was the pope who officially approved the Society of Jesus in 1540, the Farnese family were proprietary about the Jesuits, and the relationship proved both fruitful and problematic for the new order. On the one hand, it encouraged Alessandro to lavish extraordinary wealth on the Gesù, thereby allowing it to become the most important church of its time and one that the other leading orders of the city – including the Oratorians and Theatines – struggled to match in their own mother churches. On the other hand, it put most of the crucial architectural decisions in Alessandro's hands, from the size of the church to the decoration of its facade, so that, in the words of Clare Robertson, 'If we are to speak of a style for the Gesù in Rome, it is surely a Farnese style rather than a Jesuit one.'[23] There was considerable strife between the Jesuits and their patron during the planning and building of the church, and most scholars now agree that the Gesù we see today was far more ostentatious than the Jesuits, with their preference for flat, wooden roofs and plain facades, would have liked.[24]

The Gesù was under the shadow of the Farnese from the very beginning. Immediately after he approved the new order, Paul III gave Ignatius of Loyola a small existing chapel called S. Maria della Strada on the Piazza degli Altieri, which was adjacent to the Palazzo Venezia, the Farnese pope's residence at the time.[25] S. Maria was perfectly located, at a crucial crossroads, close to the pope and also to the seat of the civic government in the Campidoglio, in a diverse neighbourhood where all kinds of humanity – rich and poor, prince and beggar, Christian and Jew – lived side by side. The first church ever held by the Jesuits, S. Maria was an ideal location for their ministries, whether public preaching or charitable work, 'ideal for men whose commitment to preaching and other ministries led them consistently to place their churches and houses as near as possible to the hub of the cities in which they found themselves.'[26] The church also became Ignatius's final resting place after his death in 1556. Nevertheless, like all the churches handed over to the Jesuits, this little one quickly proved too small for the burgeoning order, and the Society grew desperate for funds to erect a larger building. As early as 1550, Ignatius had hired the architect and sculptor Nanni di Baccio Bigio to draw up a plan for a new church, a three-aisled basilical structure that may reflect an interest in Palaeochristian style.[27] But the Society of Jesus did not have enough money even to begin the project.

It was at this point that Cardinal Farnese stepped in to help the young order and to enable them to build the first large church in Rome since the Sack of 1527 – the first really new church of any size for well over a century. He offered to pay for the church as early as 1561, but he was in no hurry, and thanks also to some delays in purchasing part of the land the church was to be built on, construction did not start until 1568, the same year that the Jesuits were able to purchase an adjacent house from the Altieri family for their Casa Professa.[28] During the famous negotiations that followed, Alessandro made it clear who was in charge. Nanni's plan was abandoned, and the Jesuit brother architect Giovanni Tristano, who the Jesuits hoped would oversee the project, ended up being little more than the executor of the Farnese's project. Nevertheless, the idea of a large, open church seems to have been promoted even before Alessandro took over, 'showing clearly that the huge dimensions of both were ordained from the beginning.'[29] Tristano may already have drafted his own version of the plan, a surviving drawing that may have been corrected by Michelangelo, who at one point offered to design the Gesù himself for free.[30] This project was for a large, single-aisled hall with side chapels and a shallow apse, which would be ideal for preaching to large congregations. Pirro Ligorio, the antiquarian and architect for Pope Pius IV, also prepared a plan for the Gesù, perhaps at the invitation of the Farnese since he had worked for Alessandro before, and his design was also for a monumental single-aisled structure.[31]

At least the basic idea of an open, acoustic church survived in the structure eventually built, a project by the Farnese architect Jacopo Barozzi da Vignola, who had already built the villa at Caprarola in the later 1550s.[32] Although Vignola had played with the idea of an oval church, he eventually settled on the existing plan for a Latin cross with a single nave, deep apse, and cupola; three rectangular side chapels on either side of the nave; and an additional circular enclosure at each of the four corners of the crossing – this was the church that was built with the assistance of the Jesuit architectural supervisors Giuseppe Valeriano (until 1590) and Giovanni de Rosis, the architect (1590–9).[33] As is well known, the Jesuits did not want a barrel vault in their church, since they were afraid it would create echoes and be unsuitable for preaching, even though Alessandro wrote that that it 'does not seem very probable to me from the example of other churches of even greater capacity.'[34] Alessandro also decided to reorient the church so that its facade and not its side faced the square, giving it a much more imposing and dramatic appearance. Dissatisfied with Vignola's facade design, Alessandro first sought the advice of Galeazzo Alessi and then hired Giacomo della Porta in 1571 to execute the austere, focused facade that exists today. Although Alessandro had intended to spend only 25,000 scudi, he ended up lavishing as much as 100,000 scudi on the church, according to one report.[35]

The church was so immense that it greatly impressed contemporary visitors even when half finished, and the Jesuits put it to use well before the final stone was laid. Typical is this description of the Jesuits' 'very large and fayre' church by the English Catholic traveller Gregory Martin (1581): '[The church] being but halfe built [they] had forthwith Masses, and preaching, and confessions, etc.; bycause thy wil leese no time, whiles the rest is a building: and thou wouldest have thought this halfe part to have been a very goodly Church.'[36] Descriptions in Jesuit letters from the early 1570s give a vivid idea of the slow and uneven character of the construction at the Gesù, and also reflect something of the conflict between the Society and the cardinal. The Annual Letter of 1571 (31 December) describes the church at a time when only the nave chapels had been erected:

> The fabric of our church has grown considerably since the beginning ... [the workers] having begun the other three chapels corresponding to the three that last year were roofed along with their vaults, and they have been built above in such a manner that this part of the fabric is already higher than [that] on the other [side]. The facade is being built with great skill in beautifully worked stone, and has reached a level almost as high as [that of] the actual construction [of the church], with the great diligence and care it has had, and with the continual efforts of the brother masons.[37]

An Annual Letter in Spanish for the following year also emphasizes that much of the work on the Gesù was done by Jesuit brothers, so many of them that almost every Jesuit mason in Rome was occupied with its construction: 'I will only say that it has been almost entirely our own brother masons who have augmented the building so much this year, one which with time will be a grand edifice, and very expensive, much more than is necessary for our ministries, and according to the Most Illustrious Cardinal Farnese.'[38] This letter also reveals that the Jesuits were less than pleased with Alessandro's pretentions, and hints that their labourers could be better employed elsewhere than in this extravagant monument to Farnese glory.

It was in the interior that the Jesuits were able to exercise control. Although the high altar and tribune area were under direct Farnese jurisdiction, the side chapels represent the Jesuits' wishes. The Society had more say about the side chapels because they were the product of a different kind of patronage. Here, instead of relying on powerful and wealthy patrons, they begged from older and poorer aristocratic families such as the Mellini, Caetani, and Orsini, people who would be less inclined to make stylistic or iconographic demands. Hibbard comments: 'Despite the irregular progress of decoration, records that survive show that the Jesuits controlled the ornamental and iconographic program: although the chapels were painted with funds from private patrons, the dedications were already set at the time of transfer and are often mentioned in the earliest documents; Jesuit decorators remained in charge; and the money paid to the artists, even of the altarpieces, was paid through Jesuit intermediaries ... The coherence of the chapel iconography did not allow room for much independent choice of subject.'[39] Several of these patrons, a number of them clerics, seem to have been hand-picked by the Jesuits for their chapels, no doubt because they or their families had been sympathetic to the Society; the group may have included people whom the Jesuits served as confessors or counselors.[40] Such was Gasparo Garzonio, original patron of the Angels' Chapel, whose father had been the first to open his doors to Ignatius in Rome, and who enjoyed an intimate relationship with the Jesuits. Even Giulio Folco, Alessandro Farnese's agent and the patron of the Martyrs' Chapel, showed an appreciation for the Society and took their side in some of his mediations between them and his patron.[41] This reliance on families who were already supporters recalls their appeal to Isabella della Rovere at S. Vitale. As with S. Vitale and S. Andrea, too, there was a reliance on women, the kind of 'widowed, childless and affluent' patrons who Maria Conelli has shown were a favoured target of the Society.[42] Prominent Roman women financed the two lateral chapels flanking the apse, which are among the most important places in the church.

The General Scheme of the Gesù Paintings

Any reconstruction of the original Gesù decorations must rely on the assistance of contemporary descriptions and archival documents, since several of the paintings were replaced or moved in the seventeenth century and later. Only two of the original altarpieces are in place today, and even some of the chapel dedications have changed. Nevertheless, a substantial number of the original decorations survive, unlike in most of the other buildings treated in this book. In the 1580s the six nave chapels were dedicated (beginning at the west door) to Sts Peter and Paul (or the Apostles) and St Andrew (the Martyrs); to the Nativity and the Passion; and to the Trinity and the Angels. The high altar depicted the Circumcision, and the transepts were dedicated to the Crucifixion and the Resurrection. The small circular chapels flanking the apse were assigned to the Madonna della Strada and St Francis of Assisi, whereas the corresponding circular openings at the west of the cupola were not chapels, and served instead simply as passageways and vestibules into the church. In addition, there was a crypt chapel under the high altar (destroyed in 1843) that was dedicated to the early Christian martyrs Sts Abundius and Abundantius in 1584, when their relics were transferred in a grand procession to the Gesù.

The dedications of two of the chapels were concessions to the location of the church. To the left of the apse was the Chapel of the Madonna della Strada, named in honour of the original church on the site given to Ignatius of Loyola. On the opposite side aisle the St Andrew (Martyrs') Chapel was dedicated in honour of a small oratory dedicated to the apostle that once had existed on the site. A seventeenth-century Jesuit report recalls, 'The Chapel of the Madonna and that of St Andrew were made because before they so greatly expanded [the building] there were two little churches on the site of the [present] church, the one of Santa Maria della Strada, whose image is conserved in the same Chapel of the Madonna, and the other of St Andrew.'[43] The Jesuits themselves chose the rest of the dedications, certainly by the early 1580s and probably as early as under the generalate of Francis Borgia (1565–72). It is likely that Borgia selected the dedication of the chapel opposite the Chapel of the Madonna della Strada, to his patron saint, Francis of Assisi, and during the early construction of the church, in the 1550s, he was an especially zealous donor.[44] As at S. Vitale, where there was a painting of St Ignatius of Antioch, and at SS. Annunziata, where there was another chapel of St Francis of Assisi, this St Francis Chapel conveniently served to call to mind a Jesuit candidate for sainthood, Francis Xavier. Ignatius himself especially revered Francis of Assisi as a model for his ministry, and it is possible that the dedication derives from him. In fact, there is evidence that the dedications of both chapels flanking the apse may have been approved by Ignatius, since, as Hibbard points out, the Virgin Mary played a crucial role in his conversion, and he modelled his life and his new order on those of St Francis of Assisi.[45]

As Hibbard has shown in his ground-breaking article on the painted decorations of the Gesù, the chapels participate in an integrated and consistent iconographic program that he relates to the meditative methods outlined in the *Spiritual Exercises*.[46] What he and other scholars have not acknowledged is that the Gesù decorations were not only consistent within themselves, but also relate closely to the painting cycles of the Novitiate and the collegiate churches as well as to printed works such as Nadal's Gospels. In fact, the programmatic method of the Gesù was tested out in these earlier interiors and publications before it was used in the mother church. This tightly integrated and coordinated iconographic web unites all the Jesuit interiors in Rome, and in every case is characterized by the 'mystical pilgrimage' format, a progressive journey through thematically interrelated areas culminating in an overall moment of conversion and experience of the divine. The ultimate goal was for the viewer to undergo a phenomenal transformation through his or her interiorization of the sacred narrative. Although this notion of a controlled mystical pilgrimage was influenced by the devotion associated with the Sacro Monte and other practices promoted by orders such as the Observant Franciscans, the degree to which it was coordinated and scripted in Jesuit foundations in Rome is unique. Also unique is the number of inscriptions, or captions, that provide viewers with a rich range of scriptural, patristic, and other commentary to assist them with their journey. In the case of the Gesù this pilgrimage is built around a progression of paired themes.

I will briefly paraphrase Hibbard's interpretation of the Gesù decorations.[47] The high altar subject, unusual as the main theme of a church, represents the moment Jesus was named, and is therefore a symbol of the name not only of the church itself but of the Society of Jesus.[48] It was also at the Circumcision that the name of Jesus was first associated with his blood. The transepts show the key events of his redemptive history on earth, the Crucifixion and Resurrection, and reinforce the christological theme of the church. The side chapels collaborated in the separate but related theme of Christ's redemption, starting at the entrance with the historical and earthly and then moving to the life of Christ and, finally, to the heavenly and the theological at the church crossing. The initial pair, St Andrew and Sts Peter and Paul, illustrate the work of the first men to preach Christ's name and to die for the faith, offering a clear model for contemporary Christians and Jesuits. Unlike the Oratorian Chiesa Nuova, which had a more traditional chronological program arranged in a counter-clockwise circle, the Gesù had a cross-nave pairing of chapels so that the altarpiece subject on the left-hand side would be completed by that on the right (the Nativity Chapel found its conclusion in the Passion Chapel, and the Apostles' Chapel was completed by the Martyrs' Chapel).

The message of the side chapels is that we must work here on earth to attain salvation. The first two chapels, with their themes of apostolate and martyrdom, stress earthly ministry and the victory over paganism and heresy. The central pair of chapels relate directly to Jesus, further underscoring the dedication of the church. They stress that humankind has received the gift of redemption only through Christ's sacrifice, and that we must follow his example in our lives and work. The final pair of chapels, Trinity and Angels', take us into heaven itself. The Trinity Chapel celebrates God's influence in the human world, and the Angels' Chapel depicts humanity's troubled path to God. This heavenly theme led nicely into the appropriately well-lit cupola area, which was painted with many more angels, as well as toward the Church Fathers in the pendentives, the whole nave area 'attempt[ing] to furnish a progressive religious experience.'[49] I would add to Hibbard's analysis the remark that the middle pair of nave chapels, related to Christ's life and passion, act as a parallel to the transept altars, and help anchor the entire body of the church to a christological theme.

Hibbard has also related the nave paintings to the *Spiritual Exercises*.[50] He associates the progression of chapel pairs from door to cupola with the Three Colloquies in the *Exercises*, where the exercitant prays in turn to Mary (represented in the vault paintings of the first pair of chapels), to Christ (the central theme of the second), and to God the Father (the focus of the third). The Trinity is also a crucial element in Ignatius's manual, since it forms the subject of the First Contemplation of the First Day of the Second Week. Hell, which appears in the Angels' Chapel, forms the subject of the Fifth Exercise of the First Week. The chapel pairs also interact across the nave in subtle ways. The St Andrew and Sts Peter and Paul chapels interrelate not only because both represent the world of humankind, but also because Peter was Andrew's brother and all three saints are apostles as well as martyrs. To this I would add that Peter's and Paul's bodies were supposedly buried in Rome, as was Andrew's head after being brought to the city following the Ottoman conquest of Constantinople in 1453; the two chapels had a solidly Roman identity.[51] Similarly, the two chapels closest to the cupola interrelate, since the archangels in the Angels' Chapel are shown revering the Trinity, and the Trinity chapel is filled with angels.

Alexandra Herz has refined and expanded Hibbard's interpretation.[52] She reminds us that the Jesuit monogram for the name of Jesus, IHS, was created by the Franciscan Bernardino of Siena (1380–1444) and points out that there was a confraternity of the Holy Name established by Bernardino in 1427 under Martin V on the very site of the Gesù, probably in the Chapel of the Madonna della Strada. She suggests, convincingly, that it was no coincidence that Ignatius adopted the monogram in 1541, the same year in which he took over the church of the Madonna della Strada. Seen in this light, the Circumcision relates more directly to the name of Jesus and less to the blood of Christ per se: 'The name is not just the Name of Christ – it literally means salvation. Though the Gesù decorations indeed emphasize bloody sacrifice, the program clearly states that martyrdom is not undertaken merely because Christ had done so, but because Christ's road alone leads to salvation.'[53] She concludes that like the martyrdom cycles in the collegiate churches, the Gesù cycle does not promote martyrdom for its own sake but instead asks all Christians to follow the way of Christ, a 'far more optimistic and joyful' message than is usually acknowledged.[54] The IHS emblem also has an early Christian connection. According to the *Golden Legend*, when the executioners tore out the heart of St Ignatius of Antioch, they found the name of Christ inscribed on it in gold letters. Later Jesuit writers associated this story with Ignatius of Loyola's adoption of his name and of the Jesuit monogram. So the use of the monogram here suggests that the Gesù decorations participate in the same interest in the Palaeochristian as the collegiate chapels and S. Vitale.

Scholars so far have overlooked that the Gesù side chapels also work as a compendium of 'All Saints.' At S. Apollinare, S. Vitale, and, in the most complete form, the dormitory of the Novitiate, the Jesuit painting cycles attempted to provide a panorama of sainthood that would permit novices and students to venerate different kinds of saints in the Litany of the Saints. The Gesù nave allows the same practice, with chapels to the Trinity and the Virgin Mary (Nativity), to the apostles and martyrs (Sts Peter and Paul and Andrew), and to the angels (Angels'), as well as to the prophets, patriarchs, confessors, and virgins also depicted in these chapels (the virgin saint Catherine of Alexandria is depicted in the Martyrs' Chapel, for example). As we have seen, Jesuit communities recited the Litany daily by this time, and the students of at least some of the collegiate residences venerated the different kinds of saints on different days of the week. The nave area served as a constant reminder of the role of the saints and angels as companions, models, and intercessors in the life of the Christian, a central tenet of the reformed Catholic church.

While the dedications of the Gesù chapels may date from the 1560s or earlier, their decorative cycles mark the end of the first era of Jesuit church decoration in Rome. Work on the interior began only in the mid-1580s, when the collegiate chapel cycles and the first phase of the Novitiate cycle had already been completed, and except for the tomb of Ignatius the paintings of the Gesù chapels were finished only in 1604, later than those at S. Vitale and contemporary with the last phase of the decoration at the Novitiate. The death of Alessandro Farnese in 1589 and the lukewarm interest of his nephew Odoardo (1573–1626) meant that the vaults, dome, and apse of the church would remain undecorated until the 1670s, more than sixty years after the completion of the side chapels. The original paintings and sculptures at the Gesù were the last Jesuit art project of the Renaissance in Rome, and perhaps

the last major Renaissance art project anywhere in the city, as Rome moved forward
to embrace the Baroque.

The Artists of the Gesù Decorations

Two Jesuits supervised the painted decorations of the chapels, Valeriano and
Fiammeri, with the latter assuming sole responsibility after Valeriano's death in
1596; the sculptural and stucco elements were handled by de Rosis. Most of the
Gesù decoration was done by men who had worked for the Jesuits before, especially that of the vaults and tondos, which were particularly important areas since
they helped unify the iconographic themes of the various chapels. Three of the
artists were reformist painters in the circle of Santi di Tito. One was Niccolò
Circignani, the artist most responsible for creating a Jesuit iconography in Rome,
who painted the vaults and tondos of the Apostles' and Nativity chapels (figs 83,
85, 87–9). Another leading painter of the Gesù, whose work we have seen at S.
Vitale, was Agostino Ciampelli, who painted the entire Martyrs' Chapel and was
responsible for the vaults of the sacristy and for part of the Chapel of SS. Abbondio
and Abbondanzio (figs 95–8). Similarly, Andrea Commodi, who painted the tribune
area of S. Vitale, did a canvas for the Chapel of SS. Abbondio and Abbondanzio,
and a cycle of the life of Ignatius of Loyola – perhaps the first in Italy – for
Ignatius's tomb on the right of the apse of the church and now in the Chapel of
Odoardo Farnese (ca. 1605–8) (fig. 116). Gaspare Celio, a close friend of Valeriano's
who may have worked at the Novitiate and at S. Vitale, also made an important
contribution in his paintings for the Passion Chapel, following designs by Fiammeri
(figs 100–3). Other old Jesuit standbys include Durante Alberti, the painter of the
altarpieces at S. Andrea, S. Apollinare, and S. Tommaso, who did a fresco of the
Transfiguration for the Gesù (Trinity Chapel) (fig. 93); and Paul Brill, one of the
most sought-after landscapists in Rome, who had worked for the Jesuits at the
Collegio Romano and possibly S. Vitale, and who painted the *paesi* in the St Francis
Chapel (fig. 110).

Most of the other painters were new. Scipione Pulzone (ca. 1550–88), whose
style has been virtually equated with the Jesuits' *modus procedendi* by Federico Zeri
and Sydney Freedberg, here worked for the first time for the Jesuits. He painted
the altarpiece of the Passion Chapel (fig. 99), the original altarpiece and vaults of
the Angels' Chapel (both overpainted in less than a decade), and some of the
drapery on the figures in the Chapel of the Madonna della Strada (figs 108–9).[55]
Pulzone was best known as a portrait painter but had executed altarpieces in a
number of Roman churches, such as S. Silvestro al Quirinale and S. Caterina dei
Funari. From 1582 the rector of the Confraternità dei Virtuosi al Pantheon, Pulzone
was celebrated for a polished, somewhat icy style of court portraiture that has
been compared with that of Jacopino del Conte (fig. 1); a minute attention to detail;
and an extraordinary facility with rendering fabrics and drapery, derived from
contacts with Venetian painting. His religious painting was marked by a slightly
archaizing trend in the spirit of the Palaeochristian Revival. Another leading
painter of the Palaeochristian Revival movement who worked on the Gesù was
Baldassare Croce (1553–1628). He is responsible for a critical martyrdom cycle at

the church of S. Susanna and also worked for Cardinal Alessandro de' Medici at S. Prisca. At the Gesù he painted frescoes in both the St Francis Chapel and the Chapel of SS. Abbondio and Abbondanzio.[56] Baldassare's is a monumental style that uses bulky figure types inspired by Michelangelo and openly refers to Raphael's *stanze* in the grandness of the compositions and architectural settings.

Many painters who contributed to the Gesù interior ranked among the most celebrated and best employed of their time. Such were the Cavaliere d'Arpino (Giuseppe Cesari, 1568–1640), who painted a canvas in the transept to accompany the Crucifixion sculpture. The Cavaliere may have been the busiest fresco painter of the late Cinquecento, having contributed since his arrival in Rome in 1582 to the Vatican Logge and other parts of the Vatican Palace, SS. Trinità dei Monti, S. Lorenzo in Damaso, S. Prassede, the Palazzo dei Conservatori, the Lateran transept, the Pauline Chapel at S. Maria Maggiore, and the mosaic decorations of the cupola of St Peter's.[57] One of the great prodigies of his age, the Cavaliere introduced greater clarity and naturalism into his work, including a pronounced tenebrism in the 1590s, and he moved away from the decorative toward the descriptive. The Cavaliere's younger brother, Bernardino Cesari (1571–1622), may also have worked at the Gesù as a teenager, in the late 1580s.[58] Federico Zuccaro (ca. 1540–1609), who is responsible for the entire Angels' Chapel (figs 104–7), was almost equally ubiquitous, thanks primarily to Farnese patronage. Federico painted at S. Lorenzo in Damaso, the Villa Farnese at Caprarola, the Villa d'Este at Tivoli, the Oratorio del Gonfalone, and S. Caterina dei Funari, and completed Vasari's cupola fresco in the Duomo in Florence, among many other commissions.[59] He was especially close to the Jesuits, and his son Orazio joined the order in 1605 (see chapter 2). As we saw in chapter 1, Federico and his brother Taddeo Zuccaro were the leaders of one of the reformist schools of sacred painting and combined courtly elegance with devotional sobriety.

Giovanni de' Vecchi (1536–1615), responsible for the lantern and pendentives (fig. 114), was also a leading fresco painter, having worked on such major commissions as the Oratorio del Gonfalone, the Sala del Mappamondo and Camera degli Angeli at Caprarola, the Oratorio del SS. Crocifisso, and the church of S. Eligio degli Orefici.[60] Deeply influenced by Federico Zuccaro, his precursor at Caprarola, de' Vecchi nevertheless brought a greater humanity and richer palette to his frescoes, inspired by Barocci; in his later work he showed a predilection for dramatic shading, although the lack of naturalism in his figures and settings often gives his scenes the appearance of a supernatural vision. The *marchegiano* Andrea Lilio d'Ancona (1570–after 1631), who painted the Four Evangelists in the drum of the main dome and contributed a canvas to the Chapel of SS. Abbondio and Abbondanzio, worked on many of the most critical commissions during the reign of Sixtus V and later, including the Sixtine Chapel and the main nave at S. Maria Maggiore, the Biblioteca Sistina, the Scala Santa at the Lateran, the Lateran Palace, and the papal apartments in the Vatican.[61] A close follower of Barocci's mystical style, Lilio also favoured emotion and effects of light over solidity and naturalism.

Ventura Salimbeni (1568–1613), who worked in both the Trinity and the Angels' chapels, was a leading figure in the Sienese Cinquecento whose Roman work includes contributions to the Biblioteca Vaticana, the Lateran Palace (including an *Allegory of Faith* in the Benediction Loggia), and a *Magdalene* in the church of S. Agostino.[62] His work shows the tendency among several Sienese painters of the period to adopt Barocci's shimmering colours and sentimentality. Another artist who worked on the Gesù and who collabrated with both Lilio and Salimbeni at the Lateran Palace and the Scala Santa was the Faenza painter Ferraù Fenzoni (1562–1645) (fig. 92).[63] Fenzoni, who also worked in the Biblioteca Vaticana, the apartments of Pius V, and the nave of S. Maria Maggiore, was stylistically very close to his collaborators, all of whom had a common predilection for bright, flickering colours in the Barocci vein.

As we saw in chapter 1, few artists of the late Cinquecento had as much impact on the movement toward simplicity and sobriety in sacred art as Girolamo Muziano (1532–92), a Brescian influenced both by the Florentine reform and by Venetian painting. Muziano was active in Rome throughout the second half of the Cinquecento, especially under Gregory XIII, and executed large canvases for S. Maria Maggiore and S. Maria degli Angeli and an *Ascension* for the Chiesa Nuova.[64] He painted the most critical painting of the Gesù, the high altar *Circumcision* (fig. 112). The Roman painter Giovanni Baglione (1566–1644), Caravaggio's rival and the author of *Le vite de' pittori* (1642), painted one of the last pictures for the church, the transept altarpiece *Resurrection* (fig. 113), a commission for which Caravaggio competed, as we have seen; the result was Baglione's lifelong hatred for the Lombard artist and his abandonment of Baglione's style.[65] Baglione was very active in Rome under Sixtus V and later, having contributed to the decorations at the Scala Santa, the Biblioteca Vaticana, and the Lateran Palace, as well as at churches such as S. Maria del Orto, SS. Quattro Coronati, and S. Cecilia in Trastevere, which he was working on at the same time as on his Gesù altarpiece (1601–3). Baglione adopted Caravaggio's tenebrism (dramatically contrasting light and shadow) and theatricality for his Gesù commission, although none of that artist's intense realism. Another artist who fell under the influence of Caravaggio's tenebrism was the Sienese painter Antiveduto Grammatica (1571–1626), whose shop in Rome specialized in genre scenes and small religious pictures, and whose canvas for the left transept chapel was an important early public commission.[66]

Giovanni Battista Pozzo (1561–89), who painted ceiling frescoes in the Chapel of the Madonna della Strada, participated extensively in the commissions of Sixtus V, including the Scala Santa, the Lateran Benediction Loggia, and the Sixtine Chapel at S. Maria Maggiore, as well as the chapel of S. Lorenzo in S. Susanna, a crucial work of the Palaeochristian Revival movement.[67] Although his narrative frescoes follow the style of the Zuccaro school, with more restrained shading and bright colours, his ceiling frescoes with cloudbursts and angels (such as those at the Sixtine Chapel) also pay homage to the painterly effects of Correggio. The Luccese polymath Paolo Guidotti (1560–1629), who was an architect, sculptor, and poet as well as a painter and who worked on the Scala Santa and the Lateran Palace, executed a canvas for the Chapel of SS. Abbondio and Abbondanzio.[68] Guidotti was a reformist painter who brought solidity to his figures and simplicity to his compositions, but gave them a humanity through soft effects of light, ethereal colours, and a devout, if somewhat restrained, sense of emotion.

The artist whose style differs the most from that of the others is Francesco dal Ponte Bassano (1549–92), son of the celebrated Venetian master Jacopo Bassano, whose commissions include the Palazzo Ducale in Venice and S. Luigi dei Francesi in Rome. Francesco is responsible for the main altar of the Trinity Chapel, a work that would bring him considerable renown in the city (fig. 90).[69] Characterized by the moody darkness and sharp highlights of his father and of late Titian, and thronged with crowds in the grand manner of Titian's work for Charles V of Spain, Bassano's works bring the monumentality and painterly effects of Venice to the heart of the Gesù. The Jesuits also hired Northerners to paint important canvases for the Gesù, including Hans von Aachen (1552–1615; in Rome from 1575), who executed the altarpiece in the Nativity Chapel (fig. 86), and either Joseph Heintz the Elder (in Italy 1584–9, 1591–9) or Maarten Pepijn (in Italy 1595–1600), who painted the figures of St Francis in the canvases in which the landscapes were by the Fleming Brill (figs 110–11).[70] Both von Aachen and Heintz would soon become luminaries at the Habsburg court of Rudolf II in Prague. Although Heintz adapts to Roman reformist trends in his Gesù canvases, Hans von Aachen's altarpiece possesses all the lightness, grace, and wit of the Rudolfine style – and like the Bassano it stands out from the rest of the decoration. The Jesuits may have acquired a taste for these Rudolfine artists through Alessandro Farnese, who had hired Bartolomäus Spranger to work on the fresco cycles at Caprarola.[71]

Although the vast majority of the decorations of the Gesù were paintings, we know of four sculptors who worked on the campaign, two of whom were Jesuits. The Roman sculptor Flaminio Vacca (1538–1605), who carved the angels in the Angels' Chapel, also executed a *St Francis* to flank the tomb of Sixtus V in S. Maria Maggiore, statues of St John the Evangelist and St John the Baptist for the Chiesa Nuova, and an angel in St John Lateran, and contributed to some public fountains in Rome.[72] Vacca came to specialize in the restoration of antique sculptures, something that brought him to work at the ducal court in Florence as well. The *stuccatore* Camillo Mariani da Vicenza (1567–1611), who worked on the stucco around the vault in the Angels' Chapel (fig. 105), had contributed to the chapel of the Annunciation and to the area near the organ in St John Lateran, and had also done work at S. Bernardo a Termini, the Cappella Clementina at St Peter's, and the sacristy at S. Maria Maggiore, and executed marble sculptures at St John Lateran and elsewhere.[73] The Florentine Jesuit woodworker Bartolommeo Tronchi (1529–1604), who worked with Fiammeri and Clemente at the Florence college (see chapter 2), is responsible for the magnificent ceiling (mostly destroyed in a fire in 1989) and a wooden crucifix at the Gesù in Perugia, and also made tabernacles for SS. Annunziata and the Jesuit church in Nola.[74] Tronchi built a tabernacle and also executed the angels in the high altar area for the Roman Gesù. Known as a sculptor as well as a carpenter, Tronchi entered the Society at the age of 29.[75] He had a family in Florence: in 1586 he left 50 Roman scudi to the Banco di Guadagni in Florence to be administered by the Jesuit college of S. Giovannino as a trust fund for his nieces Domenica and Francesca.[76] His fellow Jesuit Francesco Brunelli (1572?–1635), from Forlì, carved a wooden crucifix, two angels, and a wardrobe for the Gesù sacristy, all of which survive today, before going on to do work for the Society in Sezze, Ancona, and Forlì.[77] The little-known Sicilian sculptor Lodovico del Duca, brought to the Gesù by a patron from his homeland, cast a monumental bronze crucifix for the left transept in 1593. The last sculptor to work on the early decoration of the Gesù was Michelangelo Macherini, about whom nothing is known except that he carved the emblem of the Society of Jesus over the main entrance to the church.[78]

Although many of the artists who worked on the Gesù had been hired by the Jesuits elsewhere, a few had also worked previously for Alessandro Farnese and may have come to the Gesù in consequence of Alessandro's involvement. The most obvious example is de' Vecchi, who worked on one of the areas most directly under Farnese control, the dome and pendentives. De' Vecchi contributed to the Caprarola frescoes and did the main canvas for Alessandro's titular church of S. Lorenzo in Damaso.[79] Federico Zuccaro, who directed the Caprarola decorations after the death of his brother Taddeo and also worked on S. Lorenzo in Damaso, was one of Alessandro's leading painters. Pulzone himself may have come to the Gesù through his Farnese connections, since in 1579 he had painted a portrait of Alessandro, now in the Galleria Nazionale d'Arte Antica in Rome. Even Circignani worked for the Farnese (S. Lorenzo in Damaso, 1587), although it was most likely the Jesuits who introduced him to Alessandro and not the other way around, since his Jesuit martyrdom frescoes were earlier than his work at S. Lorenzo. Although Girolamo Muziano had not worked previously for the Farnese, he had in fact been Alessandro's first choice for the decorations at Caprarola (Taddeo Zuccaro was eventually hired), and the cardinal had evidently been keen on employing him for some time.[80] Finally, the Cavaliere d'Arpino, who had also contributed to S. Lorenzo in Damaso, may have been persuaded to fit the Jesuits into his busy schedule through the exertions of Alessandro.

The Nave Chapels: Left Side

The decorations in all six nave chapels were begun between 1584 and the early 1590s. One of the first was the Apostles' Chapel (now dedicated to St Francis Borgia), the first chapel on the left, in which the initial painting activity dates from 1585 (figs 83, 85). The Jesuits paid for the initial work themselves, and only later found a private benefactor, Paolo Morelli, who intended that the chapel should house his family tomb and who paid for all the decorations.[81] Unfortunately, Morelli's heirs were less enthusiastic. The patronage was taken over by a wealthy Genovese banker, Francesco Ravenna, in the seventeenth century, and sometime after 1642 he replaced the paintings of the side walls with new works by Pier Francesco Mola (1612–66) and added to the marble revetments.[82]

Except for the altarpiece, all the original paintings on the walls and vaults of the chapel were done by Niccolò Circignani, as is attested in several sources, including an anonymous seventeenth-century description in the Jesuit archives, and re-marks by Gaspare Celio, Giovanni Baglione, Giulio Mancini, and Filippo Titi.[83] According to the account books, Circignani began work on 1 September 1585, when he was given his initial payment of 20 scudi, and his first phase of activity in the chapel lasted until 22 January of the next year.[84] After a brief hiatus Circignani was back to finish the frescoes in July and November 1586, and again in April and June 1587, and the accounts that survive add up to a total of 110 scudi in eight instalments for all his work, although this must be only a partial figure since he made over twice that for the same amount of work on the next chapel.[85]

Celio, who is the earliest of the sources, also mentions an anonymous Flemish painter, 'N. Fiamengo,' who may have painted the high altar either of the Apostles' Chapel or of the Nativity Chapel (his text is unclear).[86] This reference was overlooked by Hibbard and Lewine, who assumed the painting was never executed.[87] The best-known painters referred to as 'Fiamenghi' who worked on the Gesù – other than the Jesuit brothers Gisbert – were Heintz (or possibly Pepijn) and Brill, although their work on the St Francis Chapel is much later, dating from around 1599. Other mysterious Northerners who worked on the Gesù side chapels include 'Antonio Fiamengo' and 'Pietro Fiamengho,' both of whom we will meet below. On the other hand, it is possible that Celio is referring to the Nativity Chapel, the altarpiece of which we know was done by the German painter Hans von Aachen. Italians in the late Renaissance were usually not very specific about whether Northerners came from Germany or from the Low Countries, so such a mistake is quite plausible.

The second chapel to the left, the Nativity Chapel (now the Chapel of the Holy Family), was begun slightly earlier, in 1584 (figs 86–9). The first patron was Agostino Braghieri of Tortona, most likely a foreigner whose name had been italianized, who was granted permission to use the chapel as his family tomb.[88] As with the Apostles' Chapel, Braghieri's patronage ended with his death, as he died without heirs. In around 1639, Father General Vitelleschi handed over responsibility for the chapel to the rich Lombard prelate Antonio Cerri, who had made his fortune in Rome as the legal adviser to the Barberini family and was thus on close terms with the papal family under Urban VIII (1623–43). Cerri lavished the princely sum of 6,000 scudi on the chapel, an extraordinary amount for a side chapel (remember that Giovanna d'Aragona gave the same amount in 1566 for the entire Novitiate), and after his death in 1643 his son Cardinal Carlo Cerri spent an additional 1,000 scudi on the decorations.[89] Circignani was again selected to paint the vaults and walls of the chapel, and Hans von Aachen was commissioned to paint the altarpiece. Although the wall paintings were overpainted in oil under the Cerri by Giovanni Francesco Romanelli (1617–62), the Romanelli overpaintings have somehow disappeared and left us with Circignani's original frescoes. Other later additions include four sculptural works by four different sculptors including Domenico Guidi (1625–1701), which were added around 1658–60. The altarpiece was replaced in 1890, when the chapel was rededicated. Hans von Aachen's image survives only in an engraving by another favourite of the Rudolfine court, Aegidius Sadeler (1588).[90]

Circignani's participation in the chapel is attested by Baglione and Titi as well as the Jesuit account books.[91] At least part of the decorations were overseen by Rutilio Clemente, who paid the labourers their wages for gilding and other non-artistic activities.[92] The first payment for chapel decorations dates from 11 March 1584, when a certain 'Niccolò scultore' (not Circignani) was paid 8 scudi for making stucco cherubs on the architrave of the walls and angels and a figure of Jesus on the facade and on a shield. The artist was given his final payment on 17 June (not 20 June, as Zuccari notes), for a total of 35 scudi, 55 giulii, slightly more than the 27 scudi that had been budgeted.[93] Niccolò Circignani (referred to in the account books as 'Mastro Nicolò pittore') worked on the chapel between 12 May and 9 August 1584, and received the final payment a month before beginning work on the Apostles' Chapel. Circignani was paid a handsome lump sum of just over 250 scudi in six instalments.[94] It is remarkable how much more Circignani was paid at the Gesù than he was at the collegiate chapels. Evidently his work as a *buon e pratico maestro* came at a higher price than his work as a *maestro ordinario*, and clearly the Jesuits were willing to pay it when they had the donors. The gilt wooden frame for the altarpiece was completed ten years after the canvas was painted, in 1598, at a cost of 120 scudi; the amount covered the cost of various other items, such as the fabric of the drapery and the confessional, and wax candles.[95] The unpublished source also mentions a 'Mastro Antonio fiamengo pittore,' paid 18 scudi for unspecified work in finishing the chapel, who has so far been overlooked. Perhaps he is the mysterious 'N. Fiamengo' mentioned for the Apostles' Chapel.

The last chapel on the left side is the Trinity Chapel. It was one of the earliest to have a patron, Monsignore Pirro Taro, in 1583. Taro, however, died on 1 August of that year.[96] Unlike the heirs of those who had extended patronage to the other two chapels on this side, Taro's heir, Pompeo Arrigoni (later a cardinal, d. 1616), carried out his predecessor's obligations in the chapel and completed its decoration (figs 90–3). The Taro arms are still on the tabernacle today. The altarpiece in the Trinity Chapel was executed by Francesco Bassano, and the frescoes were done by Giovanni Battista Fiammeri, Ventura Salimbeni, Durante Alberti, Bernardino Cesari (?), and Ferraù Fenzoni, with landscapes by Pietro Fiamengho. The paintings by Cesari, Fenzoni, and possibly Alberti were based on designs by Fiammeri, who evidently supervised the entire cycle closely. All the sources agree about Bassano's participation, which is recorded in Baglione and the other chronicles of the time. His original altarpiece survives today and is a version of one of his father's works (fig 90).[97] In contrast, there has been considerable confusion over which frescoes should be assigned to which painters, much of it arising from inconsistency in recent scholarship.

The chroniclers mention only Fiammeri, Salimbeni, and Alberti by name. Celio writes that Fiammeri painted the tondo fresco *Creation* (fig. 91) and the paintings below the cornice, but attributes the rest of the vault, including the pendentives and oval lunettes, to Salimbeni – although we would not know this from reading Hibbard, who does not mention that Celio assigns anything to Salimbeni.[98] Baglione is more specific, in recording that Fiammeri painted the tondo himself, while *Baptism of Christ* (fig. 92) was done by another artist after Fiammeri's design.[99] Although the passage is confusing, Baglione attributes the oval paintings *God the Father and Angels* and *Apparition of the Angels to Abraham* to Salimbeni, as well as the angels with scrolls in the pendentives; and he attributes the *Transfiguration* (fig. 93) to Durante Alberti.[100] Mancini mentions Salimbeni as the author of only one oval painting, a 'gloria d'angeli,' while Filippo Baldinucci says merely that Salimbeni 'worked in the Gesù,' without specifying where.[101] Titi, who although writing late provides one of the most detailed descriptions, attributes the *Baptism of Christ* and *Creation* to Fiammeri, assigns the oval *God the Father and Angels* to Salimbeni, and agrees that Durante Alberti executed the wall painting *Transfiguration*.[102] Our anonymous late seventeenth-century Jesuit source, which in general follows Titi very closely, also agrees with him here, in assigning *God the Father and Angels* to Salimbeni, *Transfiguration* to Durante, and all the rest, including *Creation* in the tondo, to Fiammeri.[103] This source agrees with Baglione that only the designs of the remaining frescoes were by Fiammeri and that the frescoes themselves were executed by others. Most of these sources agree on the key paintings, even though there are some inconsistencies about the details; and there is no disagreement on the principal painters involved.

With contemporary scholarship we run into trouble. Hibbard introduces confusion by involving a new artist, Romano Alberti, the author of the minutes of the Accademia di San Luca that we looked at in chapter 1, and Lewine credits some of the work to a fictitious artist 'G.B. Valeriano called Il Fiammeri,' created by combining Valeriano and Fiammeri into one person.[104] Hibbard then suggests Celio as possibly the anonymous painter who executed Fiammeri's designs, although he admits that he can provide no evidence to support such a hypothesis, especially since Celio himself does not mention the matter.[105] Hibbard also mentions an 'Ottavio pittore' listed in the Jesuit account books as an assistant of Fiammeri in 1602, but the passage refers to Giovanni Baglione's altarpiece *Resurrection* and therefore to a part of the church in which Fiammeri did no painting whatsoever. There is no reference to an Ottavio working at the Trinity Chapel. The account books for the Trinity Chapel list someone quite different, a 'Mastro Bernardino,' whom Alessandro Zuccari identifies as Bernardino Cesari (1571–1622), the younger brother of the Cavaliere d'Arpino.[106] But Laura Russo disagrees and instead introduces the obscure Bolognese painter Bernardino Baldi (b. 1557), for whom there is little evidence that he ever went to Rome.[107]

Four more painters are mentioned in the account books. Zuccari has found a reference to Ferraù Fenzoni, an Emilian painter who apparently assisted Bernardino with one of his paintings in the chapel, and I have found a second one, which shows that he worked for a total of seven days on the project. Zuccari convincingly attributes the woods and the angel on the far right side of the *Baptism of Christ* to Fenzoni's hand.[108] Ferraù was called in only for a small intervention in Mastro Bernardino's painting, perhaps because Fiammeri was not happy with something in the younger artist's work. A second painter mentioned in the accounts is a Flemish painter called 'Pietro Fiamengho,' paid to paint landscapes in the backgrounds of scenes; incidentally, Russo ignores him altogether.[109] In addition, I have found very brief mentions of two other artists so far overlooked in the scholarship whose identity remains a mystery, including Giovanni Battista da Forlì, who like Ferraù Fenzoni worked for seven days, and a certain Giuseppe Barici or Darici – the writing is extremely difficult to read. Zuccari transcribes this last name as 'Giovanni Battista Fiammeri' and claims that it is the only payment to the Jesuit brother specifically for painting.[110] Yet this cannot be so, since the name is clearly prefixed by 'Mastro' and not 'Fratello,' the name itself cannot be read as 'Giovanni Battista,' and no Jesuit would have been paid for his labour, only for supplies.

Nor is the problem of identifying 'Mastro Bernardino' easily solved. Zuccari proposes Bernardino Cesari, since his strong Florentine connections (his brother's first major commission was to work with Circignani, Roncalli, and others at the Vatican Logge) would have made him attractive to Fiammeri.[111] The identification of Mastro Bernardino with Cesari is even more tempting when we note that Baglione says Bernardino 'made few works by himself' and was more capable of copying the works of others.[112] One thing for certain is that if Mastro Bernardino is Bernardino Cesari, he did not get the job because of his more famous brother's work at the Gesù, since the Cavaliere did not work there until the very end of the century. Zuccari also sees in *Baptism of Christ* (fig. 92) some of the naturalistic tendencies of Santi di Tito (fig. 7), especially in the pronounced roundness and veracity of the figures, something one would expect of a young artist working within Tuscan circles.

But here we run into the limitations of connoisseurship, since Russo disagrees with Zuccari's attribution, commenting that the *Baptism of Christ* is 'spacious, classical, evolved and independent in every respect from the typical mannerist handwriting' – it could be argued that these are features of Santi's work – yet feels the need to attribute it to an Emilian painter because it 'seems to anticipate Guido Reni and the Carracci.'[113] For this reason, she chooses the Emilian Baldi, and relates the Gesù panel to an *Annunciation* by Baldi, his only dated work (1600), in the Pinacoteca Civica di Forlì. Russo also believes that Bernardino at 18 would have been too young to supervise Ferraù Fenzoni. But Bernardino did not supervise Fenzoni; he merely handed him one of his payments on behalf of Fiammeri as Fiammeri's assistant – and besides, Fenzoni was only in his late twenties himself. It would seem to me even less likely that an artist of Baldi's age and experience (he was 31 at the time) would have been paid less per *giornata* than Ventura Salimbeni, who was only 20. I think, given that Bernardino Cesari was known to be working in Rome at the time and tended to execute the designs of others, and given his brother's connections not only with Circignani but with Alessandro Farnese, he is a more likely 'Mastro Bernardino' than is an Emilian artist who may never have been to Rome at all. But the jury is still out.

One other problem with Mastro Bernardino has to do with what he painted. Zuccari and Russo both maintain that he was responsible solely for the *Baptism of Christ* panel.[114] Yet, as I will soon show, he worked for more than one hundred days on the chapel – more than ten times as long as some of the other artists – and clearly worked on more than a single panel, a space with which he was assisted by Fenzoni anyway and which took Ventura Salimbeni (on the panel opposite) about twenty-four days, working by himself. Mastro Bernardino must have served as a general assitant to the other artists working in the chapel, including Fiammeri, Salimbeni, and Alberti, since his payments continued throughout the period of the decorative campaign. He himself may have contributed to other parts of the chapel, such as some of the lunette paintings (after all, the sources directly credit Salimbeni with only one of them), although probably only in the details.

In summary, Fiammeri was in charge of the chapel decorations, and painted the *Creation* tondo and designed some of the other frescoes, at least *Baptism of Christ*. He was assisted throughout the chapel by Bernardino (Cesari?), who acted as a sort of general manager and also executed the *Baptism of Christ* panel, in which he was assisted in some details by Ferraù Fenzoni. Pietro Fiamengho painted landscape details in some of the frescoes, possibly only the *Baptism of Christ* and the *Creation*, since there is not much landscape in the *Transfiguration*, and Giuseppe Barici (?) and Giovanni Battista da Forlì also helped out in more minor matters. Durante Alberti painted the *Transfiguration*, possibly to Fiammeri's design, although there is no direct evidence that the invention is Fiammeri's. Ventura Salimbeni was called in to do the vault pendentives and the lunettes, and Bassano did the altarpiece (although not on site).

Fortunately, the chronology of the paintings is less complicated. All the wall and vault paintings date from 1588–9 (not having seen the account books, Hibbard proposed the much later date of 1596–7).[115] Although Bassano's contract and payments do not survive, as Hibbard points out the Bassano altarpiece must have been executed before 1591, when the artist threw himself from a precipice and died a slow and miserable death over the course of eight months.[116] The first payments for painting supplies were made to Fiammeri on 9 May 1588, and the last on 4 March 1589, totalling just over 14 scudi for petty cash expenses such as reinforced paper for the cartoons, lapis, modelling wax, paints, and brushes, and the services of a certain Cesare to grind pigments.[117] The younger artists were paid per *giornata*, while Durante Alberti was paid a lump sum in instalments, in the same way that Circignani had been paid in the other two chapels on the left side. The mysterious Giuseppe Barici or Darici, the first artist mentioned by name, was paid 10 scudi for his work on 20 May 1588.[118] Mastro Bernardino was active longer than any other painter in the chapel, between 17 July 1588 and 4 January 1589, for a total of 101 *giornate*.[119] For his work Bernardino received just over 63 scudi, at a rate of between 60 and 80 giulii per *giornata* – a low rate, befitting a young artist. Ventura Salimbeni worked for around 24 *giornate* between 12 August and 24 September of the same year at a slightly higher rate, of between 80 and 90 giulii per *giornata*, for a total of 20 scudi, 70 giulii.[120] Ferraù Fenzoni worked for a brief 7 *giornate* at a rate of between 60 and 80 giulii per *giornata*, for which he was paid a total of 5 scudi, 8 giulii between 2 August and 17 September 1588, the latter payment via Mastro Bernardino.[121] Giovanni Battista da Forlì worked for 7 *giornate* between 4 and 16 January 1589, for which he was paid 60 giulii per *giornata*.[122] Pietro Fiamengho worked at a higher rate, of 80 giulii per *giornata*, between 13 October 1588 and 4 January 1589, for a total of 15 scudi, 25.5 giulii.[123] Durante Alberti is mentioned only in one brief entry, dated 28 January 1589, where he is paid 12 scudi in what appears to be a single payment for all his work on the *Transfiguration*.[124] Durante's low pay is consistent with his fees at S. Stefano Rotondo and S. Tommaso di Canterbury, and once again probably reflects a charitable cut rate from an artist who felt an affinity with the Society.

According to two loose folios discovered by Zuccari, the total amount spent on painting in the chapel is either 252.23 scudi or 414.23 scudi; neither of the folios, however, necessarily refers to this chapel (the first seems most likely to concern the St Francis Chapel, since it is on the reverse of a notation of the dimensions of one of the St Francis panels).[125] I have found another amount indicated for paintings that definitely refers to the Trinity Chapel, giving the amount as 439.49

scudi.[126] Decorative stucco work and gilding was carried out by Andrea Aretino between May 1588 and March 1589, with the assistance of 'Mastro Hipolito.'[127]

The Nave Chapels: Right Side

The first chapel on the right, the Chapel of St Andrew or Martyrs' Chapel, was decorated initially under the patronage of Giulio Folco (Folchi), best known as Alessandro Farnese's agent in his dealings with the Jesuits during the construction of the Gesù (figs 95–8).[128] Folco ran up a bill of 600 scudi to get things started, but he died in 1591 before he could pay it, and as usual his heirs could not complete the work.[129] The Jesuits soon found a Roman gentlewoman, Salustia Cerrini, the wife of Cavaliere Ottaviano Crescenzi, to take over, and together with some money finally obtained by the Jesuits from Folco's heirs, her contribution helped finance the chapels both of St Andrew and of SS. Abbondio and Abbondanzio. Cerrini acquired the chapel so that it would become her family tomb, as is indicated in a surviving deed of trust with her heirs, which records that the total amount spent on the Chapel of St Andrew, 'namely in paintings, stucco work, gilding, and every other expense made in the service of the said chapel,' was 3,790 scudi.[130]

All the contemporary chronicles attribute the paintings in the Chapel of St Andrew to Agostino Ciampelli. Gaspare Celio says unequivocally that 'everything is by the hand of Agostino Ciampelli Fiorentino,' as does Mancini.[131] Baglione and Titi are more specific, in stating that Ciampelli painted the altarpiece of the *Martyrdom of St Andrew* (fig. 95), the wall paintings of the *Martyrdom of St Stephen* (fig. 96) and the *Martyrdom of St Lawrence* and the oval lunettes above them, and the vault tondo *Mary, Queen of Martyrs* (fig. 98).[132] Two anonymous later seventeenth-century sources in the Jesuit archives also assign all the paintings to Ciampelli, including the altarpiece.[133] The account books show that most of the work on the stucco and architectural decoration of the chapel was carried out between April 1588 and October 1590, with a final payment to a *stuccatore* in December 1590.[134] Unfortunately, no payments whatever are recorded for the paintings, which we can nevertheless date to around the same time. There are two enigmatic references to a certain 'Cellio,' who receives extremely paltry amounts for an unspecified job, but it does not seem reasonable to associate these references with Gaspare Celio, who was working during the late 1590s on the Passion Chapel.[135]

The Passion Chapel was the site of some of the most influential paintings in the Gesù (figs 99–103).[136] The patroness of the chapel was Bianca Mellini, the wife of Giovanni Lomellini, a member of an old Roman family who were long-time benefactors of the church; she assumed rights to the chapel in 1588.[137] Mellini was also patron of a chapel in S. Maria sopra Minerva. She paid her first instalment of 190 scudi in three segments – 50 scudi in November 1588, 60 scudi in April 1589, and, finally, 80 scudi later in April.[138] Over the course of nine years Mellini paid a total of 2,000 scudi for the chapel, with the funds being administered not directly by her but by the Jesuit Giovanni de Rosis.[139] The chapel was consecrated in 1593 by Cardinal Luis de Torres.[140] The altarpiece of the *Lamentation* (fig. 99), now in the

Metropolitan Museum in New York, was painted by Scipione Pulzone, as is attested by the contemporary chronicles. But, as with the Trinity Chapel, there has been considerable disagreement, not over the authorship of the frescoes and canvases, which everyone agrees were executed by Gaspare Celio, but about their designs, which have been variously attributed to Giuseppe Valeriano and Giovanni Battista Fiammeri.

The earliest source, an anonymous Jesuit memorial from around 1616, attributes the altar to Pulzone and the frescoes to Celio, without mention of either of the Jesuit artists.[141] Celio himself, writing around the same time, also assigns the altarpiece to Pulzone and takes credit himself for the frescoes, but does not say anywhere that he worked from the designs of another artist: 'The paintings of the Chapel of the Passion of Christ, from the cornice upward in fresco, and from the cornice downward in oil, [are] by the Roman Gaspare Celio of the habit of Christ, the painting of the altar [is] by Scipione Gaetano, which is the *Pietà* in oil.'[142] Mancini, who is also one of the earliest sources (1614–21, 1630), assigns the whole chapel to Celio, and also does not mention that anyone else was responsible for the designs.[143] Baglione (1642) is the only source to credit Valeriano with the designs of the frescoes executed by Celio; he mentions specifically the side canvases *Christ on the Road to Calvary* (fig. 100) and *Christ Nailed to the Cross* (fig. 101), as well as the four images of 'Christo appassionato' (fig. 103), the tondo, the lunettes, the pendentives with the evangelists, and the pilasters with the prophets.[144] His passage 'assist[ing] Valeriano in various things, and especially in the vault' suggests that Celio worked side by side with Valeriano, a man who had been dead for two weeks before Celio even started. He confirms this in his entry on Celio, in which he writes that 'all the frescoes [are] after the designs of the Father [Valeriano].'[145] Two sources introduce another person as the author of the designs, by crediting not Valeriano but Fiammeri. The first is the anonymous seventeenth-century source from the Jesuit archives, which says in no uncertain terms that the designs of the frescoes painted by Celio are by Fiammeri; the other is Filippo Titi, writing at the end of the century, who declares that the frescoes 'were coloured by Cavaliere Gasparo Celio from designs by Father [*sic*] Fiammeri the Jesuit.'[146] He confirms this attribution in another memorial: 'The vault and the other figures were coloured by Cavaliere Gaspero Celio with designs by Father Fiammeri the Jesuit.'[147]

Almost without exception, twentieth-century scholars have accepted Baglione's assertion uncritically. Carlo Galassi Paluzzi denied Fiammeri's authorship on the basis of what he felt was the Jesuit brother's inferior style, so different from that of the frescoes executed by Celio – 'a manifestly inferior artist, and stylistically different from these paintings executed by Celio.'[148] Federico Zeri, as is well known, attributed the designs to Valeriano, the man whom he credits (together with Pulzone) with being one of the inventors of the abstracted kind of sacred painting he calls 'art without time.'[149] Pietro Pirri, the author of Valeriano's biography, and Pio Pecchiai also attribute the designs to Valeriano, going so far as to say that Celio is the weaker artist and is enlivened by Valeriano.[150] More recently, Hibbard and Lewine have followed the now traditional attribution to Valeriano, which continues to be maintained in work of the 1990s and early 2000s by Richard

Bösel, Laura Russo, and Maria Calì, although Hibbard admits that there has been considerable confusion between Valeriano and Fiammeri (think of Lewine and the Trinity Chapel).[151] However, Fabrizio d'Amico has recently played down Valeriano's role in these paintings by citing their striking disparity in style with the Jesuit painter's earlier work, using essentially the same reasoning that had led Galassi Paluzzi to rule out Fiammeri.[152]

Celio's paintings exhibit a vigour and originality, with prominent painterly effects, far removed from the comparatively static, idealized work of either Valeriano or Fiammeri – which Galassi Paluzzi says is 'more along eighteenth-century lines than sixteenth' – and clearly the credit for the stylistic innovation they show is due to their painter.[153] Yet there is considerable evidence that the underlying composition and design were created not by Valeriano but by Fiammeri, who had taken over as sole supervisor of the Gesù paintings just before Celio began the cycle. The principal confirmation of his role can be found in the close relation of his two oil paintings *Christ on the Road to Calvary* (fig. 100) and *Christ Nailed to the Cross* (fig. 101) to illustrations 125 and 127 in Nadal's *Evangelicae historiae imagines* (see figs 12, 13), which I will discuss in more detail in chapter 7. Hibbard, Buser, and Calì all have noted the similarities between Celio's canvases and the illustrated Gospel series, but no one has considered that Fiammeri was one of the principal designers of and the final arbitrator for the Nadal drawings.[154] Even if Fiammeri did not provide new sketches for Celio's two canvases per se, their close adherence to the Nadal series allows us definitively to attribute the invention of these panels to Fiammeri. Fiammeri, not Valeriano, was the Jesuit artist behind the Passion Chapel frescoes.

The first artists' payments were made to Scipione Pulzone and date from 7 and 9 February 1590, when Valeriano handed out a total of 100 scudi to the artist for his 'immagine della pietà.'[155] The chapel decoration was then suspended for six years before Gaspare Celio carried out his frescoes and canvases, for which he received an initial payment of 100 scudi on 1 August 1596.[156] He worked again on the paintings between 12 May and 25 June of the following year, for which period Giovanni de Rosis paid him an additional 141.30 scudi, in total about what Circignani was paid to fresco the Apostles' Chapel.[157] In addition Celio received a much later final payment of 46.90 scudi, in December 1611, perhaps for restoration of his paintings.[158] The hiatus between the completion of Pulzone's picture and the beginning of Celio's frescoes owed something to the declining health of the supervisor of the Gesù decorations, but there was also a delay because Celio was busy painting the Angels' Chapel in the early 1590s. The chronically overworked Valeriano finally went to Naples in February 1596, hoping to recuperate from his illness, but he died there on 15 July, the very day Celio was hired. Just one month before his death, Giacomo Domeneci, the secretary of the Society of Jesus, had written a desperate letter to the ailing Valeriano, begging him to hurry up and hire Gaspare Celio, since he was worried that Mellini would die and the chapel would lose its patronage – as had happened so many times before – but the Father General did not want to bother a sick man with such matters.[159]

Perhaps because Valeriano was no longer there to supervise, Celio himself seems to have assumed some of the more mundane responsibilities: he disbursed money to workers such as Mastro Gioseppe the gold-beater, Mastro Hercole the gilder, Mastro Jiacomo Brioso the glazer, and Mastro Andrea the blacksmith, and he made payments for scaffolding, for gold leaf for gilding, and for other practical necessities of the decoration.[160] The accounts even refer to the Passion Chapel as 'sua cappella.'[161] Celio handled 803 scudi in this manner – more than three times his own salary – from the very day Valeriano died, 15 July 1596, to 13 May 1597, a month before his paintings were finished. It is unusual for the Jesuits to have given a layman so much responsibility for the decoration of one of their chapels, but Celio was an overtly devout man and a close companion of Valeriano during his lifetime and so would do in a pinch.

The last reference to Pulzone's *Lamentation* (fig. 99) is from a Visitor's report issued by Pope Clement VIII at the end of the sixteenth century, and it is noteworthy. Clement's inspection of the Roman churches, made in preparation for the 1600 Jubilee, was the most thorough Visitation ever conducted in the city and one that also had repercussions for another Pulzone picture in the Angels' Chapel, as we shall soon see.[162] Directed at reviving the pastoral duties of the pope, Clement's reform efforts were conservative in nature and drew heavily on the precepts of the Council of Trent. An important aspect of his Visitation was the reform of ecclesiastical buildings: under the rubric of what he called 'decoro,' the pope strove to make existing churches as functional as possible for the conduct of the liturgy.[163] More important for our purposes, Clement also attended to the decoration of church interiors, especially the apse and the more conspicuous areas of the nave and side chapels. The pope ordered corrections in many side altars throughout the city with a view to accuracy and decorum. Daniele da Volterra's *Deposition* in the church of SS. Trinità dei Monti, which depicted the Virgin in a swoon, was considered inappropriate, and elsewhere the pope showed a prudish distaste for nudity.[164] Any family chapels that Clement found lacking in decorum had to be restored, decorated, or provided with appropriate liturgical furniture on pain of excommunication. Clement began his Visitation of twenty-four churches and three basilicas at the basilica of St John Lateran in June 1592, and he examined the Gesù on 4 January 1594. Upon visiting the Passion Chapel, which at the time was completely bare except for Pulzone's *Lamentation*, the pontiff remarked that the figure of the Magdalene should be 'altered to have a more devout appearance.'[165] We may never know whether Pulzone (or another artist) heeded the pope's wishes and changed the Magdalene's appearance, but if he did he also changed the Magdalene in his *Crucifixion* at the Chiesa Nuova (1590), since the same model has been used and the two figures are equally modestly clothed.[166] I doubt he did; after all, Daniele da Volterra's altarpiece at SS. Trinità dei Monti was never altered.

The last chapel on the right side of the nave, the Angels' Chapel (figs 104–7), had a patronage history of a pattern all too familiar to the beleagured Jesuits.[167] Gasparo Garzonio, the son of a Roman nobleman named Quirino who had been the first to offer Ignatius hospitality in the city, assumed responsibility for the chapel in 1588 but went bankrupt in the early 1590s.[168] Father de Rosis handed over the chapel to Curzio Vittorio, a relative of Pope Paul V Borghese, and his wife, Settima Delfini, and it is their family crest on the tabernacle.[169] The altarpiece – the original is long since missing – is shrouded in mystery, and may have the dubious honour of being the most retouched painting in the Gesù. All sources agree that the original was by Scipione Pulzone, and that it was replaced by a panel by Federico Zuccaro, although Zuccaro's painting was also retouched by Domenico Passignano (ca. 1558–1638) and reworked in the eighteenth century by the Jesuit painter Vincenzo Dandini (fig. 104).[170] Celio does not mention that Pulzone painted the first canvas, but mentions the replacement by Zuccaro and writes that it was 'ruined' by Passignano, a comment echoed by the anonymous late seventeenth-century Jesuit source ('then the Cavaliere Passignani, trying to retouch the panel, destroyed it'), which also mentions Pulzone's canvas, and by Titi ('the Cavaliere Passignano wanting to retouch it, destroyed it').[171]

The sources all agree that the frescoes are by Federico Zuccaro. Mancini and Baglione attribute all the fresco work in the chapel to Zuccaro.[172] Some sources, including Baglione, the anonymous late seventeenth-century Jesuit chronicle, and Titi, assign the lunette fresco *Abraham Adoring Three Angels* and the angels in the pendentives of the chapel to Ventura Salimbeni.[173] Finally, Baglione records that Celio sketched out two side panels for this chapel, but that the paintings were left unfinished at the time of Valeriano's death in 1596 and the walls were taken over by Zuccaro.[174] The marble angels in the chapel were attributed by the seventeenth-century chronicler and by Titi to Silvia Lungo di Vigiù and Flaminio Vacca, and some of the stucco angels in the vault to Camillo Mariani da Vicenza.[175]

The reasons for the vicissitudes suffered by the altarpiece are as obscure as is the authorship of the painting. Certainly the most notorious painting among the early Gesù decorations, it was declared inappropriate by the same papal initiative that censured Pulzone's other picture in the Gesù, the *Lamentation* (fig. 99). During his Visitation of 1594, Clement VIII remarked that Pulzone's original altarpiece, *Seven Archangels*, 'should be more decently covered,' a remark that became something of a cliché after the Council of Trent, and that was essentially what the pope said about the Magdalene in Pulzone's *Lamentation*.[176] Contrary to the version of the story accepted by most scholars, I think the pope's decree had no effect on the painting whatever. It remained in place for six more years – Zuccaro's replacement is dated 1600 – and since the *Lamentation* was surely never retouched, I see no reason to believe *Seven Archangels* was altered. Zuccari has recently remarked on the unlikelihood that the Jesuits would follow the pope's orders six years too late.[177] Besides, a print by Hieronymus Wierix that may be based on Pulzone's picture survives, and his angels can hardly be seen as scantily clad, unless bare feet are offensive (fig. 26).

Baglione and Titi give us a slightly different story concerning the rejection of the picture, this time related to another pronouncement of Trent – namely, that sacred images should not resemble living persons.[178] Baglione writes dramatically: 'And there used to be in the Chapel of the Angels, over the altar, some of these angels standing, very beautiful, but since they were portraits from life, representing diverse people known by everyone, they were removed in order to put an end to the scandal; and they were so beautiful that they seemed to breathe with life, and move.'[179] Most likely Baglione was merely garbling the story of the papal commandment from his perspective more than forty years later, since nowhere in the Visitation notes is there any reference to the angels' resembling living people. Baglione's hyperbole in describing the picture's lifelike effects makes this hypothesis even more likely. In fact, the whole story looks like a version of one of the Apelles legends, literary exaggerations of artists' abilities taken from Greek sources and preserved by Roman writers such as Pliny the Elder in his *Encyclopaedia*.[180] One of the most common of these literary topoi, in which a painting is so realistic that it fools the viewer into thinking it alive, is used in the accounts of the lives of Apelles, Protogenes, and Zeuxis, not to mention innumerable later artists.

Zuccari proposes that the painting was switched for more theological reasons, since it was an example of the prohibited imagery of the Seven Archangels, which I discussed in chapter 2.[181] Zuccari even believes that Federico Zuccaro may have painted the replacement picture directly over the Pulzone, which would explain why no one has been able to locate the earlier work. But, again, I am not convinced – and besides, the original altarpiece was on canvas, while Zuccaro's replacement is on wood panel (see below). If the apocryphal angels had been the problem, the Jesuits could much more easily (and cheaply) have painted over the offending angels' names (which still survive in the Wierix print), since there was nothing wrong with depicting seven angels per se, even *with* their attributes. As we have already seen, such pictures were common throughout the seventeenth century in Italy. In fact, the Zuccaro painting there today (fig. 104) has seven angels. I think instead that the Pulzone was rejected for aesthetic reasons. The Jesuits simply did not like it – which is ironic, since scholars such as Zeri and Freedberg have made Pulzone out to be the poster-boy for Jesuit 'anti-Maniera.' Maybe Pulzone did not reflect Jesuit taste after all. The Jesuits even got rid of the other Pulzone, the *Lamentation* in the Passion Chapel, before the end of the next century.

We are still left wondering why Passignano had to 'retouch' the picture, and when he did it. Passignano was a Tuscan painter (from Passignano, south of Florence) who had worked since the mid-1570s as an assistant to Federico Zuccaro, for example when the two of them completed the dome decorations in the Duomo in Florence begun by Vasari.[182] Since Passignano was not in Rome until 1609–16, he must have done his restoration of Zuccaro's painting during those years. Perhaps it was Zuccaro's painting that had the offending names and attributes and that had to be corrected by his long-time collaborator. Or perhaps it was just a case of water damage or damage from a wayward devotional candle.

The Jesuit account books record no payments to either Ventura Salimbeni or Federico Zuccaro, nor is there mention of the later restorations of Zuccaro's panel. The only artists noted are Pulzone and a 'young painter,' presumably Celio, and the payment records end with the handover to Vittorio and Delfini in 1592.[183] It is unclear why the painters were changed along with the patronage, but Zuccaro would still have been working for King Philip II at the Escorial when Garzonio started the chapel decorations in 1588, and perhaps the Jesuits jumped at the chance to hire this leading painter after his return to Rome. Zuccaro's close relationship with Alessandro Farnese (he became the principal painter at Caprarola upon his brother's death in 1566) may also have helped win the artist for the Jesuit commission.

The payment records paint a different picture of this early phase of decoration from the one traditionally described by scholars. Pecchiai and Hibbard and their successors have written that Pulzone had painted only the altarpiece, that Valeriano had made sketches for the frescoes and wall panels, and that Celio had started working on those panels when they were all dismissed by the new patrons, Pulzone with a final payment of 50 scudi for the work he had already done.[184] The accounts, on the other hand, show that Pulzone was working on much more than just the altarpiece and that he was assisted (presumably in the frescoes and wall panels) by Celio, and make no mention of sketches by Valeriano. The main evidence is that Pulzone was paid a lump sum of 300 scudi for 'imagini' (note the plural) between 27 July 1589 and 17 February 1590 – three times what the Jesuits normally paid for an altarpiece (Pulzone received just 100 scudi for the *Lamentation*) and more than they usually paid artists for an entire chapel.[185] Pulzone received a second round of payments totalling 65 scudi between 17 March and 8 June 1591, when his young assistant was also paid 8 scudi.[186] Since Celio was in a subordinate role, he was not paid on the scale he would be paid for the Passion Chapel. It is quite clear, therefore, that the paintings of the side panels were well under way, and perhaps even complete, at the time of the change in patronage. Moreover, all these payments predate the beginning of Pulzone's altarpiece, which was one of the last works to be completed during this first phase. According to a notation that so far has gone unnoticed, the canvas and stretching tape for the 'Altarpiece of the Angels' was purchased only on 12 March 1592, so the work was painted only at the very end of the era of the Garzono patronage.[187]

In summary, it seems that the Jesuits rejected not only Pulzone's altarpiece, but also Pulzone's (and Celio's) work on the side wall panels. In place of those painters they hired Federico Zuccaro, who was at the zenith of his career. Zuccaro was elected to the presidency of the Accademia di San Luca in 1593, the year after the change in patronage; he was the court painter of the king of Spain and of Alessandro Farnese; and his work at the Florence Duomo had brought many to regard him as the successor to Giorgio Vasari. Clearly, Pulzone was not good enough for the Jesuits, who, far from being unconcerned with aesthetics, could be as fickle as the most fashion-conscious cardinal patron when they had a chance to hire someone with greater aesthetic prestige.

The Apse and Crossing Area

There were three other separate chapels in the Gesù, not including the transepts and apse area. Two of them are located in the eastern pair of the four round chapels that surround the crossing of the church, located to either side of the choir. On the left side is the Chapel of the Madonna della Strada, the dedication of which, as we have seen, was transferred from an earlier church on the site (figs 108–9). The chapel also housed the miraculous image of the Madonna della Strada, a fifteenth-century fresco painting, now much restored, that was taken from a wall of the original church.[188] The chapel was acquired in the autumn of 1584 by three Roman gentlewomen, all members of the Caetani family, Portia Anguillara Orsini Cesi and the two sisters Giovanna Caetani Orsini and Beatrice Caetani Cesi, each of whom contributed 700 scudi and are buried there.[189] Maria Conelli has recently shown that the patronage of this chapel and the one on the other side, dedicated to St Francis, is an example of dynastic clustering. The women were all related by marriage, and Beatrice's daughter-in-law, Olimpia Orsini Cesi, commissioned the

St Francis Chapel to house the family crypt.[190] Conelli proposes that the family's desire to flank the choir has more to do with a desire to be connected with Farnese patronage than with their relationship with the Jesuits: 'Through their architectural patronage, women who were powerless in their marriages achieved an independent public profile.'[191]

The marblework, among the most magnificent in the early Gesù and including *giallo antico, corallina, pietra santa,* and other precious materials, was complete by 1587, although the vault was finished only in 1588.[192] The architect traditionally was assumed to have been della Porta, but Galassi Paluzzi assigned it to Valeriano, and his attribution is confirmed by the documents. There exists a contract of 1 December 1584, for example, with the *scarpellino* Bartolomeo Bassi, for the marble revetments, which cost a staggering 2,500 scudi, including the carved marble frames for the six panel paintings (not yet painted) and principal icon, and panels of *affricano scuro* with gold lettering for the inscriptions below the pictures.[193] This same contract suggests that the three patronesses paid unusually close attention to the aesthetic aspect of their chapel, although there is no evidence that they had a role in choosing artists to do the paintings.

The principal artists responsible for the Chapel of the Madonna della Strada were Valeriano and Giovanni Battista Pozzo. All the chroniclers agree that Valeriano executed the six panel paintings in oil, and that Pozzo painted the ceiling fresco with the choir of angel musicians.[194] Baglione maintains that Scipione Pulzone participated in the same paintings, and refers to 'some drapery painted in a very lifelike manner, which you could not have wished to be painted with more skill.'[195] His reference to Pulzone is echoed later by Titi, who generally used Baglione as his source, although only in his *Descrizione delle pitture* and not the *Studio di pittura*.[196] None of the other published chronicles mention Pulzone, and there is absolutely no reference to him in the archival sources. The painters worked from 6 May 1586 to 21 November 1588. Valeriano spent 165.13 scudi on the seven wood panels for the paintings, stucco work, and painting supplies, as well as – presumably – Pozzo's fee, of which only 12 scudi are specifically mentioned as being destined for 'Giambattista pittore.'[197]

Scholars today have made much of this participation by Scipione in the decoration of the Chapel of the Madonna della Strada. Federico Zeri equates Pulzone's adornment of Valeriano's figures using 'silk of shrill colours and of true-to-life illusionism' with the dressing up of religious statues with 'glittering drapery of rare and gaudy cloth' in churches today, and dismisses them as anti-intellectual 'mannequins.'[198] Following on his heels, Freedberg is sloppier, referring to the paintings as done 'to designs by Valeriano,' and attributing to Pulzone a 'sympathetic and precise accommodation to the Padre's thought,' an attribution that would become standard in later works.[199] More recently, Maria Calì has likewise maintained that Pulzone must not have 'limited his intervention to just the drapery,' although she provides no convincing evidence to support her theory.[200] The facial features and figures closely resemble those in Valeriano's work elsewhere, such as his *Ascension* in S. Spirito in Sassia and his *Holy Family and St John* in the Galleria Spada, and in no way relate to Pulzone's more precise and aristocratic style (see chapter 7).[201] If Pulzone had anything to do with these pictures, he most likely only added a few of the virtuosic drapery passages, places where the silk seems to shimmer in the light.

On the opposite side of the choir was the St Francis Chapel, since 1920 dedicated to the Sacred Heart (figs 110–11).[202] As I have noted, the patroness of this chapel was Olimpia Orsini, daughter-in-law of Beatrice Caetani, married to her son Federico Cesi, duke of Acquasparta.[203] The sources agree that the vaults were painted by Baldassare Croce, the panels by a group of Northerners ('diversi Fiamenghi'), the figures by 'Gioseppe Peniz' (Joseph Heintz the Elder or Maarten Pepijn), and the landscapes and birds by Paul Brill, with additional contributions by unnamed Flemish painters.[204] Perhaps the 'diversi Fiamenghi' included Pietro and Antonio, whom we saw earlier, or 'Adamo Fiamengho,' who was mentioned in the books in 1583.[205] The sources disagree as to the author of the altarpiece (now in the sacristy); Celio attributes it to Durante Alberti, and the anonymous seventeenth-century Jesuit source and Filippo Titi assign it to Giovanni de' Vecchi.[206] Recently, Patrizia Tosini has disputed both attributions, suggesting that this modest painting is more likely by the artist responsible for *Apparition of the Saint to Brother Giovanni* on the side wall of the vestibule of the same chapel, and is therefore the work of Heintz or Pepijn.[207] Recently there has been much discussion about the attribution of the St Francis panels, with Jürgen Zimmer and others attributing them to Heintz and Nicole Dacos, Rosario Nappi, and Raffaello Russo calling them the work of Pepijn. Since neither of these names appears in the documents, the attributions are based entirely on connoisseurship and on the relationship of their names to the 'Giuseppe Penitz' mentioned by Baglione (much more tenuous in the case of Pepijn).[208] The attributions have been difficult to prove, and, once again, the jury is still out. The only artist mentioned in the accounts is Baldassare Croce, who received two payments for a total of 35 scudi for his frescoes, on 6 and 18 September 1599.[209] The small amount of Croce's fee reflects the small size of the cupola compared to the frescoed area of the nave side chapels.

The smallest chapel in the apse and crossing area of the Gesù probably had the latest dedication. The crypt chapel of SS. Abbondio and Abbondanzio, built directly under the high altar, was the product of the same vogue for Palaeochristian martyrs that inspired Circignani's frescoes for the Jesuit collegiate churches.[210] In 1583 the relics of these obscure early Christian saints were discovered in the church of SS. Cosma e Damiano in the Roman Forum, and in 1584 they were transferred in a solemn ceremony to the Gesù, an event immortalized in a commemorative volume printed in the same year with an illustration of the procession.[211] The acquisition of these two saints' bodies gave the Gesù extra prestige, and allowed it to participate in the spirit of the Palaeochristian Revival movement even though it was a new church. Marc'Antonio Ciappi described the event in heroic terms in his biography of Clement VIII (1596): 'The bodies of Sts Abundius and Abundantius, marytrs, were discovered, and were handed over to the Jesuit fathers, to be placed in the high altar of their new church, built from the foundation and finished by Alessandro Farnese, nephew of Paul III, and dedicated to the Most Holy Name of Jesus, where consequently they were transported with noteworthy ecclesiastical magnificence, together with an infinite number of other holy relics.'[212] This chapel and its decorations are now entirely lost, but originally it was one of the parts of the Gesù that bore the greatest resemblance to the collegiate churches, in which the fresco cycles were litanies of early Christian martyrs.

Despite the enthusiasm of the procession, which was paid for by the pope himself and attended by the most prominent churchmen of the city and by members of the Society from all the Roman foundations, the Jesuits had to pay for the decoration of the chapel themselves – even though they had sent letters to the Farnese family in 1583 and 1584 angling for a donation.[213] As we have seen, Father General Acquaviva eventually found the money in the surplus for the Chapel of St Andrew, after Salustia Cerrini took over and Giulio Folco's heirs paid his debts.[214] The paintings, all oil on panel, were directed by Fiammeri, who may also have designed them. Three of them were executed by men who would soon be especially known for martyrdom paintings, Agostino Ciampelli, Andrea Commodi, and Baldassare Croce; *Sts Abundius and Abundantius Led before the Tyrant* is Commodi's work.[215] The other two panels were commissioned from Andrea Lilio d'Ancona and Paolo Guidotti, the former of whom painted a miracle in which the saints revive a dead man.[216] Most of the work was done in 1602–3; Ciampelli and Croce, however, were already active here in the spring of 1600. The Jesuits spent 600 scudi on the decorations, of which Croce received 23 and Ciampelli 10 on 25 May 1600 (Ciampelli was paid an additional 10 scudi on 12 March 1603), Lilio d'Ancona received 10 on 2 August 1602, and Guidotti received three times as much on 22 September 1602.[217] There are no notations in the account books of payments to Commodi. The variations in the artists' fees for what appear to have been paintings of the same size may relate to their age and reputation, since the senior artists Guidotti and Croce, both of whom were in their forties, were paid more than Lilio d'Ancona and Ciampelli, who were in their thirties.

The most important single work in the entire church, and the one most closely linked to Farnese patronage, is the high altarpiece, *Circumcision* (fig. 112).[218] Originally Alessandro had intended to make the apse area of the church a palatial interior that would rival the Sixtine Chapel at S. Maria Maggiore, with a rich altarpiece, a floor of precious marbles, a marble balustrade and tabernacle, and mosaic decoration in the apse. The apse mosaic, which may have resembled the one Alessandro commissioned from Giovanni de' Vecchi and Francesco Zucci at S. Maria Scala Coeli in 1588–9, at least reached the cartoon stage, since Fiammeri was working on the design in August 1581, at the same time he was adapting the Nadal illustrations.[219] Only the altarpiece, the lantern and pendentive frescoes, and the tabernacle were under way when the cardinal's death in 1589 brought the entire project to a halt. A document published by Pecchiai listed the state of the decorations at the time, showing that neither of the painters had yet been paid in full, and that the Jesuits decided to paint the tribune instead of using mosaics 'because it could be done faster and with less expense.'[220] Little did they know that it would take almost a century for them to do so. The tabernacle, by Giacomo della Porta and gilded in 1583 by Giovanni de' Vecchi, has now found a home in the cathedral in Thurles.[221] Farnese had originally intended to hire de' Vecchi, the painter responsible for the lantern and pendentives of the church, to paint the altarpiece. But the cardinal changed his mind, much to the chagrin of de' Vecchi, and handed the commission over to Girolamo Muziano, an artist he had wanted to hire for some time, in 1587.[222] De' Vecchi wrote bitterly to Alessandro in 1588 asking for payment for the cartoons he spent five months preparing, and saying that he had 'never wanted to accept this third commission [the altarpiece], for which I was not responsible in the contract.'[223]

Muziano's original contract, dated 1 August 1587, stipulated that the artist would paint a large oil painting, on a panel measuring 15 *palme* by 24 *palme*, of Christ's circumcision, 'with every diligence and perfection,' under the supervision of Giulio Folco and Giuseppe Valeriano, for the handsome amount of 700 scudi, in three payments of 200 scudi plus an extra 100 scudi at the beginning of work for supplies, and that the cardinal would supply not only the panel but the costly ultramarine blue pigment.[224] The contract stipulated that Muziano had to finish the work by 1589. Muziano signed a receipt saying that he had been paid his first instalment of 100 scudi to begin work on that same day.[225] The memorial written upon Farnese's death remarks that Muziano had been paid only 200 scudi in 1589; although Acquaviva asked for the remaining amount from Alessandro's heir Ranuccio Farnese, the records do not show whether the Jesuits were ever able to pay the painter the rest of his fee.[226]

After Alessandro's death only the most incidental projects were pursued for the high altar area, mostly involving sculptures for the tabernacle and around the altar. A number of references survive for payments to sculptors working on bronze angels for the tabernacle and for work on the choir between April 1592 and April 1593, for a total of 40 scudi.[227] We know that these were finished at least by October 1596, since 1.20 scudi was spent on that date to have them cleaned.[228] The sculptor Bartolommeo Tronchi was also paid for gilt bronze angels, including two candleholders for the high altar, between September 1596 and May 1597, and again between May 1599 and October 1600, for a total of just over 25 scudi for supplies.[229] There is a reference to a small 'cena' (Last Supper?) to adorn the altar of the crucifix by an anonymous Flemish painter, who was paid 10 scudi for his efforts in June 1591.[230]

The transept chapels were second only to the high altar in size and importance, and their patrons accordingly were wealthy and influential. The left transept, now the location of the altar of St Ignatius by Andrea Pozzo, was acquired by Cardinal Giacomo Savelli, grand-nephew of Paul III and cousin of Alessandro, and consequently squarely within the Farnese camp.[231] As well as being one of the richest cardinals of his day, Savelli was the vicar of Rome. The chapel originally featured a work of sculpture on its altar, a wooden crucifix of a naturalism so intense that it quickly became a favourite object of popular devotion, and remained so even after it was removed from the church and placed in the sacristy. After arranging for Giacomo della Porta to execute a grand altar of coloured marbles to house the sculpture, Savelli ordered a bronze copy of the wooden crucifix to be made, the metal being a richer material befitting the location of the crucifix (and his patronage).[232] After initial wavering, he chose the Brescian sculptor Prospero Antichi, who began a wax model. But before the work could begin, Savelli died (in 1587), and then Prospero died in 1592. After a hiatus the heir, Giovanni Savelli, wrote up a contract with the Sicilian sculptor Lodovico del Duca to finish the work.[233] The choice of the Sicilian was no coincidence: Savelli himself was from Sicily, and the sculptor had already carved the family arms over the west door of the Gesù.

This extremely detailed contract gives us tremendous insight into the way in which the Jesuits supervised the artistic projects in the Gesù, even beyond the side chapels. Dated 30 August 1593, the contract stipulates that del Duca must finish the wax model begun by Prospero 'according to the taste and satisfaction of Fr. Giuseppe Valeriano ... and another [person] whom the said Father will choose as a companion in such a judgment, and should one be lacking the said Father Giuseppe would like the superior of the Most Reverend Jesuit fathers to elect one or two others in his place.'[234] This supervision by Valeriano and his companion applied to even the most minute details, such as completing the lacunae left in Prospero's original wax model: 'Master Lodovico is obliged first and foremost to fix the said wax [model], filling in all the lacunae that are left in it, such as the head, the arms, the flanks, the knees, the legs, and the feet, which are still unfinished, along with a few other little details that are unfinished, to the satisfaction of the said Father Giuseppe and his companion.' The contract goes on to stipulate that del Duca must make a plaster cast and then cast the metal in a single piece, not counting the crown and diadem; that should either the cardinal or Valeriano be dissatisfied with his work, he must melt it down and cast it anew at his own expense; and that he must also clean it and prepare it for gilding to the satisfaction of his supervisors. His total fee, made in three equal payments, was 439 scudi, and del Duca was to complete his work within eighteen months.

As well as with del Duca's bronze crucifix, the left transept chapel soon was adorned with two paintings, a canvas by the Cavaliere d'Arpino, *Jesuit Martyrs in Japan*, most likely inspired by a Japanese painting of the same subject still in the collection of the Casa Professa, and a canvas by Antiveduto Grammatica, *Francis Borgia Praying to the Blessed Sacrament*, in which the Sacred Host is carried by angels. Although none of the payment records survive for either of these paintings – and therefore we have no date for them – they are discussed in the major secondary sources of the time.[235] Mancini is guilty of hyperbole (not to mention a glaring anachronism) in attributing the design of the altarpiece to Raphael.[236]

The competition for the altarpiece of the right transept chapel, dedicated to Christ's resurrection (fig. 113), has gone down in history as the source of Caravaggio's rivalry with Giovanni Baglione. But Baglione's victory in the contest can best be described as pyrrhic: not only was he branded a plagiarist by one of the most vocal artists in the city, but his patron pulled out before he was paid more than two instalments. This patron was Cardinal Girolamo Rusticucci, who had been assigned the transept by Clement VIII during his Visitation of 1594. Architectural plans were carried out and a competition held for the altarpiece in 1602. At first everything went well. In 1602, Fiammeri purchased colours for the painting, and Mastro Ottavio the painter, perhaps the young Ottavio Padovano, was paid 5 scudi to help Baglione with the commission.[237] In January 1604, Baglione was paid one of his first two instalments of 100 scudi, for what would be the largest single painting commission of the Gesù, a staggering 1,000 scudi for one canvas.[238] But 200 scudi was all he received. The cardinal chose to devote all his energies and his funds to his titular church of S. Susanna, and left not another scudo to the Jesuit chapel.[239] Five years later, Baglione was reduced to writing a letter to the pope, begging him to have the Jesuits pay their debt to the painter:

> Most Holy Father: From the year 1602, Giovanni Baglione painted by order of the Father General of the Jesuits a large painting of the Resurrection for a chapel of the Church of the Gesù, and for his wages he received two hundred scudi, which were received in good faith, and the Jesuit Fathers have always made promises to him about the rest, that he would be satisfied, excusing themselves that they did not have the funds, and this speaker having several times insisted that they pay the said residual, after having held back [wages] for five years, the said Father General has ultimately replied to him that he would not give him any more. And since the painting is valued at one thousand scudi, and has been made by this speaker with much study and care, as indeed the quality of this painting demonstrates, he should be paid for his labours. Therefore he humbly requests that Your Reverence deign to require Monsignor A.C. to pay him right away.[240]

We may never know whether Baglione was paid his back wages, since the only subsequent payment recorded in the Jesuit ledgers is a paltry single scudo paid to an unidentified painter nine years later, in 1616, 'to repair the altar of the Resurrection.'[241] Whatever happened, Baglione was left with no hard feelings toward the Jesuits; in his autobiography he makes no mention of insufficient payment, and records merely that he painted for Claudio Acquaviva a Resurrection 'represented with love, and studiousness.'[242]

The grandest part of the apse and crossing area was the crossing itself, and its giant cupola. Falling solidly within the Farnese part of the church, the cupola was pushed ahead in 1582–3 by an impatient Cardinal Alessandro, who perhaps sensed that he was nearing the end of his life. Writing to Bartolommeo Ammannati in August 1582, Acquaviva vents his frustration at having all his best *maestri* at work on making the cupola ready for decoration: 'These few masters whom we have are now working on the cupola of our church here in Rome, on which they cannot lose time, since the Most Illustrious Cardinal Farnese desires to see it as soon as possible brought to completion.'[243] The *maestri* evidently came close to making the cardinal's deadline, since the lantern and pendentives were decorated early the next year by Giovanni de' Vecchi, 'Alessandro's great protégé.'[244] On 12 January 1583, de' Vecchi began frescoing the lantern with 'diverse ornaments and cherubs, quite sumptuous,' and one week earlier, on 7 January, Andrea Lilio d'Ancona began his painting of the *Four Evangelists* in the drum.[245] Lilio d'Ancona's evangelists were painted in false niches in grisaille. De' Vecchi also frescoed the four pendentives below the drum with *Doctors of the Church*, which are visible in Andrea Sacchi's 1639 painting of the Gesù interior (fig. 114). According to a letter written to Alessandro by de' Vecchi and published by Robertson, two of the frescoes had been completed by 1583, and de' Vecchi had been paid only 300 scudi for the lantern and pendentives, an amount with which he was very unhappy.[246] His problems stemmed largely from his dealings with the Farnese agent, Giulio Folco, with whom de' Vecchi was still expressing discontent in 1585: 'Not being able to achieve satisfaction with Messer Gulio Folco, I am forced to await the return of your Most Illustrious Lordship, in order that in Your presence we should be able to finish this and bring it to completion.'[247] Despite his complaints that he was not suitably recompensed for his labours, de' Vecchi had assistance in his work on the cupola. Celio records that he merely designed the decorations, and that the dome was 'painted by diverse [others],' an arrangement echoed by the anonymous late seventeenth-century Jesuit source.[248]

Giovanni de' Vecchi did not fare well at the Gesù. After being underpaid for his dome paintings and summarily fired in favour of Muziano for the altarpiece, he had his contributions to the dome condemned by Alessandro's heir, Odoardo Farnese, who found them old-fashioned and planned for them to be painted over by his own protégé, Annibale Carracci.[249] Had Odoardo's plans been carried through, the Gesù might have had the first Baroque dome painting, the ecclesiastical equivalent of Annibale's ceiling in the Farnese Palace (begun 1597). Instead, that honour went to the Gesù's rival, S. Andrea della Valle, with Lanfranco's 1625–7 dome fresco *Virgin in Glory*.

The West Wall, Sacristy, Confraternity Chapels, and Miscellaneous Minor Commissions

The only other area to be decorated within the church proper was the inside of the west wall. Since the Jesuits could not rely on outside patronage for a part of the church that was not a separate chapel, they employed artists from within the order so that they would have to pay for nothing more than materials. The Society accordingly called upon Fiammeri to design a Jesuit monogram to go over the door and a series of oil paintings of unidentified saints to surround it.[250] These were executed by two Flemish Jesuit brothers, very likely Michele and Gisberto Gisbert.[251] Hibbard presumes they are martyrdoms, although there is no evidence to prove or disprove his claim.[252] The doors themselves were made of precious wood from the Indies (it is impossible to say whether Asia or Brazil) presented to Cardinal Farnese by the king of Portugal, Don Sebastião, and would serve as a reminder of the worldwide extent of the Jesuit enterprise and the Church's mission.[253]

Finally, the sacristy vault paintings were also executed during this period.[254] The building itself, which would be one of the largest sacristies in Rome, was not given much thought by the original planners of the Gesù, and was built only in 1599, under Odoardo Farnese, by Girolamo Rainaldi (1570–1655) at the same time that the new Casa Professa was being erected. The sacristy was first used in 1610.[255] It quickly became a repository for paintings and other art objects donated to the Society, and was also the final resting place of the original wooden crucifix from the left transept.[256] Unfortunately, no references to the sacristy survive in the account books. The principal secondary sources of the day indicate that the vault fresco, *Angels Adoring the Blessed Sacrament* (fig. 115), was painted by Agostino Ciampelli, but Pecchiai's attribution of other works in the sacristry to Lanfranco cannot be taken seriously.[257] Baglione more credibly assigns all these works to Ciampelli's hand. Another artist who may have painted in the sacristy is Francesco Vanni (ca. 1563–1610); according to Baldinucci, he painted a *Martyrdom of St Cecilia* in an unspecified part of the church.[258] A painting of 'S. Cecilia' is listed in a 1701 inventory of the sacristy and may be Vanni's picture.[259]

The only other spaces in the Gesù and Casa Professa complex to be finished during this period were the chapels belonging to the six lay congregations that gathered here, although there are no clues concerning their decoration before the mid-seventeenth century.[260] Among them was the Congregation of the Assumption, which originally met in a chapel in the first Casa Professa, rebuilt by Acquaviva in 1602. The chapel, which was entered via the courtyard, was rectangular with a choir loft and sacristy. In 1594 the Congregation of the Annunciation began to meet in a chapel constructed over the three lateral chapels of the south side of the Gesù, a space that was taken over by the Congregation of Merchants in 1761. In 1597 a space on the opposite side, over the lateral chapels of the north, became the chapel for the Congregation of the Immaculate Conception, another artisans' congregation. That chapel is still used by the Congregation of the Purification. Although presumably all these groups had at least an altarpiece depicting their patron saint, nothing survives from the period.

One of the chapels in the Casa Professa, the so-called Cappellina di Odoardo Farnese, was hung with earlier paintings taken from the Gesù – six canvases of different sizes depicting the life of Ignatius of Loyola painted to adorn his tomb between 1605 and 1608 by Baccio Ciarpi and Andrea Commodi, before his beatification in 1609 (fig. 116).[261] Gianni Papi has recently shown that these pictures were directly inspired by a Life of Ignatius printed in Antwerp in 1610, with illustrations drawn as early as 1601 by Juan de Mesa.[262] Their original location at Ignatius's tomb in the left transept is confirmed by Mancini, who writes that Commodi 'executed here in Rome several things for the Gesù, at the tomb of the Blessed Ignatius, in good style.'[263] Commodi's series replaced a simple portrait of Ignatius that had adorned the tomb since 1599, when the Oratorian cardinal Cesare Baronio placed it there during a ceremony in which Bellarmine also participated.[264] Another chapel in the Casa Professa that may have a painting contemporary with the first phase of decoration at the Gesù is the Cappella dei Nobili, a confraternity chapel built to house a Marian congregation dedicated to the Assumption of the Virgin that had been founded in 1593. Pecchiai publishes an archival reference, which he does not cite, stating that a 'Mastro Giuseppe pittore' (Cesari?) had painted the altarpiece of the Assumption that was set in place on 5 August 1595.[265]

The prestigious artists were not the only ones to work on the Gesù, although they are the only ones remembered in studies today. The account books are full of miscellaneous small painting and sculpture commissions for unspecified parts of the church, some of them temporary, such as the coats of arms executed by the painter Mastro Biagio in March 1568 to adorn the Piazza degli Altieri when Alessandro Farnese laid the first stone of the new church, for which he was paid 1 scudo.[266] This Mastro Biagio Fiorentino worked regularly for the Jesuits as an all-purpose painter, for example during 1583, when his name appears regularly in the Gesù account books for small amounts of a scudo or more.[267] Another commission connected with the foundation of the church is the 150 medallions of the Madonna (probably the Madonna della Strada) cast in 1570 on the order of Father Lorenzo Amodei.[268] In that same year a 'painter related to Vignola' was given 44 scudi to buy lime for an unspecified project.[269] His identity is unclear, as Vignola had many artist relatives, but since the notation says 'relative' and not 'son' we can probably rule out his son, Giacinto Barozzi (ca. 1535/40–after 1584), who in any case was an architect. It was more likely his brother, Gian Angelo, a *capomastro-scalpellino* who worked with Vignola at Caprarola; his other brother, Guarnerio, a painter known from documents dated 1545 and 1554; or his cousin Lazzaro Barozzi, a painter and gilder who married in 1558.[270]

Other painters, most of them anonymous but one known as Mastro Andrea, took care of odd jobs in the early 1590s, among them preparing two hundred large and small engravings of Jesus; small paintings of the monogram of the name of Jesus; small images of angels; and other minor commissions, such as the eighteen scenes of the Crucifixion painted for the confessionals in April 1592, at a rate of 2.5 scudi a picture, for a total of 45 scudi.[271] These notices give insight into a fascinating world of ephemera that is usually overlooked. Similarly, in the first two decades of the 1600s the painter Giovanni Battista Vanaro (also spelled Vanner; perhaps he was a German) received 24 scudi, 80 giulii for a royal coat of arms for an altar frontal; another artist executed a papal arms; an anonymous artist was given a gratuity of 5 scudi for a painting of Jesus; a Mastro Tomasso was hired to make a model of a Holy Week sepulchre; another unknown artist painted two canvases of the church; and pigments were purchased to paint the lattices and cornice of the choir.[272] Some artists are listed in the accounts not for jobs done but for gifts made to the treasury, such as Durante Alberti and another painter called Mastro Giovanni (Pozzo? de' Vecchi?), both of whom gave just over 7 scudi on 13 April 1593, and the sculptor Giovanni Paolo, who left a donation of 1 scudo, 20 giulii on 22 October 1606.[273]

These small jobs were not without their patrons. Claudia Mattei, from one of the oldest and richest families in Rome, kinswoman to Asdrubale Mattei and to his brother Ciriaco Mattei, who would be one of Caravaggio's greatest supporters, paid 45 scudi for a copy of the popular Florentine image of the Madonna dell'Annunziata in the summer of 1602.[274] That fall, Claudia, who was also related to Francis Borgia, spent 10 scudi on a painting of 'All Saints' ('tutti i santi') and 60 scudi on one of angels, as well as sums on the frames for all three pictures.[275] It is likely, given their date, that these paintings were made for the newly constructed Casa Professa, the first stone of which was laid by Odoardo Farnese in 1599. Although no records survive in the Jesuit archives for artists who worked in the Casa Professa in this period (it was not finished until 1623), the Casa contained a number of chapels that were adorned with paintings in the third decade of the seventeenth century.

7

The Church of the Gesù in Rome: Description and Interpretation

Chapter 6 was devoted to the documentary evidence surrounding the first painted and sculpted decorations in the Church of the Gesù and the Casa Professa, between the 1580s and about 1610. In that chapter I was concerned primarily with dating, patronage, economics, and attribution, and with the chronology of the church's original decorations. Because those topics draw upon an extraordinarily large number of sources, I have chosen to devote a separate chapter to a discussion of the iconography, inscriptions, and style of the Gesù cycle. Here we will take an imaginary walk through the church as it stood in 1610, passing through each of the nave chapels in turn, and then the apse and crossing area, including the two lateral chapels at the east end. I will describe each of the paintings and statues, relate them stylistically to earlier works and to each other, and reflect on the relationship between their imagery and their captions. The consideration of style is crucial to an understanding of the Jesuits' goals in decorating the Gesù, since they were extremely concerned with nuances of style and how differences in style affected different viewers. This concern is more apparent in the Gesù than in any of the Society's previous commissions in Rome. As well as considering the ideological goals of the Jesuits and their artists, I will ask who the audiences were, and how they perceived and made use of the imagery in their spiritual lives. The chapter will conclude with an examination of the legacy of the Gesù decorations in Rome, elsewhere in Italy, and in Northern Europe. For the paintings of the Gesù cycle formed a template that was copied in part or in whole in places as diverse as Florence, Perugia, and Antwerp, both with respect to its style and with respect to its iconography alone.

As we take our virtual walk through the Gesù, we must not lose sight of the fact that the Gesù paintings form only part of a decorative ensemble that is framed and accented by lavish coloured marbles, gilding, and stuccowork. These marble and sculptural surrounds provide variety and opulence of the sort employed slightly later by Pope Sixtus V for his more public commissions, such as the work at the Lateran Palace in 1588–9, and they convey the same ecclesiastical triumphalism, along with overtones of palatial splendour and the glory of antiquity.

Each of the six nave chapels at the Gesù is rectangular in shape and is separated into three principal divisions: the vault of the ceiling, the lunettes below it, and the walls below the entablature. The vaults consist of a central oval-shaped semi-dome surrounded by four pendentives, so that there are five major sections to be frescoed, although sometimes, as in the Apostles' Chapel, the pendentives are further divided, in this case into four sections each. On the next level down are the four lunettes, which rise from the entablature to the base of the dome. Only the two lateral ones contain paintings. They either frame single fresco panels, as in the St Andrew Chapel, or are themselves further divided, as in the Trinity Chapel, where they enclose an oval that reflects the oval of the main vault, or in the Apostles' Chapel, where they are divided into three panels vertically. In place of a lunette on the end wall there is a lunette-shaped window, and there is no lunette on the wall facing the nave, since it is opened up to form the entrance archway, the soffit of which is also decorated and divided into panels.

Below the entablature, which forms the base of the lunettes, are the three main walls of the chapel (again, there is no fourth wall, since the chapel opens directly onto the nave). Usually everything on this level is painted in fresco, except the pilaster panels, which can be relief sculpture. Exceptions include the Passion Chapel, the lateral panels of which are on canvas. The smallest divisions are found on the four pilasters, on which are mounted one larger and one (or more) smaller rectangular panels, not only on the four pilasters inside the chapel but on the two inside the entrance archway. The largest sections are the grand rectangular panels on the two lateral walls, just over the doors that communicate with the adjacent chapels; they are so large that the door actually penetrates a little into their frame at the bottom. The end wall is taken up almost entirely by the altar, formed of a pair of pilasters capped by a pediment, which encloses the main altarpiece, a vertical rectangle.

The chapels were overwhelmed with narrative action. As in the collegiate chapels, there are strikingly few symbolic or allegorical images, and where they exist they tend to be relegated to the smaller sections such as the pilasters and the pendentives. The unusually static altarpiece of the Angels' Chapel was, as we have seen, a later addition. The subjects and themes of the paintings are also extremely tightly interrelated. The principal narrative scene on the altarpiece is echoed throughout the chapel, first in the two main lateral panels, which treat related episodes or figures in the life of the principal dedicatee(s), and then in the lunettes, which feature lively and often crowded narratives also in some way related to the main action. The last major section of the interior, the dome vault, almost invariably features the dedicatee(s) in an apotheosis, surrounded by heavenly approbation in the form of cloudbursts and angels. The pendentives and pilasters tend to be decorated with more symbolic or iconic figures, generally without backgrounds, who also relate to the main action or dedicatee(s). Such are the Four Evangelists in the Passion Chapel pendentives, who represent the Gospels and therefore quite literally the story of Christ's passion; the four main pilaster panels feature passive and meditative images of Christ at four different stages of the Passion, and two Old Testament figures who prefigure his coming. Even some of the smallest panels contain narratives; the four smaller ones above the prophets, for example, depict events in the lives of those figures.

The Nave Chapels: Left Side

The first chapel on the left, the Apostles' Chapel, originally may not have had an altarpiece, and all the canvases below the entablature are mid- to late-seventeenth-century replacements. Scholars have speculated as to the subject of the altarpiece and have suggested a variety of titles, among them *The Calling of Peter and Andrew, Christ Giving the Keys, Christ Charging Peter, Paul Preaching at Athens,* and *Domine Quo Vadis?*[1] Perhaps it was a *Christ Walks upon the Waters,* depicting the moment in Matthew (14:22–3) when Christ appears while a storm buffets the boat carrying his disciples and asks Peter to step onto the waves and come to him. This moment is given as one of the Mysteries of the Life of Our Lord in the *Spiritual Exercises* (par 280).[2] The lateral panels once contained paintings by Circignani, which may have featured the same subjects as the panels by Mola that replaced them. These latter depict two scenes from Acts, each representing a moment of conversion featuring one of the two dedicatees, *St Peter Baptizing Sts Processus and Martinianus in Prison,* and *Conversion of St Paul.*

Above the entablature, all the frescoes are intact. The lunettes, divided into one main panel flanked by two smaller ones, introduce the theme of martyrdom, with *Martyrdom of St Peter* and *Faith* and *Hope* on the left, and *Martyrdom of St Paul* and *Religion* and *Charity* on the right. This representation of the theological virtues (Faith, Hope, and Charity, here grouped with Religion for the sake of symmetry) is highly appropriate, since Paul was the first to enumerate them (1 Cor. 13:13). The allegorical figures reflect the Jesuits' self-consciously humanistic mission, in that they closely recall classical models. As Macioce has recently pointed out, intellectuals in the period were engaged in making a 'prudent recovery of the Renaissance,' following the spiritual crises of the Tridentine period, in which they reset classical imagery in a Christian key, and such allegorical emblems were a central part of the revival.[3] Cardinal Bellarmine was especially active in reintroducing classical literary and figural forms in a new Christian mode, and wrote about allegories in his *Disputationes de controversiis christianae fidei* (Ingolstadt, 1586–93), around the time this chapel was being decorated. As we saw in chapters 3 and 4, the Jesuits were very fond of emblematica and made use of such symbolic devices in their teaching and preaching. Although these frescoes in the Gesù predate Cesare Ripa's catalogue of allegorical emblems by almost ten years, the composition of the allegories recalls those in Ripa's book – a female figure accompanied by angels and by symbols of her identity such as scales, a sword, and a jug of water. Giovanni and Cherubino Alberti soon would paint very similar allegories for Clement VIII on the ceiling of the Sala Clementina in the Vatican (1596–1600), where can be found some of the same allegorical figures, among them Justice, Charity, and Religion (fig. 30).[4]

In the vault is the scene one would most expect in a chapel dedicated to the apostolate, entitled *Pentecost* (fig. 83). This central panel is surrounded by four more personifications, this time of the four cardinal virtues (Prudence, Justice, Fortitude, and Temperance), which were regularly contrasted with the theological virtues. Below these are angels holding scrolls with the names of the virtues written on them, and between each pair of virtues is a pair of even smaller monochrome scenes from the lives of the apostles. These little narrative scenes include *Peter Liberated from Prison* (liberally inspired by Raphael's version in the Vatican) and *Christ's Charge to Sts Peter and Andrew. Pentecost* represents the moment in Acts when the apostles (not including Paul, who had not yet been converted) had gathered and were empowered by the Holy Spirit to speak so that they could be understood by persons of many different languages. As Hibbard points out, the message is clearly a missionary one and serves as a metaphor for the worldwide Jesuit missions.[5] It both celebrates Jesuit activities and exhorts viewers to follow in their path, either literally, by joining the Society, or symbolically, by living a Christian life.

The style of Circignani's main vault painting is more opulent than that of his S. Stefano murals, in its brighter colours, golden light, and greater emphasis on the palace setting; it resembles more closely the paintings of the life of St Francis that he executed in 1583–5 for S. Giovanni de' Fiorentini, *St Francis in Front of the Sultan* (fig. 84) and *St Francis Seeks the Approval of the Order from Pope Honorius III.* The Gesù *Pentecost* shares certain features with those frescoes: the setting on a descending staircase, with architectural framing devices rising past the limits of the frame; the arrangement of the figures in a vague semicircle around the main figure in the middle ground; and the size of the figures relative to that of the architecture. In this painting we see something we have not yet seen much of in Circignani's work for the Jesuits – a view of heaven. The S. Stefano murals and their progeny were notably devoid of angels and cloudbursts. But in the Gesù, where the ceiling paintings suggest an apotheosis, Circignani allows the upper part of his scene to burst forth with a brilliant light that originates in an image of the Holy Spirit and extends to the edges of the frame, and that is surrounded with rolling clouds and cherubs, some in an attitude of prayer and others mere heads with wings.

Curiously, unlike in most images of the Pentecost – such as Federico Zuccaro's version in the *retablo mayor* at the Escorial, where they appear over the heads of the apostles – Circignani gives us no overt depiction of the tongues of flame, but only a slight suggestion in the rays of sunlight.[6] Closer versions include Santi di Tito's *Pentecost* in Dubrovnik (1575), the Madonna in which is strikingly similar to Circignani's; Vasari's *Pentecost* (1568) in S. Croce in Florence, which also minimizes the tongues of flame and has a similar arrangement of figures; and Girolamo Muziano's *Pentecost* (1578) in the Vatican, though this work has a horizontal format.[7] Circignani's Gesù version may even have borrowed the two flanking figures from Muziano's painting. But the Tuscan painter gives the Virgin more prominence, by separating her from the crowd. One thing Circignani's painting shares with many contemporary versions of this subject is its representation of crowds. As Carolyn Valone has recently shown, images of the Pentecost underwent a transformation in the later sixteenth century, whereby they moved from the traditional depiction of the twelve apostles and the Virgin Mary to depicting all the male and female disciples mentioned in Acts.[8] This expansion of the image reflected the missionary ideals of Gregory XIII, and was favoured by Signora Vittoria della Tolfa, the Marchesa della Valle, an important Roman patron and the original founder of the Collegio Romano, who in the 1580s commissioned a family chapel in S. Spirito in Sassia dedicated to the Pentecost.

The elongated profiles and twisted poses of the two foreground figures are standard late Cinquecento Florentine fare, but Circignani carries the approach to an extreme rarely reached by other artists. The figures carry little believable weight, and the whole scene is marked by a floating, ethereal quality suitable to its heavenly subject. Circignani is not concerned with naturalism or even rationality, but with creating a visionary experience. What is extraordinary is the degree of symmetry in this painting. The balance of figures between left and right gives the painting the appearance of a design used in a Rorschach test, thereby enhancing the impression that divine energy and light are exploding outward from the image of the Holy Spirit. Typical of Circignani are the tiny heads on the bodies, which are balanced well below the waist, and the oval faces with their tiny, puckered mouths. The figure and gesture of the Virgin are of a type repeated elsewhere by Circignani, for example in his *Coronation of the Virgin* in the Pinacoteca Civica in Volterra (ca. 1592).[9]

In the martyrdom frescoes in the centre of the lunettes, Circignani returns to familiar territory, and here he draws directly from his work at S. Stefano. The *Martyrdom of St Peter* (fig. 85) repeats almost exactly the central figure and the position of the cross in fresco III at S. Stefano (fig. 40), although here the painter arranges the figures much more cleverly. At S. Stefano he crowds the three executioners, who are raising the cross, to one side, and balances them only by a single standing figure on the left, and he places the action so low that the upper third of the scene is almost empty. But at the Gesù he shifts the axis of the cross to the exact centre, so that its twisting X-shape itself becomes the anchor and motif of the whole picture. All the principal figures respond to the shape of the cross in different ways. Peter's body, naturally, reflects the shape of the cross since he is tied to it. The two executioners, one on either side, respond to its geometry: by having one reach up and the other down, Circignani makes them mimic the twisting motion of the cross. Finally, the two flanking figures stand in *contrapposto* in such a way that the convex outlines of their bodies are matched by the cross's concavities. A similar rotating movement can be seen in Michelangelo's version of the scene in the Pauline Chapel (fig. 53), but it is not as tightly controlled as Circignani's, which is more sparing with background and allows the figures to dominate. Again, there is an overriding sense of symmetry.

The *Martyrdom of St Paul* is not as balletic as the scene opposite, although it too uses the two flanking standing figures to balance the whole scene, and the main executioner and a column behind him as the fulcrum of the action. The saint, however, seems oddly off centre. There was no version of this scene at S. Stefano for Circignani to refer to, but the poses of the saint and the executioner are very similar to those of their counterparts in other martyrdoms in earlier Circignani cycles, such as that of St Thomas of Canterbury in the English College (print XXV) (fig. 69). In her discussion of the allegorical figures – all female – Laura Russo points to the influence of Beccafumi, and compares the small grisaille scenes, in which the figures generally stand forward as in a frieze, toward the front of the picture plane, with certain effects in the work of Perino del Vaga.[10] The resemblance to Perino's relief-like style is particularly clear, but there is also a closer and more obvious model – Circignani's own grisaille scenes of the life of

St Stephen that surround the high altar at S. Stefano Rotondo and were painted in 1583 (see chapter 4).

Like those in the Novitiate infirmary, S. Stefano, and S. Vitale, the Gesù decorations used inscriptions to guide viewers – in this case members of the general public as well as Jesuits and students – in their meditations and reflections. The inscriptions found in the cartouches on the vault underscore the missionary theme of the Apostles' Chapel. The four separate panels make up a quotation from Psalm 19 that emphasizes the global nature of the Jesuit enterprise and echoes the missionary message of the Pentecost scene: IN OMNEM TERRAM EXIVIT SONUS EORUM ET IN FINES ORBIS TERRAE VERBA EORUM (Their sound is gone out through all the earth, and their words to the end of the world [Ps. 19:4]). There are also inscriptions identifying the theological virtues, RELIGIO, CHARITAS, FIDES, and SPES, and the cardinal virtues, PRUDENTIA, FORTITUDO, IUSTITIA, and TEMPERANTIA.

The paintings of the next chapel on the left, the Nativity Chapel, are just as tightly interwoven. The altarpiece by Hans von Aachen, *Nativity of Christ*, which no longer exists but is reproduced in an engraving by Aegidius Sadeler, featured the key protagonist and central event commemorated in the chapel. The lateral wall panels were overpainted in oils by Romanelli, but fortunately for us his restorations have mysteriously vanished and left the originals by Circignani. They are *Adoration of the Magi* on the left and *Presentation of Christ at the Temple* on the right, two narrative scenes closely related to the birth of Christ. In the lunettes Circignani painted two more popular episodes belonging to the infancy of Christ, *Massacre of the Innocents* on the left and *Annunciation to the Shepherds* on the right. As in the Apostles' Chapel, the lunette level is the site of martyrdom imagery. The pendentive paintings feature Old Testament prophets who foretold Christ's coming – David, Isaiah, Zechariah, and Baruch – and the vault painting is another vision of heavenly approbation, *Heavenly Celebration of the Birth of Christ* (not of the Immaculate Conception, as Lewine records).[11] The four allegorical reliefs in the internal pilasters, made by mid-seventeenth-century sculptors but probably reflecting the original plan for the chapel, represent the four cardinal Virtues again – Temperance and Prudence on the right, and Fortitude and Justice on the left. Small decorative angels and putti make up the rest of the tiny panels in the arch soffits. The Nativity is the subject of the Second Contemplation of the First Day of the Second Week in the *Spiritual Exercises* (pars 110–17).[12]

Hans von Aachen brings the stylish grace of the imperial Habsburg court to the Gesù in *Nativity* (fig. 86). Although he had not yet moved to Rudolf II's Prague when he worked on this commission (he was to do so in the early 1590s), his work already demonstrated the aristocratic litheness of Bartolomäus Spranger, Adrien de Vries, and the other painters who helped create the Rudolfine brand of a courtly late 'Maniera' style.[13] Von Aachen's style echoes Circignani with its light, dancelike poses, elongated bodies, tiny puckered mouths, and sweet expressions, but it lacks the latter's mystical abstraction and is planted firmly in a world of secular sensuality. Like von Aachen's work at the imperial court in the 1590s and early 1600s, the figures in the *Nativity* have characteristic dimpled elbows and knuckles, long and languid eyelids, hair bundled in knots at the top or pointed headdresses, and elegant, impossibly long fingers held in dancers' gestures. The

Virgin, whose breasts ride high on her chest, bears more than a passing resemblance to the pagan nudes painted often by von Aachen at Prague, and the artist gives us a glimpse of the eroticism of his Venuses and nymphs by revealing her erect nipples beneath her tunic. We lose the best part by not having the picture in colour, since von Aachen was above all a colourist. Gone are what must have been the shimmering cold tones of his greens and blues, skin tones that are both chilly and sensual, rosy cheeks, and, above all, the Venetian-inspired fabrics with their rich, warm colours and glittering highlights.

In the lateral fresco panels *Adoration of the Magi* (fig. 87) and *Presentation of Christ at the Temple*, Circignani again increases the scale of the figures, perhaps in deference to the horizontal format, although here the architectural and even landscape element is still prominent. In the friezelike disposition of the figures and their classical setting, there is more than an echo of Perino del Vaga, for example his *Visitation* in the Pucci Chapel in SS. Trinità dei Monti (ca. 1523); and the panels also recall Circignani's own frescoes on the S. Stefano balustrade. Here, the main action is in the middle, and the painter uses a pair of standing figures on either side of the picture to serve as a framing device. The two standing figures in the *Adoration*, seen from the back and with twisting poses, recall the pairs of flanking executioners in the S. Stefano series. The principal figures, the members of the Holy Family, are moved slightly to the left so that not they but the act of reverence becomes the actual focus of the painting (the same focus on reverence is also present in the altarpiece of the St Andrew Chapel, on the other side of the nave) (fig. 95). The approach is quite different from that of von Aachen's painting in what is after all a very similar scene, where the body of Christ is the focus. The powerful horses on the upper right, with their giant necks, barrel-like bodies, and raised left hooves, closely resemble the horses painted by Circignani in the Palazzo Corgna in Castiglion del Lago in Umbria (begun 1575).

Of the lunette frescoes *Massacre of the Innocents* (fig. 88) is more directly inspired by the S. Stefano murals, although this time by Antonio Tempesta's work (fig. 60). The Gesù version copies one of the figures exactly, a woman falling headlong over her dead child, who appears just behind the woman in the foreground in Tempesta's version and is second to the left in Circignani's.[14] The Gesù fresco is very different in spirit, however, in substituting the dramatic verticality of Tempesta's prototype for a more classical, friezelike formation with most of the figures at the picture plane. As he does in the main panels below, Circignani frames the figures of the centremost victims with his favourite motif of a pair of flanking executioners, and his powerful symmetricality turns the two women at the centre into almost exact reflections, their arms and babies linked at the fulcrum. Circignani conceived two other versions of this scene, one a painting now in the Galleria Nazionale d'Arte Antica in Rome and the other a drawing in the Gabinetto Nazionale delle Stampe, both of which are characterized by smaller figures and more crowded composition and bear little resemblance to the stately classicism of the Gesù version.[15] Here again we see a symmetricality stricter than Circignani used in his collegiate frescoes, and that makes the scenes colder and more mechanical, even relentless – reflecting a draining of every last drop of emotion and humanity from the scenes and a moving closer to the goal of an abstracted and impersonal visionary state.

Circignani is especially sensitive to von Aachen's style in his *Heavenly Celebration of the Birth of Christ* (fig. 89), although he submits von Aachen's grace to an almost robotic symmetry – so much so that the two halves of the scene are virtually exact mirror opposites of each other. This binary division leaves the fresco nearly empty at the centre, with the figures concentrated on the sides and especially in the lower two-thirds. As in his vault in the Apostles' Chapel, Circignani alludes to the kind of heavenly dome pioneered by Correggio in Parma in *Vision of St John of Patmos* (1520–1) at S. Giovanni Evangelista. Unlike Correggio, however, Circignani shifts the perspective so that we are looking at the angels not from below, with the focus on the centre, but as though we are sitting among them, with the balance at the base of the foreground stage. A similar perspective – on a completely different subject – appears in the oval-shaped heavenly dome in Taddeo Zuccaro's vault of the Camera dell'Aurora at Caprarola (1564–5), and Zuccaro's prototype may have served as a model here. The Gesù model for a heavenly dome would quickly be copied elsewhere in Rome, for example in Cristofano Roncalli's *Gloria* in S. Silvestro in Capite (1605).[16] Hibbard has noted that this chapel manifested an early form of 'Baroque spatial involvement,' in which the different painted sections seem to respond to one another beyond the limits of their frames.[17] In particular the angels in the ceiling vault look down to adore Christ in the Nativity altarpiece, as do the pendentive figures of Isaiah and David. This treatment of space was standard in all the Gesù side chapels, and also in the Novitiate infirmary (see chapter 3).

The Nativity Chapel, like the others, is punctuated with inscriptions. The angels in the altarpiece carry a banner with a quotation from the Christmas story: GLORIA IN EXCELSIS DEO ET IN T[ERRA PAX HOMIN]IBUS (Glory to God in the highest; and on earth peace to men of good will [Luke 2:14]). This is a song of triumph, sung at the moment when the angels proclaim the joyful news of Christ's birth to the shepherds below. The quotation serves double duty since it is the text of the Angelic Hymn or Greater Doxology, the prayer known as the Gloria, proclaiming the Trinity and sung after the Kyrie on Sundays and certain feast days, and the reference to the Trinity here helps make the transition between this chapel and the next, which is dedicated to the Trinity. The tone of the altarpiece inscription is carried through to the ceiling vault, where putti hold aloft a banner with words from 1 Chronicles 16:31: LAETENTUR CAELI ET EXULTET TERRA (Let the heavens be glad, and let the earth rejoice [and let men say among the nations that the Lord reigneth]). Each of the prophets in the pendentives is accompanied by angels who hold tablets with the figure's prophecies about the coming of Christ. David is accompanied by a tablet reading, HOMO NATUS EST IN EA ET IPSE FUNDAVIT EAM ALTISSIMUS (That man is born in her: and the Highest himself hath founded her [Ps. 86:5]), and Isaiah is flanked by two tablets reading, PUSILLANIMIS CONFORTAMINI ET NOLITE TIMERE; DEUS IPSE VENIET ET SALVABIT NOS ([Say to them that are of a fearful heart,] Be strong, fear not: [behold, your God will come with vengeance, even God with a recompence;] he will come and save us [Isa. 35:4].) This last inscription has altered the biblical text to give it universal applicability: it ends not with 'save you,' as in the original, but with 'save us.'

After the pulpit comes the Trinity Chapel, the last nave chapel on the left side of the church. Despite the differences in style between the mostly Tuscan painters of the vaults and lateral panels and the Venetian altarpiece, the Trinity Chapel maintains the most closely interrelated iconographic scheme of the nave chapels. Bassano's canvas, *Holy Trinity Adored by Saints* (fig. 90), an extraordinarily crowded statement of heavenly glory, derives from a version of the same scene by his more famous father, Jacopo Bassano, in the Museo Civico di Bassano (ca. 1576), which shares its basic composition and many of the figures.[18] Originally painted for the church of the Ognissanti in Bassano, the canvas also shows signs of having been worked on by Francesco. Francesco Bassano planned to paint another version of the same scene for the Palazzo Ducale in Venice; that version, however, was to have been completely different in composition and format. The figures in the Gesù painting also relate to earlier figure types developed by Jacopo.

The Trinity is displayed at the very top of the painting, with Mary and John the Baptist flanking the three Persons on a slightly lower level. Directly at the feet of the Trinity are symbols of the evangelists, and below them are figures from the Old Testament, such as David, Moses, and Noah, who foretold Christ's coming. In a cluster below them at the centre are the twelve apostles with the cross, with Peter and Paul at the front. The apostles are flanked on the left by female martyrs and on the right by male martyrs, among them Catherine of Alexandria and Lawrence. On the lowest level, at the eye level of the viewer, are ecclesiastical saints, including Francis of Assisi, flanked by other churchmen and by kings. The figures of St Catherine and of the two male saints at the bottom on the left were taken from Jacopo Bassano's version, but there are significant differences between the two paintings that suggest the Jesuits maintained close control over the iconography. Jacopo's picture features the Glory of Christ instead of the Trinity and does not include the apostles or as many of the martyrs, and it lacks the St Francis figure at the bottom and has a different group of ecclesiastics. The Jesuits evidently asked Francesco to include more references to their missionary apostolate using depictions of the apostles and martyrs.

Another model for Bassano's canvas is the *Trinity*, better known as the 'Gloria,' by Titian, painted around 1551–4 for Charles V of Spain.[19] The basic arrangement of the Bassano picture is based on Titian's model, although Titian's version is emptier in the middle and has fewer figures. Titian's picture also includes nudes, unlike Bassano's, which focuses instead on the clothing as a way of differentiating the figures. The Trinity group itself is close to Titian's, except that the Son and the Father share a large orb rather than each holding one, and their heads are slightly lowered. The painting has the obscure tones that Francesco made something of a specialty; he frequently painted night scenes, such as *Agony in the Garden* in the Williams College Museum of Art.[20] This murky sobriety was popularized in Venetian painting by Tintoretto (1519–94). The brushwork is typically heavy, but it is offset with bright highlights, which shed an almost eerie light over Bassano's rich greens, golds, pinks, and purples.

Émile Mâle was the first to note the close relationship of the other paintings in the chapel to the Trinity theme stated in the altarpiece, even though at first they appear not to have much to do with it.[21] The vault painting, *Creation* (fig. 91), represents the work not just of God the Father but of the entire Trinity. *Baptism of Christ* (fig. 92), on the right lateral wall, has the words of the Father written above it and includes the Holy Ghost above Christ's head. In *Transfiguration* (fig. 93), on the left lateral wall, the Father's voice again sounds out, proclaiming his son's divinity, and the luminous cloud stands for the Holy Ghost. The oval painting of the three angels in *Apparition of the Angels to Abraham*, on the right, is a clear reference to the Trinity, as is the triple Sanctus in *God the Father and Angels*, on the left. The theme is equally clear in the pendentive paintings, which feature triple angels holding inscriptions in cartouches. Incidentally, there are also cherubs and angel heads inside all four arch soffits and six full-length angels in the pilasters supporting the arches. Hibbard has also related the *Creation* scene to the First Principle and Foundation in the *Spiritual Exercises*, where the exercitant is told, 'Man is created to praise, reverence, and serve God our Lord, and by this means to save his soul. The other things on the face of the earth are created for man to help him in attaining the end for which he is created' (par. 23).[22] The passage goes on to say that we must therefore make ourselves indifferent to created things and the material world. Another reference to the *Exercises* is found in the dedication of the chapel itself, since the Trinity is the subject of the First Contemplation of the First Day of the Second Week.[23] This understanding of the created world as a means through which to discover God's glory has much in common with the underlying philosophy of the S. Vitale landscape paintings, as I discussed in chapter 5.

Since the Bassano altarpiece is quintessentially Venetian in style, with the solidity of the figures yielding to diffuse colour and light, there is less of a blending with the vault frescoes and lateral paintings in this chapel than in the Nativity Chapel. The tiny figures of the altarpiece, lost in the crowd and the vaporous half-darkness, also contrast sharply with the giant, bright figures of the dome and lateral panels. The only real similarity between the altarpiece and Fiammeri's vault is that both are crowded with figures and both use heavy shading. Fiammeri's *Creation* (fig. 91) preserves the perspective of Circignani's two ovals, with God the Father riding on a cloud in the centre and a glimpse of heaven above and of the earth below, although the figure of God the Father here is more monumental. The artist assimilates his composition to those in the other side-chapel tondos, most notably to Ciampelli's *Mary, Queen of Martyrs* in the St Andrew Chapel (fig. 98), in which the position and scale of the Virgin Mary almost match those of Fiammeri's God the Father. As one of the supervisors of the Gesù decorations, Fiammeri may in fact have determined the format and perspective of all the vaults. Angels play a crucial role here, both supporting God's cloud and encircling him like a garland, and their presence introduces angels as a second leitmotif for the chapel. In the lower level Fiammeri presents a diverse sampling of animals set in a rich glade surrounded by mountains, water, and trees – these probably painted by Pietro Fiamengho. This Eden is identified by a small pair of nude figures, Adam and Eve, depicted at the very moment of their fall, as Adam moves the apple toward his lips. There is no doubt about Fiammeri's authorship of at least the figures in this fresco, since their bulky bodies and large, bulging eyes, with outlined eyelids, are clearly in his style. The garland of angels, done in exactly the same perspective around a lunette figure of the Virgin Mary, appears also in a drawing by Fiammeri, now in the Uffizi, for a tondo fresco, and God's face closely resembles the face in another sketch he made of God the Father, also in the Uffizi.[24]

The lateral paintings are done in a much sparer style and have fewer ancillary figures, although the monumental scale of the protagonists is consistent with the God of Fiammeri's *Creation*. The effect is also more friezelike, with the figures evenly spaced out, primarily at the front of the picture plane. Both frescoes feature weighty figures with twisting, strongly foreshortened poses. The similarities end here, however, since Mastro Bernardino's figures are solider and more three-dimensional than Durante's; and his *Baptism of Christ* (fig. 92) is set against a rich landscape, with a dense oak forest attributed to Ferraù Fenzoni, while Durante Alberti's *Transfiguration* (fig. 93) minimizes landscape detail and sets the principal actors against a background of bright cloudbursts. Bernardino's also emphasizes the nude flesh of the central figures, while Durante stresses their heavy drapery. In fact, Durante seems to be re-creating the style of a Trecento fresco painting, with static, linear figures and plain background. His bright colours, now faded, have the clarity of hue and the balance of medieval frescoes. A Trecento example of the same scene that is strikingly close to Durante's Gesù fresco can be seen on the right side of the nave of the Collegiata at San Gimignano (ca. 1380) (fig. 94). Both *Transfigurations* have their protagonists evenly spaced out, with plain backgrounds accentuated by a burst of divine light, and both feature heavy, angular drapery. Bernardino's *Baptism of Christ* reiterates the angelic sub-theme of the chapel by means of the flanking angels, who hold towels at the ready for Christ after his baptism.

The lunette ovals, by Ventura Salimbeni, use a looser brush and have a generally lighter effect, with luminous colours inspired by Barocci – although here, too, they are darkened by grime – and with less substantial figures. The colouristic effects are seen especially in *Apparition of the Angels to Abraham*. Nevertheless, he makes concessions to other paintings in the chapel. His God the Father in *God the Father and Angels* closely follows Fiammeri's figure in the tondo, and the costume of the angels recalls that of Bernardino's and Fenzoni's angels below. Salimbeni's pendentive angels, here putti grouped in threes, ride on small globes each of which has three zodiacal signs representing the months of the year.

The Trinity Chapel is exceptionally rich in inscriptions, and all are closely related to its main theme. The pendentive inscriptions, divided appropriately into three words each, are names for the Trinity: UNUS VERUS BONUS / IMMUTABILIS AETERNUS IMMENSUS / PROVIDUS MISERICORS IUSTUS / POTENS SAPIENS AMATOR (One, True, Good / Unchangeable, Eternal, Boundless / Provider, Compassionate, Just / Powerful, Wise, Lover). In the lunette oval *God the Father and Angels* is another three-word inscription, SANCTUS, SANCTUS, SANCTUS (Holy, Holy, Holy), written backwards, the first words of the hymn of praise that follows the Preface at the celebration of the Eucharist. Over both lateral paintings are the words HIC EST FILIUS MEUS DILECTUS (This is my beloved Son), stressing the role of the Son over that of the other two Persons in the Trinity, an emphasis consistent with the dedication of the church. The cartouches in the piers contain a passage from Revelation 5:12: DIGNUS EST AGNUS QUI OCCISUS EST ACCIPERE VIRTUTEM ET DIVINITATEM ET SAPIENTIAM ET FORTITUDINEM ET HONOREM ET GLORIAM ET BENEDICTIONEM ([Saying with a loud voice,] Worthy is the Lamb that was slain to receive power, and riches, and wisdom, and strength, and honour, and glory, and blessing). The six angels on the piers to the right bear the inscription SANCTUS

DEUS / SANCTUS FORTIS / SANCTUS IMMORTALIS (Holy God, Holy Strength, Holy Immortal One), and the pairs of angels to the left repeat the words in Greek (ἅγιος ὁ θεός ἅγιος ισχυρός ἅγιος αθάνατος). As Hibbard points out, this is a quotation from the Improperia (Reproaches) of the Good Friday liturgy, and its appearance on both the right and the left side of the chapel reflects the antiphonal singing of the Reproaches, by two choirs, alternately in Latin and in Greek, during the Veneration of the Cross.[25] This set of reproofs, addressed to the Good Friday congregation by the crucified Christ, contrasts his compassion with the outrages he suffers at the hands of his people. The inscription here is one of only two in Greek in the Gesù; the other is in the sacristy. The inscription in the tondo, VERBO DOMINI COELI FIRMATI SUNT: ET SPIRITU ORIS EIUS OMNIS VIRTUS EORUM (By the word of the Lord were the heavens made: and all the host of them by the breath of his mouth) is Psalm 32:6; it was part of the mass sung on the Second Sunday after Easter.

The Nave Chapels: Right Side

The theme of missionary apostolate is expressed most clearly in the first chapel on the right, the St Andrew Chapel, also known as the Martyrs' Chapel, made famous once again by Émile Mâle, who saw it as the paradigm for the Jesuits' interest in martyrdom.[26] All the paintings in this chapel except the altarpiece are in fresco, and all were painted by Agostino Ciampelli in a self-consciously classicizing and Raphaelesque mode, with the solid figures and clarity of Santi di Tito. Here the theme uniting the scenes is not St Andrew but martyrdom, a leitmotif that makes the chapel fit closely into the iconography developed for the Novitiate and collegiate chapels. The altarpiece is *Martyrdom of St Andrew* and the vault fresco *Mary, Queen of Martyrs*; the lunettes are *Martyrdom of St Agnes* on the left and *Torture of St Lucy* on the right; and the lateral panels below are *Martyrdom of St Lawrence* on the left and *Martyrdom of St Stephen* on the right. The pendentives show the martyred bishops Sts Clement, Ignatius of Antioch, Cyprian, and Polycarp. The pilasters and soffit panels bear the figures of other martyrs – on the soffit, Sts Pancras, Celsus, Vitus, and Agapitus; on the left front pier, Sts Agatha and Lucy; on the right front pier, Sts Christina and Margaret; on the left back pier, St Cecilia; and on the right·back pier, St Anastasia – standing placidly with their palm branches. We meet many of these martyrs in other Jesuit cycles: Clement, Polycarp, Vitus, Margaret, Cecilia, Anastasia, Agatha, Lucy, and Christina all appear in the S. Stefano cycle; and Ignatius appears at both S. Stefano and S. Vitale. The relics of St Anastasia were housed at the Jesuit church of S. Saba; Ignatius, here as elsewhere, is used to stand in for Ignatius of Loyola; and Polycarp serves once again as a symbol for the war on heresy.

Ciampelli's *Martyrdom of St Andrew* (fig. 95) is unlike most images in Jesuit martyrdom cycles, including that at the high altar at S. Andrea al Quirinale, in that it depicts the moment just before the martyrdom rather than the martyrdom itself. In fact, there is a noticeable disjunction between the protagonist and his executioners, who appear not to be paying attention to the saint but to be existing in a world of their own. This disjointed quality, as well as the depiction of the principal figure as engaged in fervent prayer to God, transforms the picture from a narrative into a meditative image, or a version of what Pamela Askew, referring to a slightly different phenomenon in the sacred painting of Caravaggio, calls a 'double-drama based on a symbiosis of history and meditative prayer.'[27] In works such as *Cruci-fixion of St Peter* and *Conversion of St Paul*, Caravaggio suggests that the protagonist inhabits a world different from that of the secondary figures. His St Peter and St Paul enact their drama without looking at or touching the surrounding figures, and instead of actually witnessing the action the secondary figures seem to be reliving the event in their minds, looking inward to behold the action the viewer beholds in the foreground. Askew's comments on the executioners in Caravaggio's *Crucifixion of St Peter* are also apt for Ciampelli's *Martyrdom of St Andrew*. In her interpretation the executioners can be regarded as nothing more than present-day carpenters, who, while working on a construction project, are reminded of the crucifixion of Christ or of Peter: 'May one not ... suppose that summoned up in this builder's mind, in the course of his daily work, is the action of those who in the historical past raised the wooden beam on which St. Peter was crucified?'[28]

In Ciampelli's altarpiece the principal subject is not the martyrdom itself but Andrew's faith, expressed in his prayer, and his submission to God – a focus on reverence that echoes the focus of Circignani's *Holy Family* across the nave (fig. 87). Ciampelli's composition is very classical, with large figures placed close to the picture plane, and recalls his work at S. Vitale. Ciampelli uses colour metaphorically, to differentiate between the figures: he reserves the originally garish reds and blues for the executioners and the more modest browns and earth tones for the saint. The two flanking executioners, perhaps inspired by the Circignani motif at S. Stefano, here exhibit the powerful torsion and sculpted musculature that Ciampelli would use throughout the chapel and that herald his return to High Renaissance models.

A greater dramatic intensity characterizes the lateral panels and lunettes, which show narratives of violent martyrdom strikingly different from the meditation on martyrdom of the main altarpiece – and especially from Circignani's mechanized martyrdoms across the nave. The *Martyrdom of St Stephen* (fig. 96) on the right and *Martyrdom of St Lawrence* on the left return to the classicism of Raphael's tapestry cartoons, with a horizontal format, large and sculptural figures close to the picture plane, and a dynamism created by powerful torsion and windswept drapery. Ciampelli assembles his figures into meaningful, anchored groups, usually in the pyramidal form most favoured by High Renaissance artists. Only occasionally does he fall into a late Cinquecento capriciousness, such as in the trio of figures at the lower left of *Martyrdom of St Catherine* (fig. 97), who constitute a delightful but artificial play, with the three figures rotated around an axis – homage in reverse to Rosso Fiorentino's *Moses and the Daughters of Jethro* (1523–4), itself derived from Michelangelo's *Battle of Cascina* (1504–5). Even this group, however, has a believable three-dimensionality and is executed with great care and virtuosity.

The compositions are Ciampelli's own, although the St Stephen panel borrows the figure of the main lapidary from Circignani's fresco II at S. Stefano (fig. 39), and the St Lawrence panel adapts the basic positions of the main protagonists in fresco XVII (fig. 47). The action in the St Stephen scene moves forcefully from right to left, an appropriate direction given that the painting is on the right side of the chapel; it leads the eye toward the altar wall, which is the direction of Stephen's and the viewers' prayer. Correspondingly, the St Lawrence panel moves from left to right. Unlike in the S. Stefano series, here Ciampelli has shown divine redemption in the form of the Persons of the Trinity, who appear in the St Stephen panel in a cloudburst above Stephen's head. Their inclusion makes for a link with the Trinity Chapel, diagonally opposite, on the other side of the nave.

In his vault fresco *Mary, Queen of Martyrs* (fig. 98), Ciampelli breaks with the monumental style of the walls. Here he follows the perspective, general organization, and scale of the other vaults in the nave, presumably dictated by Fiammeri and standardized by Circignani; and he reverts somewhat to the lithe, elongated figures and complexity of Circignani's style, although his Madonna is more substantial than that in his compatriot's Pentecost vault. This tondo shows a general tendency, broken only in the Passion Chapel, to homogenize the vault paintings.

The inscriptions are located in the painted cartouches below the vault and below the lateral panels. The cartouches make a proclamation from Revelation 7:14 that, like the Jesuit martyrological cycles elsewhere in the city, emphasizes the christological basis of martyrdom: QUI VENERUNT EX MAGNA TRIBULATIONE LAVERUNT STOLAS SUAS AGNUS REGET ILLOS IN SANGUINE AGNI (These are they which came out of great tribulation, and have washed their robes, and made them white in the blood of the Lamb). Underneath the *Martyrdom of St Stephen* panel is a quotation from St Augustine's commentary on Psalm 57 – EFFUSUS EST MARTYRUM SANGUIS QUO EFFUSO TAMQUAM SEMINATA SEGES ECCLESIAE FERTILIUS PULLULAVIT (The blood of martyrs flows and from this flowing the sown field of the Church grows with more fertility) – and from St Gregory's *Moralium* (VIII:xii): MARYTRES TOLERANT SCISSURAS VULNERUM ET ALIIS PROFERUNT MEDICAMENTA SANITATIS (Martyrs endure tearing of wounds and give to others the medicine for health), the same passage that adorned Ciampelli's painting of the martyrdom of St Vitalis at S. Vitale (see chapter 5). Under *Martyrdom of St Lawrence* is inscribed another quotation from St Augustine, this time from his commentary on Psalm 118 – QUI PRO VITA VERITATEM DESERERE NOLVERUNT MORIENDO PRO VERITATE VIXERUNT (Whoever refuses to abandon truth in exchange for his life, by dying for the truth lives) – and a quotation from a sermon attributed to St Ambrose: SS MARTYRES ET SI VOCE TACENT VIRTUTE NOS EDOCENT ET SI LINGUAE SILENT MARTYRII PASSIONE PERSUADENT (And if the Holy Martyrs are silent in their voices they teach us by their virtue, and if their tongues are silent they persuade us by their suffering).

The Passion Chapel, the second chapel on the right side, makes the most revolutionary artistic statement of the entire Gesù. The subjects, however, are consistent with the closely integrated programs of the other five nave chapels. The dedication is to Christ's passion, and Pulzone's altarpiece, *Lamentation*, shows a meditative moment during the Passion. The narrative lateral canvases, *Christ Nailed to the Cross* and *Christ on the Road to Calvary*, depict other episodes in the Passion, and the vault tondo becomes an apotheosis of the cross and the instruments of the Passion. The lunettes are *Agony in the Garden* on the left and *The Taking of Christ* on the right. The pendentives display the Four Evangelists, who recorded the story of the Passion. The four inner pilasters are decorated with more meditative images of Christ during his passion: they are *The Mocking of Christ, Christ before Herod, Christ at the Column*, and *Ecce Homo*. The two entrance pilasters are divided into small panels at the top with narrative scenes, and larger iconic panels below. These larger panels are *David and Goliath* and a standing prophet on the right and *Judith and Holofernes* and a standing prophet on the left, all of which appear to be a later addition. The entire chapel becomes a Stations of the Cross, with most of the major scenes of Christ's passion depicted in an arrangement that allows the viewer to visit them in order, reciting prayers and meditating on each episode. The Stations of the Cross were popularized in the late Middle Ages by the Franciscans and were based on the devotional practice of pilgrims in the Holy Land.

More important, however, the iconography of this chapel relates to the Third Week in the *Spiritual Exercises*, devoted to the Passion. Although several scholars have noted the connection, the degree of integration with Ignatius's text has been insufficiently stressed.[29] In fact, the chapel is designed specifically as a guide for someone making the Third Week of the Exercises. To begin with, the lunettes represent both scenes depicted in the Second Contemplation of the First Day:

> Christ our Lord descended with the eleven disciples from Mt. Sion, where the supper was held, to the Valley of Josaphat. Eight of the disciples were left at a place in the valley, and the other three in a part of the garden. Then Jesus began His prayer, and His sweat became as drops of blood. Three times He prayed to His Father and went to rouse His disciples from sleep. After His enemies had fallen to the ground at His word, and Judas had given Him the kiss, after St. Peter had cut off the ear of Malchus, and Christ had healed it, Jesus was seized as a malefactor, and led down through the valley and again up the slope to the house of Annas [par. 201].[30]

The figures on the pilasters and the episodes on the lateral walls and altarpiece are all subjects of contemplation during the Second Day through the Sixth Day of the Third Week:

> Second Day: At midnight the contemplation will be on the events from the Garden to the house of Annas inclusive ... In the morning, from the house of Annas to the house of Caiphas inclusive ... Third Day: At midnight from the house of Caiphas to the house of Pilate inclusive ... In the morning from Pilate to Herod inclusive ... Fourth Day: At midnight, from Herod to Pilate ... using for this contemplation only the first half of what occurred in the house of Pilate, and afterwards in the morning, the remaining part ... Fifth Day: At midnight, from the House of Pilate to the Crucifixion ... and in the morning, from the raising of the cross to His death ... Sixth Day: At midnight from the taking down from the cross to the burial exclusive ... [par. 208].[31]

On the Seventh Day the exercitant reviews the entire Passion at midnight, and again in the morning, and is exhorted to contemplate the 'most Sacred Body of Christ' throughout the day. The exercitant could therefore look first at the lunettes and then at the four pilaster paintings, which provide images aiding contemplation on Ignatius's Second through Fourth Day; then at the narratives on the lateral walls, which lead to the nailing of Christ to the cross; and finally at the altarpiece, with its image that can be interpreted as either the deposition or the burial of Christ. The emphasis on Christ's body is stressed not only in the four pilaster images, where nothing but Christ's body is shown, but also in Pulzone's canvas, where his body is displayed to all at the moment when, in Ignatius's words, 'the most Sacred Body of Christ our Lord remained separated from the soul' (par. 208).[32]

Pulzone's *Lamentation* (fig. 99) shows the moment of Christ's removal from the cross by Joseph and Nicodemus before the eyes of his grieving mother, and corresponds to another passage in the *Exercises*: 'First Point. He was taken down from the cross by Joseph and Nicodemus in the presence of His sorrowful Mother. Second Point. The body was borne to the sepulcher, and anointed, and buried' (par. 298).[33] The connection with the *Exercises* is underscored by the presence of Nicodemus, who is mentioned only in the Gospel according to John, on which this passage in Ignatius's work is based. Nicodemus, incidentally, is also present in the depiction of this event in Nadal's *Evangelicae historiae imagines* (plate 132). In accordance with Ignatius's 'composition of place,' a call to the exercitant to imagine the physical setting of the scenes contemplated, Pulzone has placed the action in a verdant but generic landscape that encourages individual amplification. The figures are large and clearly defined, and close to the picture plane. Their restrained and conventional poses, soft sentimentality, careful integration, and balanced composition recall Raphael, whose *Entombment* (1507), while representing a different episode in the Passion story, conveys a similar sense of the sacramental presentation of the body.[34] This familiar High Renaissance classicism, together with the ahistorical costumes, is precisely the timeless quality described by Zeri's expression *arte senza tempo*. Pulzone's picture arrives at something akin to the visionary abstraction of Circignani's frescoes on the other side, but achieves it in a very different way, with compositional clarity and, especially, humanity and emotion.

Each of the principal figures in the *Lamentation* seems to react to the death in an individualized way and to appeal to the viewer to do so as well. Marcia Hall notes that Pulzone's picture 'demonstrates a becalmed grief, enacted by figures who show no awareness of being observed.'[35] Noteworthy is the figure of the Virgin, who is shown actively grieving but not in the swoon belonging to an earlier convention that post-Tridentine thought pinpointed as deviating from the New Testament narrative.[36] The prominent displaying of the body of Christ – Joseph of Arimathea actually tilts it so that it faces the spectator – is symbolic of the new importance of the Eucharist in post-Tridentine Catholicism. In fact, given its location over the altar, Christ's body here can be regarded as symbolically placed directly over the spot where the priest elevates the Sacred Host during the mass. The body also relates to the tabernacle below, in which is reserved the real presence of Christ. The represented body thus provides a contrast with the 'real' body.

The emotional pathos of Pulzone's picture may not be as overt as that in pictures by contemporaries such as Caravaggio, but neither does it deserve the comment made by Loren Partridge, who discards it as 'the basis of much saccharine religious art to this day, designed to evoke pious devotion in a maximum number of unsophisticated worshippers with minimal aesthetic means.'[37] There is, for example, a compelling sweetness in the Virgin's expression, and that expression, together with the ritualized gestures of the other figures, imbues the painting with the rhythmic cadence of a musical *lamentatio*. Instead of over-sentimentalizing the scene or overpowering us with emotion, Pulzone comforts us while remaining detached. His detachment, or abstraction, is highlighted by his use of cooler colours, especially in the landscape, which has none of the *sturm und drang* common in scenes of Golgotha, especially in Northern European painting. This tension between intensity of feeling and constraint is extremely poignant. In its classical harmony, descriptive realism, and appeal to the senses, Pulzone's work for the Gesù was a harbinger of the classicizing currents of Caravaggio and Annibale Carracci.

On the other hand, Celio's narrative paintings on the walls and vault (figs 100–2) have a 'violently asserted pathos' that contrasts sharply with Pulzone's serenity.[38] These visceral depictions of the cross, with their powerful foreshortening and forceful visual impact, bring to the Gesù a fervent mysticism in which forms dissolve and colour and light take over, a vision of earthly horror and divine vengeance that bears more than a passing resemblance to the work of William Blake (especially fig. 102). The paintings have none of the solidity and classicism of Ciampelli, nor the quiet devotion of Pulzone, and are dominated instead by a sweeping sense of movement. Fabrizio d'Amico refers to the figures as 'deboned,' since they hang like rag dolls and are borne aloft by an elemental fury that seems to derive from within.[39] There is an almost menacing quality, especially in the struggle between lights and darks and between the bright reds and blues that punctuate this predominantly bichromatic atmosphere. Celio's dynamism and chromatic interplay, especially in the tondo painting and *Agony in the Garden*, have prompted scholars to refer to his style variously as possessing 'extraordinary modernity' and as constructed 'more along eighteenth-century than sixteenth-century lines.'[40] The tondo of the Passion Chapel even breaks free of the model used in the other five chapels and replaces their harmonious symmetry with chaos. Instead of being lined up in choirs, the angels make a frenzied rush toward the centre of the scene, and the cross itself thrusts downward into the chapel like a dagger. A twisting movement energizes the fresco: the trio of angels holding the cross at the centre appear to be turning on an axis, since each one looks at the next and their drapery and hair follow the direction of their movement. This group evokes the Trinity, thereby linking the chapel with the Trinity Chapel on the opposite side. The scale of the figures, which are much larger than those in the other tondos, helps create the impression that the scene is bursting from its frame.

The lateral panels, while based on the same two scenes in Nadal's *Evangelicae historiae imagines*, give the episodes drama by sharpening the focus on the central figures, removing many of the secondary players, and cutting the background in half. Celio adds action also by introducing rearing horses not present in Nadal's series. Nevertheless, some of the figures from Nadal are quoted directly, such as the two flanking centurions seen from behind in *Christ on the Road to Calvary* (fig. 100); they are taken from Nadal's plate 125 (fig. 12) but clothed in a slightly different manner. A master of composition, Celio organizes the entire scene into the form of a cross saltire (the shape of an X) not unlike Circignani's organization in the *Crucifixion of St Peter* lunette in the Apostles' Chapel, but with infinitely more energy. The diagonal body of the Roman centurion on the left forms one arm, and the charging horse and the emphatic pointing gestures of the rider and his men form the second, leading our eyes to Christ's body, which forms the axis. We find the third arm of the cross when we follow Christ's right arm through the dog and the right foot of the centurion at the lower right, and the fourth when we follow the trajectory of Christ's gaze, past the group of women and horsemen at the upper right.

A similar, if less strict, geometry underlies *Christ Nailed to the Cross* on the opposite wall (fig. 101; see also fig. 13). In that painting Celio also introduces the instruments of the Passion, just above the doorway, thereby giving the scene both a narrative and a symbolic meaning. John Paoletti and Gary Radke have noted this dual function in the Christ figure itself: 'The dramatically lit body of Christ nailed to the cross is pushed forward and isolated at the center of the composition, becoming a devotional icon within the historical narrative.'[41] Like Ciampelli's paintings in the next chapel, Celio's retain traces of 'Maniera' devices, such as the graceful but artificial reaction of the soldier on the right in *Christ Nailed to the Cross*, and, in figure 100, the two centurions with their twisting torsos seen from behind. His figures, too, are stretched out of proportion and support small heads, but this only adds to their windswept movement. The violent passion of the lunette panels is heightened by dramatic details, such as in the lower right section of *The Taking of Christ*, where Peter cuts the ear off the servant of the high priest. Even the pendentive paintings seem to want to burst from their confines. In a manner that anticipates the Baroque, some of the evangelists focus their attention beyond the frame, looking intently toward the *Apotheosis of the Instruments of the Passion* above (fig. 102). Their massive bodies, twisted in an exaggerated torsion inspired by Michelangelo's Sistine prophets and sybils, add to the sense of restlessness in the chapel.

In striking contrast, the figures of Christ on the pilasters (fig. 103) recall the passive martyrs in Circignani's S. Stefano series. Quiet and still, they seem to have just emerged from the darkness that surrounds them and that is made even more intense by the darkness of the chapel itself. The colours are muted except in *Ecce Homo*, the red wounds and scarlet clothing of which provide a shocking reminder of Christ's blood. As Mâle points out, there is a hint of the Palaeochristian Revival in Christ's column, which replicates the form of the one, kept since 1223 at S. Prassede, that became the focus of Cardinal Alessandro de' Medici's attention during his restoration of the church in the late 1590s.[42] These images are mute icons and objects of contemplation, without backgrounds and ancillary figures. Maria Calì notes that their sombre simplicity recalls the Passion imagery of the early reformer of sacred painting Sebastiano del Piombo (fig. 3), although here it is reduced to an 'almost academic purism.'[43] The images allow exercitants or casual viewers to use their senses by imagining a setting for them in the manner of Ignatius's 'composition of place.' Ignatius writes concerning the Third Week of the Exercises, 'In the Passion it is proper to ask for sorrow with Christ in sorrow, anguish with Christ in anguish, tears and deep grief because of the great affliction Christ endures for me' (par. 203).[44] The inscriptions in the Passion Chapel all date from the nineteenth century, and consist of biblical passages related to the various scenes of the Passion.

The last of the nave chapels on the right is the Angels' Chapel, described by d'Amico as 'like an homage' to Federico Zuccaro, 'the prince of the reborn Academy [of St Luke].'[45] Painted entirely by Zuccaro, perhaps with the assistance of Ventura Salimbeni, the chapel contrasts sharply with the Passion Chapel. It features uniformly smaller figures and returns to a sunny elegance and stability, 'a level of sublime, rarefied formal brightness ... more than ever allied with the "reform" of Santi di Tito.'[46] The only exception is the altarpiece itself, *Seven Archangels in Adoration of the Trinity* (fig. 104), which was so heavily overpainted by Vincenzo Dandini that it now has the pale tonality and careless *chiaroscuro* of eighteenth-century painting. Dandini has especially ruined the delicacy of Zuccaro's faces, which here are clumsy and repetitive, though without destroying the Palaeochristian spirit of the subject evident in the iconic, archaizing figures. The painting shows seven archangels on their knees under an alpha-omega symbol in a triangle surrounded by a sunburst. The number seven has been retained from the cult of the apocryphal angels, although only the orthodox angel Michael has been given a symbol of his identity, the quotation QUIS UT DEUS? Ventura Salimbeni, Zuccaro's collaborator in this chapel, painted a version of this same image for the Duomo in Pisa (the third altar on the left) that has the seven archangels on their knees below an image of God the Father, but Salimbeni gives all the angels their symbols, including the four apocryphal ones we considered in chapter 2, the other six being a bouquet of flowers, lilies, a sword, a sword and scales, a fish and chalice, and a crown.

Elsewhere, the chapel glows with Zuccaro's bright colours, which harmonize with the brilliantly coloured marble revetments. In his vault fresco Zuccaro presents an apotheosis of the Virgin, *Triumph of Mary* (fig. 105), which combines her assumption and her coronation. The lateral panels are *Fall of the Rebel Angels* (fig. 107) on the right and *Angels Freeing Souls from Purgatory* (fig. 106) on the left. Thus, the three largest fresco panels in the chapel represent heaven, purgatory, and hell. The smaller panels deal with the angelic presence in the world of humankind. The lunettes above are, on the left, *An Angel Leads the Prodigal Son to His Father*, and, on the right, *Angels Bringing the Prayers of Mankind to God*. The pendentives are unusual in that they contain narrative scenes, here illustrating four Old Testament stories in which angels give some kind of help to people on earth: in *Habakkuk and the Angel* an angel leads Habakkuk to Daniel in the lions' den; in *Shadrak, Meshak, and Abednego in the Fiery Furnace* the three boys are comforted by an angel after being thrown into the fire by Nebuchadnezzar; in *Jacob's Ladder* Jacob dreams about a ladder to heaven that angels use to climb up and down; and in *Tobias and the Angel* Raphael helps Tobias find a cure for his father's blindess. In the main arch soffit Zuccaro painted three other Old Testament scenes featuring angels, *Lot Fleeing Sodom*, *The Healing of Tobit*, and *Destruction of Jericho*. The healing of Tobit, in which the Angel Raphael is associated with healing, is a subject we have encountered in Room Five of the Novitiate infirmary (see chapter 3). Four marble angels in attitudes of ecstasy are placed in the interior pilasters, and two stucco angels flank the window above the cornice.

This was not the first Jesuit chapel devoted to angels; S. Giovannino, the Jesuit church in Florence, had an Angels' Chapel in the mid-1580s (the first on the left). It was painted by Jacopo Ligozzi (1547–1626), a Veronese painter who was one of the main proponents of Santi di Tito's classicizing manner. Since it is a Florentine niche chapel and therefore much smaller than the side chapels in the Gesù, the S. Giovannino Angels' Chapel has only three main panels for paintings. The subjects depicted on the three panels were later repeated in versions at the Gesù, although the two sets of paintings are unalike in their composition: *Jacob's Ladder* on the left, *Fall of the Rebel Angels* on the right, and an altarpiece, *Seven Archangels*, without the names but with the symbols, as in Salimbeni's version at the Duomo in Pisa.

As noted in chapter 2, the Jesuits promoted the cult of angels as intermediaries between humankind and the divine; especially active were Robert Bellarmine, who wrote at length about angels, including them even in a discussion of the Prodigal Son, and Aloysius Gonzaga, who wrote a treatise on guardian angels, *Meditazione sopra gli angeli santi e particolarmente sopra gli angeli custodi* (Rome, 1606), describing how each person has an angel companion from before birth until after death.[47] Alessandro Zuccari and Kristina Fiore have recently shown that the subjects of the Angels' Chapel paintings correspond quite closely with Gonzaga's meditations.[48] A passage in the *Meditazione* is reminiscent of the ceiling vault: 'Consider, then, the marvellous order with which Divine Providence has arranged and organized these glorious spirits, as much toward their Creator as among themselves and toward the other creatures of this world ... This spiritual and invisible heaven, with the most marvellous and divine order, has in itself in the guise of so many clear stars so many varieties of angels ... through whom, as with so many planets, the Lord of the Universe sends to our earth the influences of their gifts and spiritual grace.'[49] Elsewhere he discusses the fall of the rebel angels, Jacob's ladder, Tobias and the angel, the healing of Tobit, and the angel who leads the Prodigal Son to his father, all of which subjects are depicted in the chapel. The remaining scenes in the Angels' Chapel are treated in another Jesuit treatise on angels, Francesco Albertino's *Trattato dell'angelo custode* (Rome, 1612), which is based on Gonzaga's work and considers Habakkuk and the angel, Lot fleeing Sodom, and the destruction of Jericho. Since Gonzaga had died only in 1591 (his book was posthumously published), just a couple of years before Zuccaro took over the chapel decoration, the Angels' Chapel can be interpreted on one level as reflecting homage to Aloysius Gonzaga.

The Jesuits also chose their artist well, since Federico Zuccaro was profoundly interested in angels himself, and discussed them in his own writings, especially their relation to art theory. As Kristina Fiore has revealed in a fascinating recent study, Zuccaro merged religious and professional imagery to present angels as beings who inspire artists, invisible muses who help artists visualize and give expression to the inner idea of their work. A Neoplatonic notion inspired by St Augustine and by a 1576 treatise on angels by the Florentine Giovanni Maria Tarsia, Zuccaro's concept of 'disegno angelico' (angelic design) appears in his *Idea dei pittori scultori ed architetti*:

God the Highest Artificer and Painter, created, devised, and ornamented this World ... but he also created, painted, and ornamented another world, spiritually in the mind of the Angel ... Now from these principles I argue that it is necessary that before the

> Angel understands entirely, he not only contemplates this intelligible world that he
> has in himself, and all the things represented by this kind – but further, in order that
> the operation be brought to completion, and perfection – that when he sees these
> things he forms in himself an Idol or Design of them, using which, and understanding
> which, he has cognition of it. I add that the Angel needs this Design not only in order
> to understand, for the reason given, but also in order to act, since he cannot act on that
> which is outside without first looking into the mind at the Design, so as to find out
> how much he should act. And since some of these spirits are delegated to men – and
> there is not a man who does not have an Angel for a guardian and defender; and
> others are sent for other reasons to Kingdoms, to Provinces, and to the City, as one
> reads in Holy Scripture in an infinite number of places – they take on bodies made in
> imitation of ours, though still gossamer, which makes men believe they are human
> bodies, as we read concerning the Angel Raphael who led Tobias ...[50]

In Zuccaro's theory angels possess an inner design (*disegno interno*) and an external design (*disegno externo*) that mirror those of humankind. In humans the former is based on intellectual capacities and the senses and helps fashion the latter, the action, or, in the case of an artist, the work of art. As we saw in chapter 2, the Aristotelian basis of this theory inspired the writings of Richeôme. Zuccaro's treatise moves beyond visual experience to explore the world of the spiritual illustration of ideas, a mystical world abstracted from concrete visual data. Its meditations are striking in a painter who was highly accomplished precisely in painting reality and nature, as his brilliant depictions of animals, plants, and landscapes attest. Zuccaro's conception of a spiritualized *disegno interno* would find its way into Gabriele Paleotti's *Discorso* and into Giovanni Battista Agucchi's *Tratatto della pittura* (1607–15).[51] Zuccaro's son, the Jesuit Orazio Zuccaro, also wrote a paean to the guardian angel in his 1628 *Idea de' concetti politici, morali e christiani di diversi celebri autori*, which emphasizes the religious aspect of angels rather than their function as artists' muses.[52]

Federico and his brother Taddeo had already painted several images featuring angels, such as Taddeo's *Angels' Pietà*, executed for Alessandro Farnese at Caprarola (1566), which shows the dead Christ held up by five angels with tapers. This altarpiece became extremely popular and was frequently copied; there were two versions by Federico himself. Alessandro Farnese, an advocate of angelic intercession, dedicated a room at Caprarola to the angels, the Sala degli Angeli, which was decorated by Jacopo Bertoja, Zuccaro's collaborator at the villa, in 1572. The most noteworthy angel painting was Federico Zuccaro's contribution to the monumental *Last Judgment* dome in the Duomo in Florence (1575–9), which Giorgio Vasari had left unfinished upon his death in 1574. This vast empyrean throngs with as many devils as angels.[53] Cristina Acidini Luchinat has recently shown that Zuccaro referred to his Florentine fresco in the Gesù paintings in his chromatic range and his use of skilful *quadratura*; on several occasions the artist directly quoted one or more of his earlier figures. A major difference, however, is that the Florence dome includes allusions to Dante's *Inferno*, a text with which Zuccaro was very familiar, having illustrated it while he was in Spain; these references are lacking in the Gesù version.[54] Luchinat proposes that this lacuna can be attributed partly to the Jesuits' disapproval of the structure of Dante's purgatory, though she gives no documentation to support her hypothesis. John W. O'Malley and I doubt that the Jesuits would have disapproved of Dante.[55]

The Jesuits may have been concerned with orthodoxy in this matter because they were great promoters of the doctrine of purgatory; Laínez and Bellarmine defended it against Protestant criticism with particular ardour. The Jesuits may have wanted to present a clean and simple vision of the doctrine accessible to all audiences.[56] Christine Göttler has suggested that the juxtaposition of *Fall of the Rebel Angels* with *Angels Freeing Souls from Purgatory* had a particularly anti-Protestant message, with the fallen angels serving as a metaphor for heresy and its falling away from the papacy.[57] Zuccaro's symmetrical arrangement in the former painting sharply contrasts the ugliness of the fallen with the beauty of the angels. The juxtaposition of the two paintings also evokes a point of theology discussed in St Augustine's *De doctrina christiana*, according to which God created humankind to take the place of Lucifer and his fallen angels after their expulsion. On the right, therefore, we see the angels hurled from heaven into the abyss below, while on the left we see human souls rising from that abyss into the clouds above. The unifying element is the angels, who deliver the punishment to their fellow angels on the right and assist in the salvation of humankind on the left.

The tondo vault painting, *Triumph of Mary* (fig. 105), follows the model of Circignani and Fiammeri in both its perspective and the scale of its figures. In the centre, above the figure of the Madonna, is the Trinity, which follows the iconography of Bassano's altarpiece in the Trinity Chapel (fig. 90). The Madonna is probably based on Ciampelli's slightly earlier figure in the vault of the St Andrew Chapel (fig. 98), which it reproduces in reverse with a slightly different headscarf. The golds and reds of the background, and the bright blue of the Virgin's dress and of some of the angels' garments, recall the colours of the Florence dome. A preparatory drawing for this fresco now in Ottawa shows that Zuccaro had originally intended to represent the Trinity in a less orthodox way as three adult men, an iconography that appeared in Flemish engravings in the 1570s and later enjoyed a long afterlife in places such as South America.[58] He had also meant some of the painted clouds to extend over the frame; the blurring of divisions thereby created would become mainstream only late in the seventeenth century, when it was adopted by artists such as Baciccio and Pozzo. Federico had painted a *Coronation of the Virgin* in the chapel at Caprarola, with which this work shares the golden background and the basic organization of the Trinity figures; but the Gesù version also shows the Assumption, and consequently the Madonna appears far below the Trinity, not yet having attained her heavenly throne.

The left lateral panel (fig. 106), a statement of God's compassion, shows the Madonna acting on behalf of the souls burning in purgatory, who are comforted in their anguish by angels below. Christ presides over the painting in the upper middle, and below him two angels present him with two small humuncula representing souls. Luchinat has noted that Zuccaro borrowed his angel figures from the Florence dome, and that the Christ here also resembles the Christ in that earlier work.[59] The colours of the angels' garments make a self-conscious reference to Michelangelo's *cangiantismo*, running the gamut from blue to yellow, from green to white, and from blue to rose. Similar colour schemes were used in the Florence dome. Émile Mâle has pointed out that Zuccaro's painting is one of the oldest autonomous representations of purgatory in art.[60]

There is far more action in the right panel, *Fall of the Rebel Angels* (fig. 107). Here Zuccaro has given us a more expansive scene, the figures in which seem to extend beyond the limits of the frame, tumbling from above and hurling into the depths below. He makes the most of his foreshortening skills, which had been used to such advantage in the hell section of the Florence dome, where people are thrown into the flames just above the drum of the dome. At the Gesù, Zuccaro creates the illusion that the scene is an open window in the chapel and that the figures are tumbling into the church. Zuccaro once again repeats some of the figures in his earlier work, including the male figure on the lower right, who appears in the Florence dome among the envious, where he is shown pulling the hair of a female nude. Notably absent from the Florence dome are the nudes, with their often frankly depicted genitalia; the devils, with their spotted skin and cat ears, are unique to the Gesù painting. The fall of the rebel angels was discussed in the Catechism of Peter Canisius (*Summa doctrinae christianae*, 1554), and Alessandro Zuccari has shown that Zuccaro's interpretation at the Gesù was inspired by one of the engravings in that book.[61] It presents the rebel angels as a symbol of pride, and along with Zuccaro's painting gives an impression like that of a snapshot, with the angels falling into the abyss below.

In the left lunette Zuccaro illustrates the notion, made popular in Canisius's Catechism, that the angels bring the prayers of humankind to God. The people below are meant to represent all walks of life; among them are a pope, a king and other nobles, women, and children. Luchinat has identified the praying male figure on the left and the woman below him as portraits of the donors Curzio Vittorio and Settima Delfini.[62] This unusual scene is also illustrated in the 1589 edition of Canisius's Catechism, and Alessandro Zuccari has noted that Zuccaro was inspired in his Gesù painting by that engraving as well as by the illustration *Communion of the Saints*.[63] Bellarmine also discussed this scene: 'The second office of the Angels is that of presenting to God the prayers of mortals and of confirming their intercesion.'[64]

The opposite lunette shows the Prodigal Son comforted by angels, another symbol of the forgiveness of God; like *Angels Freeing Souls from Purgatory*, it shows the angels helping contrite sinners to attain divine grace. The pigs are especially delightful in this painting, and demonstrate Zuccaro's extraordinarily keen eye for naturalism. The composition of the lunette recalls that of Celio's *Agony in the Garden* in the adjacent chapel. Of the pendentive paintings *Jacob's Ladder* is noteworthy in that it repeats a subject treated earlier by Jacopo Bertoja in the Stanza dei Sogni (Room of Dreams) at Caprarola (1569–71). Bertoja's version shares with Zuccaro's the wooded landscape in the background, but the composition is more vertical, and God the Father appears at the top to welcome the angels into heaven.[65]

A marvellous footnote to the decoration of this chapel, provided by Ottavio Navarola in his history of the Novitiate, indicates one of the ways in which the Jesuits expected the chapel decorations to operate.[66] He writes that a young nobleman by the name of Salvatore Spinelli was having a hard time deciding whether to join the Society of Jesus, the Capuchins, or the Theatines. The matter was settled when, one morning in 1605, Spinelli, who happened to be in the Angels' Chapel while attending mass, looked up at Zuccaro's panel *Fall of the Rebel Angels* and at the opposite scene of the souls in purgatory. The representation of hellfire and damnation in these 'frightening picures seen by him' persuaded the young man to join the Jesuits immediately, a miracle Navarola notes not without a certain smugness; he comments that Spinelli was 'helped by the example ... of these two images also ... to settle and come to a decision about the desires for an Eternal Life.'

There are four inscriptions under the dome in the Angels' Chapel. The first, over the altar, is based on Psalm 97: ADORATE EUM OMNES ANGELI EJUS (Adore him, all his angels). This quotation is from verse 7: 'Confounded be all they that serve graven images, that boast themselves of idols: worship him, all ye gods'; as Hibbard points out, it is unintentionally ironic since its message is iconoclastic and it originally adorned a painting with an apocryphal iconography (Pulzone's *Seven Archangels*).[67] Over the right wall is inscribed a free interpretation of Revelation: FUMUS INCENSORUM DE ORATIONIBUS ANGELI (The smoke of the incense of the prayers of the angels); it is derived from a passage that reads, 'And another angel came and stood at the altar, having a golden censer; and there was given unto him much incense, that he should offer it with the prayers of all saints upon the golden altar which was before the throne. And the smoke of the incense, which came with the prayers of the saints, ascended up before God out of the angel's hand' (Rev. 8:3–4). The inscription over the entrance arch is IN CONSPECTU ANGELORUM PSALLAM TIBI (Before the angels will I sing praise unto thee); it is adapted from Psalm 138:1, 'I will praise thee with my whole heart: before the gods will I sing praise unto thee.' Over the painting of the Prodigal Son is a reference to his story in Luke (15:7): GAUDIUM CORAM ANGELIS DEI SUPER UNO PECCATORE POENITENTIAM AGENTE (Joy will be in the presence of the angels of God over one sinner that repenteth); the inscription is based on a passage that reads, 'I say unto you, that likewise joy shall be in heaven over one sinner that repenteth, more than over ninety and nine just persons, which need no repentance.' No one has yet noted that the text of each of these inscriptions alters the original scripture to include the word 'angel' or 'angels.' This deliberate tampering with Sacred Scripture is unusual in the Gesù chapels and indicates the degree of the Jesuits' enthusiasm for the cult of angels.

The Apse and Crossing Area

The organization of the two round chapels flanking the apse is very different from that of the six nave chapels. Both the Chapel of the Madonna della Strada and the St Francis Chapel are approached via narrow corridors, themselves decorated. On the end opposite the corridors is a rectangular recess for the altar. There are also openings onto the choir, which are balanced on the opposite side of the chapel by another rectangular recess. Thus, although the main body of the chapels is round, the circular chapel is superimposed onto a cross form. The seven paintings on the walls are rectangular and of uniform size; they fit into panels in the wall, which is divided by eight engaged columns. Two of the panels fit into the side walls of the entrance corridor, four into the walls of the chapel, and one into the niche opposite the doorway to the choir. The altarpiece fits into the recess opposite the entrance and is flanked by columns and enclosed in an aedicule. The cupola, which is divided into eight panels by ribs corresponding to the engaged columns below, is adorned with gilded stuccoes and frescoes. The rest of the chapel interior is decorated with lavish coloured marbles (*breccia, mischio affricano, portasanta, giallo antico*) and gilding, with inscription panels in *affricano scuro* and gold lettering below the paintings. Few places in the early Gesù so closely resemble a jewel box or an extravagantly decorated reliquary; the resemblance is appropriate, since at least the Chapel of the Madonna della Strada was an important depository of relics.

The Chapel of the Madonna della Strada survives almost intact from the sixteenth century. The upper part of the altarpiece is the original fifteenth-century fresco *Madonna della Strada*, much overpainted in later centuries; it is set like a relic into the altar aedicule. The painting was itself a holy relic. It recalls the Italo-Byzantine Madonnas revered elsewhere in the city as part of the Palaeochristian Revival movement, especially the icon in the Borghese Chapel in S. Maria Maggiore, whose cult was promoted by Francis Borgia. The seven panels by Valeriano treat events in the Virgin's life. Running counter-clockwise from the right entrance panel, they are *Immaculate Conception, Birth of the Virgin, Presentation of the Virgin at the Temple, Marriage of the Virgin, Annunciation* (fig. 108), *Visitation,* and *Assumption of the Virgin* (fig. 109). Although the seven panels would have given the Jesuits an opportunity to present the Seven Sorrows or the Seven Joys of the Virgin, only three of the Seven Joys (four, if we include the altarpiece) and none of the Seven Sorrows appear here. The Jesuits were strong promoters of the cult of the Immaculate Conception, the iconography of which predated the Reformation but was renewed with great zeal by Catholics afterward.[68] Pozzo's frescoes in the ceiling show a choir of angels celebrating the Virgin's life from above. On either side of the altar are two seventeenth-century panels, *Assumption of the Virgin* and *Assumption of St Joseph.*

Valeriano, as is well known, has chosen a plain and generic style for these paintings, with large figures close to the picture plane, little emphasis on background, and repetitive poses and gestures. But any austerity in the composition of the paintings is offset entirely by their brilliant, jewel-like colours, which combine the artificial brightness of Florentine *cangiantismo* with Venetian surface and light effects. Golds, pinks, blues, and greens dominate in a way that seizes the attention of the visitor long before he or she enters the chapel. Each picture becomes a variation on a theme, a rhythmic restatement of a central principle, musical in spirit. The artist has removed supplementary figures and unnecessary props, thereby focusing attention on the scene at hand, and this reduction to essential elements, combined with the universal, muted emotions, gives the scenes a sense of timelessness and abstraction similar to that of Pulzone's *Lamentation* in the Passion Chapel (fig. 99), but much more of a human sense than that in Circignani's works. A meditative stillness, akin to that in Fra Angelico's cell frescoes in S. Marco in Florence, is especially evident in the *Assumption,* in which the scene is confined to the Virgin and angels, without reference to earth, to the Virgin's tomb, or to the grieving apostles. It is present also in the *Annunciation* (fig. 108), which presents only the Angel Gabriel and the Virgin, set against a smoky grey background that makes the Virgin look as though she is kneeling on a cloud. Valeriano's paintings are instilled with an infectious sweetness and emotional warmth that in spirit, if not in method, recall the affective style of Federico Barocci.

Scholars have recognized in these paintings a crucial moment in the development of sacred art, one they have associated with the piety and authoritarianism of the 'Counter-Reformation' and seen as the death knell of 'Mannerism' before painting was rescued by Annibale and Caravaggio. Federico Zeri was the first to advance this point of view, and it has been argued with special passion by Sydney Freedberg. Zeri, less negative than others, compared the idealism and populism of Valeriano's paintings with the Utopian social experiments of the Jesuit reductions in Paraguay (1609–1768):

> The paintings of the Cappella della Madonna della Strada constitute an act of great importance in the history of painting. With these seven paintings – in which the painter annulled the presence of his personality – painting touched for the first time a state of absolute anti-poeticalness and anti-emotiveness, an abstract immobility, in which every passion is spent, and which falls beyond the corrosive action of hourglasses, clocks, and points of the meridian. These seven panels are the exact parallel in the pictorial camp of the astonishing results the Society of Jesus began to realize at the end of the sixteenth century and during the course of the seventeenth: results gained by the triumph of a reasoning so perfect and brilliant as to mark the superimposition of Utopia on reality, as in the social experiments of the missions of Paraguay, which preceded by almost three centuries every other similar attempt.[69]

For Zeri, Valeriano's paintings in the Chapel of the Madonna della Strada were the first and clearest example of his *arte senza tempo* ('art without time'), imagery detached from the specificity of time or place and the cares of the temporal world. Zeri compared the figures to dolls, the 'levelling anonymity' of which combines an extraordinary number of visual sources, from the Quattrocento to Titian to Michelangelo, into 'the most binding, rich, and conscious example of that "regulated mixture" which Gilio invoked as the remedy to the crisis of sacred painting.'[70] The reference is to Giovanni Andrea Gilio da Fabriano, an art theorist of the post-Tridentine era whom we met in chapter 1. Gilio wrote in his *Degli errori dei pittori* (1564), a book dedicated to Alessandro Farnese, that religious painting should be more illustration than art, and should combine the most felicitous mixture of earlier and modern styles to produce one that elicits the maximum response of piety from the viewer. This mixture Zeri traces to a veritable bouquet of sources, including Spanish painting (Valeriano had recently returned from a sojourn in Spain when this chapel was painted), engravings, and High Renaissance masters,

> an incredibly vast repertoire of notes, cues, and themes: engravings of the Quattrocentro and Cinquecento, Michelangelo, Raphael, and Sebastiano del Piombo are next to reminiscences of the trip to Spain, with Morales, Yanez y Llanos, Navarrete

'el mudo,' with Pedro Machuca, whose *Virgin in Purgatory* presents a clear relationship with certain parts of the *Assumption*. And Pietro Perugino stands next to Garofalo and even to Bianchi Ferrari, Baccio Bandinelli, and Titian. But everything is reduced to a uniform discourse, without sudden changes or terribly violent stresses, which turns incessantly toward the pole of the impersonal or the anonymous, even though the painter, incapable of avoiding certain handwriting traits, cannot get to the heart of it completely.[71]

Maria Calì relates Valeriano's series to the devotional spirit that seized Florence at the end of the Quattrocento, during the ascendency of Savonarola. Although I do not agree with her implication that Valeriano's approach to painting is akin to Savonarola's authoritarianism, I find her comparison of Valeriano's style with that of Fra Bartolommeo and Fra Paolino of Pistoia quite compelling, and I believe that Valeriano's reference to those artists was explicit.[72]

Freedberg is much more caustic, and blames these paintings for all the faults of late Cinquecento painting.[73] As outlined in chapter 1, he cites these works as the beginning of the descent into 'slick, intentionally witless' imagery, which he calls 'Counter-Maniera,' and which he sees as ultimately the progenitor of the lithographed holy cards of the nineteenth century. For Freedberg the greatest transgression is that Valeriano's painting is directed toward a common audience, the exact opposite of the cultured, aristocratic viewers addressed by the high 'Maniera.' Freedberg traces Valeriano's sources past Michelangelo and Sebastiano del Piombo directly to Raphael, but for him this legacy is 'taken in an aspect in which a nineteenth-century Nazarene might see him [i.e., Raphael], and with a similar false assumption of sentiment and simplicity.'[74]

Whether we like his painting or not, Valeriano is undoubtedly a revolutionary. He is one of the first Italian painters of the Cinquecento to attempt to address a universal audience, a goal that for the most part had been ignored in artistic circles in Italy but had been achieved for some decades past in the art sent to the world missions. Valeriano may have learned from his experiences in Spain and Portugal, where much of this mission art was produced and exported, and, as I suggested in chapter 1, he probably produced paintings for the overseas missions himself.[75] D'Amico has commented that the popular appeal of Valeriano's paintings lay 'in the oils so rich in colour and in seduction, in moving outbursts, and in good feelings, which tell the story of a Virgin so much closer and more available to the world of the faithful ... with the intent of rendering it universally comprehensible.'[76] Even though theorists such as Gabriele Paleotti called for art that could be understood by different levels of society, few late Cinquecento painters actually attempted to produce it, and instead addressed specific audiences, primarily learned and aristocratic ones.[77] Even the Jesuits were guilty of this transgression; their collegiate frescoes were saturated with erudite and obscure references accessible only to a learned young Jesuit scholastic or his secular equivalent in the university. The universal accessibility pioneered by Valeriano's series would go on to inspire greater painters in the early years of the Baroque, when appealing to a diverse audience became one of the principal obsessions of the age. Valeriano also achieved a stylistic revolution, as Zeri pointed out. Zeri sees Valeriano's contribution to sacred painting as that of a leveller, who wove the eclectic threads of late Cinquecento painting and its antecedents into a uniform fabric. A unification of diverse elements also created early Baroque painting, with its combination of High Renaissance classicism, Venetian colour and texture, and fresh interest in naturalism. Valeriano's synthesis anticipated a stylistic solution that soon would mark a new chapter in the history of Italian painting.

The inscriptions below the paintings in the Chapel of the Madonna della Strada, in gold letters on large black panels, are equally simple, brief mottos that summarize the essence of the scene like the labels on emblems. They have nothing of the complexity and erudition found in the Novitiate, the collegiate chapels, or elsewhere in the Gesù. Under the *Immaculate Conception* are found words from the Song of Songs: TOTA PULCHRA ES, AMICA MEA, ET MACULA NON EST IN TE (Thou art all fair, my love; there is no spot in thee [Song of Sol. 4:7]). The *Birth of the Virgin* too is accompanied by words from the Song of Songs: QUAE EST ISTA QUAE PROGREDITUR QUASI AURORA CONSURGENS? (Who is she that cometh forth as the morning [Song of Sol. 6:10]). The *Presentation of the Virgin at the Temple* is summarized with a paraphrase of Psalm 45:14, a slightly longer version of the one in the church of S. Vitale above *Holy Virgin Martyrs*: ADDUCENTUR REGI VIRGINES POST EAM. ADDUCENTUR IN TEMPLUM REGIS (The virgins shall be brought to the king after her. They shall be brought into the temple of the King). Beneath the *Marriage of the Virgin* is an inscription concerning Christ's genealogy: DESPONSATA MATER JESU MARIA VIRO CUI NOMEN ERA JOSEPH DE DOMO DAVID (The mother of Jesus married a man whose name was Joseph, of the House of David). The *Annunciation* bears a quotation from Sacred Scripture: ECCE VIRGO CONCIPIET ET PARIET FILIUM ET VOCABITUR NOMEN EIUS EMMANUEL (Behold, a virgin shall be with child and bring forth a son; and they shall call his name Emmanuel [Matt. 1:23]). The next inscription, accompanying the *Visitation*, also quotes from the Gospels: UT AUDIVIT ELISABETH SALUTATIONEM MARIAE, EXULTAVIT INFANS IN UTERO EIUS (And it came to pass that, when Elizabeth heard the salutation of Mary, the infant leaped in her womb [Luke 1:41]). The *Assumption* carries the motto QUAE EST ISTA QUAE ASCENDIT DE DESERTO DELICIIS AFFLUENS? (Who is she that goeth up by the desert, as a pillar of smoke? [Song of Sol. 3:6]).

One point never considered in the scholarship is the impact of the location of these pictures within the Gesù. The simplicity of Valeriano's paintings and the brevity and clarity of their inscriptions lead me to suspect that this chapel was deliberately calibrated to address a more general audience than most of the others in the church. Since the devotion to the Madonna della Strada was a long-standing one, which predated the arrival of the Jesuits, the chapel may have had a more public function than did the rest of the church; it may have served as a neighbourhood shrine without a particularly Jesuit identity. It was also the repository of many of the church's holy relics. All seven of the panels hid relics housed in niches behind them, which were opened on special occasions to allow for veneration by the faithful.

The Jesuits' notion of 'public' art was different from that reflected in the major papal commissions of the period. Interiors such as Clement VIII's Lateran Transept, in the decoration of which some of the Gesù artists participated, are directed toward an elite audience, of statesmen, nobles, and churchmen who would understand their complex proclamations of papal authority in the temporal and spiritual worlds.[78] The Jesuits were both able and willing to address such an audience when necessary, as witness the obscure theological references in the Angels' Chapel or the Gregorian pomp of the Collegio Romano. But the Society was also committed to addressing the very people who were the focus of their ministries in the city of Rome – 'children and unlettered persons,' beggars and prostitutes, peasants and even infidels – a commitment that gave the early Jesuits the sense that they had a unique role in the world.[79] The fine adjustment of style and subject matter to a general audience found in the Chapel of the Madonna della Strada can also be seen in the opposite chapel, dedicated to St Francis.

The St Francis Chapel is also remarkably intact, especially given the change of dedication in the nineteenth century. Although the altarpiece is no longer in place, a triptych survives in the sacristy, *St Francis Receiving the Stigmata*, the most likely choice for the altar since it emphasized Francis's connection with Christ.[80] This central panel is flanked by the figures of St Clare and St Elizabeth of Hungary, both Franciscan saints. The style and scale of the triptych panels make it clear that they were originally painted for the St Francis Chapel. The four wall panels and three wall canvases are by Heintz or Pepijn with landscapes by Brill, and show scenes from the life of the saint. In the small vestibule leading from the transept are *St Francis Returns His Clothes to His Father*, in which the saint renounces the world, and *Death of St Francis* (fig. 111), in which he departs from the world. There is also a landscape fresco on the ceiling of the entrance, *Temptation of St Francis*, that appears to be by Brill alone. Its main figure, posed on a ledge, recalls St Clement in the S. Vitale fresco of his martyrdom (fig. 80). On the wall facing the tribune is *St Francis in Egypt*, showing him defending the faith before the sultan of Egypt; the painting makes a reference to missionary work and the battle against paganism. On the side walls are found smaller panels, *St Francis and the Wolf of Gubbio*, *St Francis Preaching to the Birds* (fig. 110), *St Francis Appearing to His Brothers*, and *St Francis Appearing to Brother Giovanni*; the first two stress the saint's affinity with all Creation, and the second two celebrate visions, a major interest in the post-Tridentine period.[81] Most of these scenes were common in traditional Francis cycles, such as the early fourteenth-century Giottesque series at Assisi and Giotto's own cycle in the Bardi Chapel at S. Croce in Florence (after 1305); but the more narrative scenes were rarer in the post-Tridentine period, when artists tended to focus on Francis's stigmata, ecstasy, and visions.[82]

The colours are more muted than in the corresponding chapel of the Madonna della Strada; browns and earth tones dominate, although *cangiante* reds, golds, and blues pierce through this sobriety in some of the paintings, especially in the scene in which Francis disrobes and in the scene before the sultan. Here, as in Ciampelli's *Martyrdom of St Andrew*, the earthier colours serve as a metaphor for the goodness of the friars and contrast with the brilliance of the worldly nobility and of the sultan and his court. The scene with the sultan is also full of imaginative Orientalist detail, including the Mamluk costumes of the Muslims and the elaborate tents, made of shimmering fabrics and crowned with crescents, in their encampment. The paintings in the St Francis Chapel also reveal the Northern propensity for detail, especially in their rich landscapes and delightful animals and birds (the birds in *St Francis Preaching to the Birds* are a masterpiece); the images are strikingly different from Valeriano's abstractions on the other side of the tribune.

Such a wholehearted embracing of Franciscan imagery would never have taken place after the 1622 canonizations of Ignatius and Xavier, especially as relations between the two orders became strained in the mission field in places such as China in the late sixteenth century.[83] At this period, however, the Jesuits felt an affinity with Francis's original charism, and also with his insistence on living a life in Christ, a point made especially clear in the painting *Death of St Francis* (fig. 111), in which the figure of Francis looks for all the world like that of Christ himself. Even here, however, there is a noticeable absence of imagery related to the Franciscan order; in particular the confirmation of the Franciscan Rule, a subject found in both the early fourteenth-century cycles, makes no appearance. The dedication of the chapel may have attracted the patron, Olimpia Orsini Cesi, who enjoyed close relations with the Capuchins.[84]

The dome is more complex than that of the Chapel of the Madonna della Strada, in that it has windows on the main axes at the base of the dome alternating with four depictions of the Doctors of the Church, above which there is a second tier of pictures, of angels standing over each of the Doctors. The Four Evangelists are painted over the windows. These subjects are somewhat generic, constituting a rare exception to the closely knit iconographic programs found in the other chapels. The angels, however, are there representing heavenly approbation on the ceiling, as elsewhere in the church, and their appearance supports the importance of angels throughout.

If the St Francis cycle paintings are indeed by Heintz, the Swiss painter reveals nothing of the style he would develop at Rudolf's court in Prague. These paintings are far removed from the elongated figures, sensuality, and lightness of his work in Prague such as *Venus and Adonis* (1603), or of his religious pictures such as *Adoration of the Shepherds* (1590).[85] His figures in the St Francis Chapel are stockier and earthier, and the sharp folds of their drapery have none of the calligraphic smoothness he would later employ in Bohemia. Like those in the Chapel of the Madonna della Strada, the pictures here show large figures placed close to the picture plane, although many of the scenes are set against a rich natural setting, by the master landscape painter Paul Brill. The most exceptional is *St Francis Preaching to the Birds* (fig. 110), in which a diverse crowd of birds of identifiable species line up in front of the saint. The St Francis Chapel has no inscriptions.

Nothing survives of the small chapel of SS. Abbondio and Abbondanzio, and we have no idea of the subjects of the paintings there, except that in one the saints are led before the tyrant, and in another the saints revive a dead man. Presumably their martyrdom ranked high in the cycle. From the entire crossing area only a single painting survives, the *Circumcision* by Girolamo Muziano (fig. 112), the great promoter of reform in sacred painting. This canvas, removed from the high altar in 1841 and now kept in the hallway next to the sacristy, has just been magnificently restored, so that once more it is dominated by the brilliant blues, turquoises, and greens that so long were muted with a grime that deceived scholars into speaking of its 'poverty of colour.'[86] Particularly stunning is the bright yellow cloak worn by the figure in the foreground. The composition is notably spacious, with a dramatic use of orthogonals and a monumental architectural setting and atmospheric landscape inspired by Venetian painting, and it is difficult not to agree with Ugo da Como that it is a 'grandissima e mirabile tavole.'[87] Still, it is a curious picture. Although Muziano was a champion of large figures positioned centrally and unambiguously, this painting is empty in the centre, and it lacks conviction and drama in its depiction of the central event (which is shown in the middle ground), especially when seen from a distance as it originally would have been seen (compare with figs 6, 34). A similar mood and composition can be seen in some of the other late works of Muziano, such as his representations of Sts Jerome and Romuald in S. Maria degli Angeli.[88] And despite the richness of the colours, the picture is dominated by a melancholy and a coldness, a mood also communicated by the poses of the distant and statuesque figures. Muziano hushes the emotions and drama of the scene, thereby reducing the narrative almost to a symbol or an emblem, in keeping with the abstracted devotion we have seen in the work of Pulzone, Valeriano, and even Circignani elsewhere in the church. This stillness is especially evident when we compare the painting to the one Muziano did for the Chiesa Nuova, the *Transfiguration*, in which the protagonist is centrally situated, the crowd below him is strictly symmetrical in its arrangement, and the figures are larger and more prominent in relation to the setting. It is not surprising that Muziano's *Circumcision* did not weather the taste of the nineteenth century.

Giovanni Baglione's altarpiece of the *Resurrection* did not last even that long. No longer extant, the giant painting was removed from the right transept in the 1670s, when the Jesuits replaced it with Carlo Maratta's *Death of St Francis Xavier*. But an oil bozzetto surviving in the Louvre demonstrates that Baglione planned a grandiose composition divided into heavenly and earthly realms, focusing on Christ at the top with his banner unfurled and flanked by an orchestra of angels (fig. 113). The most noteworthy feature of Baglione's project is the heavy tenebrism that makes the figures stand out starkly against the background, although the light source is inconsistent. Both the tenebrism and the monumental soldier figures dominating the lower half of the painting were inspired by Caravaggio's *Martyrdom of St Matthew* (1599–1600) in S. Luigi dei Francesi, and they provoked the Lombard painter and his followers to slander Baglione and the painting in a series of scatological verses and again during the ensuing trial for libel. Nevertheless, with its disproportionate, idealized figures the sketch gives no indication that Baglione intended to emulate Caravaggio's naturalism or the violence of his action.

Of Giovanni de' Vecchi's and Andrea Lilio d'Ancona's frescoes for the dome area, only glimpses of the drum and pendentives survive, in the Andrea Sacchi painting of the celebrations of the centenary of the Jesuit order (fig. 114) and in an engraving by Valérien Regnard recently published by Klaus Schwager.[89] De' Vecchi's pendentive Church Fathers are each shown sitting with a book in hand, and are each surrounded by three angels holding inscriptions on banderoles. The angel trios simultaneously revive both the angel theme and the theme of the Trinity, to which the two nave chapels closest to the crossing are dedicated. There is a hint of Barocci's ethereal colours and shimmering light in the drapery of the pendentive figures.

The Sacristy and the Tomb of Ignatius

The sacristy painting, Agostino Ciampelli's *Angels Adoring the Blessed Sacrament* (fig. 115), is another example of the Jesuits' adjustment of iconography to a particular audience. Just as the paintings in the Chapel of the Madonna della Strada were simplified to address a general audience, this painting, intended to be seen only by priests officiating at the church, gives pride of place to the figures of young Jesuit priests and, for a single painting, contains an extraordinary number of inscriptions, including one in Greek. The priests are shown at the bottom of the picture, together with young acolytes, who are participating in a mass at which a richly garbed priest in the centre presides. A few men, a woman, and two children sit behind them, representing their duty to the congregation. The exact centre of the scene is taken up by the chalice itself, set in a rich aedicule and behind an altar bearing the Jesuit monogram. Two choirs of angels flank this altar, and more angels, including musicians, glorify it from above. The prominence of the Jesuit figures, along with the angels who assist at the Eucharist, recalls the kind of imagery we encountered at the Novitiate of S. Andrea al Quirinale. The presence of the wine rather than the wafer emphasizes the blood of Christ, a theme raised by the *Circumcision*, Muziano's painting at the high altar.

At the top of the panel, angels carry a banderole with an inscription from Hebrews (12:22): ACCESSISTIS AD MULTORUM MILLIUM FREQUENTIAM ANGELORUM (Ye are come ... to the company of many thousands of angels). Aside from welcoming the reader into the Heavenly Jerusalem, this chapter of Hebrews also speaks of the Eucharist, in verse 24: 'And to Jesus the mediator of the new covenant, and to the blood of sprinkling, that speaketh better things than that of Abel.' At the top of the aedicule in a false cartouche is a motto referring to the Eucharist: VISCERA MISERICORDIAE (The flesh of mercy). Below the chalice another choir of angels holds a second banderole draping over the altar, which carries a song of praise for the bread of the Eucharist: LAUDEMUS COMMUNEM DOMINUM QUO COMMUNI PANE VIVIMUS (Let us praise the universal Lord through whose universal bread we live). The final inscription, at the bottom of the painting, is a Greek quotation from St John Chrysostom's twenty-fourth homily on 1 Corinthians 10:13, a sermon that devotes considerable attention to the Eucharist. The passage refers to the Eucharistic table, that is, the altar, and follows a stern warning that only famine and death result from neglecting the mystical supper: ʽυπόθεσις τῆς παρρησίας ʽη ʼελπίς ʽη σωτηρία τό φῶς ʽη ζωή (The foundation of our confidence, our hope, our salvation, our light, our life).

The last paintings to consider are the six illustrations of the life of Blessed Ignatius by Baccio Ciarpi and Andrea Commodi, which were painted around 1605–8 to adorn Ignatius's tomb in the left transept, and which are now housed in the Cappella Farnesiana in the Casa Professa.[90] They are *St Peter Appears to Ignatius in a Vision, Senator Marcantonio Trevisan Gives Hospitality to Ignatius under the Portico of S. Marco in Venice, Mass at Manresa, Apparition of the Madonna to Ignatius, Apparition of the Trinty to Ignatius at the Entrance to a Church,* and *Death of Ignatius* (fig. 116). The largest canvas is the one in which Peter appears to Ignatius during his convalescence. Adapted from Juan de Mesa's engraved series of Ignatius's life, these narrative scenes provide a Jesuit response to the Franciscan narratives in the St Francis Chapel and were the first painted series of Ignatius's life to appear in Rome. Some scenes are exact parallels: *Death of Ignatius,* for example, matches *Death of St Francis* (fig. 111), and the two scenes of visions correspond to the two apparitions of St Francis. But the Ignatius series differs sharply from its St Francis counterpart in costume and setting, since here the action takes place in the present. The scene in which the Trinity appears to Ignatius features a church facade that closely resembles that of SS. Annunziata or S. Andrea al Quirinale, and, even more, that of the nearby S. Caterina dei Funari (1564).

In a penetrating study of these paintings Papi has shown that two of them have political overtones.[91] The scene in which Ignatius is welcomed by Marcantonio Trevisan emphasizes the welcome given the first Jesuits by Venice at a time when, after 1606, they had been forced to leave the city owing to a dispute between Venice and the pope over jurisdiction. Papi has also pointed out that *Mass at Manresa* is set not in the historical church in Manresa but in the contemporary Gesù, and that it therefore stresses the contemporary mission of the Society of Jesus. The picture also includes what are most likely portraits of prominent individuals, including members of the Farnese family and Filippo Neri, in celebration of their association with the Jesuits and as a further legitimization of the order. The style of these two canvases, attributed to Commodi alone, demonstrates a keen eye for detail, and *Mass at Manresa* in particular expresses a Venetian-inspired pageantry and monumentality, especially in the soaring architectural elements and the rich tapestries and carpets. Speaking of Commodi's 'meccanismi oculari,' Papi suggests that the painter has feasted on the specific yet allowed the entire scene to blend together through his masterful use of light. He compares the picture to Commodi's *Consecration of the Church of SS. Salvatore* in the Duomo in Cortona, which has the same luminosity of colour, attention to detail, and interest in architecture and vestments.

The Legacy of the First Gesù Decorations

Like the building they adorned, the original painted cycles of the Gesù exerted a profound influence on sacred art in Rome, in Italy, and throughout the world for decades to come. This legacy was felt on two levels. On the one hand, individual paintings, known through engravings or visits to the church, inspired artists at a time when they were working out a clear, systematic approach to devotional imagery after the crisis of Trent. On the other, whole iconographic cycles were adopted, usually because they were associated with devotions especially promoted by the Society, such as the cult of angels, or because they related to Jesuit-inspired catechetical or liturgical practices. Even more influential was the treatment of space at the Gesù, which Hibbard was the first to recognize as anticipating a major preoccupation of Baroque interiors. In the Gesù chapels the vault frescoes and altarpiece are related spatially, so that, for instance, the angels in the vault of the Nativity Chapel seem to praise the Christ child in his manger in the altarpiece below, and the prophets in the pendentives also look down upon him, bearing appropriate quotations from scripture that foretell his coming. Hibbard traces this development in 'Baroque spatial involvement' to Baldassare Croce's paintings in the crypt of S. Susanna (ca. 1595) and then to Guido Reni's Cappella dell'Annunziata in the Quirinale (1610–12); from there, spatial relatedness became a standard aspect of Bernini's mature style, as seen, for example, at the new church of S. Andrea al Quirinale.[92]

Naturally, the legacy of the Gesù paintings was felt most strongly in Jesuit churches and in the churches of other religious orders and of confraternities. Particularly influential was the intimate relationship between imagery and devotional practices. Thus, as Jeffrey Chipps Smith has recently shown, Jesuit churches in German cities such as Neuburg an der Donau and Düsseldorf were adorned in the early seventeenth century with iconographic cycles based on the Litany of Loreto, associated with both the Jesuits and Peter Canisius; with structured litanies of the saints; and, toward the middle of the century, with the life of St Ignatius.[93] The Jesuit Michaelskirche in Munich (1583–97), the decorations of which are exactly contemporary with those of the Gesù and give similar emphasis to martyrdoms, used a conceptual framework based on the *Spiritual Exercises* that allowed the worshipper to use the church to guide him or her through a process of self-examination: 'A pilgrimage of discovery potentially leading to salvation ... gradually unfolds as one moves through the church. Art focuses prayer, especially mental prayer. As arranged here, the art offers a coherent framework for personal meditation. The individual controls his or her own pace and course. Just as the formal giving of the *Spiritual Exercises* took from one to four weeks, the artistic program is not designed to be absorbed in a single trip. It unfolds over time.'[94] What is uniquely Jesuit about these interiors in Germany is the episodic, structured presentation of imagery designed to lead the worshipper through a specific program of prayer.

Perhaps the most distinguished follower of the integrated kind of iconographic cycles begun in the Gesù was the Jesuit church in Antwerp, the original ceiling of which was painted by the young Peter Paul Rubens. As we saw in chapter 2, Rubens painted three altarpieces for the Jesuit church of SS. Trinità in Mantua under the patronage of the Gonzaga family (1604–5), canvases the themes of which repeat three of the subjects in the Trinity Chapel of the Gesù – *Adoration of the Trinity, Baptism of Christ*, and *Transfiguration*. The Jesuit church in Antwerp was one of the first churches dedicated to the new St Ignatius; it was constructed between 1615 and 1622, the year of the canonization (it is now dedicated to St Charles Borromeo).[95] Rubens executed two monumental changeable altarpieces for the church, *Miracles of St Ignatius of Loyola* and *Miracles of St Francis Xavier* (both 1615–17), as well as thirty-nine ceiling paintings of saints (including martyrdoms) and biblical subjects (1620–after 1623, destroyed by fire in 1718).

Recent work by Antien Knaap has shown that the original program of the Antwerp ceiling worked together with the altarpieces in a way that recalls the integrated spatial relationships of the paintings in the Roman Gesù chapels. According to Knaap, as the visitor proceeded through the church, he or she encountered both biblical, mostly christological, scenes and depictions of saints on the ceiling, and these culminated in the altarpieces showing the miracles of the recently canonized Jesuit saints; there was created, therefore, 'a visually structured spiritual hierarchy that reinforced the ties between the newly canonized Jesuit saints and the spiritual heritage of the Catholic church.'[96] Several of the ceiling paintings also had subjects that had been used in the Gesù, most notably the *Fall of the Rebel Angels* and the *Nativity*. Two of these panels, known through copies, reflect the influence of figures or compositions in the Gesù paintings. The *Fall of the Rebel Angels* adapts the figure at the lower left from Zuccaro's version in the Angels' Chapel; the strong foreshortening of the fallen angels, who seem to tumble into the viewer's space, may also have been inspired by the earlier chapel. Rubens may have looked at Zuccaro's dome in the Angels' Chapel when designing his *Coronation of the Virgin* panel, since both scenes combine the coronation of the Virgin with her assumption, although Rubens has integrated the figures in a much more compelling way.

Although such programs seem to have been especially popular in the North, Italian Jesuit churches also had thematic cycles of the kind introduced in the Roman Gesù. No systematic studies have yet dealt with the iconography of these early Jesuit churches in the peninsula, but a brief survey of early descriptions and recent works on their architecture reveals significant affinities with the Gesù. I have already noted that there was an Angels' Chapel in S. Giovannino in Florence that shared all its imagery with the Gesù chapel of the same name. S. Giovannino also had a Passion Chapel (across from the Angels' Chapel and focusing on Girolamo Macchietti's *Crucifixion*), a Nativity Chapel, and a Martyrs' Chapel (with an altarpiece of the *Martyrdom of St Catherine*).[97] As at the Gesù, the Martyrs' Chapel was directly across from one with an apostolic dedication, here to St Bartholomew, the patron saint of Ammannati, who paid for the chapel.

At Pellegrino Tibaldi's church of S. Fedele in Milan (nave built 1568/9–1595), where, as Stefano Della Torre and Richard Schofield have recently shown, the Jesuits maintained strict control over the iconography, the two side altars decorated in the sixteenth century were dedicated to the Coronation of the Virgin and the Transfiguration.[98] Not only were both these scenes featured in the Gesù, the former in the Angels' Chapel and the latter in the Trinity Chapel, but, as in Milan, they were featured in chapels immediately across from each other. In Milan both these altarpieces were accompanied by clusters of smaller paintings representing a diverse group of saints (the Transfiguration Chapel had Sts Michael, John the Baptist, Cecilia, and Catherine) and thereby resembling the images of 'All Saints' we have seen in various Jesuit foundations in Rome. Of the two side chapels added in the seventeenth century one was dedicated to the Passion and featured a *Lamentation* as its altarpiece, as in the Roman Gesù. Even the paintings themselves betray the influence of the Gesù versions. Giovanni Ambrogio Figino's canvas of the *Coronation of the Virgin* (1581–7) shares its nebulous background and sense of *arte senza tempo* with Valeriano's exactly contemporary paintings in the Chapel of the Madonna della Strada in the Gesù, and the position of the Virgin and treatment of God the Father are strikingly similar to those in Valeriano's *Annunciation* in that series. Camillo Procaccini's *Transfiguration* (before 1590) also shares its basic concept with the Gesù version, in having the same luminous cloud behind Christ, flanking apostles in similar positions, and a Christ using the same arm gestures.

Although the decoration of the Gesù in Perugia was begun in the first decade of the seventeenth century and so concentrates largely on Jesuit *beati*, the high altar featured a *Circumcision* (Durante Alberti, 1613), and there was also a heavy emphasis on angels around the crossing area, which had Rutilio Clemente's *Christ in Benediction among Angels* in the tribune, and in the chapel left of the crossing, which had an altarpiece *Francis Borgia Contemplating the Eucharist Borne by Angels, Aloysius Gonzaga with Angels*, and *Stanislas Kostka with Angels*.[99] On the right side of the nave was a painting *Francis Xavier Embracing a Cross Brought by an Angel* (1614), an iconography that played into the Jesuit interest in the cult of the guardian angel. The Jesuit church in Turin, SS. Martiri, which was also decorated in the first decades of the seventeenth century, appropriately had a Martyrs' Chapel, with a canvas of St Paul by Federico Zuccaro (1607) and narrative scenes of the life of Sts Paul and Stephen by his assistants, as well as an All Saints Chapel (ca. 1607) featuring Francis Xavier, Aloysius Gonzaga, and Sts Charles, Octavius (a patron martyr of the church), and Brigid.[100]

The impact of the Gesù decorations was felt not only in Jesuit churches. The vaults in the Gesù nave chapels, with their distinctive treatment of perspective and angelic imagery, inspired imitations beyond the Society, from two-dimensional treatments such as the altarpiece of the *Coronation of the Virgin* by the Faenza painter Bartolomeo Garminanti (active 1587–1621) to Cherubino Alberti's vault fresco of the *Triumph of the Cross* in the Aldobrandini Chapel in S. Maria sopra Minerva, the tomb chapel of Pope Clement VIII. Alberti's tondo is a simplified and more symmetrical version of the Celio-Fiammeri *Apotheosis of the Instruments of the Passion* in the Passion Chapel (fig. 102; see also fig. 120).[101] Stefania Macioce, the first to draw this connection, comments on the difference in style that nevertheless existed between the two: 'To the hot, *pastoso*, vibrant style of Celio ... is contrasted this neat, calligraphic, draughstmanlike [style] of Cherubino. For the dynamic vortex of Valeriano [*sic*], which exalts the dislocation of the angels grappling with the cross, almost using them to demonstrate the possibility of salvation, is substituted the rigorous elevating vision of Cherubino, in which the putti have abandoned the impassioned active role played by the angels painted by Celio, who seem almost to speak together of a communal piety.'[102] The intellectualizing style of Cherubino has drained all dynamism and emotion from Celio's model to create something more akin to an emblem. This abstraction brings the image closer to Circignani's and Pulzone's work in the Gesù, and is also more demonstrative of the stylistic changes generally at play at the end of the century.

Individual paintings in the Gesù also served as models. Often their legacy was felt in iconography, composition, and pose rather than in style. Federico Barocci used Valeriano's paintings in the Chapel of the Madonna della Strada as the departure point for a number of paintings, including the *Visitation* in the Chiesa Nuova (1586) and his *Assumption* in Urbino (before 1612) (fig. 117). A recent study by Dante Bernini has shown that although Barocci borrowed the settings, scale, and basic gestures of his figures from Valeriano's prototypes, he did not give them the stylistic anonymity the Jesuit artist aimed for in his desire to reach a universal audience.[103] Barocci, by contrast, always strove for a personal, more individual kind of devotion, using a style that contrasted sharply with that of Valeriano. Federico Zuccaro also responded to Valeriano's series, which he would have had ample time to see while executing his own paintings at the Gesù. In his *Assumption* in the Pucci Chapel at SS. Trinità dei Monti, begun by Taddeo Zuccaro but altered radically by Federico in the late 1580s (fig. 118), the upper part of Valeriano's *Madonna* (fig. 109) appears almost verbatim, borne aloft at the top by angels.[104] The inclusion of this Valeriano-inspired figure took place quite late in the execution of the picture, since she was not present in a 1571 version immortalized in an engraving by Cherubino Alberti; Zuccaro must have had access to Valeriano's drawings, since the actual painting was not completed until 1588. Valeriano's image of God the Father in *Immaculate Conception* reappears with a slight adjustment of gesture and drapery in Ferraù Fenzoni's *Conversion of St Paul with Sts Luke and Egidius* (1597–9), part of a six-canvas series he executed for the cathedral in Todi and now in the Museo Civico in that city.

But the most significant legacy of Valeriano's *Assumption* (fig. 109) is one that so far has escaped detection. In his monumental *Assumption* of 1601 for the Cerasi Chapel in S. Maria del Popolo (fig. 119), Annibale Carracci surely pays homage to the late Jesuit artist in the figure of his Madonna, which is very close in position, pose, scale, and expression to Valeriano's. Posner cites Raphael's Vatican *Transfiguration* as the primary model for Annibale's painting, and to that I would add Titian's *Assumption* of 1518; but Valeriano's *Assumption* is a much closer prototype than either of these, and must have served as a model for the Emilian artist. Valeriano's *arte senza tempo* may also have had an impact on the style of Annibale's panel. The painting marks an abrupt change in Annibale's style, toward a detachment that leads Donald Posner to refer to Annibale's Madonna as a 'frontal, quasi-hieratic image.'[105] Posner has attributed this 'cold, hyper-idealized' stylistic development to Annibale's confrontation in the same chapel with Caravaggio's dramatic hyper-realism, and Sydney Freedberg has identified the change as a return by Annibale to the style of his early work.[106] Although Annibale's picture dominates with an almost explosive bulk in the figures, which are very different from Valeriano's lithe protagonists, the mystical pietism of the expressions and poses surely took their cue from the Chapel of the Madonna della Strada.

8

Conclusion: A New Sacred Art for a New Era

By 1600 the Jesuits and their artists had offered Roman society a showcase of new approaches to sacred painting, one of the most extensive and diverse since the 1563 decree on painting at the Council of Trent. And as we have seen, these approaches were extremely influential in their day, especially during the last two decades of the sixteenth century and the first decade of the seventeenth, when they provided a paradigm for painters of religious pictures from Milan to Naples and beyond. Yet, as fate would have it, these exercises in devotional art were not destined to have a direct impact on the *style* of Roman painting in the early seventeenth century, since the artistic world was soon dominated by a school of Emilian painters who had achieved their own stylistic solutions largely independently of Rome or Florence, and who had the backing of influential intellectuals and patrons who were even capable of stifling the legacy of Caravaggio. These men were Annibale (1560–1609) and Agostino Carracci (1557–1602) and their followers Domenichino (1581–1641), Guido Reni (1575–1642), and Lanfranco (1582–1647), among others.

Nevertheless, the Jesuit painting cycles anticipated many of the developments that would coalesce into early Baroque painting, and their authors can justly be described as pioneers. Particularly crucial was these artists' recognition of the importance of affective art, of using emotions to address the viewer – even if that meant, in some circumstances, consciously withholding emotion for maximum effect. At the same time the Jesuit painting cycles in Rome had a direct impact on the *iconography* of seventeenth-century church interiors, and they were the first – at least in Rome – to make the decoration of the different walls and that of the ceiling interact, to create a spatial relationship that would be one of the salient characteristics of the High Baroque interior at the middle of the century. But the most important legacy of the first Jesuit painting cycles was their concern for audience. The Jesuits may have been the first patron in Rome to adjust the style and sumptuousness of their interior decorations to suit particular viewers, from the princely and ecclesiastical to the public at large, and to match specific functions and locations. This attention to the decorum of imagery according to function or location was quickly adopted by Sixtus V and made characteristic of papal commissions for the rest of the century, as has been explored by Alessandro Zuccari, Steven Ostrow, and Marcia Hall (see chapter 1). The Jesuits were also the first to attempt a style of painting that could appeal to all groups at once, demonstrating a concern for universality that reflected their commitment to education and their worldwide mission enterprise. The Jesuits were extraordinarily sensitive to audience response.

I must stress again that the Jesuits did not do this on their own. Whatever solutions they achieved in their painting cycles were as much the product of the artists as of the Society itself. Although the Jesuits maintained firm control over the iconographic program of their church and college interiors, they never told their artists how to paint. Even the Jesuit brother artists, such as Giovanni Battista Fiammeri, did not have stylistic blinkers imposed on them, as we can conclude from the diplomatic letter from Father General Acquaviva concerning the interior of S. Vitale, which tentatively suggests some changes but ultimately relies on Fiammeri's judgment. It is a testament to the Jesuits' *lack* of authoritarianism that their first painting cycles are so diverse and 'eclectic.' There can be no doubt that the Jesuits chose certain artists because their style pleased them, but these artists were allowed virtually free reign – stylistically, though not iconographically – once the contract was signed. Because the styles of the Jesuits' first painting cycles were entirely the invention of their painters, they give us valuable insight into the minds of their creators and the artistic climate of the time. In these Roman paintings we can see, gathered in one place, a broad spectrum of independent approaches to religious art made during this period of artistic soul-searching, a compendium of personal spiritual journeys. Although many of them share characteristics with the approaches and emphases of the *Spiritual Exercises* and other Jesuit tracts, the artists arrived at the affinities themselves, making the partnership between patron and artist all the more remarkable.

How can we summarize the reaction of the artists of the Gesù, the collegiate chapels, colleges, and the Novitiate to the new spiritual climate of Early Modern Catholicism? Although there was much variety in their work, their products also had many features in common. The artists who really do not belong with the rest are those, such as Hans von Aachen and Francesco Bassano, who were commissioned off site and made no attempt to fit in with their surroundings. Most painters who worked for the Jesuits, especially from the mid-1580s onward, tried to reduce the number of figures, or at least the complexity of the backgrounds and compositions, to create an art with a legible didactic message. Most of them also feature larger figures than were common in later Cinquecento painting. Even in Circignani's crowded martyrdoms of 1581–3, the scene usually focuses on only a handful of protagonists, who are depicted on a much larger scale than the rest. In addition, like so many reformist painters at the end of the century, most of them made great use of deep shading, or *chiaroscuro*, as a way of enhancing the drama of the scene and of adding the sense of solemnity that was considered appropriate in devotional imagery and that distinguished it from contemporary mainstream secular painting. Many of the artists, such as Zuccaro and Commodi, also showed great interest in a naturalistic use of light, as part of an attempt to return to visual veracity and spiritual truth.

Hand in hand with this use of light was the treatment of colour. Although they arrived at very different results from those of early Baroque painters, the artists of the Jesuits' painting cycles were unanimous in their recognition of the value of colour in enhancing a work's devotional or didactic function. Since most of the artists were Central Italian, with a preponderance of Tuscans, most of them used the brilliant and varied colours perfected in the Florentine High Renaissance. These hues give the paintings a visual delightfulness that catches the viewer's attention in accord with the Ciceronian oratorical principle *delectare, docere, movere* (to delight, to teach, to move). Colour was an especially effective means by which an altarpiece or fresco in a darkened side chapel could capture the attention of visitors passing through the nave and draw them inside. These Tuscan colour modes included above all the *cangiantismo* of Michelangelo, with its irridescent drapery effects, but also the naturalistic mode of Raphael, and, where there was influence from Barocci, the *sfumato* of Correggio and Leonardo.

Most of these characteristics had already been introduced in Italian painting before the Jesuits came on the scene, but others are unique to the Jesuit commissions. One of the most salient is the abstracted, visionary state, which, as we have seen, relates not only to meditative practices of the time but also to the *Exercises*. By altering the physical aspect of the figures and their gestures and expressions so that they appear to be somewhat removed from reality, the painter spirits us away from the cares of the physical world into an exalted state beyond it. The artists achieve this effect in a variety of ways. Circignani does so by exaggerating the proportions of his figures, so that they have the elongated, ethereal profiles of Gothic painting, and by depicting them with artificial gestures and expressions drained of emotion, so that even the greatest horrors of this world are given the quality of ritual actions performed in preparation for the attainment of salvation. The movements are more liturgical than narrative or real. This abstracted quality is enhanced by Circignani's bodies, which despite their twisting torsos carry no real weight, and instead seem to float in a mystical world separate from our own. That world itself is made as generic and non-specific as possible, so that, as in the *Spiritual Exercises'* 'composition of place,' the viewers can project themselves onto the scene and fill it with the creations of their own imaginations. Like all successful meditative art, it is an imagery inviting participation.

In the painting of Durante Alberti and Giovanni Battista Fiammeri and in some of Circignani's frescoes, this abstraction is achieved by self-conscious reference to Trecento and early Renaissance paintings, with their iconic stillness, brightness of colour, and purity of line. Like the 'restorations' of the Palaeochristian Revival movement, their works equate the devotional with the simplicity and immediacy of the art of the past. A similar motive prompted Federico Zuccaro to explore High Renaissance classicism, out of which he brought to his paintings something of Raphael's sense of idealized detachment. Muziano creates abstraction in his *Circumcision* through a sense of emotional emptiness and cool monumentality, emphasized by the frigid greens and blues of the landscape. This chill is pierced only – startlingly – by the infant Jesus' almost reproachful glance at the Madonna as his first blood is shed, a glance that sends a shudder through mother and viewer alike. Valeriano's 'art without time' shares this sense of disengagement with the work of the other painters, but he adds a modicum of emotion, an infectious sweetness – not enough to disturb the placidity of the image but sufficient to seize the attention and sympathy of the viewer. He achieves this effect especially through the warmth of his colours, which are dominated by golds and saturated reds, and through the tenderness and sentimentality of his facial expressions. The same can be said of Scipione Pulzone's hushed evocation of emotion, despite his use of cooler colours in paintings such as the *Lamentation*. In the marvellous landscapes at S. Vitale, perhaps by Brill or a close follower, the abstraction is achieved by an almost total stifling of the human element. Like Circignani's pictures but in an entirely different way, this series of frescoes depicts gruesome horrors with an ironic absence of horror, using the language of pastoral imagery to create a sense of divine peace and harmony.

But meditative abstraction was not the only technique used by the Jesuits' artists. Many of them made more powerful appeals to the emotions, in an approach that was becoming common in reformist circles but that was promoted early on by the Jesuits. At the opposite end of the spectrum from Circignani's abstraction are Gaspare Celio's paintings in the Passion Chapel, which is rent asunder by a whirlwind of elemental anger at Christ's torture and death. By reducing colour and making some of his figures almost transparent as they fuse with the background, Celio distils his scenes into an almost purely bichromatic battle between Good and Evil. Few Catholic viewers at the time would not be deeply moved to penitence by Celio's turbulent vision. But Celio is also able to create images of almost iconic serenity, such as his individual paintings of Christ, which are as removed and abstracted from the profane world and as drained of emotion as Circignani's images of martyrs. The Jesuits' artists used emotion to express anger and to bring viewers to a sense of sinfulness, but they also used it to instil in viewers a sense of purpose and mission. Agostino Ciampelli's almost confrontational scenes of martyrdom at S. Vitale, for example, together with the triumphal tribune painting by Andrea Commodi, quicken in their audience a sense of vengeance and duty and thereby exhort them to positive action.

The Jesuits and their artists also had an interest in landscape and geography that was prodigious for its time. In an age when the figure ruled and extensive landscapes in painting were seen as a Northern intrusion, the Jesuits painted the interiors of the Collegio Romano, S. Stefano, S. Tommaso, and S. Vitale with expansive natural settings, and in the last of these the decorations approached pure landscape painting – in which all expression is delegated to the trees, hills, and valleys. The emphasis on landscape, like everything else in the early painting commissions, is the product of collaboration. On the one hand were the Jesuits, for whom landscape and geography had been a crucial concern since the time of Ignatius, a deepening concern as they gained more experience of world geography in their overseas missions. On the other hand were the mostly Northern painters they hired to do the work, who brought to Rome the naturalistic traditions of their homelands.

I hope this book has shown that the Jesuits were greatly concerned with style. No one as keenly conscious as they of the value of the visual arts in meditation and liturgy could afford to ignore it. The Jesuits did not hire anyone; they hired painters who worked in a limited number of styles, and these styles approached sacred painting in ways that resonated with Jesuit spirituality. The Society was not content to express that spirituality through iconography alone, and to leave matters of aesthetics to the Oratorians. They were extraordinarily acquainted with the intellectual climate of the time and well apprised of the taste of the nobility and churchmen of Rome and of the critical reception of art. As a new order in an era of political turbulence, one continually having to raise funds and establish connections not only in Italy but around the world, the Jesuits recognized the importance of making a good impression. They were not naively content to hire their own brother artists and to ignore matters of quality and style at a time when art theory was the talk of the day and cardinal patrons and other orders were vying for the best painters for their own projects. And although the artists they chose have not found favour in present-day criticism, they were sought-after in their time and were remarkably representative of the various approaches to devotional painting. These artists and their Jesuit patrons demonstrated a consciousness of stylistic difference that was almost postmodern, as is evident in their sense of decorum according to location, and in the 'regulated mixture' created by combining references to the Early Christian, the Trecento, Fra Bartolommeo, a panoply of High Renaissance artists, and – yes – even courtly 'Maniera.'

This last word raises another matter I have discussed before but would like to return to. The painters of the Jesuits' Roman commissions borrowed from many earlier traditions, but we cannot describe the end product either as 'Maniera' or as 'Mannerist,' even if we are willing to accept the meaning of these terms in contemporary scholarship. Certainly 'Maniera' elements were there, such as Circignani's calligraphic way of drawing and the artificial grace of some of Ciampelli's secondary figures. But these features are merely quotations of vocabulary and do not represent a coherent language or integrated system. Gone is Smyth's relief-like style, the flat light, the courtly sense of caprice, the delight in difficulty and complexity, and the self-conscious exploitation of the strain between two and three dimensions, which are so much a part of that courtly, Florentine tradition. Much more fundamental in most of these artists' work are High Renaissance principles of unity and clarity, a taste for Early Christian and medieval iconography, and the sobriety of *chiaroscuro*. If these paintings are guilty of being eclectic, it is precisely this eclecticism that keeps them from being defined as true 'Maniera.'

Yet how were Jesuit paintings different from products of the reform of Annibale Carracci and his Emilian followers? Again, the difference had more to do with syntax than vocabulary. The Emilians quoted many of the same models that were quoted by their counterparts working on the Jesuit commissions. Moreover, they had a goal similar to that of several of the Gesù painters – to create an art that appealed directly to the spectator and presented a lucid, comprehensible message. Like many of the artists who worked for the Jesuits, the Emilian painters went back to High Renaissance models to solve their formal and compositional problems, and evoked the structural clarity, simplicity, and honesty of Raphael; and both schools tended toward larger figures and greater monumentality. They also demonstrated along with some of the Gesù painters an appreciation of Barocci and

Correggio, at first by flirting with their painterly colour effects and *sfumato* and finally by acknowledging the importance of their essential humanity and affective power. In fact Annibale and Ludovico Carracci's first contacts with Barocci's style date from about the same time that Ventura Salimbeni and his half-brother Francesco Vanni were adopting Barocci's style for the same reasons, the early 1580s, and were probably inspired by their Tuscan colleagues.[1] In addition, the Emilians and the Jesuit painters collaborated in reviving the study of nature and landscape, an enthusiasm that led Annibale and his followers, especially Domenichino, to have self-contained landscapes accepted as a legitimate genre of Italian painting in the early seventeenth century. Also of Northern origin, the enthusiasm for still-life and genre reverberated through the two camps, and both Annibale and Federico Zuccaro included illusionistic features and other details of everyday reality in their devotional scenes.

Despite the similar projectories of the Jesuit painters and Annibale's academy, the two groups arrived at different results. The Carracci and their followers fused the formal and compositional stability and emotional warmth with a *consistently* rational and natural treatment of light, in which hue was combined more logically with *chiaroscuro*. The combination was perfected later on, when the Emilian school borrowed the warm, glowing palette, the broken and textured brushstroke, and the harmonizing, atmospheric light effects of the Venetian painters, a model few of the Jesuits' painters explored. They also laid a new emphasis on life figure drawing, another element still absent from the work of most of the Jesuit painters, with their interest in mystical abstraction. The result was a style more prosaic and earthy. It was also more naturalistic, in light effects, colour, volume, gesture, and anatomy; it was less so in the faces, which retain the idealized features of their classical or High Renaissance models, and – especially in Annibale – the liquid, doelike eyes of Correggio.

Few deny that the Jesuits were iconographical pioneers. One of their most important contributions in iconography was in the martyrdom cycles, which exercised a profound influence on religious painting at the turn of the century. The Jesuits were also among the first in Rome to popularize the 'heavenly dome,' with its suggestion of apotheosis. Decades before Giovanni Lanfranco brought Correggio's prototypes of this form to Rome at S. Andrea della Valle (1627), Fiammeri and Circignani had caused the ceiling of every side chapel in the Gesù to be decorated with an illusionistic view of heaven, containing cloudbursts, angels, and divine light. Finally, as we have seen with reference to every commission discussed in this book, the Jesuits' complex iconographic schemes achieved a closer and more integrated relationship between art and meditation and liturgy than was achieved in the devotional schemes of most other religious patrons of the time.

Another iconographic feature that unified the work of the various artists of the Jesuit commissions was a spirit of triumphalism. Since long before Freedberg, scholars have characterized the devotional painting of the second half of the sixteenth century as dominated by a sombre pessimism, a dark mood that reflected the crisis in and anxiety of the Church during and after Trent, and that had its ultimate expression in the martyrdoms of Circignani at S. Stefano and S. Tommaso.[2] They have seen the Jesuits as one of the primary forces behind this sombreness. Francis Haskell even used early Jesuit art and architectural commissions as an austere foil for the more celebratory projects undertaken by the Society in the second half of the seventeenth century under Father General Giovanni Paolo Oliva.[3] Yet, as we have seen, Circignani's martyrdoms are not painted on the walls of these churches to inspire remorse or regret but to emphasize the legitimacy and glory of the Church; strongly victorious in tone, they echo the triumphal imagery of ancient Rome. The same goes for all the other paintings in the Roman Jesuit cycles. They are, above all, positive and celebratory. They reaffirm the papacy, Rome, and the example of Christ, but they also resurrect the legacy of humanism and of learning. Even the goriest tortures and executions are meant less as a lament and more as a battle cry.

Hand in hand with this triumphalist spirit comes a taste for visual opulence that is far from the austere, almost puritan inclinations scholars traditionally have assigned to the early Jesuits. The Society may not yet have had the means to encase every chapel in porphyry and lapis, but they covered every square inch with painting – including false marble and statuary of palatial pretensions – and, where they could afford it through outside patronage, they showed no hesitation in including enough coloured marbles, stucco work, and gilding to recall the most extravagant projects of Sixtus V or Clement VIII. Had they finished the Gesù by 1610, the interior would have looked something like the Sixtine or the Pauline Chapel at S. Maria Maggiore. This sumptuousness in their churches did not go against their commitment to austerity in their residences, and one need only read Richeôme's loving descriptions of Stanislas Kostka's tomb or Francis Xavier's clothing upon meeting the Japanese *daimyo* to realize the important role that visual richness played in Jesuit spirituality.[4]

The Jesuits' enthusiasm for sumptuous church interiors is governed by their profound commitment to the classical notion of decorum. Several of the treatise writers in the wake of Trent dealt with the importance of using style and imagery adapted to the location and function of a picture. The most famous promoter of this concept was Gilio, whose 1564 treatise dedicated to Alessandro Farnese revived the Horatian idea that the style of a painting should match its subject, location, dignity, and era, among other things.[5] He wrote, for example, that a scene of martyrdom or of the Passion should be terrifying, so as to evoke an appropriate horror in the viewer, whereas a joyful scene such as the Nativity should display beauty, elegance, and grace. Similarly, quoting directly from Horace, Gilio wrote that sacred art should be different from profane, and private from public. Although scholars have tended to overestimate the immediate impact on the practice of painting of treatises such as Gilio's, there can be no doubt that when designing their Roman painting cycles the Jesuits were clearly motivated by a sense of decorum similar to that promoted by Gilio.

Thus, with Gilio, the Jesuits encouraged their artists to be unstinting in their depiction of the horrors of martyrdom at S. Stefano and S. Tommaso, and equally unstinting in their depiction of the beatific grace associated with the Virgin Mary in the Chapel of the Madonna della Strada. Their concern with location and audience also led them to keep their orthodox imagery, especially that equating uncanonized Jesuits with saints, inside their Novitiate, and to place the more complex imagery, along with its erudite inscriptions, in the Novitiate, the colleges, and the collegiate churches, where a learned audience would be guaranteed. Themes having to do with the duties of priests and missionaries were placed where they would be seen by novices and seminarians. More public art, such as that at the Collegio Romano, adorned the places that would be visited by the greatest variety of people. The ethnic origin of the audience was sometimes kept in mind, as at S. Tommaso, where the frescoes deal specifically with English and Welsh martyrdom. At S. Vitale geographical breadth is emphasized in the settings of the scenes, in an acknowledgment of the multi-ethnic congregation. This subtle appreciation of differences in audience is found even within the same building, so that the iconography in the Gesù sacristy or inside the altar balustrade at S. Stefano addresses ecclesiastics while that in the more public parts of the church appeals to a general audience. It is a testament to the resilience of the Jesuits' program that the iconographic schemes of these various foundations were able to maintain thematic unity in the face of such a variety of audiences.

The first generation of Jesuit art enjoyed its most direct legacy in the Society's own paintings, sculptures, and stuccoes during the next century, a legacy built on the iconographies and characteristics we have looked at. Scholars have tended to overstress the difference between Jesuit interiors of the later seventeenth century and their late sixteenth-century predecessors, seeing in the later works an example of an increasing superficiality and interest in mundane things. According to Rudolf Wittkower, 'In the course of the seventeenth century the Order of the Jesuits itself went through a characteristic metamorphosis ... Mundane interests in wealth, luxury, and political intrigue, and a frivolity in the interpretation of the vows replaced the original zealous and austere spirit of the Order.'[6] Certainly, the early Jesuit commissions have nothing comparable to the lavishness of the St Ignatius altar of Andrea Pozzo (1696–9), with its coloured marbles, lapis, silver, and gilt bronze ornament, or of Pozzo's interior at the Jesuits' new church of S. Ignazio (1691–4). The Jesuits could afford more in later years and placed their wealth in precious materials and sculpture, elements less obvious in the original decorations of the Gesù and other foundations. Yet the impulse toward sumptuous interior decoration was there from the beginning – after all, the nave and tribune of the Gesù were not left bare because the Society wanted them that way. The spirit of the original Gesù decorations did not differ significantly from that of its late Baroque vaults and embellishments.

We can even trace the idea of illusionistic ceiling paintings to the early Gesù. Baciccio's ceiling fresco the *Triumph of the Name of Jesus* (1674–9), showing the Jesuit monogram surrounded by a blast of divine light and churning clouds and angels, can be seen as the ultimate expression of the heavenly tondo vaults of the late sixteenth-century side chapels. Even Baciccio's device of having the painting spill out of the frame was anticipated by Federico Zuccaro's sketch for the Angels' Chapel tondo, although in the end he chose not to use it. This fascination with illusionistic domes and ceilings became something of a Jesuit cliché toward the end of the seventeenth century, and found its greatest promoter in Andrea Pozzo, who painted perspective ceilings and false domes for S. Ignazio and churches elsewhere in Italy and Austria. In Northern Europe, from Bavaria and the Tyrol to Switzerland, Pozzo's creations lived on through the end of the eighteenth century.

Another link between the first and the second generation of Jesuit painting was the importance given to exotica, especially in images relating to the Jesuits' overseas missions and to the life of St Francis Xavier. Again, the crowning example is a ceiling painting, Pozzo's *Allegory of the Missionary Work of the Society of Jesus*, at S. Ignazio. Other key examples are Carlo Maratti's *Death of St Francis Xavier* and Anthony Van Dyck's *St Francis Xavier before Otomo Sorin, Daimyo of Bungo* (ca. 1641). This Jesuit imagery, combined with the Jesuits' sponsorship of two Japanese embassies in 1585–90 and 1613–20, with the fundraising efforts of Nicholas Trigault on behalf of the China mission in the second decade of the seventeenth century, and with the Society's zealous advertising of the Paraguay reductions a few decades later, helped inspire a fashion for exotica in painting throughout Baroque Europe.[7] Similarly, the 'Baroque spatial involvement' to which I have frequently referred found one of its most influenial expressions in Bernini's new church for S. Andrea al Quirinale (1658–70), the paintings, sculpture, and architecture of which join forces in a three-dimensional performance reminiscent not only of the Gesù side chapels but of the Novitiate rooms in the same complex.

Two final types of imagery present in the first Jesuit painting cycles that would come to their full flowering in the Jesuit art commissions of the seventeenth century were emblematica and the iconography of Jesuit saints. Jesuit emblem books by people such as Jeremias Drexel, Henricus Engelgrave, Jacques Callot, Jan David, and Antoine Sucquet proliferated in the early years of the century, especially in the North of Europe, and found their most influential expression in the volume published by the Jesuits in celebration of their first centenary, *Imago primi saeculi Societatis Jesu* (Antwerp, 1640); its extensive series of erudite emblems was used as a copybook by artists throughout the world.[8] Although the Jesuit painting cycles were inspired by emblem books and not vice versa, they offer one of the first examples of emblematica used in interior decoration and were themselves highly influential. The emblematic treatment of the living patients in the Novitiate infirmary represents an especially creative interpretation of the idea.

Although pre-1622 painting cycles could include no Jesuit saints, the omnipresence of Ignatius, Francis Xavier, and various Jesuit martyrs in the Novitiate and in S. Tommaso anticipated the iconography of Jesuit saints in the seventeenth and eighteenth centuries, which saw a revolution in Jesuit imagery that would change the standard Jesuit church interior forever. Beginning with Ignatius of Loyola and Francis Xavier in 1622 and later including Francis Borgia, Aloysius Gonzaga, and Stanislas Kostka, the iconography of Jesuit saints was fully developed in the later seventeenth century in the work of Carlo Maratta (1625–1713), Baciccio, Pozzo, Ciro Ferri, and others. The most extensive use of such imagery in a Roman interior was in the Corridoio delle Camerette di S. Ignazio, a delightfully illusionistic corridor outside the private rooms of Ignatius at the Casa Professa, by Giacomo Cortese and Andrea Pozzo, which features not only scenes from Ignatius's life but his posthumous miracles.[9]

The Jesuits did not invent the Baroque, nor did they create the reform movement in later Cinquecento religious painting. Yet neither would have been the same without them. Their greatest contribution to the two movements was their peculiar brand of programmatic and meditative interior decoration. Using the *Spiritual Exercises* as a model but not relying on it exclusively, the Jesuits created a tightly integrated network of imagery that extended throughout the city and addressed all walks of life, taking the visitor on a sequenced mystical pilgrimage from repentance to salvation. The Jesuits enhanced this devotional experience by harnessing emotion and meditative abstraction, and by drawing from a storehouse of pedagogical erudition in a fashion that championed the return of humanism and the primacy of the liberal arts, not to mention the importance of science and medicine. This irresistible blend of classical learning and spirituality appealed to prince and pauper, to cleric and student alike, and inspired imitations throughout the city and around the world for centuries to come. Like their more celebrated successors in the later seventeenth century, the Jesuits of the first fifty years used the visual arts to re-create a vision of the splendour of the Heavenly Jerusalem, that place given to humankind through the sacrifice of the Son, to whom the Church of the Gesù and the Society of Jesus are dedicated.

Notes

Abbreviations

ACGU	Archivio del Collegio Germanico-Ungarico, Rome
ARSI	Archivum Romanum Societatis Iesu, Rome
ASF	Archivio di Stato di Firenze
ASPar	Archivio di Stato di Parma
ASPer	Archivio di Stato di Perugia
ASR	Archivio di Stato di Roma
BAV	Biblioteca Apostolica Vaticana
BNR	Biblioteca Nazionale, Rome
VEC	Archives of the Venerable English College, Rome

1: Introduction

1 Federico Zeri used the term 'art without time' (*arte senza tempo*) to describe a style developed by the Jesuits in the first decorations of the Gesù. See Federico Zeri, *Pittura e controriforma* (repr. Vicenza, 1997).

2 The quotation is from Sydney Freedberg, *Painting in Italy, 1500–1600* (repr. New Haven, 1993), p. 14. For recent critiques of the notion of High Renaissance unity, see Alexander Nagel, *Michelangelo and the Reform of Art* (New York, 2000), p. 19; David Franklin, *Painting in Renaissance Florence* (New Haven and London, 2001), pp. 1–3.

3 The comment was made by the Baroque art critic Giovanni Pietro Bellori in his *Le vite de' pittori, scultori et architetti moderni* (Rome, 1672), pp. 19–20.

4 A very recent example, Marcia Hall's insightful volume on the Cinquecento, called *After Raphael* (Cambridge, 1999), devotes only the last of seven chapters to the period after 1580, with the preceding chapters giving the barest glimpse of the 1560s and 1570s.

5 Walter Friedländer's 'anti-Mannerism,' on the other hand, refers to early Baroque painting. For the origins of these labels, see Zeri, *Pittura e controriforma*, pp. 53–4; Freedberg, *Painting in Italy*, pp. 429, 499, 657ff; Craig Hugh Smyth, *Mannerism and Maniera* (Vienna, 1992), p. 34. Hall, whose *After Raphael* is the most lucid and subtle treatment of the subject to appear in years, succumbs to this vogue for labels, even adding to the list (pp. xiv–xv). See Caroline P. Murphy's review of Hall's book in *Catholic Historical Review* 86:2 (April 2000): 323–4.

6 Cristina Acidini Luchinat, *Taddeo e Federico Zuccari: Fratelli pittori del cinquecento*, 2 vols (Milan, 1998); Andrea Emiliani, *Federigo Barocci*, 2 vols (Bologna, 1985); Paola di Giammaria, *Girolamo Muziano* (Brescia, 1997); Simona Lecchini Giovannoni, *Alessandro Allori* (Torino, 1991).

7 Most books on patronage in the period 1560–1600 have appeared only in the last decade. They include Alessandro Zuccari, *Arte e committenza nella Roma di Caravaggio* (Torino, 1984); Stefania Macioce, *Undique splendent: Aspetti della pittura sacra nella Roma di Clemente VIII Aldobrandini* (Rome, 1990); Clare Robertson, *'Il Gran Cardinale': Alessandro Farnese, Patron of the Arts* (New Haven and London, 1992); Jack Freiburg, *The Lateran in 1600: Christian Concord in Counter-Reformation Rome* (Cambridge, 1995); Maria Luisa Madonna, ed., *Roma di Sisto V: Le arti e la cultura* (Rome, 1993); and Steven F. Ostrow, *Art and Spirituality in Counter-Reformation Rome: The Sistine and Pauline Chapels in S. Maria Maggiore* (Cambridge, 1996).

8 Gauvin Alexander Bailey, *Art on the Jesuit Missions in Asia and Latin America, 1540–1773* (Toronto and Buffalo, 1999).

9 John W. O'Malley, *The First Jesuits* (Cambridge, MA, 1993), p. 239; O'Malley, 'Introduction,' in *Ratio Studiorum: Jesuit Education, 1540–1773*, ed. John Atteberry and John Russell (Boston, 1999), pp. 7–11.

10 See John W. O'Malley, 'The Historiography of the Society of Jesus: Where Does It Stand Today?' pp. 3–37, and Gauvin Alexander Bailey, '"Le style jésuite n'existe pas": Jesuit Corporate Culture and the Visual Arts,' pp. 38–89, in John W. O'Malley et al., eds, *The Jesuits: Cultures, Sciences, and the Arts, 1540–1773* (Toronto and Buffalo, 1999). In this article I discuss the history of the notion of 'Jesuit style' and its place in the contemporary art historiography of the Society of Jesus. The quotation is from O'Malley, p. 8.

11 Freedberg, *Painting in Italy*, pp. 599–600.

12 Ibid., p. 486.

13 Rudolf Wittkower, 'Introduction,' in Rudolf Wittkower and Irma Jaffe, eds, *Baroque Art: The Jesuit Contribution* (New York, 1972), p. 8.

14 Francis Haskell, *Patrons and Painters* (New York, 1963), p. 68; Howard Hibbard, *Caravaggio* (New York, 1983), p. 146.

15 Maria Calì, *Da Michelangelo all'Escorial* (Torino, 1980), pp. 296–7. My translation.

16 Calì, *Da Michelangelo*, p. 295.

17 Wittkower, 'Introduction,' p. 8.

18 Pierre-Antoine Fabre, 'Les visions d'Ignace de Loyola dans la diffusion de l'art jésuite,' *MLN* 114 (1999): 822. On Ignatius and imagery, see also Ilse von zur Mühlen, 'Imaginibus honos – Ehre sei dem Bild: Die Jesuiten und die Bilderfrage,' in Reinhold Baumstark, *Rom in Bayern: Kunst und Spiritualität der ersten Jesuiten* (Munich, 1997), pp. 163–4.

19 The scholarship on the *Spiritual Exercises* is so extensive that it has become a veritable cottage industry. For an extensive bibliography of work in English on the *Exercises*, see Paul Begheyn and Kenneth Bogart, 'A Bibliography on St. Ignatius' Spiritual Exercises,' *Studies in the Spirituality of Jesuits* 2:33 (1991), and O'Malley, *The First Jesuits*, pp. 37–50. For an indispensable account of the way Early Modern Europeans used the *Exercises*, see Ignacio Iparraguirre, *Historia de la práctica de los Ejercicios Espirituales de San Ignacio de Loyola*, 3 vols (Rome, 1946–73). There has also been much scholarship on the impact of the *Exercises* on art, beginning with Walter Weibel's classic text, *Jesuitismus und Barockskulptur in Rom* (Strasbourg, 1909), which proposed a direct connection between

the *Exercises'* emphasis on the senses and the sculpture of Gianlorenzo Bernini. Other early works on the subject include Diego Angeli, *Sant'Ignazio di Loyola nella vita e nell'arte* (Lanciano, 1911); and Walter Sierp, *Das Exerzitienbuch des hl. Ignatius von Loyola* (Freiburg am Breslau, 1925). Recent work by Pierre-Antoine Fabre on the *Spiritual Exercises* and early Jesuit imagery has considerably refined our notion of Ignatius's conception of imagery and its relationship to the imagination. See Pierre-Antoine Fabre, 'Les "Exercises Spirituels" sont-ils illustrables?' in Luce Giard and Louis de Vaucelles, eds, *Les jésuites à l'âge baroque, 1540–1640* (Grenoble, 1996), pp. 197–212; Fabre, *Ignace de Loyola: Le lieu de l'image* (Paris, 1992); Fabre, 'Les visions d'Ignace de Loyola,' pp. 816–47. I would like to thank Pierre-Antoine Fabre for kindly providing me with these references and offprints. Heinrich Pfeiffer and Lydia Salviucci Insolera have studied an early series of illustrations published in the seventeenth century to accompany the *Exercises,* a more literal link between Ignatius's text and pictures: Heinrich Pfeiffer, 'Die ersten Illustrationen zum Exerzitienbuch,' in Michael Sievernich and Günther Switek, eds, *Ignatianisch: Eigenart und Methode der Gesellschaft Jesu* (Freiburg, Basel, and Vienna, 1990), pp. 120–30; Lydia Salviucci Insolera, 'Le illustrazioni per gli Esercizi Spirituali intorno al 1600,' *Archivum Historicum Societatis Iesu* 60:119 (January–June 1991): 160–217. For other recent work on imagery and the *Exercises,* see Josef Sudbrack, 'Die Anwendung der Sinne als Angelpunkt der Exerzitien,' in Sievernich and Switek, *Ignatianisch,* pp. 96–119; and Friedrich Polleross, 'Nuestro modo de proceder: Betrachtungen aus Anlass der Tagung "Die Jesuiten in Wien" vom 19. bis 21. Oktober 2000,' *Früh Neuzeit Info* 12:1 (2001): 103–8. I would like to thank Friedrich Polleross for sending me an offprint of this article. There is an exceptionally detailed and accessible discussion of the *Exercises* in Jeffrey Chipps Smith, *Sensuous Worship: Jesuits and the Art of the Early Catholic Reformation in Germany* (Princeton, 2002), pp. 25–36.

20 O'Malley, *The First Jesuits,* p. 4.

21 Ibid., p. 46. On the impact of the *Meditationes* on art, see John Shearman, *Only Connect: Art and the Spectator in the Italian Renaissance* (Princeton, 1992), p. 85.

22 For a thorough treatment of the application of the *Exercises* in the Early Modern period, see Iparraguirre, *Historia de la práctica de los Ejercicios.* See also O'Malley, *The First Jesuits,* pp. 127ff.

23 Insolera, 'Le illustrazioni per gli Esercizi Spirituali intorno al 1600.'

24 Maria Calì, *La pittura del cinquecento,* 2 vols (Torino, 2000), I, p. 218; Bailey, 'Le style jésuite,' pp. 42–3; Gauvin Alexander Bailey, 'The Jesuits and Painting in Italy,' in Franco Mormando, ed., *Saints and Sinners: Caravaggio and the Baroque Image* (Boston and Chicago, 1999), p. 153, Smith, *Sensuous Worship,* p. 33. On Caravaggio and Ignatius, see P. Francastel, 'Le réalisme de Caravage,' *Gazette des beaux-arts* 80 (1938): 57; Walter Friedländer, *Caravaggio Studies* (Princeton, 1955), pp. ix, 121–2; Richard Spear, *Caravaggio and His Followers* (Cleveland, 1971), pp. 5–6; Joseph F. Chorpenning, 'Another Look at Caravaggio and Religion,' *Artibus et historiae* 16 (1987): 149–58; Catherine Puglisi, *Caravaggio* (London, 1998), pp. 248–9. On Ignatius and Bernini, see Weibel, *Jesuitismus und Barockskulptur;* Irving Lavin, *Bernini and the Unity of the Visual Arts* (New York and London, 1980), p. 4 n3.

25 Ignatius of Loyola, *The Spiritual Exercises,* trans. and ed. Louis J. Puhl (Chicago, 1951), p. 52.

26 For Ignatius and imagery in general, see Fabre, *Ignace de Loyola*; Fabre, 'Les "Exercises Spirituels" sont-ils illustrables?'; and Fabre, 'Les visions d'Ignace de Loyola.' Fabre goes further, and writes that Ignatius's final goal was to obliterate all imagery from the imagination and purify the mind of its need for images. I am not convinced by this part of Fabre's hypothesis.

27 Quoted in Fabre, 'Les "Exercices Spirituels,"' p. 198.

28 Ignatius of Loyola, *Spiritual Exercises*, p. 158.

29 J. Waterworth, ed., *The Council of Trent: Canons and Decrees* (Chicago, 1848), p. 234.

30 Maj-Brit Wadell, *Evangelicae historiae imagines: Entstehungsgeschichte und Vorlagen* (Göteborg, 1985), p. 10; Fabre, 'Les "Exercises Spirituels,"' pp. 202–3.

31 O'Malley, *The First Jesuits*, p. 164; Fabre, 'Les "Exercises Spirituels,"' pp. 202–3.

32 See Steven Ostrow, *Art and Spirituality in Counter-Reformation Rome*, pp. 126–32; Bailey, *Art on the Jesuit Missions*, pp. 70–2.

33 See Hans Belting, *Likeness and Presence* (Chicago, 1994).

34 O'Malley, *The First Jesuits*, p. 164. See also Jerónimo Nadal, *Adnotationes et meditationes in evangelia*, 3 vols, trans. Frederick Homann, ed. Walter S. Melion (Philadelphia, 2002); Mühlen, 'Imaginibus honos,' pp. 164–5; Dietmar Spengler, 'Die Ars Jesuitica der Gebrüder Wierix,' *Wallraf-Richartz-Jahrbuch* 57 (1996): 161–94; William V. Bangert and Thomas M. McCoog, *Jerome Nadal, S.J., 1507–1580* (Chicago, 1992); Fabre, *Ignace de Loyola*; P. Rheinbay, *Biblische Bilder für der inneren Weg: Das Betrachtungsbuch des Ignatius-Gefährten Hieronymus Nadal (1507–1580)* (Engelsbach, 1995); Wadell, *Evangelicae*; Maj-Brit Wadell, 'The Evangelicae Historiae Imagines: The Designs and Their Artists,' *Quaerendo* 10 (1980): 279–91. On their influence outside Europe, see Bailey, *Art on the Jesuit Missions*, p. 93. On their influence in France, see Marie Mauquoy-Hendrickx, 'Les Wierix illustrateurs de la Bible dite de Natalis,' *Quaerendo* 6 (1976): 60–3. Walter S. Melion has done much recent work on Nadal's text and its audiences, such as in his paper '"In conspectum Hierusalem venit Jesus": Divine Spectacle and Spectatorship in Jerónimo Nadal's Annotations and Meditations on the Gospels,' delivered at the symposium 'Image of the Invisible God: Picturing Jesus Christ from the 8th to the 20th Century,' Metropolitan Museum of Art, New York, 9 March 2001.

35 See Fabre, *Ignace de Loyola*, 'Les "Exercises Spirituels,"' and 'Les visions d'Ignace de Loyola.'

36 Quoted in Fabre, 'Les "Exercises Spirituels,"' pp. 197–8.

37 Thomas Buser, 'Jerome Nadal and Early Jesuit Art in Rome,' *Art Bulletin* 58 (1976): 424–5; Wadell, *Evangelicae*, pp. 11–17.

38 Buser, 'Jerome Nadal,' p. 424. The technique had already been used in the Polyglot Bible printed by the Plantin Press of Antwerp between 1568 and 1572, which itself inspired fresco paintings such as those in the marvellous library at the Abbazia di S. Giovanni Evangelista in Parma, which were painted by Giovanni Antonio Paganino and Ercole Pio in the early 1570s.

39 These are listed in his will of 23 January 1611: '... frati meo ... restituatur imago, seu quadri Clementis 8' Pont. Max., nepoti meo Angelo detur imago seu quadri Roberti card. De Nobili, et unum ex duobus quadris S.ti Caroli Borromei, et una ex parvis crucibus, quas ad pectus gero cum reliquiis' (ASPar, Epistolario scelto, b. 25).

40 Polleross, 'Nuestro modo de proceder,' p. 104; Macioce, *Undique splendent*, p. 42; Valeria de Laurentiis, 'Immagini ed arte in Bellarmino,' in Romeo de Maio et al., eds, *Bellarmino e la Controriforma* (Sora, 1990), pp. 581–608; Paola Barocchi, 'Nota critica,' in

Trattati d'arte del cinquecento fra manierismo e controriforma, 2 vols (Bari, 1960–2), II, pp. 532–42.

41 Polleross, 'Nuestro modo de proceder,' p. 104; Christine Göttler, *Die Kunst des Fegefeuers nach der Reformation* (Mainz, 1996), pp. 310–11; Mühlen, 'Imaginibus honos,' p. 162; *Ratio Studiorum*, ed. Atteberry and Russell, p. 60.

42 Macioce, *Undique splendent*, pp. 49–54; John Patrick Donnelly, 'Antonio Possevino, S.J., as a Counter-Reformation Critic of the Arts,' *Journal of the Rocky Mountain Medieval and Renaissance Association* 3 (1982): 153–64; Paolo Prodi, 'Ricerche sulla teorica delle arti figurative nella riforma cattolica,' *Archivio italiano per la storia della pietà* 4 (1962): 123–88.

43 J.F. Moffit, 'A Christianization of Pagan Antiquity: Giovanni Andrea Gilio da Fabriano, Antonio Possevino, and the *Laocöon* of Domenico Theotocopoli El Greco,' *Paragone* 417 (November 1904): 44–60.

44 'Con questa sarà dato à V.S. ragguaglio d'un opera d'imagini et meditationi sopra gli evangelij di tutto l'anno fatta da un padre della Compagnia, chi contiene la vita e miracoli del Nostro Salvatore, cavata da i quattro evangelisti, la quale per essere la migliore et maggiore, che in questo genere d'imagini è uscita insino adesso, et per la utilità spirituale, che se ne spera, desideriamo che sia intagliata da' migliori artifici che si troveranno' (ASPar, Carteggio Farnesiano Roma, b. 403).

45 'T'immaginerai di vedere la Beatissima Vergine in quella cappanuccia hora stare inginocchiata davanti all'Incarnato verbo, hora prederselo in seno, e tal hora darlo a tenere in braccio al glorioso San Gioseppe'; 'T'immaginerai di trovarti presente nel tempio, e contempla la commotione grande di tutta quella gente che vi si trovava quando il vecchio Simeone con tanto devotione, e lacrime viglia nelle sue braccia il figlio di Maria' (BNR, Fond. Ges. 1295 [Claudio Acquaviva, *Esercizi Spirituali*], 93a, 109a].

46 Alessandro Nova, '"Popular" Art in Renaissance Italy: Early Responses to the Holy Mountain at Varallo,' in Claire Farago, ed., *Reframing the Renaissance* (New Haven and London, 1995), p. 117.

47 '… Ha illustrato i Martiri, et altri Beati della Compagnia, de quali nelle sue stanze haveva i ritratti, e con particolare affetto li contempleva e riveriva' (ARSI, Vitae 144 I [Claudio Acquaviva], 74a).

48 'Ultimamente perche l'indispositione lo sforzava a trattenersi in letto molte giorni, massimamente l'inverno, si era fatto dipingere con chiaro oscuro i misterij della Passione, et porve in camera in alto, dove potesse haverli di continuo avanti a gl' occhi' (ARSI, Vitae 144 I, 69b). On this source, see also Pieter-Matthijs Gijsbers, 'Claudio Aquaviva, Louis Richeome, and Dante Alberti's Altarpiece for Sant'Andrea al Quirinale,' in Anna Gramiccia, ed., *Docere, Delectare, Movere* (Rome, 1998), p. 33.

49 John Padberg et al., eds, *For Matters of Greater Moment: The First Thirty Jesuit General Congregations* (St Louis, 1994), p. 98.

50 For example, see Sandro Benedetti, *Fuori dal classicismo* (Rome, 1984); and Leif Holm Monssen, 'Rex gloriose martyrum: A Contribution to Jesuit Iconography,' *Art Bulletin* 63 (1981): 130. Derek Moore, 'Pellegrino Tibaldi's Church of S. Fedele in Milan,' PhD dissertation, New York University, 1988, p. 301, was one of the first to point out this frequent mistake. See also Moore, 'The Sixteenth Century in Italy,' *Journal of the Society of Architectural Historians* 45 (1986): 172. For a recent study that stresses the ideal of

poverty in Jesuit architecture, see Giovanni Sale, *Pauperismo architettonico e architettura gesuitica* (Milan, 2001).

51 See John W. O'Malley, *Trent and All That: Renaming Catholicism in the Early Modern Era* (Cambridge, MA, and London, 2000).

52 Ibid.; O'Malley, 'Historiography,' pp. 21–2; Prodi, 'Ricerche sulla teorica'; Zeri, *Pittura e controriforma*; Hubert Jedin, *Katholische Reformation oder Gegenreformation?* (Lucerno, 1946).

53 On the origins of the Catholic reform of the visual arts, see G. Scavizzi, *The Controversy on Images from Calvin to Baronius* (New York, 1992); Scavizzi, *Arte e architettura sacra, cronache e documenti sulla controversia tra riformati e cattolici (1500–1550)* (Rome, 1981); Scavizzi, 'La teologia cattolica e le immagini durante il XVI secolo,' *Storia dell'arte 2* (1974): 171–212; Anthony Blunt, *Artistic Theory in Italy, 1450–1600* (London, 1940), pp. 103–36.

54 Waterworth, *The Council of Trent*, pp. 234–5.

55 The original texts of many of these treatises have been compiled in Barocchi, *Trattati d'arte del cinquecento*. For a thorough bibliography on post-Tridentine image theory, see Pamela Jones, *Federico Borromeo and the Ambrosiana* (Cambridge, 1993), pp. 117–26. On imagery after Trent, see also Mühlen, 'Imaginibus honos.'

56 On Gilio and Michelangelo, see Bernardine Barnes, *Michelangelo's Last Judgment: The Renaissance Response* (Berkeley, Los Angeles, and London, 1998), pp. 98–101. For a translation of Borromeo's treatise, see Evelyn Carole Voelker, 'Charles Borromeo's *Instructiones Fabricae et Supellectilis Ecclesiasticae, 1577,*' PhD dissertation, Syracuse University, 1977. For a classic study of Jan Molanus, see Sydney Freedberg, 'Johannes Molanus on Provocative Paintings,' *Journal of the Warburg and Courtauld Institutes* 34 (1971): 229–36.

57 On the notion of causality, or the impact of treatise writers on art (specifically, of Gabriele Paleotti on the Carracci), see A.W.A. Boschloo, *Annibale Carracci in Bologna: Visible Reality in Art after the Council of Trent* (The Hague, 1974). See also Dempsey's new introduction in Charles Dempsey, *Annibale Carracci and the Beginnings of Baroque Style*, 2nd ed. (Fiesole, 2000), pp. vii–viii; Calì, *La pittura del cinquecento*, vol. 1, p. 152; Freedberg, *Circa 1600*, pp. 6, 88. Denis Mahon had already noted in 1947 that the theories of the art academies of the Seicento had no marked effect on the practice of art (Mahon, *Studies in Seicento Art and Theory* [London, 1947], p. 6).

58 See Jones, *Federico Borromeo*.

59 Hall, *After Raphael*, pp. 173–5; Calì, *La pittura del cinquecento*, vol. 1, p. 145; Alexander Nagel, *Michelangelo and the Reform of Art* (Cambridge, 2000), pp. 3–16; Calì, *Da Michelangelo*.

60 Belting, *Likeness and Presence*; Sylvie Deswarte-Rosa, 'Francisco de Holanda: Maniera e Idea,' in *A pintura manierista em Portugal: Arte no tempo de Camões* (Lisbon, 1995), pp. 59–105; Nagel, *Michelangelo*, pp. 14, 75.

61 Like many scholars, Blunt declares that artists were 'forced in general to follow' Trent and the treatise writers (*Artistic Theory in Italy*, p. 120).

62 'Oratorians,' in *Oxford Dictionary of the Christian Church* (Oxford, 1997), pp. 1186–7.

63 For example, Haskell, *Patrons and Painters*, p. 68.

64 Ian Verstegen, 'Federico Barocci, Federico Borromeo, and the Oratorian Orbit,' *Renaissance Quarterly* 66:1 (Spring, 2003): 56–87; Josephine von Henneberg, 'Cardinal

Caesar Baronius, the Arts, and the Early Christian Martyrs,' in Mormando, *Saints and Sinners*, pp. 136–50; Daniele Ferrara, 'Artisti e committenze alla Chiesa Nuova,' in *La regola e la fama: San Filippo Neri e l'arte* (Milan, 1995), pp. 108–9; C. Barbieri et al., *Santa Maria in Vallicella* (Rome, 1995); Macioce, *Undique splendent*, p. 6; Joseph Connors, *Borromini and the Roman Oratory* (Cambridge, MA, 1982), pp. 1–2, 9–10.

65 Ferrara, 'Artisti e committenze,' p. 109; Barbieri et al., *Santa Maria in Vallicella*, pp. 89, 117; M. Jaffé, *Rubens in Italy* (Ithaca, 1977), p. 94.

66 Verstegen, 'Federico Barocci,' pp. 56–7; Hall, *After Raphael*, p. 445; A. Cistellini, *San Filippo Neri. L'Oratorio e la Congregazione oratoriana: Storia e spiritualità* (Brescia, 1989); Stuart Lingo, 'The Capuchins and the Art of History,' PhD dissertation, Harvard University, 1998, pp. 264–5; Alessandro Zuccari, 'La politica culturale dell'Oratorio Romano nella seconda metà del cinquecento,' *Storia dell'arte* 41 (1981): 77–112; Zuccari, 'La politica culturale dell'Oratorio Romano nelle imprese artistiche promosse da Cesare Baronio,' *Storia dell'arte* 42 (1981): 171–93.

67 Verstegen, 'Federico Barocci,' p. 64.

68 Ibid., p. 6; Harald Olsen, *Federico Barocci* (Copenhagen, 1962), p. 29, cat. no. 27a.

69 Henneberg, 'Cardinal Caesar Baronius,' pp. 136–8; Zuccari, *Arte e committenza*, pp. 13–14; Zuccari, 'Cesare Baronio, le immagini, gli artisti,' in *La regola e la fama*, pp. 80–97; Scavizzi, *Arte e architettura sacra*, pp. 83–113, 154–78.

70 For a recent study of Paleotti's treatise, see Pamela Jones, 'Art Theory as Ideology: Gabriele Paleotti's Hierarchical Notion of Painting's Universality and Reception,' in Farago, *Reframing the Renaissance*, pp. 127–39.

71 On the origins and diffusion of the imagery of St Filippo Neri, see Olga Melasecchi, 'Nascità e sviluppo dell'iconografia di S. Filippo Neri dal cinquecento al settecento,' in *La regola e la fama*, pp. 34–49.

72 Angeli, *Sant'Ignazio*; Julius Held, 'Rubens and the *Vita beati P. Ignatii Loiolae* of 1609,' in John R. Martin, ed., *Rubens before 1620* (Princeton, 1972), pp. 93–104; Ursula König-Nordhoff, *Ignatius von Loyola: Studien zur Entwicklung einer neuen Heiligen-Ikonographie im Rahmen einer Kanonisationskampagne um 1600* (Berlin, 1982); Gianni Papi, 'Le tele della cappellina di Odoardo Farnese nella Casa Professa dei gesuiti a Roma,' *Storia dell'arte* 62 (1988): 71–80; Otto von Simson, *Peter Paul Rubens: (1577–1640)* (Mainz, 1996); Baumstark, *Rom in Bayern*, cat. nos 34, 35.

73 Held, 'Rubens,' pp. 93–134; Simson, *Peter Paul Rubens*, pp. 165ff.

74 Held, 'Rubens,' p. 125.

75 Jaffé, *Rubens and Italy*, plates 239, 246–7, 249; Simson, *Peter Paul Rubens*, pp. 79ff.

76 Melasecchi, 'Nascità e sviluppo,' pp. 41–4.

77 See Gauvin Alexander Bailey, 'Creating a Global Artistic Language in Late Renaissance Rome: Artists in the Service of the Overseas Missions, 1542–1621,' in Pamela Jones and Thomas Worcester, eds, *From Rome to Eternity: Catholicism and the Arts in Italy, ca. 1550–1650* (Leiden, 2002), pp. 225–52.

78 See Jones, 'Art Theory as Ideology.'

79 For a bibliography of the history of Jesuit architecture, see Bailey, 'Le style jésuite.'

80 See Francis Haskell, 'The Role of Patrons: Baroque Style Changes,' in Wittkower and Jaffe, *Baroque Art*, p. 53.

81 See Bailey, 'Le style jésuite,' pp. 42–4; 63–71.

82 See the bibliographies at the beginning of the appropriate chapters.

83 Jeroen Stumpel, 'Speaking of Manner,' *Word and Image* 4 (1988): 248.

84 Hessel Miedema, 'On Mannerism and Maniera,' *Simiolus* 10 (1978–9): 19–45.

85 John Shearman, *Mannerism* (Harmondsworth, 1967), pp. 18–19.

86 Stumpel, 'Speaking of Manner,' p. 248.

87 There is a vast literature on Mannerism and *Maniera*. For recent surveys of the literature, see Elizabeth Cropper, 'Introduction,' in Smyth, *Mannerism and Maniera*, pp. 12–
21; Stumpel, 'Speaking of Manner,' pp. 246–64; A. Pinelli, 'La maniera: definizione di
campo e modelli di lettura,' *Storia dell'arte italiana*, part 3, vol. 2, book 1 (Torino, 1981):
88–181. On Wölfflin's discussion of 'Mannerism' as a 'decline' and 'distortion' of
High Renaissance ideals, see Smyth, *Mannerism and Maniera*, p. 22; Henri Zerner,
'Observations on the Use of the Concept of Mannerism,' in Franklin W. Robinson and
Stephen G. Nichols, eds, *The Meaning of Mannerism* (Hanover, 1972), p. 105; Heinrich
Wölfflin, *Classic Art: An Introduction to the Italian Renaissance* (repr. Ithaca, 1986),
pp. 202–4. The most recent assessment is in David Franklin, *Painting in Renaissance
Florence* (New Haven and London, 2001), especially pp. 1–17.

88 Smyth, *Mannerism and Maniera*, p. 24.

89 Walter Friedländer, 'The Anticlassical Style,' in Friedländer, *Mannerism and Anti-
Mannerism in Italian Painting* (New York, 1957), pp. 3–53. This is a translation of an
article written in German and published in 1925.

90 Arnold Hauser, *Mannerism: The Crisis of the Renaissance and the Origin of Modern Art*
(London, 1965).

91 Ernst Gombrich, 'Introduction,' in Gombrich, ed. *The Renaissance and Mannerism*
(Princeton, 1963), pp. 1–68.

92 Cropper, 'Introduction,' pp. 14–15; Bailey, 'Le style jésuite,' p. 39.

93 Mahon, *Studies in Seicento Art and Theory*.

94 John Shearman, 'Maniera as an Aesthetic Ideal,' in Gombrich, *The Renaissance and
Mannerism*, pp. 200–21; Craig Hugh Smyth, 'Mannerism and Maniera,' ibid., pp. 174–
99; Shearman, *Mannerism*; Smyth, *Mannerism and Maniera*.

95 Cropper, 'Introduction,' p. 14; Zerner, 'Observations,' p. 107.

96 Smyth, 'Mannerism and Maniera,' pp. 39–49.

97 Cropper, 'Introduction,' p. 14.

98 See n2 to this chapter, above.

99 For a survey of recent scholarship on the period 1520–50, see Cropper, 'Introduction,'
and Hall, *After Raphael*, pp. xii–xv.

100 See Cropper, 'Introduction,' p. 17; Zerner, 'Observations,' p. 115; Hauser, *Mannerism*,
p. 11–16.

101 Freedberg, *Painting in Italy*, p. 428.

102 Ibid., pp. 429–50, 657–61.

103 Cropper, 'Introduction,' pp. 12–21; Franklin, *Painting in Renaissance Florence*, pp. 1–17.

104 Hall, *After Raphael*, pp. xiii, xiv.

105 Freedberg, *Painting in Italy*, pp. 495–6; Hall, *After Raphael*, pp. 194–5; Calì, *La pittura del
cinquecento*, vol. 1, pp. 185–6.

106 Hall, *After Raphael*, p. 185. For an excellent and extremely thorough catalogue
raisonnée of both Zuccaro brothers, see Luchinat, *Taddeo e Federico Zuccari*. See also
Calì, *La pittura del cinquecento*, vol. 1, p. 188.

107 On Zuccaro and the academy, see Mahon, *Studies in Seicento Art and Theory*, pp. 157–91.

108 Barbara Wisch, 'The Archiconfraternita del Gonfalone and Its Oratory in Rome: Art and Counter-Reformation Spiritual Values,' PhD dissertation, University of California at Berkeley, 1985; Wisch, 'The Passion of Christ in the Art, Theater, and Penitential Rituals of the Roman Confraternity of the Gonfalone,' in Konrad Eisenbichler, ed., *Crossing the Boundaries: Christian Piety and the Arts in Italian Medieval and Renaissance Confraternities* (Kalamazoo, 1991), pp. 237–62.

109 Giammaria, *Girolamo Muziano*; Ugo da Como, *Girolamo Muziano* (Bergamo, 1930). See also Calì, *La pittura del cinquecento*, vol. 1, p. 199.

110 Calì, *La pittura del cinquecento*, vol. 1, p. 199.

111 I would like to thank Maura Giacobbe Borelli for giving me access to the paintings in the collection of the Opera del Duomo in Orvieto, which are currently being restored.

112 Hall, *After Raphael*, p. 198.

113 Freedberg, *Painting in Italy*, p. 620; Gunter Arnolds, *Santi di Tito: Pittore del Sansepolcro* (Arezzo, 1934); Jack Spalding, 'Santi di Tito,' PhD dissertation, Princeton University, 1976, pp. 36ff. See also Gauvin Alexander Bailey, 'Santi di Tito and the Florentine Academy: *Solomon Building the Temple* in the Capitolo of the Accademia del Disegno (1570–1),' *Apollo* (February 2002): 2–8.

114 Olsen, *Federico Barocci*; Emiliani, *Federigo Barrocci*.

115 See Hall, *After Raphael*, pp. 8–9.

116 Madonna, *Roma di Sisto V*; Ostrow, *Art and Spirituality*; Hall, *After Raphael*, pp. 257–91; Alessandro Zuccari, *I pittori di Sisto V* (Rome, 1992).

117 See Bailey, *Art on the Jesuit Missions*, pp. 46–51.

118 Bailey, 'Le style jésuite,' pp. 44–5.

119 Padberg et al., *For Matters of Greater Moment*, p. 129.

120 Bailey, *Art on the Jesuit Missions*, p. 46; Richard Bösel, *Jesuitenarchitektur in Italien, 1540–1773* (Vienna, 1985–), vol. 1, pp. 11ff; Jean Vallery-Radot, *Le receuil de plans d'édifices de la Compagnie de Jésus conservé à la Bibliothèque Nationale de Paris* (Rome, 1960), pp. 6ff.

121 Calì, *Da Michelangelo*, p. 283. My translation.

122 Federico Zeri, 'Giuseppe Valeriano,' *Paragone* 61 (1955): 35ff; A. Rodríguez Gutiérrez de Ceballos, 'Juan de Herrera y los jesuítas Villalpando, Valeriani, Ruiz, Tolosa,' *Archivum Historicum Societatis Iesu* 23 (July–December 1966): 287ff; Gutiérrez de Ceballos, *Bartolomé de Bustamente y los origines de la arquitectura jesuítica en España* (Rome, 1967); Pietro Pirri, *Giuseppe Valeriano S.I. architetto e pittore, 1542–96* (Rome, 1970). A major reassessment of Valeriano's architectural work is currently being undertaken by Maria Ann Conelli: *The Gesù Nuovo in Naples: Politics, Property, and Religion* (forthcoming).

123 Pirri, *Valeriano*, pp. 1–3.

124 Zeri, *Pittura e controriforma*, pp. 49–50; Calì, *Da Michelangelo*, p. 283.

125 Hall, *After Raphael*, pp. 183–4.

126 Zeri, *Pittura e controriforma*, p. 51.

127 Giovanni Baglione, *Le vite de' pittori, scultori, et architetti* (Rome, 1642), p. 83.

128 Calì, *Da Michelangelo*, p. 284.

129 Ibid., p. 285.

130 Pirri, *Valeriano*, pp. 221, 235, 239.

131 Ibid., pp. 225, 228.

132 The first letter is from Claudio Acquaviva to Valeriano, written upon receipt of two of

his letters, on 26 October 1580: 'Habbiamo ricevuto le due vostre lettere, et ci siamo rallegrati intendere per esse il miglioramento di vostra sanità ... M'è piaciuto intendere le buone qualità di quel curato, di cui mi scrivete, et lodo il desiderio, che nella vostra mostrate del suo aiuto spirituale per mezzo de' nostri essercitij' (ARSI, Rom. 12 II, 85a). The second is from Father Manareo to Valeriano from Recanati on 4 January 1581: 'Mi son rallegrato nel Signore d'intendere dalla vostra lettera il commodo viaggio che havete havuto, et insieme che vi trovate consolato nell'animo et con sanità nel corpo. Spero che cotesta aria vi habbia ad aiutare e ricoverare interamente la sanità. Et per questo rispetto mi pare, che vi tratteniate più presto costì, che in Loreto, per la strettezza grande che hanno di luogo; stimo che quell'aria non vi sarebbe così giovevole. Intanto potrete andarvi rinfrescando le cose della lingua, et insieme fare qualche essercitio intorno alli casi, perché per profittarsi bene della prattica è necessario prima havere li principii della scienza, et al suo tempo poi non si mancherà darvi aiuto ancora in questo. Mi fu caro che si rimandesse consolato il vostro cugino. Et con questo mi raccomando alle vostre orationi' (ARSI, Rom. 13 I, 29b; Pirri, *Valeriano*, pp. 256–7).

133   In a letter of 21 November 1580, Father Oliveiro Manareo described Valeriano's regime to the vice-rector of Recanati, Giovanni Giorgio: 'Viene il fratello Gioseffo Valeriano, del quale già scrissi a V.R. l'esercitio suo è di pingere, et ha in ciò buona mano. Ma perché il P. Generale di buona memoria disegnò farlo sacerdote et il P. Vicario sta nel medesimo, conviene ch'egli attenda agli studi della lingua et de' casi. Pertanta basterà che in pingere qualche bella icona per le chiese si occupi due o tre hore del giorno, come egli s'inclinarà, et il resto del tempo V.R. glie lo lasci libero, procurando che alcuni de' nostri costì l'aiuti. E glie lo racommando' (ARSI, Rom. 13 I, 16a; Pirri, *Valeriano*, p. 256).

134   Personnel records in the Jesuit archives give the date of his ordination as 15 August 1589 (ARSI, Rom. 53 I, 43a, 66a).

135   Milton Lewine, 'The Roman Church Interior,' PhD dissertation, Columbia University, 1960), p. 252; Michael Keine, *Bartolomeo Ammannati* (Milan, 1995), p. 169 n9.

136   Vasari calls him 'Battista di Benedetto' and says he is 'a youth who has already given evidence of future success, was also the disciple of Ammannato; his many works produced thus early show him to be in nowise inferior to the above mentioned Andrea [Calamec of Carrara], or to any other of the young sculptors who are Academicians, whether in genius or judgment' ('e Batista di Benedetto, giovane che ha dato saggio di dovere, come farà, riuscire eccellente, avendo già mostro in molte opere che non è meno del detto Andrea, nè di qualsivoglia altro de'giovani scultori accademici, di bell'ingegno e giudizio') (Giorgio Vasari, *Vasari's Lives of the Painters, Sculptors, and Architects*, trans. and ed. Mrs Jonathan Foster, 5 vols [London, 1883], V, p. 489; Vasari, *Le vite de' piu eccellenti pittori, scultori, ed architettori scritte da Giorgio Vasari*, ed. Gaetano Milanesi, 8 vols [Florence, 1881], VII, p. 626).

137   'che levando il superfluo alla pietra, riduce le forme de' corpi all'Idea dell'artifice, conformi; & usando la misura, ma co'l giuditio però dell'occhio accompagnata, comparte a gli ornamenti & alle figure proportione, e gratia; E su egli buon scultore' (Baglione, *Le vite de' pittori*, p. 98).

138   The account books for the Florence college include a reference dated June 1592 to a small trust placed by 'M.a Lisabetta Fiameri vedova' and delivered by 'Giulio Parigi

suo nipote' for 40 Florentine lire. This amount was to be invested with the Collegio Romano in Rome as a dowry for her daughter (ASF, Comp. Rel. Sopp. 990, #74, 3b].

139 Giulio Parigi was the son of the architect Alfonso Parigi and the grand-nephew of Bartolommeo Ammannati. A pupil of Bernardo Buontalenti, Parigi became very active in court circles and designed, among other important *apparati*, the set for the 1608 marriage of Cosimo II to Maria Maddalena of Austria (*La pittura in italia: Il seicento*, 2 vols [Milan, 1988], II, p. 837).

140 ARSI, Ital. 40, 422a. For the reference to 'Lisabetta Fiameri,' see n138 to this chapter, above.

141 Fiammeri witnessed a receipt for a loan from Ammannati to Giovanni Figiollo di Francone dated 26 June 1557: 'Io batista di benedetto fui presente a quanto di sopra si chontiene' (ASF, Comp. Rel. Sopp. 1036, #240, 102a).

142 ASF, Accademia del Disegno 24 (Giornale di Negozi, 1563–71), 2a, 9a, 21a; Accademia del Disegno 25 (1571–3), 11b, 25b; Accademia del Disegno 101 (Entrate e Uscite, 1562–85), 5a, 14b, 20b, 24a, 29a, 32a, 33a, 36b; Accademia del Disegno 123 (Entrate e Uscite, 1568–77), 7b, 8a, 27a, 28a, 53b, 54a. For a history of the Florentine Academy, see Karen-edis Barzman, *The Florentine Academy and the Early Modern State* (Cambridge, 2000).

143 Barzman, *The Florentine Academy*, pp. 52, 70; Zygmunt Wazbinski, *L'Accademia medicea del disegno a Firenze nel cinquecento*, 2 vols (Florence, 1997), II, pp. 95–103; Rudolf Wittkower and Mary Wittkower, *The Divine Michelangelo and the Florentine Academy's Homage on His Death in 1564* (New York, 1950), pp. 12, 22–3. See also Bailey, 'Santi di Tito and the Florentine Academy.'

144 The references to these two commissions are in three letters, the first from Don Vincenzo Borghini to Duke Cosimo de' Medici (Pisa, 4 November 1564), the second from Giorgio Vasari to Duke Cosimo (Pisa, 5 November 1564), and the third from Borghini to the Duke (Pisa, 29 December 1564) (ASF, Cart. Med. Un. 510, 586a, 1486a). The full texts are published in Karl Frey, *Der literarische Nachlass Giorgio Vasaris*, 2 vols (Munich, 1940), II, pp. 116–23, 138–89. See also Pietro Pirri, 'L'architetto Bartolomeo Ammannati e i gesuiti,' *Archivum Historicum Societatis Iesu* 12 (1943): 25–6; Keine, *Ammannati*, p. 161.

145 Annamaria Petrioli Tofani, *Gabinetto isegni e stampe degli Uffizi: Inventario 2. Disegni esposti* (Forence, 1987), p. 924e; Wadell, *Evangelicae*, Abb. 228.

146 ASF, Accademia del Disegno 25, 11b. Fiammeri's name is crossed out and substituted with that of Domenico di Francesco di Siena. In the book of *Entrate e Uscite*, Fiammeri pays his dues up to May 1577 in advance, in a lump sum in 1575, the year before he entered the novitiate (ASF, Accademia del Disegno 123, 27a, 28a, 53b, 54a).

147 The register of new novices from 1576 reads, 'Gio. Batt.a Fiammiero Fiorenza 3 Marzo' (ARSI, Rom. 169, 12a). Another notice of new novices for 1576 reads, 'Giovanni Battista Fiammeri Fiorentino. Pittore assai valoroso. 3 Marzo' (ARSI, Rom. 162 I, 45b).

148 The catalogue entries read: '[1579] Io. Baptista Flamerius/Florentinus/Annorum 33/ Sanus/admissus est Romae anno 1576/pictor/ coadjutor Formatus Temporalis'; '[1584] Gio: Batt.a Fiammeri/Florentinus/1550/bonas/1576 in Febr./pictor'; '[1586] Gio. Batt.a Fiammere pittore'; '[1590] Jo: Bap.ta Flammerius/Florentinus/Annos 47/ Satisfirma/Annos 14/ Pictor et statuarius sculptor' (ARSI, Rom. 53 I, 38b, 63a, 105b, 165a; Pietro Pirri, 'Intagliatori gesuiti italiani dei secoli XVI e XVII,' *Archivum Histor-*

icum Societatis Iesu 21 [1952]: 37 n66; Carlo Galassi Paluzzi, 'Note di storia e d'arte su le cappelle e gli altari del Gesù,' *Roma* 7 [1929]: 393); '[1600] pictoris officio fungitur, praeterea nihil' (ARSI, Rom. 54, 129b, 263a; Pirri, 'Intagliatori,' p. 37 n66); '[Fiammeri is] aptus ad pingendum et imprimendas imagines, et sculpendas in aere ... mediocris iudicii et prudentiae: habet aliquam experientiam. Collericae complexionis' (ARSI, Rom. 55, 57a; Pirri, 'Intagliatori,' p. 37 n66). For references to Fiammeri in his old age, see ARSI, Rom. 55, 16b; Rom. 78, 42a; Rom. 143, 120.

149 'e particolarmente era bravo in far cartelle di diversi sorti di chiaro, e scuro con varii capricci, e belle bizzerrie, sì come se ne mirano per il Collegio, e nella Casa del Giesù, & in altre luoghi di quella Compagnia' (Baglione, *Le vite de' pittori*, p. 98).

150 For a complete study of the original paintings of S. Giovannino, see Gauvin Alexander Bailey, 'The Florentine Reformers and the Original Painting Cycle of the Church of S. Giovannino,' in Thomas M. Lucas, ed., *Spirit, Style, Story: Essays Honoring John W. Padberg, S.J.* (Chicago, 2002), pp. 135–80. See also Pirri, 'Ammannati,' pp. 22, 26–7; Pirri, 'Intagliatori,' p. 37 n66; Bösel, *Jesuitenarchitektur in Italien*, p. 82; Wadell, *Evangelicae*, p. 28; Michael Keine, 'Bartolomeo Ammannati e i Gesuiti,' in Niccolò Rosselli del Turco and Federica Salvi, *Bartolomeo Ammannati: Scultore e architetto* (Florence, 1995), pp. 187–94; Mario Bencivenni, *L'architettura della Compagnia di Gesù in Toscana* (Florence, 1996), pp. 27–44; Vieri Franco Boccia, 'La chiesa di San Giovanni Evangelista a Firenze,' pp. 105–11, and Pietro Matracchi, 'Il collegio di S. Giovannino a Firenze,' pp. 111–17, in Giuseppe Rocchi Coopmans de Yoldi, ed., *Architettura della compagnia ignaziana nei centri antichi italiani* (Florence, 1999).

151 See ASF, Comp. Rel. Sopp. 990, #74, 154b–155b.

152 See Bailey, 'The Florentine Reformers' for the complete list with documentation. Only Giulio Parigi (January 1591 to April 1593) and Giovanni di Rafaello (April 1592) are mentioned in the Jesuit accounts (ASF, Comp. Rel. Sopp. 990, #74, 151b, 156a, 173b, 175a, 222b).

153 ASF, Comp. Rel. Sopp. 1064, #336, 28a, 29a, 43a, 45b.

154 Fiammeri and Clemente were accompanied by the gilder Vincenzo Maria, the sculptor Bartolomeo Tronchi, and the carpenter Antonio de Sanctis (ARSI, Rom. 53, 108b; Pirri, 'Ammannati,' p. 22). See also ASF, Comp. Rel. Sopp. 1000, #111, 87b, 89a, 96a.

155 ASF, Comp. Rel. Sopp. 999, #104, 238a; Comp. Rel. Sopp. 1000, #111, 95a, 95b, 96a, 106b.

156 ASF, Comp. Rel. Sopp. 1064, #335 (Rome, 12 August 1582): 'Intorno all'historie che si potrebbono dipinger in quelli spatii, piaccia al S.re che si spedisca così presto il restante della chiesa, come queste si troveranno senza difficoltà.'

157 ASF, Comp. Rel. Sopp. 999, #104, 238a;

158 ASF, Comp. Rel. Sopp. 999, #104, 238a; Comp. Rel. Sopp. 998, #98, 111b, 151a; Comp. Rel. Sopp. 1000, #111, 96b.

159 ARSI, Rom. 13 I, 120a, 176b, 177b; Rom. 13 II, 250a, 390a; Pirri, 'Ammannati,' pp. 27–8, 50, 52.

160 His final vows read as follows: 'Io Giovanbattista Fiammeri prometo all'omnipotente Dio in presentia della Beatissima Vergine sua madre Maria, et di tutta la corte celeste, et a voi Reverendo Padre Preposito vener.e dalle Compagnia di Giesù che tenete il loco di Dio, et à Vostri successori perpetua povertà, castità et obbedenzia secondo il modo espresso nelle lettere Appostoliche, et constitud.e di detta Compagnia. In Roma

nella Chiesa della Casa Professa di detta Compagnia à dì 15 d'Agosto 1587' (ARSI, Ital. 40, 211a).

161 Baglione, *Le vite de' pittori*, p. 98.

162 '[1617] Joan: Bap.a Flammerius ibid [Rome] 23 Aug.'; '[1620] Laurentius Fiammerius Viterbij – 20 Sept' (ARSI, Hist. Soc. 43 [Defunti], 6b, 7a).

163 Wadell, *Evangelicae*, plates 207–32.

164 See ibid., p. 30.

165 Ibid., pp. 25–30.

166 Acquaviva mentions in two letters, dated 1581 and 1599, the work Fiammeri did on Nadal's illustrations (ARSI, Neap. 2, 89v; Neap. 6 I, 5b; Pirri, 'Intagliatori,' p. 37 n66). See also chapter 6.

167 Wadell, *Evangelicae*, pp. 15–16; Mauquoy-Hendrickx, 'Les Wierix,' pp. 28ff.

168 See Fabrizio d'Amico, 'Una grande "nazione" di pittori a Roma: I toscani,' in Giuseppe Zander, ed., *L'arte in Roma nel secolo XVI*, 2 vols (Bologna, 1992), II, pp. 279–87; and Macioce, *Undique splendent*, p. 83.

169 Mahon, *Studies in Seicento Art and Theory*, p. 157. On the Florentine Accademia del Disegno, see Bailey, 'Santi di Tito and the Florentine Academy.'

170 Romano Alberti, *Origine, et progresso dell'Accademia del Dissegno de' pittori, scultori, e architetti di Roma* (Pavia, 1604; repr. Bologna, 1978), pp. 84–7.

171 Ibid., p. 79; Mahon, *Studies in Seicento Art and Theory*, pp. 174–5.

172 'Il detto M. Durante capo dell'Academia, che così volsero i Superiori, che si nomasse, condusse nell'Academia per prima sua tornata un'Rever. Padre ... della Compagnia del Giesù, à fare un'essortatione à tutti li fratelli Academici ad essere avertiti al dipengere cose honeste, e gere una lettera in materia d'una Cleopatra, vista già figurata poco honestamente, in reprensione della quale pose molte ragioni, & avertimenti, che furono cosa assai gustosa; onde diede speranza di far qualche cosa, ma in resolutione questo fù quanto egli fece, e spirò l'anno senza far mai altra cosa di momento' (Alberti, *Origine, et progresso*, p. 79).

2: The Novitiate of S. Andrea al Quirinale

1 Jones, 'Art Theory as Ideology,' p. 129.

2 See Nova, '"Popular" Art in Renaissance Italy,' pp. 113–26; and Luciano Vaccaro and Francesca Riccardi, *Sacri Monti: Devozione, arte e cultura della Controriforma* (Milan, 1992).

3 Nova, '"Popular" Art in Renaissance Italy,' p. 116.

4 Ibid. The classic study of this relationship is Henry Thode, *Franz von Assisi und die Anfänge der Kunst der Renaissance in Italien* (Berlin, 1885).

5 Randi Klebanoff, 'The *Vita* and the *Morte*: Making the Sacred in Renaissance Bologna,' paper delivered at the Sixteenth Century Studies Conference, Toronto, 24 October 1998; Klebanoff, 'The Material of Imagination: The Early Sacri Monti of Varallo and San Vivaldo,' unpublished paper. I am grateful to Randi Klebanoff for providing me with this text.

6 Riccardo Ghidotti, *Il Santuario delle Sette chiese di Monselice* (Vicenza, 2000).

7 See Bailey, *Art on the Jesuit Missions*, pp. 35–41.

8 ARSI, Rom. 167, 1b; Rom. 167a, 5a. For the history of the early patronage of S. Andrea,

see Carolyn Valone, 'Women on the Quirinal Hill: Patronage in Rome, 1560–1630,' *Art Bulletin* 76:1 (March 1994): 130–1; Bösel, *Jesuitenarchitektur in Italien*, pp. 212–22; Christof L. Frommel, 'S. Andrea al Quirinale, genesi e struttura,' in G. Spagnesi and M. Fagiolo, eds, *Gian Lorenzo Bernini e l'architettura europea del sei-settecento* (Rome, 1983), pp. 211–53; Joseph Connors, 'Bernini's S. Andrea al Quirinale: Payments and Planning,' *Journal of Architectural Historians* 41 (1982): 15–37; G. Giachi and G. Matthiae, *Sant'Andrea al Quirinale* (Rome, 1967). Maria Ann Conelli also is doing research on the female patrons of S. Andrea. See also Giovanni Careri, *Bernini: Flights of Love, the Art of Devotion*, trans Linda Lappin (Chicago, 1995), pp. 87–101. The first Jesuit novitiate was in Messina, Sicily, and was founded in 1550 (O'Malley, *The First Jesuits*, pp. 360–1).

9 See David R. Coffin, *The Villa in the Life of Renaissance Rome* (Princeton, 1979), pp. 181–214.

10 Letizia Lanzetta, *Sant'Andrea al Quirinale* (Rome, 1996), pp. 15–16.

11 Lanzetta, *Sant'Andrea*, p. 17. The description comes from F. Martinelli, *Roma ex ethnica sacra sanctorum Petri et Pauli predicatione apostolica profuso sanguine publicae veneratione exposita* (Rome, 1653), p. 58.

12 Thomas M. Lucas, *Landmarking: City, Church, & Jesuit Urban Strategy* (Chicago, 1997), p. 23.

13 ARSI, Rom. 163 [a 1566 letter entitled 'Informazione d'alcune cose della nova casa de probatione'], 224a; Rom. 167, 1b; Valone, 'Women on the Quirinal,' pp. 130–1; Luciano Patteta, 'Le prime costruzioni del Noviziato di Sant'Andrea al Quirinale,' in Luciano Patetta and Stefano Della Torre, eds, *L'architettura della Compagnia di Gesù in Italia, xvi–xviii secolo* (Milan, 1990), p. 88.

14 Padberg et al., *For Matters of Greater Moment*, p. 115; see also O'Malley, *The First Jesuits*, pp. 360–2.

15 For literature on the training regimen of Jesuit novices, see Gijsbers, 'Claudio Aquaviva,' p. 32 n21.

16 The Navarola text is in ARSI, Rom. 164 and FG 1033; three versions of Sisti are Rom. 167, 167a, and 168. The Sisti text (ARSI, Rom. 167a) has been published recently in Patetta, 'Le prime costruzioni,' pp. 87–90.

17 ARSI, Rom. 167, 4b, 6a. See also Rom. 127 I, 70a; Rom. 167a, plate 2.

18 Patteta, 'Le prime costruzioni, p. 87; Pietro Pirri, *Giovanni Tristano e i primordi della architettura gesuitica* (Rome, 1955), pp. 95–8.

19 ARSI, FG 1033, 37b; Rom. 167, 6a.

20 G.A. Brutio, *Theatrum Romanae Urbis sive romanorum sacrae aedes: Chiese de canonici* (BAV, Vat. Lat. 11886, 291a–b; quoted in Gijsbers, 'Claudio Aquaviva,' p. 29 n5). My translation.

21 See Pirri, *Tristano*, tav. XV (a); Milton Lewine, 'The Roman Church Interior,' figs 14, 15, 17.

22 There is some confusion about the date. The Sisti text (1733) and another late source say the church was consecrated in 1568 (Patetta, 'Le prime costruzioni,' p. 98; ARSI, Rom. 163 [Historia Dom. Probat. Rom.], 217b), whereas the older Navarola version (1612) clearly says 2 February 1569 (ARSI, Rom. 162 I, 16b; FG 1033, 2a). Gijsbers gives a third date of 1570 ('Claudio Aquaviva,' p. 34).

23 ARSI, Rom. 162 I, 16b; Rom. 127, 70a.

24 Lanzetta, *Sant'Andrea*, p. 19; Gijsbers, 'Claudio Acquaviva,' p. 34.

25 ARSI, Rom. 167, 9a; Rom. 163, 219a.

26 ARSI, Rom. 162 I, 20b–21a. This price included all the furnishings for the refectory and kitchen, which had to be made 'di nuovo.'

27 ARSI, Rom. 167, 9a, 20b–21a; Rom. 167a, plate 3; FG 1033, 3a.

28 ARSI, Rom. 162 I, 42a; Rom. 167, 14a; FG 1033, 4a. The account books list payments to a carpenter to do work on the door and windows of the sacristy on 28 June 1573: 'per pagar al falegname il modelo del formato & la finestra della sacristia & porte tutte tre, scudi 1.50' (ARSI, FG 1048, 58b). The accounts record a considerable amount of building activity in 1576, as well, with many payments to *muratori* and *scarpellini* (ARSI, FG 1048, 108a–31b).

29 ARSI, Rom. 167a, plate 4.

30 ARSI, Rom. 162 I, 53a–b, where Navarola states that immediately after his inauguration, Acquaviva made it his goal to 'allargar l'habitazione ... [che] havessero miglior commodità.'

31 ARSI, Rom. 167 I, published in Patetta, 'Le prime costruzioni,' p. 90. See also ibid., pp. 87–8; Pirri, *Tristano*, p. 84; and Bösel, *Jesuitenarchitektur in Italien*, p. 213. For the reference to the gift by Farnese, see ARSI, Rom. 162 I, 59a.

32 'Ha ricevuto Santo Andrea da Marcello Palavicino scudi tremila per fabricare parte per mezzo del Collegio Romano come incontro si scrive' (ASR, Patrimonio Ex-Jesuitico, Entrate e Uscite 1578–90 [S. Andrea al Quirinale], 138a).

33 Different sources contradict themselves on the chronology. Navarola, who is the earliest, gives the date of Pallavicini's rectorate as 1581–7 and credits him with building the infirmary during those years (ARSI, Rom. 162 I, 53a–b; Bösel, *Jesuitenarchitektur in Italien*, p. 213). The eighteenth-century Sisti text, however, states very clearly that Acquaviva's renovations began in 1591, and does not mention the infirmary until later (ARSI, Rom. 167a, plate 7; Patetta, 'Le prime costruzioni,' p. 90). The account books show that there was extensive building activity in 1581–3, with many payments to masons, woodworkers, and *scarpellini* and for lime, wood, and stone (ARSI, FG 866 A [Libro della Fabrica della Casa a S. Andrea, 1581–94], no folio).

34 ARSI, Rom. 162 I, 94b–107b.

35 ARSI, Rom. 162 I, 109a; Rom. 163, 231a–236a; FG 866 A, no folios. On Valeriano's activity at S. Andrea, see Pirri, *Valeriano*, pp. 179–83. The account books for S. Andrea demonstrate extensive building activity in the years 1593–4 [ARSI, FG 866 A, no folio).

36 Again, all the sources do not agree. Navarola says there were only 15 rooms, whereas Sisti and the published Annual Letter of 1593 by Orazio Torsellino say 17 (ARSI, Rom. 162 I, 117a; Rom. 167a, 22a, plate 8; Patetta, 'Le prime costruzioni,' p. 90; Torsellino, *Annuae Litterae Societatis Iesu anno 1593* (Florence, 1601), p. 18; Pirri, *Valeriano*, p. 180). The account book shows that construction on the infirmary began in 1594 (ARSI, FG 866 A, no folio).

37 ARSI, Rom. 162 I, 59a, 117a; 167, 18a; 167a, 26a, plate 10; FG 866 A [Libro della Fabrica della Casa a S. Andrea, 1581–94], 26a, 30a. See also Patetta, 'Le prime costruzione,' p. 90.

38 ARSI, Rom. 162 I, 117a.

39 Pirri, *Valeriano*, p. 180.

40 ARSI, Rom. 162 II, 284b; Rom. 167a, plate 11.

41 ARSI, Rom. 163, 277b. A plan of the Novitiate as it appeared in 1649, before Bernini's

church was built, is in the ASR, Collezione piante e disegni I, cart. 84, n477 II, and was published by Johannes Terhalle, '... ha della Grandezza de padri Gesuiti: Die Architektur der Jesuiten um 1600 und St. Michael in München,' in Baumstark, *Rom in Bayern*, Abb. 10.

42 ARSI, Rom. 162 I, 39a. In 1571, the history of S. Andrea records, 'fu finita la fabrica incominciata l'anno precedente depinto il coro' (ARSI, FG 1033, 3a).

43 ARSI, FG 1048, 29a, 67a–b; FG 1033, 3a. The first payment recorded to a painter was made on 8 October 1569, 'per giesso per il pittore, scudo 1.' Other payments listed in the accounts are as follows: '[4 November 1574] per colori per dipingere il Gesù, scudi 0.85'; '[14 November] per colori da dipingere [and other petty expenses] ... scudi 0.28; per colori, scudi 0.20'; '[28 November] per colori da dipingere, scudi 0.30; per colori da dipingere [and other petty expenses] ... scudi 0.75'; '[1 December 1574] per colori da dipingere, scudi 0.30.' In addition to these payments for pigments, there is a payment on 1 October 1574 for a glass to place over a painting: 'per un vetro per l'imagine, scudi 0.20' (ARSI, FG 1048, 66b). No payments to artists of any kind are listed in FG 938 (S. Andrea accounts for 1571–97).

44 ARSI, Rom. 162 I, 74b.

45 Payments for painting supplies range from December 1582 to October 1584: '[9 November 1583] colori [among other things], scudi 0.92'; '[12 November 1583] colori [among other things], scudi 6.3'; '[17 October 1584] colori [among other things], 7.60' (ARSI, FG 1048, 102b, 105a); '[December 1582] A dì 9 per giesso, scudi 18'; '[February 1583] A dì 3 per ... giesso, scudi 1.21'; '[March 1583] A dì 19 per giesso, scudi 20'; '[April 1583] A dì 22 per giesso, scudi 14'; '[3 September 1593] E più b. 30 al pittore per il disegno delle fenestre ..., b. 30'; '[7 September 1593] b. 50 per 10 fogli di carta papale per dipinger li sportelli, b. 50; e più al pittore per li disegni fatti in carta ... sessanta, b. 60'; '[31 October 1593] Spesi in due libretti d'oro per servire della pittura della fabrica, b. 30'; '[27 November 1593] b.30 spesi in due libretti d'oro per la pittura, b. 30'; '[26 February 1594] per 2 decine di gesso, b. 20'; '[15 April 1594] E devono dare b. 32 spesi in decine 3 di gesso, b. 32' (ARSI, FG 866 A, no folio).

46 See Bailey, 'The Florentine Reformers.'

47 The following are some references to Clemente in Jesuit annual catalogues, listing such things as his name, origin, birthdate, health, date of entry into the Society, and profession: '[1584] Rutilio Clemente/ Peruginus/ 1558/ mediocres/ 1579/ pictore, stuccatore, scultore & orifice' (ARSI, Rom. 53 I, 65a); '[1590, Roman College] Rutilius Clemens/ Perusinus/ 32/ mediocres/ 1579/ pictor' (ARSI, Rom. 53 I, 151a); '[1594, S. Andrea] Rutilius Clemens/ Perusinus/ mediocres/ 14.6.Xbris 1579/ Pictor/ Coad. form. Xi. 9bris 1596' (ARSI, Rom. 53 II, 188b); '[1597, S. Andrea] Rutilius Clemens/ Perusinus/ Pictor/ Nat.s An.o 1558/ adm.s 6 Decembris 1579/ Ex.a pictor/ Coad. Form. Xi 9bris 1596' (ARSI, Rom. 53 II, 258a, 301a). His obituary is listed in the book of deaths for 1640–9: 'Rutilius Clemens Perusiae 26 Februarij 1643 Romanae' (ARSI, Hist. Soc. 47 [Defuncti, 1640–9], 62a. See also Pirri, 'Ammannati,' p. 25, who cites other records, but says Clemente died in Perugia.

48 '[27 December 1593] b. 10 pagati al fratello Rutilio per comprare cerchi, b. 10 ...'; '[19 January 1594] deve dare per tre moneta pagati al battiloro, per l'oro dato al frattello Rutilio Clementi per le pitture, scudi 3'; '[11 February 1594] Scudi 2 sinò a dì

11 detto al F. Rutilio per comprare di colori per le pitture, scudi 2'; '[13 April, 1594]
b. 90 pagato conto Rutilio Clementi fino al primero del presente disse per pagare colorj,
b. 90' (ARSI, FG 866 A, no folio).

49 Serafino Siepi, *Descrizione topologico-istorica della Città di Perugia*, vol. 1 (Perugia, 1722),
p. 412; ASPer, Perugia II 167 5 (Annibale Mariotti, *Memorie storiche delle chiese della Città
di Perugia*, 1819), pp. 191–206.

50 The foundation stone of the Jesuit church at Tivoli was laid on 8 July 1582 (ARSI, Rom.
12 II, 100b). However, the paintings were not executed until late in the following
decade. On 18 February 1599, Acquaviva wrote in a letter to Sebastiano Sicinio that he
was pleased with Rutilio Clemente's work at the church: 'Mi rallegro poi che il nostro
fratello Rutilio habbia fatto buon effetto alla sua cappella il tutto sia a gloria del Signore da cui prego a V.S. grand'abondanza di gratia et ogni felicità' (ARSI, Rom. 14 II,
403a).

51 For example, ARSI, Rom. 53 I, 63a, 65a. Jesuit artists found themselves in an even more
drastic situation in the world missions, where they might have to serve not only as
artists but as architects, pastoral counsellors, doctors, and farmers. See Bailey, *Art on
the Jesuit Missions*, pp. 46–51.

52 This topos was frequently used in descriptions of the world missions. See Bailey, *Art on
the Jesuit Missions*, pp. 31–5.

53 'Piacque il Signore che costui capitasse in questa casa con occasione di dipingere alcune
cose della vita di N.B.P. et altri Beati, e martiri della Compagnia per adornar con essi la
sala del Noviziato, come fu fatto con molta spesa, dove essendosi intrattenuto alcuni
mesi con forse particolar diligenza in osservar come le cose passassero, trovò tutto
il contrario di quello, che imaginato s'era ... Et vedendo in particolare che li Novitij
stavano sempre tanto allegri' (ARSI, Rom. 162 II, 271a–b). Zuccari, *Arte e committenza*,
pp. 165–6, publishes another version in the Archivio della Provincia Romana della
Compagnia di Gesù (ARPG, E. 71, 118b–119a).

54 ARSI, 162 II, 286 a–b. In a list of clothing owned by the two brothers, they are described
as follows: '[1605] Gisberto Gisberti di Anversa fiammingo di anni 29. Venne a Santo
Andrea l'ultimo di Agosto. Porto seco doi capelli di feltro, un mantillo di saia scotto,
un'altro di panno verde ...; Michele Gisberti di Anversa di anni 21 fiammingo venne a
Sto Andrea al Ultimo di Agosto. Porto seco un capello di feltro un manzillo di panno
verde mischio' (ARSI, Rom. 172 [Ingressus Novitiorum ab anno 1594 usq. ad 1630],
90a). Michele's obituary reads as follows: 'Michael Gisbertus, Antverpiae in Belgio
natus, Temporalis Coadiutor formatus, pingendi artem, quam apprimem callebat,
excrevit in felicitate: in qua viginti vixit annos cum magna pietatis commendatione.
Tibure mortuus est Aprilis dix 1.a Anno Domini MDCXXIII. Suae vero aetatis octavo
supra trigesimum. Felicitatem ingressus est Romae Anno MDCIII (ARSI, Rom. 188 I
[Romana: Necrologia], 217a).

55 Pirri, 'Intagliatori,' p. 16.

56 See *Arte e committenza*, p. 166; Pio Pecchiai, *Il Gesù di Roma* (Rome, 1952), pp. 106, 242;
E. Lamalle, 'La propagande du P. Nicolas Trigault en faveur des Missions de Chine
(1616),' *Archivum Historicum Societatis Iesu* 9 (1940): 96 n20; Gaspare Celio, *Memoria delli
nomi dell'artefici delle pitture che sone in alcune chiese, facciate, e palazzi di Roma* (Naples,
1638), p. 42.

57 ARSI, Rom. 162 I, 18a, 45b; Rom. 53 I, 38b, 43a, 65a.

58 See Bailey, 'Creating a Global Artistic Language.' See also Ruben Vargas Ugarte, *Ensayo de un diccionario de artifices coloniales de la America Meridional* (Lima, 1947), pp. 62–4; Martin Soria, *La pintura del siglo XVI en Sudamerica* (Buenos Aires, 1956), pp. 45–72; George Kubler and Martin Soria, *Art and Architecture in Spain and Portugal and their American Dominions* (Baltimore, 1959), pp. 321–2; José de Mesa and Teresa Gisbert, *Bernardo Bitti* (La Paz, 1961); Mesa and Gisbert, *Historia de la pintura cuzqueña* (Lima, 1982), pp. 56–62. Bitti's entry into the novitiate at S. Andrea al Quirinale in 1568 is recorded in ARSI, Rom. 162 I, 18a.

59 ARSI, Rom. 171c, 30. Although none of Bitti's European work survives, he is known to have painted a canvas for a woman when he was in Seville en route to Lima. Mesa and Gisbert note that it was very unlikely he had much opportunity to paint during his years as a novice, between 1568 and 1570 (*Historia*, p. 57), but this may not be true.

60 ARSI, FG 1488, 22a.

61 The catalogue listing for Rudellux is as follows: '[1579] Joannes Rudellux Ulissipanensis/ 29/ mediocres/ 1576 in 8bre/ ... sculptor per an.6' (ARSI, Rom. 53 I, 43b); and for Benedetti (who is not to be confused with Giovanni Battista di Benedetto Fiammeri): 'Joannes di Benedictus/ Bononiensis/ 35/ bonus/ 1585 in 7bre/ ex pictor et miles' (ARSI, Rom. 53 I, 44a). Fioravante/Francischetti is described as follows: '[1586, S. Andrea] Giulio Cesare Fioravante/ Perugia/ anni 23/ pittore/ in Novembre' (ARSI, Rom. 53 I, 88a); '[1595] Julius Cesar Francischettus/ Perusinus/ an 34/ bonae/ ingressus xi 9bris 1563/ ex.a Pictor in Soc.te adituus an. 6 infirmarius an. 3 ianitor' (ARSI, Rom. 53 II, 210a). Melcetti/Miletti is listed as '[1587, S. Andrea] Bernardus Melcettus/ Faentinus/ An: 20/ optimas/ pictor/ prim.a Novemb.' (ARSI, Rom. 53 I, 116a]; and '[1597, Florence College] Bernardus Milettus/ Faentibus/ Ann. 30/ bonae/ admissus 1 Nov. 1586/ pictor, infirmar. Aeditus' (ARSI, Rom. 53 II, 312b).

62 'Vincenzo Maria di Massa del Regno di Napoli d'età di 23 anni, entrò nella compagnia in Roma, sono da sette anni, stette in novitiato da otto mesi prima et la seconda volta da un mese et mezzo, fece i voti semplici qualche un'anno et mezzo doppo di esser entrato per coadiutore temporale, è dispensiero, et pittore mediocre, è sano, et gagliardo' (ARSI, Hist. Soc. 41, 88a; Pirri, *Tristano*, p. 244). For the definition of *dispensiero* I am indebted to John O'Malley and Stanley Morrow.

63 The catalogue listing for 1584 is as follows: 'Giosef Roncalli/ Florentinus/ 1567 in Martio/ bonas/ 1584 in 7bre/ artes picturae, suterire, et pharmacopoli' (ARSI, Rom. 53 I, 67b). On his more famous namesake, see Freedberg, *Painting in Italy*, pp. 664–5; Louise Rice, *The Altars and Altarpieces of New St. Peter's* (Cambridge, 1997), p. 28.

64 ARSI, Rom. 162 II, 276a-b; Rom. 112 (Catalog. Novitior. 1565–1657), 136. See also Zuccari, *Arte e committenza*, pp. 166–7, who cites another source on Zuccaro in the Archivio della Provincia Romana della Compagnia di Gesù (ARPG, E. 71, 120b–121a). For Baglione's biography of Zuccaro, see Baglione, *Le vite de' pittori*, pp. 121–5; and for his work at Caprarola, see Robertson, *Il Gran Cardinale*, pp. 104–30.

65 See the chronology in Pirri, *Valeriano*, pp. xxxiv–xxxv, 179–83.

66 P. Totti (1638) and G.A. Brutio attribute the *Martyrdom of St Andrew* altarpiece and the painting *Adoration of the Magi* to Durante Alberti, while Filippo Titi (whose account is much later, 1674) says that all three are by Alberti (Gijsbers, 'Claudio Aquaviva,' p. 30

n6). Pirri states that Giovanni Baglione attributes these paintings to Alberti, but I cannot find any reference in Baglione (Pirri, *Tristano*, p. 97; Baglione, *Le vite de'pittori*, pp. 118–19).

67 *La pittura in Italia: Il seicento*, vol. 2, p. 608; Baglione, *Le vite de'pittori*, p. 118; Coffin, *The Villa in the Life of Renaissance Rome*, p. 317.

68 Macioce, *Undique splendent*, pp. 117–18.

69 Alberti, *Origine, et progresso*, p. 56.

70 Richeôme is believed to have been at work on his book in 1608–9, at which time the painting must have been in place. Gijsbers believes that the picture was completed under Acquaviva. ('Claudio Aquaviva,' p. 30). According to Gijsbers, the painting is last mentioned in an inventory in 1733. Although Gijsbers agrees that there is no evidence to date the painting, he maintains, without referring to a source, that Alberti's main altar painting, *Martyrdom of St Andrew*, was introduced into the church around 1600, and replaced an earlier painting of the same subject probably depicting the apostle standing and accompanied by a cross saltire ('Claudio Aquaviva,' p. 34).

71 *La pittura in Italia: Il cinquecento*, 2 vols (Milan, 1988), II, p. 675; Baglione, *Le vite de' pittori*, p. 377. See also chapter 4. Baglione records his work at Tivoli, in a chapel of the church frescoed by Rutilio Clemente in 1599: 'Andò egli per li medesimi Padri a Tivoli, e vi dipinse una Cappelletta nella loro Chiesa a mano manca con varie pitture a fresco; ma come talvolta l'eta, e l'occorrenza porta, invaghissi di una giovane di quel luogo, e di nascosto de' Padri Giesuiti per moglie la si tolse, e poi da loro rihavuti i suoi danari, di questi in Tivoli ne comperò un'oliveto' (Baglione, *Le vite de' pittori*, p. 378).

72 '[6 June 1595, among a list of funds for the garden] S. 300 ... da Gasparo Celio pittore a 6.0 p. mano di d.o [Francesco] Silla'; '[13 June 1598] Censo estinto da Celio Pittore p. s. 150; poscià che con s. 150 d'essi a ... in estinto un censo, che si era renduto a Gaspare Celio Pittore' (ARSI, Rom. 162 I, 134a, 168a); '[23 December 1597] per estinzione d'un Annuo conto di s. 150 à bon conto di s. di trecento m.ta presi l'anno pasato a di 6 giugno a 6 ½ per oto duo, s. 150'; '[13 June 1598] A Gasparo Celio ... per estinzione d'un Annuo conto di s. 19 rendutogli per s. 300 de quali s. 150 furono resi del 1596, per resto altri 150' (ARSI, Rom. 167 I, 14b–15a. Published differently in Zuccari, *Arte e committenza*, p. 165).

73 'Restò Gasparo Celio a servire i Padri Giesuiti, & in varie opere l'impiegarono; e loro diede intanto qualche intentione di volersi fare di quella Compagnia, anzi alcuni danari, che dalle sue fatiche havea ragunato, lasciò loro in serbo, mostrando unita con essi ogni sua voluntà' (Baglione, *Le vite de' pittori*, p. 378).

74 Richeôme's book is discussed in H. Brémond, *Histoire littéraire du sentiment religieux en France*, vol. 1 (Paris, 1929), pp. 18–67; it is mentioned and partly paraphrased in Émile Mâle's *L'art religieux après le Concile de Trente* (Paris, 1932), p. 120; and it is discussed in Marc Fumaroli, *L'âge de l'éloquence: Rhetorique et 'res literaria' de la Renaissance au seuil de l'époque classique* (Geneva, 1980), pp. 262–3, and in Kristof van Assche, 'Louis Richeome, Ignatius, and Philostrates in the Novice's Garden: Or, the Signification of Everyday Environment,' in John Manning and Marc van Vaeck, *The Jesuits and the Emblem Tradition* (Leiden, 1999), pp. 3–10. Many scholars have referred to this book, but only in passing; no one has made an in-depth study of this incredibly rich and delightful treatise on art history and spirituality.

75 Mühlen, 'Imaginibus honos,' pp. 162–3.
76 Quoted in Bernard Dompnier, 'La Compagnie de Jésus et la mission de l'intérieur,' in Giard and Vaucelles, *Les jésuites à l'âge baroque*, p. 174 n57.
77 Gijsbers, 'Claudio Aquaviva,' p. 35.
78 Fumaroli, *L'âge de l'éloquence*, p. 258; van Assche, 'Louis Richeome,' p. 3. See also Gijsbers, 'Claudio Aquaviva,' p. 37. Philostratus's grandson Philostratus the Younger (third century) wrote a second series of *Imagines*.
79 Fumaroli, *L'âge de l'éloquence*, pp. 262, 678–9.
80 Ibid., p. 262. My translation.
81 For a recent, if short, study on the garden section, see van Assche, 'Louis Richeome.'
82 See Gijsbers, 'Claudio Aquaviva,' p. 30.
83 In addition to the sources listed above, see, on the gardens, Stefania Macioce, 'Aspetti simbolici nel giardino del noviziato di S. Andrea al Quirinale in Rome,' in P.C. Ioly Zorattini, ed., *Memor fui dierum antiquorum: Studi in memoria di Luigi De Biasio* (Udine, 1995), pp. 381–95; David R. Coffin, *Gardens and Gardening in Papal Rome* (Princeton, 1991), pp. 100–2; and van Assche, 'Louis Richeome.
84 Richeôme, *La peinture spirituelle* (Lyon, 1611), p. 138. The quotations in the paragraph below are from pp. 138–46.
85 Ibid., p. 146.
86 Mark S. Weil, 'The Devotion of the Forty Hours and Roman Baroque Illusions,' *Journal of the Warburg and Courtauld Institutes* 37 (1974): 223–5.
87 Alison Simmons, 'Jesuit Aristotelian Education: The *De Anima* Commentaries,' in O'Malley et al., *The Jesuits*, pp. 522–37.
88 Ibid., pp. 528–9.
89 Ignatius of Loyola, *Spiritual Exercises*, pp. 54–5.
90 Richeôme, *La peinture spirituelle*, pp. 11, 21–2.
91 Ibid., p. 14.
92 Gijsbers, 'Claudio Aquaviva,' p. 30.
93 Ibid., p. 32.
94 Careri, *Bernini*, p. 93.
95 See Bailey, 'The Jesuits and Painting in Italy,' pp. 158–60.
96 Gijsbers, 'Claudio Aquaviva,' p. 38.
97 Bailey, 'The Jesuits and Painting in Italy,' fig. 13.
98 Gijsbers maintains that the SS. Nereo ed Achilleo fresco focuses on a slightly different moment in the story, when the executioners are still tying the apostle to the cross; but that remains open to interpretation since both pictures clearly show at least one executioner tying Andrew's foot (Gijsbers, 'Claudio Aquaviva,' p. 38).
99 Richeôme, *La peinture spirituelle*, p. 22.
100 Mâle, *L'art religieux*, p. 301. Churchmen also believed that Christ's blood flowed not only for humankind but also for angels.
101 Monsignor Filippo Caraffa, ed., *Bibliotheca sanctorum*, 13 vols (Rome, 1968), xi, pp. 1369–71.
102 Josephine von Henneberg, 'Saint Francesca Romana and Guardian Angels in Baroque Art,' *Religion and the Arts* 2–4 (1998): 470.
103 See Pamela M. Jones, 'The Power of Images: Paintings and Viewers in Caravaggio's Italy,' in Mormando, *Saints and Sinners*, p. 32; and Alessandro Zuccari, 'Bellarmino e

la prima iconografia gesuitica: La Cappella degli Angeli al Gesù,' in de Maio et al., *Bellarmino e la controriforma*, pp. 612–13.

104 'Subito che fu approvato dal Pontefice Paolo V l'offizio dell'Angelo Custode, l'abbracciò con molta allegrezza, e con ugual divozione ogni anno lo disse, recitando ogni dì l'orazione, che all'istesso Angelo ivi si pone. Visitando una volta in Tivoli una chiesa Parrochiale di S. Michele Archangelo dentro l'istessa città, vide che non vi era altra imagine di quel glorioso Principe, che una roza, e vecchia figura di carta, cosi attaccata al muro: dalla qual vista commosso, subito che tornò a Roma, da un nostro fratello pittore fece fare un quadro in tela bello, e grande, e donollo à quella chiesa, dove hoggi è riverito' (ARSI, Vitae 144 I [Claudio Acquaviva], 73a).

105 Ostrow, *Art and Spirituality*, pp. 46ff.

106 Macioce, *Undique splendent*, plate LXIIa–b.

107 Richeôme, *La peinture spirituelle*, p. 26.

108 Ignatius of Loyola, *Spiritual Exercises*, p. 50.

109 Ibid., pp. 49–50.

110 On the Holy Family as an earthly Trinity, see Mâle, *L'art religieux*, pp. 309ff.

111 Richeôme, *La peinture spirituelle*, pp. 26–7.

112 Ibid., p. 37.

113 Ignatius of Loyola, *Spiritual Exercises*, p. 117.

114 Mâle, *L'art religieux*, p. 250.

115 Richeôme, *La peinture spirituelle*, pp. 47–64.

116 Pope Clement VIII beatified Stanislas on 17 February 1604, and in 1605 Paul V allowed a painting of the young man to be placed on his memorial (ARSI, Rom. 168, 43a; Rom. 162 II [Ottavio Navarola, Hist. Dom. Probat. Rom. II], 261b). See also Gijsbers, 'Claudio Aquaviva,' p. 29.

117 ARSI, Rom. 162 II, 263a.

118 ARSI, Rom. 162 II, 417a.

119 'essendo stato ornato il sepolcro con due portieri del Cardinale Montalto di valore di 1600. Fu posto sopra l'imagine un bellissimo baldacchino, e sotto compriva il tumolo del santo un frontale di raso branco tutto ricamente di tela d'oro con l'imagine dell'istesso in atto di esser communicato dagl'Angeli alla presenza di S. Barbara ... sopra il quale erano molti belli fiori, e dabasso intorno alla predella avanti al tumolo 6. candelieri d'argento mezani, e 2. grandi della statura d'un huomo con le candeli ardenti divisi con altri fiori' (ARSI, Rom. 162 II, 263a). See also ARSI, Rom. 163 (Hist. Dom. Prob. Rom.), 15a.

120 Richeôme, *La peinture spirituelle*, pp. 48–9.

121 Haskell, *Painters and Patrons*, p. 68. See also Haskell, 'The Role of Patrons,' p. 56.

122 Richeôme, *La peinture spirituelle*, p. 49.

123 See *Jesuit Art in North American Collections* (Dobbs Ferry, 1991), plate 17.

124 Marcus B. Burke, *Jesuit Art and Iconography: 1550–1800* (Jersey City, 1993), cat. no. 35.

125 O'Malley, *The First Jesuits*, p. 358. I am grateful to John O'Malley for pointing out this reference.

126 Richeôme, *La peinture spirituelle*, pp. 65–137.

127 Ibid., p. 76.

128 Ibid., p. 106.

129 Ibid., p. 122.

130 See Franco Mormando, 'Teaching the Faithful to Fly: Mary Magdalene and Peter in Baroque Italy,' in Mormando, *Saints and Sinners*, pp. 107–35.

131 Richeôme, *La peinture spirituelle*, pp. 148–50.

132 Ibid., pp. 149–50.

133 Ibid., p. 153.

134 See, for example, Alexandra Herz, 'Imitators of Christ: The Martyr-Cycles of Late Sixteenth Century Rome Seen in Context,' *Storia dell'arte* 62 (1988): 59; and Evonne Levy, 'A Noble Medley and Concert of Materials and Artifice: Jesuit Church Interiors in Rome,' in Thomas J. Lucas, ed., *Saint, Site, and Sacred Strategy* (Vatican City, 1990), p. 48. Leif Holm Monssen cites the Jesuits' rejection of lavish adornment in their houses (1558) as the reason why the martyrdoms were painted in the recreation room and not the church; he argues that the Jesuits wanted to keep the church plain. He dates the martyrdom paintings to 1570 ('Rex gloriose martyrum,' p. 130). In reality, the situation was the opposite. The proclamation concerning austerity had nothing to do with churches, and everything to do with places like the recreation room. See Bailey, 'Le style jésuite,' pp. 64–5; Bailey, *Art on the Jesuit Missions*, pp. 44–5.

135 Careri, *Bernini*, p. 88.

136 Angeli, *Sant'Ignazio*; Milton Lewine, 'The Sources of Rubens's *Miracles of Saint Ignatius*,' *Art Bulletin* 45 (1963): 143–7; Held, 'Rubens,' pp. 93–104; Ursula König-Nordhoff, 'Zur Entstehungsgeschichte der *Vita beati P. Ignatii Loiolae Societatis Iesu fundatoris Romae* 1609 und 1622,' *Archivum Historicum Societatis Iesu* 45 (1976): 306–17; König-Nordhoff, *Ignatius von Loyola*, pp. 21–5, 118–21, 277–321; Joaquim Oliveira Caetano, 'Uma brevíssima nota acerca das fontes da Vida de Santo Inácio de Loyola na Igreja de S. Roque de Lisboa,' in *O púlpito e a imagem: Os jesuítas e a arte*, ed. Nuno Vassallo e Silva (Lisbon, 1997), p. 49; Baumstark, *Rom in Bayern*, pp. 324–6.

137 Lucas, *Saint, Site*, p. 92.

138 O'Malley, *The First Jesuits*, p. 33.

139 Richeôme, *La peinture spirituelle*, p. 163.

140 For an illustration, see Oliveira Caetano, 'Una brevissima nota,' p. 49.

141 Richeôme, *La peinture spirituelle*, p. 171.

142 Vitor Serrão, 'Quadros de Vida de S. Francisco Xavier,' *Oceanos* 12 (November 1992): 56–69; *O púlpito e a imagem*, ed. Vassallo e Silva, p. 22. The same church has an Ignatian cycle from a slightly later date, based on the images in the *Vita beati Ignatii*.

143 *St. Francis Xavier – His Life and Times* (Tokyo, 1999), cat. no. 50. See also cat. no. 49 for a similar image from Portugal.

144 Richeôme, *La peinture spirituelle*, p. 179.

145 Ibid., p. 179.

146 Ibid., p. 181.

147 Bailey, *Art on the Jesuit Missions*; Lucas, *Saint, Site*, p. 130.

148 See Dauril Alden, *The Making of an Enterprise: The Society of Jesus in Portugal, Its Empire, and Beyond, 1540–1750* (Stanford, 1996), p. 74; for information about the death of Rodolfo Acquaviva, see Edward Maclagan, *The Jesuits and the Great Mogul* (London, 1932), pp. 64–5.

149 Claudio's support of his young nephew is discusssed in his *Vita* (ARSI, Vitae 144 I, 19a ff).

150 Richeôme, *La peinture spirituelle*, p. 226.

151 Alexandra Herz, 'Cardinal Cesare Baronio's Restoration of SS. Nereo ed Achilleo and S. Cesario de' Appia,' *Art Bulletin* 70 (1988): 607.

152 Ibid., p. 613.

153 Herz notes this regarding the victory angel figures ('Imitators of Christ,' p. 59).

154 Richeôme, *La peinture spirituelle*, p. 225.

155 Ibid., p. 237.

156 Bailey, *Art on the Jesuit Missions*, pp. 6ff.

157 Richeôme, *La peinture spirituelle*, p. 233.

158 ARSI, Rom. 162 I, 94a. On the Japanese embassy, see Bailey, *Art on the Jesuit Missions*, p. 63.

159 Robert Parsons, *An Epistle of the Persecutions of Catholickes in Englande* (Douai, 1582), p. 28 (margin).

160 Richeôme, *La peinture spirituelle*, pp. 191, 211.

161 See Bailey, 'The Jesuits and Painting in Italy,' p. 160.

162 Richeôme, *La peinture spirituelle*, p. 237.

163 Ibid., p. 237.

164 See Francis Haskell, *History and Its Images* (New Haven and London, 1993), pp. 32–3.

165 Richeôme, *La peinture spirituelle*, pp. 193, 238.

166 Herz, 'Imitators of Christ,' p. 67.

167 Mâle, *L'art religieux*, pp. 298–301; Zuccari, 'Bellarmino e la Cappella degli Angeli,' pp. 611–28; Ramón Mujica Pinilla, *Ángeles apócrifos en la América virreinal*, 2nd ed. (Lima, 1996), pp. 19–37; *La regola e la fama*, pp. 506–11.

168 Early examples include fresco paintings in the Convento de las Descalzas Reales in Madrid by Bartolomé Román (1596–1659), a canvas painting after the Wierix engraving by the same painter in San Pedro in Lima, and an early version in the Santuario de Ocotlán in Mexico (Mujica Pinilla, *Ángeles apócrifos*, p. 29).

169 *La regola e la fama*, p. 507.

170 Ibid., p. 503.

171 *La regola e la fama*, cat. no. 66d.

172 Mujica Pinilla, *Ángeles apócrifos*, 43; *La regola e la fama*, p. 506.

173 Mujica Pinilla, *Ángeles apócrifos*, pp. 55–7.

174 *La regola e la fama*, pp. 510–11.

175 Ibid., p. 507.

176 Ibid., pp. 510–11.

177 Mujica Pinilla, *Ángeles apócrifos*, p. 30.

178 *La regola e la Fama*, cat. no. 66d.

179 Ibid., p. 503, cat. no. 61.

180 Hibbard, 'Ut picturae sermones': The First Painted Decorations of the Gesù,' in Wittkower and Jaffe, *Baroque Art*, p. 38; Hibbard, *Caravaggio*, pp. 146–7; Zuccari, 'Bellarmino e la Capella degli Angeli,' pp. 612 ff. For similar images of the Seven Archangels in the Oratorian circle, see *La regola e la fama*, cat. nos 61–7.

181 Richeôme, *La peinture spirituelle*, p. 244.

182 *La regola e la fama*, cat. no. 67b.

183 Richeôme, *La peinture spirituelle*, p. 244.

184 Ibid., p. 252.
185 Ibid., p. 256. On the supposed travels of the apostles to Asia and the Americas, see Bailey, *Art on the Jesuit Missions*, pp. 32, 60, 153.
186 Richeôme, *La peinture spirituelle*, p. 265.
187 Ignatius of Loyola, *Spiritual Exercises*, p. 7.
188 Richeôme, *La peinture spirituelle*, p. 273.
189 O'Malley, *The First Jesuits*, p. 268. I am grateful to John O'Malley for bringing this reference to my attention.
190 See Leif Holm Monssen, 'The Martyrdom Cycle in Santo Stefano Rotondo, Part Two,' *Acta ad archaeologiam et artium historiam pertinentia*, series 3, 3 (1983): 63; Monssen, 'Rex gloriose martyrum,' p. 131. See also chapter 3.

3: The Novitiate Infirmary

1 Both Ignatius and Nadal stressed that as a way of encouraging chastity Jesuits were to sleep one to a bed, even if they had to pay more while travelling, a rule that almost certainly would have applied to the Jesuit infirmary as well (O'Malley, *The First Jesuits*, p. 349).
2 Throughout this book I will use the Douai-Rheims translation of the Vulgate Bible for the biblical quotations (*The Holy Bible, Douay Version* [London, 1956]).
3 As mentioned in chapter 2, the sources disagree as to the number of rooms in the infirmary, some saying 15 and others as many as 19. Richeôme mentions only 13 plus a refectory, which at least means that these were probably the only ones with paintings.
4 See A. Lynn Martin, *Plague? Jesuit Accounts of Epidemic Disease in the 16th Century* (St Louis, 1996), pp. xii–xiii; and James Dean Clifton, 'Images of the Plague and Other Contemporary Events in Seventeenth-Century Naples,' PhD dissertation, Princeton University, 1987, pp. 75–6.
5 ARSI, Rom. 162 I, 152b.
6 Clifton, Images of the Plague, p. 107.
7 Martin, *Plague?* p. 92.
8 Ignatius of Loyola, *The Constitutions of the Society of Jesus*, ed. George E. Ganss (St Louis, 1970), pp. 292–306; quoted in Martin, *Plague?* p. 60.
9 W.W. Meissner, *Ignatius of Loyola: The Psychology of a Saint* (New Haven, 1992), p. 223. See also Martin, *Plague?* p. 60.
10 Martin, *Plague?*
11 Richeôme, *La peinture spirituelle*, p. 283.
12 Ibid., pp. 283–470.
13 The reference is dated 15 April 1594 (ARSI, FG 866 A, no folios).
14 Richeôme, *La peinture spirituelle*, pp. 285–95.
15 Hippocrates, *The Genuine Works of Hippocrates*, trans. and ed. Francis Adams (Baltimore, 1939), p. 292.
16 Katharine Park, *Doctors and Medicine in Early Renaissance Florence* (Princeton, 1985), p. 62, n47. Hippocrates' *Aphorismata* was listed on the medical curriculum at the University of Bologna in 1405 (*Doctors and Medicine*, p. 245).
17 ASF, Comp. Rel. Sopp. 999, #104, 39a.

18 Martin, *Plague?* pp. 90–2.

19 Ibid., p. 89.

20 Ibid., pp. 92, 106–7.

21 Ibid., p. 112.

22 On the role of Galen in medieval and Renaissance culture, see Owsei Temkin, *Galenism: The Rise and Decline of a Medical Philosophy* (Ithaca, 1973). See also Rudolf E. Siegel, *Galen on the Affected Parts* (Basel, 1976), pp. 1–5.

23 Hibbard, 'Ut picturae sermones,' p. 37.

24 Sergio Rossi, ed., *Scienza e miracoli nell'arte del '600* (Milan, 1998), cat. no. D55.

25 For the Lucca bozzetto, see *La pittura a Lucca nel primo seicento* (Lucca, 1994), cat. no. 8. The version in S. Egidio is still there today. The Castiglion Fiorentino canvas, which had been transferred to S. Agostino in 1695, is now in the Pinacoteca.

26 Richeôme, *La peinture spirituelle*, pp. 295–308.

27 St Augustine, *Sancti Aurelii Augustini Enarrationes in Psalmos III* (Brussels, 1956), Ps. 103:4.

28 Hippocrates, *Genuine Works*, p. 292.

29 Lois N. Magner, *A History of Medicine* (New York, 1992), pp. 71–2. See also Zirka Z. Filipczak, *Hot Dry Men, Cold Wet Women: The Theory of Humors in Western European Art, 1575–1700* (New York, 1997), pp. 14–27; Stefania Macioce, 'Melanconia e pittura nel seicento,' in Rossi, *Scienza e miracoli*, pp. 134–45; and Martin, *Plague?* pp. 112–14.

30 Filipczak, *Hot Dry Men*, p. 15.

31 Pliny the Elder (Gaius Plinius Secundus), *Pliny: Natural History I* , trans. and ed. H. Rackham (Cambridge, MA, 1963), pp. 284–5.

32 Ibid.

33 For example, a volume of the *Natural History* was listed in an inventory of the Florentine college of S. Giovannino in 1579 (ASF, Comp. Rel. Sopp. 999, #104, 38a).

34 Christine M. Boeckl, 'Plague Imagery as Metaphor for Heresy in Rubens's *The Miracles of St. Francis Xavier*,' *Sixteenth Century Journal* 27:4 (1996): 979–95; Boeckl, *Images of Plague and Pestilence: Iconography and Iconology* (Kirksville, 2000), pp. 125–9.

35 Clifton, 'Images of the Plague,' pp. 35ff.

36 Bailey, 'The Jesuits and Painting in Italy,' p. 160.

37 See Macioce, *Undique splendent*.

38 'Una vergine con habito bianchissimo sopra una pietra quadrata, con la destra terrà elevata una Croce, & con essa un libro aperto' (Cesare Ripa, *Iconologia*, ed. Erna Mandowsky [Hildesheim and New York, 1970], p. 149).

39 Bailey, 'Le style jésuite,' p. 71.

40 Richeôme, *La peinture spirituelle*, pp. 309–24.

41 Caraffa, *Bibliotheca sanctorum*, vol. 8, pp. 349–54.

42 Augustine, *Psalmos*, Ps. 103:4.

43 Hippocrates, *Genuine Works*, p. 295.

44 Macioce, *Undique splendent*, plates IX (b), X; Ripa, *Iconologia*, p. 64.

45 Richeôme, *La peinture spirituelle*, pp. 324–41.

46 Augustine, *Psalmos*, Ps. 103:4.

47 Hippocrates, *Genuine Works*, p. 293.

48 Richeôme, *La peinture spirituelle*, p. 327. Richeôme may be using hyperbole. In his catalogue of diseases named by Pliny in the *Natural History*, W.H.S. Jones lists only

about 140 (*Pliny: Natural History VIII*, trans. and ed. W.H.S. Jones [Cambridge, MA, 1963], pp. 578–85).

49 Richeôme, *La peinture spirituelle*, p. 329. The actual sentence in Plutarch is 'I have heard that Tiberius Caesar once said that a man over sixty who holds out his hand to a physician is ridiculous' (Plutarch, *Plutarch's Moralia II*, trans. and ed. Frank Cole Babbitt [Cambridge, MA, 1971], p. 287). An edition of Plutarch's *Lives* is listed in the 1579 inventory of the collegiate library at S. Giovannino in Florence (ASF, Comp. Rel. Sopp. 999, #104, 38a).

50 Richeôme, *La peinture spirituelle*, p. 331. The fox is the crafty hero of many of Aesop's fables, who outwits lions, crows, and donkeys with aplomb. See Aesop, *Fables of Aesop*, trans. and ed. S.A. Handford (Harmondsworth, 1973), especially fables 1–15.

51 Seneca the Elder (Lucius Annaeus Seneca), *Seneca: Moral Epistles I*, trans. and ed. Richard M. Gummere (Cambridge, MA, 1917), p. 355.

52 Such as the Florentine college, inventoried in 1579 (ASF, Comp. Rel. Sopp. 999, #104, 37b).

53 Richeôme, *La peinture spirituelle*, pp. 335–6; Pliny, *Pliny: Natural History III*, trans. and ed. H. Rackham (Cambridge, MA, 1963), pp. 70–4.

54 W.H.S. Jones, 'Popular Medicine in Ancient Italy,' in Pliny, *Natural History VIII*, pp. 569–75.

55 See Book XXVIII:1 and Book XXIV:1, Pliny, *Natural History VIII*, p. 3; and Pliny, *Pliny: Natural History VII*, trans. and ed. W.H.S. Jones (Cambridge, MA, 1966), p. 3.

56 Pliny, *Natural History VII*, p. 3.

57 Pliny, *Natural History III*, pp. 70–1.

58 Ibid., p. 71. See also Magner, *A History of Medicine*, p. 190. This habit of the ibis is also recorded by the Roman encyclopaedist Aelian (Claudius Aelianus, ca. 170–235 AD) in his *On the Characteristics of Animals*, Book II:35: 'The Egyptians assert that a knowledge of clysters and intestinal purges is derived from no discovery of man's, but they commonly affirm that it was the Ibis that taught them this remedy. And how it instructed those who were first to see it, some other shall tell' (Aelian, *Aelian on the Characteristics of Animals I*, trans. and ed. A.F. Scholfield [Cambridge, MA, 1958], p. 133). I am grateful to Peta Gillyatt for bringing this source to my attention.

59 Virgil (Publius Vergilius Maro), *The Aeneid*, trans. and ed. John Dryden (New York, 1965), Book XII. The Florentine college of S. Giovannino had an edition of the *Aeneid* in its libraries as early as 1579 (ASF, Comp. Rel. Sopp. 999, #104, 37b).

60 Pliny, *Natural History III*, p. 71 (all these references are to Book VIII:41). Pliny makes further remarks about great celandine and dittany in Book XX:55 (Pliny, *Pliny: Natural History VI*, trans. and ed. W.H.S. Jones [Cambridge, MA, 1961], p. 91). On mandrake as a soporific agent, see Magner, *A History of Medicine*, p. 283.

61 On the history of the illustrated herbal, see Minta Collins, *Medieval Herbals: The Illustrative Traditions* (London and Toronto, 2000).

62 Salvatore Pezzella, *Un erbario inedito dell'Italia centrale* (Perugia, 2000), p. 112.

63 Richeôme, *La peinture spirituelle*, p. 340.

64 'Donna vestita di gialdo, con un'arboscello fiorito in capo, la veste farà tutta piena di varie piante, & nella sinistra terrà un'anchora' (Ripa, *Iconologia*, p. 470).

65 Richeôme, *La peinture spirituelle*, p. 341–61.

66 Augustine, *Psalmos*, Ps. 102:4.

67 Hippocrates, *Genuine Works*, p. 293.

68 Ezia Gavazza et al., eds, *Bernardo Strozzi* (Milan, 1995), cat. no. 59. See also the discussion in Rossi, *Scienza e miracoli*, pp. 119–22.

69 Richeôme, *La peinture spirituelle*, pp. 362–83.

70 Augustine, *Psalmos*, Ps. 102:17.

71 Hippocrates, *Genuine Works*, p. 298.

72 Richeôme, *La peinture spirituelle*, p. 373.

73 St Gregory, *Saint Gregory the Great: Dialogues*, trans. and ed. Odo John Zimmerman (New York, 1959), Book IV, chap. 40, p. 244.

74 Richeôme, *La peinture spirituelle*, pp. 384–92.

75 Augustine, *Psalmos*, Ps. 102:17.

76 Hippocrates, *Genuine Works*, p. 296.

77 I am grateful to Steven J. Harris for his notes on the contents of Kircher's books, prepared as part of an exhibition I curated with him at the John J. Burns Library at Boston College in May 1997 entitled 'Ad Maiorem Dei Gloriam: Jesuit Books from the Old Society in the John J. Burns Library.' The exhibition was remounted, with some alterations, in 1999–2000, together with a published catalogue, *Ratio Studiorum: Jesuit Education, 1540–1773*, ed. Atteberry and Russell.

78 Richeôme, *La peinture spirituelle*, p. 386.

79 Park, *Doctors and Medicine*, 99–100.

80 O'Malley, *The First Jesuits*, p. 344.

81 Park, *Doctors and Medicine*, p. 60.

82 ASR, Patrimonio Ex-Jesuitico, Entrate e Uscite: S. Andrea al Quirinale, 1578–90 45a, 164b, 165a; ARSI, Rom. 156 I (Histor. Colleg. Anglor. Hibern. et Scotor.), 64b.

83 Richeôme, *La peinture spirituelle*, p. 388.

84 Ibid., pp. 392–404.

85 Richeôme incorrectly cites this passage as Job 10.

86 Augustine, *Psalmos*, Ps. 102:17.

87 Hippocrates, *Genuine Works*, p. 295.

88 Dante Alighieri, *The Divine Comedy: Hell*, trans. and ed. Dorothy L. Sayers (repr. Harmondsworth, 1980), Canto XIX:115, Canto XXVII:94.

89 Jones, *Federico Borromeo*, p. 79.

90 Ibid., p. 381.

91 Richeôme, *La peinture spirituelle*, p. 403.

92 Ibid., pp. 404–12.

93 Augustine, *Psalmos*, Ps. 141:4.

94 Hippocrates, *Genuine Works*, p. 295.

95 Richeôme, *La peinture spirituelle*, p. 404.

96 Ibid., p. 405.

97 Plutarch, *Plutarch's Moralia I*, trans. and ed. Frank Cole Babitt (Cambridge, MA, 1986), p. 233.

98 Richeôme, *La peinture spirituelle*, p. 406.

99 Ibid., pp. 413–24.

100 Hippocrates, *Genuine Works*, p. 292.

101 Richard Burton, *The Anatomy of Melancholy* (London, 1652), p. 164.

102 Richeôme, *La peinture spirituelle*, p. 418.

103 Ibid., p. 420.

104 Richeôme claims that the story is from Book III of Galen's *De locis affectis* (On the Affected Parts) – an apparently appropriate attribution since the work deals with neurological functions and disorders – but the story does not appear in that text. Richeôme is frequently mistaken about a specific book or line of a reference, but rarely about a source itself. Galen's treatise has been translated in Galen, *Galen on the Affected Parts*, ed. Rudolph E. Siegel (Basel, 1976), pp. 71–103. On Galen, see also Arthur J. Brock, *Greek Medicine* (London, 1929), p. 165.

105 Magner, *History of Medicine*, pp. 83–6. In 1579 the Florentine college of S. Giovannino had a copy of Celsus's *De re medicina* (ASF, Comp. Rel. Sopp. 999, #104, 39a).

106 Plutarch's text runs as follows: 'Once upon a time a dire and strange trouble took possession of the young women of Miletus for some unknown cause. The most popular conjecture was that the air had acquired a distracting and infectious constitution, and that this operated to produce in them an alteration and derangement of mind. At any rate, a yearning for death and an insane impulse toward hanging suddenly fell upon all of them, and many managed to steal away and hang themselves ... The malady seemed to be of divine origin and beyond human help, until, on the advice of a man of sense, an ordinance was proposed that the women who hanged themselves should be carried naked through the market-place to their burial. And when this ordinance was passed it not only checked, but stopped completely, the young women from killing themselves. Plainly a high testimony to natural goodness and to virtue in its desire to guard against ill repute' (Plutarch, *Moralia III*, p. 509).

107 Richeôme, *La peinture spirituelle*, p. 423.

108 Ibid., pp. 424–32.

109 Hippocrates, *Genuine Works*, p. 296.

110 For Hippocrates, disease was a natural process, and in order to cure it the physician had to determine its relation to food, drink, and way of life. Dietetics was therefore fundamental in the art of healing, and the physician set diets and regimens for the patient. Richeôme uses Hippocrates' very literal statement about purging the body as a metaphor for penitence (see Magner, *A History of Medicine*, pp. 68–9).

111 St Augustine, *De civitate Dei*, 2 vols (Brussels, 1955), II, Book XXII, chap. 8.

112 Ibid. The second boy also lost part of his sight. He had his eyeball torn out by a vengeful devil who possessed him while he was watering his horse; the eye was healed after he bound it with a handkerchief.

113 Augustine, *De civitate Dei*, vol. 2, Book XXII, chap. 8.

114 Richeôme, *La peinture spirituelle*, p. 432.

115 Ibid., pp. 433–46.

116 Richeôme incorrectly cites this passage as Matthew 25.

117 Richeôme incorrectly cites this passage as Psalm 107.

118 Hippocrates, *Genuine Works*, p. 295.

119 Richeôme once again claims that the passage is from *De locis affectis*, and once again he is mistaken.

120 Again, Richeôme claims that the passage is from Galen's *De locis affectis*, but it does not appear there.

121 Galen, *Claudii Galeni Opera Omnia*, ed. C.G. Kühn (Hildesheim, 1965), VII:60. The Latin title is *De symptomatum differentiis liber*, and the text is as follows: '... quaemodum et

Theophilo medico aegrotanti contigit in caeteris quidem prudenter et differere et praesentes exacte noscere, sed tibicines quosdam angulum domus, ubi decumbebat, ocuppasse assidueque tibia modulari ac sonos edere putabat; atque hos se intueri arbitrabatur, alios quidem illic stantes, alios autem sedentes ita continue tibia canentes, ut neque noctu quicquam remitterent, neque omnio interdiu vel minimum tempus quiescerent; proinde exclamabat, perpetuo jubens eos domo ejici.'

122 Horace, *The Complete Works of Horace*, ed. Charles E. Passage (New York, 1983), p. 354.

123 Ibid.

124 Richeôme, *La peinture spirituelle*, p. 443.

125 Ripa, *Iconologia*, pp. 499–501.

126 Richeôme, *La peinture spirituelle*, pp. 446–68.

127 Hippocrates, *Genuine Works*, p. 295.

128 Ignatius of Loyola, *Spiritual Exercises*, p. 60.

129 Richeôme, *La peinture spirituelle*, p. 455.

130 Herz, 'Cardinal Cesare Baronio's Restoration,' p. 615.

131 Richeôme, *La peinture spirituelle*, pp. 458–61.

132 Ibid., pp. 462–8.

133 Ignatius of Loyola, *Spiritual Exercises*, pp. 61–2.

134 Jeffrey Chipps Smith, 'The Art of Salvation in Bavaria,' in O'Malley et al., *The Jesuits*, pp. 571–72. See also Smith, *Sensuous Worship*, pp. 7–21.

135 Park, *Doctors and Medicine*, p. 103.

136 Eunice D. Howe, 'The Hospital of Santo Spirito and Pope Sixtus IV,' PhD dissertation, The Johns Hopkins University, 1977, pp. 162–6.

137 Howe, 'The Hospital of Santo Spirito,' p. 164. In the late Middle Ages there was a tremendous growth in the number and size of hospitals in Italy. See Park, *Doctors and Medicine*, pp. 100–1.

138 There is a rich literature on the Scala Hospital, including Alessandro Orlandini, *Gettatelli pellegrini: Gli affreschi nella Sala del Pellegrinaio dell'Ospedale di Santa Maria della Scala di Siena* (Siena, 1997); Gualterio Bellucci and Pietro Torriti, *Il Santa Maria della Scala in Siena* (Genoa, 1991); Pietro Torriti, *Il Pellegrinaio nella Spedale di Santa Maria della Scala in Siena* (Siena, 1987); *Spedale di Santa Maria della Scala: Atti del convegno internazionale di studi* (Siena, 1986); Daniela Gallavotti Cavallero, *Lo spedale di Santa Maria della Scala in Siena: Vicenda di una committenza artistica* (Siena, 1985).

139 Cavallero, *Lo spedale della Scala*, p. 156; Howe, 'The Hospital of Santo Spirito,' p. 170.

140 Howe, 'The Hospital of Santo Spirito,' p. 172.

141 Luchinat, *Taddeo e Federico Zuccari*, vol. 2, fig. 116. The work was formerly attributed to Federico Zuccaro.

142 Laura Cavazzini, 'Dipinti e sculture nelle chiese dell'Ospedale,' in Lucia Sandri, ed., *Gli innocenti e Firenze nei secoli: Un ospedale, un archivio, una città* (Florence, 1996), pp. 113–45.

143 *Gli innocenti*, fig. 15.

144 Gallery of the Accademia, Inv. 1890 no. 9385.

145 Howe, 'The Hospital of Santo Spirito,' pp. 173–5; Ralph Quadflieg, *Filaretes Ospedale Maggiore in Mailand* (Cologne, 1981); Giuliana Albini, 'La gestione dell'Ospedale Maggiore di Milano nel quattrocento: Un esempio di concentrazione ospedaliera,' in Allen J. Grieco and Lucia Sandri, eds, *Ospedale e Città* (Florence, 1997), pp. 157–78.

146 Howe, 'The Hospital of Santo Spirito,' p. 175.

147 Ibid., p. 368.

148 *Lo Spedale Serristori di Figline* (Figline Val d'Arno, 1982); *Contributi per la storia dello spedale del Ceppo di Pistoia* (Pistoia, 1977).

4: The Jesuit Collegiate Foundations of the Collegio Romano, the Seminario Romano, and the German-Hungarian College

1 Buser, 'Jerome Nadal,' p. 428.

2 O'Malley, *Trent and All That*.

3 They are referring specifically to the S. Stefano Rotondo murals. See John Paoletti and Gary Radke, *Art in Renaissance Italy* (Upper Saddle River, 1997), p. 429.

4 Herz, 'Imitators of Christ,' pp. 67–8.

5 See Buser, 'Jerome Nadal'; Monssen, 'The Martyrdom Cycle in Santo Stefano Rotondo, Part Two,' p. 77; Lydia Salviucci Insolera, 'Gli affreschi del ciclo dei martiri commissionati al Pomarancio in rapporto alla situazione religiosa ed artistica della seconda metà del cinquecento,' in Hugo Brandenburg and József Pál, eds, *Santo Stefano Rotondo in Rom* (Wiesbaden, 2000), p. 133.

6 ARSI, FG 866 A (Libro della Fabrica della Casa a S. Andrea, 1581–94), no folios.

7 In as early as 1560, Juan Alfonso de Polanco wrote in General Laínez's name that education had become the primary ministry of the Society of Jesus. For the early history of Jesuit schools, see O'Malley, *The First Jesuits*, pp. 200–42.

8 O'Malley, 'Introduction,' in *Ratio Studiorum*, ed. Atteberry and Russell, p. 9.

9 O'Malley, *The First Jesuits*, p. 204.

10 O'Malley, 'Historiography,' p. 9; Lucas, *Landmarking*, pp. 116–17.

11 Francesco C. Cesareo, 'The Jesuit Colleges in Rome under Everard Mercurian,' in Thomas McCoog, ed., *Mercurian Studies* (forthcoming).

12 O'Malley, 'Introduction,' p. 10.

13 Paul F. Grendler, *Schooling in Renaissance Italy: Literacy and Learning, 1300–1600* (Baltimore, 1989), p. 379.

14 O'Malley, *The First Jesuits*, pp. 220–2.

15 Ernesto Rinaldi, *La fondazione del Collegio Romano* (Arezzo, 1914), pp. 74–5.

16 Lucas, *Landmarking*, p. 160.

17 O'Malley, *The First Jesuits*, p. 222; Karel Porteman, *Emblematic Exhibitions at the Brussels Jesuit College (1630–1685)* (Brussels, 1996), pp. 10–11. For similar exhibitions on the worldwide missions, see Bailey, *Art on the Jesuit Missions*, pp. 68–71.

18 Judy Loach, 'The Teaching of Emblematics and Other Symbolic Imagery by Jesuits within Town Colleges in Seventeenth and Eighteenth Century France,' in Manning and Vaeck, *The Jesuits and the Emblem Tradition*, pp. 161–86.

19 Rinaldi, *La fondazione*, p. 74.

20 'Cum autem R.P. Generalis universae congregationis multitudine comitatus ad Collegium venit, tot versibus emblematisq. quae superiorem & inferiorum deambulationem ornabant, exceptus est' (*Annuae Litterae Societatis Iesu anni MDLXXXI* [Rome, 1583], p. 19).

21 Paulette Choné, 'Domus optima: Un manuscrit emblématique au collège des jésuites de Verdun (1585),' in Manning and Vaeck, *The Jesuits and the Emblem Tradition*, pp. 35–86; Bailey, *Art on the Jesuit Missions*, p. 69.

22 Louise Rice, 'Jesuit Thesis Prints and the Festive Academic Defence at the Collegio Romano,' in O'Malley et al., *The Jesuits*, pp. 148–69.

23 Rinaldi, *La fondazione*, pp. 55–6.

24 Cesareo, 'Jesuit Colleges,' p. 6; O'Malley, *The First Jesuits*, pp. 232–3.

25 Cesareo, 'Jesuit Colleges,' p. 2. See also Francesco C. Cesareo, 'The Collegium Germanicum and the Ignatian Vision of Education,' *Sixteenth Century Journal* 24 (1993): 829–41.

26 O'Malley, *The First Jesuits*, p. 205; Lucas, *Landmarking*, p. 160; Giovanni Martinetti, *Sant'Ignazio (Le chiese di Roma illustrate, 97)* (Rome, 1967), pp. 11–20; Rinaldi, *La fondazione*, p. 31.

27 Rinaldi, *La fondazione*, pp. 57–8.

28 BNR, Fond. Ges. 1526, 24a–33a. See also Rinaldi, *La fondazione*, pp. 61–7; Pirri, *Tristano*, p. 11.

29 O'Malley, *The First Jesuits*, pp. 232–3; Cesareo, 'Jesuit Colleges,' pp. 11–12.

30 Lucas, *Landmarking*, p. 160; Rinaldi, *La fondazione*, p. 53.

31 Cesareo, 'Jesuit Colleges,' pp. 2, 10–14; Rinaldi, *La fondazione*, p. 18.

32 Rinaldi, *La fondazione*, pp. 50, 53, 75.

33 'in Roma, et alle missioni da' paesi fuori alle parti settentrionali, delle Indie' [undated letter, BNR, Fond. Ges. 1526, 17a; see also 17b–24a).

34 Cesareo 'Jesuit Colleges,' pp. 1–2; Rinaldi, *La fondazione*, p. 92. For the colleges in Japan, see Bailey, *Art on the Jesuit Missions*, pp. 52, 59, 63.

35 Pirri, *Valeriano*, p. 54; Ludwig von Pastor, *The History of the Popes from the Close of the Middle Ages*, 40 vols (London, 1924–53), XX, pp. 586–9; Rinaldi, *La fondazione*, pp. 81–4.

36 Marc'Antonio Ciappi, *Compendio delle heroiche et gloriose attioni, et santa vita di Papa Gregorio XIII* (Rome, 1596), pp. 25–6.

37 'Ma che diremo della sontuosissima fabrica per lo Collegio Romano, retto dalli Padri della Compagnia di Giesu, fatta l'anno decimo del suo Ponteficato, con sì meravigliosa architettura, & spesa, con molte scole capacissime, & quelle di facoltà, scienze, & lingue diverse, non ad altro fine, che per dar commodità à tutti li poveri, giovani, & fanciulli, non solo di Roma, ma d'Italia tutta, & fuori di venire à farsi dotti nelle lingue, scientifiche, & in ogni scienza, & instruirsi insieme ne' costumi Christiani sotto la dottrina, & disciplina di que' Padri, i quali ogni giorno più si mostrano utili, & fruttuosi alle Chiesa di Dio, & Republica Christiana' (Ciappi, *Compendio delle heroiche*, p. 16).

38 Cesareo, 'Jesuit Colleges,' p. 17; O'Malley, *The First Jesuits*, p. 234.

39 Allan P. Farrell, 'Colleges for Extern Students Opened in the Lifetime of St. Ignatius,' *Archivum Historicum Societatis Iesu* 6 (1937): 89.

40 Quoted in Cesareo, 'Jesuit Colleges,' p. 17. See also Peter Schmidt, *Das Collegium Germanicum in Rom. und die Germaniker* (Tübingen: 1984), p. 13.

41 The quotation is from a letter from Diego Laínez to Alessandro Farnese, dated 21 October 1556: '... raccomandandole la souventione del Collegio Germanico di Roma; et anchorche la Compagnia nostra, non ha preso assunto, d'aiutare quella Santa Opera nel temporale; ma solamente nel spirituale, quanto alla buona istitutione in lettere e' virtu de gli scholari Germani; la charità ci hà obligato affar quanto havemo potuto etiam nel temporale, aumentando assai nostri debiti, per suvenirla' (ASPar, Epistolario scelto, b. 26).

42 O'Malley, *The First Jesuits*, p. 135. The quotation from Laínez is from a letter dated 30 January 1557 addressed to Alessandro Farnese: 'Questi mesi hò dato aviso à V. S.

R.ma del stretto bisogno, nel qual si trovava il collegio Germanico con questi travagli delli tempi' (ASPar, Epistolario scelto, b. 26).

43 Cesareo, 'Jesuit Colleges,' p. 19; O'Malley, *The First Jesuits*, p. 236; Pastor, *History of the Popes*, vol. 19, p. 238.

44 Cesareo, 'Jesuit Colleges,' p. 21.

45 Ibid., p. 22. See also Istvan Bitskey, 'The Collegium Germanicum Hungaricum in Rome and the Beginning of the Counter-Reformation in Hungary,' in R.J.W. Evans and T.V. Thomas, eds, *Crown, Church, and Estates: Central European Politics in the Sixteenth and Seventeenth Centuries* (London, 1991), pp. 110–14.

46 Leif Holm Monssen, 'Triumphus and Trophaea Sacra: Notes on the Iconography and Spirituality of the Triumphant Martyr,' *Konsthistorisk Tidskrift* 51 (1982): 11.

47 Bösel, *Jesuitenarchitektur in Italien*, p. 243.

48 Waterworth, *The Council of Trent*, pp. 233–4.

49 O'Malley, *The First Jesuits*, p. 237. For the history of the Seminario Romano, see Guerrino Pelliccia, *La Preparazione ed ammissione dei chierici ai santi ordini nella Roma del secolo XVI* (Rome, 1946), pp. 257–303; and Pio Paschini, 'Le origini del Seminario Romano,' in Paschini, ed., *Cinquecento romano e riforma cattolica: Scritti raccolti in occasione dell'ottantesimo compleanno dell'autore* (Rome, 1958), pp. 1–32. The most thorough history of the Seminario exists only in manuscript copy: Girolamo Nappi, *Diario del Seminario Romano* (1640s), (ACGU, Hist. 145). There is also a copy at the Gregorian. See also ARSI, Rom. 155 I (Seminarium Romanum), 93a ff, an 'Informatione del Seminario di Roma' dated 1 January 1609.

50 O'Malley, *The First Jesuits*, p. 236.

51 Rice, 'Jesuit Thesis Prints,' pp. 149–50.

52 O'Malley, *The First Jesuits*, p. 237.

53 Padberg et al., *For Matters of Greater Moment*, p. 116.

54 O'Malley, *The First Jesuits*, p. 237.

55 'per dar comodità a quei giovini della n.ra Comp.ia, che finito il loro Novitiato erano inviati agli studij in questo Coll.o Rom.o' (BNR, Fond. Ges. 1669 [Breve notizia della S.a Cappella ..., 1701], 152a).

56 ARSI, Rom. 150 I (Historia Veteris Collegii Romani, 1817), 8b–9a; BNR, Fond. Ges. 1526, 78b; Rinaldi, *La fondazione*, pp. 61–2. On the history of the Church of the Annunziata, see Sandro Benedetti, 'La prima architettura gesuitica a Roma: Note sulla chiesa dell'Annunziata e sul Collegio Romano,' pp. 57–68, and Isabella Di Resta, 'Il Collegio Romano,' pp. 81–5, in Patetta and Della Torre, *L'architettura della Compagnia di Gesù*.

57 In an undated report of the negotiations between the Jesuits and the Marchesa, the church is described as 'già cominciata, e fatti i fondamenti sino al pian di terra' (BNR, Fond. Ges. 1526 [Collegio Romano], 24a).

58 The original contract stated, 'che il Collegio fabricasse a tutte spese nostre una chiesa in una parte del medesimo sito, che lei [the Marchesa] era obbligata a fabricare, il che fece il Collegio spendendo in grosso, come si può vedere.' Elsewhere the conditions are repeated, and stress that the Jesuits use their own labourers: 'La prima fù che noi fabricassimo una chiesa a spese nostre, il che fù fatto non solo con molta spesa, ma con molta fatica de' nostri' (BNR, Fond. Ges. 1526, 26a, 31a).

59 Bösel, *Jesuitenarchitektur in Italien*, p. 181; Lewine, 'The Roman Church Interior,' p. 155; Martinetti, *Sant'Ignazio*, p. 22; Pirri, *Tristano*, pp. 27–30.

60 Lewine, 'The Roman Church Interior,' p. 157. Benedetti points out that it was unusual at the time to have two chapels per side, and relates their appearance here to the four Cardinal Virtues of the Madonna (Benedetti, 'La prima architettura,' p. 58).

61 'de' quali il maggiore ha una tribuna a volta dov'è dipinta l'Annunciata, alcuni Profeti, i chori degl'Angeli, Dio padre di sopra con gran varietà et artificio, fatta per disegno et opera di Federico Zuccaro pittor eccellente; gli altri hanno i suoi quadri fatti da diversi maestri, cioè del Crucifisso, della Madonna, di S. Bastiano e S. Francesco' (Girolamo Francini, *Le cose maravigliose dell'alma città di Roma* [Rome, 1580], p. 71; quoted in Pirri, *Tristano*, p. 30].

62 An excerpt from the letter reads, 'le stanze di sopra dove saranno gelosie sonno quasi fatte, et presto si comincierà la volta della Capella grande' (Quoted in Pirri, *Tristano*, p. 28). See also Lewine, 'The Roman Church Interior,' p. 157.

63 BNR, Fond. Ges. 1526, 26a.

64 Benedetti, 'La prima architettura,' p. 58.

65 Ibid., p. 57.

66 'ha fatto un coro di molti Angeli e variati splendori, con Dio Padre che manda lo Spirito Santo sopra la Madonna, mentre è dall'angelo Gabriello annunziata, e messa in mezzo da sei Profeti, maggiori del vivo, e molto belli' (Vasari, *Le vite de' più eccellenti pittori*, ed. Milanesi, vol. 7, p. 102)

.67 Rinaldi, *La fondazione*, pp. 93–4; Lewine, 'The Roman Church Interior,' p. 160; Martinetti, *Sant'Ignazio*, pp. 24–5; Bösel, *Jesuitenarchitektur in Italien*, p. 182. According to Lewine, the work survives also in preparatory drawings; and Rinaldi claims that the bust of the Virgin survives, having been transferred to canvas.

68 Luchinat, *Taddeo e Federico Zuccari*, vol. 1, p. 256, fig. 59. They are in the National Gallery in Washington and the Hermitage in St Petersburg.

69 'Colorì, e compì Federico la bella opera dell'Annuntiata nel Collegio Romano; e fece le due altre historie della Natività, e della Circoncisione di Giesù a fresco con buona maniera' (Baglione, *Le vite de' pittori*, p. 121).

70 Hibbard, 'Ut picturae sermones,' p. 32.

71 Taddeo Zuccaro's authorship is attested to by Gaspare Celio: 'L'Adamo, & Eva nelli triangoli dell'arco à fresco, di Tadeo Zuccari. La tribona, & il di sotto à fresco, dipinti da Federico suo featello [sic]' (Celio, *Memoria delli nomi*, p. 24).

72 Robertson, *Il Gran Cardinale*, pp. 88–90, 105.

73 'Nell'Annunziata del Collegio Romano sopra uno degli altari sta San Francesco, che receve le stimmate assai spiritoso a olio formato' (Baglione, *Le vite de' pittori*, p. 50). See also Robertson, *Il Gran Cardinale*, p. 88; Giammaria, *Girolamo Muziano*, pp. 109–23; Coffin, *The Villa in the Life of Renaissance Rome*, pp. 204–6, 317.

74 Giammaria, *Girolamo Muziano*, pp. 143–8.

75 BNR, Fond. Ges. 1526, 98a–b; Martinetti, *Sant'Ignazio*, pp. 22–3.

76 'Quod attinet ad locum sepulture libenter iacere corpus meum voluissem ad pedes B. Aloysij Gonzaga mei quondam spiritualis filii, et tum superiores societatis ubi voluerint corpus meum ponant' (ASPar, Epistolario scelto, b. 25).

77 Lucas, *Saint, Site*, pp. 164–8; Martinetti, *Sant'Ignazio*, p. 16; Pirri, *Tristano*, p. 14; Rinaldi, *La fondazione*, p. 102.

78 Pirri, *Valeriano*, pp. 57–62. On the question of the architect's identity, see also Benedetti, 'La prima architettura,' pp. 59–60; Di Resta, 'Il Collegio Romano,' pp. 81–2.

79 The accounts are in ARSI, FG 1070 (Libro della Fabrica del Collegio), 109b–163a, and
were published in Pirri, *Valeriano*, pp. 278–81. I reproduce them here: '[4 February
1584] pagati per mano del detto [Fr. Giovan Iacomo Rossa], cioè scudi 5.20 a Mastro
Bartolomeo Sogliani pittore per 13 giornate, e scudi 0.50 a Mastro Andrea Aretino pittore per una giornata per dipingere in la sala e sopra la scala, e scudi 0.82 per portatura
di 300 tavole d'olmo e per uno straccio, e altro, scudi 6.52' (f. 109b); '[10 March 1584]
pagato scudi 6.75 a Mastro Matteo [Neroni da Siena] pittore per giornate 7½ a g. 9 il
giorno e sc. 2.40 a Mastro Bartolomeo pittore per giornate 6 a g. 4 il giorno per dipinger
la sala, scudi 9.15' (f. 109b); '[21 April 1584] pagati a Cesare [Rossetto] e Bartolomeo
[Sogliani] pittori per X giornate a giuli 4 il giorno che questa settimana hanno dipinto
in la sala, scudi 4' (f. 138a); '[21 July 1584] pagato a Cristofano [Roncalli] pittore per sua
mercede di 4 giornate in dipingere in la sala, scudi 3.60' (f. 138b); '[11 August 1584]
pagato a Mastro Andrea Aretino, Cristofano dalle Pomarancie, Paulo [Brill] fiammengo e
Bartolomeo Sogliani pittori per lor mercede di giornate 19 ½ a vari prezzi che sono stati
a dipingere nella sala grande e nella sala della teologia, scudi 12.15' (f. 138b); '[18 August 1584] pagato per mano di Giovan Battista [Fiammeri] pittore per conto di tanti
colori compri, scudi 2' (f. 138b); '[24 August 1584] pagato scudi 4.50 a Cristofano dalle
Pomarancie per giornate 4 ½; scudi 2,69 a Mastro Andrea Aretino per 5 giornate compreso b. 19 per colori; scudi 2,50, a Bartolommeo Sogliani per 5 giornate [fatte al Giesù
della Teologia, che l'altre di sopra sono alla sala] e la sala grande e al teolog[ato], scudi
9.24' (f. 138b); '[24 August 1584] Mastro Ambrosio Bonvicino scultore de dare ... scudi 3
di moneta pagato contanti a buon conto del prezzo dell'arme di stucco che ne fa sopra
'1 piano di mezza scala, scudi 3' (f. 151a); '[7 September 1584] scudi 11 moneta pagato
contanti per resto di scudi 14 per il prezzo di detta arme, scudi 11. [Total] scudi 14' (f.
151a); '[7 September 1584: they liquidate the account] delle arme di stucco fattaci sopra
la scala, cioè acanto a la volta sopra il piano che è a mezza scala' (f. 151b); '[11 September 1584] pagato per mano del fratello Rutilio [Clementi, S.J. from Perugia] pittore per
tanti colori comprati, scudi 0.20' (f. 151a); '[15 September 1584] pagati scudi 4.50 a
Mastro Cristofano [delle Pomarancie] pittore per 5 giornate, e scudi 3.69 a Mastro
Andrea [Aretino] e altri pittori per giornate [sei], compreso b.69 per colori. In tutto,
scudi 8.19' (f. 151a); '[20 September 1584] pagato a Alexandro de Magistris alias Cald-
erola per a buon conto di sua merciede de versi scrive [nelle cartelle], scudi 3' (f. 151a);
'[22 September 1584] pagato a Mastro Cristofano pittore per 4 giornate per dipingere in
la sala, scudi 3.60' (f. 151a); '[28 September 1584] pagato scudi 4.50 a Mastro Cristofano
e scudi 2.55 a Mastro Andrea [Aretino] pittori per giornate 5 per uno, scudi 7.5' (f. 151a);
'[6 October 1584] pagato scudi 3.10 a Mastro Andrea Aretino pittore per 6 giornate e
scudi [5.50] a Mastro Anton Francesco Verocchi per pittura di 30 arme in carta, in tutto,
scudi 8.60' (f. 151a); '[13 October 1584] pagato scudi 3.7 a Mastro Andrea per 6 giornate
e per colori, scudi 0.90 a Cristofano pittore per una giornata, e b.48 a Pietro Lombardi
per spesa di colori et altro per le tavolette fatte, scudi 4.45' (f. 151b); '[27 October 1584]
pagato a tre pittori per lor giornate di haver dipinto in la sala e altri luoghi, cioè scudi
4 a Mastro Andrea per la pittura di 6 porte finte, scudi 2 a Mastro Paulo [Brill] per la
pittura di dua paesi in la facciata della sala a la parte del papa, e scudi 0.50 per una
giornata a Mastro Bartolomeo [Sogliani] per dipingere le 2 porticelle di color di noce al
principio della scala, scudi 6.50' (f. 151b); '[16 January 1585] spesi per mano del fratello
Rutilio pittore da dì 24 di ottobre sino a questo dì in cinque partite per colori per gesso

e altro comprati per dipingere nel quadro della Madonna della Congregatione de
piccolli e per dipingere l'adornamento fattoli [di nuovo], scudi 3.30′ (f. 163a); '[1 February 1585] per pittura di una tavoletta per la 4a classe, scudi 16′ (f. 163a).

80 Freedberg, *Painting in Italy*, p. 657; Macioce, *Undique splendent*, pp. 111–12, 129–31;
Baglione, *Le vite de' pittori*, p. 296; Caterina Limentani Virdis, 'Flemish Winds on the
Roman Landscape: The Bril Brothers and Other Painters in Rome at the Time of Pope
Gregory XIII,' in Nicole Dacos, ed., *Fiamminghi a Roma, 1508–1608* (Florence, 1999),
pp. 67–78; Calì, *La pittura del cinquecento*, vol. 2, p. 201.

81 Freedberg, *Painting in Italy*, pp. 664–5; Baglione, *Le vite de' pittori*, pp. 288–9.

82 Freiberg, *The Lateran in 1600*, p. 81; Rice, *The Altars and Altarpieces*, p. 28.

83 The account book makes further reference to the gilding and curtains of this painting:
'[7 March 1582] b. 90 per la duratura dello adornamento del quadro d'una Madonna, et
b. 20 per il ferro che tiene la cortina d'esso, qual fu donato a monsignor Passamonte,
scudi 1.10′ (ARSI, FG 1070, 45a; Pirri, *Valeriano*, p. 274).

84 'In fondo alla sala subito l'occhio del visitatore è attratto dall'immagine di Gregorio
XIII seduto in trono, circondato da una numerosa schiera di cardinali, nell'atto di
benedire un buon numero di nostri collegiali prostrati ai suoi piedi, insieme ad un
gruppo dei più distini alunni in rappresentanza dei rispettivi collegi. Se volgiamo
intorno lo sguardo sulle pareti dell'aula, vedremo da ogni parte raffigurate bellissime
immagini di fabbriche. Sono i collegi gregoriani costruiti dallo zelante pontefice nelle
varie parti del mondo per la propagazione della Religione, sei a destra e sette a sinistra.
A destra si vedono i collegi di Vilna in Lituania e di Claudiopoli in Transilvania, e altri
tre in Giappone, col seminario di Fulda. A sinistra i collegi di Vienna in Austria, l'Illirico
nel Piceno, e infine i cinque romani, cioè, oltre agli altri già esistenti, il seminario dei
Neofiti greci e ultimo quello dei Maroniti. La parete di prospetto reca in fronte l'immagine del Collegio Romano più grande di tutti gli altri, e di fronte a questo nella
parete d'ingresso si vedono altri cinque collegi, minori di proporzione e di opere, quelli
cioè di Pont-à-Mousson in Lorena, di Braunsberg in Prussia, di Olmütz in Moravia,
di Graz in Stiria e infine di Praga in Boemia. Tutte queste svariate figure si vedono
rappresentate intorno alla sala come in un grande arazzo spiegato, e per dar vita ad
esse è stato messo in ciascuna un breve ed elegante epigramma latino che in poche
parole indica le caratteristiche di essa' (ARSI, Opp. NN. 326 [memorial of Gregory XIII
by Possevino], 20a; *Annuae Litterae 1584* [Rome, 1586], pp. 11–12. The complete text has
also been published in Pirri, *Giuseppe Valeriano*, p. 69).

85 See Bailey, *Art on the Jesuit Missions*, p. 59; John McCall, 'Early Jesuit Art in the Far East
V: More Discoveries,' *Artibus Asiae* 17 (1954): 52–3.

86 See the reconstruction in Madonna, *Roma di Sisto V*, tav. XIX–XXIII. For the Salone
Sistino in the Vatican Library, see ibid., pp. 77–90; and Freiburg, *The Lateran in 1600*,
pp. 24–5. The Salone Sistino was decorated by a team led by Giovanni Guerra and
Cesare Nebbia.

87 Macioce, *Undique splendent*, tav. IV (b).

88 Lucas, *Saint, Site*, cat. nos 94, 95.

89 'Fu fatto un apparato bellissimo di pitture e composizioni per tutto il cortile e per tutte
le scale. Venne il Papa, vide e godè molto di tutto: fu portato al salone già dipinto
attorno con pitture rappresentanti le fabbriche di diversi collegi fatti da sua S.tà. Nel
fondo del salone era stato dipinto lo stesso papa Gregorio con a fianco molti cardinali e

con a' piedi diversi giovani di diverse devise secondo gli abiti de' loro collegi, in atto di benedirli, come ancor presentemente si vede. In faccia a questo quadro era alzato il trono per il Papa col baldacchino ... Partì poi il Papa tutto sodisfatto e animò i padri a dar principio alli studi' (ms. Origini del Collegio Romano, pp. 68–9, quoted in Rinaldi, *La fondazione*, p. 104). A papal *avviso* describing the same event but without reference to the paintings is published in Lucas, *Saint, Site*, p. 170.

90 'A 28 d'Ottobre [1584] l'istesso Pontefice andò à vedere il Collegio Romano da lui fabricato dove fu invitato ... A visto il Papa nel salone dipinto come si vede hoggi con la Pittura in faccia di Gregorio, dove si trovava un Trono ... poi andò girando tutto il collegio fabricato di nuovo, et ornato con vesti per ultimo girò le scuole che en qual giorno furono tutti ornati di vesti et emblemmi' (ACGU, Hist. 145 [Nappi, *Diario del Seminario Romano*], 286a).

91 '[25 November 1581] Bartolommeo Argentires da Turino scultore de dare ... sc. XX di moneta pagato contanti per parte e a buon conto del prezzo delle medaglie che fa per questo collegio cioè dua medaglie cioè dua forme da gettare medaglie di dua sorte, scudi 20'; '[17 December 1581] b. 50 di moneta pagato contanti che sc. 26 sono per resto di sc. 46 per il prezzo delle sopradette dua medaglie o forme per gettar medaglie, e sc. 2.50 sono per il prezzo della medaglia gettata di argento in tutto sono, scudi 28.50'; '[23 December 1581] scudi II. b. 60 di moneta pagato contanti per il prezzo di una medaglia d'argento gettata dataci, scudi 2.60'; '[29 November 1581] b. 40 pagato per mano del pittore per olio di noce, per biacha, e oro macinato per li cartoni delle imprese si fanno per la fondatione del collegio, scudi 0.40'; '[30 March 1582] Bernardino Passero scultore di contro de havere addì 30 di marzo sc. 75 di moneta se li fanno buoni che sc. 71 sono per il prezzo delle tre medaglie fattoci, cioè delle cere fattone da improntare medaglie di tre sorte, e sc. 4 sono per una medaglia d'argento gettataci e finita del tutto con suo argento, posto dar medaglie f., scudi 75'; '[30 June 1583] scudi 120.50 di moneta fatti buoni a Mastro Flaminio Vacca scultore per valuta delle due armi del Papa, fatteci per detto prezzo d'accordo per metter sopra le scale del cortile delle scuole, scudi 120,50' (ARSI, FG 1070, 21b, 25a, 30a, 97a; Pirri, *Valeriano*, pp. 270, 273, 275).

92 'Circa le camere, se non quelle del sup.re de' Procuratori, del spenditore, et de la Matematica. In ogni camera ci e un vaso d'acqua benedetta alla porta. Ciascuno habbi due imagini una appresso il letto, dove fa' orazione, l'altra alla tavola' (ARSI, Rom. 150 I, 36a).

93 '[7 January 1586] ho dato al F. Gio. Batt.a Fiammeri per comprare colori per il Coll.o Romano scudi due alla romana, [scudi] 1.6.6.8'; '[1587] Coll.o Rom.o deve havere scudi 2 alla romana, quali ha portato il F. Gio. Batt.a Fiammeri, quando è venuto di Roma in ricompensa delli 2 scudi si erano dati al detto Fratello per comprare colori per detto Collegio, che sono alla fiorentina, [scudi] 1.6.6.8' (ASF, Comp. Rel. Sopp. 998, #98, 111b; Comp. Rel. Sopp. 1000, 96b).

94 '[24 September 1587] ho dato al F. Rutilio p. comprare colori p. portare all'Abbatia del Coll.o Rom.o y. 10, et p. opere 3 di Ms Muratore à B. [soldi] 35 il di, et opere 3 di manuale à b. 18 p. la facciata di fuore, [scudi] 2.3.19'; '[26 September 1587] ho dato p. viatico al F. Rutilio Clemente quando si è partito di questo Coll.o per ire all'Abbatia di Chiaraualle giuli 25 et p. un opera di manuale, b. 15, [scudi] 2.3.6.8' (ASF, Comp. Rel. Sopp. 1000, #111, 102a, 102b). A canvas of the *Annunciation* still at the abbey today may be the work of Fiammeri.

95 Bösel, *Jesuitenarchitektur in Italien*, p. 223; Paschini, 'Le origini,' p. 26; ARSI, Rom. 155
   I [Seminarium Romanum, after 1622], 7a, 84b. There is a surprising paucity of
   documentary material in the Jesuit archives on the early years of the Seminario
   Romano, a problem noted by Bösel.

96 Paschini, 'Le origini,' p. 29.

97 'Le habitationi del Seminario sono stati varii Palazzi per Roma, i quali per il gran
   numero de convittori si andavari mutando, sinche furono comprati due Palazzi
   contigui alla Chiesa di S. Bartolomeo de Bergamaschi, e ridotti con la nuova fabrica
   ad habitatione alta e sofficiente per sempre, sicome si è sperimentato per lo spatio di
   anni 56' (ARSI, Rom. 155 I, 7a). Another history reads: 'Paolo V comprò due palazzi
   vicini alla chiesa di S. Bartolomeo de Bergamaschi per il Seminario Romano. Alli 13
   giugno andarono ad abitarlo' (BNR, Fond. Ges. 1526, 82b).

98 For example, the letters of Polanco from 1565 and 1567, recording the earliest years of
   the Seminario's existence (Paschini, 'Le origini,' pp. 27–9).

99 'E divisa tutta la presente habitazione in una gran sala che serve per le fonzioni
   pubbliche di Dispute di filosofia e Teologia private e publiche, addottoramenti,
   recitamenti di orationi e poemi, attioni tragichi, o altre rappresentationi solite à farsi
   nel Carnevale, per adunanza de seminaristi all'hore proprie secondo la diversità delle
   classi, quando descono andare allo studio del vicino Collegio Romano, e finalmente
   per udir' messa ogni mattina con la solita musica, e per la frequenza de sagramenti
   ne'i giorni festivi' (ARSI, Rom. 155 I, 8a–b).

100 Paschini, 'Le origini,' p. 28.

101 '... giachè ogni mese sono tutti obligati a communicarsi secondo le Regole del Semi-
    nario, e di più ogni 15 giorni per obligo delle congregationi, le quali sono 4 oratorij al
    piano della porta maggiore e cortile del Seminario. Il primero è sotto il titolo della
    Visitazione della Santissima Vergine per li convittori mezzani. Il 2 sotto il titolo della
    Natività per li convittori grandi. Il 3 sotto il medesimo titolo per li convittori piccoli.
    Et il 4 per li chierici sotto il titolo della Concettione Immaculata dell'istessa Madre di
    Dio; la quale è riverita in quelli ogni giorno di festa con varie divotioni et essercitij
    spirituali con l'acquisso di varie Indulgentie' (ARSI, Rom. 155 I, 8b).

102 'In contro poi all'oratorio de' chierici sotto alla sala sudetta è situato il Refettorio
    capace di 200 e più persone, ornato ... con pitture, come anco la volta di sopra è ornata
    con pitture e stucchi dorati. V'e anco il pulpitino, da cui si legge hora da' chierici'
    (ARSI, Rom. 155 I, 8b–9a).

103 'Dividesi poi il Seminario oltre l'officine e camere de' padri, e scrittori in nove came-
    roni, cioè otto per li convittori, e due per li chierici. La prima dei convittori maggiori
    chiamasi della Madonna; la 2a di S. Giovanni Battista; la 3a di S. Bartolomeo; la 4a di
    S. Andrea; la 5a di S. Paulo; la 6a di S. Michele; la 7a di S. Giovanni Evangelista; la 8a
    di S. Francesco Xaverio. La Prima de' chierici grandi chiamasi di S. Gregorio, la 2a de'
    chierici mezzani e piccoli di S. Pietro' (ARSI, Rom. 155 I, 9a).

104 'In ciascuno camerata vi è il suo Padre Prefetto che di continuo inviglia all'applica-
    zione et osservanza de' giovani tanto circa la divozione e pietà, quanto circa lo studio,
    et ogni buona Disciplina. Et in oltre v'e un' cameriere assegnato per la polizia, e
    servitù personale de' giovani, per tenere e ricomporre i letti, postare acqua, et altre
    cose secondo il bisogno di tutti, e di ciascuno ... [after getting up in the morning and
    going to their rooms to pray with the priest in honour of the Immaculate Conception]

Doppo che son' levati tutti in ginocchioni in fila avanti l'Imagine del Santo Protettore e Titolar della loro camerata cioè li convittori per un quarto d'hora' (ARSI, Rom. 155 I, 9b–12b).

105 In addition to a quite sizeable literature on the church's early Christian and even Roman archaeology, there is an extraordinarily extensive bibliography on the paintings alone. On the paintings, see Mara Nimmo, 'Santo Stefano Rotondo: La recinzione dell'altare di mezzo,' pp. 97–109, and Veronika Biermann, 'Die Vita der Heiligen Paulus von Theben und Stephanus: Ein neuentdeckter monochromer Gemäldezyklus des 16. Jahrhunderts in der Portikus von Santo Stefano Rotondo in Rom,' pp. 111–27, in Brandenburg and Pál, *Santo Stefano Rotondo in Rom*; Leslie Korrick, 'On the Meaning of Style: Nicolò Circignani in Counter-Reformation Rome,' *Word and Image* 15:2 (April–June 1999): 170–89; Insolera, 'Gli affreschi,' pp. 129–37; Kristen Noreen, 'Ecclesiae militantis triumphi: Jesuit Iconography and the Counter-Reformation,' *Sixteenth Century Journal* 29:3 (1998): 689–716; Herz, 'Imitators of Christ,' pp. 53–70; Mara Nimmo, 'Alcune precisazioni su Santo Stefano Rotondo,' *Ricerche di storia dell'arte* 25 (1985): 91–102; Leif Holm Monssen, 'Antonio Tempesta in Santo Stefano Rotondo,' *Bolletino d'arte* 67 (1982): 107–20; Monssen, 'The Martyrdom Cycle in Santo Stefano Rotondo, Part One,' *Acta ad archaeologiam et artium historiam pertinentia*, series 2, 2 (1982): 175–319; Monssen, 'The Martyrdom Cycle in Santo Stefano Rotondo, Part Two'; Antonio Vannugli, 'Gli affreschi di Antonio Tempesta a S. Stefano Rotondo e l'emblematica nella cultura del Martirio presso la Compagnia di Gesù,' *Storia dell'arte* 48 (1983): 101–16; Monssen, 'Rex gloriose martyrum,' pp. 130–7; Monssen, 'Triumphus and Trophaea Sacra,' pp. 10–20; Buser, 'Jerome Nadal,' pp. 425–33; Herwarth Röttgen, 'Zeitgeschichtliche Bildprogramme der katolischen Restauration unter Gregor XIII,' *Münchener Jahrbuch der bildenden Kunst* 26 (1975): 89–122. For recent literature on the early Christian and medieval history of the church, see Lorenz Weinrich, *Das ungarische paulinerkloster Santo Stefano Rotondo in Rom (1404–1579)* (Berlin, 1998).

106 Charles Dickens, *American Notes and Pictures from Italy* (repr. London, 1997), p. 415.

107 Ibid., p. 415.

108 Sade, Donatien-Alphonse-François de, *Oeuvres complètes du Marquis de Sade*, vol. 6 (Rome) (Paris, 1967), pp. 288–9.

109 On the anti-aesthetic paradigm and twentieth-century treatments of Jesuit art projects, see Bailey, 'Le style jésuite,' pp. 42–6; and on the martyrdom cycles, see Bailey, 'The Jesuits and Painting in Italy,' pp. 158–9. For the comparison with Nazi Germany, see *Santo Stefano Rotondo auf dem Caelius in Rom* (Munich, 1991), p. 24. See also Korrick, 'On the Meaning of Style,' p. 180.

110 Derek Moore maintains that the Jesuits' reuse of older churches should be seen as a purely practical solution made necessary by poverty and unrelated to the revival of Palaeochristian churches by titular cardinals (Moore, 'Pellegrino Tibaldi's Church of S. Fedele,' p. 303). While it may be true that the Jesuits themselves did not choose to renovate these churches, the buildings were handed over to them by the pope, and they were expected to repair them just as the cardinals were expected to repair their titular churches. The stylistic similarities between the frescoes commissioned by the Jesuits and those commissioned by the titular cardinals, and the ideological goals shared by both groups, indicate that both were part of the same movement. On the Palaeochristian Revival movement in general, see Freiburg, *The Lateran in 1600*,

pp. 161–76; Macioce, *Undique splendent*, pp. 9–75; Herz, 'Imitators of Christ'; Herz, 'Cardinal Cesare Baronio's Restoration'; Zuccari, *Arte e committenza*, pp. 31–147; Morton Abromson, 'Painting in Rome during the Papacy of Clement VIII,' PhD dissertation, New York University, 1981, pp. 121–219.

111 Freiburg, *The Lateran in 1600*, p. 38; Zuccari, *Arte e committenza*, pp. 34–6; Abromson, 'Painting in Rome,' p. 123.

112 Henneberg, 'Cardinal Caesar Baronius,' pp. 137–8; Zuccari, 'Cesare Baronio, le immagini, gli artisti,' pp. 82–9.

113 Zuccari, *Arte e committenza*, p. 111. My translation.

114 Abromson, 'Painting in Rome,' p. 126.

115 Henneberg, 'Cardinal Caesar Baronius,' p. 137.

116 Erasmo Vaudo, *Scipione Pulzone da Gaeta, pittore* (Gaeta, 1976), pp. 11–12.

117 Henneberg, 'Cardinal Caesar Baronius,' p. 157; Zuccari, 'La politica culturale dell'Oratorio romano,' p. 101; Buser, 'Jerome Nadal,' p. 432.

118 Zuccari, *Arte e committenza*, p. 36.

119 Charles Dempsey, 'The Carracci and the Devout Style in Emilia,' in Henry Millon, ed., *Emilian Painting of the 16th and 17th Centuries* (Bologna, 1987), pp. 75–8.

120 Robertson, *Il Gran Cardinale*, p. 166; Lewine, 'The Roman Church Interior,' pp. 52ff.

121 See Abromson, 'Painting in Rome,' p. 63.

122 Lewine, 'The Roman Church Interior,' p. 65. See also Robertson, *Il Gran Cardinale*, p. 166.

123 Lewine, 'The Roman Church Interior,' p. 323.

124 On the history of S. Saba, see P. Testini, *San Saba (Le chiese di Roma illustrate, 68)* (Rome, 1961).

125 Francini, *Le cose maravigliose*, p. 17a. The passage reads, '... vi è una fontana, nella quale è il scapolario di San Saua: della quale esce maravigliosa virtù in sanare molte infermità, & specialmente il flusso di sangue.'

126 Testini, *San Saba*, p. 14.

127 Monssen, 'The Martyrdom Cycle in Santo Stefano Rotondo, Part Two,' p. 14.

128 Testini, *San Saba*, pp. 14–15. Francini records that the bodies of two Roman emperors lay within the church as well: 'Et in sepolchro di marmo appresso il choro ivi sono li corpi di Vespasiano & Tito Imperatori' (Francini, *Le cose maravigliose*, p. 17a).

129 Zuccari, *Arte e committenza*, pp. 37, 46 n28; Testini, *San Saba*, p. 15. The reference is as follows: 'le quali scatole dal Rettore del Collegio suddetto [Germanico] che fu il Rev.do padre Michele Lauretano, furono rinnovate e poste nell'istesso luogo' (ms. Casanatense, Sulle Chiese di Roma, vol. X, cod. 2186, 2–3). Terribilini lived from 1709 to 1755. For Ciappi, see n139 to this chapter, below.

130 'P. repara[zion]e della chiesa di S. Saba, [scudi] 886–86' (ARSI, Rom. 51 I [Visitors Report, Roman Province, 1576–83], 9a).

131 On Di Loreto's life, see Nimmo, 'Santo Stefano Rotondo: La recinzione,' p. 103.

132 Mara Nimmo, '"L'Età perfetta della virilità" di Nicolò Circignani,' *Studi romani* 3–4 (1984): 200. The standard reprint edition of Paleotti's tract is Barocchi, *Trattati d'arte del cinquecento*, vol. 2, pp. 117–509. On Paleotti, see also Jones, 'Art Theory as Ideology,' pp. 127–39.

133 Paleotti visited S. Stefano to celebrate mass on several occasions in 1582 and 1583, precisely when the frescoes were being painted, and expressed his pleasure with them (ACGU, Hist. 103, 31, 39, 51). See also Nimmo, 'Alcune precisazioni,' p. 92.

134   O'Malley, *The First Jesuits*, pp. 235–6.

135   Cesareo, 'Jesuit Colleges,' p. 18.

136   O'Malley, *The First Jesuits*, p. 220.

137   'Nella chiesa di S. Sabba si farà fare un tabernacolo decente per tenere sopra l'altare grande il S.mo Sacram.to quando vi si vuol tenere' (ARSI, Rom. 51 I, 66a).

138   For example, the Annual Letter of 1582 by Di Loreto reads: 'Di queste tre chiese, doi quest'anno son state tutte depinte, la una vi è la vita di S. Apollinare, al quale è dedicata, nell'altra, che è dedicata à Santo Stefano, et è molto maggiore, et molto più bella per esser di forma rotonda et per haver in doi circoli che si sono, 56 colonne di marmo tra grosse e piccole. Hanno fatto depingere le persecutioni della Chiesa, che furono nelli primi 400 anni, che sono distribuite nel circolo maggiore in 31 quadro, servando sé per l'ordine delli imperatori Romani sotto quali furono con applicatione Italiana, et Latina' (ARSI, Rom. 126b I, 287a). A very similar passage appears in Di Loreto's *Diario*: 'Di queste 3 chiese il Collegio ne ha fatto depingere quest'anno doi. In una vi è la vita di S. Apollinare, al quale è dedicata, nella altra, che è di S. Stefano protomartire, et è molto maggiore, et più bella, et di forma rotonda, et doi circoli di colonne di marmo quali tra grande, et picole sono cinquanta sei, vi sono dipinte le persecutioni della Chiesa, che furono sotto diversi Imperatori, nelli primi 400 anni ab incarnazione Christi distribuite tutte in 31 quadri' (ACGU, Hist. 103, 49a; published in part in Monssen, 'The Martyrdom Cycle in Santo Stefano Rotondo, Part Two,' p. 19). A published source confirms that a Father from the college was responsible for the series: 'Itaque a Moderatoribus eiusdem Collegij religiosissimis Patribus Societatis Iesu merito excogitatum est, ut circumquaque parietes templi, Martyrum hystorijs pro varietate temporum ac persecutiorum exornarentur' (Giulio Rossi da Orte, *Triumphus martyrum in templo d. S. Stephani Caelii Montis expressus* [Rome, 1587], introduction; published in Monssen, 'The Martyrdom Cycle, Part Two,' p. 19).

139   Ciappi, *Compendio delle heroiche*, p. 27. The entire passage reads: 'L'Anno secondo a dunque del suo Ponteficato, havendo sua Beatitudine di nuovo fatto congregare un Collegio della natione Vngara, le parue per degni rispetti unirlo al Collegio Germanico, & perche erano molti di numero, concesse loro per habitatione, & residenza il Palazzo, & Chiesa di S. Apollinare, & anco una buona somma di denari per ristorare esso palazzo, & chiesa, & per sostètamento, & vitto de' collegiati, unì à detto Collegio le Abbatie, & Chiese di San Sauo, & di San Stefano Rotondo, le quali furono da i Rettori similmente con la mano adiutrice del Prencipe ristorate, & quella di San Stefano in particolare (richiedendo il Santo titolare, & anco la forma della Chiesa fabricata in cerchio) fù fatta ornare tutta di nobili pitture con l'historie più celebri de' santi Martiri di Christo' (pp. 26–7).

140   The entire passage reads: 'Et è cosa che il gran numero de' Martiri, et infinite sorti di tormenti, che qui sono depinti, et per esser la pittura mediocre, ma molto devota, ha dato grand' edificazione à tutti, et nome al Collegio, et molti sono che non possono risguardarle senza lagrime. Il Papa di continuo si mostra molto affettionaro à questa opera, et ne resta molto contento, et quest'anno il giorno che fu la stattione à Santo Stefano, andò à visitare quella chiesa, et fu riceuto da molti Alumni, massimamente sacerdoti, che l'andorno in contro con le cotte, et qui stette un pezzo à sentir la messa cantata, con grande sua allegrezza, et contento, come lo mostrò de poi' (ARSI, Rom. 126b I, 10b). A similar passage appears in Di Loreto's *Diario*: 'Et è cosa che move molto à divotione per vedere infinite sorti di tormenti, et tanto gran numero de' Martiri, et per

esser la pittura mediocremente bella, ma molto divota, molti non la possono vedere senza lagrime, et moti spirituali' (ACGU, Hist. 103, 49a; published in Monssen, 'The Martyrdom Cycle in Santo Stefano Rotondo, Part Two,' p. 19). I am following Leslie Korrick's lead in identifying 'mediocremente bella' as 'modest' or 'restrained' rather than 'of mediocre quality.' See Korrick, 'On the Meaning of Style,' p. 177.

141 'Circa l'istesso tempo [November 1582] il Cardinal Farnese andò a vedere S. Stefano, et vidde tutte le pitture, et ne restò molto soddisfatto, et contento' (ACGU, Hist. 103, 32; Monssen, 'The Martyrdom Cycle in Santo Stefano Rotondo, Part Two,' p. 19; Vannugli, 'Antonio Tempesta,' p. 101). The same source, Di Loreto's *Diario*, mentions a papal visit: 'Il Papa si mostra di continuo molto affezzionato à quest'opera, et ne resta molto contento et quest'anno il giorno che fu la stattione à S. Stefano andò à visitare quella chiesa et nel entrare ... incontro molti sacerdoti, et che erano in sacris, con le cotte, et quivi stette un pezzo a sentir la Messa cantata, con gran' gasto suo como lo mostrò dipoi' (f. 49). Another history of the college mentions a 1583 papal visit made during a pilgrimage to the Seven Churches of Rome: 'Visitò insieme la Chiesa di S. Stefano Ritondo nel di della Statione che è il Venerdi auanti le Palme' (ARSI, Hist. 126 [Dell'Origine del Collegio Germanico, 1587], 121a; Vannugli, 'Antonio Tempesta,' p. 102). See also the reference in the Annual Letter for 1583 in ARSI, Rom. 127 I, 154b. Cardinal Farnese was a donor of the German-Hungarian College, having given 120 scudi annually to the institution (ARSI, Rom. 53 I, 52b). For a discussion of eminent churchmen who frequented the Germanicum, including Cardinals Altemps, Albani, Caraffa, Boncompagno, and Borromeo, see A. Steinhuber, *Geschichte des Kollegium Germanicum in Rom*, vol. 1 (Freiburg, 1906), p. 174.

142 'è stata questa chiesa di S. Stefano si vagamente adornata et illustrata, che non vi è forse in Roma chiesa di più bella et più gioconda vista. Per cioche tutto il muro che attorno chiude e circonda la chiesa vi hanno fatto depingere con l'historia de santi Martiri cominciando da i santi Innocenti primitie di quelli, et poi à Christo venendo Re glorioso de i medesimi Martiri. Indi per S. Stefano che è tutti gl'altri fece la strada d'imitar Christo, seguitando per l'ordine de i tempi et per le varie persecutioni del nome Christiano infino all'età nostra' (Pompeo Ugonio, *Historia delle stationi di Roma* [Rome, 1588], pp. 290–1; Monssen, 'The Martyrdom Cycle in Santo Stefano Rotondo, Part Two,' p. 24; Vannugli, 'Antonio Tempesta,' p. 103). The text is repeated almost verbatim by Brutio (1667): '... PP della Compagnia del Gesù ... hanno fare depingere con l'historie de SS Martiri cominciando dai SS. Innocenti primitie di quelli poi a Christo venendo Re glorioso de'medisimi martiri, onde poi S. Stefano, che e tutti gl'altri fece la strada d'imitar Christo seguitando per l'ordine de' tempi e per le varie persecuzioni del nome Christiano infino all'età nostra' (BAV, Vat. Lat. 11886, 24b–25a).

143 'Huic pio desiderio suo, aliquà ut ratione satisfaceret, et aliquis viam procuret, hystoriam B. Apollinaris in suis Templi parietibus curavit conspicue depingi. Deinde in monte Celio in Augustà, ac Rotundà aede S. Protomartyris Stephani, ceu in theatro quodam, nobiliora Martyrum trophaea secundum temporum ex historiae feriem digesta, ordinatissimè pingi fecit. Bonum factum pià aemulatione plures accendit: proximè enim infectum est Collegium Anglicanum, quod templum etiam suum praeclare, tam veterum quam recentiorum Martyrum suorum victorijs depictum mirificè illustravit. Similiter B. Laurentij Martyrum in Ecclesià (quae ab fundatore suo in Damaso dicitur) Illustrissimis Cardinalis Alexandri Farnesij sumptu depictum est, imitatus hoc exemplum est Cardinalis Sfondrata (qui postmodum Gregorius Decimus

quartus Pontifex fuit) Chorum S. Caeciliae Virginis ac Martyris depictà Martyris ipsius Historià exornavit' (ARSI, Vitae 6 [Life of Michael Lauretanus by P. M. Schrick] 39a–b). This source is mistaken in that it credits Gregory XIV with the renovations at S. Cecilia, which were in fact the work of his *nipote*. A similar description appears in the obituary of the Roman province: 'Huic desiderio ut aliquà ratione satisfaceret, coepit ipse primum exemplo praeire B. Apollinaris historiam in parietibus templi conspicuè pingi curavit, tum in monte Coelio nobiliora Martyrum secundum ordinem temporis digesta, in rotundo velut theatro S. Prothomartyris Sephani templo, repre-sentari. Bonum factum pia aemulatione plures accendit, proxime enim insecutum est Collegium Anglicanum, et templum suum praeclaris tam veterum, quam recentio-rum suorum Martyrum victorijs depictum, mirificè illustravit; Subinde B. Laurentij martyrium in aede sua quondam B. Damasi impendio exstructa celeberrimi Car-dinalis Farnesij sumptu depictum est, quaemadmodum etiam in Santa Martyris Caeciliae, per illustrissimi Cardinalis Sfondrati qui postmodum Greg.o XIII Pontifex fuit, liberalitatem, eius historiae depicta visitur, atque in bis ordinatè disponendis consilium atque industria Patris Michaelis requisita fuit' (ARSI, Rom. 188 I [Romana: Necrologia], 81b–82a). The latter reference is mentioned fleetingly by Haskell in *Patrons and Painters*, p. 67 n2, but he does not mention the references to the non-Jesuit churches; it is cited also by Zuccari, *Arte e committenza*, p. 139. On the S. Lorenzo commission, see Robertson, *Il Gran Cardinale*, pp. 162–8. See also Francis Haskell's review of Zeri's *Pittura e controriforma* in *Burlington Magazine* 100 (1958): 398–9.

144   '... desiderabat, in suis quemque sanctorum ecclesijs quam solemnissime celebrari, et illustria martyrum trophaea expressa coloribus exponi ad conspectum hominum, ut illorum excitati facinoribus induerent animos ad imitamenta institutis. Ipse ut condocefaceret alios ad optimam aemulationem, collegij templum Divi Apollinaris Patroni praeclare factis circum Depictis ornavit, et in Caelio Monte S. Stephanè Rotundà aedè gestis martyrum iuxta temporum et historiae seriem expressis illus-travit. Nec operae suae pretio, nec spe sua frustratus est, nam post paulo et Anglorum templum, et S. Laurentij in Damaso, et aedes S. Caeciliae paribus studijs, et picturis condecoratae sunt' (ARSI, Rom. 188 I, 127a–b).

145   *Il seicento fiorentino*, 3 vols (Florence, 1984), I, p. 96; See also *La Compagnia della Santissima Annunziata a Firenze: Gli affreschi del chiostro* (Florence, 1989).

146   'Fu il primo che io sappia che cominciasse à far depingere nelle chiese li martirij patiti da Santi Martiri per la confessione di Christo con le sue note che dichiarano le' per-sone et le qualità de tormenti come si vede in Santo Stefano Rotondo, et dopo fu seguitato et imitato da molti altri' (ARSI Rom. 185 [Fr Fabio de Fabiis, 16 August 1610, Necrologio del P. Michele Lauretano], 25a; published in Haskell, *Painters and Patrons*, p. 67 n2; Monssen, 'The Martyrdom Cycle in Santo Stefano Rotondo, Part Two,' p. 20).

147   'Vidi ... quomodo pii Padris exemplum hoc in genere, usque in Aquilonares Ger-maniae partes pensaverit, nimirum in Cathedralis Hildesiensis ecclesiae parietibus, eadem serie Martyrum trophaea quae in Monte Celio praeclarè depicta diximus, expressa representare' (ARSI, Vitae 6 [Life of Michael Lauretanus by P. M. Schrick], 38b–40a). The obituaries report runs along similar lines: 'Nam ad ipsas usque Aquilonares Germaniae partes exemplum persuasit, magna etenim cum animi mei voluptate conspexi parietes Cathedralis Ecclesiae Hildesiensis, eadem Martyrum

trophaea, quae in Monte Celio in D. Stephani visuntur praeclarè ad modum repraesentare' (ARSI, Rom. 188 I [Romana: Necrologia], 81b–82a).

148 The order of the paintings of the second phase of renovation at the German-Hungarian College (and of those at the Venerable English College) was exactly the opposite of that given by Thomas Buser, who wrote that S. Tommaso was the first cycle and was followed by S. Stefano and S. Appolinare (see Buser, 'Jerome Nadal,' p. 427).

149 P. Santini, 'Com'era S. Apollinare,' *L'Osservatore romano*, 19 March 1937; Claudio M. Mancini, *S. Apollinare: La chiesa e il palazzo (Le chiese di Roma illustrate, 93)* (Rome, 1967), p. 8; Francini, *Le cose maravigliose*, p. 8a.

150 Mancini, *S. Apollinare*, p. 11.

151 'Per questo effetto ancora hanno fatto nella chiesa del Collegio due volte l'oratione delle 40. hore con gran concorso di gente, et massime in una volta, che si fece le feste di Pasqua alla quale vi concorse quasi tutta Roma' (ARSI, Rom. 127 I [1583 Annual Letter], 153b–154a).

152 Santini, 'Com'era S. Apollinare,' p. 5; Mancini, *S. Apollinare*, fig. 1; Lucas, *Saint, Site*, cat. no. 105. The shelf number of the drawing is ACGU, Disegni 10.

153 Ugonio, *Historia delle stationi di Roma*, 285v–286r. Translation published in Lucas, *Saint, Site*, p. 118.

154 Mancini, *S. Apollinare*, pp. 13–17; Lucas, *Saint, Site*, cat. no. 106.

155 Both Celio and Mancini mention Durante's painting. Celio writes, 'La pittura dell'altare con mezze figure ad olio di Durante dal Borgo' (*Memoria delle nomi*, p. 23). Giulio Mancini agrees but mistakenly calls him 'Giovan dal Borgo': 'Nell'Apolinare ... l'altar di quei santi Padri di Giovan dal Borgo' (*Considerazioni sulla pittura*, p. 282).

156 The passages are cited in Monssen, 'The Martyrdom Cycle in Santo Stefano Rotondo, Part Two,' p. 63. See also Monssen, 'Rex gloriose martyrum,' p. 131.

157 For the archival documents, see below where I discuss the chronology of the S. Apollinare paintings. See also Mâle, *L'art religieux*, p. 113; Nimmo, 'Alcune precisazioni,' p. 95; Nimmo, 'L'Età perfetta della virilità,' p. 201.

158 Many of the images in this book, which was also reprinted in 1585 and 1589, were published in reverse. Cavallieri later published his octavo version with cruder prints, *Triumphus martyrum in templo d. S. Stephani caelii Montis expressus*, with verses by Giulio Rossi da Orte; it was reprinted in 1589 (see Anne Liénardy, '*Ecclesiae militantis triumphi* – Rome, 1585,' *Bulletin de l'Institut historique Belge de Rome* 55–6 [1985–6]: 85–95).

159 Noreen, 'Ecclesiae militantis triumphi: Jesuit Iconography,' pp. 692–3; Lucas, *Saint, Site*, p. 188 (which mentions only three of them); Herz, 'Imitators of Christ,' p. 53; Nimmo, 'L'Età perfetta della virilità,' p. 204.

160 Giulio Mancini (1614–21) attributes the paintings to Circignani: 'Nell'Apolinare si vedono quelle pitture di Niccolò dalle Pomarancie' (*Considerazioni sulla pittura*, p. 282). Gaspare Celio (1620) agrees: 'La pittura à fresco à torno la Chiesa, atti del Santo, di Nicolao dalle Pomeranie' (*Memoria delli nomi*, p. 23). Baglione confirms his participation in his biography of Circignani: 'A S. Apollinare, dov'è'l Collegio Germanico, ornò di figure intorno tutta la chiesa con historie di quel Santo. E l'altar maggiore con sua tribuna a fresco egli colorì' (*Le vite de' pittori*, p. 41). The reference to Orazio is in the account book of the German College, dated 3 June 1580, where he is called 'Ms Oratio depintore' (ACGU, Libro del Collegio Germanico di Roma – B [1580–3], 44a;

published in Nimmo, 'L'Età perfetta della virilità,' p. 203). On Gentileschi, see Baglione, *Le vite de' pittori*, pp. 359–60. I am grateful to Pamela Jones for identifying 'Orazio' as Gentileschi.

161 *La pittura in Italia: Il cinquecento*, vol. 2, p. 680; Nimmo, 'L'Età perfetta della virilità,' pp. 194–214.

162 He signed the *Resurrection* (1569) in this series with the words 'Nicholaus Florentius me pinxit.'

163 For a study of the Torre de' Venti, see Nicola Cartright, 'Gregory XIII's Tower of the Winds in the Vatican,' PhD dissertation, New York University, 1990.

164 Robertson says about the S. Lorenzo paintings: 'A striking feature of the decorative scheme of S. Lorenzo in Damaso is the number of scenes of torture and martyrdom ... Such scenes were very much in vogue at this date, most notably in the Jesuit churches, and it is conceivable that their appearance here may reflect Cardinal Alessandro's close links with the order' (*Il Gran Cardinale*, p. 168).

165 Baglione writes: 'Et in una vigna de'Padri Giesuiti, dietro le Therme Diocletiane, colorì una Cappella, & una soffitta con quantità di figure, a olio, & a fresco terminate' (*Le vite de' pittori*, p. 302); Mancini comments: 'suo figlio, il quale adesso in Roma è in buona riputatione, havendo fatto una cappella alla Transpontina di buon colorito, e nella vigna di Giesuiti sopra Termini. E di costumi simil al padre, ma in questo differente che questo, per obligo d'un'heredità, veste di longo et con gravità dottoresca o sacerdotale, et il padre vestiva con semplicità antica toscana (*Considerazioni sulla pittura*, p. 207).

166 Baglione, *Le vite de' pittori*, p. 42. Mancini writes about Circignani: 'venendo in Roma, hebbe due pennelli: uno da maestro ordinario, l'altro da buon e pratico maestro; col primo operò negl'Inglesi, S. Apollinare, S. Stefano Rotondo et altrove, con l'altro operò nella Minerva, nel Giesù e S. Lorenzo in Damaso. Fu huomo di grand'inventione e prestezza, come si vede in S. Stefano Rotondo, che dicono che tutte quelle pitture fece in un'estate, facendone un quadro il giorno' (*Considerazioni sulla pittura*, p. 206). See also Röttgen, 'Zeitgeschichtliche Bildprogramme,' p. 109; Monssen, 'Rex gloriose martyrum,' 132.

167 See Röttgen, 'Zeitgeschichtliche Bildprogramme,' p. 108.

168 On 19 February 1580, *muratori* were paid for work on both S. Stefano and S. Apollinare. On 3 June of the same year the account book reads, 'scudi 12.60 fattone mandato a M. Rocco spenditore sono per tanti pagati a Mastro oratio depintore per resto di haver depinto la tribuna della chiesa a Sto Apolinare, va per Cosmo Vacano. Scudi 12.60' (ACGU, Libro del Collegio Germanico di Roma – B [1580–3], 43a, 44a; cited in part in Nimmo, 'L'Età perfetta della virilità,' p. 203).

169 '[8 July 1581] scudi 60 fattone mandato a Mastro Nicolao Circiniani depintor per havere depinto la tribuna dal cordone in giù del'altar maggiore della nostra chiesa, va per Cosmo Vacano. Scudi 60 ... Scudi 60 a Mastro Nicolo Circiniano depintore in spesa di chiesa. Scudi 60' (ACGU, Libro del Collegio Germanico di Roma – B, 91a, 108a). The first reference is cited in Nimmo, 'L'Età perfetta della virilità,' p. 203.

170 '[12 August 1581] scudi 20 di moneta ... pagati a Mastro Niccolo pittore a buon conto della pittura della cappella sudetta [di. S. Apollinare]' (ACGU, Libro del Collegio Germanico di Roma – B, 91a). This reference is cited in part in Nimmo, 'L'età perfetta della virilità,' p. 203.

171 '[18 May 1582] Mastro Nicolo Circiniano Pittore ... dieci scudi 130 moneta pagatili per il Padre Nicolo Bencivenni depositorio de la cassa de li scolari in tre partiti a buon conto dele pitture fatte a Sto Stefano et a Sto Apollinare vi.o per la cassa. Scudi 130' (ACGU, Libro del Collegio Germanico di Roma – B, 162a).

172 '[28 August 1582] ditto scudi 100 se fanno boni al detto Nicolò per quadri dieci dipinti nella chiesa di Sto Apollinare, vi.o per esso Nicolò. Scudi 100 ... scudi 10 se li fanno boni per il stendardo dipinto de Sto Apollinare, vi.o in Chiesa. Scudi ... ditto scudi 10 se fanno boni al detto per la pittura del stendardo di Sto Apollinare, vi.o per esso Nicolò. Scudi 2.10 ... scudi 100 se li fanno boni per dieci quadri dipinti in Sto Apollinare, vi.o in spese di Chiesa. Scudi 100' (ACGU, Libro del Collegio Germanico di Roma – B, 137b, 162a–b). Published in part in Nimmo, 'L'Età perfetta della virilità,' p. 205.

173 Bösel, *Jesuitenarchitektur in Italien*, p. 229; Lucas, *Saint, Site*, pp. 173–4.

174 Monssen, 'The Martyrdom Cycle in Santo Stefano Rotondo, Part Two,' pp. 66–7. Monssen uses Di Loreto's *Consuetudini del Collegio Germanico, et Hungarico* (ACGU, Hist. 274). The document dates from 1587.

175 'Le camere sono dedicate tutte, à qualche santo, et nella sua festa acconciano molto bene il suo altare, che hanno in camera, con versi, et altri ornamenti, et la vigilia oltre modi altri di devozione, chiamano le altre camere, et doppo d'haver cantato qualche motetto, tutti di quella camera fanno insieme una disciplina in qualche loco vicino' (ACGU, Hist. 103, p. 48). A similar description was published in Monssen: 'Quando viene la festa d'alcuna camera, sogliono ornar l'Altare loro con varij intagli, et lavori di carta il che se li concede accioche tutti imparino a far simili cose per il tempo che ne haveranno bisogno nelle loro Chiese rominare et ornare tutta la Camera con frondi versi, alcuni panni verdi ... Hanno cura di ornare l'Altare della Chiesa, di quel Santo ponendovi panni di seta et altri ornamenti secondo la festa, procurando che ivi siano sempre da fiori' ('The Martyrdom Cycle in Santo Stefano Rotondo, Part Two,' p. 67. The quotation is from ACGU, Hist. 274, 15b–16a).

176 '... ivi quei virtuosi Padri, & giovani di detto collegio havevano fatto archi trionfali, & apparato nobilissimo, con un numero infinito d'inscrittioni, distici & altri sententiosi versi in Greco, & Latino' (Ciappi, *Compendio delle heroiche*, p. 20).

177 Monssen, 'The Martyrdom Cycle in Santo Stefano Rotondo, Part Two,' pp. 11–12; *Santo Stefano Rotondo auf dem Caelius in Rom*, pp. 4–7.

178 Monssen, 'The Martyrdom Cycle in Santo Stefano Rotondo, Part Two,' pp. 13–14.

179 See Biermann, 'Die Vita der Heiligen Paulus,' pp. 111–27.

180 'In S. Stefano Rotondo, nel portico è un chiaro scuro forsi di Baldassare' (Mancini, *Considerazioni sulla pittura*, p. 274). Brutio also describes these paintings: '... Sopra la Porta arcuato che guarda à tramontana vi è nel vano una Pietà depinta tra S. Stefano Protomartiro e S. Paulo primo Eremita, e vi si leggono queste lettere: PP. Nicolaus V. Nelle pareti di esso Portico sono da uno parte dipinti à chiaro oscuro gli atti di S. Stefano, e dall'altra di S. Paulo primo Eremita' (BAV, Vat. Lat. 11886, 24b–25a). See Biermann's recent article on these frescoes, discovered during restorations, 'Die Vita der Heiligen Paulus,' pp. 111–27.

181 Biermann, 'Die Vita der Heiligen Paulus,' pp. 113–14.

182 See BAV, Vat. Lat. 11886, 24b. Francini writes: 'San Stefano Rotondo ... essendo ruinata Nicolò Quinto la restaurò, & è titolo di Cardinale, & vi è statione il venerdi

dopò la quinta domenica di quaresima, & nel giorno di San Stefano, & vi sono li corpi di San Primo, & S. Feliciano, & delle reliquie di S. Domitilla Agostino, & Ladislao, & di molti altri. Et vi stanno frati bianchi Vngheri' (*Le cose maravigliose*, p. 16b).

183 For example, this mass held on the Second Sunday of Lent on 6 March 1583: 'Dominica di Quaresima, in questo giorno per esser la stattione à S. Maria della Navicella concorre gran gente à S. Stefano (il che cominciò à esser doppo che quella chiesa venne in mano del Collegio, et massime doppo che fu cominiciata à depingere) et però in questo di, non se canta niente à S. Apollinare, ora in S. Stefano si fà tutto l'officio, secondo la bolla del'unione di quella chiesa' (ACGU, Hist. 103, 63).

184 As well as the references in the Jesuit archives, the principal biographies of artists of the period assign these paintings to Circignani. Celio writes, 'Le pitture à fresco à torno, martirii de Santi, di Nicolao dalle Pomerancie, vi hà da essere in Altare una Madonna con il Putto che dorme in tavola, ad'olio, di Pierino del Vaga' (*Memoria delli nomi*, p. 90). Mancini agrees: 'In S. Stefano Rotondo ... tutte le pitture della chiesa sono di Niccolò dalle Pomarancie' (*Considerazioni sulla pittura*, 274). Baglione also assigns the main cycle to Circignani: 'Figurò co'l suo pennello nella chiesa di S. Stefano Rotondo diverse historie, e numerosi martirii di varii Santi a fresco con buona prattica condotti' (*Le vite de' pittori*, p. 41). Brutio also credits Circignani with the main cycle: 'Questa trionfo de SS. Martirij lo devono pinto da Nicolò Circiniano' (BAV, Vat. Lat. 11886, p. 24b).

185 Monssen, 'The Martyrdom Cycle in Santo Stefano Rotondo, Part Two,' pp. 19, 30; Josephine von Henneberg, *L'Oratorio dell'Arciconfraternità del Santissimo Crocifisso di San Marcello* (Rome, 1974), p. 71.

186 In his biography of Matteo da Siena, Baglione writes: 'E particolarmente in S. Stefano Rotondo sù'l Monte Celio, nelle storie da Nicolao dipinte, furono dal suo penello quelli lontani felicemente a fresco terminati. E tutta l'opera, ch'è di trentadue quadri sù'l muro coloriti, che tutta la chiesa circondano, poi a beneficio del publico è stata intagliata, e data alle stampe con elogii in versi di Giulio Roscio da Orte' (*Le vite de' pittori*, p. 44). He also mentions it in his discussion of Circignani's work on the church: 'ma le prospettive, e li paesi sono, di mano di Mattheo da Siena in questo genere valent'huomo, e degno di molta stima' (p. 41).

187 Leif Holm Monssen, 'An Enigma: Matteo da Siena, Painter and Cosmographer?' *Acta ad archaeologiam et artium historiam pertinentia*, series 8, 7 (1989): 209–313.

188 Leif Holm Monssen, 'St. Stephen's Balustrade in Santo Stefano Rotondo,' *Acta ad archaeologiam et artium historiam pertinentia*, series 8, 3 (1983): 107–82. Monssen dated the frescoes to 1581 or 1583, and Nimmo later published a document proving the date to be 1583 (see n198 to this chapter, below).

189 Baglione is the only early source to mention Tempesta by name: '[Antonio Tempesta] fece a fresco le strage degl'Innocenti e la Madonna con i sette dolori nelle due facciate dell'altar maggiore in Santo Stefano Rotondo' (*Le vite de' pittori*, p. 314). G.F. Cecconi also names Tempesta as the author of the fresco cycle in the chapel of Sts Primus and Felicianus (*Roma sacra e moderna* [Rome, 1725], p. 43). Ugonio discusses these chapel paintings, but does not mention Tempesta by name: 'Nell'entrar della chiesa à man sinistra, è la cappella del santissimo Sacramento, dedicata anticamente da S. Simplicio in honore de santi Martiri Primo e Feliciano, dei quali novamenti vi è stata sotto Gregorio XIII. in essa depinto il Martirio' (*Historia delle stationi di Roma* [Rome, 1588],

pp. 290–1). For a similar text, see Brutio in BAV, Vat. Lat. 11886, pp. 25a–b. For a discussion of most of these sources, see Monssen, 'The Martyrdom Cycle in Santo Stefano Rotondo, Part Two,' p. 24; Vannugli, 'Antonio Tempesta,' p. 103. See also Monssen, 'Antonio Tempesta,' pp. 14–15, where Monssen convincingly attributes the chapel paintings to Tempesta for stylistic reasons.

190 Vannugli, 'Antonio Tempesta'; *La pittura in Italia: Il cinquecento*, vol. 2, p. 849; Freedberg, *Painting in Italy*, 657; Baglione, *Le vite de' pittori*, pp. 314–16.

191 Macioce, *Undique splendent*, p. 91; Zuccari, *Arte e committenza*, p. 112; Mâle, *L'art religieux*, p. 112.

192 'Adi vetoto dotobre 1581 io nicholaio cicignani pitore iroma ho ricevuto R padre ministro de colegio germanico escudi cinquata di moneta e quali mi li a pagati per a buochoto dele pitture che o fatte e che si fano e Santo Stefano ritodo da me e mie ... tati (aiutanti?) e fede de vero ho fatta la presete di mia propria mano – scudi 50 jo nicholaio di mia propria mano e scriti' (ACGU, Busta Ricevute 1580–3, 'Ricevuto di Mastro Nicolò pittore di scudi cinquanta di moneta,' no folios. This document is cited in Nimmo, 'Alcune precisazione,' p. 101, but apparently has gone missing since then; the archivist and I were unable to locate it in an intensive search in 1999).

193 The account books list this payment twice: '[31 December 1581] Scudi 9 ... sono per barili 9 di vino venduto a Mastro Niccolo pittore agli X l'uno, va in esso 121. Scudi 9 ... Mastro Niccolo Circiniano pittore deve dare ... scudi nove di moneta sono per barili nove di vino havuto di casa va per visita pittore a Sto Stefano rotondo. Scudi 9' (ACGU, Libro del Collegio Germanico di Roma – B, 79a, 121a).

194 In chronological order, the payments recorded are as follows: 'Io Nicholaio Cicignani ho ricevuto questo dì tredici di marz 1582 scudi cinquanta di moneta a bon cho[n]to delle pitture che si fan[n]o a Santo Stefano e di fede ho fatto la prese[n]te e sotto scrit[t]a di mia propria mano questo dì e an[n]o sopradetto – io nicholaio sopradetto scris[s]i scudi 50. E più io Nicholaio sopradetto ho ricevuto questo dì 12 di aprile 1582 scudi tre[n]ta di moneta da padre Nicolo Be[n]civenni procuratore di detto Chol[l]egio pure a buo[n] cho[n]to delle pit[t]ure fatte e da fa[r]se a santo Stefano rito[n]do e di fede ho fatto la prese[n]te e sotto scrit[t]a di mia propria mano questo di ed an[n]o detto – io Nicholaio scri[s]i scudi 30' (ACGU, Busta Ricevute 1580–3, no folio; Nimmo, 'Alcune precisazione,' p. 101. This document is now missing); '[23 May 1582] Scudi 200 à Mastro Nicolò Circiniano c.o inesso. Scudi 200'; '[28 August 1582] Havere scudi 320 se li fanno boni per trendadoi quadri dipinti à Sto Stefano à ragione de scudi 10 il quadro, vi.o in spese di chiesa. 320 scudi; scudi 2.10 se li fanno boni per ritoccatura di molte pitture, vi.o in Chiesa. Scudi 2.10 ... Scudi 320 se fanno boni à Mastro Nicolò Circiniano Pittore per quadri trenta doi dipinti à Sto Stefano, vi.o per esso Nicolò. Scudi 320'; '[13 September 1583] Scudi 66 jattone mandato à Nicolò Circiniano pittore inesso. Scudi 66'; '[17 October 1582] Scudi 30 à Mastro Nicolò Circiniano pittore vi.o in esso. Scudi 30'; '[20 October 1582] Scudi 9 si jano boni à Mastro Nicolò pittore per storno di una partita che ja dupplicata vi.o pesso. Scudi 9'; '[31 December 1582] Scudi 37.50 pagati à Mastro Nicolò Circiniano Pittore, vi.o in esso. Scudi 37.50' (ACGU, Libro del Collegio Germanico di Roma – B, 163b, 162b, 137b, 264a, 177b, 125b, 182b). For an 18 May 1582 payment of 130 scudi for both S. Stefano and S. Apollinare, see n171 to this chapter, above, and the following: '[18 May 1582] Scudi 130 pagati à Mastro Nicolò Circin. Pittore vi.o inesso. Scudi 130';

(f. 158a). An anonymous payment on 16 June 1582 handed out '19.35 pagati per diversi colori di fare pitture in chiesa v.o in spese di chiesa. Scudi 19.35' (f. 158a).

195 Monssen, 'The Martyrdom Cycle in Santo Stefano Rotondo, Part Two,' pp. 21–4.

196 Nimmo, 'Alcune precisazioni,' pp. 94–5.

197 Röttgen, 'Zeitgeschichtliche Bildprogramme,' p. 111.

198 Nimmo, 'Alcune precisazioni,' p. 92. The source is transcribed on p. 101, appendix D. The other source, a reference from Michele Di Loreto's diary dated 20 March 1583, records: 'Circa questo tempo si cominciò a fare il circolo di muro intorno all'altar di mezzo in S. Stefano' (ACGU, Hist. 103, 64a; published in Nimmo, 'Santo Stefano Rotondo: La recinzione,' p. 98).

199 The original reads, '[13 September 1583] scudi 40 boni p(er) 24 jstoriette fatte in Sto Stefano intorno al altare maggiore, vi.o in spese di chiesa. Scudi 40' (ACGU, Libro del Collegio Germanico di Roma – B, 162a. In Nimmo's version, the words 'a Ms Nicolo circiniano Pittore' are inserted between '40 boni' and 'p(er)'; Nimmo, 'Alcune precisazioni,' p. 101). For Monssen's opinion on the *chiaroscuri*, see 'St. Stephen's Balustrade,' p. 146.

200 Monssen, 'The Martyrdom Cycle in Santo Stefano Rotondo, Part Two,' p. 17.

201 Vannugli, 'Antonio Tempesta,' pp. 103–5; Monssen, 'Antonio Tempesta,' p. 118.

202 The references in the account book are as follows, in chronological order: '[16 June 1582] Mastro Durante pittore dieci scudi 10 pagateli la cassa deli depositi per li mani del Padre ministro dipositario v.o per la cassa. Scudi 10'; '[16 June 1582] Scudi 10 pagati à Mastro Durante pittore v.o inesso. Scudi 10'; '[7 December 1582] Scudi 12 moneta pagateli per la cassa deli depositi per mani del P. Nicolò Bencivenni Depositario, v.o per essa cassa. Scudi 12; Havere scudi 22 se li fanno boni per un Sto Stefano dipinto in tela d'argento, v.o in Chiesa. Scudi 22'; '[7 December 1582] Scudi 22 se fanno boni a mastro Durante Pittore per un Sto Stefano dipinto in tela d'Argento, v.o per esso. Scudi 22'; '[7 December 1582] Scudi 12 pagati à Mastro Durante Pittore per mani del P. Nicolò Bencivenni, v.o desso Mastro Durante' (ACGU, Libro B, 169a, 158a, 169a, 169b, 182a, 158a).

203 Monssen, 'The Martyrdom Cycle in Santo Stefano Rotondo, Part One' and 'Part Two'; Vannugli, 'Antonio Tempesta.'

204 I am not the first to suggest a link between the Nadal series and S. Stefano, although no one has raised the issue of Fiammeri's participation. See Buser, 'Jerome Nadal'; Monssen, 'The Martyrdom Cycle in Santo Stefano Rotondo, Part Two,' p. 77. On mnemonics, see Korrick, 'On the Meaning of Style,' pp. 173–4.

205 Noreen, 'Ecclesiae militantis triumphi: Jesuit Iconography,' pp. 696–7. Noreen's conclusions were taken largely from Monssen, 'The Martyrdom Cycle in Santo Stefano Rotondo, Part Two,' p. 35.

206 Monssen, 'The Martyrdom Cycle in Santo Stefano Rotondo, Part Two,' p. 85.

207 Ibid., p. 74.

208 Ibid., pp. 38–47; Vannugli, 'Antonio Tempesta,' pp. 111, 115.

209 Buser, 'Jerome Nadal,' p. 432. Korrick makes the intriguing suggestion that the 'pennello ordinario' refers to a devout style characterized by restraint, clarity, and an archaic air ('On the Meaning of Style,' p. 177).

210 Monssen, 'The Martyrdom Cycle in Santo Stefano Rotondo, Part One,' pp. 175–7.

211 Ibid., p. 197.

212 For published images of the Renaissance ideal cityscapes, see Richard Krautheimer,

'The Panels in Urbino, Baltimore, and Berlin Reconsidered,' in Henry Millon, ed., *The Renaissance from Brunelleschi to Michelangelo* (New York, 1997), pp. 233–57.

213 Monssen, 'Triumphus and Trophaea Sacra,' p. 12.

214 Monssen relates them to two contemporary series of decorations in the Vatican, including one by Circignani (Gregory XIII's Loggia III, facing the Corte San Damaso, 1582) and the vault of the Galleria delle Carte Geografiche (1580–3) ('The Martyrdom Cycle in Santo Stefano Rotondo, Part Two,' p. 30).

215 Other quotations from the Gonfalone cycle include a figure of an old man in fresco VII, which Monssen relates to a figure in the anonymous *Capture of Christ* (1570s) ('The Martyrdom Cycle in Santo Stefano Rotondo, Part One,' p. 208).

216 The Circignani version is now in the Pinacoteca Comunale in Città del Castello. I would like to thank the helpful staff at the Museo Civico in Todi for bringing this picture to my attention. The Santi is reproduced in Spalding, 'Santi di Tito,' fig. 48.

217 Although Monssen proposes that the SS. Nereo ed Achilleo series is also by Circignani, the styles are very different. The figures in the later series are cruder and more ungainly than Circignani's, and the scenes are less crowded and with fewer landscape elements. As further evidence against Circignani's participation, Zuccari has published a document showing that Cerroni was likely the painter of at least a part of the series (Monssen, 'The Martyrdom Cycle at S. Stefano Rotondo, Part Two,' p. 47; Zuccari, *Arte e committenza*, p. 83).

218 Monssen shows that the Crucifixion surrounded by martyrs is a rare image, but that this representation with the Holy Innocents is unique ('Rex gloriose martyrum,' pp. 130–7, and 'The Martyrdom Cycle in Santo Stefano Rotondo, Part One,' p. 183).

219 Monssen points out that the church itself is sublimated to a cross plan, with the four altars on the cross axes (one of which is dedicated to the Holy Cross) and the central altar being dedicated to St Stephen ('The Martyrdom Cycle in Santo Stefano Rotondo, Part Two,' p. 29).

220 Herz, 'Imitators of Christ,' p. 64.

221 Ibid., p. 68. For a discussion of the role of Germanic and Central European Jesuits in the world missions, see Bailey, *Art on the Jesuit Missions*, pp. 46–51, and Gauvin Alexander Bailey, 'The Jesuits and the Non-Spanish Contribution to South American Colonial Architecture,' in Hilmar M. Pabel and Kathleen M. Comerford, eds, *Early Modern Catholicism: Essays Presented to John O'Malley* (Toronto, 2001), pp. 211–40.

222 The figure is lacking in his original 1580 drawing for the project, as is the judge figure at the upper right, who may have been inspired by Circignani's fresco XVII. What is interesting about these changes in Barocci's project, made after the patrons asked for 'more figures,' is how quickly the impact of Circignani's paintings was felt throughout Italy. Barocci was probably exposed to the Circignani cycle in Cavallieri's engraved version. For the Barocci painting and its history, see Olsen, *Federico Barocci*, cat. no. 34.

223 I cannot agree with Monssen's suggestion that Caravaggio's *Crucifixion of St Peter* in the Cerasi Chapel in S. Maria del Popolo (1600–1) was influenced by Circignani's version, since it has virtually nothing in common compositionally and was itself inspired more directly by Michelangelo's fresco (Monssen, 'The Martyrdom Cycle in Santo Stefano Rotondo, Part One,' p. 189). For the Caravaggio version, see Hibbard, *Caravaggio*, fig. 82. Hibbard makes the connection between Caravaggio's and Michelangelo's versions of the scene.

224 Zuccari, *Arte e committenza*, p. 148.
225 Monssen also notes similar composition in Perino del Vaga's *Martyrdom of St John the Evangelist* in S. Spirito in Sassia (ca. 1547), with the two executioners reversed, although the saint himself is much younger in Perino's version and the setting is a palace interior ('The Martyrdom Cycle in Santo Stefano Rotondo, Part Two,' figs 9, 10).
226 Monssen, 'The Martyrdom Cycle in Santo Stefano Rotondo, Part One,' pp. 202–7.
227 Zeri, *Pittura e controriforma*, p. 67.
228 The print, which was reissued in 1602, is published in *La regola e la fama*, cat. no. 72a.
229 The print is published in Patricia Lee Rubin, *Giorgio Vasari: Art and History* (New Haven and London, 1995), fig. 36. The Salviati is in the Cappella del Pallio in the Palazzo della Cancelleria in Rome (1548–50), and the Macchietti is a reversed version of the scene in S. Maria Novella in Florence (1573).
230 Circignani worked on the same Casamari commission (Madonna, *Roma di Sisto V*, p. 336). For the S. Susanna painting, see Zander, *L'arte in Roma nel secolo XVI*, vol. 2, tav. CLXXXIII.
231 Monssen, 'The Martyrdom Cycle in Santo Stefano Rotondo, Part One,' p. 151.
232 Ibid., p. 255.
233 Herz, 'Imitators of Christ,' p. 64.
234 The painting is illustrated in Rossi, *Scienza e miracoli*, cat. no. D35.
235 Monssen, 'The Martyrdom Cycle in Santo Stefano Rotondo, Part One,' p. 265. This scene is also very similar to one Circignani used later at S. Tommaso.
236 Monssen identified the Vesta temple (ibid., p. 284).
237 Ibid., p. 295.
238 Ibid., p. 300. Circignani would use the same model for his depiction of Constantine in the S. Tommaso cycle.
239 Vannugli, 'Antonio Tempesta,' p. 106.
240 Ibid., p. 107.
241 Monssen, 'Antonio Tempesta,' p. 109.
242 Ibid., fig. 10; Eduard A. Safarik, ed., *Galleria Colonna in Roma: Dipinti* (Rome, 1981), cat. no. 138.
243 The Galleria delle Carte Geografiche fresco is illustrated in Monssen, 'Antonio Tempesta,' fig. 24, and in Vannugli, 'Antonio Tempesta,' fig. 25.
244 Monssen, 'The Martyrdom Cycle in Santo Stefano Rotondo, Part One,' p. 117.
245 Monssen, 'Triumphus and Trophaea Sacra,' pp. 11–12.
246 Fulvio Cardulo, *Sanctorum martyrum Abundii presbyteri Abundantii diaconi Marciani* (Rome, 1584).
247 Donald Attwater, *The Penguin Dictionary of Saints* (Harmondsworth, 1980), p. 292.
248 Walter L. Strauss, ed., *The Illustrated Bartsch* (New York, 1985), vol. 3, p. 264, cat. no. 536 (142).
249 Herz, 'Imitators of Christ,' pp. 58–60.
250 For the catalogue of the paintings with illustrations, see Monssen, 'St. Stephen's Balustrade.' See also Nimmo, 'Santo Stefano Rotondo: La recinzione,' pp. 98–102.
251 Nimmo, 'Santo Stefano Rotondo: La recinzione,' p. 108.
252 Monssen, 'St. Stephen's Balustrade,' p. 118. See also Nimmo, 'Santo Stefano Rotondo: La recinzione,' pp. 98–9.
253 Cavallieri was a popular printmaker who published several picture books in the 1580s, including books on the architecture and sculpture of Rome, and a series of

portraits of the popes. He published, together with Antoine Lafréry, *Speculum romanae magnificentiae* (Rome, 1575), with 148 plates; and by himself, *Romanum imperatorum effigies* (Rome, 1583); *Antiquarum statuarum Urbis Romae* (Rome, 1585), in two volumes with over 200 plates; and *Pontificum romanorum effigies* (Rome, 1588). These were some of the first illustrated art books as we know them. For more on Cavallieri, see Liénardy, *'Ecclesiae militantis triumphi* – Rome, 1585,' pp. 85–95.

254 In the Keir Collection in Ham, Surrey, there is a Mughal painting of ca. 1590 that copies fresco VIII (folio 8) at S. Stefano Rotondo (Inv. no. V.55).

255 See Noreen, 'Ecclesiae militantis triumphi: Jesuit Iconography.'

5: The Collegiate Church of S. Tommaso di Canterbury and the Novitiate Church of S. Vitale

1 Histories of the Venerable English College are Cardinal Gasquet, *A History of the Venerable English College, Rome* (London, 1920); Rev. H.E.Q. Rope, *The Schola Saxonum, the Hospice, and the English College in Rome* (Rome, 1951); Luigi and Pier Luigi Lotti, *La comunità cattolica inglese di Roma* (Rome, 1978); and Michael E. Williams, *The Venerable English College, Rome* (Dublin, 1979). See also Joseph Cartwell, 'The Church of St. Thomas of the English,' *The Venerable* 3:1 (October 1926): 31–40; Anthony Laird, 'The College Church,' *The Venerable* 24:1 (October 1968): 28–38; 24:3: 159–73; Thomas H. Clancy, 'The First Generation of English Jesuits, 1555–1585,' *Archivum Historicum Societatis Iesu* 57 (1988): 137–62.

2 Cesareo, 'Jesuit Colleges,' p. 24; Clancy, 'The First Generation,' p. 137.

3 Gasquet, *A History*, p. 62.

4 June Hager, 'The Venerable: The English College and Church in Rome,' *Inside the Vatican* (May 1999): 66; Gasquet, *A History*, pp. 1–61.

5 Gasquet, *A History*, pp. 70–1. On the Welsh-English problems, see also ARSI, Rom. 156. I [Historia Colleg. Anglor. Hibern. et Scotor.], 1a–27a.

6 Williams, *The Venerable English*, p. 6.

7 The words of one of the English students, recorded in Gasquet, *A History*, p. 71.

8 Ibid., pp. 72–8. The English students did not settle down, however, and another major upheaval during the years 1585–96 was directed toward the Jesuit rectors, who they believed were stealing their diocesan priests for the Jesuit order. Sixtus V was so concerned that he ordered a Visitation in 1585. See ibid., pp. 88–106.

9 Cesareo 'Jesuit Colleges,' p. 30; Hager, 'The Venerable,' p. 68.

10 Cesareo 'Jesuit Colleges,' p. 31.

11 Gasquet, *A History*, p. 86.

12 Hager, 'The Venerable,' p. 68; Gasquet, *A History*, pp. 118–46.

13 John Foxe, *Actes and Monuments of These Latter and Perillous Dayes ...* (London, 1563). On this work, see Buser, 'Jerome Nadal,' p. 429, and J.F. Mozley, *John Foxe and His Book* (New York, 1940). On the S. Tommaso series, see also Mâle, *L'art religieux*, p. 111.

14 John Foxe, *Actes and Monuments*, introduction.

15 Mozley, *John Foxe*, p. 177.

16 Buser, 'Jerome Nadal,' p. 429 n30.

17 Parsons, *An Epistle of the Persecutions*, pp. 5–6.

18 Buser, 'Jerome Nadal,' pp. 429–30.

19 Lewine, 'The Roman Church Interior,' p. 490. Lewine includes the church in his dissertation as a new church of the Cinquecento, and writes, 'The church was evidently begun and finished in 1575.'
20 Gasquet, *A History*, p. 85.
21 'Reliquarii 6 di legno indorati et vi sono le infrascritte reliquie: un pezzetto del velo della B. Virgine; un dente di S. Andrea Apostolo; un deto delli Innocenti; capelli di S. Maria Maddalena; un pezzo di osso di S. Vittorino; reliquie di S. Lucia; un pezzo di osso di S. Pietro Confess.; un pezzetto de una costa di Philippo Apostolo; un pezzo del braccio di S. Thomas Cantuar. con il braccio di legno indorato. Tabernacolo grande vecchio dove stava il santissimo sacramento in chiesa all'altare maggiore et sta adesso in guardaroba et il nuovo sta in chiesa et e molto bello et ornato de belle figure' (VEC, 34 [Inventory of Sacristy, 1585], no folio).
22 Gasquet, *A History*, p. 122.
23 The quotation is from a 1585 Annual Letter: 'La chiesa et sacristia si tiene con tanta diligenza et politezza che molti forastieri vengano giornalemente in celebrare in chiesa nostra, fra quali ci sono quattro, tre di molta importanza che ogni giorno celebrano qui, et le feste cene. Viene delli altri vescovi et prelati oltre a i semplici sacerdoti. A Vesperi poi et alle messe la festa ci concorre tanto populo che molte volte non può capire in chiesa' (ARSI, Rom. 126b I, 353b).
24 '... s'aggiusti l'altar maggiore decentemente con le reliquie di sopra indorare e fiori; all'altare della Madonna si ponghino l'argenti con la sua lampada e à gl'altri altari li quattro fiori per ciasche d'uno, all'altar maggiore il paliotto biancho fiorato' (VEC, 34 [Inventory of Sacristy, 1585], no folio). The account books also list gifts of fabrics destined for the high altar, including a 'taffetta turchino' purchased by Michele Rafaelli to adorn the altarpiece of the Trinity on 1 July 1581 (VEC, 91 [Entrata e uscita, 1579–83], 86a).
25 'Collegii onera: ex onere Collegij per Alumnos et Patres quotidie celebrantur in Altari S.ti Johannis pro anima bo.me. Cardinalis Poli. In altari S.mi Crucifixi pro anima Benefactoris Angli ter in hebdomada. In Capella S.ti Edmundi ter in hebdomada. Pro Benefactore qui domum Collegio legant, semel in hebdomada. Pro Benefactoribus vivis semel in hebdomada cum recitatione rosarij sive corone ut aiunt. Idem servatur pro Benefactoribus defunctis ... Quod autem Patres et Alumni pro Benefactoribus vivis atque defunctis et pro sum. Pontifice praestant, id sua sponte faciunt, piam tamen institutionem hanc se perpetuo servaturos promittunt. Diebus autem Dominicis, alijsque solemnibus festis, quae ex ecclesiae praecepto sanctificantur, Missa decantatur, sacerdoti adhibitis ministris, diacono scilicet et subdiacono, magistro ceremoniarum, canonicis sex vel octo (ita enim appellantur qui superpelliceis induti in ecclesia deserviunt) duobus acolythis et thuriferario ultra' (VEC, Scr.39.19.1 [Visitations, 1585]).
26 'Angeli 2 che tengano le candelle di legno indorati' (VEC, 34, no folio).
27 VEC 246, Horatio Torriani: Descrittioni delle Case ... sotto la proprietà del Venerabile Collegio Inglese di Roma, 1630, 4a.
28 'La chiesa si, è ... devisa in tre navi con pilastri e colonne, à quattro altare piccoli, et l'altar maggiore ... La nave di mezzo soffittala con suoi intagli, et le due nave piccole sono soffittate semplice; et nella nave di mezzo nel fine di essa vi è il choro per la musica' (VEC, 246, 3a–4a).
29 'La chiesa del detto Collegio è dedicata alla Santissima Trinità e à San Tomaso Martire:

Hà il choro, organo, sacristia, e campanile con tre campane, et un horologio. Hà cinque altari, e due sepolture comuni, con alcune altre de' particolari' (VEC, Scr. 31.5.1 [Status of the College, 1662]).

30 Gasquet, *A History*, p. 210.

31 Both Baglione and Titi assign the martyrdom cycle to Circignani. Baglione writes: 'Dipinse di sua mano a fresco tutta la chiesa della Trinità del Collegio Inglese con le storie del regno d'Inghilterra, e de'molti martirii di que catholici, e con altre figure' (*Le vite de' pittori*, p. 41). Titi is more effusive: 'Della SS. Trinità, ò S. Tommaso degl'Inglesi. Questa Chiesa fù concessa da Gregorio XIII al Seminario da lui fatto per istruttione nella Fede Cattolica à Giovani della Natione Inglese, à quali assegnò molte rendite per sostentamento, e deputò alla lor cura li PP. della Compagnia di Giesù, che s'impiegarono à questo con ogni diligenza, come anche ad ornare la Chiesa di belle pitture fatte à fresco con l'historie del Regno d'Inghilterra, e de' molti martirij di quelli Cattolici da Nicolò Pomarancio' (Filippo Titi, *Studio di pittura, scoltura, et architetura, nelle chiese di Roma (1674–1763)*, 2 vols [repr. Florence, 1987], I, p. 65).

32 '... l'assiduità dell'orationi et della meditatione, cosi di giorno come di notte, il desiderio di vedersi avanti il conspetto di Dio ... la divotion singolare che teneva al santissimo sacramento dell'Altare, l'affetto ch'egli haveva a' santi, l'honore che portava alle lor reliquie, la riverenza che teneva alle lor imagini' (ARSI, Angl. 7 [Anglia Necrologia, 1578–1732], 43b).

33 Gasquet, *A History*, p. 122.

34 For example, 207.80 scudi were given to Charles Basset, who was a young relative of St Thomas More who had come to Rome with Gilbert, in January 1584, and in the same year 690 scudi were paid to Robert Parsons in France (VEC, 37 [Libro Mastro 1579–83], 227a–b; VEC, 38 [Libro Mastro 1584–5], 1a, 37a). See also VEC, 92, Giornale 1584–7, 39a.

35 An eighteenth-century Visitor's report itemizes the altarpieces: 'Giorgio Gilbert fece à sue spese dipingere i laterali della Chiesa, ed i quadri degli Altari, due dei quali, cioè quello della croce, e l'altro di S. Giovanni Evangelista furono consagrati dal Vescovo Apatense, Tommaso Godwele' (VEC, 324 [Visitation, 1739], 17a). A college report from 1582 also mentions the chapel of St John the Evangelist by name (VEC, 91 [Libro di Entrata e Uscita A, 1579–83], 113b).

36 Gasquet is cautious, dating the paintings 'somewhere about 1582, and certainly between 1580 and 1583' (*A History*, p. 121). Lewine goes even further, saying that the series was painted sometime between 1573 and 1583 ('The Roman Church Interior,' p. 493). Herz dates the series to 1583, and Buser suggests as much when he proposes that Circignani copied Allen's engravings (Herz, 'Imitators of Christ,' p. 59; Buser, 'Jerome Nadal,' p. 469).

37 Quoted in Gasquet, *A History*, p. 210.

38 '[16 August 1581] detto scudi 20 per mandato a Mastro Durante pintore v.o in spesa di chiesa scudi 20' (VEC, 37 [Libro Mastro 1579–83], 131b).

39 Herz, 'Imitators of Christ,' p. 65 n114; Lewine, 'The Roman Church Interior,' p. 493.

40 See Madonna, *Roma di Sisto V*, tav. XXV and p. 229.

41 See Freedberg, *Painting in Italy*, p. 261; Zander, *L'arte in Roma nel secolo xvi*, vol. 2, tav. clxix; Madonna, *Roma di Sisto V*, p. 233.

42 Herz, 'Imitators of Christ,' p. 65.

43 'Nella Trinità de gl'Inglesi medesimamente sopra l'altar maggiore stavvi un Dio Padre, che ha in braccio N. Signore Giesù Christo morto con Angeli, e da basso altri santi; una delle belle opere, che egli mai habbia fatto' (Baglione, *Le vite de' pittori*, p. 118).

44 The reference to the *scarpellino* Andrea Luchesino is the following: '[16 January 1584] Reparatione devono scudi venti di moneta fattone mandato à Mastro Andrea luchesino scarpellino per saldo di un suo conto de' lavori fatti in Collegio dalli 12 di Jugno, 1581 per il termino Xbre 1583 come per il conto in filza vagliono per cenoli. Scudi 20' (VEC, 92 [Giornale, 1584–7], 7a).

45 '[30 October 1584] Scudi 64 moneta havuti da Mastro Ambrosio falignamo per il canone di dui anni, nel conto che ha con il Collegio per il Tabernacolo banchi et alteri lavori fatti in questo modo. Scudi 64' (VEC, 38 [Libro Mastro 1584–7], 74a).

46 VEC, 37 (Libro Mastro, 1579–83), 227b.

47 The references to paint materials are cryptic: '[9 August 1582] scudi 82 pitture mandato sino a dì 17 agosto 1581 a Mastro Droschonio Ottonasio vi.o per in [Tiberio] Cenoli scudi 82'; '[1582] Spese di libri dieci scudi 20 pitture mandato sino a dì 16 di Agosto 1581 per libri datti in collegio vi.o in Cenoli scudi 20' (VEC, 37 [Libro Mastro 1579–83], 157a, 170a). Tiberio Cenoli was the banker used by the college.

48 According to this list of expenses of the English College, the following amounts in scudi were spent on the 'Chiesa' in the following years: (1579) 64.53; (1580) 657.51; (1581) 518.11; (1583) 1234.35; (1584) 294.22; (1585) 389.47.1/2 (ARSI, Rom. 156 I, 68b–76b).

49 ARSI, Rom. 126b I, 302a.

50 'et è dipinta con diversi stori delli santi de santi [sic] de Inghilterra fatte l'anno 1583' (VEC, 246, 3a–4a).

51 '[2 March 1591] A Mastro Simone Pittore per 2 Arme, scudi 1.10'; '[13 September 1591] A Mastro Simone per pittura d'un Baldachino, scudi 0.60'; '[23 November 1591] A Mastro Simon Pittore per la cartella grande racconcia, scudi 0.70'; '[16 April 1592] Intaglio d'un Giesu in osso, scudi 0.7'; '[1 June 1592] Un'Agnus Dei d'osso con cristalli di montagna, scudi 0.35' (VEC, 166 [Giornale del 1591–3], 6a, 36b, 46b, 63b, 70b).

52 Lewine, who did not have the Gilbert quotation about the paintings being over the columns, surmised that the paintings were 'probably painted around the side walls of the aisles and perhaps across the front wall as well' ('The Roman Church Interior,' p. 494). Monssen too believed that the paintings covered the walls of the side aisles in addition to the walls above the columns of the nave ('Rex gloriose martyrum,' p. 131; Lucas, *Saint, Site*, p. 186).

53 The quotation is from Cardinal Wiseman and is published in Gasquet, *A History*, pp. 210–11. The paintings were praised in a 1585 Visitation report as making the church most beautiful in aspect: '... Templum hoc ... ex divertorum Dei martyrum expressis imaginibus iucundissimum esse' (ARSI, Rom. 156 I [Histor. Colleg. Anglor. Hibern. et Scotor.], 44a).

54 'L'anno quinto del suo Ponteficato istituì il Collegio Inglese nella Chiesa della Trinità, vicino alle carceri di Corte Savella, havendosi fatto fare delle case vicine commode habitationi per li collegianti, & fatto depingere la Chiesa con l'historie de' Santi Martiri dell'istessa nazione' (Ciappi, *Compendio delle heroiche*, p. 28).

55 'Tra gl'altri santi portava grandissima venerazione a i martiri, per l'ardente desiderio che haveva di farseli compagno nelle pene e morte. Di qui nacque che il santo huomo

fece con gran fatica una raccolta di tutti li martiri Inglesi, tanto antiqui, come moderni, et fece dipingere il lor martirio in quadri, con li quali ornò tutta la chiesa di questo Collegio di quella maniera che V.P. hà visto, ponendo anco' i santi confessori fra l'un quadro et l'altro, et sopra i capitelli delle colonne; nel che spese da sette cento scudi, havendo à questo effetto raccolte alcune elimosine da varij gentilhuomini Inglesi suoi amici. Soleva egli dire che non solo haveva procurato questo per l'honore di quei gloriosissime martiri, et per manifestare al mondo la gloria et lo splendore della Chiesa d'Inghilterra, ma anco per che li scolari ci questo collegio si spechiassero nel'essempio, di questi loro predecessori, et s'accendessero anch'essi al martirio, et anco acciò che con l'imagini dei novelli martiri mettesse di nostri à gl'occhi di roma, et di tutto il mondo, il misero stato della sua patria, et cosi si movesse la gente à raccommandarla à Dio' (ARSI, Angl. 7, 44a–b). A very similar but not identical version appears in the history of S. Andrea al Quirinale, where the staining of the ink makes the text virtually impossible to read: 'Tra gl'altri santi portava gran veneratione a Martirij per l'ardente desiderio che haveva di farli compagni nella morte. Fu qui nacque, che il santo huomo fece un gran fatica una raccolta di tutti i Martirii Inglesi, tanto antichi, come moderni, e fece dipingere loro martirio di quadri con li quali ornò la chiesa tutta di questo Collegio di quella maniera, come V.P. ha visto, ponendo anco'i SS. Confessori tra l'un quadro, e l'altro, e sopra i capitelli delle colonne: nella quel' tota spese da 700 scudi, havendo a questo effecto raccolta alle limosine da varii gentilhuomini Inglesi suoi amici. Soleva egli dire, che non solo haveva agli procurator.o il honore di quei gloriossissimi Martirii, e per manifestare al mondo la gloria, e lo splendore della chiesa d'Inghilterra; ma anco' per li scolari di questo Collegio li specchiassero nell'essempio di quali loro predecessori, e accendessero anc'essi; e per mettere di nostri agl'occhi di Roma, e di tutto il mondo con l'imagine dei novelli Martiri il misero stato della sua patria, onde li movesse la gente a raccomandarla à Dio' (ARSI, Rom. 162 I, 95a). A version of this letter was also published in Henry Foley, *Record of the English Province of the Society of Jesus III* (London, 1878), pp. 697–8. See also this remark from the introduction to Cavallieri's illustrated volume of the S. Tommaso frescoes: 'Merito in illo suorum cum priscae tum huius aetatis martyrum certamina exprimi curarunt: ut alios ad laudes, precesque, se vero etiam ad parem animi constantiam, maiorum et sociorum exemplis, excitarent' (Giovanni Battista da Cavallieri, *Ecclesiae anglicanae trophaea ... Romae in collegio Anglico per Nicolaum Circinianum depictae* [Rome, 1584]).

56 'Ci fu tra gl'altri quadri uno di San Giorgio protettore d'Inghilterra, dove era dipinto il suo martirio, et quando liberò quello figliuola del Rè amazzando il dragone. Alcuni pregarono il pittore che facesse l'effigie di questo santo simile al S[ignor] Giorgio, meritandolo la sua virtù, et essendo al santo tanto simile in ogni cosa. Egli avedutosi di questo, non voleva più cosi spesso comparire in presenzia del Pittore mentre lavorava quel quadro perche non dipingere il santo à se simile, giudicandosi molto dissimile ne'costumi. Non puo poter far' tanto ch'il pittore non li disse qualche aria et sembianza di lui. Il che accorgendosene il Santo Giorgio li disse, com'è avete dipinto voi un'huomo armata et in atto di combattere, senza la visiera? Di gratia fateli la visiera. Il pittore si oppose alquanto, et fu accommodata la cosa in questo modo, che si li facesse un'elmo in testa, ma egli non restò sodisfatto, et voleva per coprir più la faccia che si dipingessero due piastre che sogliano coprir' le orecchie, et allacciarsi sotto il mento, ancor che il Padre Ministro se li oppose, et non voleva in modo alcuno che li fusse in

ciò sodisfatto, acciò l'effigie di questo signore per consolazione di tutti restasse in Collegio' (ARSI, Angl. 7, 44a–b). The other version is very close: 'Ci fu tra gl'altri quadri uno di S. Giorgio Prottetor d'Inghilterra, dove ero dipinto il suo martirio, e q[ua]n[do] liberò quella figliuola del re ammazzando il dragone: alcuni pregarono il pittore, che facesse l'effigie di questo Santo simile al S[ignor] Giorgio, meritandolo la sua virtù, essendo al Santo simile in ogni cosa: egli avvendatosi di ciò, non voleva, giudicandosi molto dissimile nei costumi; ma non può poter far tanto, che il pittore non li disse qualet aria e sembianza di lui. Il che accantoli egli li disse, come havete dipinto un'huomo armato, et in acto di combattere senza la visiera, di gratia fateli la visiera: il pittore si oppose al quanto e fu accommodata la cosa a questo modo: che si li facesse un'elmo in testa, ma egli non restò sodisfatto, e voleva che coprir più la faccia, che si gli depingessero due piastre, et sogliarono coprire gl'orecchi, et allacciarsi sotto il [m]ento. Ma il Padre Ministro si gli oppose e non voleva rimandali che fine fù ciò sodisfatto, accio l'effigie di questo Padre per consolazione di tutto restasse in Collegio' (ARSI, Rom. 162 I, 95a). See also Foley, *Record of the English College*, p. 698.

57 The St George story is referred to only in the manuscript version of the Annual Letter, from which the quotation is also taken: 'Et hoc [Gilbert] in martires amore processit quod omnes qui a prima Angliae conversione ad hodiernum usque diem ex hac natione pro fide mortem perpessi sunt, pulcherrimis in templo huius collegij imaginibus exprimi suis sumptibus curarit ... cumque sancti Georgij Anglorum patroni curaret depingi imaginem, et quosdam pictori suasisse intellexisset, ut eam ad illius faceret similitudinem: se quo ad illa imago omnium esset perfecta et conspectu pictoris subtraxit, ne honor iste merito aliquid detraheret' (ARSI, Rom. 126b I [Annuae 1570–85], 302a). It is not repeated in the published version of the letter: 'quotquot iam inde à prima Angliae conversione ad hanc usque aetatem vità pro religione dedissent, eorum imagines in Collegij templo pulcherrime depingendas exprimendasq. curavit' (*Annuae Litterae Societatis Iesu anni MDLXXXIII* [Rome, 1585], p. 22).

58 Venerable Bede, *A History of the English Church and People* (Harmondsworth, 1979), p. 42.

59 Ibid., pp. 44–7.

60 Ibid., p. 48.

61 Ibid., p. 58. See also pp. 58–61.

62 Bede has much to say about these monarchs (ibid., pp. 114–34, 150–1, 155–63).

63 Buser, 'Jerome Nadal,' p. 429 n30.

64 These two drawings are published in Röttgen, 'Zeitgeschichtliche Bildprogramme,' figs 32, 34.

65 British Museum 1956-5-12-2. The drawing is mentioned in Lewine, 'The Roman Church Interior,' p. 494, but not reproduced. The mount has an inscription, from the nineteenth century, that relates the drawing to S. Tommaso and Cavallieri.

66 Haskell, *Patrons and Painters*, p. 47.

67 Zuccari, *Arte e committenza*, pp. 140–1. See also Abromson, 'Painting in Rome,' p. 243; Mâle, *L'art religieux*, pp. 113–14.

68 On the patronage of Isabella della Rovere, see Valone, 'Women on the Quirinal Hill,' pp. 137–8. Maria Ann Conelli also has worked recently on della Rovere and female patronage of the Society of Jesus in Naples and Rome, and delivered a talk on the

subject at the Sixteenth Century Studies Conference, Toronto, 22–5 October 1998, entitled 'Female Patronage and Piety in Sixteenth-Century Naples.'

69 Navarola writes about the year 1598: 'Fondatione della Casa di S. Vitale. Signora Principessa di Brisiano Donna Isabella della Rovere Filtria, et il Signore Giovanni Theodoro Duca di San Marco suo figlio furono riceuti per fondatori di detta casa havendo detta Signora Principessa già assegnato per ciò cosi donatione inrevocabile fatta in Napoli: ducati sessanta mila di Regno, da pagarti dalli suoi heredi, dopò la sua morto; et il valsen.to di altri 38 m[il]a simili in tanto gioie; di quali 4 m[il]a volse che servisseranno per aiuto di costa, et per pagare debbito di questo lavoro; et l'altri 34 m[il]a con l'altri 60 che si dovevano havere s'impiegassero in tanti beni stabile, dei frutti de' quali cavatam.e per m.a scudi 500 l'anno per questa casa; si facesse tre parti: una per il Novitiato; et l'altre 2 per la Casa Profesa di Napoli; sin tanto che havesse interamente finito le sue fabriche, et provisto la sacrestia delle cose necessarie dovendo poi ristare ogni cosa al novitio; quali scudi 38 m[il]a poi si sono havuti in diverse partite, come si divà apprisso. In tutto d.co scudi 38 m[il]a' (ARSI, FG 1033 [Compendio delle cose temporale di questo casa di S.o An-drea dall'anno 1565 per tutto l'anno 1609], 15a). The source mentions an amount of 98,000 Neapolitan scudi, which were worth 90,000 Roman scudi. See Valone, 'Women on the Quirinal Hill,' p. 137.

70 Bailey, 'Le style jésuite,' p. 40.

71 Conelli, 'Female Patronage,' p. 7.

72 For the early history of S. Vitale, see Luigi Huetter and Vincenzo Golzio, *San Vitale (Le chiese di Roma illustrate, 35)* (Rome, n.d.), pp. 6–15.

73 Navarola's manuscript history refers to Vestina's gift to the church, which was 'Ornata con ['edificato con' is crossed out] gemme, et ornamente di una pia, e liberal matrona Romana chiamata Vestina' (ARSI, Rom. 162 I, 134b).

74 On the foundation, see the manuscript histories in ARSI, Rom. 162 I, 134a, 166b–167a. See also Valone, 'Women on the Quirinal Hill,' p. 137.

75 See also Zuccari, *Arte e committenza*, pp. 40, 47 n39.

76 See the reference to S. Vitale in Acquaviva's *vita* in ARSI, Vitae 144 I, 73.

77 Macioce, *Undique splendent*, pp. 122–3; van Assche, 'Louis Richeôme,' pp. 3–10. The garden was destroyed in 1870 to make way for the Via Piacenza.

78 Conelli concurs: 'She did not dictate iconographic programs, artistic styles, or artists employed' ('Female Patronage,' p. 7).

79 'Rinovò la chiesa di S. Vitale, et l'abbelli con l'industria de nostri fratelli, et con le limosine degl'amici: et facendovi pingere attorno nelle mura di dentro varij martirij distinti per le Principali Provinciae; a fuori nel Portico gl'instrumenti de carnefieri adoperati ne' tormenti de' Santi; egli stesso inventò la maggior parte de' motti, che bellissimi vi sono aggiunti' (ARSI, Vitae 144 I [Claudio Acquaviva], 74).

80 'In quant' al disegno, Giovanni Battista carissimo, vi dico che mi piace assai; solamente vi significherò un mio concetto (rimettendomi pure all'arte vostra), se fussi meglio che le colonne che reggono il cornicione della tribuna fussero piutosto pilastri piani scannellati, per variare un poco, già che per tutto 'l resto della chiesa son colonne. Consideratela e giudicatela voi. Nelle figure poi della tribuna, se ben veggo che non havete voluto guadagnar luogo et fare bello scompartimento, tuctavia gusterei che la Madonna Sma e l'altre Marie fussero intere e che venissero incontro al Signore, il quale

riguardasse la madre, et ella lui, con affetto. Del resto, resto sodisfatto. In quant'al trattar con Paris per la pittura, a me la storia che voi dite di Christo N. S. alla colonna mi sodisfa, e mi par che voi possiate cominciare a negotiare con essolui; ma non concludete altro sin alla nostra venuta a Roma, che sarà presto' (ARSI, Rom. 14, 478b; published in Pirri, 'Intagliatori,' p. 40).

81 '[1597] In torno alla chiesa di S. Vitale, della quale si scrisse l'anno passato, si continuò il restauramento e fu finito il portico, dipinto dentro, e fuori, e si cominciò a dipinger la chiesa, et a fare il soffitto ornato con pitture, rosoni, fogliami, et altri lavori, che se bene sono di poca spesa, lo rendono però molto vago, e riguardevole. La tribuna si fece da fondamenti tutta di nuovo' (ARSI, Rom. 162 I, 155b; published in Zuccari, *Arte e committenza*, p. 160). Zuccari also publishes another copy of Navarola's text in the Archivio della Provincia Romana della Compagnia di Gesù: '... se bene la pittura dell'Altare, e gl'ornamenti che hoggi passono il valore di mille scudi, tuto e stato per altra via buscato e provisto dal fr[ate]llo Domenico Rinaldi, e doni per l'altare' (ARPG E.71, 74b; published in Zuccari, *Arte e committenza*, p. 160).

82 '[1598] s'ebbero due mille scudi a conto delli 4 m[ila] assegnati per aiuto stando con li quali si tirò avanti la restauratione di S. Vitale, aggiungendo due altari alli tre malandati che vi erano, e seguitando il soffitto con la pittura di tutta la chiesa, che gia cominciava ad apparire non meno nobile, che vaga' (ARSI, Rom. 162 I, 167b; published in Zuccari, *Arte e committenza*, p. 160).

83 Zuccari, *Arte e committenza*, p. 161; Macioce, *Undique splendent*, p. 124.

84 '[1598] La Casa spese nelle pitture di S. Vitale del presente anno da scudi 300' (ARSI, FG 1033, 16a).

85 'Il Fiammeri fece anche di figure, e se ne vedono di sua mano in S. Vitale, luogo dove già i Romani inalzarono il Tempio a Quirino, e da lui diedero il nome al Quirinale, hora Chiesa de' loro Padri; ove sopra l'altare ha fatto a man diritta diverse sante Vergini in piedi co' segni de' loro martirii, e con palme nelle mani; come ancora allo'ncontro v'è di suo l'altro quadro, tutti due a dio dipinti. E la facciata della chiesa, & il portico di S. Vitale fu parimente da lui colorito, dove sono diversi stromenti da flagellare i Martiri fatti in foggia di trionfi con diversi capricci espressi per rimembranza de gli stenti crudeli, co'quali conducevano a morte i Santi di Dio: e tutta questa opera fu, con gli ordini del Padre Fiammeri, fabricata, e distinta' (Baglione, *Le vite de' pittori*, p. 98). Titi agrees: 'La facciata con il Portico fù colorita dal P. Gio: Battista Fiammeri, che anche da i lati dell'Altar maggiore dipinse due Quadri à olio in uno de' quali sono diverse Vergini in piedi' (*Studio di pittura*, p. 151).

86 'Ricordi relativi alla decorazione della chiesa di San Vitale. Ricordi Jesus Maria. Le pitture delle colonne di S. Vitale si diede a pingere a Anibale priori, pittore perugino (questa parola cancellata nel documento); il quale d'accordo et con scrittura di sua propria mano sottoscritta per prezzo di 120 overo 130 scudi tutto l'opera dal soffitto fino in terra, salvo però la facciata tutta della porta, et le figure de' Profeti, poi per sua indispositione et licentia entrò in suo luogo, et nel medesimo modo, et prezzo Tarquinio Ligusti pittore; ho fatto questo ricordo imperò che la scritta sopradetta non la ritrovo, et penso che la diedi in mano del fratello Lodovico Giappi, insieme con le sue altre appartenenze, sì come hieri diedi a voi quelle dell'altro pittore Andrea Commodi' (ARSI, FG 861; published in Huetter and Golzio, *San Vitale*, p. 63). The

consecration of the altars of S. Vitale on 10 May 1600 is mentioned in the account book, ARSI, FG 1048 bis, 46b, and is published in Zuccari, *Arte e committenza*, p. 162.

87 Macioce, *Undique splendent*, p. 123.

88 In a letter of 16 August 1599, written in Tivoli to the provincial in Rome, Acquaviva requests that he send Fiammeri to the Father General in person so that he might stress how much he is needed at S. Vitale: 'Mi sarà anco caro che V.R. quanto prima mi mandi il fr. Giovan Battista Fiammeri, per dirli a bocca quel tanto ch'io desideri da lui intorno alle pitture di S. Vitale' (ARSI, Rom. 14, 474b; published in Pirri, 'Intagliatori,' p. 40). Zuccari has published two references in the account books to funds used for painting in July to September 1599: '... a di p[rim]o 9bre furono applicati da N.P. G[enerale] s. 3150 impiegati in L[uoghi] 21 del monte della religione, ch'è quanto s'ebbe di aiuto in q[uest]o anno oltre s. 410 dati per limosina ... e s. 250 cavati da pani venduti di montij e lor deposidi, li quali con qualche cosa di più furono spesi nelle pitture di S. Vitale'; '[6 July 1599] La chiesa di S. Vitale deve dare per spese diverse fatte nella da questa casa di S. Andrea ... a dì 6 di luglio 1599 dati à Stefano da Montesanto falegname lavorante di S. Vitale per saldo di un mese 1/2 scudi 3. Et più per conti dati ad un lavorante di muratore d'ordine del P. Lucio Bencio Rettore, scudi 1.20. Et più a dì 8 d'Agosto per conti dati al F. Rotilio per dare ad un pittore d'ordine del Padre sudetto, scudi 6.20. Et a dì detto [5 September 1599] al F. Rotilio chiesa S. Vitale scudi 70' (ARSI, Rom. 162 I, 175a; FG 1048 bis, 146b; Zuccari, *Arte e committenza*, p. 161. Zuccari's reading of the second quotation differs from my own).

89 '[From Tivoli, 28 January 1599] V.S. sa quant'io desidero farle cosa grata et quanto volentieri le conceda il nostro Fratello Rutilio per la cappella, ma lo domanda aperto ad un tempo nel quale egli ha un opera per le mani in S. Vitale di fretta e per havere lavorato un pezzo et presa practica l'assistenza sua saria causa di prolongare troppo'; '[from Tivoli, 18 February 1599] Mi rallegro poi che il Nostro fratello Rutilio habbia fatto buon effetto alla Sua cappella il tutto sia a gloria del Signore da cui prego a V.S. grande abbondanza di gratia et ogni felicità' (ARSI, Rom. 14 II, 392a, 403a).

90 '[May 1599] Lista delli denari che ho ricevuti io Tarquinio Ligustri pittore dallo Reverendo Padre Ludovico Ciappi nella Casa del Giesù a conto della pittura che ho fatta nella Chiesa di Sto. Vitale, come appare per una scritta fatta dal Reverendo Padre Giovambattista Fiammieri nel principio del Maggio 1599 di scudi 103 e scudi 6 per li pilastro in tutto scudi 109. A dì 6 di Maggio 1599, scudi 10; A dì 5 di Giugno, scudi 10; a dì 27, scudi 10; a dì 20 del luglio, scudi 10; a dì 5 di 7bre, scudi 10; a dì ultimo di 7bre, scudi 15; a dì 18 de 8bre, scudi 20; a dì 14 di 9bre, scudi 20. E più ho ricevuto a dì 26 di Xbre scudi 10 per la pittura che ho fatto intorno alle statue di stucco la quale non s'intende nel contenuto della scritta. E più devo havere per la facciata da basso che non si contiene nella scritta fatta senza patto, scudi 60. E più per l'Augmento delli ornamenti intorno alli paesi che nulla scritta si dichiara campo bianco, scudi 12' (ARSI, Rom. 163, 238b; slightly different in Zuccari, *Arte e committenza*, p. 163).

91 'Quietantia Tarquinii Ligustri Pictoris pro hornatu facto sua manu in Ecclesia S. Vitalis. Fuori: 8 luglio 1603. Ric.ta di Tarquinio Ligustri de s. 30. Dentro: Adì 8 de luglio 1603. Per la p.te confesso io Tarquinio Ligustri Pittore haver ricevuto dal R.do Padre Bartolomeo Parentij Proc.re scudi 30 di m.ta, quali sono p. resto et integro pagamento di tutta la pittura che ho fatto nella chiesa di S. Vitale sino al presente giorno così le tre

facciate come le atre cose che io vi havessi fatto et così fo quitanza di tutto quello
che io pretendesse, dechiarando che le figure sopra la porta ce l dono, dico s. 30. Io
Tarquinio Ligustri sopr.to m.o pp.a' (Huetter and Golzio, *San Vitale*, pp. 62–3).

92 Macioce, *Undique splendent*, p. 124.

93 'Nondimeno di quelle poche, ch'egli [Andrea Commodo] fece in Roma, rammentan-
domesene alcune; diremo, che nella chiesa di S. Vitale per li Padri Giesuiti operasse la
Tribuna, nella quale nostro Signore porta la croce al Calvario con molte figure, e
sopra vi sono Agnoli, e puttini. E da basso dalle bande vi si veggono due storie
de'martirij di Santi a fresco con buona grazia, e gran diligenza maneggiate' (Baglione,
Le vite de' pittori, p. 334). Baldinucci writes, 'In S. Vitale de' Padri Gesuiti dipinse
[Andrea Commodo] la Tribuna, ov'è il Signore portante la Croce, con assai figure, e
dai lati due Storie di S. Martiri' (Filippo Baldinucci, *Notizie de' professori del disegno*
[Florence, 1702], p. 261). Titi concurs: 'e le pitture della Tribuna, dove stà effigiato
N.S. che porta la Croce al Calvario, le condusse Andrea Commodo. Due Martirij de'
Santi, che sono da basso dalle bande, furono à fresco con buona gratia, e gran
diligenza maneggiati dal sudetto Commodo' (*Studio di pittura*, vol. 1, p. 151).

94 Gianni Papi, *Andrea Commodi* (Florence, 1994); *La pittura in Italia: Il seicento*, vol. 2,
p. 699; Papi, 'Le tele della cappellina di Odoardo Farnese'; *Il seicento fiorentino*, vol. 3,
pp. 60–1; *Arte in Valdichiana* (Cortona, 1970), pp. 54–5, fig. 83.

95 ASF, Accademia del Disegno 27, 75a–b, 56b, 59b, 138a. See Bailey, 'Santi di Tito and
the Florentine Academy.'

96 *La pittura in Italia: Il seicento*, vol. 2, p. 691; *Il seicento fiorentino*, vol. 3, pp. 60–1.

97 ASF, Accademia del Disegno 27, 58a, 59b, 60b, 79b, 127b.

98 Baglione writes, 'Mostrò anche il suo pregio in S. Vitale, titolo di Vestina, con due
storie del martirio di quel Santo, ne' lati a canto della Tribuna, con buona maniera
in fresco figurate, e vogliono, che ciò sia delle migliori cose, ch'egli co'l pennello
operasse' (*Le vite de' pittori*, p. 320). Titi concurs: '... e ne i lati accanto alla Tribuna vi
sono due historie del Martirio di S. Vitale con buona maniera à fresco figurate dal
Ciampelli Fiorentino' (*Studio di pittura*, vol. 1, p. 151). For the drawings, see Gabinetto
Disegni e Stampe degli Uffizi, *Disegni dei toscani a Roma (1580–1620)* (Florence, 1979),
cat. nos 43, 44, pp. 66–70; see also Abromson, 'Painting in Rome,' pp. 243ff.

99 'S. Vitale esteso sopra l'eculeo per havere esortato Orsicino, schifando l'adoraz.e
dell'Idolo / mostragli dal sacerd.e gentile et dal Giudice / st.a seconda' (Uffizi, GDS,
n. 5137).

100 Zeri, *Pittura e controriforma*, p. 107; Zuccari, *Arte e committenza*, p. 165. An amount of
money was lent by Celio in 1596 and was used to help construct the garden. He was
paid back, in two annual instalments of 150 scudi, by 1598. The first reference is listed
under *censi diversi* for 1595 (*sic*): 'Scudi 300 a 6 giugnio da Gasparo Celio pitture a 6.
per mano di detto [Francesco] Silla' (ARSI, Rom. 162 I, 134a). The others are quoted in
Zuccari: 'A' Gasparo Celio 23 detto [diciembre 1597] per estinzione d'un Annuo conto
di s. 150 a' bon conto di s. di trecento m[one]ta presi l'Anno pasato A di 6 Giugno a 6
1/2 per oto duo, s. 150 ... A Gasparo Celio A di 13 Giugno [1598] per estinzione d'un
Annuo conto di s. 19 vendutogli per s. 300 de quali s. 150 furono resi del 1596, per
resto altri 150' (ARSI, Rom. 167 I, 14b, 15a; published in Zuccari, *Arte e committenza*, p.
165).

101 Zuccari, *Arte e committenza*, p. 164.

102 Macioce, *Undique splendent*, p. 123; Zeri, *Pittura e controriforma*, fig. 94.

103 '[28 April 1609] si finì la porta di S. Vitale a cui si lavorò circa due anni' (ARSI, Hist. Soc. 23, 2b; published in Pietro Pirri and Pietro di Rosa, 'Il P. Giovanni de Rosis (1538–1610) e lo sviluppo dell'edilizia gesuitica,' *Archivum Historicum Societatis Iesu* 44 (1975): 78.

104 For the St Francis image, see Bailey, 'The Jesuits and Painting in Italy,' pp. 151–78.

105 Huetter and Golzio, *San Vitale*, p. 53; Pirri, 'Intagliatori,' pp. 40–1.

106 Pirri, 'Intagliatori,' p. 42. My translation.

107 'Il lavoro di S. Vitale fu distinto in parti cioè: Due colonne con tutto il vano seguente per fino a l'altre colonne che seguono appresso, cioè che contiene il cornicione, fregio, architrave, capitelli, colonne à la sua base e piedistallo, dal soffitto per fino in terra: e il vano che contiene l'ornamento della finistra o' nichia dove sono i profeti, l'hornamento de paesi e tutto fino in terra. Di modo che: sei parti si fanno tutta una facciata, la faccia poi di mezzo fino alla porta che sono 7. e questa è la mita: che così tutte le parti del lavoro sono parti – 14. D'intorno intorno: da un pilastro, a l'altro[missing]. Vi è poi l'ornamento della porta e' tutto quello che e' sopra la porta, dalle figure in poi, le quali furono fatte di suo piacere e' volunta, et l'hornamento detto faremolo ancor' esso per un' altra parte: che saranno in tutto parti – 15. Et il tutto da un pilastro a' l'altro in torno tutte 3 le facciate. Le quali parti si pattui daccordo, et con iscritto di s. 6 overo otto del che no' mi ricordo, di modo che se a' 8, s. 120. Il pilastro datene scudi 5, s. 5. Dell'ornamento della porta e sopra porta senza le figure, le quali non si mettono a conto datene scudi 10 overo 15 al più, s. 15. La pittura che è intorno alle statue di stucco, non sò io che se ne sia fatto patto determinato: pero datene, s. 5. Sua satisfatt[ione] e prezzo sia, s. 145 il tutto. Et di più quella cortesia è bene andata che si co[n]verrà. Ha ricevuto in questo foglio s. 109 fare a me serbare questo conto e servitevi dell'altro' (ARSI, Rom. 163, 238a; published in Zuccari, *Arte e committenza*, pp. 162–3). A very similar but undated description was published earlier by Golzio: 'Il lavoro di S. Vitale fu distinto tutto in parti equali et daccordo p. iscritta, cioè: Le due colonne insieme con tutto il seguente perfino alle altre due colonne contiene una parte: dal soffitto fino in terra dai paesi in poi. E tutte le parti del lavoro intorno intorno [sic] sono parti 14: l'hornamento della porta, et sopra il diritto della porta faranno a discretione: cioè che sia come valore di unaltra parte dalle figure che tengono il JHS in poi. Dimodo che tutte le parti saranno parti, s. 15. Le quali parti sono pattuite d'accordo per prezzo di s. 8 overo 6, il che non mi ricordo. Otto vie 15 fa, s. 120. Per il pilastro, che non vi è patto, s. 5. Per l'hornamento fatto intorno le statue, s. 5. Per altro et ultimo, s. 5. Devere havere in tutto, s. 135. Et per ultima satisfatt.e e cortesia, s. 10. Tutto, s. 145' (ARSI, FG 861; published in Huetter and Golzio, *San Vitale*, p. 62).

108 'La chiesa di S. Vitale e posta in luogo basso a piede alli giardini di detta casa e assai grande con cinque altari ben ornati e tutta dipinta con l'historia della vita e morte di San Vitale, Santa Valeria sua moglie e Santi Gervasio e Protasio suoi figlioli e bene soffitata ha il portone, e portici antichi con colonne con la sacrestia molto humida ne ha case contigue ma solo arti anco dirimpetto' (ARSI, FG 1033, 37b [1650]).

109 See Zuccari, *Arte e committenza*, pp. 53–6.

110 Dante, *The Divine Comedy: Hell*, Canto XXVII:7.

111 Richeôme, *La peinture spirituelle*, pp. 673–6.

112 Ibid., p. 677.

113 'le plus cruel, le plus ignominieux, & le plus abominable instrument de tous, que nostre Seigneur a voulu endurer & souffrir pour nous fere vivre' (ibid., p. 674).

114 Zeri, *Pittura e controriforma*, fig. 93.

115 Richeôme, *La peinture spirituelle*, p. 684. Richeôme does not publish the Latin inscriptions, which are still visible in the church today.

116 See Macioce, *Undique splendent*, tav. XXVIII.

117 Richeôme, *La peinture spirituelle*, p. 707.

118 Ibid., p. 706.

119 Huetter and Golzio, *San Vitale*, p. 53; Macioce, *Undique splendent*, p. 122.

120 All the inscriptions are recorded in Richeôme, *La peinture spirituelle*, pp. 696–7.

121 This picture was recently published in Baumstark, *Rom in Bayern*, cat. no. 141.

122 See the selection of Fiammeri's drawings in Wadell, *Evangelicae*, Abb. 207–32.

123 Richeôme, *La peinture spirituelle*, p. 723.

124 See Wadell, *Evangelicae*, Abb. 221.

125 The other canvas is published in Claudio Strinati, *Quadri romani tra '500 e '600* (Rome, 1979), tav. 8.

126 Smith, 'The Art of Salvation in Bavaria,' p. 582.

127 Richeôme, *La peinture spirituelle*, p. 711.

128 The inscription is preserved in Richeôme, *La peinture spirituelle*, p. 760, but is not clear on the painting.

129 Richeôme, *La peinture spirituelle*, p. 735.

130 In Richeôme's words, 'freschement massacrez' (ibid., p. 773).

131 A. Richard Turner, *The Vision of Landscape in Renaissance Italy* (Princeton, 1966), p. 153.

132 Turner, *The Vision of Landscape*, p. 170.

133 Rudolf Wittkower, *Art and Architecture in Italy, 1600–1750* (London, 1958; repr. 1991), p. 19. On Brill, see Baglione, *Le vite de' pittori*, pp. 296–7; L. Van Puyvelde, *La peinture flamande à Rome* (Brussels, 1950); Turner, *The Vision of Landscape*, pp. 170–4, 187–8; Luigi Salerno, *Pittori di paesaggio del seicento a Roma* (Rome, 1977–8), pp. 12–9; Andrea Berger, *Die Tafelgemälde Paul Brils* (Saarbrücken, 1991).

134 See Antonia Nava Cellini, 'Stefano Maderno, Francesco Vanni e Guido Reni a Santa Cecilia in Trastevere,' *Paragone* 227 (January, 1969): 18–41.

135 On the Sala Clementina, see Macioce, *Undique splendent*, pp. 169–224.

136 Ibid., p. 131.

137 Pamela Jones, 'Two Newly-discovered Hermit Landscapes by Paul Bril,' *Burlington Magazine* 130 (January 1988): 34, nn 10, 14. I would like to thank Pamela Jones for bringing this reference to my attention. See also Marco Rossi and Alessandro Rovetta, *The Pinacoteca Ambrosiana* (Milan, 1997), pp. 121–3.

138 Turner, *The Vision of Landscape*, pp. 173–4.

139 For example, Freedberg, *Painting in Italy*; Zander, *L'arte in Roma nel secolo XVI*; Calì, *La pittura del cinquecento*, vol. 1.

140 Ignatius of Loyola, *Spiritual Exercises*, p. 102

141 Jones, *Federico Borromeo*, especially pp. 78–9; Rossi and Rovetta, *The Pinacoteca Ambrosiana*, pp. 119–39.

142 Jones, *Federico Borromeo*, p. 80.

143 Ibid.

144 Ibid., p. 81.

145 In 1610 the crowds in S. Vitale regularly reached five hundred at a time, according to Navarola, and the novices preached in many languages (ARSI, Rom. 162 II, 385b).

146 'Si fa ogni settimana nella chiesa nostra di S. Vitale il giorno di mercoledi, o altro giorno, se questo viene impedito da forse la dottrina Christiana alli poveri catechizantogli per mezz'hora, cantandosi le litanie della Madonna, cose della dottrina Christiana & lo di spirituali ... et concorso continuo di 400, in circa, procendendosi in ciò con buon ordine ... di tutte le nazione, et lingue, et è più volte acceduto essersi venuti di quelli tanto ignoranti alle cose della fede che non sapovano pur forsi il segno della Santa Croce, ne il Pater Noster, o Ave Maria' (ARSI, Rom. 162 II, 371a).

147 See Samuel Y. Edgerton, *Theaters of Conversion: Religious Architecture and Indian Artisans in Colonial Mexico* (Albuquerque, 2001), fig. 2.29.

148 '... vous viennent voir les Italiens, les Allemans, les Polonois, les Bohemiens, les Hongrois, les Flamans, les Vallons, les Hibernois, les Escossois, les Anglois, les Grecs, les Espagnols, les François, & autres Nations de la Chrestienté, & toutes sont enseignees en leur langue Patriotte, & chacun de vous a sa troupe & son Escole à part en un mesme lieu, & sans confusion ... non seulement vous, mais encor tous ceux, qui sont dressez comme vous, en autres maisons semblables assises en cinq parties du Monde habitable' (Richeôme, *La peinture spirituelle*, pp. 784, 790). The resonance with Acts is quite striking: 'And how hear we every man in our own tongue, wherein we were born? Parthians, and Medes, and Elamites, and the dwellers in Mesopotamia, and in Judaea, and Cappadocia, in Pontus, and Asia, Phrygia, and Pamphylia, in Egypt, and in the parts of Libya about Cyrene, and strangers of Rome, Jews and proselytes, Cretes and Arabians, we do hear them speak in our tongues the wonderful works of God' (Acts 2:8–11).

6: The Church of the Gesù in Rome: Documents

1 See Bailey, 'Le style jésuite,' pp. 42, 68–9; Haskell, *Patrons and Painters*, p. 62.

2 See in particular Carlo Galassi Paluzzi, 'Architetti e decoratori nella chiesa del Gesù,' *Architettura ed arti decorative* IV (1924–5): 49–61; Galassi Paluzzi, *Storia segreta dello stile dei gesuiti* (Rome, 1951); Pecchiai, *Il Gesù di Roma*; Pirri, *Tristano*; Pirri and Rosa, 'Il P. Giovanni de Rosis,' especially pp. 65–79; Rudolf Wittkower, 'Problems of the Theme,' pp. 1–14, and James Ackerman, 'The Gesù in the Light of Contemporary Church Design,' pp. 15–28, in Wittkower and Jaffe, *Baroque Art*; Klaus Schwager, 'La chiesa del Gesù del Vignola,' *Bollettino del Centro A. Palladio* 19 (1977): 251–71; Bösel, *Jesuitenarchitektur in Italien*, vol. 1, pp. 160–79; Klaus Schwager, 'Concetto e realtà: Alcune precisazioni sulla difficile nascita del Gesù di Roma,' in Patetta and Della Torre, *L'architettura della Compagnia di Gesù*, pp. 69–77; Robertson, *Il Gran Cardinale*, pp. 181–96; Clare Robertson, 'Two Farnese Cardinals and the Question of Jesuit Taste,' in O'Malley et al., *The Jesuits*, pp. 134–47. There is an excellent survey of the literature in Luciano Patetta, 'Le chiese della Compagnia di Gesù come tipo: Complessità e sviluppi,' in his *Storia e tipologia* (Milan, 1989), pp. 160–201.

3 See Hibbard, 'Ut picturae sermones,' pp. 29–50; Lewine, 'The Roman Church Interior,' pp. 226–66; Alessandro Zuccari, 'Aggiornamenti sulla decorazione cinquecentesca di alcune cappelle del Gesù,' *Storia dell'arte* (1984): 28–33; Zuccari, 'Bellarmino e la

Cappella degli Angeli,' pp. 611–28; and the contributions by Patrizia Tosini and Laura Russo to Madonna, *Roma di Sisto V*, pp. 168–87.

4 Freedberg, *Painting in Italy*, p. 660. Morton Abromson also refers to 'a banal sentimentality that appealed to popular taste' ('Painting in Rome,' p. 266).

5 Francis Haskell maintained that the Jesuits had limited access to artists of 'really first-class quality' for the Gesù because the best artists were being employed on more important projects such as the Vatican, the family palaces of the reigning popes, and the titular churches (*Patrons and Painters*, p. 65).

6 Hibbard, 'Ut picturae sermones,' pp. 36–7.

7 For example, see Abromson, 'Painting in Rome,' pp. 262–7. On the decorations of the Chiesa Nuova, see Verstegen, 'Federico Barocci'; Ferrara, 'Artisti e committenze,' pp. 108–29; Barbieri et al., *Santa Maria in Vallicella*. See also Giles Knox, 'The Unified Church Interior in Baroque Italy: S. Maria Maggiore in Bergamo,' *Art Bulletin* (December 2000): 679.

8 Haskell, *Patrons and Painters*, p. 68.

9 For recent literature on this treatise, see Bailey, 'The Jesuits and Painting in Italy,' p. 171. Pietro da Cortona may also have submitted a design for the altarpiece of the Chapel of St Francis Xavier at the Gesù at the end of his life – this is a hotly contested issue (ibid., p. 164).

10 See Ferrara, 'Artisti e committenze.'

11 See Hibbard, *Caravaggio*, pp. 160–1.

12 Josephine von Henneberg comments about Cesare Baronio that 'the artists he directly commissioned were not of the highest rank' ('Cardinal Caesar Baronius,' p. 138).

13 Zuccari, 'Cultura e predicazione nelle immagini dell'Oratorio'; Hall, *After Raphael*, p. 445. Hall finds a unity in 'an understanding that the worshipper's affective participation must be solicited.' See also Verstegen, 'Federico Barrocci,' p. 4.

14 Zuccari, 'Cesare Baronio, le immagini, gli artisti,' p. 94. My translation.

15 Hibbard, 'Ut picturae sermones,' p. 40.

16 Ibid., p. 34; Hall, *After Raphael*, p. 269. See also Haskell, *Patrons and Painters*, p. 66.

17 Daniele Ferrara has recently published a 1580 document, entitled 'Conditioni cole quali si ha da conceder le Cappelle,' that demonstrates the degree of control the Oratorians had over their side chapels. The document spells out that the patrons had to adorn the chapels in a manner that had already been decided, that the altarpieces had to show one of the mysteries of the Virgin according to a previously given order, and that even the tabernacles had to conform to one of two possible designs ('Artisti e committenze,' pp. 108–9). In one case, the Oratorians offered a patron a choice between Federico Barocci and Girolamo Muziano (Verstegen, 'Federico Barocci,' p. 6).

18 Abromson, 'Painting in Rome,' p. 239; Hibbard, 'Ut picturae sermones,' p. 40.

19 Hall, *After Raphael*, p. 269.

20 Haskell, *Patrons and Painters*, p. 66.

21 Wittkower, 'Introduction,' p. 8.

22 See Robertson, *Il Gran Cardinale* and 'Two Farnese Cardinals.'

23 Robertson, 'Two Farnese Cardinals,' p. 144.

24 Bailey, 'Le style jésuite,' p. 43; Robertson, *Il Gran Cardinale*, pp. 184–96.

25 Pietro Pirri, 'La topografia del Gesù di Roma,' *Archivum Historicum Societatis Iesu* 10 (1941): 177–82; Pecchiai, *Il Gesù di Roma*, pp. 3–14; Lucas, *Landmarking*, pp. 85–104.

26 O'Malley, *The First Jesuits*, p. 36.

27 Pirri, *Tristano*, p. 138; Schwager, 'La chiesa del Gesù del Vignola,' pp. 252ff.

28 Robertson, *Il Gran Cardinale*, p. 184; Lewine, 'The Roman Church Interior,' p. 227; Pecchiai, *Il Gesù di Roma*, pp. 14–37.

29 O'Malley, *The First Jesuits*, p. 356.

30 James Ackerman, *The Architecture of Michelangelo* (London, 1961), pp. ii, 141ff; Robertson, *Il Gran Cardinale*, p. 185.

31 Robertson, *Il Gran Cardinale*, p. 187.

32 Ackerman, 'The Gesù,' p. 26.

33 Pirri, *Tristano*, p. 159; Pecchiai, *Il Gesù di Roma*, p. 89; Hibbard, 'Ut picturae sermones,' p. 34; Klaus Schwager, 'Anlässlich eines unbekannten Stichs des romischen Gesù von Valeriannus Regnartius,' in Hans-Caspar Graf von Bothmer et al., eds, *Festschrift Lorenz Dittman* (Munich, 1994), p. 308.

34 Robertson, *Il Gran Cardinale*, p. 189.

35 Ibid.

36 Quoted in O'Malley, *The First Jesuits*, p. 357.

37 'La fabrica della nostra chiesa è cresciuto molto molto [*sic*] dal principio ... essendosi inalzante le tre altre capelle corresponderà alle tre che l'hanno passato si fecero coperte insieme con le sue vuolte, et fabricatovi sopra di modo che quella parte della fabrica và hormai più in alto che l'altra. La facciata si và facendo con grande artificio di pietra molto ben lavorata, et arrivata un lato quasi tanto alto come la istessa fabrica con la buona diligenza et cura che si e havuta, et con la continua fatica de' fratelli muratori, et tempo buono che dio Nostro Signore ha dato quest'anno' (ARSI, Rom. 126b I [Annuae 1570–85], 10b). There are more descriptions of the construction of the Gesù in the same volume, for example f. 55a and f. 58a.

38 '... diré solamente que son hasta todos hermanos nuestros albañires que han augmentado este año mucho la fabrica, la qual con el tiempo será un grande edificio, y de mucha costa, mas muy al preposito para nuestros ministerios, y siguiendo el Illmo Cardenal Farnese' (ARSI, Rom. 127 I, 80b).

39 Hibbard, 'Ut picturae sermones,' p. 34.

40 Conelli, 'Female Patronage,' p. 1.

41 Robertson, *Il Gran Cardinale*, p. 194.

42 Conelli, 'Female Patronage,' p. 11.

43 'La Cappella della Madonna, et di S. Andrea furono fatte per esser state nel sito della chiesa, avvanti, che tanto ampla si fabbricasse due chiesoline, l'una di Sta Maria della Strada, la cui figura si conserva nella medesima Cappella della Maddonna, et l'altra di Sto. Andrea' (ARSI, FG 545, 5a).

44 Hibbard, 'Ut picturae sermones,' p. 34; Pecchiai, *Il Gesù di Roma*, pp. 10–11; Raffaele Russo, *Il ciclo francescano nella Chiesa del Gesù in Roma* (Rome, 2001), pp. 42–3.

45 Hibbard, 'Ut picturae sermones,' p. 34.

46 Hibbard, 'Ut picturae sermones.'

47 Ibid., pp. 29–41.

48 See also Mâle, *L'art religieux*, p. 432.

49 Hibbard, 'Ut picturae sermones,' p. 41.

50 Ibid., p. 39.

51 I am grateful to John O'Malley for drawing my attention to this relationship.

52 Herz, 'Imitators of Christ,' pp. 66–7. On the Jesuit monogram, see also Polleross, 'Nuestro modo de proceder,' p. 100.

53 Herz, 'Imitators of Christ,' p. 67.

54 Ibid., p. 66.

55 Zeri, *Pittura e controriforma*; Vaudo, *Scipione Pulzone*; Freedberg, *Painting in Italy*, pp. 657–67.

56 *La pittura in Italia: Il cinquecento*, vol. 2, p. 690.

57 Ibid., p. 677; *Il Cavalier d'Arpino* (Rome, 1973).

58 *La pittura in Italia: Il seicento*, vol. 2, p. 677.

59 *La pittura in Italia: Il cinquecento*, vol. 2, p. 868; Matthias Winner and Dietlief Heikamp, *Der Maler Federico Zuccari* (Munich, 1999); Luchinat, *Taddeo e Federico Zuccari*; Bonita Cleri, ed., *Federico Zuccari* (Milan, 1997).

60 *La pittura in Italia: Il cinquecento*, vol. 2, p. 704.

61 Ibid., p. 749; *Andrea Lilli nella pittura delle Marche: Tra cinquecento e seicento* (Rome, 1985).

62 *La pittura in Italia: Il cinquecento*, vol. 2, p. 829.

63 *La pittura in Italia: Il seicento*, vol. 2, p. 710.

64 *La pittura in Italia: Il cinquecento*, vol. 2, p. 779; Giammaria, *Girolamo Muziano*; Como, *Girolamo Muziano*.

65 *La pittura in Italia: Il seicento*, vol. 2, p. 621.

66 Ibid., p. 677; Helmut Philipp Riedl, *Antiveduto della Grammatica* (Berlin, 1998).

67 *La pittura in Italia: Il cinquecento*, vol. 2, p. 812; Ostrow, *Art and Spirituality*, pp. 87–9.

68 *La pittura in Italia: Il seicento*, vol. 2, p. 774.

69 *La pittura in Italia: Il cinquecento*, vol. 2, p. 693; Edoardo Arslan, *I Bassano*, 2 vols (Milan, 1960), I, pp. 183–226.

70 See Madonna, *Roma di Sisto V*, pp. 177–8. The attribution to Heintz was made by Jürgen Zimmer in *Joseph Heintz der Ältere als Maler* (Weissenhorn, 1971), p. 13. See also Zimmer, *Joseph Heintz der Ältere* (Munich, 1988), pp. 23ff. On Hans von Aachen, see Joachim Jacoby, *Hans von Aachen, 1552–1615* (Munich, 2000). I would like to thank Jeffrey Chipps Smith for bringing this reference to my attention. For Pepijn, see Russo, *Il ciclo*, pp. 55–6.

71 Calì, *La pittura del cinquecento*, vol. 2, p. 201; Robertson, *Il Gran Cardinale*, p. 111.

72 Baglione, *Le vite de' pittori*, pp. 72–3; Ostrow, *Art and Spirituality*, p. 57.

73 Baglione, *Le vite de' pittori*, pp. 114–15; Ostrow, *Art and Spirituality*, pp. 147, 173; Freiburg, *The Lateran in 1600*, pp. 293–5, 304–9. See also Roger C. Burns, 'Camillo Mariani: Catalyst of the Sculpture of the Roman Baroque,' PhD dissertation, The Johns Hopkins University, 1979.

74 Pirri, 'Intagliatori,' pp. 4–10. On Tronchi's ceiling for the Gesù in Perugia, gilt and painted in 1574, see the description in the 1819 manuscript gazetteer of Perugia by Annibale Mariotti, *Memorie storiche delle chiese della Città di Perugia* (ASPer, Perugia II 167 5, 205); and Siepi, *Descrizione topologico-istorica*, p. 407. For the Florentine project, see Bailey, 'The Florentine Reformers.'

75 The personnel records list him as follows: 'Bartolomeo de Tronchi da Brozzi fiorentino d'età di 40 anni, sono 11 anni che entrò nella Compagnia in Roma, fece i voti dapoi l'entrata, fu fatto coadiutore temporale formato sono da 3 anni, falegname, intagliatore, et ha buon dissegno di questa arte, di sanità mediocre et mediocre forze' (ARSI, Hist. Soc. 41, 89a). See also Pirri, *Tristano*, p. 245, and 'Ammannati,' pp. 22–3 n51.

76 ASF, Comp. Rel. Sopp. 978, #52, 34a; Comp. Rel. Sopp. 999, #104, 91a, 91b, 233a, 234b, 238a; Comp. Rel. Sopp. 998, #98, 112b.

77 Pirri, 'Intagliatori,' pp. 10–18.

78 See Pecchiai, *Il Gesù di Roma*, p. 70.

79 Robertson, *Il Gran Cardinale*, pp. 162–8.

80 Ibid., pp. 88, 196.

81 Pecchiai, *Il Gesù di Roma*, p. 94; Hibbard, 'Ut picturae sermones,' p. 42; Lewine, 'The Roman Church Interior,' pp. 250–1; Madonna, *Roma di Sisto V*, pp. 186–7. A late seventeenth-century description in the Jesuit archives records the patronage: 'La Cappella delli SS. Apostoli Pietro, e Paolo fu fatta dalli Signori Pietro, e Paolo Morelli' (ARSI, FG 545 ['Fabrica della Chiesa del Giesu di Roma, e Casa fabricata dalli Cardinali Alessandro e Odoardo Farnese'], 4a).

82 'Cappella dei Santi Pietro e Paolo: Fu ornata dal Signore Paolo Morelli, ma degli Eredi, con licenza del P. Generale ceduta al Signore Francesco Ravenna per sei luoghi di Monti Camerali impiegati per monacare non so quale zitella. Il Signore Francesco Ravenna l'ha ornata di marmi, e di pitture di Francesco Mola con pavimento di marmo. E ha fatto Candelieri d'ottone, e una lampara, quale ha dotata con obbligo alla sagrestia di tenerla accesa il giorno ... Ha lasciato ai Morelli viventi la sepoltura dalla parte dell'Epistola' (ARSI, FG 2053 [Libro delle consuetudini nelli festi che si celebrano nella Chiesa del Giesù di Roma 1666], 30; published in part in Galassi Paluzzi, 'Note di storia,' p. 385).

83 The Jesuit source records, 'La Cappella di S. Pietro, e Paolo, e loro istorie dipinta da Francesco Mola; quella della volta dirono esser del Pomerancio' (ARSI, FG 545, 2b). Celio remarks: 'La pittura della Cappella incontro di SS. Pietro e Paolo, l'altra contigua della Natività di Christo, sono à fresco, di Nicolao dalle Pomaranie. La pittura, del suo altare con il Presepio di N. Fiamengo' (*Memoria delli nomi*, p. 41). Baglione, in his entry on Circignani, agrees with Celio: 'Ou'è il Tempio del Giesù, sono due cappelle di mano di Nicolao dalle Pomarancie; la prima al lato sinistro dedicata a S. Pietro, e. S. Paolo con le storie di questi Apostoli' (*Le vite de' pittori*, p. 41). Mancini is less specific but attributes various chapels to Circignani: 'Nel Giesù varie cappelle di Nicolao del Pomarancio' (*Considerazioni sulla pittura*, p. 79). Titi, who like the anonymous Jesuit source wrote after Mola's paintings were added, also credits the vault to Circignani: 'L'historie de' SS. Pietro, e Paolo dipinte nella Cappella vicina & ultima con franchezza, e buona maniera condotte à fresco sono di Francesco Mola, quelle nella Volta dicono del Pomarancio' (*Studio di pittura*, vol. 1, p. 102).

84 '[1 September 1585] à Mastro Nicolano scudi 20'; '[12 October 1585] à Mastro Nicolo pittore a buon conto scudi dieci, scudi 10'; '[23 December, 1585] à Mastro Nicolao a buon conto della pittura scudi dodeci, scudi 12'; '[22 January 1586] à Mastro Nicolo scudi tredici à buon conto, scudi 13' (ARSI, FG 2000, 12b [Libro delle spese fatti nella Chiesa]; Zuccari, 'Aggiornamenti,' p. 31]

85 '[15 July 1586] à Mastro Nicolano Pittore scudi 15'; '[15 November 1586] à Mastro Nicolo à buon conto, scudi 10'; '[18 April 1587] à Mastro Nicolo a buon conto della pittura, scudi 20'; '[1 June 1587] à Mastro Nicolao pittore, scudi 10' (ARSI, FG 2000, 15a–16a; Zuccari, 'Aggiornamenti,' p. 31).

86 Celio, *Memoria delli nomi*, p. 41.

87 Hibbard, 'Ut picturae sermones,' p. 37; Lewine, 'The Roman Church Interior,' p. 250.

Pecchiai, *Il Gesù di Roma*, notes Celio's reference (p. 104) but does not mention the anonymous Fleming in his description of the chapel (pp. 94ff).

88 The original contract for the chapel reads: 'Nella scrittura si deve haver auerenta di porre distintamente gl'oblighi della Compagnia a quelli de Monsignor. La Compagnia si obliga a concedergli la Capella della Natività a questo solo fine di ornarla e porre le sue armi in luogo opportuno, et il Sepolcro, dove si possi sepolire esso e li suoi posteri e discendenti. Monsignor si obligherà a dare al suddetto effetto dichiarando l'una e l'altra parte che non intendare perciò dare o acquistare alcun iuspatronato o portare alcun pregiudicio alla Chiesa' (ARSI, AG Busta I, 80; published in part in Galassi Paluzzi, 'Note di storia,' p. 388). The late seventeenth-century Jesuit source also mentions Braghieri's patronage: 'La Cappella della Natività ebbe in parte della spesa l'ajuto di Signor Agostino Brachieri' (ARSI, FG 545, 4a).

89 An anonymous and unpublished Jesuit source from 1666 records the following: 'Cappella della Natività e di S. Carlo: Questa Cappella fu ornata già di elemosine dal Signore Agostino Braglier – morto senza eredi. Il Padre Muzio Vitelleschi ne volle compiacere gratis Monsignor Cerri Vecchio, il quale si obbligò di ornarla con spendervi sei mila scudi, e Monsignor Carlo Cerri Auditore di Ruota si obbligò di arrivare a scudi sette-mila per ornarla come si vede con pitture dell'Altare e pareti laterali del Sig. Romanelli' (ARSI, FG 2053, 30; incorrect fragments in Galassi Paluzzi, 'Note di storia,' p. 387). On the patronage of the chapel, see also Pecchiai, *Il Gesù di Roma*, pp. 94–5; Hibbard, 'Ut picturae sermones,' p. 43; Lewine, 'The Roman Church Interior,' pp. 251–2.

90 The anonymous late seventeenth-century Jesuit source records the following: 'La Cappella della Natività, il quadro dell'Altare e della Cornice in giù, è di Giovanni Francesco Romanelli, dalla Cornice in sù opera di Nicolò dell'Pomerancio; e le statue della medesima Cappella quella che representa la Fiortezza, la scolpi Giacomo Antonio suo fratello, e le due altre, una è di Domenico Guidi, e l'altra di Giovanni Lanzone scultori' (ARSI, FG 545, 2b).

91 Baglione writes in his entry for Circignani, 'e l'altra [cappella] a questa congiunta della Natività di Christo con sue historie, tutte a fresco con buona prattica lavorate' (*Le vite de' pittori*, p. 41). Titi concurs, also mentioning Romanelli's work: 'Nella Cappella contigua [della Natività] vi sono dipinte diverse historie di M.V. e Giesù Christo nell'Altare, e lati di essa dalla cornice in giù, tutte fatighe studiate, e colorite da Gio: Francesco Romanelli con più forza del suo solito; mà quelle dalla cornice in sù, e nella Volta furono con buona prattica lavorate da Nicolò dalle Pomarancie' (*Studio di pittura*, vol. 1, p. 101). For the references in the account books, see the following note.

92 '[11 March 1584] al fr.llo Rutilio p. doi libre de olio p. mordente, s. 0.20'; '[23 March 1584] Al Stefano nettitore di oro p. mano del fr.llo Rutilio, a bo. Conto di 18 gior.te a b. 20 una, s. 1'; [14 April 1584] A Fr.llo Rutilio p. colla e bambace, s. 0.20'; '[12 May 1584] Al fr.llo Rutilio p. pagare il lavorante p. 5 giorn.te à indorare a b. 18 il gior.e, s. 0.90'; '[19 May 1584] Al fr.llo Rutilio p. pagare geronimo nettiloro p. 6 giorn.te a b. 18, s. 1.80' (ARSI, FG 2000, 2a–3b). There are many further references to Brother Rutilio, especially relating to the gilding of the chapel, in later folios.

93 '[11 March 1584] A Nicolo scultore p. la manifatura di quatro cherubini, s. 8'; '[15 April (?) 1584] Si è fatto patto con Nicolao stucatore delli angeli et scudo del ysu in novo al muro conforme al modello p. li doi angeli delle bande et scudo nel muro p. s. ventisette di M.ta di fattura, s. 0.60' (ARSI, FG 2000, 2a–2b; transcribed differently in Zuccari,

'Aggiornamenti,' p. 30). The rest of Niccolò's payments are unpublished: '[12 May 1584] A M.s Nicolo scultore à bo. conto della fattura delli angeli et giesu di rilevo nella faciata della cappella, s. dieci d'oro in oro, e giulij 11 ½ l'uno; et li fa detti Angeli e Gesu per s. 27 moneta, [Total] scudi 11.50'; '[2 June 1584] A Nicolano scultore à buon conto delli Angeli scudi cinque d'oro in oro et scudi tre di moneta. [Total] 8.65'; '[17 June 1584] A Nicolo scultore per resto della fattura delli Angeli scudi 6.8' (ARSI, FG 2000, 3a–3b).

94 '[12 May 1584] à Mastro Nicolo pittore à conto della Cappella della Natività scudi trenta d'oro in oro à ragione di giulii 11 + ½ il patto della cappella à farla tutta scudi 250. [Total] scudi 33.75'; '[2 June 1584] à Mastro Nicolo pittore à buon conto della pittura della cappella scudi centoventi moneta. [Total] 120'; '[15 June 1584] à Mastro Nicolao Pittore à buon conto scudi 20'; '[18 July 1584] à Mastro Nicolano pittore buon conto venti. [Total] 20'; '[9 August 1584] Mastro Nicolau pittore à buon conto scudi 10'; '[18 August 1584] à Mastro Nicolao pittore per resto et intero pagamento della pittura della Natività del Signore scudi 50.30' (ARSI, FG 2000, 3a–4a; published in part in Zuccari, 'Aggiornamenti,' p. 30).

95 '[22 July 1598] Più spesi in una cornice per il quadro della cappella del Signor Agostino della Natività scudi 120; e più in tavole per fodrarlo scudi 1.90; e più in fattura scudi 0.40; e più nel indoratura della cornice scudi 3; e più a buon conto per il cristallo che va in mezzo della testa di Santo Melchiade scudi 0.60; e più per spese fatte d'Andrea scudi 0.25; e più per spesi per il parato ... da Mastro Alessandro scudi 49.50; e più in disegni per il suddetto scudi 5'; '[6 August 1598] e più in spese fatte al quadro della Natività in fodrarlo di tavole, et la cornice d'oro scudi 6.50; 13 detto datti a Andrea per saldar il conto della cera con Mastro Alessandro Pavini scudi 17; e più conti a Maestro Ambrosio a conto del confessionale scudi 15; scudi 18 pagati a Mastro Antonio fiamengo pittore scudi. [Total] scudi 120' (ARSI, FG 1233, 115b).

96 Pecchiai, *Il Gesù di Roma*, p. 95; Hibbard, 'Ut picturae sermones,' pp. 44–5; Lewine, 'The Roman Church Interior,' pp. 252–3; Madonna, *Roma di Sisto V*, pp. 181–5. The anonymous late seventeenth-century Jesuit source confirms his patronage: 'La Cappella della SS Trinità fu fatta da Monsignor Piro Taro, zio del Cardinale Arigona' (ARSI, FG 545, 4a). This anonymous report from 1666 concurs: 'Cappella della Santissima Trinità: Il Quadro di questa Cappella è del Bassano. Si dice che l'abbia ornata il Signore Pirro Taro. Vi hanno pretensione li Signori Varesi, e anco i signori Rocci. Niuno però di loro vi fa cosa alcuna' (ARSI, FG 2053, 100a; published in part in Galassi Paluzzi, 'Note di storia,' p. 390).

97 Baglione writes, 'Nel pontificato poi di Clemente viii pur da Vinegia Francesco Ponte da Bassano mandò anche del suo un'altro quadretto d'altare per la chiesa del Giesù, ed è posto nella terza cappella a mano stanca, den trovi la Santissima Trinità con li Santi, e Sante del Paradiso, con grand'amore, e diligenza operato, e dalli profesori del disegno ne riportò molta lode' (*Le vite de' pittori*, p. 64).

98 Celio's passage reads: 'Le pitture della Cappella seguente dalla cornice à basso, & il tondo nella volta con la creation, sono à fresco, e secco, del Fratello Giovan Battista Fiammeri della Compagnia di Giesù. Il resto della cornice in sù di Ventura Salinbeni Senese, la pittura del suo altare ad olio, è del secondo Bassano' (*Memoria delli nomi*, p. 42). See Hibbard, 'Ut picturae sermones,' p. 45.

99 Baglione writes in his passage on Fiammeri, 'Nel tempio del Giesù dal lato manco di esso

dentro la terza cappella, sù nella volta, il Dio Padre; e da una banda il quadro del
Battesimo del Figliolo di Dio sono suoi disegni da altri coloriti' (*Le vite de' pittori*, p. 98).

100 'Nel Giesù alla terza cappella in uno de' mezi tondi è di suo il Dio Padre con Angioli
intorno, molto belli. E nell'altare, allo'ncontro, Abramo, che adora li tre Angeli fatti a
fresco. Et ancora vi sono alcuni puttini nelli triangoli, o peducci della volta, che tengono alcune cartelle, e pure a fresco da lui furono lavorati' (Baglione, *Le vite de' pittori*,
p. 119). And for Durante: 'Dentro il Tempio del Giesù, alla piazza de gli Altieri, nella
terza cappella di tutti i Santi, alla man sinistra la storia della Trasfiguratione su'l
Tabor è di Durante' (ibid., p. 118).

101 Mancini mentions Salimbeni's participation in two places, on p. 211 – 'nel Giesù la
gloria di quegl'angeli nella capella di quel quadro del Bassano, et altro di sodisfattione agl'intendenti' – and on p. 279: 'aiutato in una gloria d'angeli da Ventura
Salimbeni e l'altare del Bassano' (*Considerazioni sulla pittura*). Baldinucci writes in his
entry on Salimbeni, 'operò nel Gesù' (*Notizie de' professori del disegno*, p. 128).

102 'Il Quadro dell'Altare, che segue passata la porta di fianco, ove è dipinta la SS. Trinità
con li Santi, e Sante del Paradiso, con grand'amore, e diligenza operato, lo mandò da
Venetia Francesco Ponte da Bassano, e dalli Professori del disegno ne riportò molte
lode ... In uno de' mezzi Tondi di questa Cappella vi è dipinto Dio Padre con Angioli
bellissimi intorno, condotti, e coloriti dal Cav. Salimbeni. Alla man sinistra si vede la
Transfiguratione di N.S. sul Tabor opera di Durante Alberti; alla destra il Battesimo
di Giesù, e nella Volta il Dio Padre, che crea il mondo, disegni del P. Gio: Battista
Fiammieri, da altri coloriti con tutto il resto' (Titi, *Studio di pittura*, vol. 1, p. 101).

103 'La Cappella della SS. Trinità, il quadro dell'Altare fece Francesco Ponte da Bassano,
e lo mando da Venetia molto lodati da Professori, in uno de mezzi fondi di questa
Cappella vi è dipinto Iddio Padre; con Angioli bellissimi coloriti dal Cavalier Salimbeni; alla mano sinistra si vede la trasfigurazione, opera di Durante Alberti. Nella
volta Iddio Padre che crea il Mondo, disegno del P. Giovanni Battista Fiammeri della
Compagnia di Giesu, da altri colorito con tutto il resto' (ARSI, FG 545, 2b).

104 Hibbard, 'Ut picturae sermones,' p. 45; Lewine, 'The Roman Church Interior,' p. 252.

105 Hibbard, 'Ut picturae sermones,' p. 45.

106 Zuccari, 'Aggiornamenti,' p. 32.

107 Madonna, *Roma di Sisto V*, p. 183.

108 Zuccari, 'Aggiornamenti,' p. 28.

109 Ibid., p. 32.

110 Ibid.

111 Ibid., p. 28.

112 Baglione, *Le vite de' pittori*, p. 147.

113 Madonna, *Roma di Sisto V*, p. 183.

114 Zuccari, 'Aggiornamenti,' p. 28; Madonna, *Roma di Sisto V*, p. 182.

115 Hibbard, 'Ut picturae sermones,' p. 45.

116 Ibid., p. 44.

117 'A 9 maggio 1588 spesa della pittura della Trinità carte reale quattri[ni] 7 per li
cartoni, s. 0.70; chiodi, s. 0.6 ½; Al fr.llo Gio. Batt.a per lapis, scudi 0.20; Carta
rinforzata per li cartoni, s. 0.5 ... A di 16 maggio al f.llo Gio. Batt.a per comprare cera
schizzo, s. 1 ... A 23 detto al f.llo Gio. Batt.a s. 3 e più p. penneli, s. 0.20; A di 28 doi
giornati di garzone [Cesare] à macinare colore a b. 7 che fanno b. 14.2 ½ gli reditte il

f.llo Batt.a, s. 0.11.½; Al f.llo Gio. Batt.a per spendere in diverse cose per dipingere, s. 1.50 … al p[rim]o luglio al f.llo Gio. Batt.a per comprare carta per usa per li cartoni, s. 1 … A di ii luglio al f.llo Giovani Batt.a p. colori, s. 2' (ARSI, FG 2000, 35b; Zuccari, 'Aggiornamenti,' p. 32). Later references to Fiammeri are not published in Zuccari: '[14 August 1588] al fratello Giovanni Battista per spendere in diverse cose et dipingere 1.50'; '[29 August 1588] al fr.llo Gio. Batt.a p. comprare colori, s. 4'; '[20 October 1588] al fr.llo Gio. Batt.a p. colori, s. 1'; '[27 October 1588] E più una quarta d'azuro piglio al fr.llo Gio. Batta, s. 0.60'; '[20 November 1588] p. colori al fr.llo Giova. Bat.a, s. 0.50'; '[4 January 1589] a fr.llo Giovan. Batt.a p. colori, s. 1'; '[4 February 1589] al fr.llo Giova. Batt.a p. colori, s. 0.60'; '[4 March 1589] al fratello Giovanni Battista per colori, scudi 0.30' (ARSI, FG 2000, 37a–b, 38a, 39b).

118 '[20 May 1588] à {M.s Giu.}m. Barici pittore à bo. Conto della pittura, s. 10' (ARSI, FG 2000, 36b). The first name, here placed in brackets, is inserted before the last name afterwards.

119 '[17 July 1588] à M[astro] Ber[nardin]o p. 10 giorn.te, s. 6'; '[2 August 1588] à M.s Ber.o p. 9 gr.te, s. 5.40'; '[10 August 1588] à M.s Ber.o p. 4 gr.te, s. 2.40'; '[14 August 1588] à M.s Ber.o pittore [giornate 3], s. 2.40'; '[20 August 1588] à M.s Ber.o g.te 4. et giulii 3 spesi in colori p. la cappella, s 3.10'; '[27 August 1588] M.s Bernardino g.te 7, s. 3.50'; '[3 September 1588] à Mastro Ber.o, g.te 5, s. 3.50'; '[17 September 1588] à M.s Ber.o una giornata, s. 0.70'; '[24 September 1588] à M.s Ber.o pittore giornate g.te 3, s. 2.10'; '[2 October 1588] à M.s Ber.o giorn.te 5, s. 3.50'; '[8 October 1588] à M.s Bernardino pitt.re g.te 6, s. 4.20'; '[15 October 1588] à M.s Ber.o pittore g.te 5, s. 4.20'; '[23 October 1588] à M.s Ber.o g.te 6, s. 4.20'; '[30 October 1588] à M.s Ber.o g.te 5, s. 3.50'; '[7 November 1588] à M.s Ber.o g.te 5, s. 3.50'; '[13 November 1588] à M.s Ber.o g.te 5, s. 3.50'; '[20 November 1588] à M.s Ber.o g.te 4, s. 3.20'; '[27 November 1588] à M.s Ber.o g.te 3, s. 2.40'; '[20 December 1588] à M.s Br.o pittore g.te 5, s. 4'; '[26 December 1588] dato à M.s Br.o, [giornate 3] s. 2.50'; '[4 January 1589] à M.s Bern.o III, s. 2.40' (ARSI, FG 2000, 35b, 36b–37b).

120 '[12 August 1588] à M[astro] Ventura pittore a b. conto, s. 3'; '[20 August 1588] à M.s Ventura g[iornate] 3, s. 2.40'; '[24 August 1588] à M.s Ventura p. giorn.te 3, s. 2.70'; '[27 August 1588] M.s Ventura g.te 2, s. 1.80'; '[3 September 1588] à M.s Ventura g.te 5, s. 4.50'; '[7 September 1588] à Mastro Ventura per resto et intero pagamento del servizio sino à questo di detto, s. 1.80'; '[24 September 1588] à M.s Ventura g.te 5, s. 4.50' (ARSI, FG 2000, 35b, 36a–b; transcribed differently in Zuccari, 'Aggiornamenti,' p. 32). Zuccari mistakenly transcribes 'giornate' as 'grossi,' and has the artist paid 20 grossi, 20 scudi, 40 giulii.

121 '[17 September 1588] à M.s Ferraù p. mano d. Br.o g.te 2, s. 1.80' (ARSI, FG 2000, 37a; Zuccari, 'Aggiornamenti,' p. 32). Zuccari transcribes 'giornate' as 'giulii.' The earlier reference to Ferraù is dated 2 August: 'à M.s Ferrau p. 5 gr.te, s. 4' (FG 2000, 36b).

122 '[4 January 1589] A Giova. Batt.a da Forli, IIIII [giornate], s. 3.60'; '[16 January 1589] M.s Giov.i Batt.a, I [giornata], s. 0.60' (ARSI, FG 2000, 38a).

123 '[13 October 1588] al fiamengho p. doi gio.ti in fare paesi, scudi 1.60'; '[27 November 1588] à M.s Pietro Fiamengho, g.te 5, s. 4'; '[20 December 1588] à M.s Pietro fiamengho g.te 4, s. 3.20'; '[26 December 1588] à M.s Pietro Fiamengho, s. 2.40'; '[4 January 1589] M.s Pietro Fiamengho pittore, III [giornate], s. 4, e più p. colori 0.5 ½' (ARSI, FG 2000, 36a–37b; mostly in Zuccari, 'Aggiornamenti,' p. 32).

124 '[28 January 1589] à M.s Durante per la pittura fatta cioè la transfiguratione, s.12' (ARSI, FG 2000, 35b; Zuccari, 'Aggiornamenti,' p. 32).

125 Zuccari, 'Aggiornamenti,' pp. 31–2. The folios are found in ARSI, FG 2000.

126 ARSI, FG 2000, 36a.

127 ARSI, FG 2000, 35b–38a; Zuccari, 'Aggiornamenti,' p. 32.

128 Pecchiai, *Il Gesù di Roma*, pp. 92–3; Hibbard, 'Ut picturae sermones,' p. 42; Lewine, 'The Roman Church Interior,' pp. 245–6; Zuccari, 'Aggiornamenti,' p. 33. For more about Giulio Folco, see Robertson, *Il Gran Cardinale*, pp. 185–94.

129 A memorial of the patronage of the Gesù records the following: 'La Cappella di S. Andrea fu principiata dal Signore Giulio Folchi, ma venuto a morte, nè ponendola gl'eredi finire, la cederono alla Signora Salustia Cerrini Crescentij, quale la finì, con pagare 600 scudi per la spesa, che vi aveva fatta il Signore Folchi, de'quali s'adornò la Cappella de' Santi tutto l'Altar Maggiore, con ordine di Nostro Padre Generale Acquaviva gli si nominasse la Cappella di Giulio Folchi' (ARSI, FG 545, 4a).

130 'La Signora Salustia Cerrini moglie del Signor Ottaviano Crescentij lasciò un ricco fidecommisso à suoi figliuoli questi morti senza successione, passò il detto fidecommisso nel Signore Francesco Serlupi figliuolo della Signora Livia Crescentij figliuola primogenita di detti Signora Salustia, ed Ottaviano. Oggi questo fidecommisso si gode dal Signore Marchero Francesco Serlupi Crescentij figliuolo della Signora Marchesa Anna Maria Bongiovanni Serlupi. E à Signora Salustia suddetta comprò, et ornò, mentre viveva con molta spesa la Cappella, di S. Andrea Apostolo nella chiesa del Giesù de' Padri della Compagnia di Giesù. Lasciò nel suo Testamento d'esser sepolta in questa sua Cappella come segui. Lasciò à Padri della Casa Professa scudi 100 per limosina, e si conserva ancor la ricevuta di detta Limosina fra le scritture in Casa Serlupi. In detto Testamento rogato da Notaro Demofonte Ferrini Comparisce la dispositione del fidecommisso, in vigor della quale è passato in Casa Serlupi. Fu fatto l'anno 1606 ad mese 8 si trova frà gli Patron. del detto Notaro Demofonte Ferrini. Nella Cappella di Sant' Andrea Apostolo nel pavimento ancor oggi si vede l'arme Cerrini. E i signori Serlupi hanno mantenuto il ius che hanno sopra questa Cappella con mandar ogn'anno alcune torcie nel giorno de' Morti. & in un libro della Sagrestia del Giesù, in cui si notano quoi, che mandano candelo, ò Torcie ad giorno de' Morti si trovano li Signori Serlupi, come heredi di detta Salustia Cerrini Crescentij. In un libro di memorie che si conserva in Casa Serlupi si trova questa partita. Cappella di S. Andrea con tutti li Santi Martiri nossa Chiesa del Giesù deve dare scudi tremila settecento novanta per tanti spesi per mano del Molto Reverendo Padre Francesco Mercati di detta Compagnia nella Casa Professa, cioè in pitture, stuccature, indorature, e ogni altra spesa fatta y servitio di detta Cappella. Scudi 3790' (ARSI, AG Busta I, 81; cited, but not transcribed, in Galassi Paluzzi, 'Note di storia,' p. 303).

131 Celio writes, 'La pittura della Cappella seguente con li atti di S. Andrea tutta da mano di Agostino Ciampelli Fiorentino' (*Memoria delli nomi*, p. 41). Mancini concurs: 'nell'entrare a man destra d'Agostin Ciampelli' (*Considerazioni sulla pittura*, p. 279).

132 Baglione writes: 'Dipinse nel Tempio del Giesù la prima cappella a man diritta, che sopra l'altare ha il quadro, entrovi la storia, quando vogliano crucifigere S. Andrea Apostolo. Dalle bande evvi il Martirio di S. Stefano, e l'altro di S. Lorenzo, e di sopra nelle lunette altre storie, e nella volta una gloria di santi, e di sante a fresco con gran-

dissima diligenza portati, & espressi' (*Le vite de' pittori*, p. 320). Titi agrees: 'Nell'Altare della prima Cappella à mano destra vi è dipinto S. Andrea Apostolo con molti manigoldi, che lo vogliono crocifiggere, e dalle bande di essa il martirio di S. Stefano, e di S. Lorenzo; di sopra nelle lunette altre historie, e nella volta una gloria di Santi, e Sante à fresco con grandissima diligenza il tutto espresso e colorito da Agostino Ciampelli' (*Studio di pittura*, vol. 1, p. 100).

133 One reads, 'La cappella di S. Andrea fu depinta da Agostino Campelli, et ancor il quadro' (ARSI, FG 545, 2a). The other is more comprehensive: 'Cappella di S. Andrea: Questa fu ornata dalla Signora Salustia Cerrini con pitture dal Campelli, ha fatti due angeli con l'ornamento della Santa Croce, e alcuni paliotti, e pianete per servizio di detta Cappella. Fu erede di il Signore Crescenzio Crescentij, e di questo il Signore Francesco Serlupi pur defonto sotto l'Altare v'è l'urna col suo Corpo Santo' (ARSI, FG 2053 [1666], 30).

134 ARSI, FG 2000, 54aff. See Zuccari, 'Aggiornamenti,' p. 33.

135 ARSI, FG 2000, 59a–b.

136 Pecchiai, *Il Gesù di Roma*, p. 93; Zeri, *Pittura e controriforma*, pp. 55–7; Hibbard, 'Ut picturae sermones,' p. 44; Lewine, 'The Roman Church Interior,' pp. 246–7; Madonna, *Roma di Sisto V*, pp. 173–4; Bailey, 'The Jesuits and Painting in Italy,' pp. 154–5.

137 Among many references to Mellini in the Jesuit archives is a memorial from the later seventeenth century that records the following: 'La Cappella della Passione fu fatta dalla Signora Bianca Millini' (ARSI, FG 545, 4a). Another is a mid-seventeenth-century report that reads, 'Cappella della Passione: Questa fu ornata dalla Signora Bianca Mellini, la quale lasciò erede sua Nipote Moglie del Signore Asbudrale Cardelli, erede del quale è rimastro il Signore Cardelli già defonto' (ARSI, FG 2053, 29). Her 'Disposizione Testimentaria' for the chapel is in ARSI, AG Busta I, 79. The Lomellini family made regular small gifts to the Gesù during the seventeenth century, as well as substantial donations to the Novitiate of S. Andrea al Quirinale from 1593 (ARSI, FG 2005 [Libro delle limosine], 38a, 47a, 54b, 62a; FG 2005a [Libro dell'elemosine], 6b, 27b, 50b; ARSI, Rom. 162 I, 153a, 155a; Rom. 163, 275a, 277b).

138 The original contract survives: 'La Signora Bianca Mellini ha' pigliato à far' fare la cappella intitolata della passione di N.S. Iesu Christo in chiesa nostra per sua devotione, lassandane la cura al P. Giovanni de Rosi: per la cui spessa quotidiana da' per mano del P. Lutio Croce al' P. Proc.re di Casa le seguenti partite di denari: Addi 27 novembre 1588 scudi cinquanta m.ta L. 50. E addi 5 Aprile 1589 ha dato per mano dell'istesso P. Lutio Croce per la spese della sua Cappella scudi sessanta di m.ta L.60. E ebbi io detto ha' dato per mano del P. Lutio Croce per detto cosa scudi ottanta di m.ta L.80. Sommatório e lilancia con la spesa per cose L.190' (ARSI, FG 2004 [Per le cappelle della Chiesa, et altri conti della fabrica], 1b; transcribed in part in Pirri and Rosa, 'Il P. Giovanni de Rosis,' p. 71; and in part in Galassi Paluzzi, 'Note di storia,' p. 304).

139 The Jesuit account books make it clear that she left all responsibility for handing out the money to de Rosis; for example, 'La Signora Bianca per contro ha speso per le mani del P. Giov. De Rosi per le occorrenze della sua cappella che fa in chiesa nostra, come per li conti particolari tenuti dall'istesso Padre si vede, li seguenti danari' (ARSI, FG 2004, 2a; Pirri and Rosa, 'Il P. Giovanni de Rosis,' p. 71).

140 ARSI, AG Busta I, 3 bis; Pecchiai, *Il Gesù di Roma*, p. 80; Hibbard, 'Ut picturae sermones,' p. 44.

141 'La cappella della Pietà posta nella Venerable Chiesa della Giesù di Roma, questa fu incominciato prima dell'anno 1595 della bo:me: della Signora Bianca Mellini Lomellini, il cui quadro dell'Altare è di Scipione Caetano, e l'altre pitture à torno, sono del'Cavaliere Gaspare Cellio pittori famosi' (ARSI, AG Busta I, 78).

142 'La pittura della Cappella della Passione di Christo, della cornice in su à fresco, e dalla cornice à basso ad olio di Gaspare Celio dell'abito di Christo Romano, la pittura del suo altare di Scipione Caetano, vi è la Pietà ad'olio' (Celio, *Memoria delli nomi*, p. 41).

143 Mancini refers to 'la seconda [cappella] del Cavalier Gasparo Celio Romano' (*Considerazioni sulla pittura*, p. 279).

144 In his section on Valeriano, Baglione writes: 'E nella seconda cappella a man diritta, dov'è sopra l'altare un Christo morto in braccio alla santissima Madre con figure di mano di Scipione Gaetano, il P. Gioseppe fece li disegni delle due historie dalle bande, una si è, quando il Salvatore del Mondo porta la Croce al Calvario; e l'altra, quando lo vogliono crocifiggere; & anche le quattro figure intorno alla cappella, che rassembrano Christo appassionato, sono suoi disegni, & inventioni; ma le lavorò Gasparo Celio, che servì il Valeriano in diverse cose, e spetialmente nella volta, ove sono nel mezo alcuni Angioli, che pigliano una Croce, e ne' peducci, o triangoli stanno li quattro Evangelisti, e dalle bande due mezi tondi, o archi con historie della Passione di N. Signore Giesù, e ne' pilastri vi si veggono due Profeti, li quali scorgonsi della maniera della volta a fresco dipinta, li quali non hanno, che fare con li quadri già detti, a olio conclusi, se bene il Padre l'aiutò con qualche disegno; ma li Profeti lavorati ne'pilastri veggonsi esser dinventione, e colorito, come fu la vera maniera di Gasparo Celio, così da tutti li Professori della pittura giudicati' (*Le vite de' pittori*, pp. 83–4).

145 'Hebbe in tal tempo il Padre a dipingere due Cappelle nella stessa Chiesa del Giesù, una fu la seconda a man diritta dedicata alla Passione di N. Signore, e il Celio volle servirsi, e gli fece lavorare, dalla cornice in sù, lo sfondato con diversi Angeli, che abbracciano una Croce, e li quattro Angoli, ove sono li quattro Evangelisti con le due mezitondi, & il sottarco con li pilastri, ove colorì diverse Historie, e figurò due Profeti, il tutto a fresco co' disegni del Padre; e da basso li due quadri grandi, uno de'quali è, quando N. Signore portò la croce al Calvario; e l'altro quadro vogliono crucifigerlo; e li quattro Christi passionati sono parimente disegni del P. Valeriano, e vi lavorò il Celio, e furono a olio condotti' (Baglione, *Le vite de' pittori*, p. 377).

146 'La cappella della Passione fu depinta da Scipione Gaetano, et anchor il quadro, la volta, e Profeti, e gli evangelisti furono coloriti del Cavagliere Gaspare Celio. Il disegno è del P. Fiammeri della Comp.a di Giesu' (ARSI, FG 545, 2a); 'Il Christo morto in braccio alla Madre, felicemente figurato nell'Altare della Cappella, che segue, è di mano di Scipione Gaetano, la Volta però dove sono dipinti alcuni Angioli, che abracciano la Croce, con tutti l'altri fatti della Passione, Evangelisti, Profeti, & altre figure, furono colorite dal Cav. Gasparo Celio con disegno del P. Fiammeri Gesuita' (Titi, *Studio di pittura*, vol. 1, 100).

147 Filippo Titi, *Descrizione delle pitture, sculture e architetture esposte al pubblico in Roma* (Rome, 1763), p. 173.

148 Galassi Paluzzi, 'Note di storia,' p. 305. My translation.

149 Zeri, *Pittura e controriforma*, pp. 54–7.

150 Pirri, *Valeriano*, pp. 212, 225, 228; Pecchiai, *Il Gesù di Roma*, p. 93.

151 Hibbard, 'Ut picturae sermones,' p. 45; Lewine, 'The Roman Church Interior,' p. 246. See Richard Bösel's entry in Baumstark, *Rom in Bayern*, pp. 454–5; Laura Russo in Madonna, *Roma di Sisto V*, p. 173; Calì, *La pittura del cinquecento*, vol. 1, p. 221.

152 Fabrizio d'Amico, 'La pittura a Roma nella seconda metà del cinquecento,' in Zander, *L'arte in Roma nel secolo XVI*, vol. 2, p. 197.

153 Carlo Galassi Paluzzi, 'La Cappella di Santa Maria della Strada al Gesù e il suo architetto,' *Architettura ed arti decorative* 4 (1924–5): 60.

154 Hibbard, 'Ut picturae sermones,' plates 29a, 29b. Buser suggests as much when he says that 'Gaspare Celio used Nadal's *Evangelicae historiae imagines* as the source for his painting of *Christ Nailed to the Cross* in a chapel of the Gesù decorated about 1594,' but he does not consider that Fiammeri may actually have made the design for Celio's image ('Jerome Nadal,' p. 427). Calì does not mention Fiammeri at all in connection with the Nadal series or the Passion Chapel, and although she points out the similarity of the two, she sees no direct causal link (*La pittura del cinquecento*, vol. 1, p. 223).

155 '[7 February 1590] dati al Padre Gioseppe Valeriano per l'imagine come disse il Padre Lutio [Croce] a buon conto, scudi 30'; '[9 February 1590] dati al Padre Giuseppe Valeriano scudi settanta per dare a Mastro Scipione Caetano pittore à buon conto dell'imagine della pietà che fa in chiesa nostra, et ne ha fatto polleza d'havere ricevuto scudi cento con gli scudi trenta sopradetti, scudi 70' (ARSI, FG 2004, 3a; published in Galassi Paluzzi, 'Note di storia,' p. 304).

156 '[1 August 1596] A Mastro Gasparo pittore à conto della pittura della sua cappella datoli con tanti scudi 100' (ARSI FG 2004, 6b).

157 '[12 May 1597] scudi 50 al pittore'; '[25 June 1597] 91.30 dati a Mastro Gasparo, scudi 91.30' (ARSI, FG 2004, 6b).

158 '[26 December 1611] a Mastro Gasparo Celio pittore pagamente per ordine di Mastro Pompeo, scudi 46.90' (ARSI, FG 2005, 65a).

159 '[10 June 1596: Letter of P. Giacomo Domeneci, segr. della Comp.a, to Valeriano, Naples] V.R. si deve ben ricordare come la Capella della Passione in questa nostra chiesa resta sospesa, né ve si attende se non a metter lo stucco senz'altro principio di pittura; et perché per quel che tocca alla chiesa l'è molto scommodo tenerla tanto tempo serrata per la commodità delle prediche e delle lettioni, stando ella in mezzo all'uditorio e dell'altre capelle della nave della chiesa, si desidera molto che quanto prima si dipinga, tanto più che vi concorre un gran desiderio di quella Gentildonna che fa la spesa. Che se la cosa andasse troppo in lungo, o si straccarebbe, o s'intepidirebbe almeno da concorrere a questa limosina, o si andarebbe a pericolo di qualch'altro disturbo, et anche morte della benefattrice, senza speranza del compimento dell'opera. Però si desidera grandemente che V.R. subito scriva a Mastro Gasparo che vi metta le mani e presto la spedischi, assicurandola che si farà cosa molto grata a molti' (ARSI, Neap.5 I [Litterae], 197a; published in Pirri, *Valeriano*, p. 378).

160 'Nota che Mastro Gasparo ha da dare conto di 803 che ha havuti per fare li palchi et altre cose per la cappella ... Per calce per accomodar li stucchi et altro a 15 di luglio 1596 al Pittore, scudi 100; dalli 12 di Settembre 96 sino adesso per 139 fogli d'oro per

indorare @ 8 il mig.r 111.20 scudi, preso da Mastro Gio: battiloro; Nel medesimo tempo per la doratura a Mastro Hercole à 4 scudi il mig. Compreso 200 fogli che se sono cavati delli libretti di più, scudi 56.40; A di 5 ottobre 96 a Mastro Jiacomo Brioso vetraio per l'invetriata, scudi 21; A di 30 Sett.br a M.o Andrea Ferraro p. li ferra della invietrata, scudi 12.60; sino a13 di Maggio 97 à Mastro Gasparo pittore ancor che ne facessi ricevuta com'impresto, scudi 3.50; e piu al detto, scudi 3.91.30 [Total] scudi 34.50' (ARSI, FG 2004, 7a–7b).

161 ARSI, FG 2004, 6b.

162 See Macioce, *Undique splendent*, pp. 13–15; Freiburg, *The Lateran in 1600*, pp. 37, 166; Zuccari, 'Bellarmino e la Cappella degli angeli,' p. 613.

163 Zuccari, *Arte e committenza*, pp. 11–12; Diego Beggiao, *La visita pastorale di Clemente VIII (1592–1605)* (Rome, 1978), pp. 48–9.

164 Zuccari, *Arte e committenza*, p. 15.

165 'Ad Cappellam Passionis. Imago Beatae Mariae Magdalena ibidem depicti in magis devotam speciem redigatur' (ARSI, FG 545, 8a).

166 Bailey, 'The Jesuits and Painting in Italy,' fig. 12.

167 Pecchiai, *Il Gesù di Roma*, p. 94; Hibbard, 'Ut picturae sermones,' pp. 46–7; Lewine, 'The Roman Church Interior,' pp. 248–50; Madonna, *Roma di Sisto V*, p. 177; Luchinat, *Taddeo e Federico Zuccari*, vol. 2, pp. 181–90.

168 'La Cappella degl'Angeli fu cominciata dal Signore Gasparo Garzoni, ma caduto in Passa fortuna, la cedè al Signore Curtio Vittorij, che gli ristituì, quanto quello c'aveva speso' (ARSI, FG 545, 4a).

169 'Cappella degli Angeli: Questa fu ornata dal Signore Curzio Vittorio, e sua Moglie di Casa Delfini' (ARSI, FG 2053 [1666], 29; Galassi Paluzzi, 'Note di storia,' p. 385).

170 For the reworking by Dandini, mentioned in ARSI, 2002 I, 37b, see *La regola e la fama*, p. 508.

171 Celio's words are 'La pittura nella Cappella dell'Angioli tutta à fresco di Federico Zuccari, quella del suo altare ad olio era sua, mà fu guasta dal Cavalier Passignani' (*Memoria delli nomi*, p. 40). The anonymous source comments, 'La cappella degli Angioli fu dipinta da Federico Zuccaro, volendo poi il Cavagliere Passignani ritoccare il quadro lo guasto, gli altri non furono toccati' (ARSI, FG 545, 2a). Titi writes, 'La Cappella contigua fu condotta à fresco con diverse storie d'Angioli fatte con vaghezza di colorito, & exquisita maniera da Federigo Zuccaro, che vi fece anco il Quadro dell'Altare, dove sono à olio dipinti molti Angioli in atto d'orare, quale volendolo ritoccare il Cav. Passignani, lo guastò' (*Studio di pittura*, vol. 1, p. 100).

172 Mancini writes, 'la terza [cappella] di Federico Zuccaro' (*Considerazioni sulla pittura*, p. 279). Baglione also mentions the altarpiece, in his entry on Zuccaro: 'Poscia colorì nella Chiesa del Giesù la cappella de' Sig. Vitorii a gli Angioli dedicata, tutta a fresco condotta; e nell'altare envi, un quadro a olio, entrovi gli Angeli in atto di far'orazione' (*Le vite de' pittori*, p. 124).

173 Baglione writes in his entry on Salimbeni: 'E nell'altare [across from the Trinity Chapel], Abramo, che adora li tre Angeli fatti a fresco. Et ancora vi sono alcuni puttini nelli triangoli, o peducci della volta, che tengono alcune cartelle, e pure a fresco da lui farono lavorati' (*Le vite de' pittori*, p. 119). The Jesuit source agrees: 'et abbramo che adora li tre Angioli, pittura a fresco, con alcuni puttini ne' tre angoli nella volta, sono opere del Cavaglier Salinbeni' (ARSI, FG 545, 2a). Basing his research on Baglione, Titi

concurs: 'Abramo, che adora li trè Angioli pittura à fresco, con alcuni puttini ne'triangoli della Volta, sono opere del Cav. Salimbeni, conforme dice il Baglioni nel libro delle Vite de' Pittori' (*Studio di pittura*, vol. 1, p. 100; see also Titi, *Descrizione delle pitture*, p. 173).

174 '[Celio] Cominciò anche due quadri per la Cappella de'Signori Vittorij; gli abbozzò, e restarono imperfetti per la morte del P. Valeriano; e la Cappella poi fu data a Federico Zucchero, gran Maestro, ad esser dipinta, come hora si vede' (Baglione, *Le vite de' pittori*, pp. 377–8).

175 The Jesuit source reads, 'Gli angioli di Marmo sono sculture di Silva Lungo da Vigiù, e di Filaminio Vacca Romano, et alcuni puttini di stucco intorno alla volta sono di Camillo Mariani da Vicenza' (ARSI, FG 545, 2a). Titi, as usual, agrees: 'e gli Angioli di marmo, che stanno nelle nicchie di detta Cappella sono scolture di Silla Lungo da Vigiù, di Flaminio Vacca Romano, e d'altri, & alcuni puttini di stucco intorno alla Volta sono di Camillo Mariani da Vicenza' (*Studio di pittura*, vol. 1, p. 100; see also Titi, *Descrizione delle pitture*, p. 173).

176 'Ad Cappellam SS. Angelos. Imagines etiam SS Angelorum decentius contegantur' (ARSI, FG 545, 8a; the same document in a copy at the Archivio Segreto Vaticano, Miscellanea, Arm. VII 3, 69b, is cited in *La regola e la fama*, p. 508, and in Zuccari, 'Bellarmino e la Cappella degli Angeli,' p. 615). See also Luigi Spezzaferro, 'Il recupero del rinascimento,' in Giulio Ballati et al., eds, *Storia dell'arte italiana* (Torino, 1981), pp. 240–1.

177 Zuccari, 'Bellarmino e la Cappella degli Angeli,' p. 614.

178 Hibbard, 'Ut picturae sermones,' p. 38; Hibbard, *Caravaggio*, pp. 146–8; Zuccari, 'Bellarmino e la Cappella degli Angeli,' pp. 612ff; *La regola e la fama*, cat. nos 61–7.

179 'E stavano nella cappella de gli Angeli sopra l'altare alcuni d'essi Angioli in piede assai belli, ma perche erano ritratti dal naturale, rappresentanti diverse persone da tutti conosciute, per cancellare lo scandalo, furono tolti via; & eran sì bella, che parevano spirar vita, e moto' (Baglione, *Le vite de' pittori*, p. 54). Titi repeats Baglione's story almost verbatim: 'Sopra questo Altare stavano per prima dipinti di mano di Scipione Gaetano alcuni Angioli in piedi assai belli, mà perche erano ritratti dal naturale, rappresentanti diverse persone da tutti conosciute, per cancellare lo scandolo furono tolti via & erano sì belli, che parevano spirar vita, e moto. Abramo, che adora li trè Angioli pittura à fresco, con alcuni puttini ne'triangoli della Volta, sono opere del Cav. Salimbeni, conforme dice il Baglioni nel libro delle Vite de' Pittori' (Titi, *Studio di pittura*, vol. 1, p. 100).

180 See Ernst Kris and Otto Kurz, *Legend, Myth, and Magic in the Image of the Artist* (New Haven, 1979), especially pp. 62ff. See also Bailey, *Art on the Jesuit Missions*, pp. 31–5.

181 Zuccari, 'Bellarmino e la Cappella degli Angeli,' p. 614.

182 Freedberg, *Painting in Italy*, pp. 625–6; *La pittura in Italia: Il seicento*, vol. 2, pp. 839–40.

183 Hibbard proposes that he is Celio, and I agree (Hibbard, 'Ut picturae sermones,' p. 64).

184 Pecchiai, *Il Gesù di Roma*, p. 94; Hibbard, 'Ut picturae sermones,' p. 46. For a more recent account along the same lines, see Luchinat, *Taddeo e Federico Zuccari*, vol. 2, p. 182.

185 'Il Signor Gasparo Garzonio ha' pigliato à far' fare per sua devotione la cappella intitolata degli Santi Angeli in chiesa nostra, lasciandone la cura al P. Giovanni de

Rosi, per la cui spesa quotidiana da al' P. Procuratore di Casa li seguenti danari: A dì 27 luglio 1589 ha' dato al P. Joseffe da Faro Proc.re di Casa Prof.a mandato al'banco di Lelio Mangili scudi centoventi di m.ta, s.120 ... A dì 17 febbraio 1590 Il P. Gioseppe da Fano Procuratore controscritto ha dato al P. Gioseppe Valeriano à bon conto delle spese della cappella del Signore Gasparo Garzonio che fa l'imagini di essa Mastro Scipione Gaetano Pittore scudi cento trentacinque b.a settanta, il quale resta di havere per il complimento di scudi trecento che dovea havesse, scudi sessanta quattro b.a trenta. Computaleri gli cento che hebbe nella prima paga ... s. 135.70' (ARSI, FG 2004, 39b–41a; published in part and incorrectly in Pirri and Rosa, 'Il P. Giovanni de Rosis,' p. 71; and published in part in Galassi Paluzzi, 'Note di storia,' p. 306).

186 '[17 March 1591] dati al P. Joseffe Valeriano per dare al pittore Caetano, scudi 15'; '[1 May 1591] dati al Padre Joseffe Valeriano per il giovane pittore del Signor Gaspero di moneta scudi 8'; '[8 June 1591] dati al Padre Giovanni de Rosis disse per dare à Mastro Scipione Caetano di moneta, scudi 50'; '[3 November 1591] dati al Padre Giovanni de Rosis disse per la cappella del Signor Gasparo Garzonio scudi 20'; '[12 January 1592] dati al Padre Giovanni de Rosis come di sopra per la cappella del Signor Gasparo, scudi 36.66' (ARSI, FG 2004, 42a; published in part in Pirri and Rosa, 'Il P. Giovanni de Rosis,' pp. 71–2).

187 '[12 March 1592] per tela per l'Altar delli Angeli, et fettuccia per la coperta detto quadro scudi 2.30' (ARSI, FG 1233 [Libro de' conti del Prefetto della Chiesa], 39b).

188 There is a reference in the archives to the transferral of this picture, as well as to a restoration: 'il quadro della Madonna della Strada con il Signore in braccio fatto rifare' (ARSI, AG Busta I [1561], 191).

189 Galassi Paluzzi, 'La Cappella di Santa Maria della Strada'; Pecchiai, *Il Gesù di Roma*, pp. 88–9; Zeri, *Pittura e controriforma*, pp. 54–5; Lewine, 'The Roman Church Interior,' pp. 258–60; Madonna, *Roma di Sisto V*, pp. 179–80; Conelli, 'Female Patronage,' pp. 8–11. Two seventeenth-century memorials mention the patronage: 'La Cappella della Madonna fu fatta insieme della Signora Donna Giovanna Ursina, dalla Signora Beatrice Gaetana, et dalla Marchesa d'Ariana' (ARSI, FG 545, 4b); 'La Cappella della Madonna fu ornata da tre Signore Romane, cioè la Signora Beatrice Gaetana, Signora Orsini, e Signora Duchessa Cesarini, le quali non solamente l'ornarono come si vede ma anco fecero Lampadi, e Candelieri d'argento, e furono grandi Benefattrici della nostra chiesa, sagrestia, e casa, e fecero anco li candelieri grandi d'argento per l'altare maggiore' (ARSI, FG 2053 [1666], 29).

190 Pecchiai, *Il Gesù di Roma*, p. 96.

191 Conelli, 'Female Patronage,' pp. 8–9.

192 Galassi Paluzzi, 'La Cappella di Santa Maria della Strada,' pp. 58–9; Pirri, *Valeriano*, pp. 80–1; Pecchiai, *Il Gesù di Roma*, pp. 89–92. For archival references to the marble revetments and roofing of the chapel, see ARSI, AG Busta I, 66–8, 70. On the silver ornament for the same chapel, see ARSI, AG Busta I, 71, 72.

193 'Die prima Decembris 1584: Havendo l'Ill.ma Signora Portia Cere de Cesis, la Signora Beatrice Gaetana de Cesi, et la Signora Giovanna Gaetana de Ursini da una parte, et m. Bartolomeo de Bassi scarpellino in Roma dall'altra parte fermati et conclusi diversi patti et conventioni sopra l'ornamento d'una cappella posta nella Venerabile Chiesa del Gesù alla piazza dell'Altieri, et sopra di ciò havendo fatto una polizia sotto scritta di lor mano, sopra le qual cose desiderando che se stipuli instrumento per maggior

sicurezza loro; Perciò questo dì primo di Xbre 1584, nell'Inditione XII, nel decimo terzo anno del pontificato del S.mo Signor nostro papa Gregorio XIII, alla presenza dell'infrascritti testimoni et di me notaro chiamati particolarmente a questo, constitute personalmente le dette Ill.me Signore Portia de Cere, Beatrice et Giovanna Gaetane principali da una parte, et m. Bartolomeo de Bassi scarpellino in Roma dall'altra parte; asserendo in prima haver fermati diversi patti, capitoli et conventioni sì come appare in una poliza sottoscritta di mano di ambe le parti, quale consignorno a me notario, di questo tenore cioè: Io Bartolomeo Bassi, scarpellino in Roma mi obligo di fare a tutte mie spese la Cappella della Madonna della Chiesa del Gesù, che sta a man dritta a l'altare maggiore, mettendo et lavorando li marmi et mischi a tutte mie spese, mettendoli in opera come hanno di stare, salvo che il pavimento, et li fondi delli stucchi sotto li architravi nelli quattro vani che sono in detta Cappella, per prezzo et integro pagamento di scudi doi millia et cento di moneta di giulii dieci per scudo, salvo la tribuna et pittura, et facendo però detti lavori di marmi et mischi a piacimento del Padre Josepho Valeriano Architetto, et del R.do Padre Lorenzo Maggio et principalmente delle Ill.me padrone di detta Cappella. Non la facendo bene et ben comessa con marmi scolpiti et mischi belli ben lustrati, voglio che sia lecito a detti R.di padri pagarmi detta opera scudi mille et novecentodi moneta simili; Prometto osservare il presente disegno di pianta et alzata fatto dal sopradetto padre Josepho Valeriano della Compagnia del Gesù et prometto come sopra ... Prometto di fare li ornamenti delle pitture di marmi gentile intagliati secondo che bisognara conforme al detto disegno, appare nella libro A ... Prometto di fare li riquadramenti per le inscrittioni sotto le pitture scritte con lettere d'oro et queste serranno d'affricano scuro et bello ... Prometto di fare tutta questa opera quanto tocca a me di marmo et mischi con tutti suoi ornamenti et lavori, salvo le pitture che saranno sei vani senza l'altare della Madonna, et salvo la volta che si la da dipingere, a costa, et gusto del padrone' (ARSI, AG Busta I, 67; cited in part in Galassi Paluzzi, 'Note di storia,' 90).

194 Celio, who is earliest, writes, 'La pittura in olio, della cornice in giù, con le ationi della Madonna, l'architettura d'essa Cappella, del Molto R. Padre Giuseppe Valeriano dell'Aquila, della Compagnia del Giesù. La pittura à fresco dalla cornice in su Angioli, disegno di esso Padre, depinti da Giovan Battista Pozzi da Milano' (*Memoria delli nomi*, p. 39]. In his section on Pozzo, Baglione writes, 'Lavorò nella chiesa del Giesù entro la cappelletta della Madonna, tra le costole della volta, chori di Angeli, che contano, e suonano diversi instromenti con tanta dolcezza condotti, che innamorano a vederli; e fanno restare manchevoli le altre pitture da basso a olio, dal Padre Gioseppe Valeriano con quale durezza, se ben con diligenza operate' (*Le vite de' pittori*, p. 40). The anonymous seventeenth-century Jesuit source records the following: 'La Cappella della Madonna della Strada, è architettura di Giacomo della Porta; gli Angioli dell'istessa che cantano, e sonano diversi instromenti furono fatti da Gio. Batt.a Pozzo Milanese, e le figure di sotto nelli quadri vita della Madonna furono dipinti dal P. Giuseppe Valeriano della Compania di Giesu' (ARSI, FG 545, 2b). Another record in the same document but by another hand says much the same thing: 'I chori di Angili che cantano, e suonano diversi instromenti furono dipinti da Giovanni Battista Pozzo Milanese in molta delicarezza, e spirito. L'istorie da basso a olio sono del P. Giuseppe Valeriano Gesuita fatte con diligenza' (ARSI, FG 545, 3a). Titi remarks, 'La Cappelletta rotonda dalla parte dell'Evangelo della maggiore,

dedicata à M.V. è architettura del Porta sudetto, e li Chori d'Angioli, che cantano, e suonano diversi instrumenti, furono dipinti da Gio: Battista Pozzo Milanese, con tanta delicatezza, che innamorando à vederli, e fanno restar manchevoli l'altre pitture da basso à olio dal P. Gioseppe Valeriano Gesuita con qualche durezza, se ben con diligenza operate' (*Studio di pittura*, vol. 1, 101).

195   In his section on Valeriano, Baglione writes, 'Sì come vedesi nella cappelletta della Madonna, ove sono diversi quadri in tavola a olio figurati con le storie di N. Donna; & in faccia da una banda, stavvi un'Annuntiata, che dicono esser la miglior cosa, ch'egli dipingesse, e nella volta sonvi formati alcuni chori d'Angeli di mano di Gio. Battista Pozzo Milanese a fresco lavorati; e mentre il P. Valeriano andava formando quest'opera, haveva amicitia con Scipione Gaetano, il quale gli fece in quei quadri alcuni drappi dipinti tanto simili al vero, che non si possono desiderare fatti con più arte; et il Padre il rimanente di sua mano con gran diligenza finì' (*Le vite de' pittori*, p. 83).

196   'La cappelleta rotonda della parte dell'Evangelio dell'altar maggiore, dedicata a Maria Vergine, è disegno del medesimo Porta; e i cori d'Angioli, che suonano, furono dipinti da Gio.Batista Pozzo Milanese con tanta delicatezza, che innamorano a vederli, e fanno restar manchevoli le altre pitture da basso a olio del P. Giuseppe Valeriano Gesuita, dove Scipion Gaetano fece alcuni panni, che pajon veri' (Titi, *Descrizione delle pitture*, pp. 174–5).

197   'Uscita per mano del Padre Joseffe Valeriano il quale terrà conto minuto delli danari seguenti per conto delle pitture'; '[6 May 1586] per pagare 7 tavolini per li imagini dabasso, scudi trentadui, scudi 32'; '[21 May 1586] al medesimo Padre Valeriano scudi dieci, scudi 10'; '[28 May 1586] al medesimo Padre Valeriano scudi dodici, scudi 12'; '[7 June 1586] al medesimo Padre Valeriano scudi dieci, scudi 10'; '[16 June 1586] scudi ventise, scudi 26'; '[23 August 1588] ho riceuto per stucco et pitture como di sopra scudi trenta moneta, scudi 30'; '[14 September 1588] Sino a 17 del istesso pago il Padre Giovanni Lavia per ordine mio mentre io stetti a Frascati per il pittore stuccatori e forni per invitriate scudi 33 giulii 13, scudi 33.13'; '[21 November 1588] ricevetti per Giambattista pittore, scudi 12' (ARSI, AG Busta I, 66; published in part in Galassi Paluzzi, 'La Cappella di Santa Maria della Strada,' p. 58; Pirri, *Valeriano*, p. 82).

198   Zeri, *Pittura e controriforma*, pp. 53–4.

199   Freedberg, *Painting in Italy*, pp. 659.

200   Calì, *Da Michelangelo*, p. 294, and *La pittura del cinquecento*, vol. 1, p. 221. See also Vaudo, *Scipione Pulzone*, p. 30.

201   Zeri, *Pittura e controriforma*, figs 55, 57.

202   Carlo Galassi Paluzzi, 'La Cappella del S. Cuore al Gesù,' *Roma* 9 (1931): 65 ff; Pecchiai, *Il Gesù di Roma*, p. 96; Lewine, 'The Roman Church Interior,' pp. 260–2; Madonna, *Roma di Sisto V*, pp. 177–8.

203   Pecchiai, *Il Gesù di Roma*, pp. 95–6. There are several references in the archives to this patronage, including the following: 'La Cappella di S. Francesco d'Assisi fu fatta dalla Signora Duchessa d'Aguasporta moglie del Signore Duca di Casis' (ARSI, FG 545, 4a); and 'La Cappella di S. Francesco d'Assisi fu ornata dalla Eccelentissima Casa Cesi aequa sparsa e ogni anno mandano le torcie essendosi sepolti i fondatori di quella' (ARSI, FG 2053, 29).

204 Celio writes: 'La pittura nella Cappella di S. Francesco, della cornice à basso, di
diversi Fiamenghi, li suoi paesi di Paolo Brillo ... Della cornice in sù sono à fresco di
Baldassarino da Bologna' (*Memoria delli nomi*, p. 40). Baglione, in his entry for Paul
Brill, comments, 'Gli uccelli, & i paesi, che sono nella chiesa della Compagnia di
Giesù dentro la cappella di S. Francesco sono suoi; & il rimanente a olio è di Gioseppe
Peniz, e d'altri Fiammighi'; and in his section on Baldassare Croce he adds, 'La chiesa
del Giesù, nella Cappelletta di S. Francesco, ha di suo la cupola tutta in fresco fatta'
(*Le vite de' pittori*, pp. 297–8).

205 His name comes up in ARSI, FG 1231 (Opere della fabrica murali & manovali).

206 Celio writes, 'quella del suo altare di Durante dal Borgo, sono ad'olio' (*Memoria delli
nomi*, p. 40). The Jesuit source records, 'La Cappella di S. Francesco di Assisi fu fatta
con l'architettura di Giacomo della Porta; il quadro dell'Altare fu dipinta da Gio. Da
Vecchi; la cuppola colorito a fresco da Balthassarre Croce, e li Paesi da Paolo Brillo ne
suoi tempi eccellente, e dalla cornice in giù da diversi Fiaminghi' (ARSI, FG 545, 2a).
Titi writes: 'Seguitando il camino, si entra nella Cappelletta dedicata à S. Francesco
fatta con l'Architettura di Giacomo della Porta che hà il Quadro del suo Altare
dipinto da Gio: de' Vecchi. La Cuppola colorità à fresco da Baldassarre Croce, e li
Paesi da Paolo Brillo in questo genere, de' suoi tempi, eccellente, e l'altre opere dalla
cornice à basso sono di diversi Fiamminghi' (*Studio di pittura*, vol. 1, p. 100; see also
Titi, *Descrizione delle pitture*, p. 174).

207 Tosini in *Roma di Sisto V*, p. 178. Russo disagrees, reaffirming the attribution to Durante Alberti (Russo, *Il ciclo*, pp. 52–3).

208 For a survey of the literature, see Russo, *Il ciclo*, pp. 53–8.

209 '[6 September 1599] Io Baldassare Croce Pittore ò ricevuto dal Padre Vincentio scudi
venti cinque di moneta à bon conto della Cappella di S. Francesco in fede del vero o
fatto la presente di mia propria mano questo dì 6 di setembre 1599. Io Baldassare
Croce mano propria. Et di più ò ricevuto dal Padre Vincentio scudi dieci di moneta à
bon conto della Cappella di S. Francesco questo dì 18 di setembre 1599. Io Baldassare
Croce mano propria ... [on the verso] Ricevuta di Mastro Baldassare pitore a conto
della capela di S.o Francesco' (ARSI, AG Busta I, 10 bis; Pirri and Rosa, 'Il P. Giovanni de Rosis,' p. 69). In addition, there is another, shorter reference: '[6 December
1599] Dati à Mastro Baldasaro pictore che pinge la cappella di S. Francesco scudi 25 di
monetta, scudi 25'; '[19 December 1599] Dati à Mastro Baldasare pictore che pinge la
cappella di S.to Francesco, scudi 10' (ARSI, AG Busta I, 10 bis; Pirri and Rosa, 'Il P.
Giovanni de Rosis,' p. 69; published in part in Galassi Paluzzi, 'La Cappella del S.
Cuore,' p. 65). A loose folio also records the measurements of the panel paintings:
'La misura delli quadri de S.to Francesco: Il quadro del altare largho palmi 5 1/4, alto
palmi 8. Li quattro quadri delli Angeli fra le colonne larghi l'uno palmi 5 alto palmi
8 1/3. Li tre quadri grandi larghi l'uno palmi 8 alto palmi 11' (ARSI, FG 2000, loose
folio, ca. 1589).

210 Pecchiai, *Il Gesù di Roma*, pp. 79, 92; Lewine, 'The Roman Church Interior,' p. 263.

211 Cardulo, *Sanctorum martyrum Abundii presbyteri Abundantii diaconi Marciani* (Rome,
1584). See also Monssen, 'Triumphus and Trophaea Sacra,' who reproduces the
engraving as fig. 3. Claudio Acquaviva refers to the transferral of 'que' corpi santi,
che stanno in S. Cosme e Damiano, cio'é del corpo di S. Abondio, et di S. Abondantio
per collocarli qui nella Chiesa di V.S. Ill.ma,' in a letter dated 13 August 1583 to

Cardinal Farnese, in which he hints that the cardinal should pay for the decorations of the chapel as well (ASPar, Carteggio Farnesiano Roma, b. 395).

212 '... vi furono ritrovati li corpi de' Santi Abundo, & Abundàtio Martiri, li quali S. Beatitudine concesse alli Padri Giesuiti, per collocarli nell'Altar maggiore della loro nuova Chiesa, eretta dà fundamenti, & finita da Alessandro Cardinal Farnese, Nepote di Paulo Terzo, & dedicata al Santissimo Nome di Giesu: ove perciò furono con celebre pompa Ecclesiastica trasportati, & collocati, insieme con altre infinite Sante Reliquie' (Ciappi, *Compendio delle heroiche*, p. 18). The translation of the relics is also mentioned in an anonymous description in the Jesuit archives dated 1666: 'Il fondatore della nostra chiesa fu il Signore Cardinal Alessandro Farnese. Il quale arrichì anco la sagrestia con le sue pianete, e altri arredi sacri. La Cappelletta sotto l'altar Maggiore dove corrisponde l'urna, nella quale sono riposti li corpi de' Santi Abondio Prete, e Abondanzio Diacono Martiri trasferiti in questa chiesa dalla chiesa di S. Adriano [*sic*], dove furono trovati, e donati dalla gloriosa memoria di Papa Gregorio Decimo Terzo al Signore Cardinale Alessandro Farnese per la nostra chiesa allora finita di fabbricare, e trasferiti con solennissima processione. Fu ornata come ora si vede dal Signore Antonio Folchi servitore di detto Sigore Cardinale Alessandro Farnese' (ARSI, FG 2053, 28a).

213 For the first letter, speaking in glowing terms about the translation of the bodies, see n211 to this chapter, above. The second letter, dated 22 July 1584, from Acquaviva to Cardinal Farnese, was accompanied by Cardulo's book on the martyrdom of Sts Abundius and Abundantius, about which he says: 'Con questa mando à V.S. Ill.ma un libretto, che s'è fatto stampare del martirio, et traslatione de' nostri santi martiri, trasferiti l'anno passato à questa sua chiesa, parendomi che sia per haver' consolatione di vederlo. Si rappresenta hora nuova occasione di ornarla con altro simil tesoro, di cui più a lungo ella sarà ragguagliata da Ms. Giulio Folco' (ASPar, Carteggio Farnesiano Roma, b. 397).

214 See also Pietro Tacchi-Venturi, *Storia della Compagnia di Gesù in Italia*, 6 vols (Rome, 1950), I, p. 605; Carlo Galassi Paluzzi, 'Note sull'altar maggiore del Gesù,' *Roma* 5 (1927): 248ff.

215 Baglione records the subject of Commodi's painting: 'Sotto l'altar maggiore della Chiesa del Giesù v'è un quadro in tavola, rappresentate i SS. Abundio, & Abundantio condotti avanti il Tiranno a olio, assai buono, e diligente; & il suo modo di dipingere era da buoni maestri tenuto in conto' (*Le vite de' pittori*, p. 334). Baldinucci notes the same subject in his section on Commodi: 'E ancora nella Chiesa del Gesù una sua Tavola de'Santi Abondio, ed Abbondanzio avanti al Tirano' (*Notizie de' professori del disegno*, p. 261). Titi also mentions Commodi and the subject of his painting: 'Un Quadretto di Tavola sotto l'Altar medesimo dipinto à olio, è opera del Ciampelli; & un'altro pur'in Tavola rappresentante li SS. Abundio, & Abundantio condotti avanti il Tiranno fatto à olio, e ben'inteso è di mano d'Andrea Comodo, il modo del dipinger del quale era da buoni maestri tenuto in conto grande' (*Studio di pittura*, vol. 1, p. 101; see also Titi, *Descrizione delle pitture*, p. 174).

216 Baglione records the subject of Ancona's picture: 'Sotto l'altar maggiore del Giesù ha egli un quadretto in tavola con un miracolo di risuscitare un morto' (*Le vite de' pittori*, p. 139).

217 'Danari per la capella sotto l'altar Maggiore: scudi 600. Il Padre Giovanni ha havuto
scudi 178. Resta d'havere sino alli 600 scudi 422. [Total] 600. Se gli assegnano li debiti
seguenti: Dal R.do Padre Generale, scudi 133. Dal Padre Giovanni Bruno, scudi 100.
Da Santo Andrea, scudi 100.' The payments to painters include: '[25 May, 1600]
Mastro Agustino pictori, scudi 10; al P. [sic] Baldasaro per coro scudi tredici, per li
balustri scudi dieci'; '[? August 1602] Reverendo Padre, ecc. Vostra Reverenza sarà
contenta di pagare a Mastro Andrea di Ancona pittore scudi dieci: quali saranno a
conto di suo lavoro fatto è da farsi in tavola a olio per la cappellina de SS Abundio e
Abbondanzio nella chiesa del Giesù. Non essendo questa per altro, alle Vostre
Orationi mi racommando. di V. R.a servo in Domino, Gianbatista Fiammeri'; '[6 September 1602] Io, Andrea Lillius Anconitano pittore a buon conto o ricevuto li sopradetti schudi dieci e in fede o fato la presete ricevuta di mano mia propria questo dì
6 di 7bre 1602 il medessimo Lillius mano propria'; '[12 March 1603] Io, Agostino
Ciampelli pittore, o ricevuto questo dì 12 di marzo 1603 scudi dieci di moneta e quali
sono per a bon conto della pittura che o fatta nella cappella sotto l'altare maggiore
nella chiesa del Giesù et anzi li ricevo per le mani del P. Giovanni di Rosa questo di
sopra detto. Io Agostino Ciampelli mano propria'; '[22 September 1603] Reverendo
Padre ecc. V. R. sarà contenta di pagare a Mastro Paulo Guidotti pittore scudi venti
quattro al solito, quali saranno per resto di tutto pagamento di suo lavoro fatto in una
tavolina a olio, dentrovi il Martirio di SS. Abundio et Abundantio per collocare nella
cappellina sotto l'altare maggiore della Chiesa del Giesù, che tanti sono per resto fino
la somma di scudi 30 come fummo daccordo. Non essendo questa per altro, alle sue
orationi mi raccommando. di V.R. servo in Domino, Gianbatista Fiammeri'; '[22
September 1603] Io Paulo Guidotti sopranominato ho ricevuto li scudi venti quattro
come di sopra si contiene, essendo di questo conto satisfatto e contento. Et in fede ho
fatto et sottoscritto la presente sotto il di sopradetto. Io Paulo Guidotti, mano propria'
(ARSI, AG Busta I, 10 bis; Pirri and Rosa, 'Il P. Giovanni de Rosis,' pp. 69–70;
published in part in Galassi Paluzzi, 'Note sull'altar maggiore,' pp. 251–2). Pirri
and Rosa mistakenly assign Agostino's payment of 25 May 1600 to the St Francis
Chapel.
218 Robertson, *Il Gran Cardinale*, pp. 195–8; Pecchiai, *Il Gesù di Roma*, pp. 80–1; Lewine,
'The Roman Church Interior,' pp. 262–3. A memorial in the Jesuit account books
makes clear Farnese's control over the east end: 'L'Altare Maggiore fu principiato dal
Signore Cardinale Alessandro Farnese' (ARSI, FG 545, 4b).
219 We know about Fiammeri's activities from a letter of Acquaviva to the rector of Nola,
P. Bartolommeo Ricci, dated 5 August 158: 'Io desidero ogni sodisfattione nel Signore
alla signora Virginia, ma m'incresce che non se le potrà concedere il fratello Giovan
Battista fiorentino, perchè, oltre che si ha da occupare nel mosaico dell'illmo Farnese
per la nostra chiesa, ha anco da intagliare l'opera del P. Natale, la quale, perchè sarà
di molto servigio del Signore, siamo risoluti che vada avanti. Nondimeno, quando
non si havesse a dipingere cosa di molto apparato, il che io desidero et raccomando a
V.R., mi pare che potrebbe supplire a questo il fratello novitio che l'anno passato si
mandò da Roma costì [Mario Bissoni]. Quì, ancora, ne abbiamo un attro, ma intendo
che non è da paragonare a codesto. Quale egli si sia, si offereisce' (ARSI Neap.2, 89v;
Pirri, 'Intagliatori,' p. 37 n66).

220 Pecchiai, *Il Gesù di Roma*, pp. 86–7.

221 'Io Antonio Francesco Verochi pitore ... scudi 4 di moneta sono a buon conto della doratura della cupola del tabernacolo die ne siamo restatti dacordo per porre di scudi venti tre di moneta questo dì 13 di marzo 1583' (ARSI, AG Busta I, 6; Pecchiai, *Il Gesù di Roma*, p. 79).

222 All the sources agree as to Muziano's authorship. Celio writes, 'La pittura ad olio nell'altare maggiore con la circoncisione di Christo, de Geronimo Mutiani' (*Memoria della nomi*, p. 39). In his section on Muziano, Baglione writes, 'Nè minor lode consegui egli nella chiesa del Giesù, nel cui altar maggiore è la circoncisione di Giesù, con diverse figure a olio ben fatte, e degne d'eternità' (*Le vite de' pittori*, p. 50). Mancini concurs: 'Nel Giesù l'altar maggiore del Muciano' (*Considerazioni sulla pittura*, p. 279), as do the anonymous seventeenth-century Jesuit source – 'Il quadro dell'Altare Maggiore della Circoncisione fu dipinto da Girolamo Muziano' (ARSI, FG 545, 2a) – and Filippo Titi: 'L'Altar maggiore con sue colonne assai nobile, e ricco, fu architettato da Giacomo della Porta, & il Quadro dove stà dipinta la Circoncisione di Giesù con diverse figure à olio ben fatte, è opera di Girolamo Mutiani, degna di molta lode' (*Studio di pittura*, vol. 1, p. 100; see also Titi, *Descrizione delle pitture*, p. 174).

223 This letter from de' Vecchi to Alessandro Farnese, from Rome and dated 28 July 1588, was published by Robertson, although the line about taking on the third commission is omitted from her transcription. The full text reads: 'Illustrissimo et Reverendissimo Signor Mio Colendissimo, Havendo inteso che Vostra Signoria Illustrissima et Reverendissima ha mandato ordine in Roma che sieno veduti li miei conti, ho creduto che questo non vengha da mala sodisfattione che lei habbia di me, perché io non habbia voluto accettare quella terza opera, alla quale io non era tenuto secondo li Capitoli, percio ché se bene io dissi da principio di non poterla fare per il prezzo dell'altra, tuttavia soggiunse poi, che farei tutto quello che Vostra Signoria Illustrissima et Reverendissima m'havesse comandato. Però io credo che l'ordine di Vostra Signoria Illustrissima sia solamente a fine che mi si paghino le fatiche mie, nelle quale la voglio pregare per l'amor d'Iddio vogla haver' consideratione alli cinque mesi che io posi nel cartone della Circoncisione, il quale se bene non ha servito, tuttavia io vi ho posto et il tempo et la fatica, et il tutto d'ordine suo, del che la supplico humilissimamente vogla scriverne a questi ministri, li quali dicono che non si travalgono, se non di quelle cose che sono passate per man loro, et questo fu per commissione di Vostra Signoria Illustrissima et Reverendissima, alla quale prego Iddio conceda ogni contento' (ASPar, Epistolario scelto, b. 19; Robertson, *Il Gran Cardinale*, p. 314, doc. 135 [Robertson publishes it as busta 20]).

224 'A dì primo di Agosto 1587. L'Ilmo Cardinal Farnese si è convenuto con Mastro Girolamo Mutiano pittore da Brescia per depingere la icona del Altar maggiore della chiesa che sua S.ia Ill.ma ha fatto fabricare del Giesù in Roma. Qual icona sará di palmi 15 larga et 24 alta; et vi ha da essere depinta la Circoncisio di Nostro Signore Giesù Christo, et sará detta pittura in tavola et ad olio con ogni diligenza et perfettione. Et detto Illmo Cardinale Farnese elegge per esecutori di questa sua voluntà il Signor Giulio Folco et il Padre Giuseppe Valeriano della Compagnia di Giesù per il presente tempo riservandosi però a sua elettione ogni altro che a sua S.ria Illma piacessi per questo effetto nominare in qual si voglia occasione o tempo: accio detti nominati, o alteri in luogo loro, diano il recapito necessario a detto Mastro Girolamo

per detta pittura e promette detto Illmo di pagare per la pittura detta al detto Mastro Girolamo scudi seicento di oro in oro in tre overo piu paghe: ciò è dugento scudi avanti l'opera, dugento alla metà, et dugento finita l'opera overo scudi cento per cominciar et comprare colori cento quando sarrà tutta abbozzata, cento quando la metà delle figure sarranno finite, et trecento in fine di tutta l'opera, come a detti nominati piacerà, et se debbano intendere scudi di oro in oro come di sopra. In oltre promette il detto Illmo di dare a detto Mastro Girolamo la tavola et l'azzurro oltre-marino de detti nominati giudicaranno necessario senza nessuna altra cosa. Dal altra parte si obliga detto Mastro Girolamo fare quest' opera a tutte sue spese, salvo la tavola et oltremarino detto et promette usare in detta pittura ogni diligenza pro-ducendola con ogni perfettioni et studio a contento di detti nominati per il detto pagamento et prezzo di sei cento di oro in oro; pagateli parte avvanti per comenciare; parte mentre si fa l'opera et parte in fine come si e detto; et promette di non pigliare nè lavorare in altre pitture che in quelle che ha tra le mano al presente sino a tanto che questa sarà finita et crede che da hoggi a doi anni e mezzo darà di tutto punto finita la detta icona del Illmo Farnese che sarrà al Natale overo Circoncisione del 1589 non occorrendo però notabile impedimento di infermità o simile et in tal caso L'Illmo Cardinale Farnese da ogni autorità a detti nominati acciò possino prolungare il tempo, secondo da loro sarrà giudicata la necessità: acciò non resti per nessuna cosa il detto Mastro Girolamo di fare detta Circoncisione con ogni sodisfatione perfettione et studio. Et quando piacessi a Dio che detto Mastro Girolamo passassi a meglior vita prima che finissi detta opera, in tal caso restando imperfecta in modo che nessun valent'homo vi volessi metter mani o pure che non fuisse l'opera tanto avanti che potessi scrivere: in tal caso detto Mastro Girolamo si contenta che si vegga da uno pittore da parte de sui heredi, et da un altro da parte del Illmo Cardinale et quando non fussero d'accordo, si possa elegere un terzo' (signed by Hieronimo Muzziano, who also notes that he got the first payment in 1587. ARSI, AG Busta 8; published in part in Carlo Galassi Paluzzi, 'La 'Circoncisione' del Muziano nella Chiesa del Gesù,' *Roma* 3 (1924), fasc. 1).

225 'Io Hieronimo Muttiano prometo a oservare quanto disopra. Io Hieronimo Muttiano mano propria. Io Hieronimo Muttiano à receuto questo di primo di Agosto schudi cento de oro in oro per mano del Reverendo Padre Josepe Valeriano del Jesù a bon conto de la sopra scrito pitura. Io Hieronimo Mutiano o riceuto questo di ultimo de decembre 1587 schudi cento de oro in oro per mano del Reverendo Padre Josepe Valeriano del Jesù a bon chonto como di sopra. Io Hieronimo Muttiano' (ARSI, FG Busta I, 8).

226 Pecchiai, *Il Gesù di Roma*, pp. 86–7 (the document can be found in ARSI, Rom. 143 II, 249a).

227 '[16 April 1592] al P. Giovanni de Rosis à buon conto delle statuette del Tabernacolo per ordine di N.P. scudi 20 et à buon costo dei chori scudi 10. [total] Scudi 30' (ARSI, FG 1233, 40a; Pirri and Rosa, 'Il P. Giovanni de Rosis,' p. 67); '[25 March 1593] cavati di cassa per dare al P. Giovanni [de Rosis] per le statue de bronzo per il tabernacolo scudi 10' (ARSI, FG 1233, 16a; Pirri and Rosa, 'Il P. Giovanni de Rosis,' p. 66). This last payment is recapitulated in a memorial from the next month: 'A dì primo d'Aprile 1593, Io, Pietro Paolo Blosio, pigliai la prefettura della nostra chiesa e nella cassa del prefetto che era stato il P. Giovanni Battista Peruschi vi trovai scudi 46 liberi: S.R.

n'havea lasciati 56 ma il P. Ministro ne pigliò dieci per darli al P. Giovanni de Rosis per le statue di bronzo del tabernacolo, come appare nel retroscritto foglio: del hora in qua in loro entrassé nella Cassa del prefetto li seguenti' (ARSI, FG 1233, 16b; published in part in Pirri and Rosa, 'Il P. Giovanni de Rosis,' p. 66).

228 '[October 1596] per nettatura delle statue di bronzo del Tabernacolo scudi 1.20' (ARSI, FG 1233, 73b).

229 '[September 1596] a Mastro Bartolommeo per l'Angeli scudi 0.10'; '[October 1596] dato à Mastro Bartolommeo per l'angeli scudi 2.10'; '[May 1597] a Mastro Bartolommeo per l'angeli scudi 1.50'; '[May 1597] dato à Vicenzo per indorar l'angeli scudi 7' (ARSI, FG 1233, 73a–b; 76a–b); '[8 May 1599] dato a Mastro Bartolomé Tronchi scudi doi per pagare la fattura del falegname per sbozzare il legno per far doi Angeli'; '[17 December 1599] dato a Mastro Bartolomeo Tronchi b. 50 per li angeli, scudi 0.50'; '[15 July 1600] Item dato a Mastro Bartolomeo Tronchi scudi doi per finimento delli Angeli dove si metano le candele, scudi 2'; '[September 1600] Item per una soma di carbone un scudo a Mastro Bartolomeo Tronchi per finire li Angeli .30 e per scope .80 e melangole e altre cose che fano in tutto scudi doi et b.10, scudi 2.10'; '[28 October 1600] a Mastro Bartolomeo Tronchi scudi dieci b. 20 per pingere doi Angeli per l'altare magiore, scudi 10.20' (ARSI, FG 2005, 66b–69a).

230 '[5 June 1591] al P. Giovanni de Rosis per la cena del tabernacolo di figure piccole, al pittore fiammengo scudi 10' (ARSI, FG 1233, 33b).

231 Pecchiai, *Il Gesu di Roma*, p. 96; Lewine, 'The Roman Church Interior,' pp. 262–3.

232 For della Porta's contracts for the altarpiece, see ARSI, FG 545, 57a–58a.

233 A memorial in the Jesuit archives records, 'L'Altare, et Cappella, oggi del Nostro S. Padre Ignazio fu cominciata dal Cardinale Savelli il vecchio, et morendo lasciò 12,000 scudi, acciò si finesse, de' quali si servì Papa' (ARSI, FG 545, 4a).

234 'Havendo Illmo Signor Cardinal Savello fatto fare un crocifisso di cera a Prospero Bresciano, per farlo gittare poi di bronzo per la sua cappella che fece nella chiesa del Gesù in Roma, et essendo detta figura di cera rimasta imperfetta per la morte dell'artifice l'Eccelentissimo Signor Duca Giovanni Savello nipote del suddetto Illmo ha fatto dimandare M. Ludovico Del Duca siciliano acciò detta opera si finisca. Hora li obliga detto M. Ludovico a detto Eccmo Signor Duca Savello di dare finita con ogni perfectione della figura di metallo con le seguenti condicioni. Prima si obliga finire detto crocifisso di cera, a gusto e contento del P. Giuseppe Valeriano della Compagnia del Giesù e d'un altro che detto Padre elegerà per compagno a tal giuditio, e mancando il detto P. Giuseppe vuole che lo superiore delli RR Padri del Gesù posse elegere uno, overo doi altri in luogo suo, acciò detta opera riesca con ogni perfettione conforme la mente et intentione dell'Ecc.mo Signor Duca Savello il quale così li ha ordinato e vuole, e però detto M. Ludovico si obliga emendare primieramente, detta cera levandone alcune imperfettioni che vi sono, come la testa, le braccia, li fianchi, li ginocchi, le gambe, e piedi, che imperfette restano, con alcune altre cosette che si veggono imperfette, a contento del sopra detto P. Gioseppe e compagno. Si obliga subito, finita detta figura di cera, come di sopra, farli la forma di gesso per posser gittare la figura, che poi l'haverà a fondare di metallo, la quale prima la rinetterà e perfettionerà conforme l'uso dell'arte. Si obliga fundere detta figura di metallo tutta d'un pezzo, salvo la corona, e la diadema, che saranno staccate e da per loro, e

con detta figura fare il suo panno attaccato et unito nell'istesso getto, e contento dell'Ecc.mo Signor Duca overo del detto P. Giuseppe in tal caso l'obliga detto M. Ludovico di rifunderlo e gettarlo di nuovo, tutto a sue spese, sino a tanto che detto getto riesca netto e recipiente, conforme dal sudetto Padre Giuseppe e Compagna serà giudicato intendendoli detto getto e opera solo per il crocifisso con il suo panno, e la Diadema e Corona, come di sopra, senza nessuna altra cosa. Si obliga detto M. Ludovico fare detta figura di bronzo e crucifisso polito, e rinetto et atto per essere indorato a gusto delli sopradetti, e tutto a sue spese salvo, che il metallo, che serà necessario per fonderlo, restituendo però quello che gli avanzerà con farseli buono li cali ad uso de funditori di figure, e salvo ducento libre di cera per li getti e sfiatatori, la quale perché d'ordinario li suole bagnare, però non l'obliga restituirne avanzo. Dall'altra parte l'Ecc.mo Signor Duca Giovanni Savello l'obliga dare a detto M. Ludovico Siciliano la sudetta figura fatta da Prospero Bresciano il metallo necessario con le condizioni sudette salvo ducento libre di cera, è per prezzo e pagamento di detto Cristo fatto gettato et rinetto a contento del sudetto P. Giuseppe et compagno, l'obliga e promette dare a detto M. Ludovico scudi quattrocento treintanove moneta a giulij dieci per scudo d'argento in paghe tre cioè 146.33 scudi avanti che l'opera l'comincia, cioè quanto la presente scrittura l'stipularà, e li serà consignata detta figura, metallo e cera. E 146.33 scudi a mezza l'opera, che serà a mese nove dopo questa presente Conventione stipulata, et a mese 18 l'ultima paga delli altri 146.33 scudi quando l'opera serà finita. E M. Ludovico sudetto l'obliga nel termine d'mesi 18 dopo detta stipulatione dare detta figura gettata, e rinetta con ogni professio.mte contento delli sopra nominati, con conditione, che se ha seconda paga l'perlongasse oltre li nove mesi, che in tal caso possa egli quel tanto prolungare l'opera, oltre li 18 nominati e posservanza delle sopradette cosa promette M. Ludovico sopra nominato dare idonea li gustà nella stipulatione che li fara dell' pnt.capti. Die 30 Augusti 1593' (ARSI, FG 545, 59b–60b; cited, but not transcribed, in Pecchiai, *Il Gesù di Roma*, pp. 97–8).

235 Baglione writes in his section on Grammatica, 'Alla piazza de gli Altieri, nella Chiesa del Giesù, presso l'altare di S. Ignatio Loiola, v'è di suo il quadro del B. Borgia orante avanti il Santissimo Sagramento, da diversi Angioli portato' (*Le vite de' pittori*, p. 293); and Baldinucci concurs in his section on the same artist: 'Fece ancora un Quadro pel Gesù, ove rappresentò il Beato Francesco Borgia in atto d'orazione avanti al Santissimo sacramento' (*Notizie de' professori del disegno*, p. 246). The anonymous seventeenth-century Jesuit memorial states, 'Il quadro de' Nostri Santi Martyri Crocefissi, è del Cavaliere d'Arpino' (ARSI, FG 545, 2b). Celio mentions the Cavaliere's painting but not the one by Grammatica: 'La pittura delli martirizzati in India collatarale all'altare ad'olio, del Cavalier Gioseppe Cesari' (*Memoria delli nomi*, p. 40). Baglione also discusses d'Arpino's contribution: 'E tutto di non mai nell'operare stancandosi, & ad ogni hora essercitandosi, dipinse nella Chiesa del Giesù un quadro di alcuni Martiri di quella Compagnia nel Giappone crocifissi, e sta vicino all'altare del loro S. Ignatio' (*Le vite de' pittori*, p. 373). Titi discusses both works: 'Il Quadro di San Francesco Borgia orante, portato da diversi Angioli, posto presso l'Altar, che segue nella Crociata è opera d'Antiveduto Grammatica, che fece molte cose assai piaciute per il Card. del Monte, hora quì è un altro Quadro col medesimo Santo, che porta il Santissimo, e quantità di figure operato con studio, e diligenza da Ludovico

Gimignani ... La pittura, che stà dall'altro lato dell'Altare con alcuni Martiri della Compagnia di Giesù nel Giappone crocefissi è di mano del Cavalier d'Arpino' (*Studio di pittura*, vol. 1, p. 101; see also Titi, *Descrizione delle pitture*, p. 175).

236 'il Salvatore della Cappella maggiore sotto la cuppola a man sinistra di Rafaello; incontro il cavalier Baglione' (Mancini, *Considerazioni sulla pitture*, p. 279).

237 '[8 December 1602] Per i colori del fr[atello] Giovanni Battista Fiamero scudi 1.60; per Ottavio pittore che aiuta à depingere, scudi 5' (ARSI, FG 2005, 88a). Ottavio may be Ottavio Padovano, later a *cavaliere*, born in Rome to Paduan parents. Padovano's main line of work was portrait painting, but he worked on several large-scale canvases in Rome, including an *Annunciation* in S. Eustachio. He later became the *principe* of the Academy of St Luke (Baglione, *Le vite de' pittori*, pp. 321–2).

238 '[28 January 1604] Per un quadro grande della Resurettione che il N.R.P. Generale fece depingere in chiesa nostra dal Signore Andrea Giovanni Baglioni pittore perugino scudi cento di moneta quali furono pigliati in prestito dal Padre Antonio Longi Ministro passati et dati a buon conto à detto Pittore. Et hora si restituiscono al Padre Giacomo Campione Ministro al presente della casa, et sono dei denari che lasso alla sacrestia la 6m del Sept. Greg.o Sabatare come si è detto nel introito à cav. 28 [Total] scudi 100' (ARSI, FG 2005, 94a).

239 A memorial in the Jesuit archives reads, 'La Cappella di S. Francesco Saverio fu offerta da Papa Clemente, quando visitò la nostra chiesa, al Cardinale Rusticuccio, allora Vicario; l'accettò, ma poi essendosi applicato a finire la chiesa di Sta Susanna, la rinunciò' (ARSI, FG 545, 4a).

240 'Beatissimo Padre: Giovanni Baglione dall'anno 1602 dipinse d'ordine del Padre Generale dei Gesuiti un quadro grande della Resurrettione per una Cappella della chiesa del Giesù, et à conto della sua mercede hebbe scudi doi cento de quali fu fatta ricevuta per a bon conto, e del restante dalli Padri Gesuiti gli son state date sempre buone parole, che saria stato sodisfato, scusandosi, che per all'hora non havevano comodità, et havendo più volte esso oratore fatt'instanza, che gli fusse pagato detto residuo. Dopò esser stato rattenuto cinque anni gli è stato risposto ultimamente da detto Padre Generale che non li vol dar altro, e perchè il quadro è di valuta di mille scudi, et è stato fatto da esso oratore con molto studio e diligenza sì come la qualità di detto quadro lo dimostra, e doverìa esser pagato delle sue fatighe. Però supplica humilmente la S.V. degnarsi d'ordinare à Monsignor A.C. che lo faccia pagare, sommariamente per giustizia che si riceverà per grazia della S.V. quam Deus' (ARSI, FG 545, 7a; Pecchiai, *Il Gesù di Roma*, p. 101).

241 '[29 October 1616] al pittore per accomodare l'altare della Resurretione scudo 1' (ARSI, FG 2005a, 104a).

242 'E per il P. Acquaviva Generale de'Giesuiti formò un grand quadro alto 35 palmi, e largo 20. entrovi a olio la Resurettione di Christo, con amore, e con studio rappresentata' (Baglione, *Le vite de' pittori*, p. 402).

243 ASF, Comp. Rel. Sopp. 1064, #335 (Rome, 12 August 1582): 'per che quelli pochi maestri che habbiamo, stanno hora occupati nella Cupola della Chiesa nostra qui di Roma, nella quale non si perde tempo, che L'Ill.mo Card.le Farnese desidera vederne quanto più presto il fine.'

244 Robertson, *Il Gran Cardinale*, p. 208.

245 'a dì 7 Gennaro 1583 si cominciò a dipingere li 4 Evangelisti sotto alla Cupula da M.
     Andrea Pittore; a dì 12 detto si cominciò a dipingere la Cupula da M. Giovanni; Li
     Capitelli del Altare Maggiore dati a fare a cotimo a scudi 60 l'uno; li Capitelli della
     Cupula intagliati a scudi 10 ½ l'uno et li squadrati a scudi sei l'uno' (ARSI, AG Busta
     V, 787; Pecchiai, *Il Gesù di Roma*, p. 76) Baglione describes the subjects of de' Vecchi's
     frescoes: 'Nel Tempio del Giesù ha dipinta tutta la cupola con diversi adornamenti, e
     puttini assai ricca, e ne'quattro peducci di essa vi sono li quattro Dottori della Chiesa
     Latina Gregorio, Ambrogio, Girolamo, & Agostino con gran maniera condotti, e
     figuroni assai grandi' (*Le vite de' pittori*, p. 127). Titi adds to his description: 'Tutta la
     Cuppola della Chiesa ricca d'adornamenti, e puttini fu dipinta con disegno di Gio: de
     Vecchi, con li quattro Dottori della Chiesa Latina nelli Peducci, figuroni grandi assai,
     e condotti con gran maestria' (*Studio di pittura*, vol. 1, p. 102).
246 '[Giovanni de' Vecchi to Cardinal Alessandro Farnese, from Rome, 4 September 1583]
     Illustrissimo et Reverendissimo Signore, Havendo finito l'altro giorno il Santo
     Agostino e Santo Girolamo, andai a trovare Messer Giulio Folco, che volessi farmi
     satisfare secondo l'ordine di Vostra Signoria Illustrissima. Mi rispose che li trecento
     scudi ch'ei mi ha dato intende havermili dati per la cupola e per questi sancti insieme,
     il che non può stare, perché oltre la discrepantia grande che vi è, per giuditio di chi se
     n'intende, Vostra Signoria Illustrissima sa che quando si parlò della cupola, non c'era
     intention veruna di fare i detti sancti da basso, si come Padre Giovanni si ricorda
     benissimo. Per tanto sono stato forzato di supplicare a Vostra Signoria Illustrissima
     che vogla scrivere a Messer Giulio, che habbia consideratione alle mie fatiche, rimet-
     tendosi a quelli della professione, dove lui habbia qualche difficultà, perché la verita
     sta come io ho detto a Vostra Signoria Illustrissima, nel voler della quale io rimetto
     però questa et ogn'altra cosa mia, raccommandandomi in sua buona gratia humilis-
     simamente' (ASPar, Epistolario scelto., b.19 [pittori]; Robertson, *Il Gran Cardinale*, p.
     310, doc. 115 [published as busta 20]).
247 The letter is dated 5 August 1585: 'Non potendo risolvere con Messer Giulio Folco
     d'esser soddisfatto, son forzato di spettare il ritorno di V.S. Ill.ma acciò che alla
     presenza sua, sia fatto capaci, per posserla finire et ultimarla, d'onde prego sempre il
     Signore Dio per ogni felice contento di V.S. Ill.ma.' (ASPar, Epistolario scelto, b. 19).
248 'Li quattro Dottori nelli peducci nella Cupola, di Giovanni di Vecchi, il resto in essa
     Cupola, suo disegno depinto da diversi, sono à fresco' (Celio, *Memoria delli nomi*,
     p. 40). The Jesuit source writes, 'la cupola pittura antica fu dipinta con disegno di
     Giovanni de Vecchi, con li 4 dottori della chiesa latina' (ARSI, FG 545, 2b). Mancini
     simply refers to 'gl'Evangelisti della tribuna di Giovanni de'Vecchi' (*Considerazioni
     sulla pittura*, p. 279). See also Robertson, *Il Gran Cardinale*, p. 195.
249 Baldinucci writes that Odoardo wanted Annibale to begin on the Gesù dome after
     he had finished the Farnese Gallery: 'Avea concetto eziandìo di farlo operare nella
     Cupola del Gesù, fatta poc'avanti dipingere dal Zio, riuscita cosa poco lodevole, e
     intanto applicava a trovare i modi di degnamente ricompensare il gran Pittore'
     (*Notizie de' professori del disegno*, p. 78).
250 Baglione credits Fiammeri with these paintings: 'E sopra la porta dell'istesso Tempio
     un tondo in tela co'l nome di Giesù, e varii Santi intorno a olio dipinti' (*Le vite de'
     pittori*, p. 98).

251 Celio writes, 'Le pitture sopra le porte dalla parte di dietro di N.N. Fiamenghi fratelli
della Compagnia di Giesù' (*Memoria delli nomi*, p. 42). The same thing is recorded in
the anonymous seventeenth-century Jesuit memorial: 'e le pitture sopra alla porta,
sono da diversi giesuiti Fiaminghi' (ARSI, FG 545, 2b). Titi, as usual, agrees with the
anonymous Jesuit source: 'le pitture sopra le Porte di dentro della Chiesa sono di
diversi Gesuiti Fiaminghi' (*Studio di pittura*, vol. 1, p. 102). Pecchiai is the first to draw
the connection between the Gisbert brothers and the west wall of the Gesù (*Il Gesù di
Roma*, p. 242).

252 Hibbard, 'Ut picturae sermones,' p. 35 n24.

253 The anonymous seventeenth-century Jesuit source reads: 'Le porte della Chiesa si
sono fatte di legno e a questo fine mandato dall'Indie, dal Rè di Portogallo Don
Sebastiano, al Cardinale Farnese, quando intese, che faceva la chiesa della nostra
Compagnia' (ARSI, FG 545, 5a).

254 Lucilla Micozzi, 'La Ratio Domiciliorum: Casa Professa,' in Luciana Gaudenzi, ed., *La
chiesa del Gesù a Roma: Gli ultimi restauri* (Viterbo, 1996), p. 86; Pecchiai, *Il Gesù di
Roma*, p. 278.

255 BNR, Fond. Ges. 1526, 83a.

256 The following memorial indicates that sculptures and paintings were transferred to
the sacristy from the main body of the church as the decorations of the church
were altered: 'La sacrestia è stata fatta dal Signor Cardinale Odoardo Farnese, li
armaij però di noce sono costati 2800 scudi in circa di diverse limosina. Il crocifisso,
ch'è in Sacrestia, stava prima esposto in Chiesa nell'altare, adesso di S. Ignazio, ed
ora di gran divozione a tutto il popolo. Li quadri, che stanno alli lati de medesimo
crocifisso de Nostri Santi sono quei, che stavano al Corno destro, et sinistro
dell'Altare Maggiore, avvanti che fussero canonizzati per moltissimi voti celebri'
(ARSI, FG 545, 4b).

257 In his entry on Ciampelli, Baglione writes: 'E nella volta della Sagrestia ha parimente
di suo una storia assai copiosa, a fresco lavorata. E sotto l'altar maggiore un quadretto
in tavola a olio, & altre cose di suo a fresco' (*Le vite de' pittori*, p. 320). Titi concurs:
'Nella Volta della Sagrestia vi è un'historia assai copiosa à fresco lavorata da Agostino
Ciampelli' (*Studio di pittura*, vol. 1, p. 103), and again: 'La volta della sagrestia è
d'Agostin Ciampelli' (*Descrizione delle pitture*, p. 179). Pecchiai is the first to suggest
that Lanfranco painted the two Passion frescoes (*Il Gesù di Roma*, p. 279). The anonymous seventeenth-century Jesuit source simply says, 'Nella sagrestia vi è una volta
molto copiosa di pitture à fresco lavorata da Agostino Campelli' (ARSI, FG 545, 3a).

258 'A Roma ... un Quadro di essa Santa [Cecilia] pe'l Gesù' (Baldinucci, *Notizie de'
professori del disegno*, p. 145).

259 The inventory is published in its entirety in Pecchiai, *Il Gesù di Roma*, pp. 331–43; the
reference to 'S. Cecilia' is on p. 339.

260 See Michael William Maher, 'Reforming Rome: The Society of Jesus and Its Congregations at the Church of the Gesù,' PhD dissertation, University of Minnesota, 1997, pp.
529–47.

261 Pecchiai, *Il Gesu di Roma*, pp. 312–13; Papi, 'Le tele della cappellina di Odoardo
Farnese.'

262 Papi, 'Le tele della cappellina di Odoardo Farnese,' p. 74.

263 'Andrea Commodi, nato in Fiorenza d'assai honesti parenti, di buon gusto, molt'anni

sono operò qui in Roma alcune cose del Giesù al sepolcro del beato Ignatio di buona maniera' (Mancini, *Considerazioni sulla pittura*, p. 248).

264 BNR, Fond. Ges. 1526, 81a.

265 Pecchiai, *Il Gesù di Roma*, p. 314.

266 '[20 March 1568] E à dì detto scudo uno per gli spesi in orpello, spago, cotone, fogli, et altr.o per mano di Mastro Biagio pittore per li scudi del parato che si fece su la piazza q.do al Cardinale Farnese misse la prima pietra' (ARSI, FG 2059, 58a).

267 ARSI, FG 1231 (*Opere delle Fabrica Murali & Manovali*, 1583).

268 'Tre scudi 50 pagati per suo ordine al Padre Lorenzo Amodei disse per 150 medagliette di rame con l'immagine della Madonna' (ARSI, FG 2059, 114a).

269 '[4 September 1570] E a dì detto scudi 44 per rubbia uno di calce bagnata accomodata à un' pittore parente del Vignola' (ARSI, FG 2059, 97b).

270 See Giovanni Canevazzi, 'Intorno a Jacopo e a Giacinto Barozzi,' in *Memorie e studi intorno a Jacopo Barozzi* (Vignola, 1908), pp. 313–46.

271 '[6 February 1590] per 24 imagini scudi 0.24'; '[20 February 1590] per à buon conto al pittore per li angeli, et candelieri di legno giulii 20'; '[6 January 1591] per la stampa di 200. giesù grandi, et piccoli scudi 0.48'; '[11 February 1591] à Andrea per diverse spese, cioè al chiavaro per la porta della Mad.a al pittore per resto delli Angeli per scope, et code, et carta azurra scudi 1.17'; '[4 January 1592] per dipingere li nomi di Giesù scudi 1.80'; '[17 April 1592] in 18 imagini di crocifisso per li confessionali à scudi 2 ½ l'una, intotale scudi 45'; '[3 November 1592] 3 imagini di crocifissi per li oratorii'; '[6 November 1592] per 6 quinterni di carta reale per stampare li nomi di Giesù scudi 0.80 ... a di 13 detto per stampatura 200 nomi di Giesù scudi 0.80' (ARSI, FG 1233, 25a, 29a, 31a–b, 42b, 43b).

272 '[21 October 1600] scudi quattro giulii 80 dati al fratello Giovanni Battista [Vanaro or Vanner] per fatura dell'arma della Regina per il suo frontale, scudi 4.80; item scudi venti dati al fr.llo Gio. Batt.a Vanaro per fare la pranza al frontale della Regina'; '[November 1601] Per otto telari di legno et tela per tre telari di depingere scudi quattordeci, scudi 14. Per l'imprimitura de quadri da depingersi et i colori dati a diversi pittori scudi dieci, scudi 10'; '[1 July 1602] per mancia del pittore che depinge il quadro del Giesù scudi cinque, scudi 5'; '[18 August 1604, for the model of the Holy Week sepulchre] E de più per contestare il detto Mastro Tomasso che e stato dato scudi dua giulii cinquanta. Disse per haver pagato un pittore à buon conto di certi capitelli di carta ... Scudi 2.50'; '[September 1605] per accomodare l'Arma del Papa al pittore, scudi 0.50'; '[30 August 1614] per colori per dipingere scudi 30'; '[7 June 1616] per dare di colore alle cornice de'chori grandi scudi 100'; '[23 July 1616] per fare dipingere le gelosie delli 2 chori et 4 tavole scudi 4'; '[25 October 1616] al F. Cornelio per comprare tela et colori per 2 quadri per chiesa scudi 10'; '[17 July 1617] al F. Cornelio per colori per li 2 quadri della chiesa scudi 4' (ARSI, FG 2005, 69a, 84a, 86b, 96a; FG 2005A, 102b, 103a, 104a, 106b).

273 '[13 April 1593] da Mastro Durante Pittore scudi 7.1.0 ... [da] Mastro Giovanni Pittore scudi 7.0.60' (ARSI, FG 1233 [Libro de' conti del Prefetto della Chiesa, 1590–7], 16b); '[22 October 1606] dal Signor Giovanni Paulo scultore, scudi 1.20' (ARSI, FG 2005, 46b).

274 '[8 July 1602] Dalla S.ra Claudia Mattei scudi cinque per mancia del pittore scudi 5'; '[24 July 1602] dalla Signora Claudi Mattei scudi dieci à buon conto per una imagine,

scudi 10'; '[25 August 1602] per una imagine dell'Annunciata di Firenze à buon conto scudi dieci, scudi 10'; '[10 September 1602] dalla Signora Claudia Mattei dieci per l'imagine dell'Annunciata, scudi 10' (ARSI, FG 2005, 20b, 86b). Asbudrale and Ciriaco also gave regular gifts to the Gesù treasury, some of them substantial. The Mattei family gave frequently from 1602 into the 1690s (ARSI, FG 2005, 20b–34b; FG 2012, 119a).

275 '[10 September 1602] dalla Signora Claudia Mattei sc[u]di dieci à buon conto per un quadro de tutti i santi, scudi 10'; '[20 September 1602] dalla Signora Claudia Mattei per le cornice dei quadri, scudi 10'; '[20 October 1602] per li cartoni degl'Angeli et quadri à buon conto scudi trenta, scudi 30'; '[25 October 1602] dalla Signora Claudia Mattei trenta per li quadri et Angeli, scudi 30'; '[20 December 1602] dalla Signora Claudia Mattei scudi 30; dalla Signora Claudia Mattei scudi dieci per l'imagine a fili al ferro, scudi 10' (ARSI, FG 2005, 21a, 87a, 21b, 87b, 21b).

7: The Church of the Gesù in Rome: Description and Interpretation

1 Hibbard, 'Ut picturae sermones,' p. 37.

2 Ignatius of Loyola, *Spiritual Exercises*, p. 123.

3 Macioce, *Undique splendent*, p. 79.

4 See ibid., pp. 174–215.

5 Hibbard, 'Ut picturae sermones,' p. 37. On Pentecost imagery in general, see Carolyn Valone, 'The Pentecost: Image and Experience in Late Sixteenth-Century Rome,' *Sixteenth Century Journal* 24 (1993): 801–28.

6 For Zuccaro's version of the scene, see Luchinat, *Taddeo e Federico Zuccaro*, vol. 2, p. 163.

7 Spalding, 'Santi di Tito,' figs 37, 183; Como, *Girolamo Muziano*, pp. 116–17.

8 Valone, 'The Pentecost.'

9 The picture is illustrated in *Dopo il Rosso: Artisti a Volterra e Pomarance* (Marsilio, 1997), p. 70.

10 Madonna, *Roma di Sisto V*, p. 186.

11 Lewine, 'The Roman Church Interior,' p. 251.

12 Ignatius of Loyola, *Spiritual Exercises*, pp. 52–3.

13 Jacoby, *Hans von Aachen*; and *Prag um 1600: Kunst und Kultur am Hofe Kaiser Rudolfs II*, 2 vols (Vienna, 1988), I, pp. 180–1.

14 It was Vannugli who first noticed that these two figures were the same (Vannugli, 'Antonio Tempesta,' p. 106).

15 Ibid., figs 6, 7.

16 Macioce, *Undique splendent*, plate LXVb.

17 Hibbard, 'Ut picturae sermones,' p. 37.

18 Arslan, *I Bassano*, vol. 2, fig. 181. See Hibbard, 'Ut picturae sermones,' p. 45; Madonna, *Roma di Sisto V*, p. 185.

19 Harold E. Wethey, *The Paintings of Titian*, 3 vols (London, 1969), I, cat. no. 149.

20 Mormando, *Saints and Sinners*, plate 9.

21 Mâle, *L'art religieux*, pp. 337–8.

22 Ignatius of Loyola, *Spiritual Exercises*, p. 12. See Hibbard, 'Ut picturae sermones,' pp. 45–6.

23 Ignatius of Loyola, *Spiritual Exercises*, p. 49. See Hibbard, 'Ut picturae sermones,' p. 45.

24 Wadell, *Evangelicae*, figs 220, 225.

25 Hibbard, 'Ut picturae sermones,' p. 46.

26 Mâle, *L'art religieux*, pp. 113–14.

27 See Pamela Askew, 'Caravaggio: Outward Action, Inward Vision,' in Stefania Macioce, ed., *Michelangelo Merisi da Caravaggio: La vita e le opere attraverso i documenti* (Rome, 1996), pp. 248–69.

28 Ibid., p. 251.

29 Ignatius of Loyola, *Spiritual Exercises*, pp. 81–8. See Hibbard, 'Ut picturae sermones,' p. 38, and Baumstark, *Rom in Bayern*, pp. 454–5.

30 Ignatius of Loyola, *Spiritual Exercises*, p. 83–4.

31 Ibid., p. 85–7.

32 Ibid., p. 87.

33 Ibid., p. 132; Baumstark, *Rom in Bayern*, pp. 458–60.

34 See Shearman, *Only Connect*, pp. 85–92.

35 Hall, *After Raphael*, p. 269.

36 Mâle, *L'art religieux*, p. 8.

37 Loren Partridge, *The Art of Renaissance Rome, 1400–1600* (New York, 1996), p. 101.

38 D'Amico, 'La pittura a Roma,' p. 197. Calì, mysteriously, sees these paintings as cold, static, and drained of emotion in the spirit of Luca Cambiaso's frescoes at the Escorial (*La pittura del cinquecento*, vol. 1, p. 223).

39 D'Amico, 'La pittura a Roma,' p. 197.

40 Ibid., p. 198; Galassi Paluzzi, 'La Cappella di Santa Maria della Strada,' p. 60. Galassi Paluzzi attributes the paintings to Valeriano.

41 Paoletti and Radke, *Art in Renaissance Italy*, p. 425.

42 Mâle, *L'art religieux*, p. 264.

43 Calì, *Da Michelangelo*, p. 295.

44 Ignatius of Loyola, *Spiritual Exercises*, p. 84.

45 D'Amico, 'La pittura a Roma,' p. 196.

46 Ibid., p. 195.

47 Zuccari, 'Bellarmino e la Cappella degli Angeli,' pp. 612–13. See also Mâle, *L'art religieux*, p. 302.

48 Zuccari, 'Bellarmino e la Cappella degli Angeli,' pp. 619–27; Kristina Hermann Fiore, 'Gli angeli, nella teoria e nella pittura di Federico Zuccari,' in Bonita Cleri, ed., *Federico Zuccari: Le idee, gli scritti* (Milan, 1997), pp. 101–2.

49 Fiore, 'Gli angeli,' p. 101.

50 'Iddio sommo Artefice e Pittore creò divise e ornò questo Mondo ... ma anco creò, dipinse et ornò un'altro Mondo spiritualmente nella mente dell'Angelo ... Hora da questi principi argumento che è necessario prima che l'Angelo intenda compitamente che non pur vagheggi questo Mondo intelligibile c'ha in lui medesimo, e tutte le cose rappresentanti per queste specie, ma di più, acciochè l'operazione sia terminata, e perfetta, che mirando queste cose formi in se stesso un 'Idolo e un Disegno di loro, nel quale, e il quale intendendo, ha cognitione di quelle. Aggiongo che non solo l'Angelo ha necessità di questo Disegno per indendere per la ragione detta, ma anco per operare, perché non si può operare al di fuori senza prima mirar nella mente il Disegno di quanto si ha da operare. Et perché di questi spiriti alcuni sono deputati e

gli huomini, e non è huomo, che non abbia un Angelo per custode, e difensore; et altre sono mandati ad altri effetti nei Regni, nelle Provincie e nelle Città come si legge nelle scritture sacre in infiniti luoghi, i quali presero corpi formati a similitudine de nostri, ma aerei però, onde gli huomini credevano che fossero corpi umani come si legge dell'Angelo Raffaele che condusse Tobia' (published in Fiore, 'Gli angeli,' pp. 90–1). My translation.

51 Calì, *La pittura del cinquecento*, vol. 2, p. 209.

52 Fiori, 'Gli angeli,' pp. 105–7.

53 Luchinat, *Taddeo e Federico Zuccari* vol. 1, pp. 76–96.

54 Ibid., p. 182.

55 John W. O'Malley, personal communication.

56 Mâle, *L'art religieux*, p. 61.

57 Göttler, *Die Kunst des Fegefeuers*, pp. 307–10.

58 Luchinat, *Taddeo e Federico Zuccari*, vol. 1, p. 188.

59 Ibid.

60 Mâle, *L'art religieux*, p. 82.

61 Zuccari, 'Bellarmino e la Cappella degli Angeli,' p. 621.

62 Luchinat, *Taddeo e Federico Zuccari*, vol. 1, p. 190.

63 Zuccari, 'Bellarmino e la Cappella degli Angeli,' p. 622.

64 Ibid.

65 The fresco is illustrated in Robertson, *Il Gran Cardinale*, fig. 107.

66 ARSI, Rom. 162 II, 276a. Published in Zuccari, *Arte e commitenza*, pp. 166–7.

67 Hibbard, 'Ut picturae sermones,' p. 47.

68 Mâle, *L'art religieux*, pp. 41–4.

69 Zeri, *Pittura e controriforma*, p. 54. My translation.

70 Ibid., my translation. See also Laurentiis, 'Immagini ed arte,' pp. 592–3.

71 Zeri, *Pittura e controriforma*, pp. 53–4. My translation.

72 Calì, *Da Michelangelo*, p. 295, and *La pittura del cinquecento*, vol. 1, p. 218.

73 Freedberg, *Painting in Italy*, pp. 599–600.

74 Ibid., p. 600.

75 See Bailey, 'Creating a Global Artistic Language.'

76 Fabrizio d'Amico, 'Uno sguardo d'assieme,' in Zander, *L'arte in Roma nel secolo XVI*, vol. 2, p. 196. My translation.

77 On Paleotti, see Jones, 'Art Theory as Ideology,' pp. 127–39.

78 See Freiburg, *The Lateran in 1600*, especially pp. 161–76.

79 O'Malley, *The First Jesuits*, pp. 5, 18–19. The quotation is from Ignatius's *Formula* (1550).

80 Russo, *Il ciclo*, pp. 60–1.

81 See Mâle, *L'art religieux*, pp. 152–92.

82 For Francis imagery of the period, see *L'immagine di San Francesco nella Controriforma* (Rome, 1982). See also Mâle, *L'art religieux*, p. 172.

83 On the relationship between the Franciscans and the Jesuits on the world missions, see Bailey, *Art on the Jesuit Missions*.

84 I would like to thank one of my anonymous readers for bringing this connection to my attention.

85 *Prag um 1600*, II, colorplate 10; I, p. 235.

86 D'Amico, 'Uno sguardo d'assieme,' p. 196.

87 Como, *Girolamo Muziano*, p. 85. See Giammaria, *Girolamo Muziano*, p. 154.

88 Como, *Girolamo Muziano*, p. 151.

89 Schwager, 'Anlässlich eines unbekannten Stichs,' pp. 295–312.

90 See Papi, 'Le tele della cappellina di Odoardo Farnese,' pp. 72–80; Strinati, *Quadri romani*, p. 10; Bailey, 'The Jesuits and Painting in Rome,' p. 160.

91 Papi, 'Le tele della cappellina di Odoardo Farnese,' pp. 73–4.

92 Hibbard, 'Ut picturae sermones,' p. 37.

93 Smith, 'The Art of Salvation,' pp. 568–99. See also Smith, *Sensuous Worship*.

94 Ibid., p. 576.

95 The most thorough history of the church is John Rupert Martin, *The Ceiling Paintings for the Jesuit Church in Antwerp (Corpus Rubenianum Ludwig Burchard)* (London and New York, 1967). For Rubens's altarpieces, see also Graham Smith, 'Rubens altargemälde des Hl. Ignatius,' *Jahrbuch der kunsthistorischen Sammlungen in Wien* 65 (1969): 39–60. Antien Knaap, a PhD candidate at New York University, is preparing her dissertation on the ceiling paintings of this church.

96 Antien Knaap, 'Envisioning a Sacred Hierarchy: Rubens' Paintings for the Jesuit Church in Antwerp,' paper delivered at the conference 'The Jesuits II' at Boston College in June 2002.

97 Giuseppe Richa, *Notizie istoriche delle chiese fiorentine*, vol. 5 (Florence, 1757), pp. 145–8; Pirri, 'Ammannati,' p. 22; Bencivenni, *L'architettura della Compagnia di Gesù*, pp. 27–44; Matracchi, 'Il Collegio di S. Giovannino.' Ammannati's original plan, with the dedications of the chapels written in, is in ASR, Collezione Mappe e Disegni I, cart. 29, n97.

98 Stefano Della Torre and Richard Schofield, *Pellegrino Tibaldi Architetto e il S. Fedele di Milano* (Milan, 1994), pp. 221–38. See also Moore, 'Pellegrino Tibaldi's Church of S. Fedele,' pp. 194ff.

99 ASPer, Perugia II 167 5, 191–206; Siepi, *Descrizione topologico-istorico*, vol. 1, pp. 405–15.

100 Giuseppe Rocchi Coopmans de Yoldi, 'Presentazione delle monografie,' in Yoldi, *Architettura della compagnia ignaziana*, pp. 80–1; Luchinat, *Taddeo e Federico Zuccari*, vol. 2, p. 259.

101 For the Garminati, see *Biblia pauperum: Dipinti dalle diocesi di Romagna, 1570–1670* (Ravenna, 1992), cat. no. 33. For the Alberti fresco, see Macioce, *Undique splendent*, plate XXIII.

102 Macioce, *Undique splendent*, pp. 96–7. My translation.

103 Dante Bernini, 'La vita devota del pittore Federico Barocci,' in *L'immagine di San Francesco nella Controriforma* (Rome, 1982), pp. 57–62.

104 For a reproduction of the painting and the Cherubino Alberti engraving, see Luchinat, *Taddeo e Federico Zuccari*, vol. 1, p. 271.

105 Donald Posner, *Annibale Carracci*, 2 vols (London, 1971), I, p. 126. See also Freedberg, *Circa 1600*, p. 65.

106 Posner, *Carracci*, vol. 1, p. 138.

8: Conclusion

1 See Dempsey, *Annibale Carracci*, pp. 6–10, 14.

2 See Freedberg, *Painting in Italy*, pp. 429ff, 649–50.

3 Haskell, 'The Role of Patrons,' pp. 51–62.

4 On the scholarly debate over the Jesuits' professed austerity in their residences vs. their churches, see Bailey, 'Le style jésuite,' pp. 64–5.

5 See the excellent summary in Hall, *After Raphael*, p. 190. For Gilio's text (entitled *Due dialoghi ... degli errori de' pittori*), see Barocchi, *Trattati d'arte del cinquecento*, especially vol. 2, pp. 40–8. See also Zeri, *Pittura e controriforma*, pp. 20–1; Calì, *Da Michelangelo*, pp. 18–20; Macioce, *Undique splendent*, pp. 52–3.

6 Wittkower, *Art and Architecture in Italy*, p. 90. See Bailey, 'Le style jésuite,' pp. 42–3.

7 On the embassies, the fundraising efforts of Trigault, and the public reception of the Paraguay reductions, see Bailey, *Art on the Jesuit Missions*, pp. 62–3, 65, 100, 144–82.

8 See Bailey, 'Le style jésuite,' p. 71.

9 Bailey, 'The Jesuits and Painting in Italy,' p. 164.

Bibliography

Abromson, Morton. 'Painting in Rome during the Papacy of Clement VIII.' PhD dissertation, New York University, 1981.

Ackerman, James. *The Architecture of Michelangelo*. London, 1961.

Aelian (Claudius Aelianus). *Aelian on the Characteristics of Animals I*. Trans. and ed. A.F. Scholfield. Cambridge, MA, 1958.

Aesop, *Fables of Aesop*. Trans. and ed. S.A. Handford. Harmondsworth, 1973.

Alberti, Romano. *Origine, et progresso dell'academia del dissegno de' pittori, scultori, e architetti di Roma*. Pavia, 1604; repr. Bologna, 1978.

Albini, Giuliana. 'La gestione dell'Ospedale Maggiore di Milano nel quattrocento: Un esempio di concentrazione ospedaliera.' In Allen J. Grieco and Lucia Sandri, *eds, Ospedale e Città* (Florence, 1997), pp. 157–78.

Alden, Dauril. *The Making of an Enterprise: The Society of Jesus in Portugal, Its Empire, and Beyond, 1540–1750*. Stanford, 1996.

Alighieri, Dante. *The Divine Comedy: Hell*. Trans. and ed. Dorothy L. Sayers. Repr. Harmondsworth, 1980.

Andrea Lilli nella pittura delle Marche: Tra cinquecento e seicento. Rome, 1985.

Angeli, Diego. *Sant'Ignazio di Loyola nella vita e nell'arte*. Lanciano, 1911.

Annuae Litterae Societatis Iesu anni MDLXXXI. Rome, 1583.

Annuae Litterae Societatis Iesu anni MDLXXXIII. Rome, 1585.

Antal, F. 'Paris Nogari.' *Old Master Drawings* 13 (1938): 40–2.

Arnolds, Gunter. *Santi di Tito: Pittore del Sansepolcro*. Arezzo, 1934.

Arslan, Edoardo. *I Bassano*. 2 vols. Milan, 1960.

Arte in Valdichiana. Cortona, 1970.

Askew, Pamela. 'Caravaggio: Outward Action, Inward Vision.' In Stefania Macioce, ed. *Michelangelo Merisi da Caravaggio: La vita e le opere attraverso i documenti* (Rome, 1996), pp. 248–69.

Assche, Kristof van. 'Louis Richeome, Ignatius, and Philostrates in the Novice's Garden: Or, the Signification of Everyday Environment.' In Manning and Vaeck, *The Jesuits and the Emblem Tradition*, pp. 3–10.

Attwater, Donald. *The Penguin Dictionary of Saints*. Harmondsworth, 1980.

Augustine, St. *De civitate Dei*. 2 vols. Brussels, 1955.

– *Sancti Aurelii Augustini Enarrationes in Psalmos III*. Brussels, 1956.

Baglione, Giovanni. *Le vite de' pittori, scultori, et architetti*. Rome, 1642.

Bailey, Gauvin Alexander, *Art on the Jesuit Missions in Asia and Latin America, 1540–1773*. Toronto and Buffalo, 1999.
– 'Creating a Global Artistic Language in Late Renaissance Rome: Artists in the Service of the Overseas Missions, 1542–1621.' In Pamela Jones and Thomas Worcester, eds, *From Rome to Eternity: Catholicism and the Arts in Italy, ca. 1550–1650* (Leiden, 2002), pp. 225–52.
– 'The Florentine Reformers and the Original Painting Cycle of the Church of S. Giovannino.' In Thomas M. Lucas, ed., *Spirit, Style, Story: Essays Honoring John W. Padberg, S.J.* (Chicago, 2002), pp. 135–80.
– 'Jesuit Art Patronage before 1580.' In Thomas McCoog, ed., *Mercurian Studies*. Rome, forthcoming.
– 'The Jesuits and Painting in Italy, 1550–1690: The Art of the Catholic Reform.' In Mormando, *Saints and Sinners*, pp. 151–78.
– 'The Jesuits and the Non-Spanish Contribution to South American Colonial Architecture.' In Hilmar M. Pabel and Kathleen M. Comerford, eds, *Early Modern Catholicism: Essays Presented to John O'Malley* (Toronto, 2001), pp. 211–40.
– 'Santi di Tito and the Florentine Academy: *Solomon Building the Temple* in the Capitolo of the Accademia del Disegno (1570–71).' *Apollo* (February 2002): 2–8.
– 'Les premières décorations du Gesù.' In Tapié, *Baroque, vision jésuite*, pp. 155–63.
– 'Le style jésuite n'existe pas: Jesuit Corporate Culture and the Visual Arts.' In O'Malley et al., *The Jesuits*, pp. 38–89.
Baldinucci, Filippo. *Notizie de' professori del disegno*. Florence, 1702.
Bangert, William V., and Thomas M. McCoog. *Jerome Nadal, S.J., 1507–1580*. Chicago, 1992.
Barbieri, C., et al. *Santa Maria in Vallicella: Chiesa Nuova*. Rome, 1995.
Barnes, Bernardine. *Michelangelo's Last Judgment: The Renaissance Response*. Berkeley, Los Angeles, and London, 1998.
Barocchi, Paola, ed. *Trattati d'arte del cinquecento fra manierismo e controriforma*. 2 vols. Bari, 1960–2.
Barzman, Karen-edis. *The Florentine Academy and the Early Modern State*. Cambridge, 2000.
Baumstark, Reinhold. *Rom in Bayern: Kunst und Spiritualität der ersten Jesuiten*. Munich, 1997.
Bede, Venerable. *A History of the English Church and People*. Harmondsworth, 1979.
Beggiao, Diego. *La visita pastorale di Clemente VIII (1592–1605)*. Rome, 1978.
Bellori, Giovanni Pietro. *Le vite de' pittori, scultori e architetti moderni*. Rome, 1672.
Bellucci, Gualtiero, and Pietro Torriti. *Il Santa Maria della Scala in Siena*. Genoa, 1991.
Belting, Hans. *Likeness and Presence*. Chicago, 1994.
Bencivenni, Mario. *L'architettura della Compagnia di Gesù in Toscana*. Florence, 1996.
Benedetti, Sandro. *Fuori dal classicismo*. Rome, 1984.
– 'La prima architettura gesuitica a Roma: Note sulla chiesa dell'Annunziata e sul Collegio Romano.' In Patetta and Della Torre, *L'architettura della Compagnia di Gesù*, pp. 57–68.
Berger, Andrea. *Die Tafelgemälde Paul Brils*. Saarbrücken, 1991.
Bernini, Dante. 'La vita devota del pittore Federico Barocci.' In *L'immagine di San Francesco nella Controriforma*, pp. 57–62.
Biblia pauperum: Dipinti dalle diocesi di Romagna, 1570–1670. Ravenna, 1992.
Biermann, Veronika. 'Die Vita der Heiligen Paulus von Theben und Stephanus: Ein neuentdeckter monochromer Gemäldezyklus des 16. Jahrhunderts in der Portikus von

Santo Stefano Rotondo in Rom.' In Brandenburg and Pál, *Santo Stefano Rotondo in Rom,* pp. 111–27.

Bitskey, Istvan. 'The Collegium Germanicum Hungaricum in Rome and the Beginning of the Counter-Reformation in Hungary.' In R.J.W. Evans and T.V. Thomas, eds, *Crown, Church and Estates: Central European Politics in the Sixteenth and Seventeenth Centuries* (London, 1991), pp. 110–14.

Blunt, Anthony. *Artistic Theory in Italy, 1450–1600.* London, 1940.

Boccia, Vieri Franco. 'La chiesa di San Giovanni Evangelista a Firenze.' In Yoldi, *Architettura della compagnia ignaziana,* pp. 105–11.

Boeckl, Christine M. *Images of Plague and Pestilence: Iconography and Iconology.* Kirksville, 2000.

– 'Plague Imagery as Metaphor for Heresy in Rubens' *The Miracles of St. Francis Xavier.' Sixteenth Century Journal* 27:4 (1996): 979–95.

Borghesi, Sergio, ed. *Nicolò Cercignani, Cristofano Roncalli: Pittori di Pomarance.* Volterra, 1992.

Bösel, Richard. *Jesuitenarchitektur in Italien, 1540–1773.* Vienna, 1985–.

Brandenburg, Hugo, and József Pál, eds. *Santo Stefano Rotondo in Rom.* Wiesbaden, 2000.

Bridgewater, John, ed. *Concertatio ecclesiae catholicae in Anglia, adversus Calvinopapistas & puritanos.* Trier, 1583.

Brock, Arthur J. *Greek Medicine.* London, 1929.

Burke, Marcus B. *Jesuit Art and Iconography, 1550–1800.* Jersey City, 1993.

Burns, Roger C. 'Camillo Mariani: Catalyst of the Sculpture of the Roman Baroque.' PhD dissertation, The Johns Hopkins University, 1979.

Burton, Richard. *The Anatomy of Melancholy.* London, 1652.

Buser, Thomas. 'Jerome Nadal and Early Jesuit Art in Rome.' *Art Bulletin* 58 (1976): 424–33.

Calì, Maria. *Da Michelangelo all'Escorial.* Torino, 1980.

– *La pittura del cinquecento.* 2 vols. Torino, 2000.

Canevazzi, Giovanni. 'Intorno a Jacopo e a Giacinto Barozzi.' In *Memorie e studi intorno a Jacopo Barozzi* (Vignola, 1908), pp. 313–46.

Caraffa, Monsignor Filippo, ed. *Bibliotheca sanctorum.* 13 vols. Rome, 1968.

Cardulo, Fulvio. *Sanctorum martyrum Abundii presbyteri Abundantii diaconi Marciani.* Rome, 1584.

Careri, Giovanni. *Bernini: Flights of Love, the Art of Devotion.* Trans. Linda Lappin. Chicago, 1995.

Cartright, Nicola. 'Gregory XIII's Tower of the Winds in the Vatican.' PhD dissertation, New York University, 1990.

Cartwell, Joseph. 'The Church of St. Thomas of the English.' *The Venerable* 3:1 (October 1926): 31–40.

Il Cavalier d'Arpino. Rome, 1973.

Cavallero, Daniela Gallavotti. *Lo spedale di Santa Maria della Scala in Siena: Vicenda di una committenza artistica.* Siena, 1985.

Cavallieri, Giovanni Battista. *Ecclesiae anglicanae trophaea ... Romae in collegio Anglico per Nicolaum Circinianum depictae.* Rome, 1584.

– *Ecclesiae militantis triumphi ... in ecclesia S. Stephani Rotundi Romae Nicolai Circiniani pictoris manu visuntur.* Rome, 1585.

Cavazzini, Laura. 'Dipinti e sculture nelle chiese dell'Ospedale.' In Lucia Sandri, ed., *Gli innocenti e Firenze nei secoli: Un ospedale, un archivio, una città* (Florence, 1996), pp. 113–45.

Cecconi, G.F. *Roma sacra e moderna*. Rome, 1725.

Celio, Gaspare. *Memoria delli nomi dell'artefici delle pitture che sone in alcune chiese, facciate, e palazzi di Roma*. Naples, 1638.

Cellini, Antonia Nava. 'Stefano Maderno, Francesco Vanni e Guido Reni a Santa Cecilia in Trastevere.' *Paragone* 227 (January 1969): 18–41.

Cesareo, Francesco C. 'The Collegium Germanicum and the Ignatian Vision of Education.' *Sixteenth Century Journal* 24 (1993): 829–41.

– 'The Jesuit Colleges in Rome under Everard Mercurian.' In Thomas McCoog, ed., *Mercurian Studies*. Rome, forthcoming.

Ceschi, C. *S. Stefano Rotondo*. Rome, 1982.

Choné, Paulette. 'Domus optima: Un manuscrit emblématique au collège des jésuites de Verdun (1585).' In Manning and Vaeck, *The Jesuits and the Emblem Tradition*, pp. 35–86.

Chorpenning, Joseph F. 'Another Look at Caravaggio and Religion.' *Artibus et historiae* 16 (1987): 149–58.

Ciappi, Marc'Antonio. *Compendio delle heroiche et gloriose attioni, et santa vita di Papa Gregorio XIII*. Rome, 1596.

Cistellini, A. *San Filippo Neri. L'Oratorio e la Congregazione oratoriana: Storia e spiritualità* (Brescia, 1989).

Clancy, Thomas H. 'The First Generation of English Jesuits, 1555–1585.' *Archivum Historicum Societatis Iesu* 57 (1988): 137–62.

Cleri, Bonita, ed. *Federico Zuccari*. Milan, 1997.

Clifton, James Dean. 'Images of the Plague and Other Contemporary Events in Seventeenth-Century Naples.' PhD dissertation, Princeton University, 1987.

Coffin, David R. *Gardens and Gardening in Papal Rome*. Princeton, 1991.

– *The Villa in the Life of Renaissance Rome*. Princeton, 1979.

Collins, Minta. *Medieval Herbals: The Illustrative Traditions*. London and Toronto, 2000.

Como, Ugo da. *Girolamo Muziano*. Bergamo, 1930.

La Compagnia della Santissima Annunziata a Firenze: Gli affreschi del chiostro. Florence, 1989.

Conelli, Maria Ann. 'Female Patronage and Piety in Sixteenth-Century Naples.' Paper delivered at the Sixteenth Century Studies Conference, Toronto, October 1998.

– *The Gesù Nuovo in Naples: Politics, Property, and Religion*. Forthcoming.

Connors, Joseph. 'Bernini's S. Andrea al Quirinale: Payments and Planning.' *Journal of Architectural Historians* XLI (1982): 15–37.

– *Borromini and the Roman Oratory*. Cambridge, MA, 1982.

Contributi per la storia dello spedale del Ceppo di Pistoia. Pistoia, 1977.

Cropper, Elizabeth. 'Introduction.' In Smyth, *Mannerism and Maniera*, pp. 12–21.

D'Amico, Fabrizio. 'La pittura a Roma,' 'Uno squardo d'assieme,' and 'Una grande "nazione" di pittori a Roma: I toscani.' In Zander, *L'arte in Roma nel secolo XVI*, vol. 2, pp. 1–196, 196–200, 279–87.

Della Torre, Stefano, and Richard Schofield. *Pellegrino Tibaldi Architetto e il S. Fedele di Milano*. Milan, 1994.

De Maio, Romeo, et al., eds. *Bellarmino e la Controriforma*. Sora, 1990.

Dempsey, Charles. *Annibale Carracci and the Beginnings of Baroque Style*. 2nd ed. Fiesole, 2000.

– 'The Carracci and the Devout Style in Emilia.' In Millon, *Emilian Painting*, pp. 75–8.

Deswarte-Rosa, Sylvie. 'Francisco de Holanda: Maniera e Idea.' In *A pintura manierista em Portugal: Arte no tempo de Camões* (Lisbon, 1995), pp. 59–105.

Dickens, Charles. *American Notes and Pictures from Italy*. Repr. London, 1997.

Di Resta, Isabella. 'Il Collegio Romano.' In Patetta and Della Torre, *L'architettura della Compagnia di Gesù*, pp. 81–5.

Dompnier, Bernard. 'La Compagnie de Jésus et la mission de l'intérieur.' In Giard and Vaucelles, *Les jésuites à l'âge baroque*, pp. 155–82.

Donnelly, John Patrick. 'Antonio Possevino, S.J., as a Counter-Reformation Critic of the Arts.' *Journal of the Rocky Mountain Medieval and Renaissance Association* 3 (1982): 153–64.

Dopo il Rosso: Artisti a Volterra e Pomarance. Marsilio, 1997.

Edgerton, Samuel Y. *Theaters of Conversion: Religious Architecture and Indian Artisans in Colonial Mexico*. Albuquerque, 2001.

Emiliani, Andrea. *Federigo Barocci*. 2 vols. Bologna, 1985.

Fabre, Pierre-Antoine. 'Les "Exercises Spirituels" sont-ils illustrables?' In Giard and Vaucelles, *Les jésuites à l'âge baroque*, pp. 197–212.

– *Ignace de Loyola: Le lieu de l'image*. Paris, 1992.

– 'Les visions d'Ignace de Loyola dans la diffusion de l'art jésuite.' *MLN* 114 (1999): 816–47.

Farago, Claire, ed. *Reframing the Renaissance*. New Haven and London, 1995.

Farrell, Allan P. 'Colleges for Extern Students Opened in the Lifetime of St. Ignatius.' *Archivum Historicum Societatis Iesu* 6 (1937).

Ferrara, Daniele. 'Artisti e committenze alla Chiesa Nuova.' In *La regola e la fama*, pp. 108–29.

Filipczak, Zirka Z. *Hot Dry Men, Cold Wet Women: The Theory of Humors in Western European Art, 1575–1700*. New York, 1997.

Fiore, Kristina Hermann. 'Gli angeli, nella teoria e nella pittura di Federico Zuccari.' In Cleri, *Federico Zuccari*, pp. 101–2.

Foley, Henry. *Record of the English Province of the Society of Jesus III*. London, 1878.

Foxe, John. *Actes and Monuments of These Latter and Perillous Dayes ...* London, 1563.

Francastel, P. 'Le réalisme de Caravage.' *Gazette des beaux-arts* 80 (1938): 45–62.

Francini, Girolamo. *Le cose maravigliose dell'alma città di Roma*. Rome, 1580.

Franklin, David. *Painting in Renaissance Florence*. New Haven and London, 2001.

Freedberg, Sydney. *Circa 1600*. Cambridge, MA, 1983.

– 'Johannes Molanus on Provocative Paintings.' *Journal of the Warburg and Courtauld Institutes* 34 (1971): 229–36.

– *Painting in Italy, 1500–1600*. Repr. New Haven, 1993.

Freiburg, Jack. *The Lateran in 1600: Christian Concord in Counter-Reformation Rome*. Cambridge, 1995.

Frey, Karl. *Der literarische Nachlass Giorgio Vasaris*. 2 vols. Munich, 1940.

Friedländer, Walter. 'The Anticlassical Style.' In Friedländer, *Mannerism and Anti-Mannerism in Italian Painting* (New York, 1957), pp. 3–53.

– *Caravaggio Studies*. Princeton, 1955.

Frommel, Christof L. 'S. Andrea al Quirinale, genesi e struttura.' In G. Spagnesi and M. Fagiolo, eds, *Gian Lorenzo Bernini e l'architettura europea del sei-settecento* (Rome, 1983), pp. 211–53.

Fumaroli, Marc. *L'âge de l'éloquence: Rhétorique et 'res literaria' de la Renaissance au seuil de l'époque classique*. Geneva, 1980.

Gabinetto Disegni e Stampe degli Uffizi. *Disegni dei toscani a Roma (1580–1620)*. Florence, 1979.

Galassi Paluzzi, Carlo. 'Architetti e decoratori nella chiesa del Gesù.' *Architettura ed arti decorative* 4 (1924–5): 49–61.

– 'La Cappella del S. Cuore al Gesù.' *Roma* 9 (1931): 65–6.

– 'La "Circoncisione" del Muziano nella Chiesa del Gesù.' *Roma* 3 (1924), fasc. 1.

– 'Note di Storia e d'arte su le cappelle e gli altari del Gesù.' *Roma* 7 (1929): 303–8; 385–94.

– 'Note sull'altar maggiore del Gesù.' *Roma* 5 (1927): 248–52.

– *Storia segreta dello stile dei gesuiti*. Rome, 1951.

Galen. *Claudii Galeni Opera Omnia*. Ed. C.G. Kühn. Hildesheim, 1965.

– *Galen on the Affected Parts*. Ed. Rudolf E. Siegel. Basel, 1976.

Gallonio, Antonio. *De SS. Martyrum Cruciatibus*. Rome, 1594.

Gasquet, Cardinal. *A History of the Venerable English College, Rome*. London, 1920.

Gaudenzi, Luciana. *La chiesa del Gesù a Roma: Gli ultimi restauri*. Viterbo, 1996.

Gavazza, Ezia, et al., eds. *Bernardo Strozzi*. Milan, 1995.

Ghidotti, Riccardo. *Il Santuario delle Sette chiese di Monselice*. Vicenza, 2000.

Giachi, G., and G. Matthiae. *Sant'Andrea al Quirinale*. Rome, 1967.

Giammaria, Paola di. *Girolamo Muziano*. Brescia, 1997.

Giard, Luce, and Louis de Vaucelles, eds. *Les jésuites à l'âge baroque, 1540–1640*. Grenoble, 1996.

Gijsbers, Pieter-Matthijs. 'Claudio Aquaviva, Louis Richeome, and Dante Alberti's Altarpiece for Sant'Andrea al Quirinale.' In Anna Gramicciia, ed., *Docere, Delectare, Movere* (Rome, 1998), pp. 29–40.

Gombrich, Ernst., ed. *The Renaissance and Mannerism*. Princeton, 1963.

Göttler, Christine. *Die Kunst des Fegefeuers nach der Reformation*. Mainz, 1996.

Gregory, St. *Saint Gregory the Great: Dialogues*. Trans. and ed. Odo John Zimmerman. New York, 1959.

Grendler, Paul F. *Schooling in Renaissance Italy: Literacy and Learning, 1300–1600*. Baltimore, 1989.

Gutiérrez de Ceballos, A. Rodríguez. *Bartolomé de Bustamente y los origines de la arquitectura jesuítica en España*. Rome, 1967.

– 'Juan de Herrera y los jesuítas Villalpando, Valeriani, Ruiz, Tolosa.' *Archivum Historicum Societatis Iesu* 23 (July–December 1966): 287ff.

Hager, June. 'The Venerable: The English College and Church in Rome.' *Inside the Vatican* (May 1999): 66–9.

Hall, Marcia. *After Raphael*. Cambridge, 1999.

Harvey, Margaret. *The English in Rome, 1362–1420: Portrait of an Expatriate Community*. Cambridge, 2000.

Haskell, Francis. *History and Its Images*. New Haven and London, 1993.

– *Patrons and Painters*. New York, 1963.

– 'The Role of Patrons: Baroque Style Changes.' In Wittkower and Jaffe, *Baroque Art*, pp. 51–62.

– Review of Federico Zeri, *Pittura e controriforma*. *Burlington Magazine* 100 (1958): 398–9.

Hauser, Arnold. *Mannerism: The Crisis of the Renaissance and the Origin of Modern Art.* London, 1965.

Held, Julius. 'Rubens and the *Vita beati P. Ignatii Loiolae* of 1609.' In John R. Martin, ed., *Rubens before 1620* (Princeton, 1972), pp. 93–104.

Henneberg, Josephine von. 'Cardinal Caesar Baronius, the Arts, and the Early Christian Martyrs.' In Mormando, *Saints and Sinners*, pp. 136–50.

– *L'Oratorio dell'Arciconfraternità del Santissimo Crocifisso di San Marcello.* Rome, 1974.

– 'Saint Francesca Romana and Guardian Angels in Baroque Art.' *Religion and the Arts* 2–4 (1998): 467–87.

Herz, Alexandra. 'Cardinal Cesare Baronio's Restoration of SS. Nereo ed Achilleo and S. Cesareo de'Appia.' *Art Bulletin* 70 (1988): 590–620.

– 'Imitators of Christ: The Martyr-Cycles of Late Sixteenth Century Rome Seen in Context.' *Storia dell'arte* 62 (1988): 53–70.

Hibbard, Howard. *Caravaggio.* New York, 1983.

– 'Ut picturae sermones: The First Painted Decorations of the Gesù.' In Wittkower and Jaffe, *Baroque Art*, pp. 29–50.

Hippocrates. *The Genuine Works of Hippocrates.* Trans. and ed. Francis Adams. Baltimore, 1939.

Horace. *The Complete Works of Horace.* Ed. Charles E. Passage. New York, 1983.

Howe, Eunice D. 'The Hospital of Santo Spirito and Pope Sixtus IV.' PhD dissertation, The Johns Hopkins University, 1977.

Huetter, Luigi, and Vincenzo Golzio. *San Vitale (Le chiese di Roma illustrate, 35).* Rome, n.d.

L'immagine di San Francesco nella Controriforma. Rome, 1982.

Insolera, Lydia Salviucci. 'Gli affreschi del ciclo dei martiri commissionati al Pomarancio in rapporto alla situazione religiosa ed artistica della seconda metà del cinquecento.' In Brandenburg and Pál, *Santo Stefano Rotondo in Rom*, pp. 129–37.

– 'Le illustrazioni per gli Esercizi Spirituali intorno al 1600.' *Archivum Historicum Societatis Iesu* 60:119 (January–June 1991): 160–217.

Jacoby, Joachim. *Hans von Aachen, 1552–1615.* Munich, 2000.

Jaffé, Michael. *Rubens and Italy.* Oxford, 1977.

Jedin, Hubert. *Katholische Reformation oder Gegenreformation?* Lucerno, 1946.

Jesuit Art in North American Collections. Dobbs Ferry, 1991.

Jones, Pamela. 'Art Theory as Ideology: Gabriele Paleotti's Hierarchical Notion of Painting's Universality and Reception.' In Farago, *Reframing the Renaissance*, pp. 127–39.

– *Federico Borromeo and the Ambrosiana.* Cambridge, 1993.

– 'The Power of Images: Paintings and Viewers in Caravaggio's Italy.' In Mormando, *Saints and Sinners*, pp. 28–48.

– 'The Recent Study of Art and Catholicism in Late-Cinquecento and Seicento Rome: State of the Question.' *Annali di storia moderna e contemporanea.* Forthcoming

– 'Two Newly-discovered Hermit Landscapes by Paul Bril.' *Burlington Magazine* 130 (January 1988): 32–4.

Jones, W.H.S. 'Popular Medicine in Ancient Italy.' In Pliny, *Pliny: Natural History VIII*, pp. 569–75.

Keine, Michael. *Bartolomeo Ammannati.* Milan, 1995.

– 'Bartolomeo Ammannati e i Gesuiti.' In Niccolò Rosselli del Turco and Federica Salvi, *Bartolomeo Ammannati: Scultore e architetto* (Florence, 1995), pp. 187–94.

Klebanoff, Randi. 'The *Vita* and the *Morte*: Making the Sacred in Renaissance Bologna.'
  Paper delivered at the Sixteenth Century Studies Conference, Toronto, 24 October 1998.
Knaap, Antien. 'Envisioning a Sacred Hierarchy: Rubens' Paintings for the Jesuit Church
  in Antwerp.' Paper delivered at the conference 'The Jesuits II' at Boston College, June
  2002.
Knox, Giles. 'The Unified Church Interior in Baroque Italy: S. Maria Maggiore in
  Bergamo.' *Art Bulletin* (December 2000): 679–702.
König-Nordhoff, Ursula. *Ignatius von Loyola: Studien zur Entwicklung einer neuen Heiligen-
  Ikonographie im Rahmen einer Kanonisationskampagne um 1600.* Berlin, 1982.
– 'Zur Entstehungsgeschichte der *Vita beati P. Ignatii Loiolae Societatis Iesu fundatoris Romae
  1609 und 1622.'* *Archivum Historicum Societatis Iesu* 45 (1976): 306–17.
Korrick, Leslie. 'On the Meaning of Style: Nicolò Circignani in Counter-Reformation
  Rome.' *Word and Image* 15:2 (April–June 1999): 170–89.
Krautheimer, Richard. 'The Panels in Urbino, Baltimore, and Berlin Reconsidered.' In
  Millon, *The Renaissance from Brunelleschi to Michelangelo*, pp. 233–57.
Kris, Ernst, and Otto Kurz. *Legend, Myth, and Magic in the Image of the Artist.* New Haven,
  1979.
Kubler, George, and Martin Soria. *Art and Architecture in Spain and Portugal and Their
  American Dominions.* Baltimore, 1959.
Lagerlöf, Margaretha Rossholm. *Ideal Landscape: Annibale Carracci, Nicholas Poussin and
  Claude Lorrain.* London, 1990.
Laird, Anthony. 'The College Church.' *The Venerable* 24:1 (October 1968): 28–38; 24:3:
  159–73.
Lamalle, E. 'La propagande du P. Nicolas Trigault en faveur des Missions de Chine
  (1616).' *Archivum Historicum Societatis Iesu* 9 (1940): 96–120.
Lanzetta, Letizia. *Sant'Andrea al Quirinale.* Rome, 1996.
Laurentiis, Valeria de. 'Immagini ed arte in Bellarmino.' In de Maio et al., *Bellarmino e la
  controriforma*, pp. 581–608.
Lavin, Irving. *Bernini and the Unity of the Visual Arts.* New York and London, 1980.
Lazar, Lance Gabriel. 'Bringing God to the People: Jesuit Confraternities in Italy in the
  Mid-Sixteenth Century.' PhD dissertation, Harvard University, 1998.
– 'E faucibus daemonis: Daughters of Prostitutes, the First Jesuits, and the Compagnia
  delle Vergini Miserabili di S. Caterina.' In Wisch and Ahl, *Confraternities and the Visual
  Arts*, pp. 258–79.
– 'The First Jesuit Confraternities and Marginalized Groups in Sixteenth-Century Rome.'
  In Nicolas Terpstra, ed., *Confraternities and Social Order in Early Modern Italy.* Forth-
  coming.
– 'Jesuit Confraternal Charity in the Missions and Jubilee.' In Thomas McCoog, ed.,
  Mercurian Studies. Rome, forthcoming.
Lecchini Giovannoni, Simona. *Alessandro Allori.* Torino, 1991.
Levy, Evonne. 'A Noble Medley and Concert of Materials and Artifice: Jesuit Church
  Interiors in Rome.' In Thomas J. Lucas, *Saint, Site*, pp. 46–61.
Lewine, Milton. 'The Roman Church Interior.' PhD dissertation, Columbia University,
  1960.
– 'The Sources of Rubens's *Miracles of Saint Ignatius.'* *Art Bulletin* 45 (1963): 143–7.
Liénardy, Anne. '*Ecclesiae militantis triumphi* – Rome, 1585.' *Bulletin de l'Institut historique
  Belge de Rome* 55/56 (1985/86): 85–95.

Lingo, Stuart. 'The Capuchins and the Art of History.' PhD dissertation, Harvard University, 1998.

Loach, Judy. 'The Teaching of Emblematics and Other Symbolic Imagery by Jesuits within Town Colleges in Seventeenth and Eighteenth Century France.' In Manning and Vaeck, *The Jesuits and the Emblem Tradition*, pp. 161–86.

Lotti, Luigi, and Pier Luigi Lotti. *La comunità cattolica inglese di Roma*. Rome, 1978.

Loyola, Ignatius of. *The Constitutions of the Society of Jesus*. Ed. George E. Ganss. St Louis, 1970.

– *The Spiritual Exercises*. Trans. and ed. Louis J. Puhl. Chicago, 1951.

Lucas, Thomas M. *Landmarking: City, Church, & Jesuit Urban Strategy*. Chicago, 1997.

– , ed. *Saint, Site, and Sacred Strategy*. Vatican City, 1990.

Luchinat, Cristina Acidini. *Taddeo e Federico Zuccari: Frattelli pittori del cinquecento*. 2 vols. Milan, 1998.

Macioce, Stefania. 'Aspetti simbolici nel giardino del noviziato di S. Andrea al Quirinale in Roma.' In P.C. Ioly Zorattini, ed., *Memor fui dierum antiquorum: Studi in memoria di Luigi De Biasio* (Udine, 1995), pp. 381–95.

– 'Melanconia e pittura nel seicento.' In Rossi, *Scienza e miracoli nell'arte del '600*, pp. 134–45.

– *Undique splendent: Aspetti della pittura sacra nella Roma di Clemente VIII Aldobrandini*. Rome, 1990.

Maclagan, Edward. *The Jesuits and the Great Mogul*. London, 1932.

Madonna, Maria Luisa, ed. *Roma di Sisto V: Le arti e la cultura*. Rome, 1993.

Magner, Lois N. *A History of Medicine*. New York, 1992.

Maher, Michael William. 'Reforming Rome: The Society of Jesus and Its Congregations at the Church of the Gesù.' PhD dissertation, University of Minnesota, 1997.

Mahon, Denis. *Studies in Seicento Art and Theory*. London, 1947.

Mâle, Émile. *L'art religieux après le Concile de Trente*. Paris, 1932.

Mancini, Claudio M. *S. Apollinare: La chiesa e il palazzo (Le chiese di Roma illustrate, 93)*. Rome, 1967.

Mancini, Giulio. *Considerazioni sulla pittura*. Rome, 1956.

Manning, John, and Marc van Vaeck. *The Jesuits and the Emblem Tradition*. Leiden, 1999.

Mariotti, Annibale. *Memorie storiche delle chiese della Città di Perugia*. Perugia, 1819.

Martin, A. Lynn. *Plague? Jesuit Accounts of Epidemic Disease in the 16th Century*. St Louis, 1996.

Martin, John Rupert. *The Ceiling Paintings for the Jesuit Church in Antwerp (Corpus Rubenianum Ludwig Burchard)*. London and New York, 1967.

Martinelli, F. *Roma ex ethnica sacra sanctorum Petri et Pauli predicatione apostolica profuso sanguine publicae veneratione exposita*. Rome, 1653.

Martinetti, Giovanni. *Sant'Ignazio (Le chiese di Roma illustrate, 97)*. Rome, 1967.

Matracchi, Pietro. 'Il collegio di S. Giovannino a Firenze.' In Yoldi, *Architetture della compagnia ignaziana*, pp. 111–17.

Mauquoy-Hendrickx, Marie. 'Les Wierix illustrateurs de la Bible dite de Natalis.' *Quaerendo* 6 (1976): 60–3.

McCall, John. 'Early Jesuit Art in the Far East V: More Discoveries.' *Artibus Asiae* 17 (1954): 52–3.

Meissner, W.W. *Ignatius of Loyola: The Psychology of a Saint*. New Haven, 1992.

Melasecchi, Olga. 'Nascità e sviluppo dell'iconografia di S. Filippo Neri dal cinquecento al settecento.' In *La regola e la fama*, pp. 34–49.

Melion, Walter S. '"In conspectum Hierusalem venit Jesus": Divine Spectacle and
    Spectatorship in Jerónimo Nadal's Annotations and Meditations on the Gospels.' Paper
    delivered at the symposium 'Image of the Invisible God: Picturing Jesus Christ from the
    8th to the 20th Century,' Metropolitan Museum of Art, New York, 9 March 2001.
Mesa, José de, and Teresa Gisbert. *Bernardo Bitti*. La Paz, 1961.
- *Historia de la pintura cuzqueña*. Lima, 1982.
Micozzi, Lucilla. 'La Ratio Domiciliorum: Casa Professa.' In Gaudenzi, *La chiesa del Gesù*,
    pp. 81–90.
Miedema, Hessel. 'On Mannerism and Maniera.' *Simiolus* 10 (1978–9): 19–45.
Millon, Henry, ed. *Emilian Painting of the 16th and 17th Centuries*. Bologna, 1987.
- *The Renaissance from Brunelleschi to Michelangelo*. New York, 1997.
Moffit, J.F. 'A Christianization of Pagan Antiquity: Giovanni Andrea Gilio da Fabriano,
    Antonio Possevino, and the *Laocöon* of Domenico Theotocopoli El Greco.' *Paragone* 417
    (November 1904): 44–60.
Monssen, Leif Holm. 'Antonio Tempesta in Santo Stefano Rotondo.' *Bolletino d'arte* 67
    (1982): 107–20.
- 'An Enigma: Matteo da Siena, Painter and Cosmographer?' *Acta ad archaeologiam et
    artium historiam pertinentia*, series 8, 7 (1989): 209–313.
- 'The Martyrdom Cycle in Santo Stefano Rotondo, Part One.' *Acta ad archaeologiam et
    artium historiam pertinentia*, series 2, 2 (1982): 175–319.
- 'The Martyrdom Cycle in Santo Stefano Rotondo, Part Two.' *Acta ad archaeologiam et
    artium historiam pertinentia*, series 3, 3 (1983): 11–106.
- 'Rex gloriose martyrum: A Contribution to Jesuit Iconography.' *Art Bulletin* 63 (1981):
    130–7.
- 'St. Stephen's Balustrade in Santo Stefano Rotondo.' *Acta ad archaeologiam et artium
    historiam pertinentia*, series 8, 3 (1983): 107–82.
- 'Triumphus and Trophaea Sacra: Notes on the Iconography and Spirituality of the
    Triumphant Martyr.' *Konsthistorisk Tidskrift* 51 (1982): 10–20.
Moore, Derek. 'Pellegrino Tibaldi's Church of S. Fedele in Milan.' PhD dissertation, New
    York University, 1988.
- 'The Sixteenth Century in Italy.' *Journal of the Society of Architectural Historians* 45 (1986):
    172.
Mormando, Franco. 'Teaching the Faithful to Fly: Mary Magdalene and Peter in Baroque
    Italy.' In Mormando, *Saints and Sinners*, pp. 107–35.
- , ed. *Saints and Sinners: Caravaggio and the Baroque Image*. Boston and Chicago, 1999.
Mozley, J.F. *John Foxe and His Book*. New York, 1940.
Mühlen, Ilse von zur. 'Imaginibus honos – Ehre sei dem Bild: Die Jesuiten und die
    Bilderfrage.' In Baumstark, *Rom in Bayern*, pp. 161–70.
Mujica Pinilla, Ramón. *Ángeles apócrifos en la América virreinal*. 2nd ed. Lima, 1996.
Murphy, Caroline P. Review of Marcia Hall, *After Raphael. Catholic Historical Review* 86: 2
    (April 2000): 323–4.
Nadal, Jerónimo. *Adnotationes et meditationes in evangelia*. 3 vols. Trans. Frederick Homann.
    Ed. Walter S. Melion. Philadelphia, 2002.
- *Adnotationes et meditationes in evangelica*. Antwerp, 1585.
- *Evangelicae historiae imagines*. Antwerp, 1593.
Nagel, Alexander. *Michelangelo and the Reform of Art*. Cambridge, 2000.

Nimmo, Mara. 'Alcune precisazioni su Santo Stefano Rotondo.' *Richerche di storia dell'arte* 25 (1985): 91–102.

- '"L'Età perfetta della virilità" di Nicolò Circignani.' *Studi romani* 3–4 (1984): 194–214.

- 'Santo Stefano Rotondo: La recinzione dell'altare di mezzo.' In Brandenburg and Pál, *Santo Stefano Rotondo in Rom*, pp. 97–109.

Noreen, Kristin. 'Ecclesiae militantis triumphi: Jesuit Iconography and the Counter-Reformation.' *Sixteenth Century Journal* 29:3 (1998): 689–716.

Nova, Alessandro. '"Popular" Art in Renaissance Italy: Early Responses to the Holy Mountain at Varallo.' In Farago, *Reframing the Renaissance*, pp. 113–26.

Oliveira Caetano, Joaquim. 'Uma brevíssima nota acerca das fontes da Vida de Santo Inácio de Loyola na Igreja de S. Roque de Lisboa.' In *O púlpito e a imagem: Os jesuitas e a arte*, ed. Vassallo e Silva, pp. 43–56.

Olsen, Harald. *Federico Barocci*. Copenhagen, 1962.

O'Malley, John. *The First Jesuits*. Cambridge, MA, 1993.

- 'The Historiography of the Society of Jesus: Where Does It Stand Today?' In O'Malley et al., *The Jesuits*, pp. 3–37.

- 'Introduction.' In *Ratio Studiorum*, ed. Atteberry and Russell, pp. 7–11.

- *Trent and All That: Renaming Catholicism in the Early Modern Era*. Cambridge, MA, and London, 2000.

- et al., eds. *The Jesuits: Cultures, Sciences, and the Arts, 1540–1773*. Toronto and Buffalo, 1999.

O púlpito e a imagem: Os jesuítas e a arte. Ed. Nuno Vassallo e Silva. Lisbon, 1997.

Orlandini, Alessandro. *Gettatelli pellegrini: Gli affreschi nella Sala del Pellegrinaio dell'Ospedale di Santa Maria della Scala di Siena*. Siena, 1997.

Ostrow, Steven F. *Art and Spirituality in Counter-Reformation Rome: The Sistine and Pauline Chapels in S. Maria Maggiore*. Cambridge, 1996.

Padberg, John, et al., eds. *For Matters of Greater Moment: The First Thirty Jesuit General Congregations*. St Louis, 1994.

Paleotti, Gabriele. *Discorso intorno alle imagini sacre et profane*. Bologna, 1582.

Paoletti, John, and Gary Radke. *Art in Renaissance Italy*. Upper Saddle River, 1997.

Papi, Gianni. *Andrea Commodi*. Florence, 1994.

- 'Le tele della cappellina di Odoardo Farnese nella Casa Professa dei gesuiti a Roma.' *Storia dell'arte* 62 (1988): 71–80.

Park, Katharine. *Doctors and Medicine in Early Renaissance Florence*. Princeton, 1985.

Parsons, Robert. *An Epistle of the Persecutions of Catholickes in Englande*. Douai, 1582.

Partridge, Loren. *The Art of Renaissance Rome, 1400–1600*. New York, 1996.

Paschini, Pio. 'Le origini del Seminario Romano.' In Paschini, ed., *Cinquecento romano e riforma cattolica: Scritti raccolti in occasione dell'ottantesimo compleanno dell'autore* (Rome, 1958), pp. 1–32.

Pastor, Ludwig von. *The History of the Popes from the Close of the Middle Ages*. 40 vols. London, 1924–53.

Patetta, Luciano. 'Le chiese della Compagnia di Gesù come tipo: Complessità e sviluppi.' In Patetta, *Storia e tipologia* (Milan, 1989), pp. 160–201.

- 'Le prime costruzioni del Noviziato di Sant'Andrea al Quirinale.' In Patetta and Della Torre, *L'architettura della Compagnia di Gesù*, 87–96.

Patetta, Luciano, and Stefano Della Torre, eds. *L'architettura della Compagnia di Gesù in Italia, XVI–XVII secolo*. Milan, 1990.

Pecchiai, Pio. *Il Gesù di Roma*. Rome, 1952.

Pelliccia, Guerrino. *La preparazione ed ammissione dei chierici ai santi ordini nella Roma del secolo XVI*. Rome, 1946.

Pezzella, Salvatore. *Un erbario inedito dell'Italia centrale*. Perugia, 2000.

Pfeiffer, Heinrich. 'Die ersten Illustrationen zum Exerzitienbuch.' In Sievernich and Switek, *Ignatianisch*, pp. 120–30.

Pinelli, A. 'La maniera: Definizione di campo e modelli di lettura.' In *Storia dell'arte italiana*, part 3, vol. 2, book 1 (Torino, 1981): 88–181.

Pirri, Pietro. 'L'architetto Bartolomeo Ammannati e i gesuiti.' *Archivum Historicum Societatis Iesu* 12 (1943): 5–57.

– *Giovanni Tristano e i primordi della architettura gesuitica*. Rome, 1955.

– *Giuseppe Valeriano S.I. architetto e pittore, 1542–96*. Rome, 1970.

– 'Intagliatori gesuiti italiani dei secoli XVI e XVII.' *Archivum Historicum Societatis Iesu* 21 (1952): 1–59.

– 'La topografia del Gesù di Roma.' *Archivum Historicum Societatis Iesu* 10 (1941): 177–82.

Pirri, Pietro, and Pietro di Rosa. 'Il P. Giovanni de Rosis (1538–1610) e lo sviluppo dell'edilizia gesuitica.' *Archivum Historicum Societatis Iesu* 44 (1975): 65–79.

La pittura a Lucca nel primo seicento. Lucca, 1994.

La pittura in Italia: Il cinquecento. 2 vols. Milan, 1988.

La pittura in italia: Il seicento. 2 vols. Milan, 1988.

Pliny the Elder (Gaius Plinius Secundus). *Pliny: Natural History I*. Trans. and ed. H. Rackham. Cambridge, MA, 1944.

– *Pliny: Natural History III*. Trans. and ed. H. Rackham. Cambridge, MA, 1963.

– *Pliny: Natural History VI*. Trans. and ed. W.H.S. Jones. Cambridge, MA, 1961.

– *Pliny: Natural History VII*. Trans. and ed. W.H.S. Jones. Cambridge, MA, 1966.

– *Pliny: Natural History VIII*. Trans. and ed. W.H.S. Jones. Cambridge, MA, 1963.

Plutarch. *Plutarch's Moralia I*. Trans. and ed. Frank Cole Babbit. Cambridge, MA, 1986.

– *Plutarch's Moralia II*. Trans. and ed. Frank Cole Babbitt. Cambridge, MA, 1971.

– *Plutarch's Moralia III*. Trans. and ed. Frank Cole Babbitt. Cambridge, MA, 1968.

Polleross, Friedrich. 'Nuestro modo de proceder: Betrachtungen aus Anlass der Tagung "Die Jesuiten in Wien" vom 19. bis 21. Oktober 2000.' *Früh Neuzeit Info* 12:1 (2001): 93–128.

Porteman, Karel. *Emblematic Exhibitions at the Brussels Jesuit College (1630–1685)*. Brussels, 1996.

Posner, Donald. *Annibale Carracci*. 2 vols. London 1971.

Prag um 1600: Kunst und Kultur am Hofe Kaiser Rudolfs II. 2 vols. Vienna, 1988.

Prodi, Paolo. 'Ricerche sulla teorica delle arti figurative nella riforme cattolica.' *Archivio italiano per la storia della pietà* 4 (1962): 123–88.

Puglisi, Catherine. *Caravaggio*. London, 1998.

Puyvelde, L. Van. *La peinture flamande à Rome*. Brussels, 1950.

Quadflieg, Ralph. *Filaretes Ospedale Maggiore in Mailand*. Cologne, 1981.

Ratio Studiorum: Jesuit Education, 1540–1773. Ed. John Atteberry and John Russell. Boston, 1999.

La regola e la fama: San Filippo Neri e l'arte. Milan, 1995.

Rheinbay, P. *Biblische Bilder für der inneren Weg: Das Betrachtungsbuch des Ignatius-Gefährten Hieronymus Nadal (1507–1580)*. Engelsbach, 1995.

Rice, Louise. *The Altars and Altarpieces of New St. Peter's*. Cambridge, 1997.

– 'Jesuit Thesis Prints and the Festive Academic Defence at the Collegio Romano.' In O'Malley et al., *The Jesuits*, pp. 148–69.

Richa, Giuseppe. *Notizie istoriche delle chiese fiorentine*. Vol. 5. Florence, 1757.

Richeôme, Louis. *La peinture spirituelle*. Lyon, 1611.

Riedl, Helmut Philipp. *Antiveduto della Grammatica*. Berlin, 1998.

Rinaldi, Ernesto. *La fondazione del Collegio Romano*. Arezzo, 1914.

Ripa, Cesare. *Iconologia*. Ed. Erna Mandowsky. Hildesheim and New York, 1970.

Robertson, Clare. *'Il Gran Cardinale': Alessandro Farnese, Patron of the Arts*. New Haven and London, 1992.

– 'Two Farnese Cardinals and the Question of Jesuit Taste.' In O'Malley et al., *The Jesuits*, pp. 134–47.

Rope, Rev. H.E.Q. *The Schola Saxonum, the Hospice, and the English College in Rome*. Rome, 1951.

Rossi, Sergio, ed. *Scienza e miracoli nell'arte del '600*. Milan, 1998.

Rossi da Orte, Giulio. *Triumphus martyrum in templo d. S. Stephani Caelii Montis expressus*. Rome, 1587.

Röttgen, Herwarth. 'Zeitgeschichtliche Bildprogramme der katolischen Restauration unter Gregor XIII.' *Münchener Jahrbuch der bildenden Kunst* 26 (1975): 89–122.

Rubin, Patricia Lee. *Giorgio Vasari: Art and History*. New Haven and London, 1995.

Russo, Raffaele. *Il ciclo francescano nella Chiesa del Gesù in Roma*. Rome, 2001.

Sade, Donatien-Alphonse-François de (Marquis de Sade). *Oeuvres complètes du Marquis de Sade*. Vol. 6 (Rome). Paris, 1967.

Safarik, Eduard A., ed. *Galleria Colonna in Roma: Dipinti*. Rome, 1981.

Sale, Giovanni. *Pauperismo architettonico e architettura gesuitica*. Milan, 2001.

St. Francis Xavier – His Life and Times. Tokyo, 1999.

Salerno, Luigi. *Pittori di paesaggio del seicento a Roma*. Rome, 1977–8.

Santini, P. 'Com'era S. Apollinare.' *L'Osservatore romano*, 19 March 1937.

Santo Stefano Rotondo auf dem Caelius in Rom. Munich, 1991.

Scavizzi, G. *Arte e architettura sacra, chronache e documenti sulla controversia tra riformati e cattolici (1500–1550)*. Rome, 1981.

– *The Controversy on Images from Calvin to Baronius*. New York, 1992.

– 'La teologia cattolica e le immagini durante il XVI secolo.' *Storia dell'arte* 2 (1974): 171–212.

Schmidt, Peter. *Das Collegium Germaniicum in Rom und die Germaniker*. Tübingen, 1984.

Schwager, Klaus. 'Anlässlich eines unbekannten Stichs des romischen Gesù von Valerianus Regnartius.' In Hans-Caspar Graf von Bothmer et al., eds, *Festschrift Lorenz Dittman* (Munich, 1994), pp. 295–312.

– 'La chiesa del Gesù del Vignola.' *Bolletino del Centro A. Palladio* 19 (1977): 251–7.

– 'Concetto e realtà: Alcune precisazioni sulla difficile nascita del Gesù di Roma.' In Patetta and Della Torre, *L'architettura della Compagnia di Gesù*, pp. 69–77.

Il seicento fiorentino. 3 vols. Florence, 1984.

Seneca the Elder (Lucius Annaeus Seneca). *Seneca: Moral Epistles I*. Trans. and ed. Richard M. Gummere. Cambridge, MA, 1917.

Serrão, Vitor. 'Quadros de Vida de S. Francisco Xavier.' *Oceanos* 12 (November 1992): 56–69.

Shearman, John. 'Maniera as an Aesthetic Ideal.' In Gombrich, *The Renaissance and Mannerism*, pp. 200–21.

– *Mannerism*. Harmondsworth, 1967.

– *Only Connect: Art and the Spectator in the Italian Renaissance*. Princeton, 1992.

Siepi, Serafino. *Descrizione topologico-istorica della Città di Perugia*. Vol. 1. Perugia, 1722.

Sierp, Walter. *Das Exerzitienbuch des hl. Ignatius von Loyola*. Freiburg am Breslau, 1925.

Sievernich, Michael, and Günther Switek, eds. *Ignatianisch: Eigenart und Methode der Gesellschaft Jesu*. Freiburg, Basel, and Vienna, 1990.

Simmons, Alison. 'Jesuit Aristotelian Education: The *De Anima* Commentaries.' In O'Malley et al., *The Jesuits*, pp. 522–35.

Simson, Otto von. *Peter Paul Rubens (1577–1640)*. Mainz, 1996.

Smith, Graham. 'Rubens altargemälde des Hl. Ignatius.' *Jahrbuch der kunsthistorischen Sammlungen in Wien* 65 (1969): 39–60.

Smith, Jeffrey Chipps. 'The Art of Salvation in Bavaria.' In O'Malley et al., *The Jesuits*, pp. 568–99.

– *Sensuous Worship: Jesuits and the Art of the Early Catholic Reformation in Germany*. Princeton, 2002.

Smyth, Craig Hugh. *Mannerism and Maniera*. 2nd ed. Vienna, 1992.

– 'Mannerism and Maniera.' In Gombrich, *The Renaissance and Mannerism*, pp. 174–99.

Soria, Martin. *La pintura del siglo XVI en Sudamerica*. Buenos Aires, 1956.

Spalding, Jack. 'Santi di Tito.' PhD dissertation, Princeton University, 1976.

Spear, Richard. *Caravaggio and His Followers*. Cleveland, 1971.

Spedale di Santa Maria della Scala: Atti del convegno internazionale di studi. Siena, 1986.

Lo Spedale Serristori di Figline. Figline Val d'Arno, 1982.

Spengler, Dietmar. 'Die Ars Jesuitica der Gebrüder Wierix.' *Wallraf-Richartz-Jahrbuch* 57 (1996): 161–94.

Spezzaferro, Luigi. 'Il recupero del rinascimento.' In Giulio Bollati et al., eds, *Storia dell'arte italiana* (Torino, 1981), pp. 185–244.

Steinhuber, A. *Geschichte des Kollegium Germanicum in Rom*. Vol. 1. Freiburg, 1906.

Strauss, Walter L., ed. *The Illustrated Bartsch*. New York, 1985.

Strinati, Claudio. '1570–1575: La situazione della pittura a Roma.' In José Álvarez Lopera, ed., *El Greco: Identità e trasformazione* (Milan, 1999), pp. 115–30.

– *Quadri romani tra '500 e '600*. Rome, 1979.

Stumpel, Jeroen. 'Speaking of Manner.' *Word and Image* 4 (1988): 246–64.

Sudbrack, Josef. 'Die Anwendung der Sinne als Angelpunkt der Exerzitien.' In Sievernich and Switek, *Ignatianisch*, pp. 96–119.

Tacchi-Venturi, Pietro. *Storia della Compagnia di Gesu in Italia*. 6 vols. Rome, 1950.

Tapié, Alain, ed. *Baroque, vision jésuite du Tintoret à Rubens*. Paris, 2003.

Temkin, Owsei. *Galenism: The Rise and Decline of a Medical Philosophy*. Ithaca, 1973.

Terhalle, Johannes. '… ha della Grandezza de padri Gesuiti: Die Architektur der Jesuiten um 1600 und St. Michael in München.' In Baumstark, *Rom in Bayern*, pp. 83–146.

Testini, P. *San Saba (Le chiese di Roma illustrate, 68)*. Rome, 1961.

Thode, Henry. *Franz von Assisi und die Anfänge der Kunst der Renaissance in Italien*. Berlin, 1885.

Titi, Filippo. *Descrizione delle pitture, sculture e architetture esposte al pubblico in Roma*. Rome, 1763.

– *Studio di pittura, scoltura, et architetura, nelle chiese di Roma (1674–1763)*. 2 vols. Repr. Florence, 1987.

Tofani, Annamaria Petrioli. *Gabinetto isegni e stampe degli Uffizi: Inventario 2. Disegni esposti*. Florence, 1987.

Torriti, Pietro. *Il Pellegrinaio nella Spedale di Santa Maria della Scala in Siena*. Siena, 1987.

Torsellino, Orazio. *Annuae Litterae Societatis Iesu anno 1593*. Florence, 1601.

Turner, A. Richard. *The Vision of Landscape in Renaissance Italy*. Princeton, 1966.

Ugonio, Pompeo. *Historia delle stationi di Roma*. Rome, 1588.

Vaccaro, Luciano, and Francesca Riccardi. *Sacri Monti: Devozione, arte e cultura della Controriforma*. Milan, 1992.

Vallery-Radot, Jean. *Le recueil de plans d'édifices de la Compagnie de Jésus conservé à la Bibliothèque Nationale de Paris*. Rome, 1960.

Valone, Carolyn. 'The Pentecost: Image and Experience in Late Sixteenth-Century Rome.' *Sixteenth Century Journal* 24 (1993): 801–28.

– 'Women on the Quirinal Hill: Patronage in Rome, 1560–1630.' *Art Bulletin* 76:1 (March 1994): 129–46.

Vannugli, Antonio.'Gli affreschi di Antonio Tempesta a S. Stefano Rotondo e l'emblematica nella cultura del Martirio presso la Compagnia di Gesù.' *Storia dell'arte* 48 (1983): 101–16.

Vargas Ugarte, Ruben. *Ensayo de un diccionario de artifices coloniales de la America Meridional*. Lima, 1947.

Vasari, Giorgio. *Vasari's Lives of the Painters, Sculptors, and Architects*. Trans. and ed. Mrs Jonathan Foster. 5 vols. London, 1883.

– *Le vite de' piu eccellenti pittori, scultori, ed architettori scritte da Giorgio Vasari*. Ed. Gaetano Milanesi. 8 vols. Florence, 1881.

Vaudo, Erasmo. *Scipione Pulzone da Gaeta, pittore*. Gaeta, 1976.

Verstegen, Ian. 'Federico Barocci, Federico Borromeo, and the Oratorian Orbit.' *Renaissance Quarterly* 66:1 (Spring, 2003): 56–87.

Virdis, Caterina Limentani. 'Flemish Winds on the Roman Landscape: The Bril Brothers and Other Painters in Rome at the Time of Pope Gregory XIII.' In Nicole Dacos, ed., *Fiamminghi a Roma, 1508–1608* (Florence, 1999), pp. 67–78.

Virgil (Publius Vergilius Maro). *The Aeneid*. Trans. John Dryden. New York, 1965.

Voelker, Evelyn Carole. 'Charles Borromeo's *Instructiones Fabricae et Supellectilis Ecclesiasticae*, 1577.' PhD dissertation, Syracuse University, 1977.

Wadell, Maj-Brit. 'The Evangelicae Historiae Imagines: The Designs and Their Artists.' *Quaerendo* 10 (1980): 279–91.

– *Evangelicae historiae imagines: Entstehungsgeschichte und Vorlagen*. Göteborg, 1985.

Waterworth, J., ed. *The Council of Trent: Canons and Decrees*. Chicago, 1848.

Wazbinski, Zygmunt. *L'Accademia medicea del disegno a Firenze nel cinquecento*. 2 vols. Florence, 1997.

Weibel, Walter. *Jesuitismus und Barockskulptur in Rom*. Strasbourg, 1909.

Weil, Mark S. 'The Devotion of the Forty Hours and Roman Baroque Illusions.' *Journal of the Warburg and Courtauld Institutes* 37 (1974): 218–48.

Weinrich, Lorenz. *Das ungarische paulinerkloster Santo Stefano Rotondo in Rom (1404–1579)*. Berlin, 1998.

Wethey, Harold, E. *The Paintings of Titian*. 3 vols. London, 1969.

Williams, Michael. *The Venerable English College, Rome*. Dublin, 1979.

Winner, Matthias, and Dietlief Heikamp. *Der Maler Federico Zuccari*. Munich, 1999.

Wisch, Barbara. 'The Archiconfraternita del Gonfalone and Its Oratory in Rome: Art and Counter-Reformation Spiritual Values.' PhD dissertation, University of California at Berkeley, 1985.

– 'The Passion of Christ in the Art, Theater, and Penitential Rituals of the Roman Confraternity of the Gonfalone.' In Konrad Eisenbichler, ed., *Crossing the Boundaries: Christian Piety and the Arts in Italian Medieval and Renaissance Confraternities* (Kalamazoo, 1991), pp. 237–62.

Wisch, Barbara, and Diane Cole Ahl, eds. *Confraternities and the Visual Arts in Renaissance Italy: Ritual, Spectacle, Image*. Cambridge, 2000.

Wittkower, Rudolf. *Art and Architecture in Italy, 1600–1750*. London, 1958; repr. 1991.

– 'Problems of the Theme.' In Wittkower and Jaffe, *Baroque Art*, pp. 1–14.

Wittkower, Rudolf, and Irma Jaffe, eds. *Baroque Art: The Jesuit Contribution*. New York, 1972.

Wittkower, Rudolf, and Mary Wittkower. *The Divine Michelangelo and the Florentine Academy's Homage on His Death in 1564*. New York, 1950.

Wölfflin, Heinrich. *Classic Art: An Introduction to the Italian Renaissance*. Repr. Ithaca, 1986.

Yoldi, Giuseppe Rocchi Coopmans de. 'Presentazione delle monografie.' In Yoldi, *Achitettura della compagnia ignaziana*, pp. 80–1.

– , ed. *Architettura della compagnia ignaziana nei centri antichi italiani*. Florence, 1999.

Zander, Giuseppe, ed. *L'arte in Roma nel secolo XVI*. 2 vols. Bologna, 1992.

Zeri, Federico. 'Giuseppe Valeriano.' *Paragone* 61 (1955): 35–65.

– *Pittura e controriforma*. Repr. Vicenza, 1997.

Zerner, Henri.'Observations on the Use of the Concept of Mannerism.' In Franklin W. Robinson and Stephen G. Nichols., eds, *The Meaning of Mannerism* (Hanover, 1972), pp. 105–40.

Zimmer, Jürgen. *Joseph Heintz der Ältere*. Munich, 1988.

– *Joseph Heintz der Ältere als Maler*. Weissenhorn, 1971.

Zuccari, Alessandro. 'Aggiornamenti sulla decorazione cinquecentesca di alcune cappelle del Gesù.' *Storia dell'arte* (1984): 28–33.

– *Arte e committenza nella Roma di Caravaggio*. Torino, 1984.

– 'Bellarmino e la prima iconografia gesuitica: La Cappella degli Angeli al Gesù.' In de Maio et al., *Bellarmino e la Controriforma*, pp. 611–28.

– 'Cesare Baronio, le immagini, gli artisti.' In *La regola e la fama*, pp. 80–97.

– *I pittori di Sisto V*. Rome, 1992.

– 'La politica culturale dell'Oratorio romano nella seconda metà del cinquecento.' *Storia dell'arte* 41 (1981): 77–112.

– 'La politica culturale dell'Oratorio romano nelle imprese artistiche promosse da Cesare Baronio.' *Storia dell'arte* 42 (1981): 171–93.

Index

Monselice: Sette Chiese, 40

Monssen, Leif Holm, 22, 135–9, 141, 143, 145, 148–9, 152

Monte, Antonio del, 69

Montenay, Georgette de: *Emblèmes et dévises chrestiennes*, 82

Monti, Antonio de,' 119

Morales, Luis de, 249

Moravia, 120

More, St Thomas, 163

Morelli, Paolo, 202

Morone, Cardinal Giovanni, 154

mosaics, 65, 124–5, 142, 149, 217

Moses, biblical figure, 72, 232

Munich: Michaelskirche, 257

music, curative powers of, 89–91

Muziano, Girolamo, 16–17, 28, 117, 189, 200, 202, 218, 227, 254; 'canon' of painting, 28; *Circumcision*, 117, 217–18, 253–5, 263, **112**; *Raising of Lazarus*, 28, **6**; *St Francis Receiving the Stigmata*, 117, **34**

Naaman the Syrian, biblical figure, 91

Nadal, Jerónimo, 77–8, 109–10; *Evangelicae historiae imagines*, 10, 11–12, 21, 32, 36, 53, 60, 140, 164, 173, 195, 210, 217, 239–40, **12–13**; and imagery, 10–11, 21, 59

Naldini, Battista: *Martyrdom of St John the Evangelist*, 143, **54**

Naples, 167; Gesù Nuovo, 167

Napoleon Bonaparte, 157–8

Nappi, Girolamo: *Diario del Seminario Romano*, 120

Nappi, Rosario, 216

Nativity of Christ, 103, 117, 122, 194, 197, 229, 257, 267

naturalism in art, 11–12, 15, 18, 24, 27, 48, 171, 173–4, 218, 244, 246, 253, 254, 262, 266

natural medicine, 85

Navarola, Ottavio: *Memorie della Casa di S. Andrea a Monte Cavallo della Compagnia di Gesù*, 41, 45, 57–8, 75, 185–6, 246–7

Navarrete, Juan Fernández, 'el mudo,' 249–50

Navesi, Giovanni, 103

Nebbia, Cesare, 27–8, 30, 126, 132; *Martyrdom of St Lawrence*, 145, **56**

Nebuchadnezzar, King, 94, 242

Negri, Giovanni Jacopo de,' 151

Nemesius of Alexandria, St, 145

Neoplatonism. *See* Aristotle

Nereus, St, 124, 143, 174

Neri, St Filippo, 16, 19, 29, 70, 124, 130, 154, 189, 256

Nero, Roman emperor, 142

Neroni, Bartolomeo, 119

Neroni, Matteo, 119

Neuburg an der Donau, 257

New York: Metropolitan Museum of Art, 87, 209

Niccolò, sculptor at the Gesù, 203

Niccolò, Giovanni, 30

Nicholas V, Pope, 134–5

Nimmo, Mara, 136, 151

Noah, biblical figure, 232

Nogari, Paris, 65, 168, 170

Nola: Gesù, 201

Noreen, Kristin, 152

Northern artists, 201, 203, 216, 218, 252–3, 264; Jesuit penchant for, 171, 173, 183

Nova, Alessandro, 40

Novitiate, Roman (S. Andrea al Quirinale), 11, 13, 18, 20, 34, 38, 41, 108, 119, 122, 153, 159, 167, 170, 177, 179, 185, 190, 195, 198, 235, 246, 251, 267–9; chronology of paintings, 44, 45, 46, 47, 48; construction, 42; dormitory, 38, 43, 76, 130, 197; dormitory paintings, 68–9, 71–3, **25**; foundation, 40–2; garden, 43–4, 48, 50, 166–7, 184, **14**; infirmary, 18, 20, 38, 43–4, 46, 74, 76, 162, 166, 178, 229, 231, 242; infirmary paintings, 75–102, 110, **27, 31**; lavatory, 38, 43; lavatory and gallery paintings, 61; recreation room, 38, 43–4, 75, 156, 163, 166; recreation room paintings, 61, 62–8, **21, 22**; refectory, 38, 43, 44, 46; refectory paintings, 59–61, **19**